THE SOCIAL PSYCHOLOGY
OF HIV INFECTION

THE
SOCIAL PSYCHOLOGY
OF HIV INFECTION

Edited by

JOHN B. PRYOR
GLENN D. REEDER
Illinois State University

LEA LAWRENCE ERLBAUM ASSOCIATES, PUBLISHERS
1993 Hillsdale, New Jersey   Hove and London

Lawrence Erlbaum Associates, Inc., Publishers
365 Broadway
Hillsdale, New Jersey 07642

Library of Congress Cataloging–in–Publication Data

The Social psychology of HIV infection / edited by John B. Pryor,
  Glenn D. Reeder.
    p.   cm.
  Includes bibliographical references and index.
  ISBN 0-8058-0991-0
  1. AIDS (Disease)—Psychological aspects. 2. AIDS (Disease)—
Social aspects. I. Pryor, John B. II. Reeder, Glenn D.
  RC607.A26S645 1992
  362.1'969792—dc20   92-18400
                                                                      CIP

Printed in the United States of America
10 9 8 7 6 5 4 3 2 1

Contents

Preface   vii

PART I: THE THEORETICAL ROOTS OF PREVENTION

Social Cognitive Views on the Perception of HIV Risks and the Performance of Risky Behaviors

1. **AIDS Risk Perceptions and Decision Biases**   5
    Patricia W. Linville, Gregory W. Fischer, and Baruch Fischhoff

2. **Perceived Risk of AIDS: Unrealistic Optimism and Self-Protective Action**   39
    J. van der Pligt, Wilma Otten, René Richard, and Frank van der Velde

3. **Perceived Vulnerability to HIV Infection and AIDS Preventive Behavior: A Critical Review of the Evidence**   59
    Meg Gerrard, Frederick X. Gibbons, Teddy D. Warner, and Gabie E. Smith

4. **Negotiating Safer Sex: Interpersonal Dynamics**   85
    Lynn Carol Miller, B. Ann Bettencourt, Sherrine Chapman DeBro, and Valerie Hoffman

Theoretical Perspectives on Intervention

5. **A General Social Psychological Model for Changing
    AIDS Risk Behavior**   127
    William A. Fisher and Jeffrey D. Fisher

6. **Persuasion Theory and AIDS Prevention**   155
    Richard E. Petty, Faith Gleicher, and W. Blair G. Jarvis

7. **Social Psychology and AIDS Among Ethnic Minority
    Individuals: Risk Behaviors and Strategies for Changing Them**   183
    John B. Jemmott, and James M. Jones

**PART II: THE DILEMMA OF THE PWA:
STIGMA, PROSOCIAL REACTIONS, AND COPING**

Understanding the Stigma of AIDS

8. **Public Attitudes Toward AIDS-Related Issues in the United States**   229
    Gregory M. Herek and Eric K. Glunt

9. **Collective and Individual Representations of HIV/AIDS
    Stigma**   263
    John B. Pryor and Glenn D. Reeder

10. **AIDS From an Attributional Perspective**   287
    Bernard Weiner

Coping with HIV Infection and Social Support

11. **Coping With the Threat of AIDS**   305
    *Shelley E. Taylor, Margaret E. Kemeny,
    Stephen G. Schneider, and Lisa G. Aspinwall*

12. **The Psychology of Volunteerism: A Conceptual
    Analysis and a Program of Action Research**   333
    Allen M. Omoto, Mark Snyder, and James P. Berghuis

Author Index   357
Subject Index   373

Preface

In the early 1980s we witnessed the birth of one of the most complex and perplexing social problems faced by modern society: the epidemic of infection with human immunodeficiency virus (HIV), which causes acquired immunodeficiency syndrome (AIDS). It began in the spring of 1981, when doctors in some metropolitan U.S. cities noticed that a few young men were dying horrible deaths from ravaged immune systems. The toll of similar deaths mounted in a dizzying spiral. It was not until 1983 that researchers isolated the virus that caused the syndrome. This virus was later labeled HIV. HIV is part of a relatively small group of viruses known as retroviruses. HIV attacks a victim's immune system and renders the person essentially defenseless against many opportunistic diseases. The most likely consequence of HIV infection is death. More than half of those diagnosed with HIV infection since it was first identified are now dead. Currently, AIDS ranks first in the most common causes of death for men between the ages 25 and 45 in the United States. It ranks fourth for women in this age range.

We now know the principal ways in which HIV is transmitted. HIV is transmitted perinatally, by intimate sexual contact, or by exposure to contaminated blood. In addition to the fears that swirl around a fatal disease, reactions to HIV have been complicated by attitudinal variables. HIV infection in the United States has occurred primarily in two large groups of people who have traditionally evoked discomfort or outright antagonism. The first cases of HIV infection to come to the attention of scientists and the general public were among gay men. Currently, more than half of the diagnonsed AIDS cases in the United States involve homosexual or bisexual men. More than one quarter are among intravenous (IV) drug users.

Currently, there is no proven vaccine to prevent HIV infection. Also, curative therapies for those infected with HIV are still in the experimental stages. Perhaps even more frightening, we know that seropositive individuals can remain asymptomatic for many years, carriers of a personal time bomb. During this time, they unwittingly may infect others as well.

With no biomedical solutions on the near horizon, society must turn to the social and behavioral sciences for guidance in dealing with the epidemic. In this context, we see two general themes underlying HIV social problems: (a) stemming the tide of HIV infection, and (b) caring for the increasing numbers of persons with AIDS (PWAs).

With regard to the first type of problem, significant strides have been made in curbing the incidence of HIV among the gay population, at least in the United States. Less success has been encountered in stopping the spread among IV drug users. Also, few inroads seem to have been made in altering the risky behaviors of potential "next generation" PWAs. How can we get people to acknowledge HIV risk in their own behaviors? What sorts of interventions might alter the frequency of risky behavior?

The other major type of social problem looming before us is responding to the increasing numbers of PWAs. Current estimates suggest that between 1.5 and 2 million Americans are infected with HIV. One aspect of this problem is the grave stigma associated with HIV infection. How can we combat the intense negative reactions that many people have to PWAs? In a related vein, how can we encourage positive or prosocial reactions to PWAs? Also, how can we help PWAs to cope with their struggle against imminent death?

The organization of this volume centers upon these two themes. The first theme concerns *The Theoretical Roots of Prevention*. The second theme concerns *The Dilemma of the PWA*. Within each of these broad themes, we present two sections of chapters, each dealing with a more specific aspect of the general theme. Within the first theme we divide the chapters into these sections: (1) Sociocognitive Views on the Perception of HIV Risk and the Performance of Risky Behaviors and (2) Theoretical Perspectives on Intervention. Within the other theme we divide the chapters into: (1) Understanding the Stigma of AIDS and (2) Coping With HIV Infection and Social Support.

As scientists, we believe that the best beginning to any solution is a thorough understanding of the problem. Because of the urgency in dealing with these important social problems, many of the solutions that have been attempted thus far were hastily concocted and had very little basis in either research or accepted theory. The goal of this volume is not to evaluate previous attempts to answer these social problems, but to provide theoretical analyses of some of the basic sociopsychological processes that underlie the problems.

The chapter authors are mainstream social psychologists who are interested in theoretically driven AIDS-related research. Our goal was to produce an edited book that will inform researchers in social psychology as well as those who are interested in AIDS, per se. Our hope was that this book would be exemplary of Kurt Lewin's often quoted maxim: There is nothing so practical as a good theory. At the same time we wanted to demonstrate the value of applied research to the building and refinement of basic social psychologial theory.

John B. Pryor
Glenn D. Reeder

THE THEORETICAL ROOTS
OF PREVENTION

SOCIAL COGNITIVE VIEWS ON THE PERCEPTION OF HIV RISKS AND THE PERFORMANCE OF RISKY BEHAVIORS

1 AIDS Risk Perceptions and Decision Biases

Patricia W. Linville
Gregory W. Fischer
Duke University

Baruch Fischhoff
Carnegie Mellon University

Until effective vaccines against human immunodeficiency virus (HIV) are avail able for general public use, the major public health strategy for limiting the spread of acquired immunodeficiency syndrome (AIDS) will be through education about the risks of AIDS and instruction in strategies for reducing that risk. But developing effective educational programs requires a deeper understanding of how people think about the risks of AIDS and how they make decisions regarding those risks. Studies of risk perception and risk-taking behavior in other domains have identified a number of systematic biases in people's risk perceptions and decision-making processes. These behavioral biases may lead people to make poor decisions that affect their risk of acquiring or spreading HIV infection. They also pose a significant obstacle to attempts to develop effective risk communications regarding AIDS and transmission of HIV.

In this chapter, we use models, methods, and findings from the field of behavioral decision research to analyze risk perceptions and decisions that affect the risk of HIV transmission. Behavioral decision research is an interdisciplinary subfield that integrates conceptions of rational decision making—from economics and statistics—with cognitive views of behavior developed in psychology. We consider three potential contributions of decision theory to the study of AIDS-related cognitions and behavior.

First, *normative* decision theory provides a set of concepts for thinking about and analyzing decisions that affect the risk of acquiring or spreading HIV. Normative decision theory addresses the question of how people should make inferences and decisions if they wish to conform to fundamental principles of logic and rational choice (Clemen, 1991; Keeney & Raiffa, 1976; von Winterfeldt & Edwards, 1986). Thus, the normative theory serves as a benchmark for evaluating the quality of the inferences and decisions that people make. In the first section of this chapter, we illustrate how the normative decision framework can be applied to several decisions affecting the risk of HIV transmission.

Second, *behavioral* decision research has revealed a variety of systematic biases in risk perceptions (e.g., Fischhoff & MacGregor, 1982; Slovic, 1987) and decision-making processes (e.g., Kahneman, Slovic, & Tversky, 1982; Kahneman & Tversky, 1984). These biases complicate the task of formulating effective HIV risk communications. In this chapter, we present empirical findings regarding college students' perceptions of the probability that they and others will acquire HIV infection. In analyzing these findings, we examine three types of cognitive bias that may adversely affect the decisions people make and that may also undermine efforts to communicate HIV risk information to the public: (a) an *accumulation bias* involving the inability to understand the relationship between the risk of acquiring HIV infection in a single sexual encounter and the risk of acquiring HIV infection in multiple sexual encounters; (b) a *framing bias* in which two logically equivalent descriptions of the effectiveness of condoms in preventing the transmission of HIV lead to systematic differences in people's willingness to use condoms; and (c) an *optimism bias* regarding one's personal risk of acquiring HIV infection. For each of these biases, we discuss implications for the composition of public health communications regarding HIV risk and protective strategies.

Third, behavioral decision research provides a set of tools for measuring perceived risk (e.g., Slovic, Fischhoff, & Lichtenstein, 1982). In this chapter, we argue that these measurement procedures are especially likely to be helpful in the case of diseases like AIDS, where many individuals perceive their personal risk to be very small. We also describe a quantitative risk-assessment instrument that we have developed and used in a number of studies of HIV risk perceptions. Valid measures of risk perception are essential for assessing the public's level of knowledge regarding risks of HIV infection. They are also needed to evaluate hypotheses about why people do or do not engage in various risky behaviors or self-protective strategies.

To preview what is to come, the first section of this chapter introduces the basic concepts of decision theory and shows how they can be applied to issues involving risks of HIV infection. The second section presents empirical data on three types of decision biases in thinking about HIV risks. The third section discusses issues surrounding the assessment of perceived risks of HIV infection.

THINKING ABOUT AIDS DECISIONS

A decision is a choice among competing courses of action. Most of the ways in which people contract and transmit HIV can be viewed as resulting from decisions. For instance, decisions about whether to have sexual intercourse and whether to use condoms largely determine who will be sexually infected with the virus. Decisions about whether to be tested for HIV antibodies influence the likelihood that infected individuals will infect others. Decisions about whether to share needles determine who will be infected by intravenous (IV) drug use. Even decisions about whether to pursue medical careers or to seek medical treatment may influence some individual's risk of HIV infection.

Public policy decisions also affect HIV transmission. Decisions about whether to provide clean needles to addicts affect the number of victims of the disease. Decisions regarding levels of funding for drug treatment and education programs may influence the rate at which the virus spreads. Decisions regarding funding levels and priorities for AIDS research, treatment, and public information programs will partially determine how many more people will become infected and what their medical prognosis will be. Finally, decisions regarding who to accept as blood donors and what criteria to use in screening public blood supplies largely determine how many people will be infected by HIV-contaminated blood.

We begin this section by discussing how concepts and tools from decision theory can be used to represent and analyze decisions such as these. Next, we address the question: How should one make decisions that influence the risk of contracting HIV? We conclude the section by addressing the question: How are intuitive decisions likely to go wrong?[1]

The Decision Theory Representation of Decisions That Affect HIV Risk

Theories of decision making use five central constructs to describe and analyze decisions: courses of action, uncertain events, subjective probability, consequences, and utility. A graphical representation known as a decision tree is used to depict the relations among these constructs. The most widely used decision theory model, expected utility theory, provides a simple rule for combining these constructs to form an overall appraisal of the best course of action. In this section, we illustrate these concepts by showing how they can be used to describe a woman's decision about whether to have sexual intercourse with a new romantic partner (who wishes to have sex with her) and, if so, whether to use a condom.

There are two possible uses of decision models like those we describe here. The first is scientific, or descriptive. Constructs in the model may represent important aspects of the decision-making process. The second use is normative, to assist in making better decisions. There are a number of decision theorists who act as agents for a variety of public and private decision makers. For instance, there is a small but thriving movement known as medical decision analysis in

---

[1] An earlier treatment of some of these issues can be found in Fischhoff (1989).

which physicians use decision theory methods to make difficult decisions regarding patient management (von Winterfeldt & Edwards, 1986).

Courses of Action.   A decision occurs when a person chooses among two or more mutually exclusive courses of action. For example, in deciding whether to have intercourse with her new romantic partner, the woman might consider three courses of action: (a) to refrain from having intercourse for the time being, (b) to engage in intercourse using a condom, and (c) to engage in unprotected intercourse. These courses of action are represented graphically as the first stage in the decision tree depicted in Fig. 1.1.

Uncertain Events.   In many decisions, the path from acts to consequences is uncertain. Physical and social events intervene between an action and its consequences. For instance, is the woman's new romantic partner HIV infected? If he is, will she contract the virus from him if she has sex with him one time with

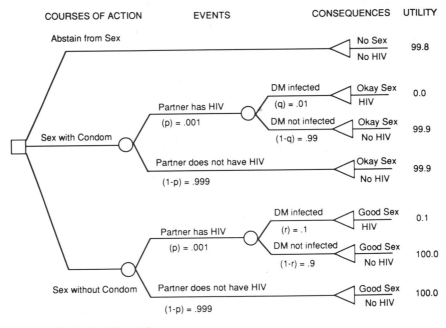

EU(Abstain) = u(No Sex, No HIV) = 99.8

EU(Sex with Condom) = pq u(Okay Sex, HIV) + p(1-q) u(Okay Sex, No HIV) + (1-p) u(Okay Sex, No HIV)
          = 0.001 x 0.01 x 0 + 0.001 x 0.99 x 99.9 + 0.999 x 99.9 = 99.9

EU(Sex w/out Condom) = pr u(Good Sex, HIV) + p(1-r) u(Good Sex, No HIV) + (1-p) u(Good Sex, No HIV)
          = 0.001 x 0.1 x 0.1 + 0.001 x 0.9 x 100 + 0.999 x 100 = 99.99

FIG. 1.1.   Deciding whether to have sex and use a condom.

(without) using a condom? Uncertainty about the occurrence of such intervening events leads to uncertainty about the final consequences of a decision.

Subjective Probability.   Decisions depend on *beliefs* about the likelihood of uncertain events like those just mentioned. If a decision maker's beliefs about the likelihoods of events conform to a few basic principles of logic, then these beliefs can be represented by numbers referred to as *subjective probabilities* that quantify the degree of perceived likelihood of an event (Savage, 1954).[2] The belief that an event is impossible is represented by a subjective probability of 0; the belief that an event is absolutely certain to occur by a subjective probability of 1; the belief that an event is as likely to occur as not by a subjective probability of 0.5; and so forth.

The decision represented in Fig. 1.1 involves three subjective probabilities. The first is p, the subjective probability that the decision maker's partner is HIV infected. For instance, our decision maker might believe that there is only a 1 in 1,000 chance ($p = 0.001$) that her prospective partner is HIV infected. The second is q, the subjective probability that the decision maker will contract HIV if she has intercourse once, with an infected partner who uses a condom. She might believe this risk to be 1 in 100 ($q = 0.01$). The third is r, the subjective probability that the decision maker will contract HIV if she has intercourse once with an infected partner who does not use a condom. She might believe this risk to be 1 in 10 ($r = 0.1$). The values of q and r used in this example imply that the decision maker believes that the risk of acquiring HIV is only one-tenth as great with a condom as without.

Consequences.   The consequences of a decision can be characterized by a set of *value attributes* reflecting the degree to which the decision results in the fulfillment (or frustration) of the decision maker's goals or objectives. In deciding whether to have intercourse with a new romantic partner, the salient value attributes describing each potential consequence might include degree of sexual pleasure, quality of the romantic relationship, embarrassment at asking one's partner to use a condom (if he does not offer to do so), becoming pregnant, and acquiring HIV. To simplify the example depicted in Fig. 1.1, only two value attributes are represented: the quality of the sexual experience (ranging from none to good) and whether the decision maker contracts HIV (yes or no).

When consequences depend on uncertain events that intervene between actions and the consequences themselves, the consequences are uncertain as well. The perception of such uncertainty contributes to subjective feelings of risk. For instance, the decision maker is uncertain as to whether having sex will lead to the

---

[2]As we discuss later, people's beliefs about uncertain events frequently violate basic principles of logical inference. In these cases, measuring the perceived likelihoods of events is complicated by the presence of inconsistency and bias.

consequence of contracting HIV. To simplify the example in Fig. 1.1, we have ignored uncertainty regarding the value attribute "quality of sexual experience." Clearly, sex without a condom is not always "good" and sex with a condom is not always "okay." We use these labels merely to summarize the decision maker's expectation that sex will be more pleasurable (on the average) without a condom.

Utility.   In decision theory, *utility* refers to a quantitative measure of the subjective desirability of a possible decision consequence. In standard practice, utility is scaled so that the worst possible outcome receives a utility of 0 and the best possible outcome a utility of 100.[3] These utility scores reflect *personal subjective preferences*. Thus, different individuals may assign different utilities to the same outcomes.

For example, assume that the woman in our example believes that the best possible consequence is one in which she has sexual intercourse without a condom, which is highly pleasurable for both her and her lover (denoted by "good sex" in Fig. 1.1), and which does not result in the transmission of HIV. To anchor the top end of the utility scale, she assigns a utility score of 100 to this consequence (see Fig. 1.1). Further, suppose that the woman believes that the worst consequence is one in which she and her partner have moderately satisfying sex ("okay sex") with a condom, but she contracts HIV infection. To anchor the bottom end of the utility scale, she assigns a utility of 0 to this consequence.

The other three decision outcomes in Fig. 1.1 receive utility scores between 0 and 100. Assume, for example, that our decision maker assigns a utility of 99.9 to the consequence "okay sex, no HIV," indicating that she sees very little difference between this outcome and the best outcome, "good sex, no HIV." She assigns a utility of 99.8 to "no sex, no HIV," indicating that it is only slightly worse. Finally, she assigns a utility of only 0.1 to "good sex, HIV," indicating that the decision maker views this outcome as being only slightly better than the worst outcome, "ok sex, HIV." Collectively, these utilities indicate that avoiding HIV infection in the future is much more important to the decision maker than having a pleasant sexual experience in the present with her new romantic partner.

On what basis can utility scores like these be assigned to potential decision outcomes? Decision theorists have developed a variety of methods for measuring decision makers' utilities for uncertain decision consequences. Some of these can be used by decision consultants (working as agents of the decision maker) or even by decision makers themselves if they wish to analyze their own decisions using the methods of decision analysis. In general, utility measurement pro-

---

[3]Expected utility theory models imply that utility can be measured on an "interval scale." Thus, the origin (zero point) and unit of measure are arbitrary. For instance, the best outcome frequently is assigned a utility of 1 instead of 100. All other utility values are simply rescaled proportionately. With an interval scale, only the relative distances between points matter.

cedures for risky decisions involve making comparisons between simple lotteries involving the consequences in question. A detailed discussion of these utility measurement procedures is beyond the scope of this chapter. (See Keeney & Raiffa, 1976, or von Winterfeldt & Edwards, 1986, for excellent descriptions.)

Expected Utility Theory. How *should* people make decisions involving uncertain consequences? This question has been investigated by economists, philosophers, psychologists, and statisticians for more than 200 years (e.g., Bernoulli, 1738). Theories regarding how people should make decisions are commonly referred to as *normative*—as contrasted with *behavioral* theories that describe actual decision-making behavior. The most widely accepted and applied normative theory is known as *expected utility theory*. This theory rests on a small set of fundamental principles of logic, rational inference, and rational choice. (For a psychologically oriented discussion of these principles, see von Winterfeldt & Edwards, 1986.)

Expected utility theory provides a simple rule for combining subjective probabilities and utilities to form an overall appraisal of the desirability of possible courses of action. The intuition behind this rule is that the more likely an outcome is to occur if a course of action is chosen, the more weight that outcome should receive in evaluating the course of action. In mathematical terms, the *expected utility*, EU, of the *i*-th course of action, A_i, is defined by the following equation:

$$EU(A_i) = \sum_{j=1}^{n} p_{ij}\, u(x_j). \tag{1}$$

Here, x_j is the *j*-th possible consequence, p_{ij} is the probability that consequence x_j will occur if action A_i is selected, and $u(x_j)$ is the utility of consequence x_j, which is defined by its value attributes. The expected utility of a course of action is a summary measure of its desirability in which the utility of each possible consequence is weighted by its probability of occurrence. According to expected utility theory, the decision maker should choose the course of action with the highest expected utility.

To illustrate, we return to our example of the woman deciding whether or not to have intercourse with her new lover. The value attributes of each decision consequence are to the immediate right of the triangular consequence nodes in the decision tree in Fig. 1.1. The utility score for each consequence is in the rightmost column. Expected utility calculations are shown at the bottom of the figure. These calculations show that *EU(no sex)* = 99.8, *EU(sex, condom)* = 99.9, and *EU(sex, no condom)* = 99.99. Thus, for the decision described in Fig. 1.1, the best course of action (from an expected utility standpoint) is to have sex without a condom, the next best is to have sex with a condom, and the worst is to abstain from sex.

In short, if having sex without condoms is perceived to be sufficiently more pleasurable than having sex with condoms, and if the perceived risk of acquiring HIV is sufficiently small, then a rational decision maker may decide that the pleasures of unprotected sex outweigh the risks. It is important to note that these conclusions depend on the specific assumptions of the model—that is, on the specific probability and utility values used. In decision theory, there is no universally correct decision for a particular situation. The best choice depends on one's assumptions about both the likelihoods of events and the utilities of consequences.

The differences between the expected utilities of the three courses of action in Fig. 1.1 appear to be very small. It may seem peculiar that all three actions have expected utility scores so close to 100, that of the best possible consequence. This happens in our example because the range of consequences is so extreme (i.e., from having pleasurable sex without negative side effects to contracting HIV). Further, the risk of acquiring HIV is very slight if one has beliefs similar to those of our hypothetical decision maker.[4] As a consequence, the expected utilities of all three options are very high. However, because the range of outcomes represented by the scale is so large, even small differences in EU are nontrivial. For example, a difference of 0.2 on the utility scale corresponds roughly to 1 chance in 500 of contracting HIV.

To see how changes in perceived risk affect decisions, imagine that the woman in our example believes that her prospective partner is from a high-risk population. As a result, she estimates that there is a 0.5 chance that her partner is infected with HIV. Making this one change in Fig. 1.1 leads to new expected utility scores of: *EU(no sex)* = 99.8, *EU(sex, condom)* = 99.4, and *EU(sex, no condom)* = 95.0. Now, abstaining from sex now has the highest expected utility, followed closely by having sex with a condom. Having sex without a condom is a distant third. (A 4.8 unit difference on our scale corresponds roughly to a 1 in 20 chance of contracting HIV.)

Decision Trees.   A *decision tree* is a graphical map of the courses of action, uncertain events, and consequences that comprise a decision. The decision tree in Fig. 1.1 displays the example we have been discussing in this chapter. It follows the standard decision theory notation: Squares denote decisions under the decision maker's control. Branches off a square denote possible courses of action. Circles denote uncertain events that are controlled by nature or by other people. Branches off a circle represent possible outcomes of this uncertain event. Triangles represent final consequences and their value attributes.

One important feature of the tree in Fig. 1.1 is that it is drawn *from the perspective of the decision maker,* not from that of an outside observer (see

---

[4]In fact, these beliefs are *pessimistic* when compared to scientific risk estimates reported by Hearst and Hulley (1988) and Gayle et al. (1990).

Clemen, 1991). That is, events and decisions are ordered, from left to right, in the sequence that information regarding these events and decisions is made known to the decision maker. This sequence need not coincide with the actual causal or temporal sequence in nature. For instance, the partner either is or is not infected at the time they have intercourse. But the decision maker is unlikely to learn conclusively about the partner's HIV status until much later, if ever. Thus, from the decision maker's perspective, the decision occurs before knowledge of the HIV status of the partner.

Decision trees are useful because they provide a compact graphical summary of the key elements of a decision. Many risky decisions are too complex to be easily understood if one relies on intuition alone. Thus, the graphical tree representation may be helpful to both decision analysts and decision makers as they grapple with the complexities of decisions. Decision trees have a second use in normative decision analysis. If drawn according to the rules described above, decision trees provide the basis for the "backwards induction algorithm," a mathematical procedure for selecting the decision strategy that has the highest expected utility (see Clemen, 1991).

Conclusion.   The normative decision analysis model is of interest for three reasons. First, it can be used as a *decision aid* for helping people to make better decisions. Keeney and Raiffa (1976) described a number of applications, including decisions regarding where to locate nuclear power plants and the Mexico City airport, rules for acquiring and disposing of blood at blood banks, and the management of patients with cleft palate syndromes. Decision analysis also could be used to help individuals make decisions like that in Fig. 1.1 or to assist policymakers confronted with risky decisions such as when to release new AIDS treatments for general use, whether to provide clean needles to addicts, what criteria to accept in screening public blood supplies, and what level of funding to provide for HIV research, treatment, and public information programs.

Second, the normative model is used as a *benchmark* for judging the quality of actual decision-making processes. Systematic deviations from the normative theory are referred to as *biases*. Later in this chapter, we use expected utility theory and probability theory as benchmarks for judging the rationality of decisions and inferences regarding the risks of acquiring HIV.

Third, the normative theory often is used as an *approximate descriptive theory,* good enough to make reasonable predictions in situations where one can assume that the average individual behaves in a rational fashion. This is the standard approach in economic analysis. In psychology, expectancy value models and the health beliefs model closely resemble expected utility theory. Even psychological alternatives to expected utility theory, such as Kahneman and Tversky's (1979, 1984) prospect theory, preserve some of the main features of the rational model.

How Can AIDS Decisions Go Wrong?

Expected utility theory provides a normative theory of how a rational individual would make decisions. In contrast, most behavioral decision research has focused on mapping out ways in which judgment and decision making depart from the normative model, and on searching for psychological explanations of these departures. Each logical requirement of the normative model provides an opportunity for the intuitive decision maker to go astray.

Incomplete or Inadequate Problem Representations.   Drawing a decision tree forces one to delineate the sequences of actions and events surrounding a decision. When people attempt to analyze decisions in their heads, problem representations and search patterns are necessarily fragmentary. Even the most skilled decision makers must limit their attention to a small subset of the possible sequences of actions and events (Newell & Simon, 1972). Later in this chapter we draw attention to one particularly damaging inadequacy in problem representations—a tendency to view risks in isolation from one another, rather than as part of a long sequence of very similar decisions. As a consequence, people fail to appreciate the cumulative risks of acquiring HIV from a series of actions (e.g., having unprotected intercourse with a low risk partner) each of which carries a very low risk of acquiring the disease.

Biased Evaluation of Decision Consequences.   Behavioral decision research has documented a wide array of systematic biases in how people evaluate decision consequences (Fischhoff, 1991; Fischhoff, Slovic, & Lichtenstein, 1980). One type drawing particular attention is referred to as *framing bias* (Kahneman & Tversky, 1984). A framing bias arises when two logically equivalent descriptions of a decision lead to systematic differences in people's evaluations of decision consequences. For example, the consequences of a policy decision could be described by the number of lives that will be saved by distributing clean needles to addicts or by the number of additional lives that will be lost if needles are not distributed. Although logically equivalent, these two ways of "framing" the decision consequences might lead to different evaluations. Later in this chapter we report an experiment asking subjects to evaluate condoms described either in terms of their success rate or failure rate in preventing the transmission of HIV. Success and failure rates are logically symmetric, but people do not treat them equivalently.

Biased Predictive Judgments and Subjective Probabilities.   Prior decision research had documented a wide array of biases in people's processing of information about uncertain events (Kahneman et al., 1982). Many biases can be traced to the use of heuristic judgment strategies that often give good results but that are subject to systematic bias. For example, people tend to overestimate the likelihood of highly visible risks (e.g., murder and car accidents), but to underestimate the likelihood of infrequently mentioned risks (e.g., suicide) (Slovic, et al., 1982). Both biases can be attributed to use of the *availability heuristic* (Tversky & Kahneman, 1973). With this strategy, events are judged to be likely (or frequent) to the extent that instances of the event are easy to recall from memory. This is a reasonable heuristic, because ease of recall is related to past frequency of occurrence. It can lead to systematic errors, however, when one is exposed to a biased sample of exemplars (e.g., more exemplars of murder than suicide) and when memory is affected by factors other than frequency of occurrence (e.g., recency). Media bias is one likely source of availability bias in judgment. For example, much has been written about both over- and underreporting of different parts of the AIDS story in the media (Shilts, 1987).

Because uncertainty plays such a key role in AIDS decision making, probability biases can have a particularly harmful impact. In this chapter, we report our own findings on two other types of probability biases that may affect HIV risk perceptions and decision making. The first is the *optimism bias,* involving the tendency to underestimate one's own level of risk. The second, which we call the *underaccumulation bias,* involves a failure to appreciate how one's cumulative level of risk grows through repeated exposures to a risk. Both biases could encourage excessive risk taking.

EMPIRICAL EVIDENCE OF JUDGMENTAL BIAS IN AIDS DECISIONS AND RISK PERCEPTIONS

The judgmental biases discussed in previous sections could distort HIV risk perceptions and lead to poor decision making. This section presents the results of several studies of college students' perceptions of the probability that they and others will acquire the HIV infection. These studies focused on three cognitive biases discussed earlier: underaccumulation of perceived risk, success versus failure rate framing bias, and excessive optimism regarding one's own level of risk.

Cumulative HIV Risk Bias

Objectively speaking, the risk of acquiring HIV in a single sexual encounter is quite small, especially if one's partner is not from a high-risk group. However, the risk of HIV infection accumulates over repeated exposures (e.g., through sex, contaminated blood) (Fineberg, 1988). Therefore, an understanding of how risk accumulates is essential to understanding one's risk of contracting HIV and to effective decision making.

Research in other contexts shows that people have difficulty judging rates of accumulation, typically underestimating how quickly risks mount up (Bar-Hillel,

1973; Ronen, 1973). For example, people fail to realize the extent to which the cumulative risk of being in a serious car accident over one's life is quite large, even though the risk on any given car trip is extremely small (Schwalm & Slovic, 1982; Slovic, Fischhoff, & Lichtenstein, 1978). Similarly, people underestimate the cumulative risk of contraceptive failure (Shaklee & Fischhoff, 1990).

Difficulties in understanding how risk accumulates can clearly lead to poor decisions. It also complicates the task of those seeking to develop effective risk communication programs. The most general way of providing AIDS risk information is in terms of the probability of HIV transmission from single exposures of various types. Doing so allows individuals to calculate the risk associated with their own exposure patterns. This communication strategy fails, however, if people fail to consider their multiple exposure risk, or if they accumulate risk inaccurately.

In order to investigate this possibility, we asked subjects to estimate the probability of acquiring HIV from an infected heterosexual partner in different numbers of sexual encounters with the same partner (Linville, Fischhoff, & Fischer, 1992). For example: "If a female student has sexual intercourse 10 times—using a condom—with a male who is infected with the AIDS virus, what is the probability that she will contract the AIDS virus?" Twelve versions of this question were created, factorially varying: the number of encounters (1, 10, and 100), whether a condom was used, and the gender of the partners. Each subject responded to all 12 versions using a quantitative probability scale. We examined these responses in terms of (a) the internal consistency of subjects' estimates for different numbers of encounters, and (b) their accuracy relative to public health estimates of risk.

Internal Consistency of Cumulative HIV Risk Estimates

How *should* one estimate the cumulative risk of having repeated sexual encounters with an HIV-infected partner? For example, if one believes that the risk in a single encounter is 10%, what is the risk associated with 10 or 100 encounters with the same partner? If one assumes the probability of acquiring HIV is constant and independent across repeated encounters (with a given partner), then the cumulative risk can be calculated using a binomial probability model.[5] This model has been used by Fineberg (1988) and others in widely reported analyses of decisions regarding AIDS risk.

Perceived Risk of HIV Infection From Single and Multiple Encounters. Based on each subject's own estimate of the risk associated with a single sexual

---

[5]If p is the probability of acquiring HIV in a single encounter, then the probability that one *will not* acquire HIV in n encounters is $(1 - p)^n$. Thus, the probability that one *will* acquire HIV is $1 - (1 - p)^n$.

encounter with an HIV-infected partner, we used the binomial model to project the risk that would arise from 10 and 100 encounters. We then compared subjects' direct estimates of multiple-exposure risks with these binomial model estimates. We repeated this analysis for each subject's estimates of male-to-female transmission without a condom, male-to-female transmission with a condom, female-to-male transmission without a condom, and female-to-male transmission with a condom. (See Linville et al., 1992, for additional details.) Table 1.1 contrasts our subjects' direct cumulative risk estimates with the model-based risk estimates.

In all four cases, subjects' risk estimates for 10 and 100 encounters were much too small, considering their own single-encounter risk estimates. For example, subjects' median estimate of the probability that a woman will contract HIV as a result of having intercourse with an infected male partner *once with* a condom was 5%. For 10 encounters, the model-predicted risk is 40.1%, compared with our subjects' median estimate of only 10%. After 100 encounters, the model-predicted risk is 99.4%, compared with our subjects' median estimate of only 20%. Both biases were highly statistically significant. Risk estimates for sex *without* a condom were also significantly biased. There were no gender differences in the degree of bias.

The magnitude of the bias is graphically illustrated in Fig. 1.2. The top panel plots median subject estimates and model predictions for male-to-female transmission without a condom; the bottom panel displays results for male-to-female transmission with a condom. (The female-to-male data followed a very similar pattern.) Although multiple-exposure risk estimates were significantly too small for both sex with and without a condom, the bias is much larger when a condom is used, a difference that was highly statistically significant.

Thus, our experiment produced two noteworthy findings. First, subjects substantially underaccumulate the risk of having repeated sexual encounters with an

TABLE 1.1
Cumulative Judged Risk of HIV Transmission
(Median Percentage Chance of Contracting HIV)

Number of Exposures	With Condom		Without Condom	
	Male-to-Female	Female-to-Male	Male-to-Female	Female-to-Male
1	5%	2%	50%	35%
10	10 (40.1)	5 (18.3)	90 (99.9)	65 (98.7)
100	20 (99.4)	10 (86.7)	99 (100)	90 (100)

Note. Numbers in parentheses are multiple-exposure estimates extrapolated from subjects' median single-encounter estimates, using a binomial model. Each table entry is the median percentage chance of contracting HIV. "Male-to-Female" refers to the chance that a female will acquire HIV from an infected male partner; "Female-to-Male" refers to the chance that a male will acquire HIV from an infected female partner. From Linville et al. (1992).

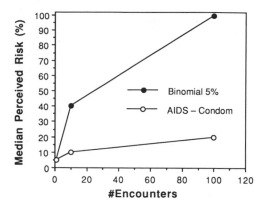

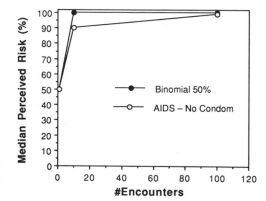

FIG. 1.2. Cumulative HIV risk judgments (source: Linville et al., 1992).

HIV-infected partner. Second, although this bias arose both for sex with and without condoms, it was much larger in the case of sex with a condom.

Why is the underaccumulation bias larger in the case where a condom is used? One hypothesis is that people believe that the risk of failure for condoms—and perhaps other protective technologies—is only weakly related (or even unrelated) to time or number of exposures. In keeping with this *protective technologies hypothesis,* 18% of our subjects assigned the same risk estimate for 1, 10, and 100 sexual exposures using a condom, saying, in effect, "There's some chance that condoms won't work for a set of sexual partners. However, if they do work once, then they will work indefinitely." By contrast, only 4.5% of our subjects gave the same risk estimates for 1, 10, and 100 encounters without a condom. A second interpretation of our results is that because single-encounter risk estimates were much greater in the no-condom condition, there was less opportunity to underaccumulate in this condition (because probability asymptotes at 1.0).

To distinguish between these interpretations, we conducted a second experiment concerning a hypothetical disease that we called KPA (Linville et al., 1992). In this experiment we created two no-condom conditions—one in which the single-encounter risk was 5% and the other in which it was 50%, thus matching the median condom and no condom single-encounter risk levels for the AIDS study. The results for the KPA-50% risk condition did not differ from those we obtained for the AIDS-no condom condition in the previous experiment. So AIDS per se seems not to be a critical factor. However, results for the KPA-5% risk condition differed strikingly from those in the AIDS-condom condition. The KPA-5% judgments displayed much *less underaccumulation* bias. Thus, low risk level per se cannot account for the extreme underaccumulation in the AIDS-condom condition. The only unique feature of the AIDS-condom condition (where extreme underaccumulation arises) is that it involves condom use. These results are consistent with the protective technologies hypothesis.

They also suggest an interesting and unanticipated problem: People may overestimate the long-run protection provided by condoms and other protective technologies. Too much faith in protective technologies can be as dangerous as too little if it leads people to expose themselves to higher risk levels out of a mistaken belief that they have more protection than they really do.

Comparison With Public Health Statistical Risk Estimates

The analysis just cited revealed that cumulative risk estimates are seriously biased in an internal consistency sense. A second interest is their *objective accuracy,* or the extent to which peoples' estimates correspond to public health data.

Single-Encounter Risk.   How accurate were subjects' estimates of a single-encounter risk with an HIV-infected partner? Using data from heterosexual couples with an HIV-infected male, public health statisticians have estimated that a woman's risk of HIV infection from having intercourse once with an infected male partner, not using a condom, is about 1 in 500 (0.2%) (Hearst & Hulley, 1988). As shown in Table 1.1, our subjects estimated this risk to be 50% for women, 35% for men.

A similar overestimation bias occurred for intercourse with a condom. Statistical estimates of the risk of HIV infection from having sex once with an HIV-infected partner, while using a condom, are on the order of 1 in 5,000 (0.02%) (Hearst & Hulley, 1988). As shown in Table 1.1, our subjects estimated this risk to be 5% for females, 2% for males.

Multiple-Encounter Risk.   How accurate were subjects' estimates of the multiple-encounter risks with an HIV-infected partner? To estimate the actual risk associated with 10 and 100 encounters with an HIV-infected partner, we applied our binomial model to Hearst and Hulley's (1988) single-encounter risk estimates. Compared with this model, our subjects greatly *overestimated* the risk of HIV transmission from 10 and 100 encounters. In the no-condom condition, subjects overestimated the 10-encounter risk by a factor of 45 (90% vs. 2%) and in the 100-encounter risk by a factor of 5 (99% vs. 18%). For the condom condition, subjects overestimated the 10-encounter risk by a factor of 50 (10% vs. 0.2%) and the 100-encounter risk by a factor of 10 (20% vs. 2%).

In short, comparison with current scientific risk estimates indicates that our subjects substantially *overestimated* the risk of HIV transmission in 1, 10, and 100 encounters with an HIV-infected partner. The bias was greater for 1 encounter than for 10 and 100 encounters, but it was substantial in all cases. It was present for both condom and no-condom risk estimates.

Condom Effectiveness.   Median single-exposure risk estimates of male-to-female transmission were 50% without a condom, 5% with a condom, implying that condoms reduce the risk of transmission by 90%. This matches the assumption used in many public health studies (Fineberg, 1988; Hearst & Hulley, 1988).

Conclusions and Implications for Risk Communication

These studies reveal two contrary biases. On the one hand, people underestimate the rate at which risks accumulate, producing multiple-episode risk estimates that are much too small relative to single-episode estimates. This underaccumulation bias is particularly pronounced when condoms are used as a protective technology. On the other hand, people greatly overestimate the single-encounter risk, relative to public health statistics. Although both biases are large, the second is so much larger that subjects' cumulative risk estimates exceed current scientific estimates.

These findings have five important implications for how risk estimates are gathered, interpreted, and communicated:

1. *Giving people better information about the single-exposure risk of HIV sexual transmission may undermine efforts to control the spread of the disease.* Most students in our studies greatly overestimated the risk of acquiring HIV from an infected partner. Although spreading the message that "AIDS is less contagious than you think" might reduce needless worry, it could also encourage more high-risk behavior. This raises the difficult ethical issue of whether consumers have the right to accurate risk information even if they may not use it appropriately.

2. *Risk communicators cannot simply give people single-encounter risk information,* then assume that they will draw the correct inferences. People are likely to underestimate the cumulative risks that they confront, leading

to excessively risky behavior. Consider, for example, the effect of informing people about Hearst and Hulley's (1988) estimate that there is only 1 chance in 500 of acquiring HIV in one encounter of unprotected sex with an infected partner. Many individuals might feel that 1 in 500 is a very small risk, and thus engage in unprotected sex with high-risk partners. In the long-run, however, the cumulative risk associated with engaging in unprotected sex can be very substantial if one has repeated sex with multiple partners from a high-risk population.

3. *It may be necessary to give people cumulative risk information,* for example, by giving 1-year, 5-year, or 10-year risk estimates. The difficulty with this approach is that it is hard to produce cumulative risk estimates appropriate to recipients' varied patterns of exposure (e.g., varied number of sexual encounters, degree of protection, partners from different risk groups). Individual counseling, similar to that provided by family planning services, might be needed to provide cumulative risk information that is tailored to the behavioral patterns of specific individuals.

4. *People will overestimate the efficacy of condoms and other protective technologies.* We found particularly great underaccumulation of risk when a protective technology was used. Overconfidence in a protective technology is dangerous if it leads one to engage in risky behaviors that one would otherwise avoid.

5. *One cannot infer people's perceptions of multiple-exposure risks from their estimates of single-exposure risks (or vice versa).* Investigators must either ask explicitly for risks of varying exposures or use results like the present ones to extrapolate from one exposure to another.

Condom Framing Bias

It is a basic tenet of rational theories of decision making that logically equivalent descriptions of a decision problem should lead to the same choices. Various investigators have demonstrated, however, that actual behavior sometimes violates this principle (Fischhoff et al., 1980; Hogarth, 1982; Tversky & Kahneman, 1981; Tversky, Sattath, & Slovic, 1988). Such violations complicate measuring people's preferences because the choices made with one description (or "framing") of a problem may not predict the choices made with a different (but formally equivalent) description. For the risk communicator, these violations may mean that it is possible to manipulate people's choices by selecting problem descriptions that favor particular alternatives.

One important class of violations arises from changing from a positive description of outcome possibilities to a logically equivalent negative description (Kahneman & Tversky, 1984; McNeil, Paulker, Sox, & Tversky, 1982). For example, actions are more attractive when described in terms of probability of success rather than in terms of probability of failure. In the case of AIDS decisions, this general tendency suggests that protective strategies such as condoms are more likely to be adopted when described in terms of their success rate rather than their (complementary) failure rate. To test this hypothesis, one group of subjects received the following "success frame":

> Suppose that a type of condom has a 90% success rate. That is, if you have sexual intercourse with someone who has the AIDS virus, there is a 90% chance that this type of condom will prevent you from being exposed to the AIDS virus.
>
> Should the government allow this type of condom to be advertised as "an effective method for reducing the risk of AIDS"? Yes [ ]   No[ ]
>
> Would you use this type of condom or encourage your partner to use it? Yes[ ]   No[ ]

Among these subjects, 86% approved advertising the method as effective, whereas 85% indicated a willingness to use it. A second group of students considered "a type of condom [that] has a 10% failure rate." This logically equivalent "failure frame" evoked a significantly lower approval rate (61%) and reported willingness to use the condom (63%).

Table 1.2 summarizes these responses, along with the analogous results obtained with additional groups receiving success rates of 95% or 99%, or the complementary failure rates of 5% or 1%. Although the magnitude of these effects varies, the general pattern is constant. Describing condoms in terms of their success rate led them to be judged more positively.

In light of these results, risk communications hoping to promote "safer sex" should describe practices like condom use in terms of their successes. A more balanced approach would present both success and failure rates, then let recipients weigh the two perspectives.

Comparative Versus Absolute Optimism Bias

Weinstein (1980, 1984) and others found that most people believe that they are less vulnerable than average to a wide range of health and safety risks (much as the inhabitants of Lake Wobegon believe that all of their children are "above average"). Of course, it is impossible for a majority of individuals to fall below the median of a population. Thus, the tendency for a majority of subjects to perceive themselves to be less at risk than average has come to be known as the *optimism bias*.[6] This definition of the optimism bias is *comparative* in nature.

---

[6]Strictly speaking, a majority cannot be at less risk than the median of the population. A majority could be at less risk than the population mean if the distribution of risks is skewed with some individuals facing extremely high levels of risk. This is likely to be the case for HIV.

TABLE 1.2
Framing Effect in AIDS Risk Communication

Should the government allow this type of condom to be advertised an "an effective method for reducing the risk of AIDS"?

Condom Effectiveness	% Yes	% No	
90% success rate	86%	14%	***
10% failure rate	61%	39%	
95% success rate	88%	12%	****
5% failure rate	42%	58%	
99% success rate	93%	7%	**
1% failure rate	71%	29%	

Would you use this type of condom or encourage your partner to use it?

90% success rate	85%	15%	**
10% failure rate	63%	37%	
95% success rate	95%	5%	*
5% failure rate	81%	19%	
99% success rate	95%	5%	
1% failure rate	92%	8%	

$*p < .05; **p < .005; ***p < .001; ****p < .0001.$
Source: Linville et al. (1992).

That is, *judgments of risk to self are compared with judgments of risk to others,* for instance, by judging how much higher/lower one's own risk is than that of the average person (Weinstein, 1980), by placing oneself in a percentile range relative to others (Weinstein, 1984), or by judging one's own risk to be lower than that of the "average person" when making separate judgments about the self and the "average person" (Weinstein, 1984).[7] For example, a great majority of people perceive themselves to be more skillful than the average driver (Naatanen & Summala, 1975; Svenson, 1981), and to be less likely than average to experience a variety of health and safety problems (Weinstein 1980, 1984), or to be harmed by various consumer products (Rethans, 1979).

Interestingly, however, in everyday usage, the word "optimism" usually has an absolute connotation—namely, that *when expectations are compared with actual outcomes,* one overestimates the likelihood that good things will happen and underestimates the likelihood that bad things will happen. To determine whether people are optimistic in this absolute sense, one can compare judgments

---

[7]Weinstein (1984) called the third type of test "absolute" because subjects made separate risk estimates for self and others. The test is still comparative, however, in that it involves comparing risk to self with risk to others.

of how likely events are with relative frequency data concerning how often these events actually occur. In the context of threats to health and safety, an *absolute optimism bias* implies that *judgments of personal risk will be lower, on the average, than actual rates of occurrence for the population in question*. In our recent work on HIV risk perceptions, we used quantitative risk assessment procedures that permitted both comparative and absolute tests of the optimism bias (Linville et al., 1992). The next two sections report our findings.

Comparative Optimism Bias: Judged Risk to Self, Friends, and Average Student

To see whether HIV risk perceptions display the traditional comparative optimism bias, we asked 135 students at the University of New Haven to complete the Risk Assessment Questionnaire displayed in Table 1.3. Subjects estimated the probability that they would be victims of seven threats to health and safety sometime in the next 3 years. The list included the AIDS virus[8] from sexual sources and the AIDS·virus from nonsexual sources. The page following the Risk Assessment Questionnaire asked subjects to estimate: (a) the probability that "the average student of your gender and sexual orientation will get the AIDS virus—as a result of sexual activity—during the next 3 years", and (b) the probability that "the average college student in your circle of friends of your same gender and sexual orientation will get the AIDS virus—as a result of sexual activity—during the next 3 years." (We discuss this questionnaire in greater detail later in this chapter.)

As one would expect, the distributions of responses to our Risk Assessment Questionnaire were quite skewed.[9] In order to reduce the influence of extreme outliers, we used medians rather than means to measure central tendency. Comparison of subjects' judgments of risk to self, friends, and the average student revealed a strong comparative optimism bias. Subjects judged that the average student had a 10% chance of acquiring HIV infection sexually, that their friends had a 3% chance, and that they themselves faced only a 0.1% risk. Each of these differences was highly statistically significant. Only 4.4% of the subjects viewed themselves as having a higher risk than the average student, whereas 78.5% saw themselves as having less risk. In short, our subjects saw themselves as facing much less than the average risk of HIV infection, and even extended some of that optimism to their friends.

---

[8]In our studies, we used the term *AIDS virus* because subjects might not be familiar with the term *HIV*.

[9]For low probability events, like contracting HIV, response distributions were concentrated on the low probability end, with a long tail to the right with a few individuals who perceived themselves to be at much higher risk.

TABLE 1.3
Risk Assessment Scale

In the following questions, we ask you to estimate your risk from a variety of sources, such as your chances of being electrocuted. For each, we'd like you to give us the probability of experiencing that risk *in the next 3 years.* Use a number from 0% (meaning that there is no chance at all of that happening to you) to 100% (meaning that it is certain to happen).

If you think that your chances of being electrocuted are between 1% and 100%, then give a whole percent. For example:

1%   5%   10%   20%   30%   40%   50%   60%   70%   80%   90%   95%   99%

If you think that your chances of being electrocuted are less than 1% (but at least 1 in 1000), then give one of the following:

.1% (or 1 in 1000)   .6% (or 6 in 1000)
.2% (or 2 in 1000)   .7% (or 7 in 1000)
.3% (or 3 in 1000)   .8% (or 8 in 1000)
.4% (or 4 in 1000)   .9% (or 9 in 1000)
.5% (or 5 in 1000)   1.0% (or 10 in 1000)

If you think that your chances of being electrocuted are still smaller (less than 1 in 1000), then give one of the following:

.01% (or 1 in 10,000)   .06% (or 6 in 10,000)
.02% (or 2 in 10,000)   .07% (or 7 in 10,000)
.03% (or 3 in 10,000)   .08% (or 8 in 10,000)
.04% (or 4 in 10,000)   .09% (or 9 in 10,000)
.05% (or 5 in 10,000)   .10% (or 10 in 10,000)

Please estimate your personal risk for the following events *in the next 3 years* by giving a percent:

___% What is the probability that you will get *electrocuted,* during the next 3 years?
___% What is the probability that you will get *cancer,* during the next 3 years?
___% What is the probability that you will get the *flu* at least once, during the next 3 years?
___% What is the probability that you will be *injured in a car accident,* during the next 3 years?
___% What is the probability that you will suffer from *genital herpes,* during the next 3 years?
___% What is the probability that you will be infected with *the AIDS virus—as the result of sexual activity,* during the next 3 years?
___% What is the probability that you will be infected with *the AIDS virus--from sources other than sexual activity,* during the next 3 years?

Source: Linville et al. (1992).

Absolute Optimism Bias: Comparison With Public Health Statistics

In testing for the presence of optimism bias in the absolute sense, we compared our subjects' judgments of personal risk with relative frequency data regarding actual risk based on public health estimates. Four samples of students completed the Risk Assessment Questionnaire: 95 from Yale University, 138 from Yale University, 135 from the University of New Haven, and 68 from Carnegie Mellon University. These three institutions draw from different populations of students. For instance, reported average SAT scores are 1,380 for Yale students, 1,202 for Carnegie Mellon students, and 1,066 for the University of New Haven students. Median risk estimates for the four samples of subjects are

TABLE 1.4
Median Responses to Risk Questions
("Please estimate your personal risk to the following events in the next 3 years.")

Risk	Study 1 (n = 95)	Study 2 (n = 138)	Study 3 (n = 135)	Study 4 (n = 68)	Scientific Risk Estimate
Electrocution	0.1	0.1	1.0	0.1	0.015
Cancer	1.0	1.0	0.7	0.3	0.06
Flu	50.0	70.0	40.0	55.0	86.2
Car injury	10.0	20.0	20.0	10.0	4.7
Herpes	0.1	1.0	1.0	0.1	4.1
AIDS virus/sexual	0.10	0.10	0.10	0.02	0.2[a]
AIDS virus/other	0.05	0.09	0.01	0.01	_[a]

Note. Subjects responded on the percent scale of Table 1.3 (e.g., 0.1% = 1 chance in 1000).
[a]The combined risk of HIV infection, from all sources, for college students is 0.2%.
From Linville et al. (1992).

displayed in Table 1.4. The rightmost column of this table presents an objective risk estimate based on public health data for people of roughly the same age as our subjects.[10]

HIV Risk Estimates.   The best available evidence regarding rates of HIV infection among U.S. college students is provided by a recent study involving HIV antibody testing performed on blood samples drawn at 19 college health clinics (Gayle et al., 1990). In this study, the overall rate of infection was 2 per 1,000 in a sample of 16,861 blood tests collected from 19 campuses. This 0.2% rate of HIV infection is cumulative of course—reflecting all those infected at any time during their lives. However, most are likely to have been infected after leaving home, so this rate provides a reasonable basis for estimating the 3-year risk confronting our college subjects.

Our subjects' median estimate of the probability of acquiring HIV sexually during the next 3 years was 0.1% for three of our four samples, and 0.02% for the fourth. Subjects believed that their risk of acquiring HIV nonsexually was smaller than their risk of acquiring it sexually, with sample medians ranging from 0.01% to 0.9% (see Table 1.4). The Gayle et al. (1990) blood sample data capture HIV infection rates from all sources. Summing our subjects' median risk estimates for sexually and nonsexually transmitted HIV in each of the four samples, we obtain total HIV risk estimates of 0.11%, 0.15%, 0.19%, and 0.03%. These are remarkably close to the 0.2% HIV infection rate found by Gayle et al. If there is an absolute optimism bias here, it is very small.

Two biases may be present in the absolute risk perceptions, however. First,

---

[10]Such a comparison is imperfect because published public health statistics are for broad categories of people. The public health statistics used in this article have been chosen to match the age range of our respondents as closely as possible.

Gayle et al. found a large difference in levels of HIV infection for males (0.5%) and females (0.02%). In our studies of perceived HIV risk, however, there were no significant differences between male and female responses. Thus, our male subjects probably were optimistic about their chances of acquiring HIV infection, whereas female subjects probably were pessimistic.

Second, subjects probably overestimated their risk of acquiring HIV nonsexually. Very few of our subjects reported being IV drug users and none reported being hemophiliacs. If they answered truthfully, their main source of HIV risk was sexual activity. Thus, although risk estimates for sexually transmitted HIV were greater than those for nonsexually transmitted HIV, the difference was probably too small.

In summary, these data suggest that subjects generally were in the right ballpark regarding their own risk of HIV infection. Thus, the optimism bias that we found for comparative HIV estimates seems to result from overestimating the risks of others rather than from underestimating the risk to oneself.   Subjects were not optimistic regarding the HIV risk they faced, they were pessimistic about the HIV risk confronted by their friends and the average student.

Other Risk Estimates.   The data in Table 1.4 present a mixed picture for the five other sources of risk included in the Risk Assessment Questionnaire (Table 1.3). Subjects' risk estimates were generally reasonable when compared to public health statistics, with no evidence of a systematic optimism (or pessimism) bias.

The greatest absolute underestimation was for the flu (see Table 1.4). For those aged 18 to 24, the chance of contracting the flu over a 3-year period is roughly 86.2% (Centers for Disease Control, 1990). Subjects' median 3-year risk estimates ranged from 40% to 70%, across the four samples, representing a modest underestimation. These estimates are in the right ballpark in order of magnitude terms, but appear too small in absolute terms. Subjects also displayed an apparent optimism bias regarding their chances of contracting genital herpes. The 3-year risk of contracting herpes is roughly 4.1% for those ages 20–24 (Centers for Disease Control, personal communication, 1991).[11] Our students' estimates of their risk of contracting genital herpes were much lower, with median estimates ranging from 0.01% to 0.1% across our four samples.

For three other risks—cancer, electrocution, and car injury—subjects' risk estimates were quite pessimistic. For cancer, the 3-year risk is only 0.06% for those ages 18–21 (Ries, Hankey, & Edwards, 1988). Our subjects estimated their

---

[11]Data for first doctor visits with initial cases of herpes among women ages 20–24 (age-adjusted data was available only for women) indicate that 4.1% will be treated for a first infection in a 3-year period—and the actual rate of infection may be higher because many are unaware that they are infected and do not seek treatment. Comparable data are not available for men. It is unlikely that they face a lower risk, however, because males generally display higher rates of sexually transmitted disease.

risk to be higher, with median estimates ranging from 0.3% to 1.0% across the four samples. For electrocution, the 3-year risk is only 0.015% for those ages 20–24 (National Center for Health Statistics, 1990). Our subjects' median estimates ranged from 0.1% to 1.0%. For car injury, the 3-year risk is only 4.7% for drivers ages 15–24 (National Safety Council, 1990). Our subjects again overestimated their risk, with median estimates ranging from 10% to 20%. Both cancer and car injury are frequently and vividly portrayed in news and film, suggesting that the availability heuristic (Tversky & Kahneman, 1973) may have elevated these perceived risks.

Perceived Risk and Worry

Is optimism (or pessimism) in risk estimates related to how much people worry about those risks? To address this question, we asked 135 subjects at the University of New Haven to rate the extent to which "any worries or any distressing or distracting thoughts" about each of seven risks "popped into your mind" during the past month (Linville et al., 1992). Their perceived risk of HIV infection was significantly related to their reported worrying about getting the infection. The correlation was .29 for sexually transmitted HIV and .28 for nonsexually transmitted HIV. We found similar modest but significant correlations for each of the other risks, ranging from .18 for the flu to .48 for cancer.

Across the seven risks, students worried most about car injury and flu, presumably because these risks had the highest estimated probability. Sexually transmitted HIV was third highest on the list of worries, despite having a very low perceived likelihood. Students worried about sexually transmitted HIV infection only slightly less than they did about a car injury and getting the flu, risks they judged to be 100 to 500 times more likely than sexually transmitted HIV. Also, students worried significantly more about sexually transmitted HIV than about other potentially fatal risks like cancer and electrocution, even though they believed HIV infection to be less likely to occur. Thus, AIDS seems to be a special source of worry among our subjects.

Discussion

Our examination of accuracy, optimism, and worry has produced three main findings. First, in a comparative sense, subjects were optimistic about their chances of acquiring HIV. They believed that they were much less at risk than either their friends or the average student, replicating past demonstrations of the comparative optimism bias (see also van der Pligt & van der Velde, in this volume). Second, in an absolute sense, however, subjects' estimates of their personal risk of acquiring HIV were remarkably close to public health statistics. Examination of the five other risks revealed no systematic tendency toward either optimism or pessimism. Finally, AIDS seems to be a special worry among students, despite their assigning a higher probability to other potentially fatal risks.

The notion that people are optimistic about health risks is now almost a truism. Our own data regarding comparative risk estimates provide additional evidence for that kind of optimism bias. However, in an absolute sense, most of our subjects' median estimates were in the right ballpark in order of magnitude, showing no systematic optimism bias. Our pattern of results in which people are systematically optimistic about HIV in a comparative sense, but not in an absolute sense, has implications for risk communication. For example, the comparative optimism bias could complicate risk communication if recipients perceived messages as applying to others, who are perceived to be more at risk, but not to themselves. Risk communicators may need to devise strategies for making risk messages feel personally relevant to the recipients.

MEASURING THE PERCEIVED RISK OF AIDS

The Centers for Disease Control, among others, have attempted to measure public perceptions of AIDS risk, both overall and in conjunction with specific behavior or events (e.g., receiving a blood transfusion, being bitten by a mosquito). Accurately monitoring the public's risk perceptions and knowledge about AIDS can guide our public policies, our risk communications, and our understanding of the factors that influence whether people engage in health damaging and protective behaviors.

Measuring AIDS risk perceptions is complicated by the fact that they vary widely—the probability of acquiring HIV from a single encounter of protected sex with a partner from a low-risk group may be only 1 in 5 million (Hearst & Hulley, 1988); whereas the cumulative risks of repeated unprotected intercourse with multiple partners from a high-risk population may be close to 100% (e.g., Fineberg, 1988). With risks ranging from near certainty to one chance in several million, a measurement procedure must permit respondents to make distinctions among a wide range of probability levels.

A Quantitative, Hierarchical-Risk Assessment Scale

To address this challenge, we developed a quantitative, hierarchically structured risk-assessment scale (Linville, et al., 1992). The scale is structured in two levels (see Table 1.3), directing subjects' attention first to a general order-of-magnitude location or ballpark of responses (1% to 100%, less than 1%, or less than .10%), then followed by more precise estimates. For small probabilities, we included a percentage as well as an "X chances in Y" format (e.g., "0.5% or 5 in 1,000") because some people experience difficulty in thinking about fractions of a percent.

Using a quantitative scale with a probability metric makes it possible to compare subjects' judgments with statistical estimates of risk. Using a hierarchical structure decomposes the task for subjects, reducing their cognitive load and making it possible to measure both large and very small probabilities on the same scale.

Subjects used this scale to judge the probability that they would experience each of seven health-related risks (listed in Table 1.3) sometime during the next 3 years.[12] The risks included contracting "the AIDS virus as the result of sexual activity" and "the AIDS virus from sources other than sexual activity" (see footnote 8). Table 1.4 summarizes the median risk judgments of our four samples of undergraduate subjects. We discussed our subject populations and a number of aspects of these results earlier in our discussions of accuracy, optimism, and worry. In this section, we focus on results that bear more directly on risk measurement methods per se.

Replicability of Risk Estimates

Because college students in general are relatively homogeneous, one would expect to observe a high degree of similarity in risk estimates across the four samples—especially, between Samples 1 and 2, both comprised of Yale students. As can be seen in Table 1.4, both the relative and absolute evaluations of risks were very similar across the four samples. Flu and car accident injuries were consistently judged to be most likely, whereas HIV infection from sexual and nonsexual causes were consistently judged to be the least likely.[13] Each group assigned a large probability to the risk of being injured in a car accident, but a very small probability to the risk of contracting genital herpes. For the risk of acquiring HIV sexually, the median risk estimate was the same in three experiments (0.1%) and slightly lower in the fourth (0.02%). This replicability lends credibility to the quantitative method.

Sensitivity to Known Risk Factors

Perceived HIV Risk and Sexual Activity.   If perceived risk is positively correlated with scientifically established risk factors, this would suggest that people possess relevant knowledge and can express it effectively using the scale. To examine the relationship between sexual activity and estimates of one's own HIV risk, we asked the University of New Haven sample (all males) to answer a series of questions regarding their sexual behavior (Linville et al., 1992). Subjects' estimates of their risk of acquiring HIV sexually in the next 3 years were significantly positively correlated with the following measures: (a) having had unprotected sex with someone at risk of HIV infection during the last 10 years, (b) the number of episodes of intercourse without a condom during the last 3 months, (c) the number of episodes of sexual intercourse during the past 3 months, (d) the

---

[12]Because most of our subjects were college freshmen or sophomores, 3 years is a natural time horizon. It corresponds roughly to the remaining years of their college experience.

[13]In some studies, these risks were tied with other risks at the top or bottom of the ranking.

number of expected episodes of intercourse with each partner in the next 3 years, and (e) the percentage of partners in the next 3 years expected to be HIV infected. Correlations were nonsignificant for number of sexual partners in the last 3 months and the percentage of time one used a condom during the last 3 months. Also, simply knowing someone with AIDS did not influence perceived risk of acquiring the virus.

Finally, it is noteworthy that no measure of sexual activity was significantly correlated with risk estimates of acquiring HIV from nonsexual sources. Thus, the positive correlations between sexual activity and risk estimates of acquiring HIV sexually cannot be attributed to a tendency of sexually active subjects to see themselves as more vulnerable to risks in general.

On balance, these correlations indicate both that subjects realized that risky sexual practices increase the risk of HIV infection and that our hierarchical risk-assessment scale captures subjects' beliefs.

Perceived Risk of HIV and Herpes.   Because both herpes and HIV infections are transmitted through sexual intercourse, risk estimates for the two diseases should be positively correlated. We found strong support for this prediction, with correlations ranging from 0.46 to 0.90 across the four experiments.

Conclusion

Several converging pieces of evidence lend credibility to this measurement instrument. First, four groups of subjects at three universities experienced little difficulty in using the scale. Second, subjects used the scale in a highly discriminating fashion, producing both very large (e.g., between 10% and 99% for risks such as contracting the flu or being injured in a car accident) and very small (between 0.01% and 0.1% for risks such as being electrocuted or contracting HIV infection) median probabilities. Third, the replicability of risk estimates across four samples of subjects (facing similar levels of risk) indicates its reliability. Finally, the positive correlations between well-known risk factors and judgments of personal HIV risk suggests that subjects were able to express their knowledge of the determinants of AIDS risk when using the scale.

Despite these favorable results, our findings also suggest minor changes in our scale. First, where very low probability events such as HIV are concerned, we suggest including even lower probability response options between 0% and 0.01%. Second, a few subjects wanted to know whether electrocution means severe electrical shock or death from electrical shock. If this item is included in future work, we suggest calling it "death from electrical shock." Finally, our findings regarding risk accumulation also raise an interesting question: What is the proper time frame for risk assessment? Where very small risks are involved, longer time periods (1 year, 3 years, 10 years) seem natural. But longer periods involve cumulating many small risks. To resolve this question, it may be necessary to discover at what level(s) people actually encode risk information.

Qualitative Versus Quantitative
Risk Assessment Scales

Qualitative Risk Assessment. Perceived risk can be measured in either qualitative or quantitative terms. Qualitative risk assessment methods rely on Likert-type scales in which subjects assign risks to a small number of labeled categories (e.g., a 7-point scale ranging from "very unlikely" to "very likely"). Quantitative assessment methods require subjects to use a clearly defined scale, such as probability or odds.

Qualitative scales are easy to construct and administer. However, they have three shortcomings: (a) They are ill-suited for risks (like AIDS) that may take on a wide range of probability levels. (b) It is impossible to judge the absolute accuracy of qualitatively measured risk perceptions (e.g., subjects' degree of absolute optimism regarding AIDS). (c) These scales are ambiguous, requiring an act of interpretation by respondents (and experimenters). For example, how should a subject using a 3-point "impossible–possible–probable" scale draw the line between risks that are "possible" and risks that are "probable"? Does "probable" mean a 10%, 50%, or 90% chance of occurrence? Research has shown that different people may interpret the same phrase differently, whereas the same person may use the same term differently in different circumstances (e.g., "likely to rain" vs. "likely to kill you") (Beyth-Marom, 1982; Wallsten, Budescu, Rapoport, Zwick, & Forsyth, 1986).

Quantitative Risk Assessment. Quantitative risk scales address all three of these problems. (a) Experimental psychological research on risk has found that subjects experience relatively little difficulty in using clearly defined quantitative risk scales. Subjects produce differentiated risk estimates, ranging over diverse probability levels. (b) Quantitative measures or perceived risk that use a probability metric can be validated against scientific risk estimates. Although there are some exceptions, events that are judged more likely also happen more often (Armstrong, 1985; Fischhoff & MacGregor, 1982; Lichtenstein, Fischhoff, & Phillips, 1982; Murphy & Winkler, 1984; Yates, 1989). (c) Finally, perceived risk is typically quite consistent across different quantitative assessment scales (Lichtenstein, Slovic, Fischhoff, Layman, & Combs, 1978; Wallsten & Budescu, 1983; von Winterfeldt & Edwards, 1986). These findings suggest that people may possess relatively consistent beliefs about risk that can be tapped by appropriate quantitative methods. Despite these potential advantages, survey investigators have typically been reluctant to use quantitative methods (e.g., Sudman & Bradburn, 1985; Wilson & Thornberry, 1987).

Quantitative risk assessment methods are not without their shortcomings. They are subject to context biases (Fischhoff & MacGregor, 1983), but so are qualitative methods. Also, quantitative methods require at least a basic understanding of the concept of probability or odds. Concern over this issue may partially explain why survey investigators have been reluctant to employ quantitative methods.

TABLE 1.5a
Comparison of Numerical and Verbal Risk Estimates

Risk Name	Median %	Median Word	Mean Word
Electrocution	0.1	1.0	1.67
Cancer	0.3	2.0	2.09
Flu	55.0	5.0	4.72
Car injury	10.0	3.0	3.38
Herpes	0.1	1.0	1.73
AIDS virus/sexual	0.02	1.0	1.41
AIDS virus/other	0.01	1.0	1.36

Source: Linville et al. (1992).

TABLE 1.5b
Relation Between Qualitative and Quantitative Risk Estimates

Qualitative Estimate	Median Quantitative Estimate (%)
1 = Very unlikely	0.01
2 = Unlikely	0.5
3 = Somewhat unlikely	5.0
4 = Somewhat likely	25.0
5 = Likely	60.0
6 = Very likely	96.0

Source: Linville et al. (1992).

An Empirical Comparison of Qualitative and Quantitative Methods. To explore the relative merits of quantitative and qualitative methods, we asked subjects to make risk assessments using a qualitative 6-point scale with labels taken from a National Center for Health Statistics survey (Wilson & Thornberry, 1987): very unlikely, unlikely, somewhat unlikely, somewhat likely, likely, and very likely. Half the subjects made these estimates before using the quantitative scale in Table 1.3, and half did so afterward (Linville et al., 1992).

The top panel of Table 1.5 displays the median quantitative and mean and median qualitative assessments for each of the seven risks (using a simple linear scale to interpret the qualitative assessments; very unlikely = 1, unlikely = 2, etc.). As this top panel reveals, the qualitative scale was not very discriminating. Four of the seven risks received a median rating of 1.0. Taking means for the qualitative assessments produced more discrimination, but this requires the assumption that the levels of the qualitative scale were linearly spaced. The quantitative scale, by comparison, produced highly differentiated responses for the seven risks, with median estimates ranging from 0.01% for HIV from nonsexual sources, to 55% for the flu. Only two risks (electrocution and herpes) had the same median assessments.

To examine the relationship between quantitative and qualitative risk assessments, we pooled across subjects and items to compute the median quantitative assessment associated with each qualitative assessment. For example, on the average, when subjects used the qualitative phrase "somewhat unlikely" to describe a risk, they assigned a probability of 5%. As seen in the bottom half of Table 1.5, the bottom two rungs of the qualitative scale were used for very low probability events. On the average, a "very unlikely" response was associated with a quantitative response of 0.01%, and an "unlikely" response with a quantitative response of 0.5%. The next two rungs of the scale were also used to denote events with less than a 50–50 chance of occurring. On the average, a "somewhat unlikely" event was judged to have a 5% chance of occurring, and a "somewhat likely" event a 25% chance. The top two rungs, "likely" and "very likely," corresponded to quantitative assessments of 60% and 96%, respectively. These results indicate that subjects used the qualitative scale in a nonlinear manner. Different steps along the scale corresponded to very unequal increments in probability. One could not have known this without also having collected the quantitative estimates.

In short, comparison of quantitative estimates with those produced using a qualitative response scale revealed several shortcomings in the qualitative scale. First, no absolute interpretation can be attached to risk perceptions measured with qualitative scales. Second, the units of the qualitative scale corresponded to vastly unequal intervals of probability. Third, the qualitative scale was very weak in discriminating among low probability risks.

GENERAL DISCUSSION

Our research has shown several potentially important biases in perceptions and decisions regarding the risk of acquiring HIV infection. The first is the *underaccumulation of risk* bias. Subjects greatly underestimated cumulative HIV risk relative to their single-episode risk estimates. Although underaccumulation occurs for encounters with and without condoms, it is especially pronounced when condoms are used. Our findings suggest that people believe that protective technologies either do or do not work, making the exposure period relatively unimportant. These findings have important implications for risk communication, implying that public health officials cannot simply provide single-encounter risk information and expect people to extrapolate to long-term cumulative risk. They also raise an interesting ethical dilemma for risk communicators. Subjects greatly overestimated the probability of acquiring HIV in a single unprotected sexual encounter with an infected partner. Providing more accurate information might actually increase feelings of invulnerability and thus increase risky sexual behavior. Does the public's right to decision-relevant information take precedence over the potentially harmful public health consequences of providing them with such information? Questions for future research include: Why do people lack the appropriate statistical intuitions regarding risk accumulation? Why is the bias so much worse with condoms? How can risk communicators overcome these difficulties?

Second, we found clear evidence of a *framing bias* in subjects' evaluations of risk communications regarding condom effectiveness in HIV transmission. Describing condoms in terms of their rates of success led to more favorable evaluations than did describing their complementary rates of failure. Such findings suggest that public health officials might be able to increase the impact of their messages by adopting appropriate ways of framing arguments about decision outcomes. But these findings also raise difficult ethical issues. Public health officials may be obliged to describe both success and failure rates in order to avoid bias.

Third, we found clear evidence of a *comparative optimism bias* in HIV risk perceptions. Subjects viewed themselves as having less risk of HIV infection than their friends, and their friends as having less risk than students in general. This finding of comparative optimism replicates that obtained in many prior studies. However, we found no evidence of an *absolute optimism* bias. Compared with public health statistics, some risk assessments for the self were too high, others too low. For HIV, perceived risk estimates were very similar to the best available public health statistics. Thus, people may be strongly optimistic in a comparative sense (e.g., I am less at risk than average) but neither systematically optimistic nor pessimistic in an absolute sense. If so, then the bias is not optimism about the self but pessimism about the fate of others. The distinction between comparative and absolute optimism was possible only because, in contrast to most past studies, we used a quantitative, probability-based risk-assessment scale.

A fourth contribution of this research concerns the measurement of perceived risk. Our measurement procedure was both quantitative and hierarchical (see Table 1.3), directing subjects' attention first to order-of-magnitude estimates, then to a more refined estimation of risk. We found that: (a) Subjects used the full range of the scale, including both very small probabilities and very large ones. (b) Four samples of college students, facing similar levels of risk, produced very similar average estimates for each of the seven risks studied. (c) Estimates of the risk of acquiring HIV varied with well-known correlates of these risks, both within and across subjects. This suggests that subjects are able to express their beliefs of the causes of risk in the responses they made using this scale. (d) Subjects' risk estimates were generally in the ballpark of the true risk magnitudes, again suggesting that they were able to use the scale in a fashion that reflected their personal knowledge of risk magnitudes. In contrast, we found serious problems with a qualitative risk-assessment scale drawn from a major national survey. Estimates generated using this scale failed to discriminate among low probability risks, and the equal-interval assumption (which is used in computing sample means for such a scale) was grossly violated.

These results suggest the need for considerable caution in formulating risk questions and risk communications. People's thinking about risk issues is complex and confused. It is not enough to put risk communications into what seems like good English. We need to know how people think about AIDS and other risks. We need to understand more about the determinants of perceived risk. Finally, we need to understand more about the interaction of perceived risk with other individual and social determinants of risk taking behaviors in the context of AIDS and other threats to health and safety.

REFERENCES

Armstrong, J. S. (1985). *Long range forecasting*. New York: Wiley.

Bar-Hillel, M. (1973). On the subjective probability of compound events. *Organizational Behavior and Human Performance, 9,* 396–406.

Bernoulli, D. (1738). Specimen theoriae novae de mensura sortis. *Commentarii academiae scientiarum imperialis Petropolitanae,* 1730 and 1731, *5,* 175–192.

Beyth-Marom, R. (1982). How probable is "probable"? Numerical translation of verbal probability expressions. *Journal of Forecasting, 1,* 257–269.

Centers for Disease Control. (1990). *1990 Division of STD/HIV Prevention, Annual Report.* Atlanta, GA: Author.

Centers for Disease Control. (1991). *National disease and therapeutic index survey* [Unpublished data].

Clemen, R. T. (1991). *Making hard decisions: An introduction to decision analysis.* Boston, MA: PWS Kent.

Fineberg, H. V. (1988). Education to prevent AIDS: Prospects and obstacles. *Science, 239,* 592–596.

Fischhoff, B. (1989). Making decisions about AIDS. In V. Mays, G. Albee, & S. Schneider (Eds.), *Primary prevention of AIDS* (pp. 168–205). Newbury Park, CA: Sage.

Fischhoff, B. (1991). Value elicitation: Is there anything in there? *American Psychologist, 46,* 835–847.

Fischhoff, B., & MacGregor, D. (1982). Subjective confidence in forecasts. *Journal of Forecasting, 1,* 155–172.

Fischhoff, B., & MacGregor, D. (1983). Judged lethality: How much people seem to know depends on how they are asked. *Risk Analysis, 3,* 229–236.

Fischhoff, B., Slovic, P., & Lichtenstein, S. (1980). Knowing what you want: measuring labile values. In T. Wallsten (Ed.), *Cognitive processes in choice and decisions behavior* (pp. 117–141). Hillsdale, NJ: Lawrence Erlbaum Associates.

Gayle, H. D., Keeling, R. P., Garcia-Tunon, M., Kilbourne, B. W., Narkunas, J. P., Ingram, F. R., Rogers, M. F., & Curran, J. W. (1990). Prevalence of the human immunodeficiency virus among university students. *The New England Journal of Medicine, 323,* 1538–1541.

Hearst, N., & Hulley, S. B. (1988). Preventing the heterosexual spread of AIDS. *Journal of the American Medical Association, 259,* 2428–2432.

Hogarth, R. (Ed.). (1982). *New directions for methodology of social and behavioral science: Question framing and response consistency.* San Francisco: Jossey-Bass.

Kahneman, D., Slovic, P., & Tversky, A. (Eds.) (1982). *Judgment under uncertainty: Heuristics and biases.* New York: Cambridge University Press.

Kahneman, D., & Tversky, A. (1979). Prospect theory. *Econometrica, 47,* 263–291.

Kahneman, D., & Tversky, A. (1984). Choices, values, and frames. *American Psychologist, 39,* 341–350.

Keeney, R. L., & Raiffa, H. (1976). *Decisions with multiple objectives: Preferences and value tradeoffs.* New York: Wiley.

Lichtenstein, S., Fischhoff, B., & Phillips, L. D. (1982). Calibration of probabilities: State of the art to 1980. In D. Kahneman, P. Slovic, & A. Tversky (Eds.), *Judgment under uncertainty: Heuristics and biases.* (pp. 306–334). New York: Cambridge University Press.

Lichtenstein, S., Slovic, P., Fischhoff, B., Layman, M., & Combs, B. (1978). Judged frequency of lethal events. *Journal of Experimental Psychology: Human Learning and Memory, 4,* 551–578.

Linville, P. W., Fischhoff, B., & Fischer, G. W. (1992). *Judging the risks from AIDS: Biases in accumulating probability, framing, and optimism.* Unpublished manuscript.

McNeil, B. J., Paulker, S., Sox, H. Jr., & Tversky, A. (1982). On the elicitation of preferences for alternative therapies. *New England Journal of Medicine, 306,* 216–221.

Naatanen, R., & Summala, H. (1975). *Road-user behavior and traffic accidents.* Amsterdam: North-Holland.

National Center for Health Statistics. (1990). *Vital statistics of the United States, 1987* (Vol. II, Mortality, Part A). Washington, DC: Public Health Service.

Newell, A., & Simon, H. A. (1972). *Human problem solving.* Englewood Cliffs, NJ: Prentice-Hall.

National Safety Council. (1990). *Accident facts, 1989 edition.* Washington, DC: Congressional Information Services.

Murphy, A., & Winkler, R. (1984). Probability of precipitation forecasts. *Journal of the American Statistical Association, 79,* 391–400.

Rethans, A. (1979). *An investigation of consumer perceptions of product hazards.* Unpublished doctoral dissertation, University of Oregon, Eugene.

Ries, L. A., Hankey, B. F., & Edwards, B. K. (Eds.). (1988). Cancer statistics review 1973–1987 (NIH Pub. #90-2789). Bethesda, MD: National Cancer Institute.

Ronen, J. (1973). Effects of some probability displays on choices. *Organizational Behavior & Human Performance, 9,* 1-15.

Savage, L. J. (1954). *The foundations of statistics.* New York: Wiley.

Schwalm, N. D., & Slovic, P. (1982). *Development and test of a motivational approach and materials for increasing use of seat belts* (PFTR-1100-823). Woodland Hills, CA: Perceptronics.

Shaklee, H., & Fischhoff, B. (1990). The psychology of contraceptive surprises: Cumulative risk and contraceptive effectiveness. *Journal of Applied Psychology* (20) 5, 385–403.

Shilts, R. (1987). *And the band played on: Politics, people, and the AIDS epidemic.* New York: St. Martin's Press.

Slovic, P. (1987). Perceptions of risk. *Science, 236,* 280–285.

Slovic, P., Fischhoff, B., & Lichtenstein, S. (1978). Accident probabilities and seat-belt usage: A psychological perspective. *Accident Analysis and Prevention, 10,* 281-285.

Slovic, P., Fischhoff, B., & Lichtenstein, S. (1982). Response mode, framing and information-processing effects in risk assessment. In R. Hogarth (Ed.), *New directions for methodology of social and behavioral science: Question framing and response consistency* (pp. 21–36). San Francisco: Jossey-Bass.

Sudman, S., & Bradburn, N. M. (1985). *Asking questions: A practical guide to questionnaire design.* San Francisco: Jossey-Bass.

Svenson, O. (1981). Are we all less risky and more skillful than our fellow drivers? *Acta Psychologica, 47,* 143–148.

Tversky, A., & Kahneman, D. (1973). Availability: A heuristic for judging frequency and probability. *Cognitive Psychology, 4,* 207–232.

Tversky, A., & Kahneman, D. (1981). The framing of decisions and the rationality of choice. *Science, 221,* 453–458.

Tversky, A., Sattath, S., & Slovic, P. (1988). Contingent weighting in judgment and choice. *Psychological Review, 95,* 371–384.

Wallsten, T., & Budescu, D. V. (1983). Encoding subjective probabilities: A psychological and psychometric review. *Management Science, 29,* 151–173.

Wallsten, T., Budescu, D. V., Rapoport, A., Zwick, R., & Forsyth, B. (1986). Measuring the vague meanings of probability terms. *Journal of Experimental Psychology: General, 115*(4), 348–365.

Weinstein, N. D. (1980). Unrealistic optimism about future life events. *Journal of Personality and Social Psychology, 39*, 806–820.

Weinstein, N. D. (1984). Why it won't happen to me: Perceptions of risk factors and susceptibility. *Health Psychology, 3*, 431–457.

Wilson, R. W., & Thornberry, O. T. (1987). Knowledge and attitudes about AIDS: Provisional data from the National Health Interview Survey, August 10–30, 1987. *Advance Data,* No. 146.

von Winterfeldt, D., & Edwards, W. (1986). *Decision analysis and behavioral research.* New York: Cambridge University Press.

Yates, J. F. (1989). *Judgment and decision making.* New York: Wiley.

2

Perceived Risk of AIDS: Unrealistic Optimism and Self-Protective Action

J. van der Pligt
Wilma Otten
René Richard
University of Amsterdam

Frank van der Velde
Municipal Health Service, Amsterdam

AIDS has produced a sense of urgency in the medical, biological, and social sciences. The scale of the AIDS epidemic and the absence of successful medical treatments justifies the necessity to assess the riskiness of specific (sexual) practices, to understand the antecedents of these behaviors, and to identify (sub)populations to be targeted for preventive programs (see also Catania, Gibson, Chitwood, & Coats, 1990).

From an individual standpoint, however, assessing one's personal risk for HIV infection tends to be complicated and unreliable. Knowledge about transmission routes is essential, but quite often the relevant risk factors remain concealed (e.g., lack of information about sexual partners). This lack of knowledge about the behavioral history and serostatus of sexual partners should lead to risk-avoiding strategies. Quite often, however, people seem to make risk appraisals on the basis of less relevant factors such as the physical appearance of their sexual partners. Moreover, even those who are likely to be relatively well-informed about AIDS-related risks often err in their subjective appraisal of the riskiness of their own behavior. For instance, Bauman and Siegel (1987) found that gay men practicing hazardous sex tend to underestimate the risks associated with their behaviors. These misappraisals of the riskiness of one's sexual practices can result in underestimating one's personal susceptibility to HIV-infection. The difficulty of adequate risk appraisals is further enhanced by the simple fact that sexual partners do not always provide correct information about their behavioral history (see e.g., Cochran & Mays, 1990).

Reducing the possible underestimation of one's susceptibility to AIDS-related risks is one of the major aims of health education programs. Many of the prevailing media campaigns designed to persuade those at risk to adopt safe-sex practices are risky, and stress the vulnerability of people who do not practice safe sex. Perceived vulnerability plays a crucial role in most models of preventive health behavior. Many of the campaigns designed to persuade those at risk to adopt less risky behaviors are based on these models of preventive health behavior.

The Health Belief Model (the framework most widely used to explain preventive health behaviors; see e.g., Kirscht, 1983) distinguishes five factors that influence the adoption of preventive, risk-reducing behavioral practices (see also Gerrard, Gibbons, & Warner, this volume). These are (a) perceived susceptibility or vulnerability to developing a health problem, (b) perceived severity of the problem, (c) perceived benefits of changes in behavior, (d) perceived barriers and/or possible negative consequences of these changes and (e) specific cues to action, such as a symptom or a health communication (see Janz & Becker, 1984). More general models focus on vulnerability and risks as threatening and fear-arousing elements that can lead to a variety of cognitive, emotional, and behavioral responses. For instance, the Fear Drive Model is based on the assumption that fear produces subjective discomfort and tension that leads to action (Leventhal, Safer, & Panagis, 1983). Janis and Mann's (1977) Conflict Theory also describes decisions in threatening circumstances and focuses on adaptive and maladaptive coping styles. More recently, Rogers and his associates (Rippetoe & Rogers, 1987; Rogers, 1975) introduced Protection Motivation Theory to account for individual reactions to information about health risks (for a more extensive review of these models, see Gerrard, Gibbons, & Warner, this volume).

All in all, most models of preventive health behavior incorporate the recognition of one's own risk status or vulnerability as an important condition for adopting behaviors that reduce these risks. Quite a few of these models focus on the role of anxiety or fear triggered by threatening information about personal risks as a motivator of behavioral action, and on adaptive versus maladaptive coping styles.

In this chapter, we focus on perceived risk. More specifically, we focus on subjective perceptions of the riskiness of one's sexual practices. We look at the accuracy of these judgments and also discuss comparative risk appraisals. These comparative risk appraisals are related to what Weinstein (1980) called *unrealistic optimism*. Weinstein argued that people tend to think they are "invulnerable"; others are more likely to experience negative health consequences than oneself. Usually it is extremely difficult to objectively assess the accuracy of an individual's assessment of his or her risk for experiencing a specific event. Each individual could be right in assuming that his or her risks are smaller than those of comparable others. On a group level, however, one could detect unrealistic optimism. If most people in a specific population rate their risk below average, a substantial part of them must be wrong.

In this chapter, we first focus on unrealistic optimism. Both the prevalence and the magnitude of unrealistic optimism about AIDS-related risks are discussed. Second, we concentrate on possible determinants of unrealistic optimism and describe empirical evidence about possible ways to reduce unrealistic optimism. Next, we take a closer look at the relationship between perceived risk of AIDS and behavioral risk reduction. In the final section we present some conclusions and possible implications for both research and practice.

NATURE AND PREVALENCE OF UNREALISTIC OPTIMISM

Risk perception has been studied for a wide variety of negative events, such as being a victim of crime (Perloff, 1982; Weinstein, 1980), divorce (Perloff & Farbisz, 1985), traffic accidents (Svenson, 1981), and natural disasters (Kunreuther, 1979). Most investigations in this area focus on health risks (e.g., Harris & Guten, 1979; Knopf, 1976; Slovic, Fischhoff, & Lichtenstein, 1978; Weinstein, 1982, 1983). A number of conclusions can be drawn from this research.

First, perceptions of risk of disease or accident vary considerably among people and often show little correspondence to epidemiological findings or accident statistics. Absolute, quantitative risk judgments are prone to a number of biases. Small probabilities are overestimated, large probabilities are underestimated. Furthermore, risks that are more available due to personal experience or media coverage, for example, tend to be overestimated. In other words, quantitative risk appraisals need to be treated with caution. This is underlined by the significant influence of the response format on risk estimates. Quantative appraisals of risk tend to be relatively unstable and influenced by the way the question is asked and by context variables such as judgmental anchors. It needs to be added, however, that people have a reasonable idea of the relative frequency of causes of death. Their orderings are similar to official statistics. Major errors occur primarily in their estimates of the magnitude of the risks.

Second, although people are quite aware of the relative risk of specific activities or behaviors, things change dramatically when this knowledge is applied to their own behavior. For instance, many smokers accept the association between smoking cigarettes and disease, but do not believe themselves to be personally vulnerable (Pechacek & Danaher, 1979). When asked to compare their risk to the "average" person or to comparable others, many more people assess their risk of experiencing a negative event as below average than as above average. This illusion of invulnerability has been obtained for a wide variety of health risks, including AIDS-related risks. Moreover, a few studies attempted to compare subjective risk appraisals with objective risk estimates based on reported sexual practices. This research also suggests an underestimation of the riskiness of one's sexual practices. For instance, Bauman and Siegel (1987) interviewed 160 gay men who were asymptomatic with respect to AIDS. The interviews included questions about the frequency of specific sexual practices and the number of different partners over a fixed time period. On the basis of epidemiological studies and available risk-reduction guidelines, the "objective" riskiness of each individual's behavior was assessed. Behaviors were classified as "risky," "low risk," and "safe." Their findings showed that 42% of the sample engaged in "high-risk" sexual activities, 33% in "low-risk" activities, and 25% in only safe sex practices. The distribution of subjective risk assessment in this sample was very different. More than 75% of the subjects rated their behavior as relatively safe. Only 9% scored their own behavior on the risky half of a 10-point scale running from "not risky at all" to "most risky." Bauman and Siegel (1987) concluded that especially those practicing risky sex underestimate the riskiness of their sexual behavior. In their study, subjects were also asked to evaluate their own risk of getting AIDS, relative to other gay men. Their results were in accordance with what Weinstein (1980) termed *unrealistic optimism,* and showed that the majority of the sample thought their own risk to be smaller than that of other gay men. Gerrard and Warner (1991) compared the mean risk estimate of becoming infected with HIV of women Marines with the actual incidence of HIV infection in the military. Their findings showed an optimistic bias. We use the term *unrealistic optimism* to refer to relative risk comparisons of self to others. Most research in this domain focuses on these self–other comparisons. Only a few studies attempted to compare people's perception of risk to their objective risk. Research by Bauman and Siegel (1987) and Gerrard and Warner (1991) are examples of the latter. These studies show an underestimation on one's own risk as compared to objective risk assessments on the basis of their behavioral practices or epidemiological findings. Given the difficulties in assessing an individual's objective risk most research deals with comparative risk appraisal.

In the following pages, we take a closer look at this phenomenon of unrealistic optimism and investigate its prevalence and magnitude in various groups. Unrealistic optimism is assessed in a variety of ways. Sometimes subjects are simply asked whether their risks are lower or higher than comparable others on a 7-point scale. In other studies, subjects are asked to indicate how much higher or lower their risk is (in percentage estimates) as compared to others. In our own studies we asked subjects to give a numerical estimate of their own risk and that of an average other of the same gender and age. These estimates could range from 0 to 100%. Table 2.1 summarizes these findings, and presents subjective risk assessments for HIV and two other sexually transmitted diseases (STDs) for a variety of groups.

A more detailed account of these findings can be found in Hooijkaas, van der Pligt, van Doornum, van der Linden, and Coutinho (1989), van der Pligt (1991), and van der Velde, van der Pligt, & Hooijkaas (1992). All samples showed significant levels of unrealistic optimism. Optimism is relatively modest in Sample D. This group consisted of visitors of the largest STD clinic in Amsterdam who participated in a longitudinal study on AIDS-related risks and the role of

TABLE 2.1
Estimated Risk (%) for Self and Comparable Others in Low-and High-Risk Groups

		Perceived Risk	
Group[1]	Risk	Self	Other
A (n = 156)	STDs	4.9	18.6*
	HIV	5.9	16.4*
	syphillis	11.1	25.9*
B (n = 85)	gonorrhoea	12.5	29.2*
	HIV	9.4	22.9*
	syphillis	22.1	35.8*
C (n = 80)	gonorrhoea	24.2	42.8*
	HIV	18.8	26.9*
	syphillis	24.2	27.3*
D (n = 535)	gonorrhoea	30.9	31,2
	HIV	26.2	28.0*
	syphillis	17.4	23.9*
E (n = 147)	gonorrhoea	18.9	27.8*
	HIV	14.8	25.2*

*$p < .05$.
[1] A heterosexual low-risk sample
  B heterosexual sample with multiple sexual partners in previous months.
  C heterosexual sample of outpatients of an STD clinic in Amsterdam (a sizeable
    proportion of subjects were prostitutes and their customers).
  D heterosexual sample of outpatients of an STD clinic in Amsterdam (with similar
    characteristics as Sample C.
  E homosexual sample of men with multiple sexual partners in previous months.

sexual practices. Subjects were tested for HIV and a variety of STDs. The sample included a sizeable proportion of prostitutes and their visitors. In this sample, subjects were asked to rate their own risk and that for an average Dutch person of their own age and gender. Although modest, the obtained optimism is still remarkable given the fact that 26% of this sample had one or more STDs at entry of the study, whereas nearly 50% had a history of STDs in the past 5 years. Moreover, nearly 70% engaged in prostitution contacts and nearly 25% had contacts with AIDS risk groups such as intravenous (IV) drug users (see van der Velde et al., 1992). All in all, these results are in accordance with Weinstein's findings and show unrealistic optimism in a variety of groups with different levels of objective risk. Results also indicate some awareness of the risk of one's own sexual practices. Group A had the lowest perceived risk for STDs and HIV infection, Group B the second lowest. All other groups were objectively more at risk than these first two samples, and also rated their risk higher. These higher levels of perceived risk were, however, accompanied by even higher estimates for others. Finally, it needs to be noted that, for all groups, the perceived risk of HIV infections was higher than that indicated by epidemiological findings. Let us now turn to the possible causes of this unrealistic optimism.

DETERMINANTS OF UNREALISTIC OPTIMISM

Unrealistic optimism has been related to a variety of possible causes. There is some conceptual overlap between these causes. Moreover, most research uses correlational designs with the usual drawbacks for conclusions about the possible causal role of specific factors. In this section, we briefly describe six possible causes mentioned in the literature. In the next section, we briefly describe experimental research on the possible effects of these causal factors. More specifically, in this section we discuss the possible role of perceived control, egocentric biases, personal experience, stereotyped beliefs about victims, self-esteem maintenance, and defensive coping styles. The first four causes refer to cognitive mechanisms, whereas the remaining two causes stress the role of motivational processes.

Perceived Control

Weinstein (1980) noted that optimism is greatest for risks with which subjects have little personal experience, for risk rated low in probability, and for the risks judged to be controllable by personal action. When rating their own risk status as compared to others, optimism tends to be greater for those risks judged to be under personal control (Weinstein, 1982). Other findings indicate that for each specific hazard those who rate its controllability higher are also more optimistic. This relation between perceived controllability and optimism is confirmed by research on risk appraisals in the context of AIDS (van der Velde et al., 1992). In their study, perceived control over the possibility of an HIV infection was significantly related to optimism. In other words, respondents who thought they could control this specific risk were also more optimistic about their chances to get infected with HIV as compared to others of their own gender and age. Bauman and Siegel's (1987) findings indicate that *illusory* perceived control is also related to optimistic risk appraisals. Their findings showed that the belief in ineffective risk-reducing practices such as showering and inspecting one's partner for lesions can result in a false sense of security.

Controllability could also be enhanced by the simple thought that social and physical appearances are good indicators of the serostatus of sexual partners. In other words, people could think it very unlikely that they would meet infected persons, and if so, that they would recognize them as such. Some indirect evidence for the role of perceived control is provided by the results described in van der Pligt (1991). When people are asked to give specific risk estimates for unprotected sexual contacts with infected partners their estimates increase dramatically and the frequently obtained optimism disappears completely. In this case subjects were not asked to give a general risk estimate of contracting an HIV infection for themselves and the average other, but were asked to assess the riskiness of unprotected sexual contact with infected others. Factors enhancing perceived control such as the idea that one simply would not meet infected persons, would "recognize" them, or would discuss each other's sexual history before deciding to have intercourse, cannot play a role in this conditional risk assessment. Table 2.2 summarizes these findings, and shows that people assess their own chances of contracting HIV after 1, 10, or 100 unprotected sexual encounters to be higher than those of others (of their gender and age) who would engage in the same number of unprotected sexual encounters with infected others.

This sample consisted of (heterosexual) first-year psychology students. As can be seen in Table 2.2 their risk estimates were far too high. Furthermore, the data reveal a lack of understanding of cumulative risks and confirm the findings obtained by Shaklee and Fischhoff (1990). Overall, these subjects were *pessimistic* about their chances of contracting the AIDS virus. This finding is in contrast with responses to more general questions about one's own risk as compared to others. As argued before, this divergence could be related to perceptions of the controllability of the risk; one simply overestimates one's control over having unprotected sexual contacts with infected partners. This divergence could also be related to stereotyped beliefs about AIDS risk groups. Before turning to that issue, however, we discuss another cognitive explanation of unrealistic optimism (i.e., egocentrism).

Egocentric Bias

Another factor that could be related to optimism is what Weinstein (1980) termed an *egocentric bias*. When people are asked to assess their risks and those of others, they simply have more knowledge about their own protective actions than those of others. It seems that people tend to focus on personal actions reducing their own risks while they tend to forget personal actions or circumstances that increase their risks. Moreover, one's own actions are more available than those of others, (i.e., one tends to forget that most other people also take protective action). This bias is also related to cognitive availability. We simply have more knowledge about our own precautionary actions than those of others. All in all,

TABLE 2.2
Risk of Getting HIV After 1, 10, and 100 Unprotected Sexual Encounters With Infected Others

	Perceived Risk (%)	
	Self	Other
1 unprotected contact	59.9	51.4
10 unprotected contacts	76.9	69.3
100 unprotected contacts	87.8	82.1

Note. Scores could range between 0-100%.

people seem to give themselves credit for factors that reduce their own risk, but often forget to assess whether other people might have as many or even more factors in their favor.

Personal Experience

Weinstein (1980, 1982) concluded that lack of previous personal experience tends to increase unrealistic optimism. Personal experience is a powerful stimulus to action (see Weinstein, 1989, for a review). Personal experience tends to be relatively vivid as compared to statistical information about risks, and enhances both availability and recall. Possible negative consequences for health and well-being that have been experienced more directly (oneself, close friends, or relatives as victims) tend to result in less optimistic risk appraisals. This effect has been obtained for a wide variety of risks such as automobile accidents and seat belt use, criminal victimization, natural hazards, and a variety of health risks. It is likely that more direct experience with the consequences of AIDS (friends, relatives) will also reduce optimism about vulnerability.

Stereotyped Beliefs

Another factor that could produce unrealistic optimism is related to stereotypical or prototypical judgment. People might have a relatively extreme image of those suffering from specific diseases. This extreme prototype is unlikely to fit one's self-image, hence the conclusion that the risk does not apply to oneself but primarily to others. The results of one of our studies are consistent with this line of reasoning. In this study (van der Pligt, 1991) we asked subjects (a relatively low-risk group) to characterize a variety of health risks on several dimensions including threat, controllability, known–unknown, and the extent to which the risk applied to specific groups. In this way it was possible to derive a risk profile for each of these risks. The risks of HIV infection and STDs showed a very similar profile: Both were seen as highly controllable and restricted to specific groups. HIV infection and STDs were seen as the two health risks (out of 12) that were most clearly associated with specific groups. Stereotypical beliefs about people at risk might induce people to think that they would simply recognize others who are HIV positive. This scenario does not apply to the more specific question discussed in the section about perceived control (see also Table 2.2). Asking people about the risk of having unprotected sexual contact with an HIV-positive partner excludes a possible (optimistic) bias due to illusory control and stereotypical beliefs. Other evidence of stereotyped beliefs or extreme prototypes is provided by Hamilton (1988), who showed that the tendency of the (U.S.) news media to link AIDS with homosexuality without refering to gender resulted in a significant overestimation of the risks of lesbians.

Self-Esteem Maintenance

Weinstein (1984) suggested that self-esteem maintenance or enhancement plays a crucial role as a determinant of unrealistic optimism. Generally, people seem to think that their actions, lifestyle, and personality are more advantageous than those of their peers. This mechanism would explain the fact that people are not optimistic about hereditary and environmental health risks. The latter do not constitute a threat to one's self-esteem. In contrast, a high-risk lifestyle implies that we are ignorant of what we should do or are simply unable to exercise self-control. These factors concern a person's ability to cope effectively with life demands and have clear-cut links to self-esteem. Self-esteem maintenance is clearly related to stereotyped beliefs. Both involve social comparison processes. Self-esteem enhancement has not been studied explicitly in the context of AIDS-related risks. One could, however, relate the findings of Bauman and Siegel (1987) to this factor. In their study, high-risk respondents could maintain their self-esteem because they were convinced that their (unprotective actions) were efficient in reducing their risks. Motivational factors also play a role in another possible antecedent of unrealistic optimism: defensive coping styles. In fact, Bauman and Siegel's findings could be interpreted as the result of a defensive coping strategy.

Defensive Coping

Under conditions of high stress or threat, denial is a response often used to protect against anxiety and worry. Denial can reduce emotional distress but can also hinder direct behavioral actions, which may be necessary to reduce one's risks. Taylor and Brown (1988) argued that exaggerated perceptions of control and unrealistic optimism are illusions that can help the individual to adapt successfully to threatening events. For instance Taylor, Lichtman, and Wood (1984) found that optimism was positively related to recovery processes after major surgery. Positive illusions such as optimism, however, are not always functional. Although these illusions can reduce emotional distress, they can also interfere with taking direct action.

There is some evidence for the role of defensive coping strategies. In a study in which optimism about each of 45 different health- and life-threatening problems was related to characteristics of these problems, Weinstein (1982) obtained a relationship between the seriousness of the different health risks and optimism. In other words, more threatening events resulted in increased levels of optimism. On the other hand, results of this study also showed that increased worry about health risks was associated with less optimism. The latter reaction seems perfectly rational and contradicts the obtained relationship between seriousness of consequences and optimism. Bauman and Siegel (1987) investigated defensive denial in a sample of gay men. They found that men who deny or underestimate their risk of an HIV infection experienced lower anxiety. On the basis of this (correlational) finding they concluded that denial is used as a strategy to manage anxiety.

Bauman and Siegel's findings suggest that defensive denial may occur primarily when people already have some reason for believing that they are at risk. This obviously poses a problem for health education. A direct confrontational approach could have potentially adverse consequences for those who perceive themselves to be at greater risk for an HIV infection. These adverse consequences include psychological distress, barriers to behavioral change, social role impairment and more intrusive worries and concerns about AIDS (see e.g., Joseph et al., 1987). The complicated dual aim of health education programs is to create and maintain a level of anxiety that is sufficient to motivate risk-reducing behaviors while at the same time these levels of anxiety should not be too high.

In our research we found defensive avoidance (one of the "maladaptive" coping styles of Janis and Mann's, 1977, Conflict Theory) to be positively related to optimism about AIDS risks (van der Velde, van der Pligt, & Hooijkaas, 1992). In another study (van der Velde & van der Pligt, 1991) we found that subjects who scored high on defensive avoidance, perceived the possible consequences of an HIV infection as less severe and were less convinced that they could exercise personal control over their actions in order to reduce their risks.

In the first study (van der Velde et al., 1992), we assessed defensive avoidance with seven items (e.g., "you leave it to your sexual partner to practice safe sex or not") scored on a 5-point scale ranging from "does not apply to me at all" (1) to "applies to me very much" (5). Cronbach's alpha for this measure was .70. Results of this study on 535 heterosexual subjects with multiple partners (STD clinic visitors) showed that a defensive coping style was one of the factors enhancing optimism.

The second study (van der Velde & van der Pligt, 1991) used a similar measure of defensive avoidance (in this instance Cronbach's alpha was .71). Heterosexual subjects with multiple sexual partners perceived the consequences of an HIV infection as less severe and scored lower on the factor self-efficacy (perceived ability to control the risks by employing safe sex techniques only). Moreover, subjects who scored higher on defensive avoidance were also less fearful of the consequences of HIV infection. Of these factors, increased fear and self-efficacy were positively related to the willingness to engage in protective actions (safe sex techniques and/or using a condom). In the same study we found that for a subsample of homosexual subjects defensive avoidance was directly related to behavioral intentions to practice safe sex. In this case, however, increased levels of defensive coping were negatively related to the intention to practice safe sex.

Both these studies focused on medium- to high-risk groups, and together with Bauman and Siegel's (1987) findings, support the view that motivational, defensive denial strategies are likely to be more pronounced if people have some reason for believing that they are at risk and the specific risk is associated with dread.

How can we summarize the possible antecedent of optimism discussed in this section? All six seem to play a role in the formation and maintenance of unrealistic optimism. Some weaknesses need to be mentioned, however. First, the six factors are obviously not mutually exclusive. Conceptually, there is considerable overlap between some of the factors. Moreover, the causal role of most factors is not well established and requires further empirical documentation. The evidence tends to be sparse and is largely correlational. All in all, it seems difficult to disentangle the various cognitive and motivational processes that could produce unrealistic optimism. Unrealistic optimism refers to a comparative risk assessment, suggesting that social comparison processes play an important role. Overestimating one's personal control and selecting stereotyped others as potential victims could be seen as mechanisms to enhance one's self-esteem. Another option is to interpret these findings as the result of a defensive coping style. Similarly, a defensive coping style could result in stereotyped beliefs about possible victims and an egocentric bias in assessing one's own risks and those of others. The overall result seems confusing. It is possible, however, to summarize the six factors under three more general headings.

1. *Positive Illusions.* People have a general tendency to overestimate their abilities, have exaggerated expectations about the future, and have optimistic illusions about the extent to which they can control life's outcomes. Taylor and Brown (1988) discussed a wide variety of these positive illusions and pointed out their functional value (e.g., in relation to well-being). Similar ideas have been put forward in the achievement-motivation literature concerning the effects of outcome expectations on behavior. The literature on self-efficacy can also be related to this general idea of positive illusions. It seems essential in all these circumstances not to be overly optimistic. Baumeister (1989) argued that there is an optimal margin of illusion. This optimal margin would have beneficial effects for behavior (e.g., persistence) and well-being. Unrealistic optimism can be seen as another example of a positive illusion. This provides an explanation of optimism in terms of its functional value. As argued before, in the context of health risks, optimism could be less functional.

2. *Availability.* Personal experience with a specific hazard and/or its consequences enhances the availability of the hazard and reduces optimism. Similarly, not having experienced negative consensus of one's life style or (sexual) practices in the past, makes possible negative consequences less available. Extreme cases of AIDS victims portrayed in the media are likely to make specific groups more available as potential victims and could result in the view that the risk does not apply to oneself. Cognitive availability due to personal experiences is likely to play an important role in risk appraisals. Availability is bound to differ be-

tween high- and low-risk groups due to confrontations with the disease in their immediate social environment. Availability is likely to lead to two separate effects. First, specific characteristics of AIDS (extreme, uncontrollable consequences that receive quite a bit of media coverage) are expected to lead to an overestimation of the absolute risk (for self and others) of contracting HIV. Personal experience is expected to affect appraisals of one's personal risk. Data presented in this chapter seem to confirm this tendency. First, risk appraisals are generally too high. Groups that are more likely to have direct experiences with AIDS victims have even higher estimates of their own risk. This increased availability cannot, however, explain the fact that individuals at risk still show an unrealistic optimism about contracting HIV.

3. *Ego-Defensive Mechanisms.* Two separate processes can be categorized under this heading. First, *self-esteem* maintenance or enhancement. We all want to be (slightly) better than most comparable others. This mechanism especially applies to controllable health risks such as HIV infection. Acknowledging that one's risks are higher than comparable others is also an acknowledgment of one's incompetence to control these risks. Such acknowledgments provide a threat to one's self-esteem. Self-esteem maintenance is likely to have an impact on comparative risk appraisals and will generally lead to an enhancement of the differences between the perceived risks for oneself vs. others. Second, *denial* strategies are likely to be prevalent under conditions of severe threat. Denial strategies do not necessarily affect comparative risk appraisals. Denial focuses on underestimating one's own risk in comparison to "objective" risk assessments.

In the next section we discuss a few studies attempting to investigate the possible *causal* role of some factors mentioned in this section.

REDUCING UNREALISTIC OPTIMISM

A few studies attempted to test the causal role of some of the variables discussed in the previous section. Weinstein (1983) examined the effectiveness of an intervention designed to eliminate unrealistic optimism. In this study, subjects (college students) rated themselves on risk factors relevant to each of a series of health problems (11 different health and safety hazards were included). Next they received information about the standing of a typical student on these risk factors and were asked to make comparative risk judgments.

Results showed that when college students describe their own standing on risk factors and are given explicit information about the risk status of their peers on these factors, optimistic biases are considerably reduced. Because the procedure had little effect on judgments for threats that do not normally evoke unrealistic optimism, Weinstein (1983) concluded that the treatment eliminated a bias and not simply created (overall) pessimism. Receiving feedback about the risk status of others was essential and reduced egocentrism by providing information about others. [Asking subjects to consider their own standing on risk factors without providing them with information about comparable others substantially increased optimistic biases.] This could be due to the fact that the manipulation increased the awareness of risk factors for which they fell into a low-risk classification. It could be argued that exclusive attention to one's own risk status may prevent people from realizing that most others fall in the same category. As argued before, self-esteem maintenance and social desirability factors might play a role in enhanced optimism when focusing on one's own risk status.

One study (van der Pligt et al., in press) attempted to investigate the effect of perceived control on unrealistic optimism. We argued that increasing the salience of the controllability and predictability of specific risk (by asking subjects to indicate to what extent these terms applied to each of 11 positive and negative life events) would enhance optimism. Focusing on the uncontrollability and unpredictability of these events (including HIV infection) was expected to reduce optimism. In the latter condition subjects were simply asked to indicate to what extent the terms *uncontrollable* and *unpredictable* applied to each of the events. Results confirmed our prediction and showed that 63% of the subjects were generally optimistic after rating the various events in terms of controllability and predictability. This percentage dropped considerably for subjects who rated the events in terms of uncontrollability and unpredictability. A third group was first asked to give risk estimates for themselves and others. Next, they were asked to select adjectives to describe each of these risks. It was predicted that optimists would show a greater preference for terms such as controllable and predictable than pessimists. Results confirmed our predictions and provide further evidence for the notion that perceived control plays an important role in optimistic biases.

Perloff and Fetzer (1986) showed that comparative risk assessment or optimism is also affected by the group or individual with which one compares one's own risk. Comparison others who are more similar tend to reduce optimism. In summary, there is evidence that optimism can be reduced. Both the reduction of egocentrism, stressing the uncontrollability and unpredictability of risks, and selecting specific comparison others reduce optimism. These effects support the claims about the causal role of egocentrism and perceived control. In the next section we focus on the behavioral consequences of unrealistic optimism.

RISK PERCEPTION, PERCEIVED VULNERABILITY, AND BEHAVIOR

All in all, there is an extensive literature about the possible *determinants* of unrealistic optimism. As argued in the previous section, the precise causal role of these antecedents remains relatively unclear. Both cognitive and motivational factors seem to play a role. Motivational factors such as defensive denial seem to be most prominent when the health threat is extreme. In this section, we focus on the *consequences* of unrealistic optimism. The basic rationale for research on the phenomenon of unrealistic optimism is that optimism could make people think they are relatively invulnerable. This perceived invulnerability, in turn, could undermine the motivation to take precautions.

There is some evidence showing that perceptions of vulnerability predict preventive health behavior (Becker et al., 1977; Cummings, Jette, Brock, Haefner, 1979; Kasl, 1975). There is less evidence, however, for the proposed relationships between unrealistic optimism, perceived vulnerability, and behavior. Lee (1989) found a direct link between risk appraisals and smoking. Smokers' ratings of the risks of smoking to the average smoker were lower than nonsmokers' ratings, and smokers' ratings of their own risk were lower still. Studies that deal with AIDS risks tend to focus on possible antecedents of unrealistic optimism and pay only marginal attention to the consequences of unrealistic optimism for behavior and psychosocial functioning.

One exception is a study conducted by Joseph et al. (1987). This study presented longitudinal analyses exploring the risk perception and behavioral, social, and psychological consequences. Data were obtained from more than 600 homosexual men living in Chicago who completed two questionnaires (time between the two interviews was six months). Although univariate analyses showed that perceived risk was related to several measures of subsequent behavioral risk reduction, these effects disappeared after adjustment for sociodemographic variables, initial behavior, and other factors such as knowledge about AIDS, perceived self-efficacy, barriers to behavioral change, and social norms. Initial sexual behavior was strongly related to subsequent behavior. Overall, their findings did not show any adverse behavioral consequences of optimism. On the contrary, those who were pessimistic and perceived themselves to be at greater risk for AIDS were more prone to a range of potentially adverse consequences such as relatively extreme anxiety about AIDS, increased barriers to behavioral change, and social role impairment. These findings suggest that there is little or no observable benefit to an increased sense of risk for existing at-risk populations. This is not supported by Bauman and Siegel's (1987) findings. Their study did not deal with the effects of optimism on future behavior but their results suggest that people at risk, who employ defensive denial as a coping strategy and are optimistic about their vulnerability, tend to engage in more risky sexual practices, and focus on irrelevant precautions to enhance their feeling of safety.

Both studies reported in this section deal with at-risk samples and provide only a partial answer concerning the relationship between optimism, perceived vulnerability, behavioral intentions, and future behavior. As described earlier, Joseph et al. (1987) did not find a relationship between optimism and subsequent risk behavior. Their findings show that increased levels of perceived vulnerability can have disfunctional, adverse consequences for the individual. Bauman and Siegel's (1987) findings deal with explanations of concurrent behavior and suggest that positive illusions and illusions of control could hinder behavioral change (see also Garrard, Gibbons, & Warner, this volume).

In a series of studies we attempted to investigate the role of perceived risk and optimism as determinants of behavioral intentions and behavior. These studies focused on low-, medium-, and high-risk groups (van der Velde & van der Pligt, 1991; van der Velde et al., 1992). Findings in the low-risk group show a clear effect of optimism on behavioral intentions to engage in safe sex techniques. This sample consisted of heterosexual subjects with multiple sexual partners. *Safe sex* was defined as using a condom when having sex with a casual partner (see van der Velde & van der Pligt, 1991). Decreased optimism led to increased intentions to use a condom. Optimism, self-efficacy (perceived personal control over AIDS-related risks), and response efficacy (belief that using a condom reduces the likelihood of HIV infection) were the prime determinants of behavioral intentions. This simple model explained nearly 50% of the variance in behavioral intentions to reduce the riskiness of one's sexual practices. When a similar model (with optimism, response efficacy, and self-efficacy as the major predictors) was tested in a high-risk sample (van der Velde & van der Pligt, 1991) its predictive power was reduced dramatically. This sample consisted of homosexual subjects participating in a longitudinal study on AIDS. In this sample less optimistic comparative risk appraisals led to lower intentions to adopt safe sex techniques. This finding seems to be in accordance with the conclusions of Joseph et al. (1987), who argued that extreme awareness of being at risk might result in maladaptive behavioral responses. Combined together, these results suggest a curvilinear relationship between (relative) optimism and intentions to reduce the riskiness of one's sexual practices with reduced willingness to change one's sexual practices at very high and very low levels of optimism.

A cautious note seems in order, however. Perceived risk seems to play a more modest role as a determinant of *actual* (safe) behavior as opposed to behavioral intentions to take precautionary measures. In the study described earlier we also attempted to relate perceived risk and optimism to actual behavior over a 4-month time span (van der Velde, 1992). This study focused on visitors of a STD clinic in Amsterdam. More than 500 subjects (mostly prostitutes and their visitors) participated in the study. After adjustment for other variables, perceived risk and optimism were not related to subsequent behavior. Our research on adolescents' risk appraisals and sexual practices confirmed these findings (Richard & van der Pligt, 1991). Factors such as self-efficacy (e.g., Bandura, 1989) and anticipated regret were far more important predictors of sexual practices. Anticipated regret is a factor based on Janis and Mann's (1977) work and refers to the worries that are associated with choosing a specific behavioral alternative (in this case, unprotected sexual intercourse with a casual partner). When the role of perceived risk and optimism was investigated in the context of both self-efficacy and anticipated regret the latter factors had a much more profound impact on behavioral expectations about both safe sex techniques and the use of condoms.

Our research shows the expected relation between optimism and behavioral intentions to engage in safe sex techniques. Unilateral analyses generally confirm predicted effects of optimism on intention to adopt safe sex techniques and/or the intention to use condoms. The picture becomes more complex when we look at individuals whose sexual behavior is relatively risky. In this case, perceived risk and optimism can also lead to maladaptive responses. A further conclusion of the research presented in this section concerns the relatively modest role of perceived risk as a determinant of sexual practices. We did obtain effects on behavioral *intentions,* but the relation between optimism and *actual* (self-reported) behavior was modest. When the role of perceived risk is tested in the context of other cognitive variables such as self-efficacy, demographic variables, and existing behavioral practices, its effect on behavior seems negligible.

CONCLUSION

There is considerable evidence showing that people have an optimistic bias in risk perception (i.e., risks apply more to others than to oneself). This unrealistic optimism has been obtained for a wide variety of health risks. Our findings indicate that this optimism also includes AIDS-related risks. On average, low-, medium-, and high-risk groups assumed their risks to be lower than average.

In this chapter we reviewed the possible causes of this optimism and tested some of these explanations in the context of AIDS-related risks. Cognitive factors such as perceived control over specific health risks, personal experience with the specific risk, the tendency to use a relatively egocentric frame of reference, and the existence of extreme prototypes of those at risk, all seem to play a role in optimism about health risks in general. Some of these have been investigated in the context of AIDS. Results of the studies suggest that both perceived control and stereotyped beliefs about AIDS victims tend to increase optimism.

Motivational factors such as self-esteem maintenance and defensive coping styles also affect optimism. These two factors have been less extensively studied in the context of AIDS. Our own findings suggest that defensive coping styles enhance optimism about AIDS-related risks. A number of experimental studies focused on ways to reduce optimism. Reducing egocentric biases and stressing the uncontrollability of health risks both tend to reduce optimism. These results confirm the findings of correlational research. The major factors causing optimism seem to have been identified. Although most research used correlational designs with the usual drawbacks for conclusions about the possible causal role of these factors, a number of factors seem to play a major role in determining optimism. Personal experience, perceived control, and egocentric biases are the prime determinants.

An important question that remains is whether optimism is related to behavior. A variety of studies underline the functional value of optimism. Moderate degrees of optimism positively affect performance, recovery processes, and well-being (see e.g., Taylor & Brown, 1988). In the present context, the crucial question concerns the relationship between optimism about AIDS-related risks, behavioral intentions, and behavior. Unfortunately, this relationship between optimism and preventive behavior is less clear. Low- and medium-risk groups' behavioral intentions can be adequately predicted by simple models that include optimism or perceived vulnerability. For these groups, perceived vulnerability is related to the intention to engage in safe sexual practices. In high-risk groups, however, the findings reveal a different pattern. First, the predictive power of these models decreases dramatically. Second, perceived risk shows an unexpected relationship with behavioral intentions. Lower levels of optimism about AIDS risks seemed to be related to increased behavioral intentions to engage in risky practices. This finding, combined with those obtained by Joseph et al. (1987) and Bauman and Siegel (1987) suggests that motivational factors play a more prominent role in situations where the risk or threat is perceived as more severe. Defensive coping styles seem to play a more pronounced role in these circumstances. Increased defensiveness is associated with high levels of risky practices. More research into the exact role of coping processes and their effects on behavior seems necessary.

Moreover, even when perceived risk and optimism are related to behavioral intentions and subsequent behavior, the role of these factors seems very modest. Previous behavior seems to be the prime determinant of future behavior, suggesting that habitual aspects of sexual practices should not be underestimated. Factors such as self-efficacy and anticipated regret seem to have a more pronounced impact on behavioral expectations about safe practices and actual safe behavior.

These findings pose some serious problems for health education programs. It seems essential to differentiate between various groups. First, high-risk and low-risk groups need a different approach focusing on the specific determinants of risky sexual practices of each group. Stressing the vulnerability of high-risk individuals who are already aware of their risk could trigger maladaptive responses. Second, after adjustment for other variables, perceived risk and optimism are related to behavioral intentions, but only marginally or not at all to actual behavior (in this instance safe sexual practices). It could well be that some level of perceived risk and/or relative optimism is a *necessary* condition for behavioral adjustment. However, perceiving risks associated with one's behavior, does not seem sufficient to produce behavioral change.

Further research is needed to investigate the effects of health education efforts that stress the risks of specific practices as opposed to approaches that attempt to increase the self-efficacy of individuals to actually insist on safe sex techniques and/or stress the possible regret they could experience due to risky sexual practices. Self-efficacy (i.e., one's perceived control over the employment of safe, protective techniques when having sex with casual or first-time partners) seems a prime determinant of (safe) sexual behavior. Next, anticipated regret about the possible negative consequences of unprotected sexual contact with casual partners, seems a more powerful predictor of safe sex behavior than the perceived risk of contracting HIV. Our findings suggest that variables such as self-efficacy and anticipated regret are more important determinants of behavioral intentions and behavior than comparative risk appraisals. Again, pointing out the risks of specific sexual practices seem a necessary but not a sufficient reason for behavioral change. Stressing anticipated regret about possible adverse consequences of unsafe practices and helping people to exercise control over the safety of their sexual encounters could make media campaigns more effective.

ACKNOWLEDGMENT

This research was supported by grant no. 88–82 and 90–038 from the Ministry of Health.

REFERENCES

Bandura, A. (1989). Perceived self-efficacy in the exercise of control over AIDS infections. In V. M. Mays, G. W. Albee, & S. F. Schneider (Eds), *Primary prevention of AIDS* (pp. 128–141). Newbury Park, CA: Sage.

Bauman, L. J., & Siegel, K. (1987). Risk perception among gay men of the risk of AIDS associated with their sexual behavior. *Journal of Applied Social Psychology, 17*, 329–350.

Baumeister, R. F. (1989). The optimal margin of illusion. *Journal of Social and Clinical Psychology, 8*, 176–189.

Becker, M. H., Haefner, D. P., Kasl, S. V., Kirscht, J. P., Maiman, L. A., & Rosenstock, I. M. (1977). Selected psychosocial models and correlates of individual health-related behaviors. *Medical Care, 15* (Supplement), 27–46.

Catania, J. A., Gibson, D. R., Chitwood, D. D., & Coates, T. J. (1990). Methodological problems in AIDS behavioral research: Influences on measurement error and participation bias in studies of sexual behavior. *Psychological Bulletin, 108*, 339–362.

Cochran, S. D., & Mays, V. M. (1990). Sex, lies and HIV. *The New England Journal of Medicine, 322*(11), 774–775.

Cummings, K. M., Jette, A. M., Brock, B. M., & Haefner, D. P. (1979). Psychological determinants of immunization behavior in a Swine Influenza campaign. *Medical Care, 17*, 639–649.

Gerrard, M., & Warner, T. D. (1991). Antecedents of pregnancy among women Marines. *Journal of the Washington Academy of Sciences, 80*, 1015.

Hamilton, M. C. (1988). Masculine generic terms and misperceptions of AIDS risk. *Journal of Applied Social Psychology, 18*, 1222–1240.

Harris, D. M., & Guten, S. (1979). Health-protective behavior: An exploratory study. *Journal of Health and Social Behavior, 20*, 17–29.

Hooijkaas, C., van der Pligt, J., van Doornum, G. J. J., van der Linden, M. M. D., & Coutinho, R. (1989). Onderschatting relatief risico op HIV bij heteroseksuelen met veel wisselende partners [Underestimation of relative HIV-risk by heterosexual respondents with multiple (sexual) partners.] *Tijdschrift voor Sociale Gezondheidszorg, 67*, 122–146.

Janis, I. L., & Mann, L. (1977). *Decision making: A psychological analysis of conflict, choice, and commitment.* New York: The Free Press.

Janz, N., & Becker, M. (1984). The health belief model: A decade later. *Health Education Quarterly, 11,* 1–47.

Joseph, J. G., Montgomey, S. B., Emmons, C. A., Kirscht, J. P., Kessler, R. C., Ostrow, D. G., Wortman, C. B., O'Brien, K., Eller, M., & Eshleman, S. (1987). Perceived risk of AIDS: Assessing the behavioral and psychological consequences in a cohort of gay men. *Journal of Applied Social Psychology, 17,* 231–250.

Kasl, S. V. (1975). Social psychological characteristics associated with behaviors that reduce cardiovascular risk. In A. J. EnsJow & J. Henderson (Eds.) *Applying behavioral science to cardiovascular risk* (pp. 173–180). Dallas TX: American Heart Association.

Kirscht, J. P. (1983). Preventive health behavior: A review of research and issues. *Health Psychology, 2,* 279–301.

Knopf, A. (1976). Changes in women's opinions about cancer. *Social Science and Medicine, 10,* 191–195.

Kunreuther, H. (1979). The changing societal consequences of risk from natural hazards. *The Annals of the American Academy of Political and Social Science, 443,* 104–116.

Lee, C. (1989). Perceptions of immunity to disease in adult smokers. *Journal of Behavioral Medicine, 12,* 267–277.

Leventhal, H., Safer, M. A., & Panagis, D. M. (1983). The impact of communications on self-regulation of health beliefs, decisions, and behavior. *Health Education Quarterly, 10,* 3–31.

Pechacek, T., & Danaher, B. (1979). How and why people quit smoking: A cognitive-behavioral analysis. In P. Kendall & S. Hollon (Eds.), *Cognitive behavioral intervention: Theory, research, and procedures* (pp. 389–422). New York: Academic Press.

Perloff, L. S. (1982). *Nonvictims' judgments of unique and universal vulnerability to future misfortune.* Unpublished doctoral dissertation, Northwestern University, Evanston, IL.

Perloff, L. S., & Farbisz, R. (1985). *Perceptions of uniqueness and illusions of invulnerability to divorce.* Paper presented at the Midwestern Psychological Association meeting, Chicago.

Perloff, L. S., & Fetzer, B. K. (1986). Self-other judgments and perceived vulnerability to victimization. *Journal of Personality and Social Psychology, 50,* 502–511.

Richard, R., & van der Pligt, J. (1991). Factors affecting condom-use among adolescent. *Journal of Community & Applied Social Psychology, 50,* 502–511.

Rippetoe, P. A., & Rogers, R. W. (1987). Effects of components of protection-motivation theory on adaptive and maladaptive coping with a health threat. *Journal of Personality and Social Psychology, 52,* 596–604.

Rogers, R. W. (1975). A protection motivation theory of fear appeals and attitude change. *The Journal of Psychology, 91,* 93–114.

Shaklee, H., & Fischhoff, B. (1990). The psychology of contraceptive surprises: Cumulative risk and contraceptive effectiveness. *Journal of Applied Psychology, (20)5,* 385–403.

Slovic, P., Fischhoff, B., & Lichtenstein, S. (1978). Accident probabilities and seat belt usage: A psychological perceptive. *Accident Analysis and Prevention, 10,* 281–285.

Svenson, O. (1981). Are we all less risky and more skillful than our fellow drivers? *Acta Psychologica, 47,* 143–148.

Taylor, S. E., Lichtman, R. R., & Wood, J. V. (1984). Attributions, beliefs about control, and adjustment to breast cancer. *Journal of Personality and Social Psychology, 46,* 489–502.

Taylor, S. E., & Brown, J. D. (1988). Illusion and well-being: A social-psychological perspective on mental health. *Psychological Bulletin, 103,* 193–210.

van der Pligt, J. (1991). Risicoperceptie, onrealistisch optimism en AIDS-preventief gedrag [Risk perception, unrealistic optimism and preventive behavior.] *Nederlands Tijdschrift voor de Psychologie, 46,* 228–237.

van der Pligt, J., de Gilder, D., Syroit, J., Brehovsky, M., Dilova, M., Georgiewa, P., Saldarelli, R., Stefanski, R., Stepper, S., & Willy, G. (in press). Dimensional salience and unrealistic optimism about future life events. *European Journal of Social Psychology.*

van der Velde, F. W., & van der Pligt, J. (1991). Aids related health behavior: Coping, protection motivation and previous behavior. *Behavioral Medicine, 14,* 429–452.

van der Velde, F. W., van der Pligt, J., & Hooijkaas, C. (1992). Risk perception and behavior: Pessimism, realism, and optimism about AIDS-related health behavior. *Psychology and Health, 6,* 23–28.

Weinstein, N. D. (1980). Unrealistic optimism about future life events. *Journal of Personality and Social Psychology, 39,* 806–820.

Weinstein, N. D. (1982). Unrealistic optimism about susceptibility to health problems. *Journal of Behavioral Medicine, 5,* 441–460.

Weinstein, N. D. (1983). Reducing unrealistic optimism about illness susceptibility. *Health Psychology, 2,* 11–20.

Weinstein, N. D. (1984). Why it won't happen to me: perceptions of risk factors and susceptibility. *Health Psychology, 3,* 431–457.

Weinstein, N. D. (1989). Effects of personal experience on self-protective behavior. *Psychological Bulletin, 105,* 31–50.

3 Perceived Vulnerability to HIV Infection and AIDS Preventive Behavior: A Critical Review of the Evidence

Meg Gerrard
Frederick X. Gibbons
Teddy D. Warner
Gabie E. Smith
Iowa State University

We all engage in behavior that is potentially harmful to our health and well-being. Ideally, our assessment of the likelihood that we will actually suffer the negative consequences associated with these risks has led us to the conclusion that we can or should proceed with the risky behavior. For example, we may decide that getting to an appointment on time is worth the risks that come with driving faster than usual, or that the thrill and excitement of downhill skiing are worth the risk of injury. For many of us, the pleasure of lying on the beach occasionally outweighs the potential risk associated with exposure to the sun's ultraviolet rays.

In each of these situations rational people are capable of obtaining relevant information and then making the necessary risk assessment in order to make a reasonable estimate of their vulnerability to the potential negative outcome. Then, based on this assessment, they can decide whether to engage in risky, or perhaps precautionary, behavior. In other words, given sufficient information, we can conduct a reasonably sophisticated, rational risk analysis by estimating the probability and severity of various potential negative outcomes of our activities. We then weigh the benefits of the risky behaviors against these potential consequences. A substantial literature suggests that this rational model is, in fact, an accurate description of many types of risk-taking and risk-avoidance behavior (for reviews see Becker & Maiman, 1983; Cleary, 1987; Pagel & Davidson, 1984; Wallston & Wallston, 1984).

A central component of this rational approach is the assumption that an individual's assessment of his or her personal vulnerability to a specific negative event is influential in the decision to engage in behaviors that decrease the likelihood of those events occurring. This assumption is reflected by the inclusion of the construct of perceived vulnerability or perceived susceptibility in virtually all models of preventive or precautionary health behavior. Two comprehensive reviews of the literature have supported this assumption: Becker (1974) concluded that perceived vulnerability predicted preventive behaviors in 10 of the 11 studies relevant to this issue published prior to 1974; and Janz and Becker (1984) reported that 20 of the 26 studies published between 1974 and 1984 supported the relationship.

Recently, however, a number of authors have questioned the empirical support for the role of perceived vulnerability in precautionary and preventive health behavior, particularly when the preventive behaviors are complex and the negative outcome (disease) is potentially extremely serious (cf. Catania, Kegeles, & Coates, 1990; Weinstein, Sandman, & Roberts, 1990, 1991). In their re-examination of the issue, Montgomery et al. (1989) suggested that the role of perceived vulnerability is qualitatively different when the behavior in question is simple (e.g., attending a screening clinic), than when it is complicated, taxing, or socially complex. These authors reported that although about three quarters of the studies reviewed by Janz and Becker did find a significant relationship between perceptions of vulnerability and preventive behavior, a large number of these studies investigated negative events that were either not very serious (e.g., influenza), or for which the preventive behaviors were not very complex (e.g., immunization, returning for a follow-up appointment). When Montgomery et al. examined only that subset of studies that investigated the relationship between perceived susceptibility to negative events with extreme threat and complex preventive behaviors (such as breast self-examination or compliance with an insulin-dependent diabetic regimen), they found that only 25% of the studies reported a significant perceived vulnerability/precautionary behavior relationship.

HIV infection presents a very serious threat to one's health. In addition, AIDS prevention requires a complex series of behaviors. This particular combination of characteristics—severe consequences and complex actions—raises the question of whether beliefs about the likelihood that one will contract HIV or develop AIDS does have an impact on one's decision to decrease sexual risk behaviors. The primary purpose of this chapter is to provide a critical review of the research that has examined this relationship. We will also discuss the differences between the motivational aspects of perceived vulnerability to HIV infection and the same motivational aspects associated with perceived vulnerability to other negative events. We begin with a brief review of the theoretical models postulating that perceptions of susceptibility motivate preventive or precautionary behavior. Then we discuss the unique nature of decisions about risky sexual behavior. These discussions provide the background for our review of the literature and assessment of the empirical support for the basic hypothesis that increases in perceived risk or susceptibility lead to increases in preventive or precautionary behavior. (In order to reduce repetitiveness we refer to this proposed relationship simply as "the hypothesis" or as the risk perception/preventive behavior hypothesis throughout this chapter.)

THEORETICAL MODELS

The Health Belief Model

The Health Belief Model was developed in the 1950s to explain and predict compliance with preventive recommendations (Becker, 1974; Rosenstock, 1966, 1974). Like many other models of health behavior, the health belief model contains four "basic ingredients" that are thought to promote (or inhibit) health relevant actions. These basic components involve subjective perceptions of the following factors: (a) severity of the negative event, (b) benefits of specific preventive actions, (c) barriers to performing those actions, and (d) likelihood that the negative event will actually occur. According to this model, after a person has assessed the severity of the negative event and his or her personal vulnerability to it, he or she weighs the relative benefits of specific preventive or precautionary behaviors against the potential barriers to undertaking those actions.

Although the model assumes that whether preventive behaviors actually result is determined by a more or less rational cost–benefit analysis, it does not ignore the possibility of irrational decisions. Both the original model and its recent reinterpretation (Becker & Rosenstock, 1987) suggest that sociopsychological variables may influence the veridicality of the person's perception of threat. These variables include traits such as compliance and emotionality. Major reviews of the relevant research have concluded that there is substantial support for the model, and in particular, for the role of perceived susceptibility in predicting preventive behaviors. For example, vulnerability perceptions have been shown to accurately predict swine flu inoculation, Tay-Sachs disease screening, and high blood pressure screening (for reviews see Becker & Rosenstock, 1987; Janz & Becker, 1984).

Roger's Protection Motivation Theory

The original formulation of Protection Motivation Theory was also designed to investigate the effects of persuasive messages on the adoption of health protective behaviors (Rogers, 1975). This model suggests that information about a health hazard stimulates a cognitive appraisal of the severity and probability of the negative event, as well as the efficacy of the recommended precautionary action. This appraisal then acts as a mediator of the persuasive effects of the communication by arousing a motivation to protect oneself. It is that motivation, according to the theory, that arouses, sustains, and directs preventive or protective behaviors. (A revision of the model [Maddux & Rogers, 1983] introduced self-efficacy as an additional component.) In a review of the literature, Rogers (1983) concluded that research has supported the major elements of the model, including the role of subjective probabilities of suffering negative health outcomes as a cognitive mediator of precautionary behavior.

The Precaution Adoption Process

More recently, Weinstein (1988) presented yet another model relevant to HIV preventive behavior, the Precaution Adoption Process. This model assumes that the steps to adopting a preventive behavior follow "an orderly sequence of qualitatively different cognitive stages" (p. 355). The final decision to engage in a precautionary behavior will not occur until a person considers him or herself to be personally vulnerable to the negative event. In this model, perceived vulnerability is described as a series of cumulative stages rather than a continuum, and these stages are defined in terms of the beliefs people hold about the risk situation. In Stage 1 people learn that the hazard (e.g., radon, HIV infection) exists. In Stage 2 they recognize that the hazard is significant for others; but they have not yet come to the conclusion that they themselves are at risk. By Stage 3 they have recognized their own vulnerability to the hazard. Achieving Stage 3 is posited to be a necessary (but not sufficient) step that precedes the decision to engage in preventive behaviors. In order for a person to decide to act (Stage 4), and then proceed with the behavior (Stage 5), the individual must also go through similar stages of belief about the severity of the disease and the efficacy of the precaution. Thus, the achievement of Stage 3 on all three dimensions—vulnerability, severity, and efficacy—is necessary before a person will begin to assess the costs of the precautionary behavior and decide whether to act.

In summary, this seemingly ubiquitous construct—perceptions of the likelihood that one will actually suffer negative consequences—plays a prominent role in each one of these major models of health behavior. More specifically, in all three models increased perceptions of susceptibility are hypothesized to precede changes (increases) in precautionary or preventive behaviors. Moreover, although it is recognized that these perceptions may reflect biased and/or faulty information-processing and emotional responses to threat, decisions about engaging in preventive behaviors are *generally* considered to be rational.

SEXUAL DECISION MAKING AND RISK BEHAVIOR

Sexual behavior presents its own unique set of risks, and there are many of them. Adolescents contemplating sexual activity, for example, must consider the threat of punishment and/or embarrassment if they get caught. Heterosexuals must think about the potential for unwanted pregnancy. Gay men and lesbian women must weigh the possibility of societal disapproval against the inconvenience and discomfort of hiding their sexual preferences. Married people must weigh the excitement associated with the novelty of an extramarital affair against the risk of discord and possible dissolution of their marriage. The unique nature of the sex drive contributes to the fact that many of these decisions are often made in the heat of the moment—while the person is emotionally and physically aroused—rather than after careful, or for that matter, even rational deliberation. In fact, one of the most consistent findings in the literature on the psychology of sexual behavior is that such decisions are heavily influenced by an emotional disposition that is likely to interfere with a rational risk assessment (i.e., one's emotional responses to sexuality).

Emotional Interference

Contraceptive Behavior.   Our own research, and that of others, has demonstrated that emotional responses to sex are strongly associated with contraceptive behavior. More specifically, there is evidence that negative emotional orientations toward sexuality (called *sex guilt* or *erotophobia;* Mosher, 1966, 1968; White, Fisher, Byrne, & Kingma, 1977) are associated with a general lack of knowledge about contraception (Mendelsohn & Mosher, 1979; Mosher, 1979). It is not surprising then that these attitudes also predict discomfort with purchasing contraceptives (Fisher, Fisher, & Byrne, 1977), and the use of ineffective methods of birth control (Fisher et al., 1979; Geis & Gerrard, 1984; Gerrard, 1982, 1987; Mosher, 1973). In addition we have demonstrated that this emotional orientation is also related to inconsistent use of effective methods, for example, among women who use oral contraceptives, those who are erotophobic are less likely to take their pills every day as prescribed than are other women, and therefore are more likely to get pregnant (Gerrard, 1977).

Risk Perception.   One of the reasons that people with erotophobia or high levels of sex guilt are less effective at avoiding unplanned pregnancy appears to be that their emotional reactions to sex interfere with their perceptions of the likelihood that they will engage in behaviors that will put them at risk. This phenomenon was demonstrated in a study of the sexual behavior of college men. Fisher (1984) asked erotophobic and erotophilic men to predict whether they would have sexual intercourse during the coming month. Even when past sexual frequency was statistically controlled, erotophilics were more likely than erotophobics to predict that they would have intercourse. Next, Fisher checked the accuracy of the men's predictions at the end of the month. He found that the erotophobic men were more likely to have underestimated their actual frequency of intercourse (and thus the probability that they would engage in risky behavior) than were erotophobic men.

Preliminary results from one of our recent studies of risk perception is also relevant here (Gerrard & Luus, 1992). In this study, sexually active women were asked to estimate the probability that they would conceive if they were to use specific methods of birth control and engage in intercourse at specific rates during the coming year. For example, they were asked to estimate the likelihood of getting pregnant if they had intercourse an average of twice a week and used condoms, and then again if they had intercourse three times a week and relied on withdrawal. Our results indicated that these women, in general, were relatively accurate in estimating the probability of conception. Those who had a negative emotional orientation toward sexuality (i.e., erotophobics), however, underestimated their vulnerability to pregnancy if they were to rely on ineffective methods of contraception. This is particularly interesting given that erotophobic people are, in fact, much more likely to use ineffective methods of contraception (Gerrard, 1977, 1982, 1987). In other words, negative emotional responses to sex can interfere with even the first step in the complicated process of protecting oneself from unwanted pregnancy—deciding prior to engaging in intercourse whether one is likely to experience the negative consequences that potentially come with it.

Summary. There is evidence, then, that emotional reactions to sex can interfere with peoples' estimates of the likelihood that they will engage in risky sexual behaviors, and with their assessment of their vulnerability to the negative consequences of unprotected sexual intercourse. More generally, it appears that decisions regarding sexual risk taking are vulnerable to emotional interference, and therefore may not be as rational as decisions involving behaviors that are less emotion-laden such as using seat belts or getting immunizations. Given that emotional responses to sexuality interfere with risk assessment as well as risk behavior, it is appropriate to question whether decisions regarding sexual behaviors that are relevant to HIV infection reflect a rational decision making process, or instead are mediated by the same type of emotional reactivity. More specifically, is HIV-relevant behavior directly related to perceived vulnerability to HIV infection?

PERCEIVED VULNERABILITY AND AIDS PREVENTIVE BEHAVIOR: EMPIRICAL EVIDENCE

A number of studies have explored the hypothesized relationship between HIV risk perceptions and precautionary sexual behavior. For the purpose of this review, these studies are grouped into three general categories based on their designs. The first category includes *cross-sectional* studies, in which risk perception and risk or preventive behaviors are measured concurrently. The authors of these studies have typically asked subjects about their current risk and preventive behaviors, or asked them to report their behavior in the recent past (e.g., for the 3 to 12 months preceding data collection). The second category includes *retrospective behavior change* studies. These studies are cross-sectional in that, like the first category, measures of perceived vulnerability and behavior are collected at the same point in time. They are distinguished from the first category, however, by the fact that the subjects are asked to describe changes in their behavior over some specified period of time rather than simply report their risk behaviors. The third category includes studies using *prospective* designs. In these studies perceptions of risk and behavior are both assessed at Time 1, and then behavior is assessed again at a later date. This procedure allows the assessment of behavior change without having to rely on subject's memory of behavior that in some instances may be quite remote, and without alerting the respondent to the exact purpose of the question.

Cross-Sectional Studies

As Table 3.1 reveals, the largest of the three categories of research is the cross-sectional group. These studies have examined the risk perception/prevention hypothesis in a variety of different populations and they have produced mixed results. In fact, only three of these studies have provided clear evidence of the hypothesized correlation. In one, Hingson, Strunin, Berlin, and Heeren (1990) employed random digit dialing to survey male and female (primarily heterosexual) adolescents in Massachusetts. This sample of 1,773 16 to 19-year-olds was asked about their condom use and perceived risk of AIDS. The authors found that the adolescents who were most likely to say that they always used condoms were those who felt most susceptible to AIDS.

In a study designed to sample a population that was engaging in relatively high-risk behaviors, Valdisseri et al. (1988) surveyed 955 homosexual men in the Pittsburgh component of the Multicenter AIDS Cohort Study (MACS) who reported having had anal intercourse within the last 6 months. Of these men 60% had been tested for HIV, and 22% of those tested were seropositive. The authors found that the men who were most concerned about their personal risk of AIDS were more likely to report always using condoms than were those who were least concerned. As might be expected, this study also revealed that underestimation of the risk was associated with persistent high-risk sexual behavior.

Finally, additional supportive evidence for the vulnerability/behavior hypothesis was provided by Campbell, Peplau, and DeBro (1990) in an examination of college students' *intentions* to use a condom with a new partner. These authors reported that worry about contracting sexually transmitted diseases (STDs) was a strong predictor of intention to use a condom. Thus, these three cross-sectional studies of homosexual men and heterosexual men and women, ranging in age from adolescence through adulthood, have reported positive correlations between perceived risk and preventive behavior (i.e., they support the hypothesis).

A number of other cross-sectional studies, however, have found evidence of either a *negative* relationship between risk estimates and preventive behaviors, or, in one case, a positive association between risk perception and risk promoting behavior. In Gerrard and Warner (1992), college women with low levels of perceived vulnerability to AIDS were more likely to claim regular use of condoms than were women with high perceived vulnerability. Baldwin and Baldwin (1988) also found that perceived risk of contracting HIV in a college student sample was positively correlated with an important risk behavior, namely number of sex partners. Kelly et al. (1990) reported similar results in a sample of

TABLE 3.1
Summary of Studies

Cross-Sectional Studies

Study	Subjects	Outcome Variables	Results
Baldwin & Baldwin (1988)	851 college students	Number of sex partners, Condom use	PR positively correlated with number of partners; PR did not predict condom use
Campbell et al. (1990)	393 college students	Intention to use condoms	Worry about STDs predicted intention to use condoms
Catania et al. (1991)	1,229 single hetero-and homo-sexual adults	Condom use	PR did not predict condom use
Catania et al. (1989)	114 female adolescents	Condom use	PR did not predict condom use
Gerrard & Warner (1992)	311 female college students	Condon use	PR negatively correlated with condom use
Hingson et al. (1990)	1,173 adolescents	Condom use	PR positively associated with condom use
Kelly et al. (1990)	481 gay men	Unprotected anal intercourse	PR estimates positively associated with reports of engaging in more unprotected anal intercourse
Pleck et al. (1990)	1,880 male adolescents	Intention to use condoms	PR did not prdict intention to use condoms
Valdiserri et al. (1988)	955 gay males	Condom use	PR positively correlated with condom use
Weisman et al. (1989)	430 female adolescents	Condom use	PR did not predict condom use

Retrospective Behavior Change Studies

Chandarana et al. (1990)	148 gay men	Reported reduction in risk behaviors	PR correlated with reduction of risk behaviors
Emmons et al. (1986)	909 gay men	Global risk behavior change, number of sex partners, number of anonymous sex partners	PR associated with global behavior change, reduction in number of sex partners, and an increase in number of anonymous sex partners
Keeter & Bradford (1988)	409 single adults	Number of partners, knowledge of potential partners, condom use	PR associated with behavior change
Klein et al. (1987)	64 gay physicians	Number of partners, anal intercourse	PR associated with decreased risk behaviors

(Continued)

TABLE 3.1
(Continued)

Cross-Sectional Studies

Study	Subjects	Outcome Variables	Results
Wolcott et al. (1990)	84 gay physicians	Number of partners, anal intercourse, fellatio	Replicated Klein et al. findings above

Prospective Studies

Study	Subjects	Outcome Variables	Results
Aspinwall et al. (1991)	389 gay men	Number of anonymous partners, frequency of unprotected anal intercourse, number of different partners	PR was not associated with decreases in number of anonymous sex partners or frequency of unprotected anal intercourse; PR-number of partners relationship was moderated by serostatus and existence of a primary partner
Joseph, Montgomery, Emmons, Kirscht et al. (1987)	637 gay men	Number of partners, anonymous partners, receptive anal, oral-genital, and/or insertive oral-anal intercourse	Positive correlation between PR and behavioral risk reduction disappears when adjusted for baseline sexual risk behavior
Montgomery et al. (1989)	495 gay men	Frequency of receptive anal intercourse, condom use, number and type of partners (multiple vs. single, primary vs. anonymous)	PR estimates did not predict precautionary or sexual behavior, regardless of prior risk behavior patterns

PR = Perceived Risk.

481 patrons of gay bars in Seattle, Washington; Tampa, Florida; and Mobile, Alabama. In that study, men with high-risk estimates reported engaging in more unprotected anal intercourse with more sex partners than did men with low estimates. Essentially identical results have been published by several other groups of researchers (Catania, Coates et al., 1991; Catania, Dolcini et al., 1989; Pleck, Sonenstein, & Ku, 1990). In these instances, then, rather than being associated with precautionary measures, perceptions that one is at risk appear to be an accurate reflection of actual risky behavior.

Conclusions From Cross-Sectional Studies.   Given the temporal dimension of the perceived risk/preventive behavior hypothesis, (i.e., perceptions of vulnerability *precede* increases in precautionary behavior), it is not surprising that the results of these studies include a mixture of positive and negative correlations. The implicit assumption behind these cross-sectional studies is that a positive correlation between risk perceptions and preventive behaviors indicates that people who think that they are at risk have decided to practice prevention, and those who do not think that they are at risk have not made that decision. Perceived vulnerability, however, means something quite different to a person who has already changed his or her risk behavior, by beginning to practice risk reduction, than it does to someone who has not yet made that change. In other words, people who believe that they are at risk may engage in appropriate behavior because of that belief. Then, having practiced preventive behaviors, they decide that they are less susceptible than they were previously, which results in a decrease and maybe even a reversal of the correlation between vulnerability and precautionary behavior. In short, one potential reason why these cross-sectional studies provide mixed results is methodological: Cross-sectional designs cannot provide an adequate test of the hypothesis that increased risk perceptions *precede* increases in precautionary behavior.

Moreover, when a positive correlation between risk perception and precautionary behaviors does exist it can be interpreted in a number of ways. The simplest (and most common) interpretation is that perceived vulnerability encourages or promotes appropriate precautionary or prophylactic behaviors. Unfortunately, it is also possible that preventive behavior may actually precede the perception of risk (cf. Ajzen & Timko, 1986; Emmons et al., 1986). Thus, people who engage in precautionary behaviors may report high-risk perceptions in order to justify their efforts (cf. Fazio & Zanna, 1981). Cross-sectional studies also cannot answer this basic chicken-and-egg question: Which comes first, the increased risk perception or the increased precautionary behavior? In order to answer this question unequivocally, it would be necessary to assess risk perception initially and then to measure risk and/or preventive behavior several times. We return to this issue later.

Retrospective Behavior Change Studies

The authors of retrospective studies have attempted to address the weaknesses inherent in the simple cross-sectional designs by asking subjects to retrospectively report *changes* in their risk and preventive behaviors. In general, these studies *do* provide support for the risk perception/preventive behavior hypothesis. For example, in a survey of high-risk males in southern California (64 homosexual physicians and 58 homosexual students at UCLA), Klein et al. (1987) found that the physicians' perceptions of vulnerability were associated with reported decreases in risk behaviors. More specifically, physicians who thought that they were members of a high-risk group (a dichotomous variable) were more likely than those in the low-risk group to report having decreased their HIV risk behavior since the onset of the AIDS epidemic. In addition, those who rated themselves as most vulnerable reported the most behavior change. A second study of 81 members of the same gay physicians' group replicated this finding (Wolcott, Sullivan, & Klein, 1990).

Keeter and Bradford (1988) reported similar results in a study in which they conducted telephone interviews with 409 unmarried, mostly heterosexual adults ages 18–39 in Richmond, Virginia. In this study, 73% of the non-monogamous subjects reported that "awareness of AIDS had influenced their sexual behavior" (p. 149). More recently, Chandarana, Conlon, Noh, and Field (1990) asked 224 homosexual men in Canada about their AIDS preventive behavior and their thoughts about AIDS. They found that worry and concern about AIDS was significantly correlated with retrospective reports of reductions in risk behaviors.

Before moving on to the prospective studies, it is instructive to examine one additional study that reported mixed results. In the first of a series of studies of homosexual men participating in the Chicago component of the MACS, Emmons et al. (1986) assessed a broad range of psychosocial variables thought to be related to homosexual men's responses to AIDS. They reported a modest positive relationship between perceived vulnerability to AIDS and two of their dependent measures: a retrospective report of "global behavioral change" and a retrospective report of "attempts to reduce the number of sexual partners" (p. 340). They found a strong negative relationship, however, between perceived risk and another dependent variable: "avoidance of anonymous sexual partners."

Summary of the Cross-Sectional and Retrospective Behavior Change Studies.   It appears that, in general, simple cross-sectional studies do not offer much support for the hypothesis that people who perceive themselves to be at relatively high risk are motivated to decrease their risk behaviors and increase their preventive behaviors. This may be due partly to an inability of this type of design to adequately capture the dynamic aspects of the hypothesis. Evidence of this is the fact that retrospective behavior change studies, for the most part, do appear to support the hypothesis. It should be noted, however, that the self-reports of behavior change in these studies are susceptible to the same bias as self-reports of preventive behaviors in the simple cross-sectional studies; subjects who report high susceptibility may do so, at least in part, in order to justify increased preventive behaviors. The purpose of retrospective studies is also particularly likely to be transparent, increasing the likelihood that respondents who perceive themselves to be at risk will be motivated to report decreasing their risk behavior.

Prospective Studies

Fortunately, three prospective studies have been conducted on gay men that provide an opportunity to assess the contribution of risk perceptions to changes in sexual behavior more directly. The first of these was a study specifically designed (among other things) to examine the relation between perceived likelihood of contracting the virus and changes in sexual behavior 6 months later (Joseph, Montgomery, Emmons, Kirscht, et al., 1987). The subjects for this study were 637 homosexual men enrolled in the MACS in Chicago. The criteria for inclusion in this research were that the men had not been diagnosed with AIDS and were not being paid for sex at the time of the study. The results appeared to be consistent with the hypothesis: perceived risk at Time 1 was positively correlated with behavior change between Time 1 and Time 2. When the authors adjusted for baseline sexual risk behavior, however, this positive relationship essentially disappeared. They concluded that "the apparent link between perceived risk and longitudinal changes in behavior is actually explained by the covariability of a sense of risk and behavior at S [time] 1" (p. 242).

This analysis suggests that initial (i.e., "Time 1") risk perceptions are a reflection of prior behavior—assuming the individual was sexually active at that time—and therefore are not true baselines. Likewise, previous risk behavior influences both initial perceived vulnerability and subsequent behavior change, and must be controlled (statistically or otherwise) when investigating the relationship between risk estimates and behavior change. Joseph et al. also explored the possibility that other behaviors could mediate the relationship between risk perceptions and risk reduction. In order to test this possibility, they examined whether persons with high perceived risk subsequently either sought more knowledge about AIDS or formed stronger affiliations within the gay community, both factors that might have mediated risk reduction. They concluded from these analyses that initial risk perceptions are not related to the development of other attitudes that facilitate behavioral risk reduction.

It is worth noting that the subjects for this study were drawn from the same Chicago MACS sample as one of the retrospective behavior change studies previously described (Emmons et al., 1986). And as the authors suggested, the "results of the longitudinal analyses . . . are dramatically different from those obtained with analyses of [retrospective behavior change] data" (Joseph, Montgomery, Emmons, Kessler et al. 1987, p. 87). More specifically, unlike their earlier retrospective behavior change study, the results of this study provided no support at all for either a direct or an indirect effect of risk perceptions on AIDS preventive behavior.

The second prospective study (conducted by the same group of researchers, Montgomery et al., 1989) also drew volunteers from the MACS sample in Chicago. This investigation was different than the first in that follow-up data on changes in risk behaviors were obtained 6, 12, and 18 months after initial data collection. Analyses were conducted separately for subjects with high- and low-risk behavioral patterns in order to examine the possibility that prior risk behaviors *moderate* the relationship between perceived vulnerability and behavior change. The results were quite similar to those obtained by these authors in their first longitudinal study—risk estimates did not predict sexual or precautionary behavior, regardless of prior risk behavioral patterns. In fact, they found that perceived vulnerability was negatively related to one of the 10 dependent variables, leading them to conclude that if anything, perceived risk of AIDS may have a deleterious effect on sexual risk reduction.

Perhaps the most thorough investigation of the role of perceived vulnerability is provided in a recent study by Taylor and her colleagues (Aspinwall, Kemeny, Taylor, Schneider, & Dudley, 1991). These authors assessed the AIDS risk perceptions of 389 exclusively homosexual men participating in the Los Angeles MACS project. All of the subjects knew their antibody status—42% were HIV seropositive, 58% were seronegative—and none of them had been diagnosed with ARC or AIDS at the time of the study. One half of the participants in this study had a primary sexual partner, and one half did not. At Time 1 in this longitudinal investigation the men were asked about their absolute risks of contracting AIDS ("Considering all the different factors that may contribute to AIDS, including your own past and present behavior, what would you say are your chances of getting AIDS?") and their relative risk ("When you compare yourself to the average gay man, what would you say are your chances of getting AIDS?"). Six months later they were asked about three specific sexual risk behaviors during the intervening 6-month period (i.e., number of anonymous partners, frequency of anal intercourse without a condom, and number of different sexual intercourse partners).

The data provided no evidence that perceived vulnerability was associated with decreases in the number of anonymous partners or the frequency of anal intercourse. There was, however, an interaction between HIV serostatus and whether the men had a primary sexual partner on a third dependent variable, number of sexual partners. Among men without a primary partner, perceptions of risk were associated with an increase in the seropositive participants' number of sexual partners, and a decrease in the seronegative participants' number of sexual partners. Perceptions of vulnerability did not predict changes in risk behavior among men with a primary sexual partner.

In two respects, the design of the Aspinwall study provided a more exhaustive search for an association between perceptions of vulnerability and risk behavior than did any of the studies previously discussed. First, the authors employed two assessments of perceived vulnerability, one that was designed to assess relative vulnerability, and one that was designed to assess absolute vulnerability. Second, three different measures of sexual risk behaviors were collected. Nonetheless, this investigation did not produce support for the hypothesis—a significant relationship was found on only one of three measures of risk behavior, it was found in only two of four cells, and the direction of the relationship was different in these two cells. Thus, it appears that none of these prospective studies provide support for the hypothesis.

RISK REDUCTION WITHOUT RISK PERCEPTION:
A PARADOX

We must conclude from this review of the literature that there is relatively little support for the hypothesis that perceptions of HIV vulnerability motivate risk reduction. This is particularly surprising in light of the fact that there have been dramatic decreases in HIV-related sexual risk behaviors, and those changes have clearly paralleled the growth in public awareness of the threat of AIDS. The largest changes have been reported among homosexual men, but modest changes have also been found in other segments of the population, including college students (Becker & Joseph, 1988; Martin, 1987; McKusick, Horstman, & Coates, 1985; Wolcott et al., 1990). Given that these changes are, as two researchers in the area have suggested, perhaps "the most rapid and profound response to a health threat which has ever been documented" (Becker & Joseph, 1988, p. 407), how can they be unrelated to perceived vulnerability? Can it be that people have altered their sexual behavior, often dramatically, but that these changes were not associated with the perception that they were at risk of contracting HIV? Although it appears that many of the studies are confusing and their findings contradictory, our review of the literature suggests that there is a distinct possibility that sexual risk taking, unlike other risk and precautionary behaviors, occurs more or less independent of relevant risk perceptions. Before settling on that conclusion, however, we think that it is important to examine some of the myriad of methodological issues that are, at least in part, responsible for much of the confusion. Some of these problems are minor, but given the frequency with which they are encountered, they are worth discussing.

Measurement Issues

Variance. To begin with, it is quite possible that many of the current methods of measuring risk perceptions—and we include some of our own methods in this category—are not sufficiently sensitive to allow for an adequate test of its association with behavior change. A perusal of the items employed in the majority of the studies reveals several problems that support this observation. For example, a number of investigators have assessed perceptions of HIV vulnerability by asking subjects to respond to items such as "What is the chance that you will get AIDS in the next 5 years?" on a 5-point scale where 1 - "very sure that it will not happen" and 5 - "very sure that it will happen" (cf. Baldwin & Baldwin, 1988; Weisman et al., 1989). When this question is asked of college students or any other relatively low-risk sample, the most reasonable reply is "1," which, of course, creates a serious problem with restricted range and variance.

Fortunately, the prospective studies cited earlier (Aspinwall et al., 1991; Joseph, Montgomery, Emmons, Kessler et al., 1987; Montgomery et al., 1989) do not suffer from this problem. For one thing, a sizable proportion (40%–50%) of the subjects in each of these studies had tested positive for HIV at the time of the survey. As a group, the subjects were clearly at least at moderate, if not high-risk of contracting AIDS, and this should have produced adequate variance. Second, each of these studies employed both absolute and comparative questions to assess perceptions of vulnerability. Responses to these two questions were then combined, producing an index with apparently reasonable range and variance.

On the other hand, too much variance can also create interpretational problems. Self-reports of both sexual behaviors and vulnerability are likely to reveal outliers who claim extremely safe or extremely unsafe sexual behavior, and/or maintain extreme perceptions of vulnerability. For example, in our recent study of women Marines (Gerrard, Gibbons, & Warner, 1991; Gerrard & Warner, 1992), individual estimates of AIDS risk ranged from 1 in 2, to 1 in over 10 million.[1] 'Likewise, reports of frequency of intercourse varied from 0 to more than 30 times per month. Although both restricted and extreme variability may reflect real differences in experience and perceptions, they can also obscure or artificially inflate actual relationships between risk perception and behavior. It is likely that the distributions of the variables in this area of research require transformation more often than has been reported in the research reviewed above.

Validity of Self-Reported Sexual Behavior.   Many people have questioned the validity of self-reports of sexual behavior and condom use (Catania, Gibson, Chitwood, & Coates, 1990). Conscious distortions can be motivated by embarrassment or fear of reprisals, or self-presentational concerns, such as the desire to conceal or embellish specific sexual behaviors. Participants' self-reports may also be affected by less conscious motivations like sex guilt or erotophobia (Mosher, 1966, 1968; White et al., 1977). In addition, people may make honest errors, not necessarily motivated by psychological factors, in recalling the frequency with which they engage in specific behaviors (cf. Catania, Gibson et al., 1990). One approach to assessing the validity of self-reports is to examine the relationship between partners' reports of how often they engage in specific sexual behaviors or use condoms over a given period of time. For example, in a study of the reliability and validity of recall measures of intercourse among gay men, McLaws, Oldenburg, Ross, and Cooper (1990) found reliability coefficients of between .73 and .98 for self-reports of number of partners and frequency of intercourse. In a similar study, Coates et al. (1986) reported reliability coefficients between .98 and .99. Evidence of reliability has also been found with older adolescents and adults in our research. In one study we had sexual partners

---

[1] Perceived vulnerability was assessed with the question "What is the likelihood that you will contract the AIDS virus? Fill in any number that you think is appropriate. For example, 1 in :1 would suggest that you think that it will definitely happen. . . 1 in: *100,000* suggests that you think that it is *extremely* unlikely."

ages 18–20 describe their contraceptive use separately in order to check on the validity of those reports (Gerrard, Breda, & Gibbons, 1989). In this sample, the intracouple agreement on current contraceptive practices was .94. Although these kinds of results are encouraging, they provide only weak estimates of the validity of the reports because they are subject to the same criticisms as individual self-reports.

Another approach to determining the validity of self-reports is to attempt to establish an external objective criterion with which to compare the self-reports. Unfortunately no "gold standard" is available for assessing the validity of self-reports of condom use or specific sexual practices (Catania, Gibson et al., 1990). There is, however, some evidence of the validity of self-report measures of sexual intercourse and contraceptive use. In our study of 955 first-term women Marines, we collected self-reports of the frequency of intercourse and the use of specific methods of birth control (Gerrard & Warner, 1990). We then projected the 1-year pregnancy rate for the sample using the proportion of the women reporting use of each method, the typical failure rate for each method, the reported frequency of intercourse for women using each specific method, and the proportion of women who were sexually active in the sample. The results of this procedure suggest that the womens' self-reports of their sexual activity and contraceptive behavior were valid—the projected 1-year pregnancy rate was less than 1% different than the number of pregnancies that actually occurred during the following 12 months. In spite of these generally encouraging results with heterosexual behavior, it should be noted that these data may not speak to the issue of validity of self-reports by gay samples, or the issue of the validity of self-reports of specific sexual behaviors.

Temporal Issues.   As we mentioned earlier, there is an additional measurement problem that has been overlooked in much of the research on the relationship between perceived vulnerability and preventive behavior. Among a sample of people who have already initiated precautionary behaviors, a negative correlation may accurately reflect the fact that engaging in preventive actions has reduced the likelihood of contracting HIV. One way to combat this confusion is to include prior risk behavior and preventive actions as covariates when examining behavior change. This technique controls for the possibility that correlations between initial risk estimates and subsequent behavior can be explained by the covariation of initial perceived risk and concurrent risk behavior (cf. Joseph, Montgomery, Emmons, Kirscht et al., 1987).

Another approach to this problem is the construction of measures that include estimates of risk assuming precautionary behavior and then again assuming no precautionary behavior. For example, "What is the likelihood that you will contract HIV if you were to continue your current level of sexual activity and use condoms?", and then ". . . if you were to continue . . . and did not use condoms?" (cf. Gibbons, McGovern, & Lando, 1991). This kind of measurement allows the investigator to control for the potentially confounding effects of the subjects' initial or current AIDS preventive behaviors. It also presents a clear indication of the respondent's perception of the risk attendant to their behavior, as well as the efficacy associated with the particular precautionary behavior. Yet another useful technique is to analyze data separately for subjects with and without prior histories of preventive behaviors. This would control for the potential confounding of perceived risk with concurrent precautionary behavior (cf. Montgomery et al., 1989). To date, most of the studies in the area have failed to incorporate these types of measures (see Linville, Fischhoff, & Fischer, this volume, for additional discussion of measurement of perceived vulnerability).

Optimistic Bias.   Yet another type of measurement problem faced by researchers in this area has to do with biases inherent in risk perceptions. People, in general, tend to underestimate their vulnerability to negative health events (Perloff & Fetzer, 1986; Weinstein, 1980, 1982, 1984). And HIV infection is certainly no exception. In our sample of women Marines, the mean HIV risk estimate was significantly lower than the actual incidence of HIV infection in the military (Gerrard, 1989). One factor that contributes to this optimistic bias about HIV infection is that people often don't give serious consideration to either their own risk behavior or to the preventive behavior of others. As a result, they tend to report that they are much less likely than others to contract HIV (i.e., they evidence an "illusion of unique invulnerability;" Perloff & Fetzer, 1986).

Data from our Marine sample once again illustrate this point. Half of our subjects were randomly selected to review their sexual and contraceptive behavior prior to estimating their vulnerability to HIV. Women in this review condition were asked to describe their sexual activity and contraceptive use in considerable detail (i.e., "Starting with your first sexual partner, indicate *all* the periods of time you were sexually active. For each [period] indicate . . . the frequency of intercourse, and the method of birth control you and your partner used."). The other half of the women provided vulnerability estimates without benefit of explicitly reviewing their behavior. This sample of women was relatively sexually active, having had an average of 5.5 sexual partners by age 19, and engaging in sexual intercourse an average of 2.2 times per week. The vast majority (85%) had not been using condoms, however, which means their sexual and contraceptive (AIDS preventive) histories reflected a relatively high degree of risk for heterosexual women.

Both the review and the no-review groups evidenced what could be considered an illusion of invulnerability to AIDS. Those women who estimated their vulnerability to HIV without reviewing their prior risk behavior, however, reported a significantly greater illusion of unique invulnerability than did those who reviewed their histories. In essence, review of their sexual and prophylactic behavior increased the women's perceived vulnerability to HIV to more realistic levels. Thus, the results were consistent with the argument that people fail to seriously consider their risk behaviors when estimating their level of risk (Weinstein, 1984). Such inattention to one's own risk status can produce measurement noise, and it can also obscure the relationship between perceived vulnerability and preventive behavior. Moreover, we suspect that this problem is exacerbated by the emotional nature of sexual risks.

Reducing Risk Behaviors Versus Increasing Preventive Behaviors.   Often the studies (and for that matter, the models) in health behavior fail to consider the possibility that the goal of reducing risk can be achieved in two distinct ways: by decreasing the frequency of risky behavior, and by increasing the frequency or efficacy of preventive behaviors. For example, a man who wants to lower the probability that he will contract HIV can do so by reducing the frequency of his exposure, perhaps by decreasing the frequency with which he engages in anal intercourse with casual or anonymous partners. Alternately, he can lower his risk by increasing the proportion of sexual encounters in which he uses condoms. And of course, he can practice both of these strategies simultaneously. The measurement problem lies in the fact that these two behaviors are not independent. Once the man has decided to use condoms, he may no longer feel that it is necessary to refrain from anal intercourse with anonymous partners. Likewise, once he decides to avoid casual or anonymous sexual partners, he may decide that condoms are not necessary. In other words, risk perceptions may motivate some behavior changes but not others. Such an effect was, in fact, reported by Fisher and Misovich (1990), who found a positive correlation between perceived vulnerability and safe sex behaviors such as condom use, but no correlation between risk perceptions and abstaining from risky behaviors. Given that a person's objective level of risk reflects both their use of prophylactics and their avoidance of high-risk partners, it would appear that both should be measured. An index combining these two different kinds of behaviors could be formed that would be more reflective of actual susceptibility than would measures of either behavior alone.

Analytic Issues

Closely related to these measurement issues are two problems associated with statistical analysis. The first is the possibility that a relationship between perceived vulnerability and HIV preventive behavior does exist, but is hard to detect because it isn't linear. In particular, the correlational techniques and covariance analyses employed in most of the studies may not be capable of adequately capturing the relationship. This would definitely be the case if the relationship involved some form of threshold effect (viz., beyond a certain level, increased perceived vulnerability does not motivate additional preventive behavior; cf. Becker & Joseph, 1988). It should be noted that none of the studies described here reported use of statistical methods appropriate for revealing such effects.

The second possibility is that a vulnerability/behavior link does exist, but it is moderated by or linked to one or more additional variables that have not been included in these studies. For example, if the vulnerability/behavior relation is moderated by such a third variable (e.g., a disposition like trait anxiety) it is possible that the association would be undetected unless this moderating variable were measured and entered into the model. A good example of this comes from the data reported by Taylor, Kemeny, Schneider, and Aspinwall (this volume), which suggest that the relation among gay men is moderated by HIV serostatus and the presence of a primary sexual partner. Likewise, if the relation between perceived vulnerability and behavior is linked (cf. Blalock, 1971) to a third variable, then the vulnerability/behavior relation can only be as strong as the relation between the product of the various links in the model. For example, the Theory of Reasoned Action (Ajzen & Fishbein, 1977; Ajzen & Timko, 1986), and the Precaution Adoption Process (Weinstein, 1988) suggest that a behavioral intention or decision to act develops after recognition of the risk, and that without this intention or decision there will be no behavior change. Thus, both of these models would predict that the relation between perceived vulnerability and precautionary behavior can only be as strong as the *product* of the relation between perceived vulnerability and intention/decision to change, *and* the relation between intentions/decisions and actual behavior. The resulting correlation between risk estimates and risk behaviors could easily be too small to be significant except in very large samples.

CONCLUSIONS

Our review of the evidence leads us to a surprising conclusion—currently, with the exception of those studies that employed retrospective reports of behavior change, there is little reliable empirical support for the hypothesis that perceptions of the risk of contracting HIV motivate precautionary behavior. There is, however, fairly compelling evidence that perceived vulnerability to other negative health events does predict a wide variety of precautionary and preventive behaviors (Janz & Becker, 1984). Thus, the most obvious conclusion to be drawn from this review is that the general hypothesis is correct, but it does not extend to AIDS preventive behavior. In fact, this argument was made by Joseph, Montgomery, Emmons, Kessler et al. (1987), in an attempt to understand the results of their prospective study (described previously) in which perceived vulnerability was not associated with decreased HIV risk behaviors. They suggest that models of precautionary health behaviors were designed to deal with nonfatal, often reversible threats, and with risk behaviors that are less central to identity than sexual behaviors. Their point is well taken in that there are a number of ways in which HIV infection and AIDS are different from other threats to one's health.

Differences Between AIDS and Other Negative Health Events

As was discussed earlier, we believe that AIDS preventive behavior, because of its sexual nature, is qualitatively different from other prophylactic behaviors such as the use of seat belts or getting immunizations. Sexual behaviors clearly have an emotional component that few other health-relevant behaviors possess. It is very likely that these emotional barriers interfere with the motivational properties of perceived risk, and do so sufficiently to mask any measurable association between perceived vulnerability and AIDS preventive behaviors. In other words, emotional responses to sex could affect AIDS precautionary behaviors in the same ways that they affect practicing effective contraception—they can reduce risk perception and interfere with the acquisition of knowledge about AIDS and safe sex. They can also inhibit both the intention to practice safe sex and the consistency of precautionary efforts.

Symptom Delay.   An additional difference between contracting HIV and many other preventable negative events is the prolonged period between exposure and the development of symptoms, currently estimated to be as long as 11 years. This delay is likely to dilute the capacity of perceived risk to motivate behavior change. More specifically, given identical perceptions of vulnerability, we suggest that preventive behavior is more likely if the consequences of risk-taking are relatively immediate. For example, consider the hypothetical situation in which a person knows that there is a 30% probability that a risk behavior will result in a specific negative consequence within 24 hours, versus a situation in which there is a 30% probability that the same risk behavior will result in the same negative consequences, but 10 years hence. In short, the greater the proximity of risk behavior to negative consequences, the stronger the relation between risk perceptions and preventive behavior. Likewise, the uncertainty and ambiguity surrounding the process of exposure, infection, and diagnosis must be considered. As in other STDs, there is not a one-to-one relationship between exposure and infection. Because transmission is a function of the infectivity of the donor, the characteristics of the recipient, and the nature and frequency of the sexual behaviors they engage in (Lawrence, Jason, Holman, & Murphy, 1991), some people who engage in high-risk behavior do not contract the virus, whereas other people appear to contract it from only a single exposure. This seemingly capricious nature of the virus is likely to further erode the motivational properties of perceived vulnerability.

Social Behavior.   Finally, as the title of this book suggests, preventive behaviors that involve sexuality, including those related to AIDS, are significantly more social than other preventive behaviors. For most people, the processes of communicating with one's sexual partner, and enlisting his or her cooperation in preventive behaviors, may be so difficult that they effectively preclude the possibility that risk perceptions will translate into modifications of sexual behaviors. Likewise, the social stigma associated with AIDS and AIDS risk behaviors (see Pryor & Reeder, this volume) may be severe enough that it encourages the formation of psychological defenses against admitting or even accepting the fact that one is at risk. Of course, if these perceptions are suppressed they cannot correlate with, or promote risk reduction. It is unclear how much each of these distinguishing characteristics of AIDS is responsible for the fact that perceived vulnerability to AIDS does not predict AIDS preventive behavior. Most likely they all contribute to some extent. It is clear, however, that the processes and the behaviors in question are very complex. Thus adequate examination of the relationships in question requires sophisticated and creative methods.

Summary and Future Research

In spite of the fact that even the most (methodologically) sophisticated studies that we have reviewed here have not provided much support for the AIDS perceived vulnerability/preventive behavior relationship, there are several reasons why we think it may be premature to simply discard the hypothesis. First among these is the strong evidence that perceived vulnerability is related to other precautionary behaviors. Second, is the fact that certain segments of the population have made major changes in their sexual behavior as knowledge of the AIDS threat has become available to the public. The coincidental nature of these two changes—in risk perception and in risk behavior—certainly cannot be ignored. And third, we also cannot overlook the serious implications associated with abandoning this hypothesis. If there is no relationship between perceived vulnerability to AIDS and preventive behavior, then how can we possibly expect to change that behavior? If convincing people that they are at risk for HIV infection does not alter their sexual behavior, than what possibly could?

The primary reason that we are unwilling to reject the hypothesis, however, is that virtually all of the studies in this area have involved methodological difficulties of one kind or another. Even the three prospective studies, which are clearly the most sophisticated in the area, are limited because they focused exclusively on gay men who knew their antibody status. We cannot be sure to what extent their results generalize beyond this particular population.

It is our belief that some relationship may well exist between people's perceptions of their risk of contracting HIV and their precautionary behavior, but that that relationship has been obscured by various methodological problems, and weakened by both the idiosyncratic nature of the virus and the emotional nature of sexuality. With this in mind, we have suggestions for a number of further research directions.

First, it is clear that longitudinal designs are necessary to determine whether perceptions of vulnerability predict subsequent risk taking, and whether changes in risk perceptions predict changes in behavior. In addition, there are a number of theoretical and practical questions that can be best addressed using longitudinal data, but not necessarily from adults. These questions have to do with the development and antecedents of perceptions of risk as individuals move from simply possessing the knowledge that HIV poses a risk for others, to recognition that they themselves are vulnerable (i.e., as they move from Stage 2 to Stage 3 of Weinstein's Precaution Adoption Model). Although the prospective studies reviewed here examine the relationship between risk perceptions and changes in risk behavior, they do not assess the impact of the *initial recognition of personal vulnerability* on behavior because they utilize adult gay samples who undoubtedly had achieved Weinstein's Stage 3 prior to the beginning of the study. In an attempt to address this problem, we are currently conducting a 3-year longitudinal study of the risk perceptions and risk behaviors of approximately 1,300 adolescents and young adults. Most of these participants were young enough at the beginning of the study that they had not yet engaged in risk behaviors, but then began or will begin to do so during the course of the study. Our goal is to trace the *development* of perceptions of vulnerability and the development of risk behaviors in this sample over a period of time when adolescents usually begin to engage in sexual intercourse. Among other things we hope to determine if risk behavior affects risk perceptions as well as vice-versa.

Our review also suggests that the measurement problems inherent in studying sexual behavior and perceptions of vulnerability dictate a multimeasure, multimethod approach. A study of optimism about AIDS by Taylor et al. (1991) can serve as an example for other investigators in this area. In this study two measures of optimism were used, one involving questions that were specific to AIDS, and the other a more general measure of dispositional optimism. The study also included three different measures of sexual risk behaviors, collected by two different research teams at different times. Although this type of approach is certainly not uniquely invulnerable to the measurement pitfalls inherent in this very difficult research area, we think multimeasure, multimethod, prospective designs will, at the very least, ameliorate many of the problems discussed here.

A third conclusion is that there are undoubtedly numerous mediators and moderators that can be useful in explaining the relationship between perceived vulnerability and risk behavior. For example, Aspinwall et al. (1991) reported that both HIV serostatus and the presence of a regular sexual partner serve as moderators for gay men. Perhaps it is time to turn our attention to a systematic examination of moderating variables in order to expand our theoretical and practical knowledge of the relationship.

Finally, we have come to the conclusion that much of the research in this area is not as theoretical or, surprisingly, as applied as it could be. As we outlined early in the chapter, there are a number of theories of health behavior that pose interesting questions about the nature of perceived vulnerability, its development, and its antecedents. These theoretical questions have largely been ignored, however. For example the Precaution Adoption Process (Weinstein, 1988) suggests that people must achieve Stage 3 (recognize their personal vulnerability to, and the severity of the negative event) and believe in the efficacy of their potential precautionary actions before they decide to engage in these actions. To date, however, there is no clear evidence that perceptions of vulnerability, severity, and efficacy are all necessary prior to movement to the decision to act.

At the same time, there are a number of applied questions related to HIV risk perceptions that beg to be answered. How can perceived vulnerability to HIV infection be changed? Are there individual differences that influence the malleability of risk perceptions and risk behaviors? Are the antecedents of risk perceptions different for gay men than for heterosexuals? Different for men than for women? The challenge to social psychology is to apply our research expertise and theoretical orientation to address these important questions. The urgency created by the rapid spread of HIV and the opportunity to examine important theoretical issues about health behavior suggests that this is a vital area for research.

REFERENCES

Aspinwall, L. G., Kemeny, M. E., Taylor, S. E., Schneider, S. G., & Dudley, J. P. (1991). Psychosocial predictors of gay men's AIDS risk-reduction behavior. *Health Psychology, 10,* 432–444.

Ajzen, I., & Fishbein, M. (1977). Attitude-behavior relations: A theoretical analysis and review of empirical research. *Psychological Bulletin, 84,* 888–918.

Ajzen, I., & Timko, C. (1986). Correspondence between health attitudes and behavior. *Basic and Applied Social Psychology, 7,* 259–276.

Baldwin, J. D., & Baldwin, J. I. (1988). Factors affecting AIDS-related sexual risk-taking behavior among college students. *The Journal of Sex Research, 25,* 181–196.

Becker, M. H. (1974). The health belief model and personal health behavior. *Health Education Monographs, 2,* 324–508.

Becker, M. H., & Joseph, J. G. (1988). AIDS and behavioral change to reduce risk: A review. *American Journal of Public Health, 78,* 394–410.

Becker, M. H., & Maiman, L. A. (1983). Models of health-related behavior. In D. Mechanic (Ed.), *Handbook of health care, and the health professions* (pp. 539–568). New York: The Free Press.

Becker, M. H., & Rosenstock, I. M. (1987). Comparing social learning theory and the health belief model. In W. B. Ward (Ed.), *Advances in health education and promotion* (Vol. 2, pp. 245–249). Greenwich, CT: JAI.

Blalock, H. M. (1971). *Causal models in the social sciences.* Chicago: Aldine.

Campbell, S. M., Peplau, L. A., & DeBro, G., C. (1990). *Women, men, and condoms: The attitudes and experiences of heterosexual college students.* Unpublished manuscript.

Catania, J. A., Coates, T. J., Kegeles, S., Fullilove, M. T., Peterson, J., Marin, B., Siegel, D., & Hulley, S. (1991). *Condom use in multi-ethnic neighborhoods of San Francisco: The population-based AMEN (AIDS in Multi-ethnic Neighborhood) Study.* Unpublished manuscript.

Catania, J. A., Dolcini, M. M., Coates, T. J., Kegeles, S. M., Greenbaltt, R. M., Puckett, S., Corman, M., & Miller, J. (1989). Predictors of condom use and multiple partnered sex among sexually-active adolescent women: Implications for AIDS-related health interventions. *Journal of Sex Research, 26,* 514–524.

Catania, J. A., Gibson, D. R., Chitwood, D. D., & Coates, T. J. (1990). Methodological problems in AIDS behavioral Research: Influences on measurement error and participation bias in studies of sexual behavior. *Psychological Bulletin, 108,* 339–362.

Catania, J. A., Kegeles, S. M., & Coates, T. J. (1990). Towards an understanding of risk behavior: An AIDS risk reduction model. *Health Education Quarterly, 17,* 53–72.

Chandarana, P. C., Conlon, P., Noh, S., & Field, V. A. (1990). The AIDS dilemma: Worry and concern over AIDS. *Canadian Journal of Public Health, 81,* 222–225.

Cleary, P. (1987). Why people take precautions against health risks. In N. D. Weinstein (Ed.), *Taking care: Understanding and encouraging self-protective behavior* (pp. 119–149). New York: Cambridge University Press.

Coates, T. J., Soskolne, C. L., Calzavara, L. M., Read, S. E., Fanning, M. M., Shepard, F. A., Klein, M. M., & Johnson, J. K. (1986). The reliability of sexual histories in AIDS-related research: Evaluation of an interview-administered questionnaire. *Canadian Journal of Public Health, 778,* 343–348.

Emmons, C., Joseph, J. G., Kessler, R. C., Wortman, C. B., Montgomery, S. B., & Ostrow, D. G. (1986). Psychosocial predictors of reported behavior change in homosexual men at risk for AIDS. *Health Education Quarterly, 13,* 331–345.

Fazio, R. H., & Zanna, M. P. (1981). Direct experience and attitude-behavior consistency. *Advances in Experimental Social Psychology, 14,* 161–202.

Fishbein, M., & Ajzen, I. (1975). *Belief, attitude, intention, and behavior: An introduction to theory and research.* Reading, MA: Addison-Wesley.

Fisher, J. D., & Misovich, S. (1990). Social influence and AIDS-preventive behavior. In J. Edwards, R. S. Tinsdale, L. Heath & Posavac. (Eds.), *Social influences processes and prevention* (pp. 39–70). New York: Plenum.

Fisher, W. A. (1984). Predicting contraceptive behavior among university men: The role of emotions and behavior intentions. *Journal of Applied Social Psychology, 14,* 104–123.

Fisher, W. A., Byrne, D., Edmunds, M., Miller, C. T., Kelley, K., & White, L. A. (1979). Psychological and situation-specific correlates of contraceptive behavior among university women. *Journal of Sex Research, 15,* 38–55.

Fisher, W. A., Fisher, J. D., & Byrne, D. (1977). Consumer reactions to contraceptive purchasing. *Personality and Social Psychology Bulletin, 3,* 293–296.

Geis, B. D., & Gerrard, M. (1984). Predicting male and female contraceptive behavior: A discriminant analysis of groups high, moderate, and low in contraceptive effectiveness. *Journal of Personality and Social Psychology, 46,* 669–680.

Gerrard, M. (1977). Sex guilt in abortion patients. *Journal of Consulting and Clinical Psychology, 45,* 708.

Gerrard, M. (1982). Sex, sex guilt, and contraceptive use. *Journal of Personality and Social Psychology, 42,* 153–158.

Gerrard, M. (1987). Sex, sex guilt, and contraceptive use revisited: Trends in the 1980s. *Journal of Personality and Social Psychology, 52,* 975–980.

Gerrard, M. (1989). *Antecedents of pregnancy and pregnancy attrition in first-term women Marines* (Technical Report ONR-89-1). Iowa State University.

Gerrard, M., Breda, C., & Gibbons, F. X. (1989). Gender effects in couples' sexual decision making and contraceptive use. *Journal of Applied Social Psychology, 20,* 449–464.

Gerrard, M., Gibbons, F. X., & Warner, T. D. (1991). Effects of reviewing risk-relevant behavior on perceived vulnerability of women Marines. *Health Psychology, 10,* 173–179.

Gerrard, M., & Luus, A. E. L. (1992). *Judgments of vulnerability to pregnancy: The role of risk factors and individual differences.* Unpublished manuscript.

Gerrard, M., & Warner, T. D. (1990). Antecedents of pregnancy among women Marines. *Journal of the Washington Academy of Sciences, 80,* 1–15.

Gerrard, M., & Warner, T. D. (1992). *A comparison of women Marine's and college women's HIV relevant sexual behaviors.* Unpublished manuscript.

Gibbons, F. X., McGovern, P. G., & Lando, H. A. (1991). Relapse and risk perception among members of a smoking cessation clinic. *Health Psychology. 10*, 42–45.

Hingson, R. W., Strunin, L., Berlin, B. M., & Heeren, T. (1990). Beliefs about AIDS, use of alcohol and drugs, and unprotected sex among Massachusetts adolescents. *American Journal of Public Health, 80*, 295–299.

Janz, N. K., & Becker, M. H. (1984). The health belief model: A decade later. *Health Education Quarterly, 11*, 1–47.

Joseph, J. G., Montgomery, S. B., Emmons, C., Kessler, R. C., Ostrow, D. G., Wortman, C. B., O'Brien, K., Eller, M., & Eshlerman, S. (1987). Magnitude and determinants of behavioral risk reduction: Longitudinal analysis of a cohort at risk for AIDS. *Psychology and Health, 1*, 73–96.

Joseph, J. G., Montgomery, S. B., Emmons, C., Kirscht, J. P., Kessler, R. C., Ostrow, D. G., Wortman, C. B., & O'Brien, K. (1987). Perceived risk of AIDS: Assessing the behavioral and psychological consequences in a cohort of gay men. *Journal of Applied Social Psychology, 17*, 231–250.

Keeter, S., & Bradford, J. B. (1988). Knowledge of AIDS and related behavior change among unmarried adults in a low-prevalence city. *American Journal of Preventive Medicine, 4*, 146–152.

Kelly, J. A., St. Lawrence, J. S., Brasfield, T. L., Lemke, A., Amidei, T., Roffman, R. E., Hood, H. V., Smith, J. E., Kilgore, H., & McNeill, C. (1990). Psychological factors that predict AIDS high-risk versus AIDS precautionary behavior. *Journal of Consulting and Clinical Psychology, 58*, 117–120.

Klein, D. E., Sullivan, G., Wolcott, D. L., Landsverk, J., Namir, S., & Fawzy, F. F. (1987). Changes in AIDS risk behaviors among homosexual male physicians and university students. *American Journal of Psychiatry, 144*, 742–747.

Lawrence, D., Jason, J., Holman, R., & Murphy, J. (1991). HIV transmission from hemophilic men to their heterosexual wives. In N. Alexander, H. Gabelnick, G. Hodgen, & R. Spieler (Eds.), *The heterosexual transmission of AIDS: Proceedings of the CONRAD 2nd International Workshop.* New York: Alan R. Liss.

Maddux, J. E., & Rogers, R. W. (1983). Protection motivation and self-efficacy: A revised theory of fear appeals and attitude change. *Journal of Experimental Social Psychology, 19*, 469–479.

Martin, J. L. (1987). The impact of AIDS on gay male sexual behavior patterns in New York City. *American Journal of Public Health, 77*, 578–581.

McKusick, L., Horstman, W., & Coates, T. J. (1985). AIDS and sexual behavior reported by gay men in San Francisco. *American Journal of Public Health, 75*, 493–496.

McLaws, M., Oldenburg, B., Ross, M. W., & Cooper, D. A. (1990). Sexual behavior in AIDS-related research: Reliability and validity of recall and diary measures. *Journal of Sex Research, 27*, 265–281.

Mendelsohn, M. J., & Mosher, D. L. (1979). Effects of sex guilt and premarital sexual permissiveness on role-played sex education and moral attitudes. *Journal of Sex Research, 15*, 174–183.

Montgomery, S. B., Joseph, J. G., Becker, M. H., Ostrow, D. G., Kessler, R. C., & Kirscht, J. P. (1989). The health belief model in understanding compliance with preventive recommendations for AIDS: How useful? *AIDS Education and Prevention, 1*, 303–323.

Mosher, D. L. (1966). The development and multitrait-multimethod matrix analysis of three measures of three aspects of guilt. *Journal of Consulting Psychology, 30*, 25–29.

Mosher, D. L. (1968). Measurement of guilt in females by self-report inventories. *Journal of Consulting and Clinical Psychology, 32*, 690–695.

Mosher, D. L, (1973). Sex differences, sex experience, sex guilt, and explicitly sexual films. *Journal of Social Issues, 29*, 95–112.

Mosher, D. L. (1979). Sex guilt and sex myths in college men and women. *Journal of Sex Research, 15*, 224–234.

Pagel, M. D., & Davidson, A. R. (1984). A comparison of three social-psychological models of attitudes and behavioral plans: Prediction of contraceptive behavior. *Journal of Personality and Social Psychology, 47*, 517–533.

Perloff, L. S., & Fetzer, B. K. (1986). Self-other judgments and perceived vulnerability to victimization. *Journal of Personality and Social Psychology, 50*, 502–510.

Pleck, J. H., Sonenstein, F. L., & Ku, L. C. (1990). Contraceptive attitudes and intention to use condoms in sexually experienced and inexperienced adolescent males. *Journal of Family Issues, 11*, 294–312.

Rogers, R. W. (1975). A protection motivation theory of fear appeals and attitude change. *The Journal of Psychology, 91*, 93–114.

Rogers, R. W. (1983). Cognitive and physiological processes in fear appeals and attitude change: A revised theory of protection motivation. In J. Cacioppo & R. Petty (Eds.), *Social psychophysiology* (pp. 153–176). New York: Guilford Press.

Rosenstock, I. M. (1966). Why people use health services. *Milbank Memorial Fund Quarterly, 44*, 94.

Rosenstock, I. M. (1974). Historical origins of the health belief model. *Health Education Monographs, 2*, 1–8.

Taylor, S. E., Kemeny, M. E., Aspinwall, L. G., Schneider, S. G., Rodriguez, R., & Herbert, M. (1991). *Optimism, coping, psychological distress, and high-risk sexual behavior among men at risk for AIDS.* Unpublished manuscript.

Valdisseri, R. O., Lyter, D., Leviton, L. C., Callahan, C. M., Kingsley, L. A., & Rinaldo, C. R. (1988). Variables influencing condom use in a cohort of gay and bisexual men. *American Journal of Public Health, 78*, 801–805.

Wallston, B. S., & Wallston, K. A. (1984). Social psychological models of health behavior: An examination and integration. In A. Baum, S. E. Taylor, & J. Singer (Eds.), *Handbook of psychology and health* (Vol. 4, pp. 23–54). Hillsdale, NJ: Lawrence Erlbaum Associates.

Weinstein, N. D. (1980). Unrealistic optimism about future life events. *Journal of Personality and Social Psychology, 39*, 806–820.

Weinstein, N. D. (1982). Unrealistic optimism about susceptibility to health problems. *Journal of Behavioral Medicine, 5*, 441–460.

Weinstein, N. D. (1984). Why it won't happen to me: Perceptions of risk factors and susceptibility. *Health Psychology, 3*, 431–457.

Weinstein, N. D. (1987). Unrealistic optimism about susceptibility to health problems: Conclusions from a community-wide sample. *Journal of Behavioral Medicine, 10*, 481–500.

Weinstein, N. D. (1988). The precaution adoption process. *Health Psychology, 7*, 355–386.

Weinstein, N. D., Sandman, P. M., & Roberts, N. E. (1990). Determinants of self-protective behavior: Home radon testing. *Journal of Applied Social Psychology, 22*, 783–801.

Weinstein, N. D., Sandman, P. M. & Roberts, N. E. (1991). Perceived susceptibility and self-protective behavior: A field experiment to encourage home radon testing. *Health Psychology, 10*, 25–33.

Weisman, C. S., Nathanson, C. A., Ensminger, M., Teitelbaum, M. A., Robinson, J. C., & Plichta, S. (1989). AIDS knowledge, perceived risk and prevention among adolescent clients of a family planning clinic. *Family Planning Perspectives, 21*, 213–217.

White, L. A., Fisher, W. A., Byrne, D., & Kingma, R. (1977). *Development and validation of a measure of affective orientation to erotic stimuli: The Sexual Orientation Survey.* Paper presented at the meeting of the Midwestern Psychological Association, Chicago.

Wolcott, D. L., Sullivan, G., & Klein, D. (1990). Longitudinal change in HIV transmission risk behaviors by gay male physicians. *Psychosomatics, 31*, 159–167.

4 Negotiating Safer Sex: Interpersonal Dynamics

Lynn Carol Miller
B. Ann Bettencourt*
University of Southern California

Sherrine Chapman DeBro
Valerie Hoffman**
The Claremont Graduate School

At the wedding, I suddenly felt very alone and wished I had somebody too. Maybe that's why I was so attracted to Amy's brother, John. At first, he acted like he didn't even notice me, so I thought—well, what a "stuck up"—forget it. But, Amy, seeing my interest, called me over. I was anxious, probably because I really couldn't take rejection right then. So, I had about four drinks. After a while, I was feeling pretty relaxed. And soon, I felt like John and I were talking like we had known each other forever; he was such a "neat guy." I could tell John was really attracted to me because when the bar started getting noisy he said, "Let's get out of here." I suggested my apartment a few miles away. I offered him another drink when we got there. I really wanted to be intimate with him. He got the idea and dimmed the lights. The next thing I knew I was on the sofa with him, passionately kissing. Our clothes came off quickly. I knew then that we were going to have sex. I thought, "If I mention condoms, will he be offended . . . I don't want him to reject me." I finally blurted out, "John, we'd both be safer if we used condoms." . . . I sounded stiff, and felt stupid, but he whispered, "Mary, don't worry" . . . I said, "please John" . . . But, holding me close, he said, "Honey, I haven't been with anyone else for a long time . . . I want you." So I thought— "well, he looks safe, he's Amy's brother, for God's sake—he's o.k." And, as I felt him pressing against me, I just wanted to lose myself in the "heat of the moment" and to feel that I was caught up in our passion. We had sex without a condom.

---
*Ann Bettencourt is now Assistant Professor at the University of Missouri, Columbia, MO.
**Valerie Hoffman is a postdoctoral fellow at the Center for AIDS Prevention Studies at the University of California, San Francisco.

Despite knowledge of the transmission modes of the human immunodeficiency virus (HIV) and AIDS education classes and programs (Baldwin, Whiteley, & Baldwin, 1990), college students continue to engage in unsafe sexual practices (Baldwin & Baldwin, 1988; Freimuth, Edgar, & Hammond, 1987; Katzman, Mulholland, & Sutherland, 1988): They are increasingly at risk for contracting and spreading HIV (Leslie, 1988). With 30 to 40 million projected carriers of HIV by the year 2000 (World Health Organization, 1992), we are left then with a crucial applied question: What keeps individuals from using safer sexual practices?

Unfortunately, we would argue that addressing this question involves understanding the tremendous complexity of ongoing intrapersonal and interpersonal processes, within which individual acts (having safer sex or not having safer sex) are embedded. Simply consider the ever changing, detailed web of individuals' perceptions, goals, and mutual influences embedded within the sexual sequence, and sexual relationship, in the example just given! For example, initially, Mary perceives that John doesn't even notice her. She attributes this to his being "stuck up." This model of John changes rapidly as John's sister, her friend Amy, calls her over to where she is talking to John. After talking to John for a while (and after a few drinks) Mary comes to a new alternative view, or mental model, of John as a "neat guy." This model is apt to be influenced by Mary's currently high level of loneliness. Mary's mental models of their interaction, of John, and of their relationship, continue to shift during the interaction. They depend on John's response to Mary, which influences Mary's response to John and his response in turn. Their continued interaction moves Mary from a mental model of John as "stuck up" to one where he is "neat." As sex becomes likely, she has the goal of wanting to have safer sex by using a condom. Her partner dissuades her by making salient other goals such as his desire not to use a condom and his desire for her. Her partner, John, even implicitly suggests a way to avoid conflict among these goals: He suggests to her that he is safe and they can have safe sex without the use of a condom. As Mary becomes more sexually aroused, her desire to avoid rejection also increases. In the face of this complex of goals, and without a viable strategy to achieve all of them, her resolve to use a condom wanes.

The process of negotiation between Mary and John is dynamic in that it involves change over time both: (a) in the construction of detailed mental models of the ongoing interaction; and (b) in how strategic actions, directed toward achieving goals, continually feed back to influence other parts of an ongoing interpersonal system. If we grant that negotiating safer sex is a fundamentally dynamic process, then studying it dynamically would seem crucial for understanding when safer sexual negotiations are apt to break down and how that process might be altered to enhance the probability that safer sex will be the emergent outcome. But, how can we study such a complex process in which even the values on predictor variables (e.g., sexual arousal, concerns about AIDS, wanting to avoid rejection) are apt to change during the very course of the interaction?

Studying dynamic processes is not straightforward. Numerous scholars historically have advocated components of a more dynamic interactional approach (Berg, 1987; Duck & Sants, 1983; Kelley, 1979, 1984; Kenny, 1981; Magnusson & Endler, 1977; L. C. Miller, 1987, 1990, 1991; L. C. Miller & Read, 1987, 1991a, 1991b; Read & Miller, 1989a; Reis & Shaver, 1988). Despite historical advocacy, this approach has barely taken root in social psychology (for an example see L. C. Miller, 1990). We suspect that one of the major stumbling blocks has been a perceived mismatch between dynamic assumptions and available methodologies.

The goal of this chapter is to suggest how we can study dynamic processes in general, and the negotiation of safer sex in particular. In doing so, we are explicit about our basic theoretical assumptions, as well as the dynamic methods, that together create a dynamic paradigm (Kuhn, 1970). Thus, our tasks become the following: First, to argue for a dynamic paradigm; second, to suggest useful units (or structures) consistent with a dynamic approach that allow us, using more traditional methodologies, to conduct research involving the interpersonal negotiation of safer sex; third, to present new methods from systems dynamics and cognitive science that fit with both the assumptions, and the structures of a dynamic paradigm; finally, to suggest how a more dynamic paradigm provides new possibilities for thinking about practical interventions and educational programs that may reduce the incidence of unsafe sexual practices.

TOWARD A DYNAMIC PARADIGM

For any paradigm, there are assumptions researchers are implicitly or explicitly making as they conduct research (Kuhn, 1970). What assumptions, for example, do we make about sexual partners and the process by which these individuals interact with and influence one another in negotiating safer sex? A number of the dynamic theoretical assumptions articulated by communications scholars (see e.g., G. R. Miller, 1983) and applied to communication processes are extremely useful here.

We would argue, in line with an actional (Cushman, Valentinsen, & Dietrich, 1982; Delia, 1977; Harre & Secord, 1972; Searle, 1983) or an actional realist perspective (Pearce & Cronen, 1980; M. J. Smith, 1982) that sexual partners are *active participants,* who each have their own set of *goals* and the ability to choose *strategies* to maximize goal achievement. The strategies most apt to be enacted also depend on the resources that the individual has available to enable successful strategic enactment, and the beliefs that the individual has about the meaning of those strategic actions. Strategic enactment also depends on the constraints and the affordances of the present situation (L. C. Miller & Read, 1987). Furthermore, individuals enact strategies in light of multiple existing and new goals made salient by the ongoing interpersonal interaction, including the mental models individuals have of the ongoing actions of their partner (L. C. Miller & Read, 1991b).

These dynamic assumptions include three sets of assumptions: One set concerns the goal-directed nature of action within a dynamic system of relationships, another concerns the dynamic construction of meaning, and the final set concerns how these dynamic processes are linked. These sets of assumptions then include the following:

Assumption Set₁

Behavioral patterns over time are the product of an interrelated, goal-directed, dynamic system of relationships among a variety of factors (e.g., intrapersonal, interpersonal, situational factors). Some subassumptions of this ontological position are listed here.

Goal-Directed Nature of Human Action.   Individuals have goals within social interactions. Discrepancies between desired salient goals and current levels of goal achievement lead individuals to enact strategies to maximize goal achievement.

For example, Mary's desire for a relationship may be a particularly salient goal to her due to Amy's wedding. As the relationship proceeds, other goals may become salient as well (e.g., wanting to avoid rejection, wanting to avoid AIDS). These goals (assuming a discrepancy between current state and desired goal), drive strategic actions. Thus, when Mary has the goal of avoiding AIDS, that goal may lead to a series of attempts to initiate condom use with her partner, John. Mary's goals (e.g., desiring safer sex) affect her strategies and subsequent behaviors (mentioning in an informative way, that they should use condoms) which in turn affect John's responses.

Dynamic Interactions Among Person and Situational Factors.   Strategic choices are influenced by the configuration of salient goals (chronic, salient due to partner, or context), resources, (chronic, partner provided, or contextually available), and beliefs (chronic, of the partner, perceived social norms) operative in the situation.

In part, some of Mary's goals become salient due to the actions of the partner and the nature of the unfolding sequence of events (movement toward sexual intimacy activates concerns about AIDS). John has his own set of goals that Mary, for the most part, has to infer. These might include wanting physical intimacy, wanting a close relationship, wanting to avoid using a condom, and so forth, that are made more or less salient as the interaction proceeds. Mary and John are both influenced by and take into account constraints imposed and opportunities afforded by changes in the social reality (e.g., perceiving mutual consent; having a private place within which to have sexual relationships; perception that they are "safe") within which their actions (e.g., having unprotected sex) are embedded.

Mutual Influence.   Within a social interaction or social relationship, individuals mutually influence one another. Partner A's behavior impacts on Partner B's perceived goals and drives strategic behavior that in turn affects Partner A's perceived goal achievement and the activation of new goals which subsequently drive new behavior.

Feedback Loops.   Actions of individuals impact on the environment. Feedback from these actions affects the assessment of goal achievement which determines whether the individual will continue efforts to reach the goal.

Let us consider an interpersonal negotiation that involves mutual influences and a feedback loop. For example, as Mary initiates attempts to use a condom, she perceives that John rejects her more and more. To reduce John's rejection of her, she decreases her initiation attempts, which reduces the rejection to the point where she initiates further attempts to use condoms. If these are met with rejection, however, this may suppress further initiation attempts unless her fear of AIDS is greater than her concerns over rejection. If Mary were to continue initiation attempts, regardless of perceived rejection, then the emergent outcome might depend upon the strength of John's desire to have sex relative to other factors (e.g., his unwillingness to use condoms).

Systems of Relationships, not the Factors Themselves, Result in Emerging Patterns of Behavioral Outcomes Over Time (Bertalanffy, 1968).   As summarized by Richmond, Peterson, and Vercuso (1987), the relative strengths of feedback loops, which are apt to shift over time, is what is important within such a framework. Thus, instead of thinking about a set of fixed-weight factors and instead of a focus on which factor is most important, a dynamic approach considers the system of relationships between factors, where the values of each factor, feeding into other factors, are not fixed over time. Within a particular system of goals, for example, different goals may play a more or less important role in predicting ongoing phenomena at different points in time. For example, perceived rejection from John is not apt to be fixed, it is apt to change over time depending on other factors feeding into it. As current level of rejection increases, for those who wish to avoid rejection, this is more and more likely to drive action. When behaviors that reduce rejection are initiated, this is apt to increase perceived rejection and with it the salience of this goal compared to other goals (e.g., wanting to avoid AIDS) in directing behavior.

Furthermore, as Richmond et al. (1987) pointed out, external forces or "shocks" may *precipitate* but do not *cause* dynamic phenomena. External forces may bring out the dynamics latent within the relationships defining a system, but it is the system that causes the person to respond as he or she does. For example, suppose we have a systems model of gay relapse behavior in which loneliness feeds into the probability of engaging in risky sexual behavior. As loneliness increases, so too does risky behavior, particularly perhaps when other factors are present (e.g., when there is an attractive male). Risky behavior might be even more likely when the last unsafe sexual encounter was a while ago and when fear associated with such an encounter (and the likelihood of contracting HIV) has had a chance to dissipate (or the individual has had a negative HIV test). Given such a system, a lonely individual could refrain from using unsafe sexual practices if he could keep his loneliness in check by engaging in a daily routine of social activities. However, the news of the death of one or more friends could suddenly cause a massive increase in loneliness that would be too great for the individual's "system" to keep in check, and the dynamic latent in the system (e.g., that if the rate of relative loneliness to fear is greater than "x" when an attractive partner is available, then unsafe sexual practices will be highly likely) may now be made manifest. The emerging dynamic of this individual's subsequent relapse behavior depends on the *interconnected web of factors* in the individual's system.

Negotiating safer sex in relationships, a dynamic perspective would argue, is apt to involve a web of interdependent factors. Therefore, a systems approach here would suggest when (within an unfolding process) individuals were most vulnerable to engaging in unsafe sexual practices and what interventions might be appropriate to keep individuals from engaging in unsafe sex. That is, if individuals are particularly vulnerable when their need for physical closeness is high and unmet, then alternative ways of meeting these needs that are "safer" might be introduced into the system at critical points in time for an individual. For example, to keep these needs reduced, an individual might typically have regular body massages, meet with a support group that gives each other hugs, and other "safe" physical touches. In addition, an individual might have a "buddy" available who he could reach by phone, who will talk with him and offer safe "touches" when that individual feels unusually lonely, or otherwise "at risk" for engaging in unsafe sex. Also, some "external shocks" (e.g., death of an HIV-infected friend) that are deemed important precipitating relapse factors for some individuals, might be anticipated by counselors in the gay community, and "emergency" support structures "built in" to provide a countervailing "force" to keep these "shocks" from temporarily overwhelming the individual.

Behavior as an Emergent Phenomena Embedded in a Process.   Instead of simply thinking about behavior at a single point in time, "a snapshot," it is argued that behavior is part of a process (G. R. Miller, 1983). That is, loneliness may peak, decline, then peak again. Although levels of loneliness are unstable, changing levels of loneliness over time could be part of the same unfolding process. To understand the process, of which the behavior is part, we need to understand the underlying system of relations among variables, and the factors that precipitated behavior.

For example, lapse behavior among gay men may show a pattern that suggests the operation of an oscillating system (e.g., vacillation between safe and unsafe behavior). Underlying such oscillation over time, may be a goal-corrected system where there are competing goal configurations (e.g., one concerned with avoiding AIDS and one concerned with wanting intimacy) that are more or less apt to drive behavior at different points over time (e.g., depending on the relative values within the system).

Assumption Set$_2$: Constructing Social Realities

Individuals construct ever changing and updated, mental models of social realities. These social constructions, often cohering around perceptions of own and other goals, are used by individuals to explain sequences of behaviors and events.

Mary's desire for a close relationship, made salient by Amy's wedding, as well as her sensitivity to rejection, are apt to affect how she construes John and the meaning of his actions. For example, Mary's sensitivity to rejection may have led her to the construction of John as "stuck up" when she perceived he didn't notice her. With his ensuing interest in her, her construction of John's behavior shifted; now, he was a "neat guy." Later, Mary and John appear to share a model that sex is mutually desired. Following this social construction, the issue of using safer sex gets discussed.

Individuals develop coherent mental models of sequences of actions, of partners, and of relationships. For example, Mary may believe that some of what John says and does suggests that they are on the road to a long-term relationship and are not having a one-night stand (i.e., John wants a committed intimate relationship too).

Meaning is Dynamic. The meaning of actions can change as individuals process new information or different facets of an interpretation are made more salient. Although there are apt to be bounds in terms of the possible or probable meanings that can be assigned to an individual action in a given culture, the act itself does not have absolute meaning. Its meaning is constructed by the individual in light of additional structures that this event or action activates that also need to be explained. The input of new information can change the meaning assigned to old information within a current mental model.

For example, after being "dumped" by John 2 weeks after they met, Mary might decide that John's actions were more indicative of a manipulative rather than a "neat" guy.

Contextualization of Meaning. The meaning of an action depends on where that action is embedded in the ongoing sequence of actions. It also depends on what structures (e.g., mental models of the sequence, person, relationship, self, other) are concurrently activated. The act "presenting a condom" means one thing when it is embedded by a partner in a sexual sequence and quite another when a counselor at a health clinic is advising women on the prevention of sexually transmitted diseases.

Assumption Set₃: Construction and Goal-Corrected Action are Interwoven Over Time

The more heavily activated a particular "explanation" is in a network of associations, the more likely that concept will play a role in determining which goal structures for the individual will remain or become activated. Once activated, these goal structures will play a role in driving strategic action that will affect the individual's ongoing mental model of the unfolding events, which will in turn affect which old goals will continue to be activated and which new goals will now be activated.

For example, heavily activated concepts may affect inferences about the goals of a partner. These inferred goals are likely to be part of the configuration of intrapersonal and interpersonal goals that guide subsequent strategic behavior. These behaviors in turn are apt to affect partner constructions and partner's subsequent actions that in turn affect our detailed constructions and so forth.

A DYNAMIC APPROACH TO STUDYING NEGOTIATING SAFER SEX: WHAT ARE THE UNITS?

Given these theoretical assumptions, how do we proceed? Our sets of assumptions suggest the nature of the questions we should be asking, and the units that we might use to pursue these. For example, understanding the role of individual goals related to dating relationships, that might conflict with using safer sex, would appear important. Understanding the obstacles to safer sex (external and internal factors) that individuals encounter in pursuing these goals and the nature of the strategies they might pursue would also appear crucial. Furthermore, sexual scripts, within which goals and strategies are embedded would seem to provide a useful framework for thinking about intrapersonal and interpersonal dynamics. Sexual scripts are apt to differ depending on the type of sexual relationship the individual is pursuing and the goals associated with these different relationships. Understanding the different sexual scripts in different sexual relationships may better enable us to devise strategies conducive to safer sex, which could be incorporated into those scripts and still serve the goals of the individual scripts. Here, we discuss research that has begun to employ such dynamic *units* as (a) goals, (b) obstacles to safer sex, (c) plans and strategies, and (d) sexual scripts. We discuss how these units provide not only insights into the sexual negotiation process for various types of sexual relationships, but also form the groundwork for moving toward a dynamic paradigm in the future.

Goals in Dating Relationships

Goals are simply something that an individual desires or wants to attain (L. C. Miller & Read, 1987, 1991a, 1991b; Read & Miller, 1989a, 1989b) and individuals differ in the strength of these goals at any one point in time. In an ongoing dating relationship, desire for sex may become part of a goal-corrected system within which sexual tension rises, needs are met, the system returns to a steady state and eventually sexual tension increases and so forth. Throughout our ongoing interaction there are apt to be moment-by-moment changes in the configuration of individual goals (e.g., wanting sex, wanting to avoid rejection, wanting to avoid AIDS) that drive subsequent actions.

As Wilensky (1983) pointed out, an individual's goals may conflict with one another (intrapersonal goal conflict) or may conflict with the perceived goals of others (interpersonal goal conflict). Although the nature and consequences of goal conflict and concordance are discussed in greater detail elsewhere (Read & Miller, 1989a), for now, it is important to point out that, for different individuals, for different relationships, the goal of wanting to avoid AIDS may conflict with other goals (both intrapersonal and interpersonal goals). Because some of these goals, which conflict with wanting to avoid AIDS, may be more immediate and salient in the sexual sequence, they may drive strategic actions that fail to enhance using safer sex. The particular types of goals that individuals have may be differentially related to the particular obstacles that they perceive in negotiating safer sex.

L. C. Miller and Bettencourt (1989) identified three composites of dating goals for primarily White college students. These tapped: (a) wanting to avoid conflict in a relationship, (b) wanting to maintain emotional intimacy and closeness with one's partner, and (c) wanting to achieve narcissistic goals (see Emmons, 1987). The narcissistic goal composite included wanting sexual intimacy, making a positive impression, keeping fit, and avoiding pain. Additional dating goals that did not load cleanly on one of these factors included: wanting to avoid embarrassment, being spontaneous, and wanting to be viewed as physically attractive (L. C. Miller & Bettencourt, 1989). In subsequent work, L. C. Miller et al. (1992), with a sample of 122 lower income African-Americans, found somewhat different clusters of dating goals. These included: (a) "needy," conflicting goals (e.g., avoiding conflict, embarrassment, and partner anger, as well as wanting acceptance and physical intimacy), (b) wanting a comfortable relationship, and (c) wanting a safe but close relationship (e.g., wanting to avoid AIDS but wanting to feel close and able to talk to the partner). Individuals for whom different goals are salient are apt to perceive different problems in negotiating safer sex. Might such personal goals predict the obstacles individuals perceive to using safer sex?

Obstacles to Safer Sex

Unfortunately, until recently, we have not known a great deal about the obstacles individuals encounter in negotiating safer sex. To rectify this situation, L. C. Miller and Bettencourt (1989) asked undergraduates to generate potential obstacles that might occur in a variety of dating scenarios for either men or women. From these student responses, a set of 101 obstacles was generated. Most of these fell into 1 of 10 conceptual categories. These categories included such things as being in the "heat of the moment," simply "talking about safe sex," the act of "buying and presenting the condom," perceiving that "condoms are unromantic," and "pressure" to have sex without the condom. In addition, subjects indicated that they would be less likely to use safer sex if they had been drinking, if their partner had been drinking, if they had never had sex before, or if they had previously had unprotected sex with a particular partner.

Were relationship goals predictive of the obstacles individuals encountered? As suggested earlier, partners enter into a sexual encounter with a number of goals particularly important to them. These goals may affect what obstacles individuals are particularly sensitive to. For example, those college students with narcissistic goals seem more concerned with desires for physical pleasure and thus they may be more likely to get "caught up" in the passion of the sexual encounter. They report that both their beliefs that the condom is unromantic, as well as their concern that using or suggesting a condom would ruin the heat of the moment, would prevent them from using safer sex. Thus, the condom itself may be a hindrance to safe sex for those college students with narcissistic goals because they may equate the condom with a reduction of sexual excitement. Thus, having safer sex for these individuals may involve an *intrapersonal* goal conflict.

On the other hand, those who want to avoid conflict in a relationship may fail to practice safe sex because they view it as a potential source of *interpersonal* conflict (they may feel that their partner may not want to use a condom). Participants in our college sample (L. C. Miller & Bettencourt, 1989) reported that they would be less likely to use safe sex because they do not want to talk about it, because they do not want to buy or present a condom, and because they fear offending their partner by implying the partner has a disreputable past. Similarly, in our African-American low-income sample (L. C. Miller et al., 1992), participants with more needy, conflicting goals were those who generally perceived more obstacles to safer sex, particularly those interpersonal obstacles that involved the risk of losing the partner, offending the partner, or talking about safer sex with the partner. Curiously, these individuals were also most likely to worry about and anticipate personally getting AIDS.

Some individuals very much desire acceptance and closeness. For college students, the most serious obstacles to safer sex were those that involve embarrassment over buying condoms, offering the condom, pressure not to use the condom, and fears of losing partner's acceptance or trust. Such concerns are primarily interpersonal in nature. In our African-American sample, both those participants who wanted a close/safe relationship and those who wanted a comfortable relationship were less likely, in general, to perceive obstacles to safer sex (although these negative correlations were not statistically significant). Those who were concerned with being safe (from AIDS) as well as having a close relationship, were most apt to report discussing safer sex and feeling greater comfort initiating condom use in their last sexual relationship. These individuals, although fearful of the disease, were more likely to report "healthier" responses to the threat of AIDS (e.g., refusing to have sex without a condom, knowing their partner before sex).

Overall, this line of research suggests that the nature of an individual's goals may greatly affect the obstacles that keep him or her from using safer sex. And, as additional research suggests (DeBro & Miller, 1992), those goals need not be chronic but may change depending on the nature of the sexual relationship that the individual is having with another (e.g., "long-term," "one-night stands," "pick-ups," "affairs," "off-and-on again relationships," and so forth). For example, when in long-term relationships, individuals are most concerned with being themselves with their partners, being comfortable and able to openly communicate, and feeling close to and accepted by the partner. In all other sexual relationships, particularly those not involving commitment (e.g., one-night stands, pick-ups, affairs, and so on), leading goals include avoiding AIDS and sexually transmitted diseases (STDs), being in control of what happens, and being physically attractive.

Once there are salient discrepancies between a goal that an individual strongly desires and what an individual has achieved, individuals are apt to enact behaviors (or refrain from behaviors) that are part of a strategy, plan, or script, to achieve their goals. We turn now to a more explicit treatment of strategies, plans, and scripts in understanding negotiation processes.

Plans and Strategies

Plans are organized sequences of behavior aimed at attaining hierarchically arranged subgoals in pursuit of the overall goal. Although plans can be quite detailed, they are often very sketchy, and several plans may be active for any given goal at the same time. For example, if we wish to get someone "to our apartment" we might "mention a party next door to our apartment that we'd like to go to, stay there for a while, and then suggest going to our apartment because the party is dull." Or, we might find out that our potential sexual partner really likes antique toys. As we have a collection of these in our apartment, this provides an opening for an alternative strategy, "Hey, I have a great collection. Would you like to see it?" Which plan is activated, then, depends on factors such as the perception of the context, the availability of resources, one's beliefs, and the judged probability that this strategy would, in fact, achieve the goal given the present partner.

Recently, a number of researchers have been exploring the different types of strategies used in sexual encounters. For example, McCormick (1979) found that men and women report more direct strategies (e.g., coercion, reward) to persuade partners to have sex, and more indirect strategies (e.g., seduction, deception) to persuade partners to avoid having sex. In addition, Perper and Weis (1987) found that women use eye contact and conversation strategically to communicate their desire to initiate or limit sexual interaction. Among dating partners, McCormick and Gaeddert (1989) found that both from the perspective of the partner persuading and the partner being persuaded, coercion was most often used to influence a dating partner to use contraception. DeBro (1988) and DeBro, Campbell, and Peplau (1990) identified a number of power strategies that individuals use to influence a partner to use and to avoid using condoms, including:

1. Reward: Power agent promises positive consequences if the partner complies,

2. Coercion: Power agent threatens negative consequences if the partner does not comply,

3. Information: Power agent presents information or logical arguments to persuade a partner to comply,

4. Relationship Building: Power agent stresses positive or negative consequences for the relationship to gain compliance,

5. Seduction: Power agent uses sexual arousal to distract partner in order to gain compliance, and

6. Deception: Power agent uses false information or deception to gain compliance.

They found that men and women were more likely to rate the power strategies as being more comfortable and effective for influencing a date to use a condom than to avoid using a condom. Although women were more likely to use coercion (threatening negative consequences such as withholding sex), men were more likely to use seduction to influence a partner to use (or allow the use of) a condom. This may fit both with men's tendency to be the sexual initiator and the partner who has more control over the application of the condom.

DeBro (1991) found that individuals use different strategies to persuade a partner to use a condom in eight different types of sexual relationships. For example, individuals in long-term relationships are less likely to use reward and coercion (tactics that might suggest more of an exchange rather than a communal relationship; see Clark & Mills, 1979) compared to those in most other types of sexual relationships (e.g., one-night stand, off-and-on again relationships, fling). And, those in long-term relationships are least likely to use deception. Perhaps, partners in long-term relationships are more secure, less concerned with rejection, and more concerned with maintaining good communication in the relationship. They might be more apt, than those in shorter term relationships, to avoid manipulative, indirect, or negative persuasion strategies, that might have long-term negative relational consequences.

Interestingly, in terms of strategy use, pick-up relationships were more similar to long-term relationships than they were to one-night stands. Pick-ups differ from one-night stands in that, in the former (as in long-term relationships), at least one of the participants wants the relationship to last. Individuals in pick-ups, like those in long-term relationships, were more reluctant to use reward or coercion; they were also more likely to use relationship-building strategies.

It seems likely that individuals (especially those most apt to be competent at safer sex negotiation) will have hierarchies of strategies, rather than single preferred strategies, that they will use as different complexes of goals become salient. The strategy chosen may be chosen to maximize one's goals (e.g., using a condom, developing a close relationship, having a good time, making a positive impression, avoid offending one's partner, avoid embarrassment, etc.). Let's consider the goal of trying to get the partner to agree to use the condom. If one strategy does not work in achieving the goal of using the condom, alternative strategies (that may be less desirable in terms of the configuration of goals one desires and wishes to avoid) may be tried in turn unless the costs of using safer sex are perceived as too great.

Perhaps we need to come up with strategies for negotiating safer sex that better take into account multiple conflicting goals of sexual partners. Adelman (1990, 1992) pointed out that there is an essential goal conflict between wanting sex on the one hand (which should be exciting, spontaneous, fun, and romantic) and wanting safer sex on the other hand (which is responsible, boring, and unromantic) and argued that humor and playfulness might provide useful strategies to resolving these tensions and apparent contradictions.

Sexual Scripts

Often, we would expect specific strategies for using or not using condoms to be embedded in broader, more stereotypical *sexual scripts*. Scripts are cognitive representations of temporally ordered sequences of behaviors. People are the actors and scripts include their qualities, motives for behavior, and their verbal and nonverbal activities (Schank & Abelson, 1977). Scripts are incomplete and are not meant to give a full and complete picture of concrete behavior. However, they can be used as a heuristic tool for examining the organization of social interaction sequences (Pryor & Merluzzi, 1985) and sexual sequences of behavior (Simon & Gagnon, 1986).

Unfortunately, until recently, there was little empirical work on sexual scripts. Hoffman and Miller (1989) had participants (many of whom were graduate students), ages 21–60, select up to 25 cards from a "deck" of 38 black-and-white photos and drawings of various "scenes" in possible scripts (e.g., made and unmade beds, couches, contraceptives of various types, telephone, bathtub, cigarettes, wine, marijuana, couples in various stages of undress and engaged in various sexual activities). Participants were asked to put the cards in order so that they could create a typical scenario for a couple that was about to have sex for the first time. Participants were asked to choose 10 of the selected photos and to answer a series of questions about them such as "What is happening in this scene?" "What happened before?" "What does he (she) feel, think?" "What is missing from this scene that you would like to add?" The order of cards was recorded on a data sheet and frequencies and ranks computed.

In general, the sexual script depicted in Fig. 4.1, is typical of the sexual scripts our participants provided. In temporal order, this typical script includes: finding a private place, "setting the scene" by trying to "get comfortable" and make the interaction "romantic," moving to a "proximal location" where individuals could gradually increase physical intimacy, a sequence of escalating sexual behavior, establishing mutual intent to progress to intercourse, and movement to a "better" location (such as a bed or floor to more comfortably engage in sexual intercourse), followed by the act of intercourse. Those subjects who mentioned using a condom typically did so only after mutual intent was established. The "window" within which to introduce and use condoms (e.g., between establishing mutual intent and having sex) may be very small and involve high levels of sexual arousal (making it more difficult to successfully negotiate safer sex at that point in time). Throughout, many subjects appeared to evaluate

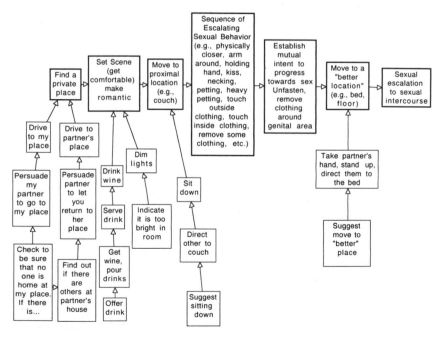

FIG. 4.1.   Typical initiator sexual script for a "one-night stand."

their partner's response (e.g., positive, negative, willingness/not) and to monitor internal sequences of events including anticipating or avoiding failure and repairing interactional "failures" if necessary. Some subjects also monitored external events and were vigilant to changes in privacy conditions. Many of the strategies mentioned were nonverbal and indirect. If sexual scripts are primarily nonverbal in nature, attempting to incorporate verbal messages within such sequences might prove much more difficult to implement, and meet with more resistance from both partners, than the incorporation of nonverbal means of conveying similar messages.

Although we are still in the process of coding this data, a number of preliminary findings are also worthy of note. Males used more photos in their scripts than females. This suggests that men may conceive of the sexual encounter in more detail, perhaps in part because males traditionally have assumed the initiator role (Hopkins, 1977). A majority of participants (68%) included "wine" in their scripts; this card appeared in significantly more scripts by men (93%) than by women (50%). The wine card also was placed significantly closer to the start of the script by females than males. These findings are consistent with work by Burns and Miller (1990) using a college sample; 70% of college men and women mentioned alcohol in their scripts for both one-night stands (79% women; 88% of men) and long-term (60% of women; 50% of men) relationships.

Hoffman and Miller (1989) also found that in contrast to other forms of contraception, which tended to be mentioned very early in the script (and typically by women), condoms tended to be mentioned relatively late, only after mutual intent was established, and prior to the act of intercourse. Surprisingly, 65% of the men and 58% of the women in this population of adults included condoms in their scripts. This contrasts, however, with the results for other samples. For example, Burns and Miller (1990) found that a much lower percentage of college students (e.g., 20% of 171) mentioned condoms in their verbal scripts (Burns & Miller, 1990). Even lower percentages of college students (3%) used condoms in a sample of 182 students in Illinois (Pryor, 1992). Perhaps the percentages in Hoffman and Miller (1989) are so high because participants tended to be older. Or, perhaps, because subjects picked from cards instead of generating their own scenes for the script, condoms were unusually salient. Differences between the Burns and Miller (1990) and the Pryor (1992) sample could reflect regional differences (e.g., southern California versus southern Illinois) in the salience of condoms and AIDS.

Let us describe the Burns and Miller work in greater detail. They asked undergraduates to construct a sexual script for one of their own personal, sexual interactions by indicating the "frames" in the sequence of events leading up to sexual intercourse starting with "my sexual partner and I are together" and ending with "I have sexual intercourse with my partner." For example, following is one male's description of the series of events that actually occurred during a one-night stand.

My sexual partner and I are together. I look deeply into her eyes. I engage in small talk; she follows along. I tell her that the bar we are in is "getting old" and that "I know of another party in the apartment next to mine." I sell the party idea to her. We leave the bar. I drive wild and fast toward my place. We both socialize at the party (10 minutes tops). I pull her outside and take the drink from her hands. With my free hand I pull her closer (firmly and gently). I press on the small of her back. She lets me pull her (tight to my body). I touch my lips to hers, drop the drink, and hold her head with her hair in my fingers. I bring her in to my room. I take her and my clothes off. I put on a condom. I mount her. I kiss her. I can't wait—I rub against her and tell her I can't wait to be inside her. *I have sexual intercourse with my partner.*

Participants were also asked to indicate, for every statement, what goals were associated with a particular action. Using the example just highlighted, Table 4.1 indicates how this participant's goals map onto the sequence of actions he depicts from an actual sexual encounter involving a one-night stand. This type of data provides insight into how the participant's goals motivate and connect to strategy choice within the sexual sequence. It is also clear from this subject's depiction that he is attending to his partner's actions and inactions (failure to withdraw, move away, refuse, show reluctance) and using his interpretation of those actions to decide whether "she's interested." Consistent with the work described earlier, much of the sexual sequence depicted is nonverbal. Of the verbal portion of the script, the verbalizations (e.g., this bar is really getting old, there's a party near my apartment tonight, do you want to go?) are often indirect, connoting more than is literally conveyed. As suggested earlier, the detailing of these scripts may suggest when, verbally or nonverbally, individuals might best negotiate the use of safer sex.[1]

We view these components as important variables within a dynamic interpersonal interaction. But, how do these units or structures (e.g., goals, plans and strategies, scripts, and so forth) come together to allow for the exploration of interpersonal dynamics? How would we study the richness of social dynamics?

Along with other social scientists (Abelson, 1968; Hastie, 1988; Hovland, 1960; Ostrom 1988; Stasser, 1988), we would argue that computer simulations provide very promising theoretical and research tools for understanding the complexities of social behavior. And, we demonstrate how two types of simulations might provide insights in the areas of negotiating safer sex.

Before proceeding, however, it might be appropriate to address some issues that sometimes surface when social scientists discuss computer simulations. Why, for example, wouldn't our traditional methods do? What are the advantages of computer simulations? Although the answers to these questions may be clearer

---

[1]Some might argue that when the man presents and uses a condom, as in Table 4.1, that no "negotiation has taken place." We would argue instead, that even the tacit agreement of the female (in not objecting to the man's use of the condom) is part of a negotiation process.

TABLE 4.1
An "Actual" Male Sexual Script for a Heterosexual One-Night Stand:
Events and Corresponding Goals

Event	Goals	
	Own	Perceived Partner's
My sexual partner and I are together	To check her out	To be checked out
I look deeply into her eyes	To begin making my move	To accept/not accept the beginning
I engage in small talk; she follows along	To "feel her out" emotionally	To see if we are compatible
I tell her that the bar we are in is "getting old"	Suggest that I am getting bored	To help me have more fun
I know of another party in the apartment next to mine	Get her to my place	Go to my place
I sell the party idea to her. We leave the bar	Get her to my place	Go to my place
I drive wild and fast toward my place	Set the "anything can happen" tone	Enjoy the ride
We both socialize at the party (10 minutes tops)	Fulfill the fake goal that I had set	Fulfill the fake goal that I had set
I pull her outside and take the drink from her hands	Get down to real business	Figure out what I am doing
With my free hand I pull her closer (firmly and gently)	First step in getting her to my room	Enjoy being handled
I press on the small of her back; she lets me pull her (tight to my body)	Let her know I want her	Let me know she wants me
I touch my lips to hers, drop the drink, and hold her head with her hair in my fingers	Romance	Romance
I bring her into my room	Second step in getting her into my room	To get into my room
I take her and my clothes off	Can't have sex with clothes on	Can't have sex with clothes on
I put on a condom	Prevent AIDS, etc.	Prevent AIDS, etc.
I mount her	Enjoy my conquest	Enjoy me on top of her
I kiss her	Romance	Romance
I can't wait—I rub against her...	Tease myself and her	To be teased
Tell her I can't wait to be inside her	Tell the truth	Say "me too"
I have sexual intercourse with my partner	Feel incredible	Feel incredible

Note. Slight modifications were made in subject protocol so that statements would be grammatically correct.

101

after we discuss some specific simulations in this domain, we provide some "temporary" answers to enable the reader to "walk over" the bridge from using traditional methods to thinking about what computer simulations can "buy us" beyond traditional methods.

WHY USE COMPUTER SIMULATIONS?

Social interaction, and sexual negotiation, is complex. Behavior, and how we construe that behavior, is constantly in flux. We perceive our partner's behavior as indicative of rejection, and we respond by feeling hurt. Perhaps we will withdraw, perhaps, if we believe we can "win them over," we may try even harder. Our constructions guide our behavior. Our partners infer our intentions from these behaviors. Perhaps, the partner infers that we are trying to be manipulative and they may respond by rejecting us all the more. In short, their perceptions guide their own next responses, those responses impact on our perceptions and behaviors, in turn. But, how do we study such changing patterns of behavior and perceptions?

As Ostrom (1988) argued, computer simulations may prove useful as a third symbol system (verbal and mathematical symbol systems being the other two) for understanding the "complexities [of social behavior that] have proven elusive to social psychological theorists." For example, Ostrom argued that we often treat social topics, and variables, in isolation without trying to examine interdependencies among latent variables. Clearly, however, "in almost any social encounter the person collectively activates many of these systems. They are not isolated from one another as the person interacts with other people. These latent variables act in unison to characterize the whole person" (p. 387).

Given current methodologies, we can specify how variables are linked in small portions of a "system." We can test with experimental methods how one variable may affect another and derive our current "best guess" of that association. But, we have not typically used methods (for an exception see Collins & Miller, 1992) that allow us to examine an entire "system" of associations that feed back to affect the level of a variable over time. Computer simulation technology could allow us to run simulated behavioral "outcomes" over time and compare these with known patterns of behavioral outcomes over time.[2] Through such a methodological process, simulation models can provide closer and closer

---

[2]Collins and Miller (1992) did something very close to that. Using "best guess" parameters from meta-analyses of experimental studies, Collins and Miller, ran a computer simulation to examine the net effects over time of a system of disclosure-liking links. That is, what would happen if the system of associations between disclosure-liking links that occur in the lab, were allowed to continue to feed into one another over a period of time. These emerging patterns for experimental interactions (among strangers) over time were compared with known disclosure-liking correlational findings from long-term relationships, which—interestingly—showed a similar pattern.

approximations or "fits" with known behavioral outcomes over time.

Furthermore, as Ostrom (1988) argued, traditional approaches that have focused on solely representing the latent variable on a continuum (e.g., attitudes pro and con; attributions high or low), and ignored qualitative shifts and movements, have been inadequate. They fail in "illuminating the dynamics through which qualitative structures come into existence and are subsequently modified. Artificial intelligence programming languages . . . provide an excellent symbol system for the theoretical representation of such structures" (p. 386). We would argue that connectionist modeling tools, discussed later, provide an excellent means of understanding networks of associations (e.g., behavior, beliefs, attributions, inferred goals, etc.) that activate and support leading explanatory structures for understanding sequences of actions, others, self, and the relationship.

However, while current methodologies at our disposal, in and of themselves, appear insufficient for exploring the dynamics of social interaction, current methods can be employed as part of a "bigger picture" of attempts to explore behavior dynamically. For example, we could use a computer simulation to simulate a system of associations based on a typical "verbal" social psychological theory concerning how variables go together. The causal links among these variables could be examined separately using traditional methods. Some or all of the links might even be examined at the same time. For some behaviors we could even use observational methods, coding behavior over time for time-series analysis. Then, the results for our computer simulation for predicting behaviors over time could be compared with the patterns of actual emerging behaviors from time-series analyses. Good "mapping" between simulation and behavioral findings would suggest that we had a plausible theoretical model of how our conceptual variables relate to one another.

Unfortunately, although it is generally difficult to study behavior dynamically given current methodologies, the problems become even more severe with sexual behaviors. There are additional ethical and feasibility constraints: Collecting interactional, observational data regarding the negotiation process, per se, is highly problematic. Computer simulations provide a particularly exciting methodological bridge to simulate the negotiation process and to explore how various variables and parameters might affect the behavioral outcomes that *can* be observed. Then studies can be set up to observe those "behavioral outcomes." Findings from these studies can be compared against theoretical expectations and can also become "input" for modifying the model.

Computer simulations also provide three additional bonuses. Because one cannot be vague about one's assumptions if the program is to run, computer simulations may force us to be more precise in our theoretical thinking. And, using dynamic tools does enable one to think more "dynamically" about social behavior in general, and sexual negotiations in particular. Such dynamic thinking provides a new, and we believe, strong theoretical and methodological paradigm for developing more effective educational programs and interventions to prevent the further spread of AIDS. Thus, we argue here that new methods in both cognitive science and systems dynamics that fit with our underlying theoretical assumptions and units provide the "glue" that makes it feasible to examine and explore the dynamic interplay among these structures.

DYNAMIC METHODS: DEMONSTRATING THE UTILITY OF COMPUTER SIMULATIONS

Here, using the example of John and Mary with which we began this chapter, we illustrate these two types of computer simulations. The first involves a computer simulation of a goal-corrected, dynamic system. This simulation incorporates many of the units and structures that we have previously discussed (e.g., goals, strategies) and can take advantage of research findings in specifying the mathematical links among such structures that feed back within the system over time. As previously mentioned, this method fits especially well with our first set of theoretical assumptions involving goal-corrected systems. We illustrate the use of this system in the section entitled, "Modeling a Dynamic System."

The second type of computer simulation, based on connectionist models of comprehension (Kintsch, 1988; Mannes & Kintsch, 1989) and other work on parallel distributed cognitive processing (Rummelhart & McClelland, 1986; Thagard, 1989), allows us to examine the current and changing activation levels of particular concepts or "nodes" around which mental models of actions, others, self, and relationships, may cohere. As new input is added, new "nodes" are activated and old "nodes" are deactivated. For example, how does Mary move from a model of safer sex that involves using a condom to a model in which sex can occur, and still be "safe" without using a condom? This computer simulation approach fits well with our second set of theoretical assumptions concerning the changing construction of meaning. We illustrate this second, very different type of computer simulation in a later section.

Modeling a Dynamic System

Consider a small part of a hypothetical sexual encounter between Mary and John. An underlying dynamic representation of the connections between some of Mary's goals, strategies, and obstacles might be as follows. Mary wants to avoid AIDS. This is a salient goal for men and women in pick-up relationships (DeBro & Miller, 1992). Because her partner is not yet using a condom, she doesn't perceive her partner as safe, a stumbling block to her having sex. This discrepancy between the goal of avoiding AIDS and the level at which she perceives that her partner is safe (which is low) drives strategic action (initiation attempts). As suggested by DeBro (DeBro, 1991; DeBro et al., 1990), Mary might be likely to engage in one of several strategies in her repertoire for getting her partner to use a condom, including an information appeal, deception, and reward. In addition to wanting to perceive her partner as safe (to avoid AIDS) she has another goal: She wants to avoid rejection. If, in initiating a strategy with her partner, Mary perceives that John's response is that he doesn't want to use a condom, this may negatively affect her perceptions of acceptance from John. This may lead to a discrepancy between wanting to avoid rejection and perceiving rejection which, if she can't come up with an alternative strategy that meets all of these goals, may lead to a decrease in attempts to initiate safer sex. To resolve the apparent conflict between wanting to avoid AIDS and wanting to avoid rejection, she may even persuade herself that John is really safe to justify her decision to have sex without a condom. Thus, from a dynamic perspective, whether a continued attempt at condom initiation would occur under these circumstances depends upon the relative values within the system over time including the levels of conflicting goals and perceptions.[3]

Thus far, our discussion of dynamic systems has been primarily at a conceptual level. Next, we model the system using a dynamic computer simulation. There are a number of computer simulation programs that can model dynamic systems, and we will illustrate only one of these, a program called STELLA (Richmond et al., 1987). For any dynamic simulation program, it is necessary to think about our variables in our models in a new way, that is we need to operationalize them within a dynamic system. For this particular dynamic simulation program, two key concepts are required in our operationalization process: stocks and flows.

Stocks and Flows.   What do we mean by the variables in our models? While for any given relationship interaction, there may be a variety of variables used in a model, for our purpose of using the opening scenario to illustrate a dynamic computer simulation, the variables for the present model are: perceived rejection, perceptions of John as unsafe, initiation attempts, and likelihood of unsafe sex. Within dynamic models, phenomena such as these involve accumulations over time. For example, over time Mary can accumulate perceptions of rejection from John. These accumulations we call *stocks* following the terminology of one dynamic systems computer simulation program, STELLA (Richmond et al., 1987). There can be increases and decreases in the level of perceived rejection from another; these increases of rejection are called *inflows* and are represented

---

[3]Which strategy Mary might employ is apt to depend on which strategy, relatively speaking, maximizes multiple goal achievement (including avoiding goals one wishes to avoid). That is, each relevant activated goal may increase and decrease, to various degrees, the likelihood of using each strategy. Which strategy "wins out" will be a function of the configuration of goals the person wishes to achieve (or avoid) and each goal's activation of each strategy. Thus, the strategy chosen need not be the very "best" strategy for any of the individual goals. Rather, it may be the best compromise (the one getting the most overall activation) among multiple goals.

by valves (inflow values) that flow into a stock. There can also be *outflows* from a stock that reduce the level of the stock over time.

Let's take a concrete look at such a simulation (Fig. 4.2). The reader is urged to follow along carefully, examining Fig 4.2, step by step, as we proceed. In the middle of this diagram at the top of the page there is a rectangular box labelled, "Rejection from John." This is a stock of Mary's perceived level of rejection from John. The valve (circle with the T on top of it) that feeds into this stock of perceived rejection is labelled "increases in rejection." A variety of factors increase perceived rejection: These feed into the inflow (increases in rejection). For example, the more attempts Mary makes to use a condom ("Initiation attempts"), the more she may perceive rejection from John. The greater the number of attempts she's made (higher level of the stock of initiation attempts), the more

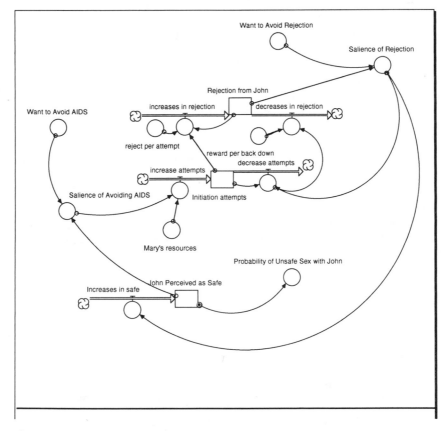

FIG. 4.2.   Dynamic modeling involving goal conflict in a heterosexual sexual sequence.

that feeds into increased "Rejection from John." Increases in perceived rejection from John should also be a function of how much rejection Mary perceives per initiation attempt. Furthermore, we might argue that as we perceive more and more rejection from another, this may bias how we construe behaviors (e.g., as indicative of greater levels of rejection). Such a bias "compounds" the level of rejection experienced that feeds into our stock of perceived rejection. To model this possibility, we have drawn an arrow from the stock, "Rejection from John," to the increase in rejection valve. Other factors decrease perceived rejection: These feed into the outflow (decreases in rejection). For example, as Mary decreases her attempts to initiate condom use, that should decrease the rejection she perceives from John; especially, if she receives rewarding behaviors (e.g., smiling) that reward her backing down.

At this point, now that we have clarified the concept of stocks and flows, let us backtrack a bit in the sequence of actions. To the left at the top of Fig. 4.2 we see a circle (called a converter in STELLA) labelled, "Want to Avoid AIDS." Because we view Mary's desire to want to avoid AIDS as a constant (e.g., what the person came into the relationship and sexual interaction with) we have modeled this variable, using the circle, or converter. The converter indicates that Mary's desire to avoid AIDS is a constant value that doesn't increase and decrease like a stock. We can set the "initial value" of wanting to avoid AIDS relatively high or low (*relative to* other initial starting values of other variables in the system).

We can also use converters (circles) when we do not wish our variables to accumulate over time. For example, consider the circle labelled, "Salience of Avoiding AIDS." If we set this value relatively high (1 on a scale from 0 to 1) then perceiving John as anything less than totally safe (e.g., a value of 1), would result in a discrepancy in our model between wanting to avoid AIDS and perceiving John as safe. Such discrepancies would feed increases (e.g., values greater than 0) in initiation attempts. For a given "cycle" through the system, let us say Cycle 1, if "Want to Avoid AIDS" is set at 1 and "John Perceived as Safe" is set at 0, that discrepancy ("Salience of Wanting to avoid AIDS" $= 1 - 0$) because it is greater than 0, would drive increases in attempts to initiate condom use. The next time through (in the next cycle), we recalculate the discrepancy anew. Because "Want to Avoid AIDS" is a constant, the value of "Salience of avoiding AIDS" rests on the current value of the stock, "John Perceived as Safe." Now the value of the stock, "John Perceived as Safe," unlike the converters, does accumulate. So if on Cycle 2, "John Perceived as Safe" $= 1$, on Cycle 3 through the system, "John Perceived as Safe" would equal the level at which John is perceived as safe (cycle 1) + increases in perceiving John as safe − decreases in perceiving John as safe. The use of converters or stocks for a variable then, is governed by a conceptualization that the variable, in any given simulation, should be thought of as "accumulating," versus not, over time. To provide another example, Mary's resources (e.g., her social skills and so forth), are treated as a constant. That constant value for resources feeds into increases in attempts to initiate condom use.[4]

Whether we perceive our partner as unsafe or not may change during the course of the interaction. And, a dynamic systems model easily allows for such a possibility. A variety of factors might affect whether we see our partner as "safe" or "unsafe." One such consideration involves other goals salient in the interaction. For example, consider the goal, "Want to Avoid Rejection," represented at the top right of Fig. 4.2.

The discrepancy between "Wanting to Avoid Rejection" and current level of "Rejection from John" is the circle marked "Salience of Rejection"; this discrepancy is apt to drive strategic action such as decreasing attempts to initiate condom use. As the level of perceived rejection from John gets greater, Mary not only reduces her attempts to initiate condom use, she may also be more likely to "see" John as safe (because he is Amy's brother, etc.). This connection is reflected by the bottom "loop" connecting "Salience of Rejection" with the flow into the "Increases in safe" valve, increasing the extent to which John is now perceived as "safe" (it feeds into the stock, "John Perceived as Safe").

The extent to which John is perceived at different times in the interaction as relatively safe or not then becomes a function of the relative importance of two factors:[5] (a) the initial starting value, relative to other factors, of "John Perceived as Safe" relative to Mary's desire to avoid AIDS; and (b) the level of John's rejection given how much Mary wishes to avoid his rejection. After the initial values of the factors in this model are specified relative to one another and the precise mathematical equations linking various factors to one another are specified, the computer simulation of this dynamic system can be "run." We have done so for the present model and this "output," represented over time, is shown in Fig. 4.3.

Over this period, we start looking at the sequence of actions following Mary's early attempt to initiate condom use, which is followed by perceived rejection from John. As this rejection from John peaks, she starts to perceive him as more and more safe, and her initiation attempts decline along with Mary's perception of being rejected by John. As this rejection declines sufficiently, Mary begins to increase her initiation attempts again. When these are met with some increased perceived rejection, her attempts diminish. During this period, the likelihood of unsafe sex (even as John himself is being perceived as more "safe") increases.

Earlier, we suggested how dynamic modeling might be useful for understand-

---

[4]It is important to note here that we are not advocating a particular, fully specified system. Rather, our intent is to advocate and illustrate a dynamic approach.

[5]To reduce the complexity of the model, we assume here that John will refuse to wear a condom regardless of Mary's initial attempts, and Mary will not have sex unless she perceives that John is safe. Then, the probability of unprotected sex increases only if John is perceived as "safe" even though he is not wearing a condom.

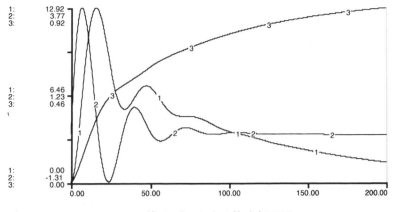

Minutes after returning to Mary's Apartment

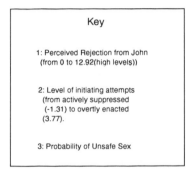

Key

1: Perceived Rejection from John
(from 0 to 12.92(high levels))

2: Level of initiating attempts
(from actively suppressed
(-1.31) to overtly enacted
(3.77).

3: Probability of Unsafe Sex

FIG. 4.3. Computer simulation output for dynamic modeling of heterosexual sexual sequence.

ing a heterosexual exchange in a pick-up given a particular idiographic configuration of individual goals and other structures. Certainly, such an approach might have important clinical applications to particular cases. In addition, it would be useful to understand more nomothetic phenomena that might apply to groups of individuals (heterosexual and gay individuals) with similar chronic goals, relationship goals, and so forth.

For example, let's consider in Fig. 4.4, a system of behavior that might operate for subgroups of gay men. When a gay man is very lonely, that loneliness may play a much greater role in directing action (including having unsafe sex). After having unsafe sex, however, for a period of time (perhaps until the next AIDS test), fear may be sufficiently up (and loneliness sufficiently reduced) that there is a marked reduction in having unsafe sex, for at least some men. After sufficient time has passed, however, fear may dissipate (and be reduced given a negative HIV test) and loneliness increase—thus, perhaps, increasing the risk of once again engaging in unsafe sexual practices. Thus, within a dynamic system,

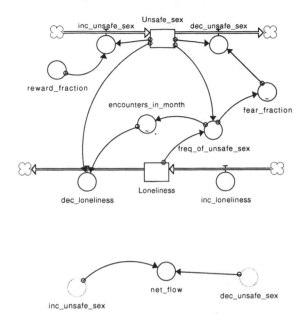

FIG. 4.4. Dynamic modeling: possible system resulting in lapse behavior.

movement between alternatively competing—but connected—subsystems can result in behavioral oscillation. Understanding such a system may thus be crucial, for example, to understanding the rise in relapse behavior in homosexual men.

Depending on the particulars of the individual case, oscillation patterns could emerge because individuals are lonely and that leads to unsafe sex which in turn decreases loneliness as well as increases fear. If unsafe sex is also rewarding then pressure to have unsafe sex mounts with increased loneliness and time elapsed from the last sexual encounter. Such a system produces a damped oscillation as depicted in Fig. 4.5.

Although dynamic systems approaches may allow us to look at the dynamics of behavior, they may not be sufficiently detailed—at least in their present form—to explore the dynamics of meaning. For example, earlier we mentioned that perceiving one's partner as "safe" or not might be an important part of the process of negotiating safer sex.

Exploring this possibility, Bowen and Michael-Johnson (1989) observed that rather than deal with the issue of negotiating safer sex directly (e.g., asking one's partner to use a condom), couples may rely on a variety of cues to evaluate the degree to which unprotected sex with their partner is apt to be "risky." The cues that sexual partners are apt to use (e.g., clothing such as wearing leather, appearance, apparent health, etc.) are clearly not reliable for accessing the likelihood that one's partner is a carrier of the HIV virus. Thus, these evaluations are likely to be incorrect and potentially dangerous.

Furthermore, as Cline and her colleagues have pointed out (Cline, 1990; Cline, Engel, Freeman, Johnson, & Gudaitis, 1989) although the surgeon general has suggested that in an era of AIDS couples should "know their partner," there are serious problems with that advice. First, the very college men who report that they are more likely to talk about AIDS and safer sex are the most likely to have more sexual partners; they are also the men who are less likely to use condoms. Second, these researchers have found that some sexual partners are willing to lie and conceal potentially problematic information regarding sexual histories. And, even if they do not lie or conceal information, couples can not know the complete histories of their past sexual partners. Thus, "talking about AIDS," if it does not lead to instrumental use of a condom, may well be dangerous: providing a false sense of security.

Because individuals are developing mental models of who is safe and who isn't, we clearly need to know more about how beliefs activate higher order

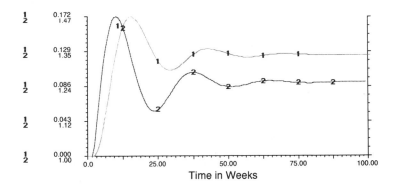

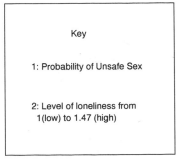

Key

1: Probability of Unsafe Sex

2: Level of loneliness from
1 (low) to 1.47 (high)

FIG. 4.5. Damped oscillation system for dynamic modeling of lapse behavior in Fig. 4.4.

cognitions (e.g., partner is safe) and what competing cognitions need to be made more salient (e.g., through interventions, media, presentations) to reinforce alternative mental models (e.g., partner might not be safe, sex could be dangerous without a condom, etc.). Unfortunately, it is unclear how one forms *coherent* mental models of one's partner as "safe" or "not safe."

In addition, during the negotiation process, what we say or do (e.g., such as mentioning AIDS) may affect our perceptions of self, other, or the relationship. Work by Collins (1990), for example, suggests that although male observers did not provide differential attributions of females who mentioned AIDS or did not mention AIDS, female observers were more likely to rate male targets who mention concern about AIDS as relatively passive, weak, and overly emotional and uptight. How might these "bits" of evidence in the array of information about one's partner "fit" with other information in developing a leading coherent model of one's partner as one with whom one could (or should) initiate and use safer sex behaviors?

Exploring the detail, coherence, and richness of individual belief systems relevant to evaluating self, one's partner, one's relationships, and using or not using safer sex, seems beyond the scope of goal-directed dynamic modeling approaches. Is there a way that we can represent and explore the detailed mental models that individuals have about their sexual partners, relationships, and about the unfolding of events in the sexual script? For this purpose another very different type of computer simulation may be needed. We elaborate such an approach here.

Developing Coherent Mental Models of Our Partner Within the Sexual Interaction

Throughout the interaction with our partner, our partner's behaviors are construed by us. We make inferences about these actions and what they mean for understanding our partner's plans and the goals that these are aimed at achieving. As new information is added, it is integrated with the preexisting construction as we continually build and add to our models of the individuals involved and the sequence of events (L. C. Miller & Read, 1991b; Read, 1987). Our interpretation of events affects our next responses and how others respond, in turn, to us. Thus, participants' interpretations of events are part of the changing flux of events as individuals mutually influence one another. Leading and coherent mental models are apt to affect how we construe our partner's new actions, these evolving constructions, in turn, are apt to impact on our subsequent action.

Coherence of Mental Models.   Coherence is a concept used by scholars in a variety of fields (e.g., linguistics, communication, cognitive science, philosophy, and psychology). Although definitions of coherence vary widely, a common theme is that coherence is a judgment of how elements (e.g., sentences in text, propositions in a network, speech acts in a conversation, person behaviors over time) at a given point in time "go together" or form a meaningful whole. But around what units do things go together or cohere? How would we measure coherence in understanding events, persons, others, and relationships? Although this is a general question with implications for a variety of phenomena, let us focus on one specific topic area: the coherence of our model of our partners as safe.

Around what units might our models cohere? L. C. Miller and Read (1991b) argued that the coherence central to social interaction and personality is provided by theories, often causal and goal-based theories, of how things are related to one another or "go together" (Murphy & Medin, 1985). These theories are embedded in complex knowledge structures such as those analyzed by Schank and Abelson (1977). Knowledge structures include goals, plans, beliefs, roles, scripts, traits, and themes. L. C. Miller and Read's (1991b) approach is concerned with the connections among these knowledge structures. We want to know how these knowledge structures are linked to one another and to the "data" (e.g., thoughts, feelings, emotions, events, etc.) that they explain for persons. What are the most heavily activated knowledge structures around which this data about the person "coheres"?

Essentially we are asking: What do these actions mean? As observers and interactants we want to understand events and so attempt to construct a coherent picture of sequences of actions, what individuals are doing, and what they are like. How can we represent how individuals construe events, and the explanatory structures used to "hold them together"?

To examine the coherence of a sequence of events, as represented in a person's memory, we need to represent the links among the knowledge structures and the "data" that they explain. One promising avenue is a recent computer simulation by Thagard (1989), which is based on connectionist modeling. Connectionism is concerned with the links (or connections) among units—or in our case—propositions (e.g., behaviors observed, speech acts, particular beliefs about what happened). Let's begin by exploring this graphically. Consider the example of Mary and John that we gave at the opening of the chapter. As is illustrated in Fig. 4.6, we can represent a "mental model" of this hypothetical sequence of behaviors, including Mary's representation of John as "safe" or "not" as a series of boxes and the links between them. Each box represents a proposition (e.g., a statement about the event, a feeling, a higher order inference, a theme, etc.). Links between propositions, and their nature, are specified using lines and arrows. An arrow from one box to another means that the higher order box contains an explanation that "explains" the box to which it is connected; these are excitatory links. A solid black line (marked with an ($-$)) indicates a contradictory link between one proposition and another. The relation among propositions may also be neutral (no relationship or links among them). Propositions in this network that are "given" in the opening scenario are considered "evidence" or "data"

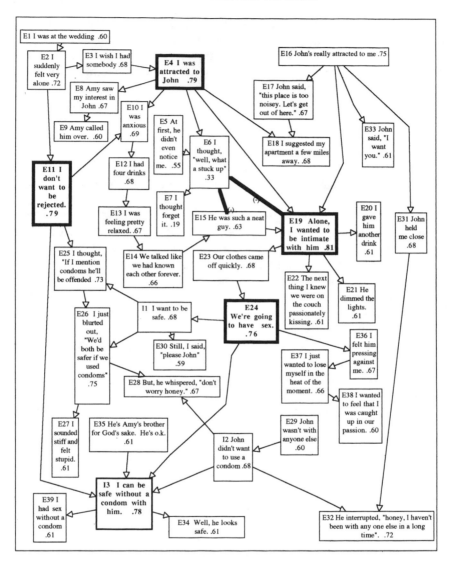

FIG. 4.6. Coherence modeling of an hypothetical unsafe sexual interaction.

and are labelled with Es. Propositions that involve more reader inference are modeled with Is.

Propositions in a network are interconnected and pass activation (positive and negative) to one another. Each unit receives activation from things it explains and things it is explained by. Higher numbers in the boxes (e.g., .81 for proposition E19) indicate higher activation levels. Because exactly how this works is explained in greater detail in a recent chapter on the coherence of mental models (L. C. Miller & Read, 1991b), we do not elaborate on this here.

However, it is important to note that this simulation uses a parallel constraint satisfaction process. This is a way of evaluating a set of constraints that are applied to the data simultaneously. Everything that is interconnected continues to send a fraction of its activation to everything else in the network, through an iterative process, until the activations asymptote.

The set of constraints that are employed in this simulation are based on the principles of coherence summarized by Thagard (1989). These include: (a) breadth, or an explanation that explains more facts is more coherent; (b) parsimony, the explanation that requires the fewest number of assumptions is more coherent; (c) an explanation that is explained by a more general principle should be more coherent; and (d) an explanation that is supported by an analogy is more coherent. Experimental work examining these principles, indicates that each plays a role in the evaluations of social explanations (Read & Cesa, 1991; Read & Marcus-Newhall, in press).

Using these constraints, Thagard's Echo Program (1989), can provide the activation levels that would result for the propositions in our example. These are provided in Fig. 4.6. Those "nodes" in the network that receive the highest activation can be viewed as the nodes around which representations of the partner, self, and the sequence of actions most cohere. The most activated or salient parts of the network then include nodes like, "I don't want to be rejected," "I was attracted to John," "We're going to have sex," and "Alone, I wanted to be intimate with him." As the sequence progresses, despite her earlier desire to use a condom that led her to initiate several attempts to get John to use a condom, Mary feels that she can be safe without a condom, and that node, "I can be safe without a condom" receives high levels of activation. In essence, she has deluded herself that "John is safe" (because she doesn't want to be rejected) during the sexual interaction, and alternative beliefs that "not using a condom is always unsafe" are not activated or salient.

Coherence analyses allow for a fine fit between a methodology that allows us to explore how incoming new inputs "fit" or do not "fit" with a representation of the sequence of events, and dynamic assumptions that argue, among other things, that individuals are constantly in the process of constructing social interactions and that these models of the interactions are constantly being updated and affected through feedback loops and new inputs into the network. Furthermore, change and stability may share an underlying dynamic. That is, on the one hand, ways of construing others may change moment by moment, sometimes dramatically. Higher order constructs may play more or less of an influential role in providing overall coherence at different points in time and this "oscillation" may mirror the oscillation of goal-corrected systems. Thus, at least some change and movement may be part of a stable process.

On the other hand, as coherence networks suggest, developing coherent mental models of interactions, self, others and relationships is conservative—and self-maintaining in that input (often with a wide latitude for interpretation; see L. C. Miller & Read, 1991b) is selectively construed and interpreted given the constraints and considerable weight of those prior structures. Ascertaining the goals of the interactants (one's own and those of one's partner) and the extent to which the goals are being met, is apt to play a central role in how we explain and construe intrapersonal and interpersonal phenomena over time.

CONCLUSIONS AND IMPLICATIONS
FOR A DYNAMIC PARADIGM

AIDS Research, Interventions, and Educational Programs

This chapter argues that behavior, such as "unsafe sexual behavior" is embedded in a dynamic process. When individuals negotiate safer sex, they are constantly constructing the meaning of actions and are responding to the perceived goals of their partner, as well as their own goals. The relative values of these perceptions, along with chronic goals, beliefs, fears, and current states, are apt to influence strategic action, action that can lead to resisting or encouraging the use of safer sexual behaviors. Suppose one buys into these dynamic assumptions, what does this suggest for AIDS interventions and educational programs?

A dynamic paradigm suggests that wanting to avoid AIDS is not enough. It is the relative level of concern with avoiding AIDS compared to other factors operating in the system that affects behavioral outcomes. Even when individuals have a strong desire to avoid AIDS, there are multiple factors that can derail their attempts to reach that goal. Each of these "weak links" suggests programs of basic research, and starting places for intervention and educational programs. Here we focus on such possibilities at the individual and dyadic levels.

Individual Level. Individuals come into sexual interactions with multiple goals and potential goal conflicts that can make negotiating safer sex more or less difficult. They have more or less detailed knowledge of sexual scripts and repertoires of plans and strategies for achieving subgoals. They have more or less extensive social and communications skills and resources for successfully enacting those strategies. And, they differ in terms of how, given preexisting belief systems, they construct meaning in social interaction. Individual differences in goals, knowledge structures, communication skills, and belief systems make it more or less difficult for persons to successfully overcome obstacles to negotiating safer sex. In a nutshell, in each of these areas we need more basic research, intervention, and educational programs.

Let us begin with goal conflicts that might reduce safer sex. Suppose we knew that the most frequent goal conflicts encountered by individuals from a particular subpopulation (e.g., gay men who were not in stable relationships) involved a conflict between avoiding loneliness and avoiding AIDS. A dynamic perspective would argue for understanding the system of relationships among these factors. We might ask questions such as: "How great would the experienced level of loneliness need to be such that, combined with other factors perhaps (e.g., attractiveness of the partner), it could override concerns about avoiding AIDS?" Answers to such questions would suggest what in the system needed to be changed or could most effectively (or economically) be changed. In the example suggested earlier, if loneliness levels acts as a critical control parameter that leads to greater likelihoods of risky sexual behavior, then loneliness levels need to be kept low. Educational programs and interventions might focus on buddy systems and support groups that such men might contact when they are feeling particularly lonely and susceptible to engaging in risky sex. Such groups might operate in a way similar to programs for recovering alcoholics. If the need for physical contact was a critical control parameter for others, educational programs might be designed to alert individuals to be aware of this need (and fluctuations in this need over time) and suggest alternative strategies for achieving such goals (e.g., therapeutic message).

At an idiographic level, clinical intervention programs aimed at enabling individuals to explore their own particular goals in sexual encounters might suggest critical "pieces in the system" that feed into risky behaviors that could be effectively controlled. For example, suppose some individuals are particularly at risk for engaging in unsafe sex when they have not had sex for a period of time. For them, relieving the sexual tension in other ways prior to going out on a date might act as the "critical control parameter" (a parameter in the system which is critical for behavior change). Diary studies and diary-based interventions in which individuals keep detailed notes regarding their sexual encounters (and other relevant behaviors, perceptions, feelings, and events), might prove a useful first step in understanding individual "control parameters."

The second general area for intervention and educational programs involves developing a knowledge base of peer recommended strategies for overcoming obstacles to safer sex. These strategies should be very specific given particular obstacles embedded in various sexual sequences. In many respects the sexual scripts that adults have used in a pre-AIDS era may be fairly automatic, and may tend to involve a large number of nonverbal behaviors. Integrating into such scripts, new—verbal behaviors—is not apt to be easy. Furthermore, individuals may not have thought about how to integrate these behaviors into the sequence, or they may not have thought about the types of obstacles and goals that might also become salient for them in negotiating safer sex.

Certainly, interventions and educational programs aimed at teaching such strategies are needed. Given the complexity and interactive nature of the types of strategies involved, some educational programs might focus on using interactive video programs in which individuals choose behaviors from various alternatives (known to vary in effectiveness) in response to various obstacles. Other educational programs might provide as "lifelike" as possible computer simulations in which individuals might respond sequentially to the nonverbal and verbal responses of their partners with behaviors of their own. Obviously, feed back and discussion of individual choices would be a critical part of such an educational program.

One useful intervention, may simply be to ask individuals to consciously go through the process of thinking about their own personal scripts and the sequence of events leading up to safer sex or not. After developing diaries of such scenarios, individuals could be asked to suggest those moments when they wanted to raise the topic and did not and finding out specifically why they did not (what were the perceived goals that they had and that their partner had that kept them from initiating action). By role-playing alternative strategies that might have overcome this obstacle and achieved the multiple goals of the interactant at that point in time, individuals may develop a more effective alternative set of idiographic strategies for overcoming such obstacles in the future. Interventions could also be designed to focus on planning behaviors (e.g., having condoms available near where you might have sexual intercourse in your apartment) and to suggest when and how individuals might most effectively initiate the topic of safer sex (in various contexts) and use verbal and nonverbal cues most effectively during the negotiation sequence. Interventions to "act out" these behaviors in as "real-life" simulations as possible could also be developed.

Furthermore, often individuals do not negotiate safer sex until there is perceived mutual intent to have sex. At that point, sexual arousal may be very high. In that context, coming up with effective, often novel ways of overcoming obstacles to safer sex "on the fly," seems relatively unlikely. Basic research exploring the role of sexual arousal and use of strategies is also needed. For example, it might be that learning strategies for circumventing obstacles under conditions of sexual arousal (e.g., induced by sexually arousing films) might enhance the use of such strategies in similarly emotionally arousing contexts.

A third area of intervention involves the enhancement of relevant communication skills and competencies. The possibilities here are complex but a good starting place might be to enhance specific communication competencies outlined by communication scholars (see e.g., Parks, 1985).

A fourth general area for work at the individual level involves the construction of social meaning. For example, in our own program of research we are interested in how individuals make sense of and construct the meaning of behaviors leading up to using or not using safer sex. We want to know in a very detailed way how individuals account for failures to enact safer sex. And, what are the implications of such accounts and attributions for subsequent changes in behavior? If different constructions of events are more or less likely to lead to instrumental planning in the future, or reductions in exposure to vulnerable circumstances, then knowledge of such constructions might lead to useful educational programs and interventions aimed at encouraging individuals to see "alternative constructions."

Dyadic Level of Analysis.   Repeatedly, we have argued that negotiating safer sex is a dyadic process involving the goals, perceptions, feelings, and behaviors of both individuals in the sequence of actions leading up to or failing to lead up to safer sex. Yet, relatively little work to date has involved looking at the negotiations among couples, either involving paper-and-pencil measures, or preferably live interactions. Currently, we are pursuing both possibilities. In one project, for example, dating individuals are asked to discuss hypothetical couples and the obstacles and problems these couples might encounter with each other and also with strangers of the opposite sex. A myriad of interventions here seem plausible. For example, perhaps the sheer act of talking to others (of the same or opposite sex) might desensitize individuals to the negotiation process and make it easier to successfully enact these behaviors in the future. Role playing possibilities for "working" on strategies in dyadic as well as group contexts would seem plausible intervention strategies.

Furthermore, in a more general way, a dynamic perspective also argues for the importance of considering change over time and collecting measures over time. For example, we could use diaries, self-reports at multiple points in time, and "beepers" to study how individuals (and potentially couples) change over time in their behaviors, perceptions, and goals with respect to using safer sex. Detailed narratives that individuals provide over time regarding their behaviors might also provide a basis for coherence analyses (of the type used for an analysis of Mary and John).

Summary and General Implications

We view the sexual interaction, embedded in a relationship, as a dynamic process. Sexual interaction involves not only the dynamic interplay of individual level phenomena (e.g., goal-corrected desires, experienced sexual arousal, activation of cognitive structures including scripts, schemas, and the development of mental models regarding—e.g., self, other, and relationship) but also the dynamics of an interpersonal process in which individuals mutually influence one another. As our ongoing research indicates, goals play an important role in the obstacles individuals perceive in negotiating safer sex. And because different sexual relationships may satisfy different goals, it is not surprising that the nature of one's relationships affects the strategies one is apt to use to persuade one's partner to use condoms. Furthermore, understanding how individuals represent the moment-by-moment fluctuations in sexual scripts and how individuals derive meaning from their own and their partner's behaviors (including the goals associated with those actions) is apt to be crucial for understanding whether particular sexual sequences result in using safer sex or not.

The blending of sophisticated methodological tools and dynamic theoretical frameworks provides the basis of a general paradigm potentially useful across a broad spectrum of phenomena and processes in the social sciences. Still, this paradigm stretches back a long way in the field of psychology. In the 1930's, for example, Kurt Lewin, in discussing his own dynamic theory of personality (Lewin, 1964) noted that "the dynamics of the processes is always to be derived from the relation of the concrete individual to the concrete situation, and, so far as internal forces are concerned, from the mutual relations of the various functional systems that make up the individual" (p. 230). Perhaps, it is time to take those insightful words seriously as we confront a dynamic problem of urgent magnitude: the AIDS crisis.

ACKNOWLEDGMENT

This work was supported by California Universitywide AIDS Research Program (Grant Number R90USC021) to the first author. Much of the research cited here was reported at a conference entitled, "Negotiating Safer Sex" funded by California Universitywide AIDS Research Program to the first author.

REFERENCES

Abelson, R. P. (1968). *Simulation and social behavior.* In C. Lindzey & E. Aronson (Eds.), Handbook of social psychology (Vol. 2, pp. 274–356). Reading, MA: Addison-Wesley.

Adelman, M. B. (1990, May). *Safer-sex talk: Negotiation or improvisation?* Paper presented at the conference on "Negotiation of Safer-Sex: Social Science Theory and Research," San Diego, CA.

Adelman, M. B. (1992). Healthy passions: Play and safe sex talk. In T. Edgar, M. A. Fitzpatrick, & V. Freimuth (Eds.), AIDS: A communication perspective. Hillsdale, NJ: Lawrence Erlbaum Associates.

Baldwin, J. D., & Baldwin, J. I. (1988). Factors affecting AIDS-related sexual risk-taking behavior among college students. *Journal of Sex Research, 25,* 181–196.

Baldwin, J. I., Whiteley, S., & Baldwin, J. D. (1990). Changing AIDS and fertility-related behavior: The effectiveness of sexual education. *The Journal of Sex Research, 27,* 245–262.

Berg, J. H. (1987). Responsiveness and self-disclosure. In V. Derlega & J. H. Berg (Eds.), *Self-disclosure: Theory, research, and therapy* (pp. 101–126). New York: Plenum.

Bertalanffy, L. (1968). *General systems theory.* New York: George Braziller.

Bowen, S., & Michael-Johnson, P. (1989). The crisis of communicating in relationships: Confronting the threat of AIDS. *AIDS and Public Policy Journal, 4,* 10–19.

Burns, D., & Miller, L. C. (1990). [*Sexual scripts and goals in different types of sexual relationships*]. Unpublished raw data.

Clark, M. S., & Mills, J. (1979). Interpersonal attraction in exchange and communal relationships. *Journal of Personality and Social Psychology, 37,* 12-24.

Cline, R. J. (1990). *Dangerous liasons: Challenging the assumptions of interpersonal AIDS prevention advice.* Paper presented at a conference supported by the Universitywide AIDS Research Program entitled, Negotiating Safer Sex: Social Science Theory and Research.

Cline, R. J., Engel, J., Freeman, K. E., Johnson, S. J., & Gudaitis, T. (1989). *Practicing sexual roulette versus practicing safe sex: Differentiating characteristics.* Paper presented at the meeting of the International Communication Association, San Francisco, CA.

Collins, B. (1990). *Identity processes in the negotiation for safer sex.* Paper presented at a conference supported by the Universitywide AIDS Research Program entitled, Negotiating Safer Sex: Social Science Theory and Research.

Collins, N., & Miller, L. C. (1992). *The disclosure-liking link: From meta-analysis towards a dynamic reconceptualization.* Unpublished manuscript.

Cushman, D. P., Valentinsen, B., & Dietrich, D. (1982). A rules theory of interpersonal relationships. In F. E. X. Dance (Ed.), *Human communication theory: Comparative essays* (pp. 90–119). New York: Harper & Row.

De Bro, S. C. (1988). *Condom power strategies: How college students influence a partner about the use of a condom.* Unpublished honor's thesis, University of California at Los Angeles.

De Bro, S. C., Campbell, S. M., & Peplau, L. A. (1990, May). *Condom Power Strategies: How heterosexual couples influence a partner about the use of a condom.* Paper presented at the conference on Negotiating Safer Sex: Social Science Theory and Research, San Diego, CA.

De Bro, S. C. (1991). *Different types of sexual relationships: How heterosexual young adults influence a partner to use a condom.* Unpublished master's thesis, The Claremont Graduate School, Claremont, CA.

De Bro, S. C., & Miller, L. C. (1992). [dating goals and sexual relationships: Influencing condom use]. Unpublished raw data.

Delia, J. G. (1977). Constructivism and the study of human communication. *Quarterly Journal of Speech, 63,* 66–83.

Duck, S., & Sants, H. (1983). On the origin of the specious: Are personal relationships really interpersonal states? *Journal of Social and Clinical Psychology, 1,* 27–41.

Emmons, R. A. (1987). Narcissism: Theory and research. *Journal of Personality and Social Psychology, 52,* 11–17.

Freimuth, V. S., Edgar, T., & Hammond, L. (1987). College students' awareness of the AIDS risk. *Science, Technology, and Human Values, 12,* 37–40.

Harre, R., & Secord, P. F. (1972). *The explanation of social behavior.* Oxford: Basil Blackwell.

Hastie, R. (1988). A computer simulation model of person memory. *Journal of Experimental Social Psychology, 24,* 423–447.

Hoffman, V., & Miller, L. C. (1989). *Sexual scripts and negotiating safer sex.* Unpublished data.

Hopkins, J. R. (1977). Sexual behavior in adolescence. *Journal of Social Issues, 33*(2), 67–85.

Hovland, C. I. (1960). Computer simulation of thinking. *American Psychologist, 15,* 687–693.

Katzman, E. M., Mulholland, M., & Sutherland, E. M. (1988). College students and AIDS: A preliminary survey of knowledge, attitudes, and behavior. *Journal of American College Health, 37,* 127–130.

Kelley, H. H. (1979). *Personal relationships: Their structures and processes.* Hillsdale, NJ: Lawrence Erlbaum Associates.

Kelley, H. H. (1984). Affect in interpersonal relations. In P. Shaver (Ed.), *Review of personal and social psychology* (Vol. 5, pp. 89–115). Beverly Hills, CA: Sage.

Kenny, D. A. (1981). Interpersonal perception: A multivariate round robin analysis. In M. B. Brewer & B. E. Collins (Eds.), *Knowing and validating in the social sciences: A tribute to Donald T. Campbell* (pp. 299–309). San Francisco: Jossey-Bass.

Kintsch, W. (1988). The role of knowledge in discourse comprehension: A construction-integration model. *Psychological Review, 95,* 163–182.

Kuhn, T. S. (1970). *The structure of scientific revolutions.* Chicago: University of Chicago Press.

Leslie, C. (1988, November 14). Amid the ivy, cases of AIDS. *Newsweek,* p. 65.

Lewin, K. (1964). A Dynamic Theory of Personality. In H. M. Ruitenbeck (Ed.) *Varieties of personality theory* (pp. 196–234). New York: E. P. Dutton.

Magnusson, D., & Endler, N. S. (1977). *Interactional psychology: Personality at the crossroads* (pp. 3–31). Hillsdale, NJ: Lawrence Erlbaum Associates.

Mannes, S. M., & Kintsch, W. (1989). *Planning routine computing tasks: Understanding what to do* (ICS Tech. Rep. #89–9). Boulder: Institute of Cognitive Science, University of Colorado.

McCormick, N. B. (1979). Come-ons and put-offs: Unmarried students' strategies for having and avoiding sexual intercourse. *Psychology of Women Quarterly, 4,*(2), 195–211.

McCormick, N. B., & Gaeddert, W. S. (1989). Power in male college students' contraceptive decisions. *Archives of Sexual Behavior, 18,* 35–48.

Miller, G. R. (1983). Taking stock of a discipline. *Journal of Communication, 33,* 31–41.

Miller, L. C. (1987). *Negotiating safer sex: 101 obstacles.* Paper presented at the Interpersonal Relations Meeting, Nags Head, NC.

Miller, L. C. (1990). Intimacy and liking: Mutual influence and the role of unique relationships. *Journal of Personality and Social Psychology, 59,* 50–60.

Miller, L. C. (1991). *Inter-personalism: A knowledge structure approach to negotiating safer sex.* Paper presented at a conference Supported by the Universitywide AIDS Research Program entitled, Negotiating Safer Sex: Social Science Theory and Research.

Miller, L. C., & Bettencourt, B. A. (1989). *Predicting obstacles in negotiating safer sex.* Paper presented at the meeting of the Iowa Conference on Personal Relationships, Iowa City.

Miller, L. C., Burns, D., Rothspan, S., Seiter, J., Washington, C., & Juarbe, M. (1992). *Predicting safe sex talk in an African American sample.* Paper presented at the Universitywide AIDS Research Meeting, San Francisco, CA.

Miller, L. C., & Read, S. J. (1987). Why am I telling you this? Self-disclosure in a goal based model of personality. In V. Derlega & J. Berg (Eds.), *Self-disclosure: Theory, research, and therapy* (pp. 35–58). New York: Plenum.

Miller, L. C., & Read, S. J. (1991a). Inter-personalism: Understanding persons in relationships. In W. Jones & D. Perlman (Eds.), *Advances in personal relationship* (Vol. 2, pp. 233–267). London: Jessica Kingsley Publishers.

Miller, L. C., & Read, S. J. (1991b). Coherence of mental models of persons and relationships: A knowledge structure approach. In G. Fletcher & F. Fincham (Eds.). *Cognition in close relationships* (pp. 69–97). Hillsdale, NJ: Lawrence Erlbaum Associates.

Murphy, G. L., & Medin, D. L. (1985). The role of theories in conceptual coherence. *Psychological Review, 92,* 289–316.

Ostrom, T. M. (1988). Computer simulation: The third symbol system. *Journal of Experimental Social Psychology, 24,* 281–392.

Parks, M. R. (1985). Interpersonal communication and the quest for personal competence. In M. L. Knapp & G. R. Miller (Eds.) *Handbook of interpersonal communication.* Beverly Hills, CA: Sage.

Pearce, W. B., & Cronen, V. E. (1980). *Communication, action, and meaning: The creation of social realities.* New York: Praeger.

Perper, T., & Weis, D. L. (1987). Proceptive and rejective strategies of U.S. and Canadian college women. *Journal for Sex Research, 23,* 455–480.

Pryor, J. B., & Merluzzi, T. V. (1985). The role of expertise in processing social interaction scripts, *Journal of Experimental Social Psychology, 4,* 362–379.

Pryor, J. B. (1992). Unpublished raw data.

Read, S. J. (1987). Constructing causal scenarios: A knowledge structure approach to causal reasoning. *Journal of Personality and Social Psychology, 52,* 288–302.

Read, S. J., & Cesa, I. L. (1991). This reminds me of the time when. . . : Expectation failures in reminding and explanation. *Journal of Experimental Social Psychology, 27,* 1–25.

Read, S. J., & Marcus-Newhall, A. (in press). *The role of explanatory coherence in social explanations. Journal of Personality and Social Psychology.*

Read, S. J., & Miller, L. C. (1989a). Inter-personalism: Toward a goal-based theory of persons in relationships. In L. Pervin (Ed.), *Goal concepts in personality and social psychology* (pp. 413–472). Hillsdale, NJ: Lawrence Erlbaum Associates.

Read, S. J., & Miller, L. C. (1989b). The importance of goals in personality: Towards a coherent model of persons. In R. S. Wyer & T. K. Srull (Eds.), *Advances in social cognition* (Vol. 2): *Social intelligence and cognitive assessments of personality* (pp. 163–174). Hillsdale, NJ: Lawrence Erlbaum Associates.

Reis, H., & Shaver, P. (1988). Intimacy as an interpersonal process. In S. Duck, D. F. Hay, S. E. Hobfoll, W. Ickes, & B. M. Montgomery (Eds.), *Handbook of personal relationships* (pp. 367–389). Chichester, England: Wiley.

Richmond, B., Peterson, S., & Vercuso, P. (1987). *An academic user's guide to Stella*. Lyme, NH: High Performance Systems.

Rummelhart, D. E., & McClelland, J. L. (1986). *Parallel distributed processing: Explorations in the microstructure of cognition. Vol 1: Foundations*. Cambridge, MA: MIT Press.

Schank, R. C., & Abelson, R. P. (1977). *Scripts, plans, goals, and understanding*. Hillsdale, NJ: Lawrence Erlbaum Associates.

Searle, J. R. (1983). *Intentionality: An essay in philosophy of language*. Cambridge: Cambridge University Press.

Simon, W., & Gagnon, J. H. (1986). Sexual scripts: Permanence and change. *Archives of Sexual Behavior, 15*, 97–120.

Smith, M. J. (1982). *Persuasion and human action: A review and critique of social influence theories*. Belmont, CA: Wadsworth.

Stasser, G. (1988). Computer simulations as a research tool: The DISCUSS model of group decision making. *Journal of Experimental Social Psychology, 24*, 393–422.

Thagard, P. (1989). Explanatory coherence. *Behavioral and Brain Sciences, 12*, 435–467.

Wilensky, R. (1983). *Planning and understanding: A computational approach to human reasoning*. Reading, MA: Addison-Wesley.

World Health Organization. (1992, July). *Global Program on AIDS World Health Organization: World AIDS Cases Quarterly Update*. Geneva, Switzerland: World Health Organization.

THEORETICAL PERSPECTIVES
ON INTERVENTION

5

A General Social Psychological Model for Changing AIDS Risk Behavior

William A. Fisher
University of Western Ontario

Jeffrey D. Fisher
University of Connecticut

Human immunodeficiency virus (HIV) and acquired immune deficiency syndrome (AIDS) have become major public health threats for our time. HIV/AIDS[1] is largely a behaviorally borne disease that is communicated via unprotected sexual intercourse, the use of contaminated needles, and other vectors for the exchange of blood and bodily fluids. As such, AIDS has affected members of many groups whose behavior has posed the risk of infection (Winkelstein & Johnson, 1990). In the United States, AIDS has had devastating effects on gay men (Centers for Disease Control, 1990), minorities (Mays, 1989; Quimby & Friedman, 1989), intravenous (IV) drug users and their sexual partners and children (Des Jarlais et al., 1989), and hemophiliacs (Stehr-Green, Holman, Jason, & Evatt, 1988). Evidence is also mounting to suggest that the general heterosexually active public is at increasing risk of AIDS as well (Burke et al., 1990; Gordin, Gibert, Hawley, & Willoughby, 1990; T. E. Miller, Booraem, Flowers, & Iverson, 1990; St. Louis et al., 1990).

Despite public awareness of AIDS risk, behavior change in the direction of risk reduction has been inconsistent in most affected groups in the United States, including gay men (Hays, Kegeles, & Coates, 1990; Kelly, St. Lawrence, Brasfield, Stevenson, Diaz, & Hauth, 1990; McCombs & White, 1990; Stall, Coates, & Hoff, 1988), minorities (Mays & Cochran, 1988), IV drug users (Des Jarlais, Friedman, & Casriel, 1990), and hemophiliacs (Centers for Disease Control,

---

[1] Both HIV infection and AIDS are of concern in this chapter. For ease of exposition, however, we use the generic term *AIDS* to refer to the spectrum that ranges from HIV infection to progression to AIDS.

1987; Clemow et al., 1989). Behavior change among heterosexually active young people, moreover, has been modest to nonexistent (DiClemente, Forrest, Mickler, & Principal Site Investigators, 1990; J. D. Fisher & Miscovich, 1990; Kegeles, Adler, & Irwin, 1988; MacDonald et al., 1990).

Given the persistence of AIDS risk behavior, it is critical to develop effective methods for encouraging AIDS risk-behavior change (Albee, 1989; Coates, 1990; Coxon & Carballo, 1989). However, in a recent review of the AIDS risk-reduction intervention literature, J. Fisher and W. Fisher (1992) concluded that research in this area has been limited by a number of conceptual and empirical shortcomings. First, risk-reduction interventions are usually based on informal conceptualizations and do not utilize sophisticated behavioral science models to illuminate either the determinants of risk behavior or the means for encouraging change. Second, risk-reduction interventions generally do not systematically identify or address the population-specific needs of the target groups they are intended to affect. Third, risk-reduction interventions generally focus singularly on the provision of information, and rarely attempt to motivate behavior change or to teach behavioral skills that are necessary for change. Fourth, risk-reduction interventions are often evaluated with little rigor. Evaluation research in this area has suffered from problems with experimental design, inappropriate control groups, high attrition rates, reactive measures, and a failure to assess the impact of interventions on factors that are presumed to mediate behavioral change. Finally, for many of these reasons, AIDS risk-reduction interventions often show little or no impact on risk behavior.

Although these shortcomings are common, several recent AIDS risk-reduction interventions prove to be positive and informative exceptions to the rule (see for example, Jemmott, Jemmott, & Fong, 1990; Kelly & St. Lawrence, 1988; Kelly, St. Lawrence, Stevenson et al., 1990; Rotheram-Borus et al., 1991; Valdiserri et al., 1989). A number of these interventions have had well-articulated conceptual bases (e.g., Kelly & St. Lawrence, 1988; Kelly, St. Lawrence, Stevenson et al., 1990), some have attempted to identify and address population-specific risk-reduction needs (Jemmott et al., 1990; Kelly, St. Lawrence, Stevenson, et al., 1990), and some have involved the provision of risk-reduction information as well as motivation and/or behavioral skills (Kelly & St. Lawrence, 1988; Rotheram-Borus et al., 1991; Valdiserri et al., 1989), and each resulted in significant AIDS risk-behavior change.

Based on this analysis of the AIDS risk-reduction literature, the present approach emphasizes the need for interventions that are conceptually based, broadly focused on the provision of risk-reduction information, motivation, and behavioral skills, and targeted at group-specific needs in these areas (J. Fisher & W. Fisher, 1992). This chapter describes a model for changing AIDS risk behavior that incorporates these characteristics, in an attempt to provide guidance for efforts to understand, promote, and evaluate AIDS risk-behavior change.

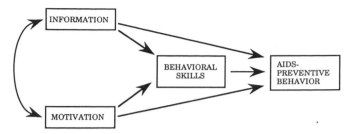

FIG. 5.1. The Information-Motivation-Behavioral Skills Model for AIDS risk reduction.

THE INFORMATION–MOTIVATION–BEHAVIORAL SKILLS MODEL OF AIDS RISK-BEHAVIOR CHANGE

In an attempt to integrate existing AIDS risk-reduction literature, J. Fisher and W. Fisher (1992) proposed a social psychological model of the determinants of AIDS risk-behavior change. The present conceptualization holds that there are three fundamental determinants of AIDS risk reduction (see Fig. 5.1). *Information* regarding AIDS transmission and AIDS prevention is a necessary prerequisite to risk-reduction behavior change. *Motivation* to modify AIDS risk behavior is a second determinant of AIDS risk reduction and influences the likelihood that the individual will act on his or her risk-reduction information. *Behavioral skills* for performing specific AIDS preventive acts represent a third determinant of whether or not even well-informed, well-motivated individuals will be capable of reducing AIDS risk.[2]

The present conceptualization assumes that risk-reduction information and motivation work through behavioral skills to affect behavior change. Essentially, risk-reduction information and motivation are believed to activate behavioral skills that are used to initiate and maintain patterns of preventive behavior. Risk-reduction information and motivation can also have direct effects on risk-reduction behavior change, when AIDS-specific behavioral skills are not necessary for the practice of preventive behavior. For example, information about monogamy as an HIV preventative strategy may have a direct effect on an individual's choice of whether or not to "play the field." Motivation to prevent infection, in terms of positive attitudes toward abstinence, and perceived social support for abstinence, may also have a direct effect on preventive behavior in relation to the decision to

---

[2]Although a number of others have addressed information, motivation, and behavioral skills as important factors in AIDS prevention (Coates, 1990; H. G. Miller, Turner, & Moses, 1990; Winett, Altman, & King, 1990), the present model (J. D. Fisher & W. A. Fisher, 1989, 1992) specifies particular content that is important to these constructs, and is the first to elaborate specific linkages among these constructs and to suggest methods for applying an information, motivation, behavioral skills conceptualization for the design of AIDS risk-reduction interventions.

remain abstinent. Finally, AIDS risk-reduction information and AIDS risk-reduction motivation are regarded as independent elements in this model.[3]

The constructs of the Information–Motivation–Behavioral Skills (IMB) model are viewed as highly general determinants of AIDS risk-reduction behavior across diverse populations of interest. At the same time, these constructs are expected to have content that is specific to particular target groups and particular preventive behaviors. Within the model, specific informational elements, motivational factors, and behavioral skills should be implicated in particular target groups' performance of particular preventive behaviors. For example, for homosexual males, the informational elements, motivational factors, and behavioral skills that are relevant for using condoms may be different than those relevant for avoiding oral sex. Furthermore, these informational, motivational, and behavioral skills elements may differ from those relevant for heterosexual males' performance of these same preventive behaviors. By the same token, it is expected that specific causal factors in the model and specific relationships among them may prove to be especially powerful determinants of behavior for particular populations and particular preventive acts. An understanding of variations in the content of the model's constructs, and in the relative strength of the relationships among them, should be helpful in conceiving strategies for modifying specific risk behaviors within specific target groups of interest.

The basic elements of the IMB model are discussed in more detail in the sections that follow.

Information and AIDS Risk-Behavior Change

The present model holds that AIDS risk-reduction information plays an important role in determining AIDS risk-behavior change. Furthermore, the model

---

[3]In the present model, information refers to basic knowledge regarding AIDS transmission and AIDS prevention, whereas motivation refers to personal attitudes toward AIDS preventive behaviors and perceived normative support for such behaviors (J. Fisher & W. Fisher, 1992). In this model, the presence of information and motivation each make it more likely that AIDS preventive behavior will occur, but there is no necessity for a strong relationship between level of AIDS information and level of AIDS prevention motivation. Well-informed individuals who are aware that AIDS can be transmitted by persons who appear to be healthy, may have very positive personal attitudes toward condom use, and may perceive strong normative support for practicing condom use. On the other hand, individuals who are well informed about AIDS transmission and prevention may have very negative attitudes about personally using condoms (they may believe that condom use dulls sensations of sex, and is embarrassing) and they may perceive little normative support for such behavior (they may believe that significant others would make negative attributions about them if they used condoms). Conceptually, then, information and motivation are each thought to influence the likelihood of preventive behavior, but they are viewed as separate entities that influence behavior in separate ways. Empirically, the many intervention studies that have increased target-group information levels without apparent increases in target-group motivation also suggest that information and motivation may be separate constructs.

specifies that risk reduction information must be relevant to preventive behavior if it is to have an impact on such behavior. For heterosexual college students, for example, information concerning the fact that it is not possible to evaluate one's partners' risk on the basis of their physical appearance, or concerning practical methods for keeping condoms readily accessible, would be regarded as relevant to preventive behavior and likely to have an impact on such behavior. In contrast, information about T cells, B cells, and the African green monkey as the possible origin of AIDS would be regarded as irrelevant to prevention and unlikely to have an impact on such behavior. Moreover, the model holds that risk-reduction information must be spontaneously accessible and involve "top-of-the-head" cognitions that the individual may easily retrieve if it is to have an impact on preventive behavior. "Recognition-only" information, such as may be assessed on close-ended measures of AIDS knowledge, is not necessarily easily retrievable by the individual nor necessarily likely to have an impact on behavior. For example, many individuals possess recognition-only knowledge about mother-to-infant (or father-to-mother-to-infant) transmission of AIDS. According to our model, it is not surprising that such recognition-only information has little impact on the behavior of young men and women who are presently practicing risky sex and nonetheless planning to have children in the future.

The present conceptualization of the relationship between AIDS information and AIDS preventive behavior may help explain why the link between the two is so often inconsistent (see for example, Catania, Kegeles, and Coates, 1990, and Emmons, Joseph, Kessler, Montgomery, & Ostrow, 1986, for observations of a knowledge–behavior link, and DiClementi, 1990, St. Lawrence, Kelly, Hood, & Brasfield, 1987, and Zielony and Wills, 1990, for failures to confirm such a link). Because much research on the relationship between AIDS information and AIDS prevention has concerned itself with information that is irrelevant to prevention, and has assessed such information using close-ended, recognition-only methodologies, it is to be expected that AIDS information and AIDS preventive behavior are found to be inconsistently related. Moreover, the IMB model stipulates that information is most likely to have an impact on behavior when it is accompanied by appropriate risk-reduction motivation and relevant behavioral skills. Because many risk-reduction interventions focus solely on the provision of information, it is not surprising that "information-only" interventions have little impact on preventive behavior (J. Fisher & W. Fisher, 1992).

Motivation and AIDS Risk-Behavior Change

According to the present model, an individual must be highly motivated to initiate and maintain AIDS risk-behavior change. Furthermore, the model specifies that there are two primary determinants of motivation to change AIDS risk: a *personal motivation* component that rests on personal attitudes toward preventive behaviors, and a *social motivation* component that rests on perceived social support for the performance of preventive behaviors (Ajzen & Fishbein, 1980; Fishbein & Ajzen, 1975). There is considerable evidence to suggest that both personal attitudes toward AIDS preventive behaviors (J. Fisher, W. Fisher, Williams, & Malloy, 1992; Jemmott & Jemmott, 1990; Pleck, Sonenstein, & Ku, 1990; Ross, 1988) and perceived normative support for such behaviors (see for example, Catania et al., 1989; DiClemente, 1990; DiClemente & Fisher, 1991; J. Fisher & Misovich, 1990; Kelly, St. Lawrence, Brasfield, Stevenson et al., 1990) are related to AIDS preventive practices in diverse samples of gay men, heterosexual adolescents, and heterosexual young adults.

The present model incorporates the constructs and operations of Fishbein and Ajzen's Theory of Reasoned Action (Ajzen & Fishbein, 1980; Fishbein & Ajzen, 1975; Fishbein & Middlestadt, 1989) to help understand and modify the personal attitudes and social norms that are thought to motivate AIDS preventive behavior. Fishbein and Ajzen's theory and methodology permit specification of whether personal attitudes and/or social norms determine particular preventive behaviors in particular populations of interest, they help identify specific factors that determine attitudes and norms regarding prevention, and they provide guidance for intervention efforts to change AIDS prevention attitudes and norms within target populations of interest.

According to the Theory of Reasoned Action, AIDS preventive behavior (B) occurs as a function of the individual's behavioral intention (BI) to perform the act in question. Behavioral intentions (BI), in turn, are thought to be a function of two factors that affect motivation to act: the individual's personal attitude toward performing the act in question (Aact), and/or the individual's subjective norm (SN) or perception of what significant others think should be done with respect to the behavior in question. Thus, the individual's intention to consistently use condoms during intercourse (BI) would be regarded as a function of his or her attitudes toward this risk-reduction act (Aact) and/or his or her perceptions of normative support for this behavior (SN). These propositions may be expressed in the following multiple regression equation in which w1 and w2 are empirically determined regression weights:

$$B \sim BI = [Aact]_{w_1} + [SN]_{w_2}$$

The Theory of Reasoned Action has also specified the basic psychological underpinnings of personal attitudes and social norms. It is held that an individual's attitude toward performing a particular preventive act (Aact) is a function of his or her beliefs about the consequences of performing the act (B_i) multiplied by his or her evaluations of these consequences (e_i). Thus, Aact = Σ $B_i e_i$. Similarly, the theory holds that subjective norms (SN) about a particular preventive behavior are a function of perceptions of specific referent others' support for performing the behavior (NB_j) multiplied by the individual's motivation to comply with these referents' wishes (Mc_j). Thus, SN = Σ $NB_j Mc_j$.

The Theory of Reasoned Action suggests that it is important to identify specific beliefs about the consequences of behavior (B_i) and specific referents for behavior (NB_j) that are salient for the particular populations and preventive acts that are of interest. Open-ended procedures for eliciting such information are used to identify the beliefs and referents that are salient in a given instance (e.g., college men's and women's beliefs about the consequences of always using condoms, and the categories of referent others whose wishes are influential in this regard). The belief and referent information obtained with open-ended procedures may then be used to conduct prospective research to determine whether personal attitudes, social norms, or both, predict a given preventive behavior, and to identify specific B_is, e_is, NB_js, and Mc_js that are the best predictors of behavior. Attitudes toward preventive acts, and/or subjective norms that predict preventive behavior, and the B_i, e_i, NB_j, and Mc_j factors that underlie them, then become important targets for intervention attempts to increase personal and social motivation to reduce AIDS risk. For example, prospective research may assess attitudes toward condom use (Aact), social norms regarding this practice (SN), beliefs and evaluations concerning the consequences of condom use (B_is, e_is), and perceptions of categories of referent other's views on this issue and motivation to comply with their wishes (NB_j, Mc_j). Subsequent assessment of condom use behavior (B) will permit inferences about whether attitudes, norms, or both are the primary determinants of condom use, and about the specific beliefs, evaluations, perceptions of referent influence, and motivation to comply that are the most strongly predictive of this behavior. This information would indicate the utility of an attitudinally and/or normatively focused intervention, and would suggest specific beliefs and evaluations, and referents and motivation to comply, that would be targets for influence attempts in an intervention to increase personal and social motivation to reduce AIDS risk.

In addition to personal attitudes toward preventive behavior and perceived social support for such behavior, numerous other factors—such as perceived vulnerability to infection—have also been investigated as possible motivators of AIDS preventive behavior (for a discussion of this literature, see J. Fisher & W. Fisher, 1992). According to Fishbein and Ajzen's theory, however, diverse motivational factors, which are external to the theory, should generally work through the components of the model (Aact, SN, B_is, e_is, NB_js, Mc_js) to indirectly affect preventive behaviors. In this fashion, the Fishbein–Ajzen model may serve as a sort of common denominator that may capture the effects of a number of possible motivators of AIDS preventive behavior.

Behavioral Skills and AIDS Risk-Behavior Change

According to the present model, risk-reduction information and motivation activate a set of behavioral skills that may be used to initiate and maintain risk-reduction behavioral change. AIDS risk-reduction behavioral skills involve the ability to enact skillfully a coherent, scriptlike sequence of preventive behaviors—the AIDS Risk-Reduction Behavior Sequence (see Fig. 5.2)—that is instrumental in reducing AIDS risk (W. Fisher 1990a, 1990b; see also Kelly & St. Lawrence, 1988). From the standpoint of the model, to reduce AIDS risk, the individual must first be able to accept the fact that he or she is a legitimately sexual being with the likelihood of future preventive needs. Second, the individual must have the skills to acquire accurate information about AIDS transmission and AIDS prevention, to discern AIDS fact from AIDS fiction, and to update relevant information as new developments occur in this rapidly evolving area. Third, the individual must be able to form a personal prevention agenda concerning the avoidance of infection and plans for doing so, based on acceptance of personal sexuality and knowledge of risk. Fourth, the individual must be skilled at bringing up his or her AIDS prevention agenda in pre-sex discussion with a partner, and must be skilled at negotiating this agenda with a partner who may be unmotivated to comply with the individual's wishes. As a corollary, the individual must be able to exit situations in which it is impossible to negotiate prevention. Fifth, the individual must be able to engage in "public" AIDS prevention activities such as purchasing condoms or seeking HIV testing. Sixth, the individual must be able to reinforce both the self and the partner for the consistent practice of AIDS preventive behaviors in order to maintain such practices over the long run. Finally, the individual must be able to monitor the quality of his or her preventive behavior, and must be able to shift preventive scripts to alternatives that occasion less anxiety, more safety, or other desired outcomes.

Beyond these specific AIDS prevention behavioral skills, it seems clear that a

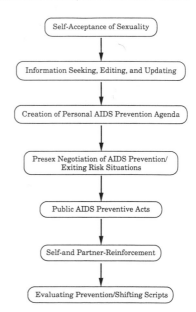

FIG. 5.2. The AIDS risk reduction behavior sequence.

sense of self-efficacy, or belief in one's ability to carry out these safer sexual behaviors, is also necessary for the practice of prevention (see Ajzen, 1990; Ajzen & Madden, 1986; Bandura, 1989, for discussions of self-efficacy and perceived control as determinants of behavior). Conceptually, level of AIDS prevention behavioral skills and sense of AIDS prevention self-efficacy may be strongly related: Possession of a high level of behavioral skill may result in the development of a strong sense of self-efficacy, which may in turn promote the effective practice of preventive behavior, further strengthening one's sense of self-efficacy, and so on (Bandura, 1989). Operationally, the assessments of behavioral skill and self-efficacy have been inextricably bound in much research on the relationship between behavioral skills and the practice of prevention: self-report assessments of whether individuals possess AIDS-related behavioral skills often measure individuals' self-perceived efficacy with respect to performing these preventive behaviors (J. Fisher et al., 1992; O'Leary, Goodhart, & Jemmott, 1991). Research in this area has documented that a strong sense of AIDS prevention self-efficacy is associated with preventive behavior in many target groups (Furgeson, Chu, & Gregory, 1989; Gibson, Wermuth, Lovelle-Drache, Ham, & Sorensen, 1989; McKusic, Coates, Wiley, Morin, & Stall, 1987; O'Leary et al., 1991). In a related vein, AIDS health locus of control scores, which assess perceptions that one can control one's AIDS risk, have been found to be associated with rates of unprotected anal intercourse (Kelly, St. Lawrence, Brasfield, Lemke et al., 1990).

In addition to these AIDS preventive behavior skill "universals," the model holds that there may be specific behavioral skills that are unique and important within particular groups that are characterized by differences in ethnicity, gender, sexual orientation, power, chemical use status, and the like. For example, in the Hispanic American population, there may be an especially significant power imbalance between the genders (Mays & Cochran, 1988; Peterson & Marin, 1988), and unique behavioral skills may be necessary to help women within this community to negotiate prevention and to minimize conflict in so doing.

Overall, then, the AIDS preventive behavior script is relatively complex, its performance requires skills that are rarely focused on in prevention interventions, and performance of the preventive behavior script will be particularly unlikely for individuals who have inadequate AIDS prevention information and/or inadequate AIDS prevention motivation (see W. Fisher, 1990a, 1990b, for extended discussions of the AIDS preventive behavior sequence).

There is considerable evidence to suggest that AIDS prevention behavioral skills are related to performance of AIDS preventive behavior. It has been found, for example, that AIDS-related communications skills (Catania et al., 1989; Polit-O'Hara & Kahn, 1985; Schinke, Gilchrest, & Small, 1979; Weisman et al., 1989), and assertiveness skills (Catania et al., 1989; Zielony & Wills, 1990) are associated with safer sexual practices. Moreover, interventions that stress the teaching of AIDS prevention behavioral skills seem to be effective in promoting sustained risk-reduction behavior change (Jemmott et al., 1990; Kelly & St. Lawrence, 1988; Kelly, St. Lawrence, Betts, Brasfield, & Hood, 1990; Valdiserri et al., 1989).

TESTING THE IMB MODEL

The relationships specified by the IMB model are consistent with the literature in this area (J. Fisher & W. Fisher, 1992), and they have been tested empirically, using structural equation modeling techniques, within two target populations of interest (J. Fisher et al., 1992). In volunteer samples of gay male affinity group members (N = 91) and primarily heterosexual male and female university students (N = 174) initial levels of AIDS risk-reduction information, motivation, behavioral skills, and behavior were assessed; two months later, the samples were retested to obtain an additional measure of AIDS preventive behavior during the intervening time period.

AIDS prevention information was assessed on the basis of responses to a number of paper-and-pencil questionnaires (e.g., Kelly, St. Lawrence, Hood, & Brasfield, 1989; Rhodes & Wolitski, 1989). From these items, several indicators of AIDS prevention information were created. For the gay male and college student samples, the HIV Transmission Scale was formed, comprising 20 items that are related to knowledge about HIV transmission (e.g., "Women can pass the AIDS virus to their male sex partners"). A General AIDS Information Scale, including 11 items that tap more general information about this disease (e.g., "Everyone who is infected with the AIDS virus has some visible symptoms"), was identified as well. Finally, a Supplementary Information Scale, involving 43 items that are especially pertinent to AIDS prevention among gay males (e.g., "Only receptive anal intercourse transmits AIDS"), was included as a third indicator of risk-reduction information for this sample.

Motivation to practice AIDS preventive behavior was assessed in accord with the principles of the Theory of Reasoned Action (Ajzen & Fishbein, 1980; Fishbein & Ajzen, 1975). A Behavioral Intentions to Practice AIDS Preventive Acts Scale assessed subjects' intentions to perform three specific preventive behaviors that were foci of this research: discussing safer sex with one's partners, using condoms consistently, and practicing only safer sex, during the next 2 months. An Attitudes Toward AIDS Preventive Acts Scale used bipolar adjective ratings to assess favorable to unfavorable attitudes toward the performance of these AIDS preventive behaviors. Finally, a Subjective Norms Concerning AIDS Preventive Acts Scale used Likert-type items to assess subjects' perceptions that significant others supported or opposed their performance of these preventive behaviors during the time frame under study.

AIDS prevention behavioral skills were assessed on two self-report measures. The Perceived Effectiveness of AIDS Preventive Behavior scale, developed by

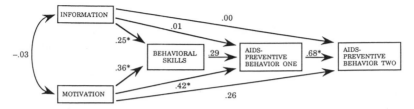

FIG. 5.3. Information, motivation, behavioral skills, and gay men's AIDS preventive behavior.

the authors, used bipolar adjective ratings to assess subjects' perceptions of how effectively they could engage in the specific preventive behaviors under study. The Perceived Difficulty of AIDS Preventive Behavior scale, derived from the Rutger's University College Health Survey, used multiple bipolar adjective scales to tap subjects' perceptions about how difficult it would be for them to engage in specific AIDS preventive behaviors.

To assess AIDS preventive behaviors, subjects' self-reports of discussion of safer sex with partners, condom use, and practicing only safer sex were obtained. At the initial assessment, performance of these behaviors was assessed relative to the preceding year; at the posttest assessment, performance of these behaviors during the past 2 months was assessed.

Results of the structural equation analysis for the gay male sample are presented in Fig. 5.3. Within this sample, AIDS prevention information and AIDS prevention motivation are statistically independent factors, and each is related to AIDS prevention behavioral skills. AIDS prevention behavioral skills, in turn, were related to AIDS preventive behavior in the anticipated direction, and at a magnitude that approached conventional levels of significance. The structural equation model also identified an independent relationship between AIDS prevention motivation and AIDS preventive behavior at Time 1, and indicated that levels of preventive behavior were stable across time. The relationships among the IMB model's components accounted for 35% of the variance in gay men's AIDS preventive behavior at the initial testing.

Results of the structural equation analysis for the university student sample are presented in Fig. 5.4. Within this sample, information and motivation are again

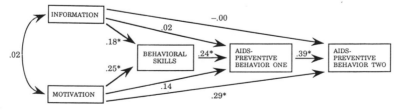

FIG. 5.4. Information, motivation, behavioral skills, and university students' AIDS preventive behavior.

independent factors, they are each linked significantly with AIDS preventive behavior skills, and AIDS preventive behavior skills are significantly associated with AIDS preventive behavior per se. The structural equation model again identified an independent relationship between AIDS prevention motivation and AIDS preventive behavior, and indicated the stability of AIDS preventive behavior across time. The relationships among the model's components account for 10% of the variance in university students' AIDS preventive behavior at initial testing.

The results of this research provide consistent empirical support for the relationship hypothesized by the IMB model, across two very different populations of interest. In both the gay male and college student samples, risk-reduction information and risk-reduction motivation appear to work through preventive behavior skills to affect preventive behavior per se. Across both populations, moreover, there is evidence of a direct link between motivation and preventive behavior, and the components of the IMB model accounted for a significant proportion of the variance in gay men's and university students' preventive behavior.

IMPLEMENTING THE IMB MODEL TO CHANGE AIDS RISK BEHAVIOR

The IMB model specifies a set of generalizable operations that may be applied to understanding, promoting, and evaluating AIDS risk reduction within target

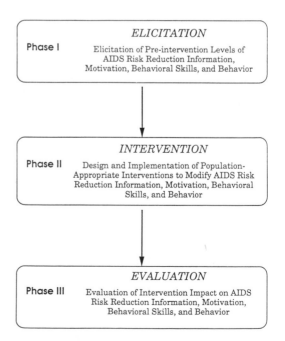

FIG. 5.5.   Three phase process for utilizing the IMB risk reduction model.

populations of interest. In practice, there are three steps in applying the present model. First, *elicitation research* must be carried out in a target population to determine preintervention levels of AIDS risk reduction information, motivation, behavioral skills, and behavior per se. Based on these findings, *population-specific interventions* are constructed and implemented to remedy population-specific deficits in risk-reduction information, motivation, behavioral skills, and ultimately behavior per se. Finally, *evaluation research* is conducted to determine whether the intervention has produced short- and long-term changes in multiple indicants of AIDS risk-reduction information, motivation, behavioral skills, and behavior. The elicitation–intervention–evaluation process specified by the IMB model is depicted graphically in Fig. 5.5, and is discussed in the sections that follow.

Elicitation Research

Eliciting a target population's existing level of AIDS risk-reduction information, motivation, behavioral skills, and behavior is a critical first step in implementing the present model.

Eliciting AIDS Risk Reduction Information.   The IMB model specifies that AIDS information that is relevant to prevention and accessible to the individual helps determine preventive behavior. In addition, the model suggests that it is critical to identify group-specific gaps in such information, in the context of elicitation research in order to structure effective, targeted interventions.

To identify group-specific gaps in relevant, accessible prevention information, both open-ended and close-ended questioning strategies may be used in research on subsamples of the target population. In our own research, for example, we have used open-ended questions concerning AIDS transmission and prevention, and focus group discussions of these topics (Krueger, 1988). These assessment procedures were supplemented by standard close-ended questionnaire inventories (e.g., Kelly et al., 1989; Rhodes & Wolitsky, 1989), to help assess group-specific levels of prevention information.

Utilizing these elicitation procedures, population-specific gaps in relevant, spontaneously accessible AIDS information may be empirically identified. These findings may then be used to target maximally effective, population-specific interventions to provide needed AIDS prevention information. For example, in our ongoing research, we have used these elicitation procedures to assess AIDS prevention information deficits in a sample of university students. Using open-ended questionnaire items that asked "How do people get AIDS?" and "How can people avoid getting AIDS?" to tap spontaneously accessible information, we found that only 3% of the college student sample indicated spontaneous awareness of spermicide use as a means to help prevent AIDS infection. By the same token, less than 14% of this sample indicated spontaneous awareness of mother-to-baby HIV transmission, despite the fact that most of this sample was engaging in high-risk sexual behaviors and planned to have children in the future. Open-ended focus group discussions, moreover, revealed that college students very commonly believed that it is easy to detect and avoid risky partners by noting how they dress, how they act, and where they are encountered. Using close-ended questionnaires, we found that 75% of college students did not know that oral sex is safer than intercourse, and that 63% did not know that saliva is unlikely to communicate HIV. The information deficits identified in this population seem relevant to its risk reduction practices, many of these information deficits would not have been detected had we relied solely on close-ended questioning, and the information deficits that were identified provide empirical guidance for targeting population-specific interventions to remedy identified information deficits.[4]

Eliciting AIDS Risk Reduction Motivation.   The IMB model holds that personal attitudes toward AIDS preventive behavior, and perceived social support for such behavior, are the primary motivational determinants of risk-reduction practices. The model utilizes the concepts and operations of the Theory of Reasoned Action (Ajzen & Fishbein, 1980; Fishbein & Ajzen, 1975) to assess attitudes toward AIDS preventive behaviors, related social norms, and the basic psychological underpinnings of these motivational factors. Beyond personal attitudes and social norms per se, the model holds that other factors may indirectly motivate AIDS preventive behavior by way of their influence on attitudes and norms.

To assess attitudes and social norms concerning specific AIDS preventive behaviors in a given population, direct measures of relevant attitudes (e.g., "Using condoms every time I have sexual intercourse during the coming year would be . . . good/bad, awful/nice, pleasant/unpleasant") and direct measures of perceived normative support ("Most people who are important to me think I should use condoms every time I have sexual intercourse during the coming year . . . very true/very untrue") may be utilized. To elicit beliefs that underlie attitudes towards specific preventive acts (Bis) and referents who are perceived to support (NBj) such behaviors, open-ended strategies are used to question a representative subsample of the target population (Ajzen & Fishbein, 1980). For example, we have elicited beliefs about the consequences of AIDS preventive

---

[4]Although we are not aware of any research that has directly tested the differential effectiveness of interventions that are targeted at identified group-specific deficits, as opposed to interventions whose content is intuitively derived, the array of unsuspected information deficits that we have detected using these elicitation research procedures persuades us on rational grounds that targeted interventions will be capable of focusing on important AIDS related material that would otherwise not be the subject of intervention attempts (see also Fullilove, Fullilove, Haynes, & Gross, 1990, for research on group-specific issues relative to AIDS prevention that have been found among Black women, and Helitzer-Allen, 1990, for an ethnographic analysis that showed that an intuitively derived health education message that ignores group-specific issues may be ineffective).

acts (Bis) with open-ended questions such as "What are all the advantages (disadvantages) of always using condoms during sexual intercourse during the next 2 months?" In response to such elicitation questions, we found that university students commonly mention the beliefs that condom use would reduce pregnancy and AIDS risk, reduce the spontaneity of sex, and result in sex that doesn't feel as good as it would without condoms. Similarly, we have elicited referents for particular AIDS preventive behaviors with open-ended questions such as "Who are the people or groups who would approve (disapprove) of you always using condoms during sexual intercourse during the next 2 months?" In response to such elicitation questions, we found that university students provide a homogeneous set of salient referent categories for this behavior that include partners, friends, parents, other family members, and health-care professionals.

Using direct measures of attitudes and subjective norms toward AIDS preventive acts, and measures of the beliefs and referents concerning such acts that have been identified, prospective elicitation research may be conducted to predict preventive behavior in a subsample of the target population. The objective of this research is to determine whether attitudes toward prevention, subjective norms, or both predict performance of preventive behaviors, and to identify specific beliefs, evaluations, perceptions of referent support, and motivations to comply that predict such behaviors. These findings will suggest whether the performance of specific AIDS preventive behaviors is under attitudinal and/or normative control in the population under study, and hence whether attitudinal and/or normatively focused interventions are most likely to create risk-reduction behavior change. Such findings will also indicate which beliefs, evaluations, referents, and motives to comply are the most powerful predictors of specific preventive behaviors, and therefore which need to be targeted for change in population-specific interventions.

Using these elicitation procedures in our ongoing research with university students, we found that both personal attitudes and subjective norms concerning AIDS preventive acts predicted performance of these behaviors across 2 months' time. Attitudes and subjective norms regarding preventive behavior, in turn, were correlated with their basic psychological underpinnings ($\Sigma B_i e_i$; $\Sigma NB_j Mc_j$). To provide but one example of these elicitation findings, it was determined that university women's attitudes toward purchasing condoms and their subjective norms in this regard predicted their condom purchasing behavior. Women's attitudes toward purchasing condoms were a function of their beliefs that doing so would reduce their risk of pregnancy, AIDS, and other sexually transmitted diseases (STDs), and of their evaluations of these consequences. Women's perceptions of normative support for purchasing condoms were related to their perceptions that sisters, parents, and health-care providers advocated such behavior and to their motivation to comply with these referents. These elicitation findings indicate the importance of focusing interventions to promote condom purchasing among university women on both attitudes and subjective norms concerning this behavior, and of targeting for change the specific beliefs and evaluations (regarding pregnancy, AIDS, and STD prevention) and perceived referent wishes and inclinations to comply (regarding parents', sisters', and health-care providers' views) that appear to motivate this risk-reduction behavior in the this population.

Open- and close-ended questioning strategies may also be used to identify additional motivational factors that may have indirect effects on preventive behavior, by way of effects on attitudes and norms. For example, in our university student research, focus group discussions revealed that few students felt personally vulnerable to AIDS, and close-ended questioning confirmed that almost all subjects felt that they were less vulnerable to infection than were most people. Such elicitation findings make a case for the inclusion of an intervention component that stresses personal vulnerability to infection. According to Fishbein and Ajzen's theory, increases in perceived vulnerability to infection should result in changes in beliefs about prevention, perceived referent support for prevention, and attitudes and norms that motivate prevention.

Eliciting AIDS Risk-Reduction Behavioral Skills.   According to the present model, an individual must possess a specific set of behavioral skills in order to initiate and maintain AIDS risk-reduction behavior change. To elicit existing levels of risk reduction behavioral skills in a target population, the present approach suggests the use of in vivo role-playing, focus group procedures, and close-ended questionnaires. In vivo role-playing procedures may be used for assessing skills at overtly performing AIDS preventive behaviors such as bringing up and negotiating prevention. Focus groups may be asked to identify behavioral tactics that work best—and those that do not work at all—in relation to AIDS risk reduction within their group. Finally, close-ended questionnaires have been developed to assess self-perceptions of how difficult it would be for respondents to engage in each step of the AIDS prevention behavior sequence, and to assess perceptions of how skillfully or effectively they feel they could execute each step (J. Fisher et al., 1992).

These elicitation procedures are designed to provide empirical guidance for targeting group-specific interventions to bolster AIDS prevention behavioral skills that are lacking in target groups of interest. For example, in ongoing research with college students, in vivo role playing has suggested that students ordinarily possess an acceptable degree of behavioral skills for the performance of critical AIDS preventive behaviors. Close-ended questionnaires, however, revealed that a majority of students perceived that it would be difficult for them to discuss safer sex with a partner, and that a substantial number would find it difficult to refuse sexual intercourse if no condom were available. Focus group discussions revealed the usefulness of nonverbal behavior skills (simply unrolling a condom on an aroused partner) and minimal interaction skills ("Here, put this on") as important supplements to verbal negotiation skills for this group. Taken together, these findings indicate the adequacy of students' ability to perform many critical AIDS preventive behaviors, the inadequate sense of self-efficacy that many nonetheless feel, and unique AIDS preventive behaviors that might prove useful in this population.

Eliciting AIDS Risk Levels.   The present model asserts that it is necessary to identify a target population's most critical AIDS risk behaviors, in order to focus a population-specific intervention on information, motivation, and behavioral skills that are relevant to the population's most significant risks. To identify AIDS risk behaviors within a target population, standard measures of sexual, needle use, and other unsafe behavior may be utilized (see for example, J. Fisher et al., 1992; Kelly et al., 1989). Measures of risky behaviors may be supplemented with open-ended investigations, such as focus group discussions, concerning group-specific factors that may exaggerate risk, including the use of alcohol or drugs, the popularity of specific sexual practices, power differences between the sexes, and the like. Finally, the model stresses the importance of employing a range of nonreactive or unobtrusive measures that may reflect a population's AIDS risk behaviors. Indices such as STD rates and pregnancy/abortion rates at target group intervention sites are examples of such indirect measures of a population's AIDS risk.

We have utilized this measurement strategy in ongoing research with college students to identify this group's areas of greatest behavioral risk and to aid in the targeting of a population-specific intervention to reduce such risk. Within the university student sample, standard measures revealed that 72% of students were coitally active during the past year; 44% of these individuals had two or more partners during this time; and only 25% of these individuals had used condoms consistently during this interval. In response to standard measures, 8% of the students reported that they had anal intercourse—modally without condoms—during this period. Open-ended focus group discussions identified alcohol use prior to casual sex as a factor that significantly exaggerated AIDS risk behavior in this population. Finally, nonreactive measures—including STD rates and a review of routine Pap tests—were used to provide unobtrusive measure of AIDS risk in this population. For example, some 10% of the Pap tests showed evidence of human papillomavirus, a viral STD, confirming the substantial risk of unprotected coitus that was present in this population. Based on these findings, it is clear that unprotected penile–vaginal and anal intercourse remain major risk behaviors in this population, and will have to be a priority focus for risk-reduction interventions in this group.

Group-Specific Intervention

Based on the findings of elicitation research, the IMB model suggests that group-specific interventions may be constructed and implemented to target identified deficits in risk-reduction information, motivation, behavioral skills, and behavior per se. The present approach strongly advocates situating interventions within intact groups that have existing social networks that are capable of producing "reverberating effects" or continuously reinforcing proprevention changes in AIDS risk-reduction information, motivation, behavioral skills, and behavior (J. Fisher & Misovich, 1990). Intervention components that focus on remediating information, motivation, and behavioral skills deficits are discussed in the following paragraphs.

Information Component of AIDS Risk Reduction Intervention.   The information component of the risk-reduction intervention is constructed to remedy group-specific deficits in information about AIDS transmission and AIDS prevention that have been identified in elicitation studies. Research indicates that a variety of teaching techniques, including the use of print media, classroom discussion, and video presentations, are effective in communicating such information to a variety of target groups (see J. Fisher & W. Fisher, 1992, for a review of this literature).

We have devised two strategies that may be used to remedy group-specific information deficits in the context of our ongoing research with college students. First, an "AIDS 101" lecture and slide show that addresses group-specific information needs has been constructed. The "AIDS 101" lecture and slide show presents relevant information about transmission and prevention and, based on elicitation research, stresses information on the relative riskiness of various sexual behaviors, the utility of spermicide use, the threat of mother-to-baby transmission, and the debunking of the notion that it is possible to identify and avoid risky partners on the basis of their dress or demeanor. Second, intervention participants may be given the opportunity to apply what they have learned in analyzing risky situations that are common in their social environment. For example, students may be given vignettes that involve individuals in various relationships (e.g., casual sex vs. living together), various sexual practices (e.g., oral sex, vaginal sex, etc.), and various preventive practices (e.g., asking about a partner's sexual history, condom use, etc.). Intervention participants then have to apply what they have learned to assess the riskiness of these situations. Specific efforts are made to sensitize students to their characteristic but inadequate safer sexual practices (e.g., vaginal sex with a live-in partner that one has come to know well is not safe, vaginal sex with an acquaintance who uses a condom would be relatively safer). Utilizing these techniques, the population-specific intervention seeks to remediate identified deficits in information that are relevant to preventive behavior in the group under study.

Motivation Component of AIDS Risk Reduction Intervention.   The motivation component of the risk-reduction intervention is based on elicitation findings concerning the attitudes, norms, beliefs, and referents that determine preventive behavior within the population under study. If attitudes toward performance of AIDS preventive behaviors are found to predict the occurrence of such behaviors, then efforts to alter such attitudes, via changes in the beliefs and evaluations that underlie them, should be effective in modifying attitudes toward preventive behaviors. If social norms regarding preventive behavior predict performance of such behavior, then efforts to alter such norms, by way of changes in perceived support from specific referent others or motivation to comply with these others, should be effective in modifying social norms regarding preventive behavior (Ajzen & Fishbein, 1980; Fishbein & Ajzen, 1975). Finally, if other motivational factors appear to be implicated in AIDS preventive behavior in the population under study, intervention attempts to change such motivational factors should ultimately improve attitudes and/or norms regarding prevention.

A number of strategies are available for modifying attitudes and norms concerning AIDS preventive behavior. According to Ajzen and Fishbein (1980), it should be possible to change negative attitudes toward preventive acts by presenting arguments that weaken the beliefs and evaluations that underlie the attitudes. The presentation of new beliefs and evaluations that are favorable to prevention may also be used to offset the influence of negative beliefs and evaluations. These persuasive communications may be presented by sources who were identified as influential referents in elicitation research. In a similar fashion, it should be possible to change perceived normative support for prevention by presenting salient referents who support prevention, and by attempting to strengthen motivation to comply with these referents' wishes. The use of peer educators to deliver intervention elements and to communicate that prevention is the norm is still another means for strengthening perceptions of normative support for AIDS prevention, provided that peers are a salient source of influence in the target population (Kelly, St. Lawrence, Stevenson, et al., 1990).

A second method for influencing attitudes and norms concerning preventive behavior involves the use of counterattitudinal advocacy and public commitment techniques (Festinger & Carlsmith, 1959; Petty & Cacioppo, 1981). Using these strategies, individuals in the target population may be induced to create strong proprevention arguments on issues where the population's prevention position is weakest (counterattitudinal advocacy), and then to endorse these arguments in public statements that are favorable to prevention (public commitment).

We have experimented with a number of these techniques in our ongoing college student intervention to modify personal attitudes and social norms that may motivate prevention. To change personal attitudes toward specific preventive behaviors, we have created videotaped "testimonials" in which empirically identified referent others (boyfriends, girlfriends, health-care providers) attack identified antiprevention beliefs (e.g., "No, condoms do not completely destroy the spontaneity and sensations of sex, and the minor difference is more than justified given the health risk at stake"). Referent others also provide testimonials that present new beliefs that are favorable to prevention (e.g., "Now that I use condoms, I can relax and enjoy sex, instead of worrying all the time"). To change norms concerning specific preventive behaviors, we have created additional videotaped testimonials in which referent others speak supportively of the behavior in question. In one testimonial segment, for example, we actually interviewed parents, brothers, sisters, and roommates at a homecoming football game, and these individuals strongly and consistently provided social support for condom use for sexually active students ("If my roommate was sexually active, and I found out she was not using condoms, I'd think she was out of her mind!"). Moreover, peer educators are used to deliver important parts of the college student intervention and to present prevention as the normative and the "in" thing to do. Finally, the college student intervention takes place within existing social networks (dormitory floors) and intervention-induced changes may therefore "reverberate" and be reinforced by prevention norms within this social network over time.

In addition to these direct attempts to alter attitudes and norms concerning prevention, elicitation findings suggested strongly the need to increase students' perceived vulnerability to AIDS as an indirect means of influencing attitudes and norms regarding prevention. To do so, we first guide intervention participants through a "Personal Risk Audit" that provides an objective self-assessment of involvement in risky sexual behavior. Second, we have created a highly impactful videotape, *People Like Us* (1992) with interviews with a number of social comparison college students and former students, who are quite similar to those in the target group, who engaged in many of the same sexual risk behaviors as those in the target group, and who now have HIV infection or AIDS. According to Fishbein and Ajzen's model, increases in perceived vulnerability to AIDS should produce changes in attitudes and norms and ultimately increase motivation to practice prevention.

Behavioral Skills Component of AIDS Risk Reduction Intervention. The behavioral skills component of the risk-reduction intervention is designed to teach individuals to perform skillfully each of the steps in the AIDS preventive behavior sequence, with special emphasis on group-specific behavior skills issues that have been identified in elicitation research.

The approach to behavioral skills training suggested by the IMB model involves teaching intervention participants directly about the steps of the AIDS preventive behavior sequence, and direct instruction concerning assertiveness and negotiation skills. Following such direct instruction, participants observe models performing critical AIDS preventive behaviors, and role-play these risk-reduction behavioral skills themselves with critique and reinforcement from peer educators and other intervention participants. This approach to teaching behavioral skills has been found to be useful in promoting AIDS prevention and related sexual health behaviors in a number of target populations (W. Fisher, 1990a, 1990b; Kelly & St. Lawrence, 1988; Kelly et al., 1989; Schinke, 1984; Schinke, Blythe, & Gilchrist, 1981).

Within our ongoing college student intervention, a number of these techniques are being used for teaching AIDS prevention behavioral skills. First, health educators provide instruction concerning the sorts of behaviors that are actually involved in AIDS prevention (e.g., acquiring information, setting a personal prevention agenda, communicating with partners about this agenda, exiting risky situations, etc.). Direct instruction is also provided concerning specific assertiveness and negotiation skills that will make these behaviors effective (e.g., bringing up safer sex during times of relatively low sexual intensity, maintaining eye contact, acknowledging resistance, restating one's position and explaining it). Next, intervention participants observe a video, *Sex, Condoms, and Videotape* (1992) that features social comparison couples who move through critical phases of the AIDS preventive behavior sequence, in several different relationship contexts. These couples rehearse the establishment of personal safer sex agendas, the communication and negotiation of these agendas to partners, the use of nonverbal techniques, overcoming resistance or leaving situations in which prevention cannot be negotiated, and self- and partner-reinforcement, within relationships that range from casual contacts to committed couples. Many of these behavioral skills (e.g., initiating discussion, nonverbal skills, refusing unsafe sex) were identified in elicitation research as relatively weak within this population. Following this, peer health educators model the performance of selected preventive behaviors. Finally, intervention participants practice these behaviors imaginatively (for behaviors such as deciding on a personal safer sex agenda), in role-play with other group members (for overt behaviors such as bringing up and negotiating limit setting or condom use, overcoming resistance, exiting unsafe situations), and in vivo behavioral performances (for overt behaviors that lend themselves to such performance, such as calling an AIDS hotline for information, or purchasing condoms from a pharmacy). Supportive peer educator and group feedback is used to reinforce successful performances and provide suggestions for improvement. Through these activities, increasing familiarity and skill at the performance of preventive behaviors is intended to increase participants' feelings that they personally can enact such behaviors when necessary, and that these behaviors will prove efficacious in reducing risk.

Evaluation Research

The present approach to AIDS risk-reduction stresses the importance of evaluation research to clarify whether risk-reduction interventions have had the desired impact on information, motivation, behavioral skills, and behavior.

Evaluating Change in AIDS Risk Reduction Information, Motivation, and Behavioral Skills. Within the IMB approach, methodology for assessing change in AIDS risk-reduction information, motivation, and behavioral skills is straightforward. Evaluation research measures of these key constructs are intended to be parallel to the measures of these constructs that were employed in the elicitation research phase. To assess changes in risk reduction information, open-ended measures of spontaneously accessible, prevention-relevant information, and close-ended measures of such information, may be utilized. To assess changes in risk-reduction motivation, measures of personal attitudes and subjective norms regarding AIDS preventive behaviors, and measures of beliefs, evaluations, referents, and motives to comply, relative to these preventive behaviors, may be collected. To assess changes in risk-reduction behavioral skills, role-plays of critical steps in the AIDS preventive behavior sequence may be recorded, and close-ended questionnaire items that assess self-efficacy in performing these behaviors may be utilized. In addition to direct measures of IMB model constructs, moreover, unobtrusive assessment techniques can be used to provide supplementary evaluation data. For example, an ostensibly unrelated "Health Survey" can be administered with embedded items that are pertinent to AIDS risk-reduction information, motivation, and behavioral skills, to provide less reactive information than that obtained via direct measurement. These direct and indirect measures should provide general assessments of risk-reduction information, motivation, and behavioral skills, and also include assessments of information, motivation, and behavioral skills elements that were identified in elicitation research as either weak, or as uniquely important, in the population under study.

Evaluating AIDS Risk Reduction Behavioral Change. Evaluation of AIDS risk-reduction behavioral change relies on both direct self-report measures and indirect, nonreactive measures of risk and preventive behavior. With respect to direct measures, standard self-report assessments of AIDS risk behavior (e.g., J. Fisher et al., 1991; Kelly et al., 1989) may be used as one criterion for judging intervention impact on behavior. With respect to indirect, less reactive measures of risk behavior, a variety of unobtrusive indicants of intervention impact may be collected, depending on the specific intervention setting involved. For example, the ostensibly unrelated "Health Behavior" survey mentioned earlier, with embedded AIDS risk-behavior and AIDS-prevention items, may be used to assess risk and preventive behavior; monitoring of STD, pregnancy, and abortion rates in target populations may provide indirect indications of intervention impact; and monitoring of redemption of condom coupons that are distributed to the target population, condom sales in nearby stores, and the number of discarded condoms in local trysting sites, may provide still other indirect measures of intervention impact. Similarly, it is possible to conduct condom "fire drills" in which members of the target population are asked unannounced to produce a condom that they have been carrying on their person; to assess knowledge of condom and spermicide price, advertising, and other point-of-sale details; and to present erotic vignettes in which AIDS risk-reduction practices are present or absent and to examine reactions to these vignettes. Taken together, such direct and indirect measures may provide convergent evidence regarding intervention impact on AIDS risk-reduction behavior change.

Evaluating Change: An Analytic Strategy.   Direct and indirect measures of risk-reduction information, motivation, behavioral skills, and behavior may be collected from intervention and control subjects, in the context of pre- and immediate- and delayed posttests. To analyze these data to assess intervention impact, a combination of analysis of covariance and structural equation modeling techniques may be used. In the analysis of covariance, pre- to posttest changes in risk-reduction information, motivation, behavioral skills, and behavior may be assessed, in relation to multiple direct and indirect measures of outcome, taken over the short and long term. Supplementing these analyses, structural equation modeling may be used to clarify the degree to which intervention-induced changes in risk-reduction information, motivation, and behavioral skills have affected behavior per se (J. Fisher et al., 1992; Joreskog & Sorbom, 1986). Overall, this analytic approach may help indicate the degree to which an AIDS risk-reduction intervention has produced changes in risk-reduction information, motivation, behavioral skills, and behavior, and the degree to which changes in each construct in the model have had an impact on behavior.

SUMMARY

This chapter conceptualizes the determinants of AIDS risk-behavior change, and proposes generalizable operations for implementing this model to understand, promote, and evaluate AIDS risk-reduction in diverse populations of interest. The model is based on the conceptual and empirical literature in the AIDS behavior change area, it has received initial empirical support in prospective research in two populations of interest, and it is hoped that the model may be applied and refined in AIDS prevention efforts in the future.

ACKNOWLEDGMENTS

Work on this chapter was supported by grants from the Social Sciences and Humanities Research Council of Canada (410-87-19333) and the National Institute of Mental Health (1-RO2-MH46224-01) to both authors, and by a grant from the Canadian Foundation for AIDS Research to the first author. The order of authorship of this chapter was randomly determined.

REFERENCES

Ajzen, I. (1990). *Attitudes, personality, and behavior.* Chicago: Dorsey Press.
Ajzen, I., & Fishbein, M. (1980). *Understanding attitudes and predicting social behavior.* Englewood Cliffs, NJ: Prentice-Hall.
Ajzen, I., & Madden, T. (1986). Prediction of goal-directed behavior: Attitudes, intentions and perceived behavioral control. *Journal of Experimental Social Psychology, 22,* 453–474.

Albee, G. W. (1989). Primary prevention in public health: Problems and challenges of behavior change as prevention. In V. M. Mays, G. W. Albee, & S. F. Schneider (Eds.), *Primary prevention of AIDS. Psychological approaches. Primary prevention of psychopathology* (Vol. 13, pp. 17–20). Newbury Park, CA: Sage.

Bandura, A. (1989). Perceived self-efficacy in the increase of control over AIDS infection. In V. M. Mays, G. W. Albee, & S. F. Schneider (Eds.), *Primary prevention of AIDS* (pp. 128–141). Newbury Park, CA: Sage.

Burke, D. S., Brundage, J. F., Goldenbaum, M., Gardner, L. I., Peterson, M., Visintine, R., Redfield, R. R., & Walter Reed Retrovirus Research Group. (1990). Human immunodeficiency virus infections in teenagers. Seroprevalence among applicants for United States military service. *Journal of the American Medical Association, 263*, 2074–2077.

Catania, J. A., Dolcini, M. M., Coates, T. J., Kegeles, S. M., Greenblatt, R. M., Puckett, J. D., Corman, M., & Miller, J. (1989). Predictors of condom use and multiple partnered sex among sexually active adolescent women: Implications for AIDS-related health interventions. *Journal of Sex Research, 26*, 514–524.

Catania, J. A., Kegeles, S. M., & Coates, T. J. (1990). Towards an understanding of risk behavior: An AIDS risk reduction model (AARM). *Health Education Quarterly, 17*, 53–72.

Centers for Disease Control. (1987). HIV infection and pregnancies in sexual partners of HIV-seropositive hemophiliac men—United States. *Morbidity and Mortality Weekly Report, 36*, 593–595.

Centers for Disease Control. (1990). *Weekly Surveillance Report*. Atlanta, GA: Author.

Clemow, L. P., Saidi, P., Lerner, A., Kim, H. C., Matts, L., & Eisele, J. (1989, August). *Hemophiliacs, AIDS & safer sex: Psychosocial issues and one-year follow-up*. Paper presented at the 97th Annual Convention of the American Psychological Association, New Orleans, LA.

Coates, T. J. (1990). Strategies for modifying sexual behavior for primary and secondary prevention of HIV disease. *Journal of Clinical and Consulting Psychology, 58*, 57–69.

Coxon, A. P. M., & Carballo, M. (1989). Research on AIDS: Behavioral perspectives. *AIDS, 3*, 191–197.

Des Jarlais, D. C., Friedman, S. R., & Casriel, C. (1990). Target groups for preventing AIDS among intravenous drug users: 2. The "hard" studies. *Journal of Consulting and Clinical Psychology, 58*(1), 50–56.

Des Jarlais, D. C., Friedman, S. R., & Novick, D. M., Sotheran, J. L., Thomas, P., Yancovitz, S. R., Mildvan, D., Weber, J., Kreek, M. J., Maslansky, R., Bartelme, S., Spira, T., & Marmor, M. (1989). HIV-1 infection among intravenous drug users in Manhattan, New York City from 1977 through 1987. *Journal of the American Medical Association, 261*, 1008–1012.

DiClemente, R. J. (1990). The emergence of adolescents as a risk group for human immunodeficiency virus infection. *Journal of Adolescent Research, 5*, 7–17.

DiClemente, R. J., & Fisher, J. D. (1991). *Social norms and AIDS-risk and preventive behavior in a sample of ethnically diverse urban adolescents*. Unpublished manuscript, University of California, San Francisco.

DiClemente, R. J., Forrest, K. A., Mickler, S., & Principal Site Investigators. (1990). College students' knowledge and attitudes about AIDS and changes in HIV-preventive behaviors. *AIDS Education and Prevention, 2*, 201–212.

Emmons, C. A., Joseph, J. G., Kessler, R. C., Montgomery, S., & Ostrow, D. (1986). Psychosocial predictors of reported behavior change in homosexual men at risk for AIDS. *Health Education Quarterly, 13*, 331–345.

Festinger, L., & Carlsmith, J. M. (1959). Cognitive consequences of forced compliance. *Journal of Abnormal and Social Psychology, 58*, 203–210.

Fishbein, M., & Ajzen, I. (1975). *Belief, attitude, intention, and behavior: An introduction to theory and research*. Reading, MA: Addison-Wesley.

Fishbein, M., & Middlestadt, S. E. (1989). Using the Theory of Reasoned Action as a framework for understanding and changing AIDS-related behaviors. In V. M. Mays, G. W. Albee, & S. F.

Schneider (Eds.), *Primary prevention of AIDS. Psychological approaches. Primary prevention of psychopathology* (Vol. 13, pp. 93–110). Newbury Park, CA: Sage.

Fisher, J. D., & Fisher, W. A. (1989). *A general technology for AIDS risk behavior change.* Unpublished manuscript, University of Connecticut, Storrs.

Fisher, J. D., & Fisher, W. A. (1992). Changing AIDS risk behavior. *Psychological Bulletin, 111,* 454–474.

Fisher, J. D., Fisher, W. A., Williams, S. S., & Malloy, T. E. (1992). *Empirical tests of an information-motivation-behavioral skills model of AIDS preventive behavior.* Manuscript submitted for publication.

Fisher, J. D., & Misovich, S. J. (1990). Social influence and AIDS-preventive behavior. In J. Edwards, R. S. Tinsdale, L. Heath, & E. Posavac (Eds.), *Applying social influence processes in preventing social problems* (pp. 39–70). New York: Plenum.

Fisher, W. A. (1990a). Understanding and preventing adolescent pregnancy and sexually transmissible disease/AIDS. In J. Edwards, R. S. Tinsdale, C. Heath, & E. J. Posavac (Eds.), *Social influence processes and prevention* (pp. 71–101). Beverly Hills, CA: Plenum.

Fisher, W. A. (1990b). All together now: An integrated approach to preventing adolescent pregnancy and STD/HIV infection. *Sex Information and Education Council of the United States, 18*(4), 1–11.

Fullilove, M. F., Fullilove, R. E., Haynes, K., & Gross, S. (1990). Black women and AIDS prevention: Understanding the gender rules. *Journal of Sex Research, 27,* 47–64.

Furgeson, J., Chu, L., & Gregory, W. L. (1989). *A motivational study of teen pregnancy from Hispanic adolescents' perspective.* Unpublished manuscript, New Mexico State University, Department of Counseling, Las Cruces.

Gibson, D. R., Wermuth, L., Lovelle-Drache, J., Ham, J., & Sorensen, J. L. (1989). Brief counseling to reduce AIDS risk in intravenous drug users and their sexual partners: Preliminary results. *Counselling Psychology Quarterly, 2,* 15–19.

Gordin, F. M., Gibert, C., Hawley, H. P., & Willoughby, A. (1990). Prevalence of human immunodeficiency virus and hepatitis B virus in unselected hospital admissions: Implications for mandatory testing and universal precautions. *Journal of Infectious Diseases, 161,* 14–17.

Hays, R. B., Kegeles, S. M., & Coates, T. J. (1990). High HIV risk-taking among young gay men. *AIDS, 4,* 901–907.

Jemmott, L. S., & Jemmott, J. B., III. (1990). Sexual knowledge, attitudes, and risky sexual behavior among inner-city Black male adolescents. *Journal of Adolescent Research, 5,* 346–369.

Jemmott, J. B., Jemmott, L. S., & Fong, G. T. (1990). *Reducing the risk of sexually transmitted HIV infection: Attitudes, knowledge, and behavior.* Unpublished manuscript, Princeton University, Princeton, NJ.

Joreskog, K. G., & Sorbom, D. (1986). *LISREL VI: Analysis of linear structural equations by the method of maximum likelihood.* Mooresville, IN: Scientific Software.

Kegeles, S. M., Adler, N. E., & Irwin, C. E. (1988). Sexually active adolescents and condoms: Changes over one year in knowledge, attitude, and use. *American Journal of Public Health, 78,* 460–461.

Kelly, J. A., & St. Lawrence, J. S. (1988). *The AIDS health crisis: Psychological and social interventions.* New York: Plenum.

Kelly, J. A., St. Lawrence, J. S., Betts, R., Brasfield, T. L., & Hood, H. V. (1990). A skills-training group intervention model to assist persons in reducing risk behaviors for HIV infection. *AIDS Education and Prevention, 2,* 24–35.

Kelly, J. A., St. Lawrence, J. S., Brasfield, T. L., Lemke, A., Amidei, T., & Roffman, R. (1990). Psychological factors that predict high risk versus AIDS precautionary behavior. *Journal of Consulting and Clinical Psychology, 58,* 117–120.

Kelly, J. A., St. Lawrence, J. S., Brasfield, T. L., Stevenson, L. Y., Diaz, Y. Y., & Hauth, A. C. (1990). AIDS risk behavior patterns among gay men in small southern cities. *American Journal of Public Health, 80*(2), 1–3.

Kelly, J. A., St. Lawrence, J. S., Hood, H. V., & Brasfield, T. L. (1989). Behavioral intervention to reduce AIDS risk activities. *Journal of Consulting and Clinical Psychology, 57,* 60–67.

Kelly, J. A., St. Lawrence, J. S., Stevenson, L. Y., Diaz, Y. E., Hauth, A. C., Brasfield, T. L., Smith, J. E., Bradley, B. G., & Bahr, G. R. (1990). *Population-wide risk behavior reduction through diffusion of innovation following intervention with natural opinion leaders.* Paper presented to the sixth International Conference on AIDS, Jackson, MS.

Krueger, R. A. (1988). *Focus groups: A practical guide for applied research.* Beverly Hills, CA: Sage.

Mays, V. M. (1989). AIDS prevention in black populations: Methods of a safer kind. In V. M. Mays, G. W. Albee, & S. F. Schneider (Eds.), *Primary prevention of AIDS: Psychological approaches* (pp. 264–270). London: Sage.

Mays, V. M., & Cochran, S. D. (1988). Issues in the perception of AIDS risk and risk reduction activities by Black and Hispanic/Latina women. *American Psychologist, 43,* 949–957.

MacDonald, N. E., Wells, G. A., Fisher, W. A., Warren, W. K., King, M. A., Doherty, J. A., & Bowie, W. R. (1990). High-risk STD/HIV behavior among college students. *Journal of the American Medical Association, 263,* 3155–3259.

McCombs, M. S., & White, K. P. (1990, August). *Gay men's risky sex relapse: Research implication, program design.* Paper presented at the 98th annual meeting of the American Psychological Association, Boston, MA.

McKusick, L., Coates, T., Wiley, J., Morin, S., Stall, R. M. (1987). *Prevention of HIV infection among gay and bisexual men: Two longitudinal studies.* Paper presented at the Third international conference on AIDS, Washington, DC.

Miller, H. G., Turner, C. F., & Moses, L. E. (Eds.). (1990). *AIDS: The second decade.* Washington, D.C.: National Academy Press.

Miller, T. E., Booraem, C., Flowers, J. V., & Iverson, A. E. (1990). Changes in knowledge, attitudes and behavior as a result of a community-based AIDS prevention program. *AIDS Education and Prevention, 2,* 12–23.

O'Leary, A., Goodhart, F., & Jemmott, L. S. (1991). *Social cognitive theory and AIDS prevention on the college campus: Implications for intervention.* Unpublished manuscript, Rutgers University, Department of Psychology, New Brunswick, NJ.

Petty, R. E., & Cacioppo, J. T. (1981). *Attitudes and persuasion: Classic and contemporary approaches.* Dubuque, Iowa: Brown.

People Like Us. (1992). [Video] Available from J. Fisher, AIDS Risk Reduction Project, Department of Psychology, University of Connecticut, Storrs, Connecticut, 06268.

Peterson, J. L., & Marin, G. (1988). Issues in the prevention of AIDS among Black and Hispanic men. *American Psychologist, 43,* 871–877.

Pleck, J. H., Sonenstein, F. L., & Ku, L. C. (1990, August). *Adolescent males' contraceptive attitudes and consistency of condom use.* Paper presented at the 98th annual convention of the American Psychological Association, Boston, Massachusetts.

Polit-O'Hara, D., & Kahn, J. (1985). Communication and contraceptive practices in adolescent couples. *Adolescence, 20,* 33–42.

Quimby, E., & Friedman, S. R. (1989). Dynamics of Black mobilization against AIDS in New York City. *Social Problems, 36,* 403–415.

Rhodes, F., & Wolitski, R. (1989). Effect of instructional videotapes on AIDS knowledge and attitudes. *Journal of American College Health, 37,* 266–271.

Ross, M. W. (1988). Personality factors that differentiate homosexual men with positive and negative attitudes towards condom use. *New York Journal of Medicine, 88,* 626–628.

Rotheram-Borus, M. J., Koopman, C., Haignere, C., Daives, M., Project Enter, & Urban Strategies. (1991). Reducing HIV sexual risk behaviors among runaway adolescents. *Journal of the American Medical Association.*

Rutgers College Health Survey. (undated). Newark, NJ: Rutgers University, Sexual Health Program.

St. Lawrence, J. S., Kelly, J. A., Hood, H. V., & Brasfield, T. L. (1987, June). *The relationship of AIDS risk knowledge to actual risk behavior among homosexually active men.* Paper presented at the third international Conference on AIDS, Washington, DC.

St. Louis, M. E., Rauch, K. J., Peterson, L. R., Anderson, J. E., Schable, M. S., Dondero, T. J., & Sentinel Hospital Surveillance Group. (1990). Seroprevalence rates of human immunodeficiency virus infection at sentinel hospitals in the United States. *New England Journal of Medicine, 323,* 213–218.

Schinke, S. P. (1984). Preventing teenage pregnancy. In M. Hersen, R. M. Eisler, & P. M. Miller (Eds.), *Progress in behavior modification* (Vol. 16, pp. 31–64). Orlando, FL: Academic Press.

Schinke, S. P., Blythe, B. J., & Gilchrist, L. D. (1981). Cognitive-behavioral prevention of adolescent pregnancy. *Journal of Counseling Psychology, 28,* 451–454.

Schinke, S. P., Gilchrist, L. D., & Small, R. W. (1979). Preventing unwanted pregnancy: A cognitive-behavioral approach. *American Journal of Orthopsychiatry, 49,* 81–88.

Sex, Condoms, and Videotape (1992). [Video] Available from J. Fisher, AIDS Risk Reduction Project, Department of Psychology, University of Connecticut, Storrs, Connecticut, 06268.

Stall, R. D., Coates, T. J., & Hoff, C. (1988). Behavioral risk reduction for HIV infection among gay and bisexual men. A review of results from the United States. *American Psychologist, 43,* 878–885.

Stehr-Green, J. K., Holman, R. C., Jason, J. M., & Evatt, B. L. (1988). Hemophilia-associated AIDS in the United States, 1981 to September 1987. *American Journal of Public Health, 78,* 439–442.

Valdiserri, R. O., Lyter, D. W., Leviton, L. C., Callahan, C. M., Kingsley, L. A., & Rinaldo, C. R. (1989). AIDS prevention in homosexual and bisexual men: Results of a randomized trial evaluating two risk reduction interventions, *AIDS, 3,* 21–26.

Weisman, C. S., Nathanson, C. A., Ensminger, M., Teitelbaum, M. A., Robinson, J. C., & Plichta, S. (1989). AIDS knowledge, perceived risk and prevention among adolescent clients of a family planning clinic. *Family Planning Perspectives, 21*(5), 213–217.

Winett, R. A., Altman, D. G., & King, A. C. (1990). Conceptual and strategic foundations for effective media campaigns for preventing the spread of HIV infection. *Evaluation and Program Planning, 13,* 91–104.

Winkelstein, W., & Johnson, A. (1990). Epidemiology overview. *AIDS, 4,*(Suppl 1), S95–S97.

Zielony, R. D., & Wills, T. A. (1990). *Psychosocial predictors of AIDS risk behavior in methadone patients.* Unpublished manuscript, Ferkauf Graduate School of Psychology and Albert Einstein College of Medicine, New York.

6 Persuasion Theory and AIDS Prevention ·

Richard E. Petty
Ohio State University

Faith Gleicher
University of California, Santa Barbara

W. Blair G. Jarvis
Ohio State University

> *AIDS is first and foremost a communication and persuasion challenge. There is no cure for AIDS at this time; there is only prevention. The answer lies in the development of persuasive interventions for use via both mass media and inter-personal communication channels.*
> —Reardon (1989, pp. 274, 289)

> *The role of mass media is often overemphasized and inappropriately suggested as a solution to serious public health issues. The mass media fantasy is, in brief, that almost any given social or health problem can be adequately addressed if the right message could be communicated to the right people in just the right way at the right time.*
> —Wallack (1989, pp. 353–354)

As these quotations illustrate, social scientists have offered both optimistic and pessimistic assessments of the utility of persuasion-based interventions for addressing the current AIDS crisis. To what extent can persuasion-based interventions via the mass media and other channels be effective in stopping the spread of AIDS? Our own view is that appropriately designed persuasive communications and interventions can be effective. Our goal in this chapter is to highlight the dominant social psychological approaches to attitude and behavior change in an attempt to summarize basic theory and research on persuasion that is of potential relevance to AIDS prevention. An appreciation of current thinking regarding the basic mechanisms by which persuasion is achieved should enhance the likelihood of selecting appropriate intervention strategies for preventing the spread of AIDS. Furthermore, an understanding of the psychological processes underlying social influence may help guard against either overly optimistic or pessimistic assessments of the prospects for changing attitudes and behaviors relevant to HIV infection.

CONTEMPORARY APPROACHES TO PERSUASION

Social scientists concerned with the study of human influence have focused on the concept of "attitudes," or peoples' general predispositions to evaluate other people, objects, and issues favorably or unfavorably. In addition to attitudes toward the AIDS disease itself (which are presumably negative for nearly all people), other attitudes relevant to the current AIDS crisis include attitudes toward: (a) oneself (e.g., low self-esteem or perceptions of personal invulnerability may encourage unsafe sexual practices), (b) authority figures (e.g., parents, government officials, and teachers who advocate safe sex), (c) peers (e.g., friends who may stigmatize those who use condoms), and (d) various AIDS-related behaviors (e.g., condom use, IV drug use). The attitude construct has achieved its preeminent position in research on influence because of the assumption that a person's attitude was an important mediating variable between the acquisition of new knowledge on the one hand, and behavioral change on the other. For example, initial AIDS educational programs were based on the view that providing the "facts" about AIDS would lead to positive attitudes toward safe sex and avoidance of risky behaviors (Becker & Joseph, 1988). In fact, assessments of AIDS prevention efforts sometimes focus on the new knowledge acquired rather than on attitude and behavior change per se (e.g., Gantz & Greenberg, 1990). Unfortunately, current research suggests that general knowledge about AIDS often has little impact on a person's own attitudes and behavior (e.g., see Fisher & Fisher, 1992; Stall, Coates, & Hoff, 1988). For example, a survey of 1,150 high school seniors included in *Who's Who Among American High School Students* in 1991 revealed that nearly all knew how AIDS was contracted, but 42% of those who were sexually active indicated that they would have sexual intercourse even if a condom was not available ("AIDS hasn't spurred teen condom use," 1992).

Over the past 50 years, numerous theories of attitude change and models of knowledge–attitude–behavior relationships have developed (see reviews by Olson & Zanna, in press; Petty, Unnava, & Strathman, 1991; Tesser & Shaffer, 1990). We review two broad approaches to persuasion and discuss their relevance to AIDS prevention in the remainder of this chapter.

Communication/Persuasion Matrix

One of the earliest assumptions of theories of attitude change (e.g., Strong, 1925), that is also evident in contemporary approaches (e.g., McGuire, 1985), was that effective influence required a sequence of steps (Petty & Cacioppo, 1984). For example, Fig. 6.1 presents McGuire's (1985, 1989) Communica-

Communication   Inputs :

Outputs:	SOURCE	MESSAGE	RECIPIENT	CHANNEL	CONTEXT
EXPOSURE					
ATTENTION					
INTEREST					
COMPREHENSION					
ACQUISITION					
YIELDING					
MEMORY					
RETRIEVAL					
DECISION					
ACTION					
REINFORCEMENT					
CONSOLIDATION					

FIG. 6.1. The Communication Persuasion Matrix Model of Attitude Change. The model depicts the various inputs to the persuasion process (e.g., source factors) as well as the various output processes that are presumed to mediate influence (e.g., interest in the message). Adapted from McGuire (1985).

tion/Persuasion Matrix model of influence. This model outlines the inputs (or independent variables) to the persuasion process that potential persuaders can control along with the outputs (or dependent variables) that can be measured to see if any influence attempt is successful.

Matrix Inputs

The first input to the influence process that one can consider is that a communication on HIV or any other topic is presented by a particular *source*. The source can be a parent, teacher, celebrity, friend, the government, or others. The source can be expert or not, admired or not, powerful or not, and so on. This source provides some information, the *message,* and this message can be emotional or logical, long or short, organized or not, directed at a specific or a general belief, and so forth. The message is presented to a particular *recipient* who may be high or low in self-esteem, intelligence, knowledge, sexual experience, and so forth. The message is presented via some *channel* of communication. That is, the message can be presented live (face to face) or via some medium (e.g., magazine, radio, etc.). Some media allow presentation of the message at the recipient's own pace (e.g., a pamphlet on AIDS), whereas other media control the pace externally (e.g., a TV public service ad). Finally, the message is presented to the recipient in some *context*. For example, the message may reach the recipient at home, in school, or in church. The environment may be pleasant or unpleasant, noisy or quiet, and so forth. Each of these inputs is under the potential control of an influence agent.

Matrix Outputs

According to McGuire (1989), to maximize influence, the inputs should be selected or controlled in order to have an impact on the various outputs depicted in Fig. 6.1. That is, the Communication/Persuasion Matrix model contends that in order for influence to occur, a number of sequential steps are required. First, a person needs to be *exposed* to some new information. Media are often selected by potential persuaders after an estimation of the number and type of people the message is likely to reach. There is no question but that exposure to messages on AIDS has increased dramatically in recent years. A survey of the content of articles in magazines showed that in the 1960s, 1970s, and early 1980s, the three most covered health-related topics were in order: cancer, pollution, and nutrition. This remained relatively stable over the 25-year period from 1960 to 1984. During the most recent four-year period surveyed, however, articles on AIDS surpassed each of these and has now become the most covered health-related topic (see Paisley, 1989).

In 1988, the U.S. government mailed an eight page brochure, *Understanding AIDS,* to every postal address in the country. Furthermore, a vigorous campaign of media public service announcements and educational programs has been initiated with the goal of stopping the spread of AIDS. During the period from 1985 to 1989, an average of more than 7,000 stories on AIDS appeared in the media each year. It is therefore likely that a wealth of facts and information have been made available to the general public about HIV infection and AIDS. Interestingly, the massive dose of AIDS messages in the media has not had much impact on people's personal perceptions of vulnerability to HIV infection, but it has been accompanied by an increased perception that an AIDS epidemic is more likely (i.e., that *others* are more susceptible; Singer, Rogers, & Glassman, 1991).

Exposure to information does not guarantee *attention* to its contents, however. Just because a person receives a pamphlet in the mail or is sitting in front of the television doesn't mean that he or she knows what specific information is presented. Even if the person does notice the information, this does not mean that the person's *interest* will be engaged. For example, in one study, only 40% of men surveyed in Los Angeles who claimed to have received the *Understanding AIDS* brochure reported reading it (Montgomery, Freeman, & Lewis, 1989). What determines whether an individual will show any interest in AIDS-relevant messages? People will generally attend to information that they perceive relevant to their lives and lifestyles. Thus, some have argued that messages advocating safe sex and condom use should be eroticized because high-risk individuals are those who enjoy sex often. For these individuals, the eroticized messages would presumably "get their attention and hold it, and strengthen cognitive–affective associations between hot sex and safe sex" (Catania et al., 1989, p. 253; see also Solomon & DeJong, 1986). On the other hand, people may avoid AIDS-related messages if they find them threatening. Thus, people who are uncomfortable with sex or their own sexuality may avoid such messages. For example, Fisher and Misovich (1990) found that acceptance of being gay was associated with seeking exposure to media AIDS messages and denial of being gay was associated with avoiding information about AIDS. One challenge in preparing AIDS-relevant messages is constructing them so that they are maximally appealing and relevant to the intended audience.

The next two output stages in the Communication/Persuasion matrix involve *comprehension* and *acquisition,* or what part of the information presented the person actually understands and learns. That is, people who are attending to and interested in the message may learn something from it, or they may not. Furthermore, just because people learn some new information does not mean that they will *yield* to or agree with it, the next step in the influence sequence. There are, of course, many determinants of whether or not a person will accept a message, and as we describe shortly, several processes that can produce yielding (e.g., identifying with an attractive source; thinking about the favorable implications of the arguments presented). The next step in the influence sequence involves *memory* or storage of the new information acquired and the attitude that it supports. The next three outputs detail the processes involved in translating the new attitude into a behavioral response. That is, at some subsequent behavioral opportunity, the person must *retrieve* the new attitude from memory (and perhaps the information that supports it), *decide* to act on it, and perform the appropriate *action*. Finally, the model notes that if the new attitude-consistent behavior is not *reinforced,* the new attitude and the behavior it supports can be undermined. If the behavior is rewarding, however, performance of the behavior may lead to attitudinal *consolidation,* making the link between the new attitude and behavior more likely to persist over time.

Variants of this general information-processing model were often interpreted in theory and in practice as suggesting that a change early in the sequence (e.g., attention) would inevitably lead to a change later in the sequence (e.g., yielding). McGuire (1989) noted, however, that the likelihood that a message will evoke each of the steps in the sequence should be viewed as a conditional probability. Thus, even if the likelihood of achieving each of the first six steps in a mass media campaign was 60%, the maximum probability of achieving all six steps (exposure, attention, interest, comprehension, learning, and yielding), would be $.6^6$ or only 5%. According to the Communication/Persuasion Matrix model then, once some researchers determined that there were no discernable changes in public knowledge as a result of the *Understanding AIDS* brochure (Singer et al, 1991), it would not be surprising that others would conclude that no behavior changes resulted either (Snyder, 1991) because the model holds that the initial steps are necessary for the later ones. Even if some initial knowledge change was produced, however, no behavior change would be expected if one of the intervening steps between knowledge acquisition and behavioral action did not occur.

Another important feature of the Communication/Persuasion Matrix model of influence is the fact that any one input variable may have different effects on the different output steps. In a cogent analysis of this point, McGuire (1968) noted that several variables might have opposite effects on the steps involving *reception* of information (e.g., exposure, attention, comprehension, acquisition, memory) versus *acceptance* of or yielding to the information. For example, recipient intelligence is related positively to reception processes, but is negatively related to yielding. The joint action of reception and yielding processes implies that people of moderate intelligence should in general be easier to influence than people of low or high intelligence (see also, Rhodes & Wood, 1992).

Additional Issues for the Communication/Persuasion Matrix Model

Although McGuire's input/output matrix model serves as a useful way to think about the steps involved in producing attitude and behavior change via the mass media or other means, it is important to appreciate a number of complicating factors. First, the accumulated persuasion literature strongly suggests that some of the steps in the postulated information-processing sequence may be independent of each other, rather than sequential. For example, although a person's ability to learn and recall new information (e.g., facts about the transmission of AIDS) was often thought to be an important causal determinant of and prerequisite to attitude and behavior change (e.g., favoring and engaging in safe sex), this is not always true (Greenwald, 1968; McGuire, 1985; Petty & Cacioppo, 1981). Rather, the existing evidence shows that: (a) message comprehension and learning can occur in the absence of attitude change, and (b) a person's beliefs and attitudes may change without the person learning the specific information in the communication.

Second, the Communication/Persuasion Matrix model tells us little about the processes responsible for yielding to a message. Even though the initial steps in the information-processing sequence were viewed as prerequisites to acceptance, McGuire did not mean to imply that people would invariably yield to all information they comprehended and learned. That is, the earlier steps were thought to be necessary but not sufficient for yielding. According to the model, just as source and other input variables determine the extent of attention to the message, they also determine the extent of message acceptance. The model does not focus, however, on how or why the various input variables have an impact on yielding or the other output variables. In contrast, current psychological research on influence has focused more on this issue (e.g., how does the credibility of the source affect yielding or resistance to a message?).

Cognitive Response Theory

Cognitive response approaches to persuasion (Greenwald, 1968; McGuire, 1964; Petty, Ostrom, & Brock, 1981) were developed explicitly to address two issues unaddressed by the Communication/Persuasion Matrix. That is, cognitive response analysis attempted to do two things. First, it aimed to account for the low correlation between message learning (e.g., as assessed by recall of facts about AIDS transmission) and attitudes and behaviors (e.g., as assessed by acceptance of and use of condoms) observed in many studies. Second, it sought to explain the specific process responsible for yielding. Cognitive response theory holds that the extent of yielding is related to the idiosyncratic thoughts (pro- and counterarguments) generated in response to the message rather than to learning of the message per se. Furthermore, the persistence of persuasion is related to memory for the cognitive responses elicited by the message rather than to memory for the specific message content. Although the cognitive response approach provides some important insights into the persuasion process, it overemphasizes the extent to which people are active processors of the information given to them. Thus, the theory does not account very well for persuasion in situations where people are not actively thinking about the message content (e.g., Petty, Cacioppo, & Goldman, 1981).

Figure 6.2 illustrates many of these points by diagramming the reactions of six hypothetical people to a television public service announcement (PSA) about AIDS. The sponsors of this PSA want young people to learn that engaging in sex without condoms is very risky and can lead to HIV infection. The spot features a popular celebrity spokesperson who serves as the source of the communication. As depicted in the figure, Person A gets nothing from the message (and will not be considered further). Persons B, C, D, and E all understand the gist of the message and would pass a typical recall or comprehension test on the specifics of the communication.

As noted earlier, current models of persuasion suggest that it is unlikely that one can judge the effectiveness of the ad solely by examining the *knowledge* acquired from the communication. Rather, an individual's idiosyncratic cognitive responses to the message are critical. Person B actively counterargues the message thinking that the message only applies to certain kinds of people—gays and IV drug users. Person C understands the message but thinks it does not apply because he is young and healthy. Thus, both B and C have learned the message, but dismiss it as irrelevant to them, although for different reasons. Persons D and E have the initial response desired by the campaign sponsors in that both come to

PERSON:

	A	B	C	D	E	F
KNOWLEDGE	none	Some people who engage in unsafe sex get AIDS and eventually die. I should use condoms to reduce the risk of AIDS.				A CELEBRITY says to use condoms.
COGNITIVE RESPONSES TO MESSAGE	(irrelevant)	This only applies to gays and IV drug users.	I'm young, healthy, and invulnerable, so I don't need to worry.	Unsafe sex could be risky for me if I don't use a condom.		A CELEBRITY approves of condom use.
		The message is irrelevant to me.		I like risk.	I dislike risk.	I like the CELEBRITY.
ATTITUDE				Condoms are bad.	Condoms are good.	Condoms are good.
BEHAVIOR				NONUSE OF CONDOMS.	USE OF CONDOMS.	

FIG 6.2.   Idiosyncratic Reactions to an AIDS PSA. The figure depicts the possible knowledge, thoughts, attitudes, and behavior of six hypothetical individuals in response to a TV commercial featuring a celebrity who says that practicing unsafe sex is very dangerous and that people should use condoms to reduce the risk of HIV infection.

think that sex without condoms could be dangerous for them. However, Individual D values risk and danger (e.g., is a high sensation seeker; Donohew, Lorch, & Palmgreen, 1991; Zuckerman, 1974), and thinks that unsafe sex might therefore be exciting. Person E, who shows the expected response of disliking danger, comes to dislike unsafe sex.

One of the puzzling findings in AIDS research has been the inconsistent relationship between perceptions of personal risk and engagement in unsafe sexual practices. In some studies of gay men, increased perceptions of risk were related to decreased engagement in unsafe sexual practices as expected (e.g., Klein et al., 1987), but in other studies the opposite was observed (Joseph et al., 1987). Thus, it is important to consider how different individuals react to perceptions of risk. For example, in one study of gay and bisexual men it was found that for those men who were HIV negative and had a primary sex partner, increased perceptions of risk were associated with increased safe sex practices, but among those who were HIV positive and had no primary sex partner, increased risk perception was associated with less safe sex practices (Aspinwall, Kemeny, Taylor, Schneider, & Dudley, 1991). The important point is that one needs to know more than whether or not a person has acquired new information. We also need to know how the person reacts to that information. In Fig. 6.2, only one (Person E) of the four people (B, C, D, E) who processed the message and would pass a typical knowledge test showed attitude change in the desired direction (see Fishbein & Middlestadt, 1989, for further discussion of the role of idiosyncratic beliefs in influencing attitudes about AIDS).

Finally, Fig. 6.2 presents Person F who misses the central point about the potential danger of unsafe sex entirely (and thus would fail the comprehension test), but does learn something—that the featured celebrity approves of condoms. Because Person F likes the celebrity, F also comes to believe that condoms are good without engaging in any thought about the content of the message itself. This result is expected by *balance theory,* which states that people feel more comfortable when they agree with people they like, and disagree with people they dislike (Heider, 1958). Note that Persons E and F have formed the same attitude, but as we explain later in the chapter, some attitudes have greater implications for behavior than others. That is, E's new attitude will tend to be more directive of subsequent behavior than F's.

In summary, Fig. 6.2 demonstrates that: (a) attitude change can occur in the absence of the presumably critical knowledge (Person F); (b) the critical knowledge can be acquired without producing any attitude change (Person B and C), (c) the same knowledge can lead to opposite attitudes (Persons D and E), and (d) attitudes that are ostensibly the same can be produced by very different processes and have different implications for behavior (Persons E and F). This analysis may help to explain why AIDS and other health intervention campaigns have sometimes found that message learning and changes in knowledge occur in the absence of attitude change and vice-versa (e.g., Gray & Saracino, 1989; Sherr, 1987).

The Elaboration Likelihood Model of Persuasion

The Elaboration Likelihood Model (ELM) of persuasion (Petty & Cacioppo, 1981, 1986) is a theory about the processes responsible for yielding to a persuasive communication that accommodates the points made by Fig. 6.2. At the most basic level, the model holds that the processes that occur during the yielding stage can be thought of as emphasizing one of two relatively distinct "routes" to persuasion.

Central Route

One route to persuasion, the *central route,* involves effortful cognitive activity whereby the person draws on prior experience and knowledge to carefully scrutinize and evaluate the issue-relevant arguments presented in the communication (whether the message appears in the mass media or comes from a friend, parent, or teacher). Consistent with the cognitive response approach outlined earlier, the message recipient under the central route is actively generating favorable and/or unfavorable thoughts in response to the message. In order for this to occur, the person must possess sufficient motivation and ability to think about the merits of the information provided. The end result of this careful and systematic processing is an attitude that is well articulated and integrated into the person's belief structure. Attitudes changed by this route have been found to be relatively accessible, persistent over time, and predictive of behavior (see Chaiken, Liberman, & Eagly, 1989; Petty & Cacioppo, 1986).

In addition, the more a person initially thinks about and has practice in defending a newly acquired attitude, the more likely the person is to resist the subsequent challenges the new attitude surely will face. That is, attitudes changed via the central route tend to be relatively resistant to counter messages (e.g., Haugtvedt & Petty, 1992). In his *inoculation theory,* McGuire (1964) used a biological analogy to suggest that just as people can be made more resistant to a disease by giving them a mild form of the germ, people can be made more resistant to attacks on their attitudes by inoculating their new opinions. The inoculation treatment consists of exposing people to a few pieces of attacking information and showing them how to refute it. Research clearly indicates that people whose attitudes are bolstered with inoculation treatments become less vulnerable to subsequent attacks on their attitudes than people whose attitudes are bolstered with supportive information alone (see McGuire, 1964). Thus, instead of providing only favorable information about the use of condoms, a message taking advantage of inoculation techniques might also contain unfavorable information along with counterarguments (e.g., yes, condoms may reduce pleasure slightly for some, but is this more important than saving your life?).

Peripheral Route

In stark contrast to the central route approach, some theories of persuasion do not place much credence on the arguments in a message or issue-relevant thinking. Instead, they postulate a *peripheral route* whereby simple cues in the persuasion context either elicit an affective state (e.g., happiness) that becomes associated with the advocated position (as in classical conditioning; Staats & Staats, 1958), or trigger a relatively simple inference or heuristic that a person can use to judge the validity of the message (e.g., "experts are correct;" Chaiken, 1987). Public service announcements attempt to employ this strategy when they rely on the audience accepting a conclusion simply because it is associated with a well-liked celebrity or sports figure rather than because the audience focuses on the merits of the arguments that are presented. We do not mean to suggest that peripheral approaches are necessarily ineffective in changing attitudes. In fact they can be quite powerful in the short term. The problem is that people's feelings about celebrities and sports figures can change dramatically over time (e.g., today's teen idol is tomorrow's fallen star), and the positive sources may become dissociated from their messages (Pratkanis, Greenwald, Leippe, & Baumgardner, 1988).

Laboratory research has shown that an attitude change based on peripheral cues tends to be less accessible, persistent, resistant, and directive of behavior than the same amount of attitude change based on careful thinking about the merits of the position presented (Petty & Cacioppo, 1986). Thus, people who hold attitudes about unsafe sex or condoms based solely on celebrity cues are less likely to resist arguments and pressure to engage in this activity than are people who have developed attitudes following careful reflection upon the personal dangers inherent in the behaviors (compare Persons E and F in Fig. 6.2). In summary, attitudes changed via the central route tend to be based on active thought processes resulting in a well-integrated cognitive structure, but attitudes changed via the peripheral route are based on more passive acceptance (or rejection) of simple cues and have a less well-articulated structure. The basic ideas of the ELM are presented schematically in Fig. 6.3.

Our discussion of the central and peripheral routes to persuasion indicates that active participation in the persuasion process is critical if one wishes to produce stable attitude changes that are influential in behavior and resistant to contrary forces. It is worth noting that drug prevention programs developed in the 1980s have incorporated a greater degree of active participation and "inoculation" by having participants discuss personal values with respect to drugs, actively question the information provided, and engage in role-playing scenarios in which drugs are refused (e.g., Botvin, Baker, Renick, Filazzola, & Botvin, 1984; DeJong, 1987). Similar strategies show promise in AIDS education programs as well (Kelly, St. Lawrence, Hood, & Brashfield, 1989).

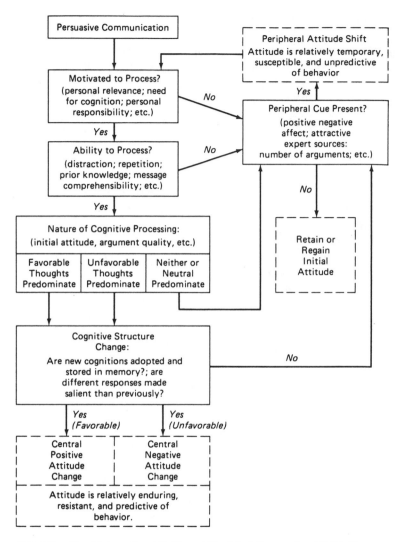

FIG. 6.3. The Elaboration Likelihood Model of Persuasion (ELM). The model depicts two routes by which attitudes may change. These routes form a continuum anchored at one end by the central route and at the other by the peripheral route to persuasion. Adapted from Petty and Cacioppo (1986).

Motivating Message Thought: Personal Relevance and Vulnerability

The ELM highlights several ways in which one can have an impact on persuasion. First, one can attempt to control the *arguments* relevant to an issue (e.g., condom use) by providing information as to the central merits of the position advocated (e.g., condoms greatly reduce the chance of HIV infection). Next, one can control the use of peripheral cues that allow favorable or unfavorable attitude formation in the absence of a diligent consideration of the true merits of the object or issue (e.g., associating condoms with liked celebrities). Whether arguments or cues have more impact on attitudes will depend on how motivated and able people are to think about the arguments. Thus, another way to influence the extent of persuasion is to modify the *extent of argument elaboration* (i.e., the intensity with which the message recipient thinks about and evaluates the central merits of the issue-relevant information presented). Finally, if a person is motivated and able to think about the arguments presented, one can attempt to influence the direction of any *bias in elaboration* (i.e., whether the thoughts generated are biased in a positive or negative direction; Petty & Cacioppo, 1990).

Personal Relevance.   As the overall likelihood of elaboration is increased (whether thinking about the arguments proceeds in a relatively objective or a more biased fashion), the perceived *quality* of the issue-relevant arguments presented becomes a more important determinant of persuasion. As the likelihood of elaboration is decreased, however, peripheral cues become more important. That is, when the elaboration likelihood is high, the central route to persuasion dominates, but when the elaboration likelihood is low, the peripheral route takes precedence. The accumulated research on persuasion has pointed to many variables that can be employed to either increase or decrease the amount of thinking about a persuasive message, but perhaps the most important variable affecting a person's general motivation to think about a message is its perceived personal relevance (Petty & Cacioppo, 1979b).

A message can be high in self-relevance because it is perceived relevant to specific values, goals, outcomes, individuals, groups, or objects that are important to the person (Petty, Cacioppo, & Haugtvedt, 1992). For example, the use of condoms may be perceived to conflict with important religious values, and thus messages on that topic will be ignored. Or, young people may not place a high value on their own personal health and may therefore be generally uninterested health communications. In one study (Radius, Dielman, Becker, Rosenstock, & Horvath 1980), for example, more than half of the adolescents surveyed reported that they were not concerned about their own health. If health was increased as a value among adolescents, attention to health messages should increase because the self-relevance of these messages would be enhanced.

Fortunately, there are a number of ways to enhance the perceived self-relevance of a message without changing values. For example, if the perceived relevance of the topic is normally low, involvement can be increased by a variety of means such as emphasizing personal connections in the text of the message (e.g., "YOU can get AIDS," rather than "PEOPLE can get AIDS"; Burnkrant & Unnava, 1989), or by having people imagine realistic ways in which they might contract AIDS (Carroll, 1978; Cialdini, Gregory, & Carpenter, 1982; Sherman, Cialdini, Schwartzman, & Reynolds, 1985). If increasing relevance is difficult, increased message thinking can be motivated by other techniques such as summarizing the message arguments as rhetorical questions rather than as statements (e.g., Isn't it a good idea to use condoms to prevent HIV transmission?" rather than "It is a good idea to use condoms to prevent HIV transmission"; Petty, Cacioppo, & Heesacker, 1981), or by employing multiple sources to present the arguments rather than a single source (Harkins & Petty, 1983).

Consistent with the laboratory research cited here, research on health communications has clearly shown that messages need to be made more motivating for people who lack interest in the topic. For example, one study (Flora & Maibach, 1990) showed that employing vivid and emotionally absorbing AIDS communications (vs. pallid presentation of facts) could enhance message processing for people who did not see the AIDS issue as very self-relevant. For high-relevance subjects, however, vivid and non vivid messages were processed to the same high degree (see also, Rook, 1986).

Perceived Vulnerability.   A potentially important factor in determining if an HIV message is seen as relevant to an individual is whether the person feels personally vulnerable to HIV infection. Not surprisingly, gay individuals feel more vulnerable to AIDS than health professionals, who feel more vulnerable than heterosexual college students (Fisher & Misovich, 1990). As Herek (1990) noted, educators may be tempted to inflate an audience's perception of risk for HIV in order to enhance the perception of vulnerability and increase attention to and thinking about the message. Will the threat or fear of vulnerability be useful or counterproductive in producing influence? Some researchers have advocated that moderate fear or personal concern can be effective in persuading people to avoid risky behaviors and to engage in preventive ones (e.g., Catania, Kegeles, & Coates, 1990). It is perhaps not too surprising that some of the largest changes in attitudes and behaviors relevant to AIDS have occurred as a result of treatment programs targeted at vulnerable populations such as the gay community (e.g., McKusick, Conant, & Coates, 1985). On the other hand, other researchers have warned that stimulating fear of AIDS or very high concern can backfire by leading to avoidance of the AIDS issue and the psychological distress it produces (e.g., Friedman, Des Jarlais, & Sotheran, 1986; Joseph et al., 1987).

Social psychologists have long been interested in the role of fear and perceived vulnerability in persuasion. Various models have developed and although the models have their important differences (cf. Janis, 1967; Leventhal, 1970;

Rogers, 1983), some common themes have emerged. For example, there is general agreement that very high levels of fear (or perceived vulnerability to a very noxious event) can produce defensive avoidance of a message, but moderate levels can be persuasive if the fear is coupled with the presentation of an effective and specific means of avoiding the threat. That is, even moderate fear of AIDS is likely to be counterproductive if the message does not leave people with the clear sense that they can do something to avoid the threat of AIDS. In his *protection motivation theory,* Rogers (1983) holds that the use of moderate fear in communications can motivate a need for reassurance that can be met by adopting the explicit recommendations in the persuasive communication.

An important issue that is unaddressed by the prevailing models, however, is whether the change induced by the use of fear is produced by the central or the peripheral route. In a study examining this issue, Gleicher and Petty (1992) hypothesized that consistent with protection motivation theory, moderate fear would induce a need for reassurance. However, the ELM holds that assurance can be obtained in one of two ways. A fearful person can simply accept the assertions of an expert that all is okay and ignore the true merits of the proposed solution to the threat, or the person can scrutinize the message itself in an attempt to seek reassurance. Gleicher and Petty found that overall, moderate fear subjects showed more acceptance of a solution to a threat than low-fear individuals, but which route to reassurance was taken depended on how the speaker introduced the solution to the threat. When the speaker, who was portrayed as an expert on the topic, indicated that the solution was highly likely to succeed, fearful subjects accepted the solution regardless of whether it was supported by strong or weak arguments. On the other hand, when the speaker indicated that the solution was only possibly effective, moderately fearful subjects processed the message and accepted the solution to a greater extent when the arguments presented were strong rather than weak.

This study suggests that an expert source presenting a proposal (e.g., using condoms) as a *certain* solution to a threatening situation (e.g., contracting AIDS) might produce considerable attitude change, but this change may not result from careful thinking about the reasons behind the solution. After all, if the solution is certain, there is little need to process this message. As a result of this non thoughtful change, the new attitude may prove vulnerable to subsequent strong counter messages because the change is based on little more than an expert's reassurance. On the other hand, if moderate fear or personal concern are raised, and an expert indicates that there is a *possible* solution, people will be motivated to actively process and think about the solution in order to obtain the desired reassurance.[1]

---

[1] It is important to note that *high* fear, in addition to producing defensive avoidance of a message, may also render a person unable to think about the merits of the solution presented.

Additional Considerations.   In summary, a number of variables that are potentially under the control of health professionals constructing AIDS-relevant communications can have an impact on persuasion by influencing the message recipients' *motivation* to think about the communication. In addition to these controllable factors (e.g., the extent of fear used in a message) it is noteworthy that there are important individual differences in people's chronic enjoyment of thinking that affect overall motivation to process a variety of messages (i.e., "need for cognition," see Cacioppo, Petty, & Morris, 1983). It is also critical to note that still other variables, such as the extent of message repetition (Cacioppo & Petty, 1989) or the nature of any distractions present (Petty, Wells, & Brock, 1976) can have an important impact on the amount of persuasion by modifying a person's overall *ability* to think about the issue-relevant arguments presented. High motivation to think will do little good if ability is impaired.

Finally, as suggested earlier, it is important to consider that some variables affect information-processing activity in a relatively objective manner, whereas others introduce a systematic bias to the information-processing activity. For example, telling a highly involved audience that a message is specifically attempting to persuade them motivates active resistance and counterarguing rather than objective processing (Petty & Cacioppo, 1979a). On the other hand, when people are motivated to think but are in a pleasant mood, they are biased in favor of generating favorable rather than unfavorable thoughts (Petty, Gleicher, & Baker, 1991).

Multiple Roles for Variables in the ELM

One of the most important features of the ELM, is that it holds that any one variable can serve in each of the roles outlined earlier, although in different situations. That is, a variable can serve as a persuasive argument in some contexts, act as a peripheral cue in others, and affect the intensity of thinking or the direction of processing bias in still other domains. For example, in separate studies, researchers have shown that the attractiveness of a message source can: (a) serve as a simple peripheral cue when it is irrelevant to evaluating the merits of an attitude object and subjects are not motivated to process the issue-relevant arguments, (b) serve as a message argument when attractiveness is relevant to evaluating the merits of the attitude object and the elaboration likelihood is high, and (c) affect the extent of thinking about the message arguments presented when the elaboration likelihood is moderate (see Petty & Priester, in press, for a review).

If any one variable can influence persuasion by several means, it becomes critical to identify the general conditions under which the variable acts in each of the different roles. The ELM holds that when the elaboration likelihood is high (such as when perceived personal relevance and knowledge are high, the message is easy to understand, no distractions are present, etc.), people typically know that they want and are able to evaluate the merits of the arguments presented and they do so. Variables such as source attractiveness have little direct impact on evaluations by serving as simple cues in these situations. Instead, they may serve as arguments if relevant to the merits of the issue, or may bias the nature of the ongoing cognitive activity. On the other hand, when the elaboration likelihood is low (e.g., low personal relevance or knowledge, complex message, many distractions, etc.), people know that they do not want and/or are not able to evaluate the merits of the arguments presented (or they do not even consider exerting effort to process the message). If any evaluation is formed under these conditions, it is likely to be the result of relatively simple associations or inferences (e.g., "I agree with people I like"). When the elaboration likelihood is moderate (e.g., uncertain personal relevance, moderate knowledge, moderate complexity, etc). people may be uncertain as to whether or not the message warrants or needs scrutiny and whether or not they are capable of providing this analysis. In these situations they may examine the persuasion context for indications (e.g., is the source credible? similar to me?) of whether or not it is worthwhile or necessary to process the message.

Consequences of the Route to Persuasion

Because any one variable can produce persuasion in multiple ways, it is important to understand why the variable has worked. As we noted previously, the ELM holds that attitudes formed or changed by the central route tend to have different consequences and properties than attitudes modified by the peripheral route (Petty & Haugtvedt, in press). For example, central route attitudes are more accessible than peripheral route attitudes. Because these attitudes come to mind more quickly and may be spontaneously accessible upon presentation of the relevant attitude object, they should be more likely to influence behavior (Fazio, 1990). If a person's favorable attitude toward condoms comes to mind spontaneously on appropriate occasions, condoms are more likely to be used (assuming they are available) than if the favorable attitude toward condoms requires considerable cognitive effort to be retrieved. In fact, studies have shown that attitudes formed as a result of effortful thinking are more predictive of behavioral intentions than attitudes formed with little thinking (Petty, Cacioppo, & Schumann, 1983; Verplanken, et al., 1991). Not surprisingly then, the attitudes of people who are highly involved with a health issue are more predictive of their health behavior intentions than the attitudes of people who are less involved (Hoverstad & Howard-Pitney, 1986).

Research also suggests that attitudes formed by the central route are more persistent over time and are more resistant to counterpersuasive attempts. For example, in two studies Haugtvedt and Petty (1992) produced similar attitude changes in individuals who differed in their need for cognition (Cacioppo & Petty, 1982). In each study, people were presented with a message containing strong arguments presented by a credible source. Both high and low need for cognition individuals become more favorable toward the position taken in the message, but presumably for different reasons. That is, high need for cognition subjects who characteristically enjoy thinking were expected to change because of their elaboration of the high quality arguments that were presented. Low need for cognition subjects who act as cognitive misers were expected to change because of the positive source cue. In one of the studies, when attitudes toward the issue were examined just 2 days after the persuasive message, recipients low in need for cognition had returned to their initial positions, but high need for cognition subjects persisted in their new attitudes. In a second study, subjects' new attitudes were challenged just a few minutes after they were created. High need for cognition subjects resisted the attacking message to a greater extent than low need for cognition individuals.

In empirical research on AIDS prevention, many source, message, recipient, and contextual variables have and will continue to be examined. The ELM notes that it is critical to understand the processes by which these variables work. For example, some have noted that peer led health programs may be superior to those led by teachers (e.g., Jordheim, 1975). Even if research demonstrates that peers are more effective than teachers in changing attitudes overall, it would be important to know if this was because a peer source was serving as a simple positive cue, or if peers enhanced attention to and processing of the substantive arguments presented. If peers work by serving as simple cues to acceptance, they may be effective in the short term, but if they work by increasing thinking about the substantive arguments raised, the attitude changes induced will be stronger.

ATTITUDE-BEHAVIOR LINKS

As noted earlier, not all attitude changes lead to behavior change. Once a person's attitude has changed (e.g., has moved from anti- to pro-condom use), it is important that the new attitude rather than old habits guide behavior. Considerable research has addressed the link between attitudes and behavior and a number of situational and dispositional factors have been showed to enhance the consistency between them. For example, attitudes have been found to have a greater impact on behavior when: (a) the attitudes in question "match" the behaviors (e.g., attitudes toward *purchasing* condoms will predict condom purchasing behavior better than attitudes toward condoms in general), (b) the attitudes in question are consistent with underlying beliefs, (c) the attitudes are based on high rather than low amounts of issue-relevant information and/or personal experience, (d) the attitudes were formed as a result of considerable issue-relevant thinking, and (e) cues in the situation indicate that the person's attitude is relevant to the behavior (see Ajzen, 1988, for a comprehensive review).

The Reasoned Use of Attitudes in Guiding Behavior

Fazio (1990) has noted that two general models of the process by which attitudes guide behavior have achieved widespread acceptance. One type of model proposes that attitudes guide behavior in a reasoned manner, and the other suggests a more spontaneous process. The former type of theory is exemplified by Ajzen's (1988) *theory of planned behavior*. This theory, along with the *theory of reasoned action* (Ajzen & Fishbein, 1980; Fishbein & Ajzen's, 1975) on which it elaborates, assumes that behavioral choices are based on an analysis of the implications of the various actions. In this model, people are hypothesized to form intentions to perform or not perform behaviors, and these intentions are based on the person's attitude toward the behavior, perceptions of the opinions of significant others (norms), and perceptions of control over the behavior (i.e., the perceived ease or difficulty in performing the behavior). The fact that each of these factors can have a direct impact on behavioral intentions suggests that behavior *change* can be produced without any change in a person's attitudes if new normative pressures can be invoked (e.g., "I'll use condoms because it now appears that everyone else wants me to, not because I personally think they are valuable"), or perceptions of control change (e.g., "Now that condoms are readily available at school, I'll use them"). In these cases, the person's behavior changes because of a desire to please important others or because of new perceptions of control rather than out of any changes in personal attitudes.

Because the theory of planned behavior views behavior as a function of attitudes, norms, and perceptions of control, it suggests that if attitudes toward some desired behavior are already highly favorable, behavior may be further influenced in a positive direction by targeting beliefs about norms and control regarding the behavior. If attitudes are not already highly favorable, however, the theory suggests that relevant attitudes can be changed by having the message recipient focus on the personal costs and benefits of engaging in some behavior. In particular, the model focuses on the perceived likelihood that certain benefits will be obtained or costs avoided, and the desirability (aversiveness) of those benefits (costs). The specific beliefs that are relevant to health-related actions have been outlined in the Health Belief Model (Janz & Becker, 1984; Rosenstock, 1974) and include beliefs about: (a) one's personal susceptibility to some negative condition (e.g., Will I get AIDS if I engage in unsafe sex?), (b) the perceived severity of the condition (e.g., Will I die?), (c) the subjective benefits of engaging in a recommended action (e.g., Can I avoid AIDS if I use condoms?), and (d) the costs (financial, psychological, etc.) of the action (e.g., Will I be embarrassed, stigmatized?). That is, people are assumed to engage in health-related actions (e.g., stopping smoking, using condoms) to the extent that they believe that some health concern is serious, relevant to them, and the likely effectiveness and other benefits of the recommended action outweigh its costs. Of course, a person need not go through this extensive cognitive analysis every time the person is confronted with the attitude object. Instead, a relevant attitude or intention that was previously formed can be retrieved and direct behavior.

The Spontaneous Use of Attitudes in Guiding Behavior

Fazio (1990) proposed that much behavior is rather spontaneous and that attitudes can guide behavior by a relatively automatic process. Specifically, Fazio argued that attitudes can guide behavior without any deliberate reflection or reasoning if: (a) the attitude is accessed (comes to mind) spontaneously by the mere presence of the attitude object, and (b) the attitude colors perception of the object so that if the attitude is favorable (or unfavorable), the qualities of the object appear favorable (or unfavorable). For example, in the midst of a passionate moment, the various costs and benefits of using condoms may not be considered at all, or may be weighed only long after sexual activity has taken place. Instead, more accessible attitudes and beliefs (e.g., I want to have fun) may guide behavior.

Fazio (1990) argued that motivational and ability factors will be important in determining whether the reasoned action or the automatic activation process occurs. That is, for behavioral decisions that are high in perceived personal consequences, attitudes are likely to guide behavior by a deliberate reflection process, but when perceived consequences are low, spontaneous attitude activation should be more important. Similarly, as the time allowed for a decision is reduced, the importance of spontaneous attitude activation processes should be increased over more deliberative processes. A teen-ager at a party who is confronted with an opportunity for sexual activity in an environment with limited time for decision making, is not likely to engage in much cogitation. Thus, the salient attitudes of the moment are likely to guide choices. Unless attitudes regarding safe sex and condom use are sufficiently strong as to come to mind spontaneously, unsafe sexual activity may be selected. To the extent that prevention programs are effective in getting teen-agers to view sexual activity as a highly consequential and personally risky activity, more thought may precede the action. Or, if safe sex attitudes are initially based on considerable cognitive activity, they may come to mind spontaneously and influence behavior.

Contributions of Social Learning Theory

In some domains an accessible attitude is easily translated into behavior (e.g., I like Candidate X, I will vote for this candidate in the upcoming election). In other domains, however, translating new attitudes into new behaviors is rather complex because other attitudes may be in conflict (e.g., I like condoms, but I don't like to buy them because it's embarrassing). In addition, in the area of safe sex, people may need to acquire new skills (e.g., How do I introduce condoms into my sexual activity?) and self-perceptions (e.g., Do I have the confidence to talk to my partner about condoms?) that allow newly acquired attitudes to be translated into actions (Bandura, 1989). Furthermore, even if a new attitude produces new behavior, this new behavior may not persist in the absence of incentives. Bandura's (1986) social (cognitive) learning theory provides a framework to understand these processes.

Like the central route to persuasion and the reasoned action approaches, the social learning perspective views voluntary behavior as determined in part by the personal consequences that an individual anticipates for various courses of action (Rosenstock, Strecher, and Becker, 1988). In addition, social learning theory notes that producing behavior change may require that a person learn new actions (skills) or new sequences of already acquired actions. Learning of new skills may occur by direct experience or by observing the behavior of others (modeling). The most effective models are people who are similar to the target or people the target admires. Unfortunately, models on television and the movies are not particularly health conscious and suggest many instances of unprotected sex (Wallack, 1989). If a person develops a negative attitude toward unprotected sex and a positive attitude toward condom use, but does not have the verbal skills to say no to unsafe sex when under pressure, or does not know when or how to introduce the subject of condoms to the partner, or where and how to buy them, any attitude change may be of little use.

Another important aspect of Bandura's framework is the idea that people do not always behave optimally, even though they know the "correct" behaviors and have positive attitudes toward them. That is, people are not always motivated to translate their acquired skills into action. One particularly important cognitive determinant of whether skills are put into action concerns people's assessments of *self-efficacy* or their behavioral competence (Ajzen, 1988; Bandura, 1982; Rogers, 1983). Judgments of self-efficacy are important because considerable research indicates that the more people see themselves as capable of engaging in various health behaviors (e.g., stopping smoking), the more likely they are to be successful in maintaining the desired behavior change (e.g., Strecher, DeVellis, Becker, & Rosenstock, 1986).

IMPLICATIONS OF ATTITUDE THEORY FOR AIDS PREVENTION

Although considerable work has shown that it is possible to change people's knowledge about AIDS, we have noted that these knowledge differences do not invariably turn into attitude and behavior changes. Our brief review of basic theory and research has emphasized that although attitudes can be changed with a simple strategy of associating a message with positive cues (e.g., attractive spokespersons), these attitude changes are unlikely to be very enduring, resistant to counterveiling pressures, or result in lasting behavior change. Rather, information will be more successful in producing consequential attitude changes if people are motivated and able to think about the information presented, and this processing results in favorable cognitive and affective reactions. Furthermore, once attitudes have changed, implementation of behavior change may require learning new skills and perceptions of self-efficacy.

Thus, current work on attitude and behavior change may help to account for some unsuccessful translations of AIDS knowledge and/or attitudes into appropriate behaviors. First, the acquired knowledge may have been seen as irrelevant by the recipients, or may have led to unfavorable rather than favorable reactions. Second, even if positive attitude changes were induced, the changes may have been based on simple peripheral cues rather than elaborative processing of the message. Third, even if attitude changes were produced by the central route, the people influenced may have lacked the necessary skills or self-confidence to translate their new attitudes into action.

Perhaps the most important issue raised in our review is that although some attitudes are based on a careful reasoning process in which externally provided information is related to oneself and integrated into a coherent knowledge structure, other attitudes are formed as a result of relatively simple cues in the persuasion environment. Although both types of processes can lead to attitudes similar in their valence (how favorable or unfavorable they are), there are important consequences of the manner of attitude change. Because the goal of persuasive communications about AIDS is to produce long-lasting changes in attitudes with behavioral consequences, the central route to persuasion appears to be the preferred influence strategy. Unfortunately, this is not simple. The recipient of the new information must have the motivation and ability to process the new information.

As noted previously, one of the most important determinants of motivation to think about a message is the perceived personal relevance of that message. When personal relevance is high, people are motivated to scrutinize the information presented and integrate it with their existing beliefs, but when perceived relevance is low, messages may be ignored or processed for peripheral cues. Many people in the population may feel that AIDS messages are not relevant to them or have few consequences for them. An important goal of any education strategy will be to increase people's motivation to think about AIDS messages by increasing the perceived personal relevance of these messages. Because people tend to think of themselves as less at risk than others for a variety of health threats including HIV infection (Weinstein, 1989), increasing perceptions of vulnerability may be an important initial step in increasing the relevance of AIDS messages. Doing this will likely require changing the pervasive stereotype of the typical HIV vulnerable person as gay, promiscuous, or an IV drug user. To the extent that this stereotype remains, and people compare themselves to this stereotype, they will continue to feel invulnerable (see Perloff & Fetzer, 1986). The stereotype of the AIDS-vulnerable person needs to change so that more people can identify with it. One note of caution, however, is that if personal fear becomes too high, people may defensively avoid thinking about AIDS messages or rely on confidently presented reassurances from experts rather than their own thoughtful assessment of the validity of the expert's recommendations.

It is also important to note that even if people can be motivated to attend to and think about AIDS-relevant communications, it is critical that they respond to these messages with favorable cognitive and affective reactions. It is likely that different types of information will be responded to favorably by different segments of the population. For example, arguments that are successful in producing favorable reactions in conservative Southern Baptists may elicit mostly counter-arguments from inner-city teen-agers. Considerable research is needed on the types of messages that will engage attention and elicit favorable thoughts and implications when presented to different audiences. Thus, campaign planners will need to engage in considerable pretesting of the content of public service messages to ensure that they elicit the appropriate responses in the target populations.

Finally, even if the appropriate attitudes are changed, a new attitude cannot influence behavior if it does not come to mind prior to the opportunity for behavior, or if people lack the necessary skills or confidence to implement their new attitudes. For example, if a person has recently come to the conclusion that condoms are useful and has formed an appropriate positive attitude, this does no good if the positive attitude is not accessible when confronted with a sexual opportunity. The new favorable attitude might be retrievable, but only if cues in the environment provoke reflection. People will need to be encouraged to think before they act so that their new attitudes rather than old habits or salient situational cues are influential. As noted earlier, people will also need to acquire the behavioral skills to implement their new attitudes.

In addition, a person may have formed a tentative favorable positive attitude toward condom use, but if the person's initial experience is unpleasant or embarrassing, two contrary attitudes are formed— "condoms are supposed to be good" and "condoms are unpleasant." Because beliefs and attitudes based on direct experience come to mind more readily than attitudes that are based solely on externally provided information, the effectiveness of the positive condom attitude is at a competitive disadvantage (Fazio & Zanna, 1981). To the extent that these effects are anticipated, prevention programs can incorporate role-playing and other direct experiences in which people receive practice in dealing with these contrary feelings, should they arise.

In summary, we note that research on social influence has come a long way from the early notion that providing factual information alone was sufficient to influence attitudes and behavior. Social influence is a complex, although explicable process. We now know that the extent and nature of a person's cognitive responses to external information may be more important than learning the information itself. We know that attitudes can be changed in different ways (central vs. peripheral routes), and that some attitude changes are more stable, resistant, and predictive of behavior than others. We also know that even apparently simple variables (such as how likeable a source is) can produce persuasion by very different processes in different situations, and that some attitude changes will need to be supplemented with skills training before they will have an impact on behavior. We hope our brief review of current thinking about attitude and behavior change processes may have some utility for developing and evaluating AIDS prevention messages.

ACKNOWLEDGMENT

This chapter was supported in part by NSF grant BNS 9021647.

REFERENCES

AIDS hasn't spurred teen condom use. (1992, February 18). *Columbus Dispatch,* p. 3A.

Ajzen, I. (1988). *Attitudes, personality, and behavior.* Chicago: Dorsey Press.

Ajzen, I., & Fishbein, M. (1980). *Understanding attitudes and predicting social behavior.* Englewood Cliffs, NJ: Prentice-Hall.

Aspinwall, L. G., Kemeny, M. E., Taylor, S. E., Schneider, S. G. & Dudley, J. P. (1991). Psychosocial predictors of gay men's AIDS risk-reduction behavior. *Health Psychology, 10,* 432–444.

Bandura, A. (1982). Self-efficacy mechanism in human agency. *American Psychologist, 37,* 122–147.

Bandura, A. (1986). *Social foundations of thought and action.* Englewood Cliffs, NJ: Prentice-Hall.

Bandura, A. (1989). Perceived self-efficacy in the exercise of control over AIDS infection. V. M. Mays, G. W. Albee, & S. F. Schneider (Eds.), *Primary prevention of AIDS: Psychological approaches* (pp. 128–141). Newbury Park, CA: Sage.

Becker, M., & Joseph, J. (1988). AIDS and behavioral change to reduce risk. *American Journal of Public Health, 78,* 394–410.

Botvin, G. J., Baker, E., Renick, N. L., Filazzola, A. D., & Botvin, E. N. (1984). A cognitive-behavioral approach to substance abuse prevention. *Addictive Behaviors, 9,* 137–147.

Burnkrant, R., & Unnava, R. (1989). Self-referencing: A strategy for increasing processing of message content. *Personality and Social Psychology Bulletin, 15,* 628–638.

Cacioppo, J. T., & Petty, R. E. (1982). The need for cognition. *Journal of Personality and Social Psychology, 42,* 116–131.

Cacioppo, J. T., & Petty, R. E. (1989). Effects of message repetition on argument processing, recall, and persuasion. *Basic and Applied Social Psychology, 10,* 3–12.

Cacioppo, J. T., Petty, R. E., & Morris, K. (1983). Effects of need for cognition on message evaluation, argument recall, and persuasion. *Journal of Personality and Social Psychology, 45,* 805–818.

Carroll, J. S. (1978). The effect of imagining an event on expectations for the event: An interpretation in terms of the availability heuristic. *Journal of Personality and Social Psychology, 36,* 1501–1511.

Catania, J. A., Coates, T. J., Kegeles, S. M., Ekstrand, M., Guydish, J. R., & Bye, L. L. (1989). In V. M. Mays, G. W. Albee, & S. F. Schneider (Eds.), *Primary prevention of AIDS: Psychological approaches* (pp. 242–263). Newbury Park, CA: Sage.

Catania, J. A., Kegeles, S. M., & Coates, T. J. (1990). Towards an understanding of risk behavior: An AIDS risk reduction model (AARM). *Health Education Quarterly, 17,* 52–72.

Chaiken, S. (1987). The heuristic model of persuasion. In M. P. Zanna, J. Olson, & C. Herman (Eds.), *Social influence: The Ontario symposium* (pp. 3–39). Hillsdale, NJ: Lawrence Erlbaum & Associates.

Chaiken, S., Liberman, A., & Eagly, A. (1989). Heuristic and systematic information processing within and beyond the persuasion context. In J. S. Uleman & J. A. Bargh (Eds.), *Unintended thought: Limits of awareness, intention, and control* (pp. 212–252). New York: Guilford.

Cialdini, R. B., Gregory, L. W., & Carpenter, K. M. (1982). Self-relevant scenarios as mediators of likelihood estimates and compliance: Does imagining make it so? *Journal of Personality and Social Psychology, 43,* 89–99.

DeJong, W. (1987). A short term evaluation of project DARE (drug abuse resistance education): Preliminary indications of effectiveness. *Journal of Drug Education, 17,* 279–293.

Donohew, L., Lorch, E., & Palmgreen, P. (1991). Sensation seeking and targeting of televised anti-drug PSAs. In L. Donohew, H. E. Sypher, & W. J. Bukoski (Eds.), *Persuasive communication and drug abuse prevention* (pp. 209–228). Hillsdale, NJ: Lawrence Erlbaum Associates.

Fazio, R. H. (1990). Multiple processes by which attitudes guide behavior: The MODE model as an integrative framework. In M. Zanna (Ed.), *Advances in experimental social psychology* (Vol. 23, pp. 75–109). New York: Academic Press.

Fazio, R. H., & Zanna, M. P. (1981). Direct experience and attitude-behavior consistency. In L. Berkowitz (Ed.), *Advances in Experimental Social Psychology* (Vol. 14, pp. 162–203). New York: Academic Press.

Fishbein, M., & Ajzen, I. (1975). *Belief, attitude, intention, and behavior: An introduction to theory and research.* Reading, MA: Addison-Wesley.

Fishbein, M., & Middlestadt, S. E. (1989). Using the theory of reasoned action as a framework for understanding and changing AILS-related behaviors. In V. M. Mays, G. W. Albee, & S. F. Schneider (Eds.), *Primary prevention of AIDS: Psychological approaches* (pp. 93–110). Newbury Park, CA: Sage.

Fisher, J. D., & Fisher, W. A. (1992). Changing AIDS-Risk behavior. *Psychological Bulletin, 111,* 455–474.

Fisher, J. D., & Misovich, S. J. (1990). Social influence and AIDS-preventive behavior. In Edwards, J., Tindale, R. S., Heath, L., & Posavac, E. J. (Eds.), *Social influence processes and prevention* (pp. 39–70). Hillsdale, NJ: Lawrence Erlbaum Associates.

Flora, J. A., & Maibach, E. W. (1990). Cognitive responses to AIDS information: The effect of issue involvement and message appeal. *Communication Research, 17,* 759–774.

Friedman, S. R., Des Jarlais, D. C., & Sotheran, J. L. (1986). AIDS health education for intravenous drug users. *Health Education Quarterly, 13,* 383–393.

Gantz, W., & Greenberg, B. S. (1990). The role of informative television programs in the battle against AIDS. *Health Communication, 2,* 199–215.

Gleicher, F., & Petty, R. E. (1992). Expectations of reassurance influence the nature of fear-stimulated attitude change. *Journal of Experimental Social Psychology, 28,* 86–100.

Gray, L., & Saracino, M. (1989). AIDS on campus: A preliminary study of college students' knowledge and behaviors. *Journal of Counseling and development, 68,* 199–202.

Greenwald, A. G. (1968). Cognitive learning, cognitive response to persuasion, and attitude change. In A. Greenwald, T. Brock, & T. Ostrom (Eds.), *Psychological foundations of attitudes* (pp. 147–170). New York: Academic Press.

Harkins, S. G., & Petty, R. E. (1983). Social context effects in persuasion: The effects of multiple sources and targets. In P. Paulus (Ed.), *Advances in group psychology* (pp. 149–175). New York: Springer-Verlag.

Haugtvedt, C., & Petty, R. E. (1992). Personality and attitude change: Need for cognition moderates the persistence and resistance of persuasion. *Journal of Personality and Social Psychology, 63,* 308–319.

Heider, F. (1958). *The psychology of interpersonal relations.* New York: Wiley.

Herek, G. M. (1990). Illness, stigma, and AIDS. In P. T. Costa & G. R. VandenBos (Eds.), *Psychological aspects of serious illness: chronic conditions, fatal diseases, and clinical care* (pp. 107–149). Washington, DC: American Psychological Association.

Hoverstad, R., & Howard-Pitney, B. (1986). Involvement in heart health issues: A field experiment. In *Advances in health care research* (pp. 18–21). Snowbird, UT: American Association for Advances in Health Care Research.

Janis, I. (1967). Effects of fear arousal on attitude change: Recent developments in theory and experimental research. In L. Berkowitz (Ed.), *Advances in experimental social psychology* (Vol. 3, pp. 166–224). New York: Academic Press.

Janz, N. K., & Becker, M. H. (1984). The health belief model: A decade later. *Health Education Quarterly, 11,* 1–47.

Jordheim, A. E. (1975). A comparison of the effects of peer teaching, and traditional instruction in venereal disease education with criterion measures of knowledge, attitudes, and behavioral intentions. *Dissertation Abstracts International, 35,* 5970B–5971B.

Joseph, J. G., Montgomery, S. B., Emmons, C. A., Kirscht, J. P., Kessler, R. C., Ostrow, D. G., Wortman, C. B., O'Brien, K., Eller, M., & Eshleman, S. (1987). Perceived Risk of AIDS: Assessing the behavioral and psychosocial consequences in a cohort of gay men. *Journal of Applied Social Psychology, 17,* 231–250.

Kelly, J. A., St. Lawrence, J. S., Hood, H. V., & Brashfield, T. L. (1989). Behavioral intervention to reduce AIDS risk activities. *Journal of Consulting and Clinical Psychology, 57,* 60–67.

Klein, D. E., Sullivan, G., Wolcott, D. L., Landsverk, J., Namir, S., & Fawzy, F. I. (1987). Changes in AIDS risk behaviors among homosexual male physicians and university students. *American Journal of Psychiatry, 144,* 742–747.

Leventhal, H. (1970). Findings and theory in the study of fear communications. In L. Berkowitz (Ed.), *Advances in experimental social psychology* (Vol. 5, pp. 120–186). New York: Academic Press.

McGuire, W. J. (1968). Personality and susceptibility to social influence. In E. F. Borgatta & W. W. Lambert (Eds.), *Handbook of personality theory and research* (pp. 1130–1188). Chicago: Rand McNally.

McGuire, W. J. (1985). Attitudes and attitude change. In G. Lindzey & E. Aronson (Eds.), *Handbook of social psychology* (Vol. 2, 3rd ed. pp. 233–346). New York: Random House.

McGuire, W. J. (1989). Theoretical foundations of campaigns. In R. Rice & W. Paisley (Eds.), *Public communication campaigns* (pp. 43–65). Newbury Park, CA: Sage.

McGuire, W. J. (1964). Inducing resistance to persuasion: Some contemporary approaches. In L. Berkowitz (Ed). *Advances in experimental social psychology* (Vol., 1 pp. 192–231). New York: Academic.

McKusick, L., Conant, M., & Coates, T. J. (1985). The AIDS epidemic: A model for developing intervention strategies for reducing high-risk behavior in gay men. *Sexually Transmitted Diseases, 12,* 229–234.

Montgomery, K., Freeman, H. E., & Lewis, C. E. (1989). Coverage and readership of the U.S. Surgeon General's AIDS pamphlet in Los Angeles. *Medical Care, 27,* 758–761.

Olson, J. M., & Zanna, M. P. (in press). Attitudes and attitude change. *Annual Review of Psychology, 44.*

Paisley, W. (1989). Public communication campaigns: The American experience. In R. E. Rice & C. K. Atkin (Eds.), *Public communication campaigns* (2nd ed., pp. 15–41). Newbury Park, CA: Sage.

Perloff, L. S., & Fetzer, B. K. (1986). Self-other judgments and perceived vulnerability to victimization. *Journal of Personality and Social Psychology, 50,* 502–511.

Petty, R. E., & Cacioppo, J. T. (1979a). Effects of forewarning of persuasive intent on cognitive responses and persuasion. *Personality and Social Psychology Bulletin, 5,* 173–176.

Petty, R. E., & Cacioppo, J. T. (1979b). Issue-involvement can increase or decrease persuasion by enhancing message-relevant cognitive responses. *Journal of Personality and Social Psychology, 37,* 1915–1926.

Petty, R. E., & Cacioppo, J. T. (1981). *Attitudes and persuasion: Classic and contemporary approaches.* Dubuque: Wm. C. Brown.

Petty, R. E., Cacioppo, J. T. (1984). Motivational factors in consumer response to advertisements. In W. Beatty, R. Geen, & R. Arkin (Eds.), *Human motivation* (pp. 418–454). New York: Allyn & Bacon.

Petty, R. E., & Cacioppo, J. T. (1986). *Communication and persuasion: Central and peripheral routes to attitude change.* New York: Springer-Verlag.

Petty, R. E., & Cacioppo, J. T. (1990). Involvement and persuasion: Tradition versus integration. *Psychological Bulletin, 107,* 367–374.

Petty, R. E., Cacioppo, J. T., & Goldman, R. (1981). Personal involvement as a determinant of argument-based persuasion. *Journal of Personality and Social Psychology, 41,* 847–855.

Petty, R. E., Cacioppo, J. T., & Haugtvedt, C. (1992). Involvement and persuasion: An appreciative look at the Sherifs' contribution to the study of self-relevance and attitude change. In D. Granberg & G. Sarup (Eds.), *Social judgment and intergroup relations: Essays in honor of Muzafer Sherif* (pp. 147–175). New York: Springer-Verlag.

Petty, R. E., Cacioppo, J. T., & Heesacker, M. (1981). The use of rhetorical questions in persuasion: A cognitive response analysis. *Journal of Personality and Social Psychology, 40,* 432–440.

Petty, R. E., Cacioppo, J. T., & Schumann, D. (1983). Central and peripheral routes to advertising effectiveness: The moderating role of involvement. *Journal of Consumer Research, 10,* 135–146.

Petty, R. E., Gleicher, F., & Baker, S. (1991). Multiple roles for affect in persuasion. In J. Forgas (Ed.), *Emotion and social judgments* (pp. 181–200). Oxford: Pergamon.

Petty, R. E., & Haugtvedt, C. (in press). Elaboration as a determinant of attitude strength. In R. E. Petty & J. A. Krosnick (Eds.). *Attitude strength: Antecedents and consequences.* Hillsdale, NJ: Lawrence Erlbaum Associates.

Petty, R. E., Ostrom, T. M., & Brock, T. C. (Eds.). (1981). *Cognitive responses in persuasion.* Hillsdale, NJ: Lawrence Erlbaum Associates.

Petty, R. E., & Priester, J. (in press). Mass media attitude change: Implications of the Elaboration Likelihood Model. In J. Bryant & D. Zillmann (Eds.), *Media effects: Advances in theory and research* Hillsdale, NJ: Lawrence Erlbaum Associates.

Petty, R. E., Unnava, R., & Strathman, A. (1991). Theories of attitude change. In H. Kassarjian & T. Robertson (Eds.). *Handbook of consumer theory and research* (pp. 241–280). Englewood Cliffs, NJ: Prentice–Hall.

Petty, R. E., Wells, G. L., & Brock, T. C. (1976). Distraction can enhance or reduce yielding to propaganda. *Journal of Personality and Social Psychology, 34,* 874–884.

Pratkanis, A. R., Greenwald, A. G., Leippe, M. R., & Baumgardner, M. H. (1988). In search of reliable persuasion effects: III. The sleeper effect is dead. Long live the sleeper effect. *Journal of Personality and Social Psychology, 54,* 203–218.

Radius, S. M., Dielman, T. E., Becker, M. H., Rosenstock, I. M., & Horvath, W. J. (1980). Adolescent perspectives on health and illness. *Adolescence, 15,* 375–384.

Reardon, K. K. (1989). The potential role of persuasion in adolescent AIDS prevention. In R. E. Rice & C. K. Atkin (Eds.)., *Public communication campaigns* (2nd ed., pp. 273–289). Newbury Park, CA: Sage.

Rhodes, N., & Wood, W. (1992). Self-esteem and intelligence affect influenceability: The mediating role of message reception. *Psychological Bulletin, 111,* 156–171.

Rogers, R. W. (1983). Cognitive and physiological processes in fear appeals and attitude change: A revised theory of protection motivation. In J. T. Cacioppo & R. E. Petty (Eds.), *Social psychophysiology: A sourcebook* (pp. 153–176). New York: Guilford.

Rook, K. S. (1986). Encouraging preventive behavior for distant and proximal health threats. Effects of vivid versus abstract information. *Journal of Gerontology, 41,* 526–534.

Rosenstock, I. M. (1974). Historical origins of the health belief model. *Health Education Monographs, 2,* 328–335.

Rosenstock, I. M., Strecher, V. J., & Becker, M. H. (1988) Social learning theory and the health belief model. *Health Education Quarterly, 15,* 175–183.

Sherman, S. J., Cialdini, R. B., Schwartzman, D. F., & Reynolds, K. D. (1985). Imagining can heighten or lower the perceived likelihood of contracting a disease: The mediating effect of ease of imagery. *Personality and Social Psychology Bulletin, 11,* 118–127.

Sherr, L. (1987). An evaluation of the UK government health education campaign on AIDS. *Psychology and Health, 1,* 61–72.

Singer, E., Rogers, T. F., & Glassman, M. B. (1991). Public opinion about AIDS before and after the 1988 U. S. Government public information campaign. *Public Opinion Quarterly, 55,* 161–179.

Snyder, L. B. (1991). The impact of the Surgeon General's "Understanding AIDS" pamphlet in Connecticut. *Health Communication, 3,* 37–57.

Solomon, M., & DeJong, W. (1986). Recent sexually transmitted disease prevention efforts and their implications for AIDS health education. *Health Education Quarterly, 13,* 310–316.

Stall, R. D., Coates, T. J., & Hoff, C. (1988). Behavioral risk reduction for HIV infection among gay and bisexual men: A review of the results from the United States. *American Psychologist, 43,* 878–885.

Staats, A. W., & Staats, C. (1958). Attitudes established by classical conditioning. *Journal of Abnormal and Social Psychology, 67,* 159–167.

Strecher, V. J., DeVellis, B. M., Becker, M. H., & Rosenstock, I. M. (1986). The role of self-efficacy in achieving health behavior change. *Health Education Quarterly, 13,* 73–91.

Strong, E. K. (1925). *The psychology of selling and advertising.* New York: McGraw Hill.

Tesser, A., & Shaffer, D. (1990). Attitudes and attitude change. *Annual Review of Psychology, 41,* 479–523.

Verplanken, B. (1991). Persuasive communication of risk information: A test of cue versus message processing effects in a field experiment. *Personality and Social Psychology Bulletin, 17,* 188–193.

Wallack, L. (1989). Mass communication and health promotion: A critical perspective. In R. E. Rice & C. K. Atkin (Eds)., *Public communication campaigns* (2nd ed., pp. 353–367). Newbury Park, CA: Sage.

Weinstein, N. D. (1989). Perceptions of personal susceptibility to harm. In V. M. Mays, G. W. Albee, & S. F. Schneider (Eds.), *Primary prevention of AIDS: Psychological approaches* (pp. 142–167). Newbury Park, CA: Sage.

Zuckerman, M. (1974). Sensation seeking. In H. London & J. Exner (Eds.), *Dimensions of personality.* (pp. 173–189). New York: Wiley.

7

Social Psychology and AIDS Among Ethnic Minority Individuals: Risk Behaviors and Strategies for Changing Them

John B. Jemmott, III
Princeton University

James M. Jones
University of Delaware

Acquired immune deficiency syndrome (AIDS) is a life-threatening disease caused by infection with the human immunodeficiency virus (HIV), which attacks the immune system and damages resistance to infection and neoplasm. Although there is no cure for AIDS, nor is a vaccine available, AIDS is preventable. HIV infection is transmitted by exposure to infected blood, semen, and vaginal secretions, usually through sexual activities or the sharing of hypodermic needles and other drug paraphernalia by injection drug users. Hence, curbing the spread of AIDS requires the development of interventions to alter the behavior of those who risk infecting themselves or other people. Such interventions are likely to be most effective if they address the determinants of risky behaviors. In this connection, social psychological factors, including beliefs, attitudes, self-regulatory processes, role constraints, social norms, and situational variables, are all likely to be important.

This chapter considers the application of social psychology to HIV risk-associated behavior among ethnic minority individuals, specifically Blacks and Hispanics. Although in the United States the largest number of reported AIDS cases have involved White men who engaged in same-gender sexual activities, AIDS has levied a heavy toll on Blacks and Hispanics. Seroprevalence surveys (Centers for Disease Control [CDC], 1990) have indicated higher rates of HIV infection among Black and Hispanic individuals as compared with White individuals.

For example, as shown in Fig. 7.1, data on civilian applicants for military service have revealed a higher cumulative seroprevalence for Blacks and Hispanics than for American Indians, Alaskan Natives, Whites, or Asians and Pacific Islanders (CDC, 1990). HIV seroprevalence surveys of women's health

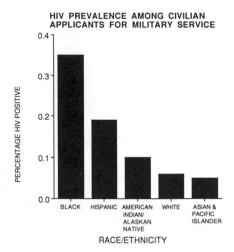

FIG. 7.1.   HIV prevalence among civilian applicants for military service, October 1985 through December 1989, United States, by race/ethnicity (source: CDC, 1990).

clinics in 39 metropolitan areas have indicated higher seroprevalence rates among Black women patients than among White and Hispanic women patients. Similarly, higher seroprevalence rates have been observed among Blacks and Hispanics than among Whites (CDC, 1990) in data on entrants to Job Corps, a residential job-training program for urban and rural disadvantaged youth ages 16 to 21 years. Blacks and Hispanics are also over represented among reported AIDS cases. Although Black individuals comprise 12% of the U. S. population,

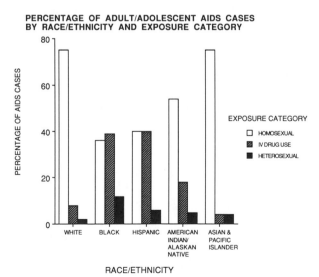

FIG. 7.2.   Percentage of adult/adolescent AIDS cases by race/ethnicity and exposure category, reported through July 1991, United States (source: CDC, 1991a).

27% of the reported AIDS cases have involved Black individuals. Hispanics represent 8% of the U.S. population, but make up 16% of persons with AIDS (CDC, 1991a). The racial and ethnic group disparity in reported AIDS cases is particularly great among women and children. As of July 1991, Black women accounted for 52% of the reported female AIDS cases, Hispanic women accounted for 20%, and White women accounted for only 26%. Moreover, 53% of pediatric AIDS cases were Black children, 25% were Hispanic children, and only 21% were White children.

The profile of AIDS among Black and Hispanic individuals differs in several important respects from the profile in Whites. HIV exposure as a result of injection drug use, heterosexual sexual activity, and perinatal transmission are far more common in the Black and Hispanic populations than in the White population, where the overwhelming majority of the reported cases of AIDS have been tied to male homosexual activities (CDC, 1991a). As shown in Fig. 7.2, as of July 1991, 76% of AIDS cases among Whites have involved HIV exposure related to male homosexual/bisexual contact, 8% have involved injection drug use, and 2% have involved heterosexual contact. In contrast 40% of cases among Hispanics have involved HIV exposure related to male homosexual/bisexual activity, 40% have involved injection drug use, and 6% have involved heterosexual contact. Among Blacks, 36% of cases have involved HIV exposure related to male homosexual/bisexual activity, 38% have involved injection drug use, and 12% have involved heterosexual contact.

Although perinatal exposure accounts for the majority of pediatric AIDS cases irrespective of race/ethnicity, perinatal exposure has been far more common among Blacks and Hispanics than among Whites. Thus, perinatal exposure has accounted for 92% of pediatric AIDS cases among Blacks and 87% of pediatric AIDS cases among Hispanics, but only 62% of such cases among Whites (CDC, 1991a). These statistics suggest that although exposure through male same-gender sexual contact is a significant risk factor, prevention efforts with Blacks and Hispanics should focus to a greater extent than for Whites, on individuals who engage in injection drug use, sexually active heterosexuals, and women of childbearing age.

HIV Risk-Associated Sexual Behavior Among Blacks and Hispanics

Epidemiological studies have identified sexual behaviors that increase risk of sexually transmitted infection (Hatcher et al., 1990), and these behaviors are risky with respect to HIV infection. Thus, HIV risk-associated sexual behaviors include having sex (vaginal or anal) that is unprotected (i.e., without a condom), having many sexual partners, and having sex with partners who engage in high-risk behaviors such as injection drug use. The best way, of course, to avoid sexually transmitted infection, including HIV infection, is to practice abstinence.

However, avoiding these high-risk sexual behaviors should decrease substantially the chances of HIV infection. Next, we review the literature on the extent to which the sexual practices of ethnic minority individuals contribute to risk of HIV infection.

Failure to Use Condoms During Coitus.   In general, there are scant data on the prevalence of sexual behaviors other than coitus and contraceptive usage among Blacks and Hispanics (Darabi, Dryfoos, & Schwartz, 1986). Data on Black and Hispanic men are particularly limited. This is problematic because males often initiate sexual activity and because the best method of preventing HIV infection, the condom, must be implemented by men. Indeed, the failure to use condoms during sexual activity is perhaps the most common HIV risk-associated behavior among heterosexuals. Although few data are available on adults, studies suggest that substantial numbers of ethnic minority adolescents engage in unprotected coitus.

More than 50% of U.S. adolescents have had sexual intercourse before they are 18 years of age (CDC, 1991b; Jones et al., 1986; Taylor, Kagay, & Leichenko, 1986; Zelnik & Kantner, 1980). National surveys of female adolescents consistently have indicated that a greater proportion of Blacks than Whites or Latinos report sexual experience (CDC, 1991b; Hofferth & Hayes, 1987; Pratt, Mosher, Bachrach, & Horn, 1984; Taylor et al., 1986), even when socio-economic background is statistically controlled (Hofferth, Kahn, & Baldwin, 1987). Similarly, in a recent nationally representative survey, nearly 81% of Black males between the ages of 15 and 19 years reported having had coitus at least once, whereas only about 60% of Latino and 57% of White males in that age group reported such experience (Sonenstein, Pleck, & Leighton, 1989).

Much of this adolescent sexual activity occurs without protection from pregnancy and sexually transmitted diseases (STDs). About 1 in 10 U.S. women become pregnant during their high school years, and roughly 85% of these pregnancies are unintended (Jones et al., 1986; Pratt, et al., 1984). Adolescents have higher rates of chlamydia, gonorrhea, syphilis, and hospitalization for pelvic inflammatory disease than any other age group (Bell & Holmes, 1984). The risks of unprotected sexual activity are particularly problematic among inner-city Black adolescents. The adolescent pregnancy rate is nearly twice as high among Blacks as among Whites. Moreover, the incidence of STDs is two to three times greater among Blacks than among Whites, and low-income people in urban areas are more likely to contract an STD than are people of higher income or those who reside in suburban or rural areas (Cates, 1987; Hatcher et al., 1990; Jones et al., 1986; Pratt et al., 1984; Zelnik, Kantner, & Ford, 1981).

More direct evidence of unprotected coitus among adolescents comes from national surveys of contraceptive utilization. In general, the first contraceptive methods that adolescents use are male methods such as the condom and withdrawal before ejaculation. As they grow older and more sexually experienced, they switch to female methods, particularly the pill (Jemmott & Jemmott, 1990; Pleck, 1989). Thus, as adolescents grow older, their risk of pregnancy declines, but their risk of sexually transmitted infection may increase. Younger adolescents who are having sex for the first time are particularly unlikely to use any contraception (Zelnik et al., 1981). Blacks are less likely than are Whites to use any contraception at first coitus. This is explained at least in part by younger age of first coitus among Blacks. However, the failure to use condoms is also common among older, more sexually experienced individuals. For instance, Jemmott and Jemmott (1991) conducted a survey of sexually active Black women who were undergraduates at a university located in an inner-city area of New Jersey and found that only 20% reported always using a condom when they had sex in the previous 3 months. A report by Mosher and Pratt (1990) on women 15–44 years of age in the National Survey of Family Growth indicated that Black women were more likely than were White women to report having intercourse in the previous 3 months without using a contraceptive method. Moreover, among those who reported using contraception, Black women were significantly more likely than were White women to use the most effective female methods—female sterilization and the pill—whereas White women were more likely to use the condom. These racial differences in condom use occurred despite the fact that women who had never married were more likely to use condoms and a greater percentage of Black women as compared with White women had never married (London, 1991).

Evidence suggests that Hispanic adolescents are less likely than are non-Hispanic Black and White adolescents to use contraceptives. Namerow and Jones (1982) found that a smaller percentage of Dominican and Puerto Ricans as compared with Black and White clients at an adolescent family planning clinic had ever used birth control before coming to the clinic. Lindemann and Scott (1982) found that fewer Mexican American, as compared with White and Black, pregnant adolescents reported previously using birth control.

It has been suggested that awareness of the AIDS epidemic may be having an ameliorative impact on condom use. Sonenstein et al. (1989) found that 58% of sexually active 17- to 19-year-old Black and White male adolescents living in metropolitan areas in 1988 reported using condoms the last time they had coitus. This represents a substantial increase from 1979 levels, when only 21% of 17- to 19-year-old Black and White male adolescents living in metropolitan areas reported condom use at last coitus. Similarly, Mosher and Pratt (1990) found a rise in condom usage among women 15–44 years of age, this time comparing 1982 levels and 1988 levels.

Taken together, these data suggest that Blacks and Latinos are at risk due to failure to use condoms during coitus. The fact that increasing percentages of adolescents and women are reporting use of condoms is encouraging. It raises the prospect that condom use is malleable and may be subject to influence by psychological interventions.

Multiple Sexual Partners.   Having a large number of sexual partners would also increase the risk of sexually transmitted infection. There is little evidence that Blacks and Whites differ in number of sexual partners. Zelnik et al. (1981) reported national survey data indicating that Black female adolescents between the ages of 15 and 19 years in 1971 and 1976 had fewer premarital sexual partners than did their White counterparts, controlling for socioeconomic status (SES), family stability, religion, religiosity, and years of sexual experience. Belcastro (1985) found no difference in total number of heterosexual partners reported by Black and White undergraduate students at a midwestern university. Wyatt, Peters, and Guthrie (1988a, 1988b) found that 52% of White women ages 18–36 years reported having had 11 or more sexual partners since age 18 years, but in a matched sample of Black women, the figure was only 29%.

Noncoital Sexual Behaviors.   Research on sexual behavior, for the most part, has focused on coitus with the aim of understanding fertility. Consequently, little is known about the dynamics of noncoital sexual behaviors such as anal intercourse and oral sex. This is unfortunate because the behavior associated with the most well-documented risk for sexual transmission of HIV is unprotected receptive anal intercourse. Although chiefly associated with homosexual men, there is growing recognition that it is a fairly common practice among heterosexuals (Reinisch, Sanders, & Ziemba-Davis, 1988). Much better data are available on the noncoital sexual behaviors of White middle-class well-educated individuals than on the noncoital sexual behaviors of other populations, but the available evidence suggests that these behaviors may be somewhat less common among Blacks than among Whites. Drawing on data from seven studies, Reinisch et al. (1988) estimated that 39% (range =20%–43%) of White middle-class women had ever participated in anal intercourse. In contrast, a study of Black college students at an east coast university revealed a relatively low incidence of anal intercourse among Black women. Only 10% of Black women reported ever experiencing anal intercourse (Thomas, Gilliam, & Iwrey, 1989). In a similar vein, Jemmott and Jemmott (1991) found that only 16% of Black female undergraduates at a university in an inner-city area of New Jersey reported ever experiencing anal sex. One of the few studies to compare noncoital sexual behaviors in Blacks and Whites was Wyatt et al.'s (1988a, 1988b) study of women ages 18 to 36 years in the Los Angeles area. The study revealed that 21% of Black women, as compared with 43% of a matched sample of White women, reported having ever experienced anal intercourse.

As in the case of anal intercourse, evidence suggests tentatively that although oral sex is common among both Blacks and Whites, it may be less common among Blacks. For instance, studying college students, Belcastro (1985) found that reports of ever engaging in heterosexual oral sex were lower among Black men and women than among their White counterparts. About 48% of the Black women, as compared with 81% of the White women, reported having engaged in fellatio. In addition, 34% of Black women, as compared with 50% of White women, reported having engaged in cunnilingus with a man. Among male students, Blacks (50%) were less likely to report having engaged in cunnilingus than were Whites (72%), although they were only nonsignificantly less likely to report experiencing heterosexual fellatio. Wyatt et al. (1988a, 1988b) also found evidence of less oral sex among Blacks: 87% of White women and 70% of Black women reported ever engaging in cunnilingus with a man, and 93% of White women, but only 65% of Black women reported ever engaging in fellatio.

The studies reviewed thus far have focused primarily on the sexual behavior of Blacks. Unfortunately, there are few studies on the sexual behavior of Hispanics (Darabi et al., 1986). In fact, many of the major nation wide studies of sexual behavior (e.g., the 1971, 1976, and 1977 National Survey of Young Women) either have not included Hispanics or have not categorized respondents as Hispanic. In addition, studies that have included Hispanics typically have aggregated different Hispanic groups. The trouble is that the risks, experiences, and behaviors of Puerto Ricans, Mexican Americans, and Cuban Americans, for instance, may be markedly different. In this connection, Selik, Castro, Pappaioanou, and Buehler (1989) reported that although the risk of AIDS is elevated among Hispanics in the United States, the cumulative incidence of AIDS in persons of Mexican ethnicity was similar to that among non-Hispanic Whites, whereas the cumulative incidence of AIDS in persons of Puerto Rican and Cuban descent exceeded that of Whites.

Cultural Sensitivity

As we have seen, HIV transmission involves behaviors that may occur with differential frequency across ethnic minority groups. The moralistic and normative interpretations of such behaviors are also likely to vary somewhat across groups. For example, sexual behavior among unmarried persons as well as contraceptive practices carry different meanings for cultural groups that are predominantly Catholic, such as many Hispanics, than for those that are Protestant. The African-American community has tended to ignore the homosexual aspects of HIV transmission and thus has rejected the threat of AIDS, in part, as a result of rejecting the reality of homosexual practices within the community. By the same token, individual African-American heterosexuals may reject risk of HIV because they may view AIDS as a disease of White gay men (Mays & Cochran, 1988).

Perhaps even more significant is the fact that many African Americans believe that the linkage of the HIV to Africa and the somewhat explosive penetration of the virus in the Black community is consistent with a racist genocide origin in White America. This belief can be understood in part as a consequence of feelings of alienation and distrust and of an escalation of hate acts perpetrated by Whites against Blacks. Ironically, rejecting messages and programs designed to modify behavior in a safer, protective direction may be one way of resisting what is perceived as manipulation by Whites. The reactions to centuries of racism cannot be ignored in attempts to understand racial, ethnic, and cultural responses to the AIDS crisis.

A number of writers have emphasized the importance of adopting a culturally sensitive approach when considering the HIV risk-associated behavior of African Americans, Latinos, and other ethnic minority individuals. The historical and contemporary experiences of Whites and members of ethnic minority groups have been markedly different; and, accordingly, different forces may underlie the behavior of ethnic minority individuals as opposed to White individuals. Although many researchers would concur that culture must have some relevance to risk behavior and to efforts to change risk behavior, the important questions of how culture is relevant and of what constitutes a culturally sensitive approach have been addressed less adequately. Several writers have pointed out the necessity of culturally appropriate interventions, but researchers have not demonstrated empirically the efficacy of such culturally appropriate interventions as compared with interventions developed on and for White populations. The issue of cultural sensitivity arises in at least three ways: ethnocentrism, generalizability of particular empirical relations, and the applicability of theories. Each has important implications of AIDS research.

First, researchers or theorists who lack knowledge about a culture may misinterpret the behavior of individuals from that culture. Research findings might be interpreted in ways that are biased toward the theorists' or researchers' own groups' perceptions of that culture. Because of past and contemporary racism, stereotyping, and segregation in United States, researchers may harbor stereotypes or may lack insight into the lives of ethnic minority individuals, and these limitations might influence unwittingly their interpretations of the behavior of ethnic minority individuals. Another way in which ethnocentrism can have an effect is in the labeling of psychological dimensions. In cases where it is possible to view psychological dimensions in value-neutral terms, racial or ethnic differences might be given an ethnocentric spin. For instance, the end of the dimension associated with Whites might be given a positive, psychologically healthy label, whereas the end of the dimension associated with ethnic minority individuals might be given a negative, psychopathologic label. The behavior of Whites is automatically normative, whereas what ethnic minority individuals do, unless Whites also do it, is abnormal or at the very least, questionable.

Quite apart from interpretations of study results, a second way in which the issue of cultural sensitivity arises is in relation to the generalizability of empirical findings on White populations to ethnic minority populations. The need to devise prevention strategies is generating a large literature on the social and psychological factors that influence the tendency to engage in behaviors that increase risk of infection with HIV (Fisher & Fisher, 1992; Kalichman, Kelly, & St. Lawrence, 1990; Kelly & Murphy, 1992). Included in this impressive body of empirical studies are cross-sectional studies, longitudinal studies, and even a few experiments that have tested the efficacy of specific risk-reduction interventions. However, the subjects in this research, for the most part, have been Whites. Much less empirical research has investigated the factors that underlie risk behavior among ethnic minority individuals. In this light, the issue of whether findings of studies on Whites generalize to ethnic minority individuals is particularly important. If the findings do generalize, then the research on Whites can be used to inform interventions for ethnic minority individuals. To the extent that findings do not generalize, however, interventions for ethnic minority individuals that are based on the results of studies of White individuals may have less than optimal impact. What is needed is an analysis of the features of African American or Latino life that might affect the applicability of findings and empirical evidence confirming where findings generalize and where they do not.

A third and closely related way in which the issue of cultural sensitivity arises is the extent to which the theories that have been used to explain the behavior of Whites have application to the behavior of ethnic minority individuals. The issue is difficult to address with the empirical data currently available because of the dearth of published comparative studies that bear on this issue directly. There is reason to believe, however, that many social psychological theories that are relevant to AIDS have broad application to both Whites and ethnic minority individuals. Indeed, social psychological theories, in some cases, may provide important insights regarding how to implement a culturally sensitive approach. This is not to say that ethnicity and culture are unimportant. The specifics of how theories apply may vary in different ethnic groups. For instance, certain determinants suggested by a given theory might prove to be more critical in one ethnic group than in another. The important point, however, is that the desire to implement a culturally appropriate intervention with ethnic minority individuals may not necessarily mean that a special theory is required. Social psychological theories might suggest different interventions for different ethnic groups. A general theory of attitude change, for instance, might provide a way of viewing similarities and differences among ethnic groups, and knowledge of theoretically relevant ethnic group differences might provide insight into the specific dynamics of attitude change in the ethnic groups.

SOCIAL PSYCHOLOGICAL MODELS OF ATTITUDE AND ATTITUDE CHANGE

Over the years, social psychologists have explored in intimate detail, the mechanisms by which an individual's evaluative orientation toward an attitude object can be modified (Hovland, Janis, & Kelley, 1953; Petty & Cacioppo, 1986). We know that source, message, and audience effects are important, as is the extent to which the individual considers the issue to be significant. Previous discussions about cultural sensitivity suggest that there may well be differential importance placed on HIV transmission, its threat to health, and the relative normative support for changing behavior as a function of racial or ethnic group membership. One of the significant implications of differential importance is the route to attitude change. Petty and Cacioppo (1986) distinguished central from peripheral routes to persuasion and showed that carefully constructed, logical, two-sided messages may be more effective for important issues that are processed centrally. However, if the issue is not important, such strong messages may be less persuasive or even may be ignored. Less important issues can be more readily influenced, according to Petty and Cacioppo, via peripheral avenues such as attractive or well-known communication sources.

More broadly, the point to consider is whether models of attitudes and attitude change can accommodate ethnic/racial differences in ways that help us understand the best approaches to changing attitudes that sustain high-risk behaviors. In the following pages, we consider how two widely known social psychological theories—McGuire's (1969, 1985) input/output model of persuasive communication and Fishbein and Ajzen's theory of reasoned action, including its extension the theory of planned behavior—might apply to HIV risk-associated behavior among Black and Hispanic individuals.

McGuire's Input/Output Model of Persuasive Communication

A central goal of AIDS risk-reduction research is to dissuade people from engaging in HIV risk-associated behavior. Although McGuire's (1969, 1985) model of persuasive communication has not been applied in such efforts, it provides some valuable insights. The model, which highlights features of successful persuasion attempts, has two key dimensions: inputs and outputs. The input variables are characteristics of communications that determine their persuasive impact. Following the classic analysis of communication as who says what, via what medium, to whom, and directed at which kind of behavior, the input variables can be divided into five broad classes: source factors, message factors, channel factors, receiver factors, and target factors.

The output variables in McGuire's (1985) model are steps in persuasion. This chain of mediating responses that leads to behavior change includes exposure to the communication, attending to it, liking for or interest in it, absorbing it, generating related cognitions, acquiring relevant skills, agreeing with the communicated position, storing the attitude change in memory, retrieving the attitude, using the attitude to make a decision, behaving in line with the attitude, and consolidating the new pattern into the individual's overall belief system. Inputs, then, are the independent variables that influence outputs, the dependent variables: behavior change and mediators of behavior change. This analysis can accommodate persuasive communications in different ethnic groups. For the present purposes, we consider input variables.

Source Factors. The attributes of the perceived source of the message, source factors, are perhaps the most salient variable in attitude change. Considerable research can be marshalled to support the view that a communicator who the receiver perceives as credible, attractive, trustworthy, and similar will induce greater attitude change than will a communicator who lacks these characteristics (McGuire, 1985). There is scant reason to believe that these basic relations would not hold among members of ethnic minority groups. Ethnic minority individuals are likely to be influenced to a greater degree by sources they find to be credible, by communicators they like and trust, and by those they perceive to be similar to themselves. The communicators who ethnic minority individuals perceive to have these characteristics, however, may be different from the communicators who Whites perceive to have these characteristics. Whites might be less persuaded by a communicator who speaks with a Spanish accent than by a communicator who does not have a Spanish accent, whereas the opposite might be true for Latinos. Owing to the greater similarity between communicator and the audience, Latinos might be more persuaded by a communicator with a Spanish accent than by a communicator without such an accent. Similarly, a Black physician, as compared with a White physician, might be perceived as more credible by low-income Black individuals. Peterson and Marin (1988) reasoned that AIDS risk-reduction programs for ethnic minority injection drug users should include ethnic minority staff, who may be more accepted by ethnic minority injection drug users because of their knowledge of ethnic minority cultural values. Many AIDS prevention interventions on Blacks and Latinos have taken source characteristics into account. The interventions may use AIDS prevention films that include Black or Latino actors (Gilliam & Seltzer, 1989; Jemmott, Jemmott, & Fong, 1992; Solomon & DeJong, 1989) or the interventions may be implemented by Black facilitators (Jemmott et al., 1992). A study of self-disclosure patterns among Anglo-American and Hispanic undergraduates indicated that self-disclosure by Hispanics was increased when the test administrator was a Hispanic woman (LeVine & Franco, 1981). However, no published studies have evaluated systematically whether matching the ethnicity of the source and the participants enhances the effectiveness of AIDS risk-reduction interventions.

Message Factors.   Another important input variable is the message itself, the content and structure of what is said. Traditionally this has included the type of arguments and appeals (e.g., logical, fear arousing), whether the conclusion is made explicit, inclusions and exclusions (e.g., one-sided vs. two-sided), ordering of material, amount and spacing of material, and extremity of advocated position (McGuire, 1985). In some cases, there is little reason to suppose that these variables would operate any differently as a function of ethnic group membership. There may be differences in details. As an illustration, consider the use of figurative language, which may enhance persuasive impact (McGuire, 1985). The choice of metaphor, for instance, should take into account the receiver. A metaphor that is effective with Whites might not be as effective with Blacks. Yet for both groups, the use of metaphor may enhance the persuasiveness of a communication. In addition, the effectiveness of different types of arguments used to encourage risk reduction may vary for different ethnic groups. This notion is consistent with Mays and Cochran's (1988) suggestion that appeals to ethnically based values of cooperation, community, family responsibility, and unity may be more powerful motivators of behavior change among African-American and Latina women than are appeals to more individualistic self-preservation. Similar suggestions have been made by Marin and Marin (1991) with respect to Latino individuals in particular. However, studies have not evaluated the effectiveness of these types of appeals among members of ethnic minority groups or whether effectiveness varies between ethnic minority individuals and Whites.

Channel Factors. The third input variable is channel factors, the paths by which the message reaches the receiver. Messages can be conveyed through the full range of mass media, including televisions, radio, newspapers, magazines, pamphlets, billboards, and mailings. But they can also be conveyed fact to face. Different channels may be differentially effective for different ethnic groups. Citing evidence that Blacks, as compared with Whites, watch more television, have less hostility toward television as a medium, view its contents as more believable, and rely on it more often as their primary source of news and information, Mays (1989) argued that televised AIDS risk-reduction messages might be particularly effective with Blacks, especially if the messages are delivered by Black actors. One channel that has been suggested as potentially effective for communicating AIDS risk-reduction messages to Black youths is rap music. Although no studies have demonstrated that television is a more effective medium for Blacks as opposed to Whites, several intervention studies on Blacks have incorporated the use of videos into their AIDS prevention programs (Gilliam & Seltzer, 1989; Jemmott et al., 1992; Solomon & DeJong, 1989), and rap also has been used in AIDS prevention programs (Rotheram-Borus, Koopman, Haignere, & Davies, 1991; Schinke, Gordon, & Weston, 1990). The important point is that a message may be most effective if it is transmitted through a channel that is likely to be monitored by the intended audience. If the receiver is not exposed to the communication or does not attend to it, persuasion is unlikely to occur. This may mean targeting channels that have large ethnic minority audiences, and some of these channels may not have large White audiences.

Receiver Factors. The fourth input factor is the receiver's characteristics. We have already discussed the ethnicity of the receiver as interacting with the other input factors. It is assumed that stable individual differences play a role in attitude change. All other things being equal, some people are less influenceable than are others. McGuire reasoned that dispositional variables, including age, gender, and self-esteem may affect the different steps in the persuasion process differentially. If so, it seems reasonable to assume that these same personality variables would operate in the same way among ethnic minority individuals.

Target Factors.   The fifth input factor is the exact target of the message. This might include the type of issue at which the persuasive message is aimed, whether long- or short-term effects are sought, and whether the objective is verbal opinion change or behavior change. For the most part, there little reason to believe that effects would vary by race. However, Marin and Marin (1991), in a discussion of the cultural value of simpatico among Hispanics, cautioned that some Hispanic individuals may be more likely to provide verbal responses that will not interfere with smooth social relations. Some such socially desirable responses may be inaccurate, although empirical evidence on differential response bias between Hispanics and other respondents is lacking.

Summary.   McGuire's input/output model of persuasion can inform efforts to change risk-associated behavior among ethnic minority individuals. The model suggests that those who would change the risky sexual behavior of ethnic minority individuals would have to consider the cultural appropriateness of the source, the message, and the channel in light of the race and ethnicity of the intended receivers. In this sense, the model itself suggests variables that might be considered in efforts to operationalize the concept of cultural appropriateness.

Fishbein and Ajzen's Theory of Reasoned Action

The second social psychological theory we consider in relation to HIV risk-associated behavior is the theory of reasoned action and its extension, the theory of planned behavior. According to the theory of reasoned action (Ajzen & Fishbein, 1980; Fishbein & Ajzen, 1975), specific behavioral intentions are the determinants of behaviors. Thus, for instance, people's use of a condom whenever they have coitus is a function of their intention to use a condom on all occasions of coitus. The theory further hold holds that a behavioral intention is determined by attitudes toward the specific behavior and subjective norms regarding the behavior. The theory is concerned not with traditional attitudes toward objects, people, and institutions, but with attitudes toward behavior. People act in accordance with not only their own attitudes, but also their perceptions of what others expect or want them to do. Thus, people intend to perform a behavior when they evaluate that behavior positively and when they believe significant others think they should perform it. The theory holds that the relative importance of the attitudes and subjective norms depends on the particular behavioral intention. For some intentions, attitudinal considerations may be more important than are normative considerations; for others, normative considerations may be the most important predictor.

A valuable feature of the theory is that it directs attention to why people hold certain attitudes and subjective norms. Attitudes toward behavior are seen as reflecting salient beliefs about the consequences of performing the behavior and the person's negative or positive evaluation of those consequences. Thus, for example, to the extent that people believe that using a condom ruins sexual enjoyment and that sexual enjoyment is desirable, their attitude toward using a condom should be negative. Subjective norms are seen as the product of salient beliefs about what specific reference persons or groups think should be done regarding the behavior and the person's motivation to comply with these referents. Thus, for example, to the extent that people believe that their friends approve of their use of a condom and their friends' opinions are important to them, their subjective norms should be more supportive of condom use.

According to the theory of reasoned action, attitudes and subjective norms are the sole direct determinants of intentions. Other variables may affect intentions; but these effects are indirect, mediated by the effects of the variables on the attitudinal component, the normative component, or both. In this way, the theory can accommodate variables that are external to it (Fishbein & Middlestadt, 1989). However, Ajzen (1985, 1991; Ajzen & Madden, 1986; Madden, Ellen, & Ajzen, 1992; Schifter & Ajzen, 1985) recently argued for an exception to the general rule that all variables external to the theory of reasoned action have their effects on intentions and behavior by influencing the attitudinal and normative components. Perceived behavioral control, he suggested, may have direct effects on intentions and behavior. A fundamental assumption of the theory of reasoned action is that its predictive power is greatest for behaviors that are fully under the volitional control of individuals. Ajzen proposed the theory of planned behavior to account for behaviors that are subject to forces that are beyond individuals' control. For instance, performance of the behavior might depend on another person's actions or the behavior might be performed in the context of strong emotions. Under such circumstances, Ajzen reasoned, prediction of intentions might be enhanced by considering not only attitudes and subjective norms, but perceived behavioral control. Defined as the perceived ease or difficulty of performing the behavior perceived behavioral control reflects past experience as well as anticipated impediments, obstacles, resources, and opportunities. Thus, for example, to the extent that people believe that they have the requisite skills and resources to use condoms, they should perceive greater control over performance of that behavior. Perceived behavioral control has affinity with the social cognitive theory construct of perceived self-efficacy or individuals' conviction that they can perform a specific behavior (Bandura, 1982, 1986, 1989; O'Leary, 1985). In fact, much of what is known about perceived behavioral control comes from research on perceived self-efficacy by Bandura and associates. What the theory of planned behavior does is to place the construct of perceived self-efficacy or perceived behavioral control within a more general framework of the relations among beliefs, attitudes, intentions, and behavior (Ajzen, 1991).

In summary, then, the theory of reasoned action and its extension the theory of planned behavior suggest that those who would intervene to change risky behavior should focus on attitudes, subjective norms, and perceived behavioral control. In addition, to change attitudes, subjective norms, or perceived behavioral control it is necessary to modify the beliefs that underlie them and the importance of those beliefs. There is little reason to believe that these theories would not apply to the behavior of members of ethnic minority groups inasmuch as such individuals' behavior is likely to be influenced by intentions, salient behavioral, normative, and control beliefs, attitudes, subjective norms, perceptions of behavioral control, evaluations of behavioral outcomes, and motivation to comply with significant referents.

An Application of a Theory of Reasoned Action.   In fact, there is some evidence bearing on the application of the theory of reasoned action/theory of planned behavior to AIDS risk behavior among ethnic minority individuals. Jemmott and Jemmott (1991) attempted to apply the theory of reasoned action to HIV risk-associated sexual behavior, specifically condom use. The subjects were 103 sexually experienced, unmarried Black women students from a university located in an inner-city area of New Jersey who completed anonymously a mailed survey. Consistent with the theory, multiple regression analysis indicated that women who expressed more favorable attitudes toward condoms and those who perceived greater support for condom use among their significant referents reported stronger intentions to use condoms. Jemmott and Jemmott (1991) also examined key determinants of attitudes toward using condoms. Hedonistic beliefs or beliefs about the consequences of safer sex practices for sexual enjoyment were important to attitudes toward using condoms. Women who believed more strongly that sex is more fun when a condom is used and who believed less strongly that sex does not feel as good if a condom is used had more favorable attitudes toward using condoms than did other women. In contrast, there was no significant relationship between AIDS knowledge and attitudes toward using condoms. To examine key referents for condoms use, the women were asked questions regarding their sexual partner, mother, father, friends, and church. Sexual partners were rated as more disapproving of condom use than any other referent. In fact, nearly 42% of respondents perceived their sexual partners as disapproving the use of condoms to some degree. Respondents rated their mother and father as the referents most strongly approving of condom use. In addition, respondents indicated they were more motivated to comply with their sexual partner's opinions regarding condom use than with the opinions of any other referent. The referent whose opinion was rated second in importance was respondents' mother, followed by their father, church, and friends. When referents' opinions were weighted by the respondents' motivation to comply, the products revealed that the referents having the strongest influence supporting the use of condoms were the respondents' mother and father, whereas the referents least supportive of condom use were the respondents' sexual partners.

This study suggests that the theory of reasoned action can help elucidate risk behavior. What is not known is how there might be differences in findings as a function of ethnicity. Ethnic groups might vary in the prevalence of particular beliefs about the consequences of HIV risk-associated behaviors or the evaluation of those consequences. Differences along these lines might cause ethnic group differences in attitudes, which might cause ethnic group differences in intentions and behavior. Similarly, the particular normative beliefs that are salient or motivation to comply with referents might vary among ethnic groups, which might cause different subjective norms and consequently different intentions and behaviors. Moreover, in one ethnic group attitudinal determinants may be most important, whereas in another, normative considerations may be paramount. The possibility of ethnic differences of this type, in fact, is very much in the spirit of Fishbein and Ajzen's discussions of the theory of reasoned action (cf. Fishbein & Middlestadt, 1989).

Normative Beliefs.   Unfortunately, little research has examined ethnic group variations in salient beliefs or attitudes, subjective norms, and perceived behavioral control. Studies of both Blacks and Whites suggest that sexual partners are key referents for sexual behavior. For example, studies of both Black and White adolescents have indicated that partner opposition to or reluctance to use birth control was a factor in respondents' nonuse of contraception (Thompson & Spanier, 1978; Zabin & Clarke, 1981).

Although sexual partners are likely to be important across ethnicity, another question is whether parents and peers are as important among Whites and ethnic minority individuals. There is some indication that peers may be less important to the sexual behavior of Blacks than to that of Whites. A longitudinal study of Billy and Udry (1985a, 1985b) revealed that White adolescent women who were virgins at an initial data collection period were more likely to have coitus between waves of the study if they had sexually experienced friends at the first wave than if they did not. White male adolescents seemed to select their friends on the basis of sexual activity rather than to be influenced by their friends' behavior. Black adolescents, however, were not influenced by friends' sexual behavior, nor did they select their friends on that basis (Billy & Udry, 1985a, 1985b). In a similar vein, Jones and Philliber (1983) found that discussions of birth control with friends were unrelated to inner-city Black female adolescents' contraceptive use.

Studies of Black and White adolescent women indicate that those whose mothers encouraged their use of birth control, especially by discussing a specific method, were more likely to use contraception (Baker, Thalberg, & Morrison, 1988; Fox & Inazu, 1980; Furstenberg, 1971; Handelsman, Cabral, & Weisfeld, 1987; Taylor et al., 1986). Considerable survey data indicate that parents are adolescents' most preferred source of sexual and contraceptive information

(Abelson, Cohen, Heaton, & Suder, 1971; Sorensen, 1973). However, the potential influence of parents and the family may be particularly strong among ethnic minority individuals (Clark, 1989). For instance, studies indicate that Black adolescents, as compared with White adolescents, were more parent-oriented (DiCindio, Floyd, Wilcox, & McSeveney, 1983) and perceived greater social support from the family (Cauce, Felner, & Primavera, 1982). Nathanson and Becker (1986), studying family and peer influences on contraceptive seeking, found striking racial differences in influence patterns. Black mothers were much more likely than were White mothers to be involved in the clinic visit decisions of their daughters; and Black female adolescents were substantially less likely than were White female adolescents to involve either a boyfriend or girlfriends in their decision.

The normative influence of parents and older family members is also likely to be greater among Hispanic than among White individuals (Marin & Marin, 1991). A study by Marin, Marin, and Juarez (1990), compared 218 Hispanic and 201 non-Hispanic White adults in San Francisco who had been recruited at health centers, public transportation terminals, or classes at adult education facilities. Results showed Hispanics were more likely to believe that the most appropriate person to speak to an injection drug user about reducing risk of transmitting HIV to his wife was an older family member. Marin et al. proposed that this may reflect the Hispanic cultural value of power distance or respect for those who are older or in authority. They suggested that messages aimed at families of drug users might usefully target older family members of either sex such as parents and grandparents.

Behavioral Beliefs.   Although other kinds of behavioral beliefs have been studied, much of the research on beliefs has focused on the role of factual beliefs relevant to the prevention of HIV infection. Indeed, such factual information is probably the most frequently proffered solution to the problem of risky behavior. The basic idea is that people who believe that HIV is transmitted during sexual activities with infected persons involving the exchange of blood, semen, and vaginal secretions should be less likely to engage in such activities. For instance, individuals who believe that condoms can reduce the risk of HIV transmission should be more likely to use condoms. It is a fairly consistent finding that ethnic minority individuals, compared with Whites, have less factual information about the cause, transmission, and prevention of AIDS (DiClemente, Boyer, & Morales, 1988; DiClemente, Zorn & Temoshok, 1986; Price, Desmond, & Kukula, 1985). For example, DiClemente et al. (1988) found that White high school students in San Francisco were more knowledgeable about AIDS than were Black students who, in turn, were more knowledgeable than Latino students. The 1988 National Survey of Adolescent Males (Sonenstein et al., 1989) revealed that, in general, AIDS knowledge was very high among respondents, but that Blacks and Hispanics scored lower on knowledge than did Whites. Similar ethnic group differences have been found for sexual and contraceptive knowledge. For example, Padilla and O'Grady (1987) found that Mexican American college students in southern California had less sexual knowledge than did Anglo students at the same state university. However, few studies have found that AIDS knowledge in general or the specific belief that condoms can prevent AIDS is related to behavior (Baldwin & Baldwin, 1988; DiClemente, Forrest, & Mickler, 1990; Fisher & Fisher, 1992; Joseph et al., 1987; Kegeles, Adler, & Irwin, 1988). For instance, Jemmott and Jemmott (1992) found that increases in general AIDS knowledge and in the specific belief that condoms prevent pregnancy, STDs, and AIDS were not significantly related to increases in inner-city Black adolescent women's intentions to use condoms.

Another type of behavioral belief is hedonistic beliefs or beliefs about the consequences of safer sex practices for sexual enjoyment. Although studies have not compared ethnic groups on the extent to which they hold hedonistic beliefs, evidence suggests that such beliefs are important among both Blacks and Whites (Catania, Coates et al., 1989; Catania, Dolcini et al., 1989; Hingson, Strunin, Berlin, & Heeren, 1990; Jemmott & Jemmott, 1991, 1992; MacDonald et al., 1990; Valdiserri, Arena, Proctor, & Bonati, 1989). For instance, Jemmott and Jemmott (1991) found that hedonistic beliefs were related to attitudes toward condom use among Black undergraduate women. In a study of White women, ages 19 to 25, recruited from a family planning clinic, Valdiserri, Arena et al. (1989) found that those who believed that they would not enjoy intercourse if their partner used condoms were less likely to report past use of condoms than were their peers who did not hold this belief. In a similar vein, Catania, Coates et al. (1989) reported that beliefs about sexual enjoyment were related to unprotected anal intercourse among White male homosexuals.

Control Beliefs.   There are several types of control beliefs that are likely to be important to perceived behavioral control regarding condom use. The belief that it would be difficult to obtain condoms or to have them available when they are needed might reduce perceived behavioral control. Beliefs about technical skill at using condoms may affect perceived behavioral control. Individuals who believe that they are not facile in their use of condoms or that they cannot use them without ruining the mood may perceive less behavioral control. Inasmuch as condoms are used in the context of strong emotional arousal and excitement, individuals who perceive that their ability to exercise restraint is relatively low may perceive less behavioral control. Condom use requires the cooperation of the person's sexual partner. This is particularly true of women, for after all it is the man who wears the condom. Perceived behavioral control may be reduced to the extent that individuals believe that they lack the ability to negotiate condom use with their partner.

As far as we know, no studies have used the theory of planned behavior as a theoretical framework to examine the relation of perceived behavioral control to

HIV risk-associated behavior. In this connection, then, a number of studies conducted within the framework of social cognitive theory are relevant because they have examined the kindred concept of perceived self-efficacy. Still, relatively few studies have focused on perceived self-efficacy in relation to safer sex practices, including condom use, among ethnic minority individuals. In addition, the available studies typically have employed global measures or have focused on only one of the several aspects of perceived self-efficacy. Thus, whether perceived behavioral control or the specific control beliefs have differential predictive power in different ethnic groups is unknown. Among adolescents, perceived self-efficacy has been related to safe sex (Hingson et al., 1990). Perceived self-efficacy to practice safer sex was significantly related to safer sex practices among college students (O'Leary, Goodhart, Jemmott, & Boccher-Lattimore, 1992). In studies of gay men, perceived self-efficacy to negotiate condom use has emerged as a strong predictor of sexual behavior change (Emmons et al., 1986; McKusick, Coates, Morin, Pollack, & Hoff, 1990). In a study of inner-city Black adolescent women, increases in perceived self-efficacy to use condoms were significantly related to increased condom-use intentions (Jemmott & Jemmott, 1992).

In summary, then, social psychological theories are likely to have application to HIV risk-associated behavior irrespective of ethnicity/race. It is the details of how the theories apply that may vary depending on ethnicity/race. In this chapter, we focused on McGuire's attitude change model and the theory of reasoned action/planned behavior, but similar arguments can be developed for other models used in AIDS research, including social cognitive theory and the health belief model (Janz & Becker, 1984; Kirscht & Joseph, 1989). The arguments regarding perceived behavioral control apply equally well to the social cognitive theory concept of perceived self-efficacy. Research using a social cognitive theory framework also has drawn attention to outcome expectancies, defined as people's beliefs about the consequences of engaging in a specific behavior (Jemmott & Jemmott, 1992; O'Leary et al., 1992). It is possible to distinguish among different types of outcome expectancies. Altered risk of harm, hedonic costs or benefits, and social sanction or approbation are all examples of possible behavioral consequences (Bandura, 1986). Thus, many of the salient beliefs that underlie attitudes and subjective norms can be seen, in social cognitive theory terms, as outcome expectancies. An application of the health belief model to HIV risk-associated behavior might include perceived susceptibility to AIDS/HIV, perceived seriousness of AIDS/HIV, perceived benefits of a behavior in reducing either susceptibility or severity of AIDS/HIV, and anticipated barriers to or cost of engaging in the behavior. Although there may be between-ethnic group differences in beliefs about susceptibility to AIDS, seriousness of AIDS, benefits of condom use, or costs of condom use, and these variables may be differentially related to risk behavior depending on ethnicity, there is little reason to believe that the health belief model would be inapplicable to ethnic minority individuals.

AIDS RISK-REDUCTION INTERVENTIONS

Based on a consideration of the importance of cultural sensitivity and the social psychological theories, a picture emerges of certain elements that may be important to the design of interventions to reduce the risk of HIV infection among ethnic minority individuals. For instance, the review of the McGuire model suggests the importance of the cultural appropriateness of the message, the structure of the message itself, and the channel in light of the intended audience. Thus, ethnically matched AIDS educators might be important, structuring a message to emphasize the impact of AIDS on the ethnic minority community or family might be particularly effective, and using channels likely to attract the attention of the ethnic group members might boost persuasive impact. The review of the theory of reasoned action/planned behavior suggests salient beliefs that might be targeted and assessed. For example, with regard to normative considerations, parents and or respected family members might be effective educators. In the next section, the published literature on AIDS risk-reduction interventions for ethnic minority individuals is considered.

AIDS Risk-Reduction Intervention Studies With Blacks and Hispanics

Although relatively few studies have tested AIDS risk-reduction interventions on Black and Hispanic populations, studies on White gay men suggest that AIDS interventions may increase condom use or decrease number of sexual partners (e.g., Coates, McKusick, Kuno, Stites, 1989; Kelly, St. Lawrence, Hood, & Brasfield, 1989; Kelly et al., 1991; Valdiserri, Lyter et al., 1989). These studies raise the possibility that similar effects might occur among ethnic minority individuals. However, this is conjecture inasmuch as the studies did not focus on ethnic minority individuals specifically. Accordingly, the small number of studies that have focused on ethnic minority individuals are of great significance. Table 7.1 summarizes those studies.

Studies of Black Adults. Three studies have been done an Black adult populations. A study by Stephens, Feucht, and Roman (1991) evaluated on AIDS education program for injection drug users, a key population with respect to HIV infection among Blacks and Hispanics. Most of the injection drug users were Black men (median age = 36 years) who were not currently in drug treatment. The intervention was presented in a one-on-one format by a professionally trained health educator and lasted from 45 minutes to 1 hour. Participants were interviewed before the intervention, and follow-up interviews were conducted beginning 3 months after the intervention. Pretest and follow-up data were obtained on 402 subjects (61% of pretest subjects). The intervention had four modules: (a) basic information about HIV and modes of transmission, (b) sexual

TABLE 7.1
AIDS Risk-Reduction Intervention Studies on Black and Hispanic Individuals

Study	Sample	Design	Data Collection	Targets of Intervention	Amount of Intervention	Key Findings
Gillian and Seltzer (1989)	278 male and female students at a predominately Black university	Experiment: AIDS film, first-aid film	Six weeks post-intervention	AIDS knowledge	One session	Students who viewed the AIDS film were less likely to believe they could get AIDS from kissing or drinking glasses, than were students who viewed the first-aid film. However, they were also less likely to mention condoms as a way to avoid getting AIDS and were not more likely to say they were using condoms when background character-istics were controlled.
Jemmott et al. (1992)	157 inner-city Black male adolescents; 150 (96%) at follow-up; mean age = 14.6 years	Experiment: AIDS intervention, career-opportunities control	Preintervention, immediately postintervention, 3-months post-intervention	AIDS knowledge, attitudes toward risky sexual behavior, negotiation skills	One 5-hour session, one 5-hour session	Controlling for preintervention measures, adolescents in the AIDS condition had greater knowledge, less positive attitudes toward risky behaviors, weaker intentions for risky behaviors immediately postintervention than did those in the control group. Controlling for preintervention measures, adolescents in the AIDS condition reported less risky sexual behavior, including more consistent condom use, fewer sexual partners, less frequent coitus, and less frequent anal intercourse 3 months postintervention than did those in the control group.

(Continued)

TABLE 7.1
(Continued)

Study	Sample	Design	Data Collection	Targets of Intervention	Amount of Intervention	Key Findings
Jemmott et al. (in press)	19 sexually active Black adolescent women from an inner-city family planning clinic	Nonequivalent groups pretest-posttest: social cognitive interventions, information along intervention, general health promotion intervention	Preintervention, immediately postintervention	AIDS knowledge, perceived self-efficacy, hedonistic beliefs, prevention beliefs	One 105-minute session	Controlling for preintervention measures, the social cognitive condition had greater interventions to use condoms, greater perceived self-efficacy, and more favorable hedonistic beliefs than did the other conditions. Although the information alone condition had greater knowledge and prevention beliefs they did not express greater intentions than did the health promotion condition.
Jemmott and Jemmott (in press)	109 sexually active, inner-city Black female adolescents; mean age = 16.8 years	One group pretest-posttest	Preintervention, immediately post-intervention	AIDS knowledge perceived self-efficacy, hedonistic beliefs, prevention beliefs	Three sessions over 3 days	Women scored higher in AIDS knowledge, prevention beliefs, hedonistic beliefs, perceived self-efficacy, and intentions to use condoms after the intervention compared with before. Perceived self-efficacy and hedonistic beliefs predicted increases in intentions, whereas AIDS knowledge and prevention beliefs did not.
Lanier and McCarthy (1989)	363 adolescents at Alabama juvenile detention facilities (87% of residents); 85% male, 56% Black	Nonequivalent groups posttest only: 5-day intervention, 3-day intervention, no intervention	Immediately postintervention	AIDS knowledge, perceived risk	Five 1-hour sessions, three 1-hour sessions, no sessions	Adolescents who received the 5-day intervention scored higher in AIDS knowledge and perceived risk of HIV infection than did those who received no intervention.

Study	Sample	Design	Assessment	Measures	Sessions	Findings
Rickert et al. (1990)	75 female adolescents at an adolescent medicine clinic in Little Rock, Arkansas; 53% Black, 47% White; ages 13–21 years	Experiment: Control (AIDS information booklet), education (lecture plus booklet), enhanced education (lecture, booklet, 25-minute film)	Immediately post-intervention	AIDS knowledge	One 15-minute to 30-minute film	Education and enhanced education conditions as compared with control condition had greater AIDS knowledge but not more positive attitudes toward prevention behavior. Enhanced education caused greater condom redemption than did the other conditions, but only among the subsample of adolescents who had previously purchased condoms.
Rotheram-Borus et al. (1991)	189 male and female runaway adolescents at two residential shelters in NYC, 145 (77%) participated in 3- and/or 6-month follow-up interviews; 63% Black, 22% Hispanic	Nonequivalent control group: intervention site (3–30 sessions), control site (two or fewer sessions)	Preintervention, 3 months and/or 6 months post-baseline	AIDS knowledge, coping skills, access to health care, attitudes	Three to 30 (M = 13) 90-minute to 2-hour sessions; two or fewer 90-minute to 2-hour sessions	Runaways who attended more intervention sessions had greater increase in reported condom use and scored lower in high-risk behavior patterns 3-months and 6-months postbaseline than did those who attended fewer intervention sessions.
Schinke et al. (1990)	60 male and female adolescents at an urban job-training program; 42% Black, 27% Hispanic; mean age = 16 years	Experiment: Self-instructional guide plus group instruction, guide only, no treatment	Preintervention, 1 month post-intervention	AIDS knowledge, decision-making skills	Three 1-hour sessions, no sessions	Adolescents in the guide-plus-instruction condition had marginally decreased permissiveness toward IVDU, whereas controls showed marginal increase. Adolescents in self-instruct plus-guide condition had increased likelihood of discussing sexual matters with friends. No significant differences on intentions to use condoms.

(Continued)

TABLE 7.1
(Continued)

Study	Sample	Design	Data Collection	Targets of Intervention	Amount of Intervention	Key Findings
Solomon and DeJong (1989, Study 1)	103 clients at an inner-city STD clinic; 82% male, 80% Black, 75% single; median age = 24 years	Experiment: AIDS film, no-treatment control	Immediately post-intervention	AIDS knowledge, attitudes toward condoms	One session	Clients who viewed the AIDS film had greater AIDS knowledge and more favorable attitude toward condoms than did those who did not view the film.
Solomon and DeJong (1989, Study 2)	182 clients at an inner-city STD clinic; 80% male, 85% Black, 86% single, median age =24 years	Experiment: AIDS film, no-treatment control	Immediately post-intervention	AIDS knowledge, attitudes toward condoms	One session	Clients who viewed the AIDS film redeemed more coupons for free condoms immediately after the intervention or by mail than did those who did not view the film.
Stephens et al. (1991)	402 intravenous drug users (60.7% of pretest subjects); predominantly ma and Black; median age = 36 years	One group pretest-postest	Preintervention, 3 months (36 to 448 days) post-intervention	AIDS knowledge, risks related to sex and drug use, HIV antibody test	One 45 minute to 1-hour session.	Reductions IV drug use and needle sharing increased needle hygiene postintervention compared with preintervention.

risk-reduction strategies, including condom use, (c) risk-reduction strategies concerning injection drug use; and (d) information about HIV antibody testing. Participants received a kit that included a bottle of bleach, condoms, and brochures about AIDS. Although the intervention seems primarily focused on providing information about AIDS and self-protection strategies, it also seems to have been designed with sensitivity to source factors and to the issue of perceived susceptibility to AIDS. The knowledge module centered on a segment from a film produced by prison inmates who were dying of AIDS, although the race of the inmates was not indicated.

Analyses revealed significant reductions in HIV risk-associated needle behavior at the follow-up, as compared with preintervention. There were reductions in the percentage of subjects who reported using injection drugs or sharing injection drug paraphernalia or "works," and there was an increase in the percentage who cleaned their works with bleach. This is the only study we could locate that evaluated an AIDS intervention program for ethnic minority injection drug users. Although the changes associated with the intervention are important and impressive, a causal impact cannot be unequivocally assigned to the intervention because there are alternative explanations in terms of history and selection because the study did not include a control group that did not receive an AIDS intervention. For example, it might be argued that factors external to the intervention that occurred during the time interval between pretest and follow-up measurements might have affected self-reports of risky behavior. However, Stephens et al. cited analyses that were inconsistent with this interpretation. Subjects whose follow-up interviews coincided with the pretest interviews of other subjects had lower reports of risky behavior. Still, approximately 39% of the original subjects did not complete the follow-up assessment. Future studies are needed to rule out the possibility that changes in risky behavior reflect not the intervention's impact, but something about the characteristics of the type of person who was willing and able to return for the follow-up session.

Another key population at risk for sexually transmitted HIV infection is individuals who have a recent history of STD. Solomon and DeJong (1989) conducted two experiments on patients undergoing treatment for STDs at an inner-city clinic. In both experiments, the subjects, primarily Black men (18 to 30 years of age), were assigned randomly either to an AIDS intervention condition where they viewed a videotape or to a control condition, where they did not receive an intervention. The intervention was sensitive to source factors, message factors, and channel factors. In addition, it addressed hedonistic beliefs, normative considerations, and perceived behavioral control. A Black cast, language characteristic of the clinic population, and realistic situations were used to make the video culturally appropriate. The video provided information indicating that both women and men might be willing to use condoms. It featured a young woman who had had STDs and who, through the support of her brother and sister, came to realize that she could persuade her boyfriend to use condoms. She was shown communicating with her boyfriend successfully and with grace and wit. The videotape was used to make condoms more sexually appealing by eroticizing condom use. It portrayed condoms as socially acceptable, normative behavior. Rather than emphasizing individualistic risk to men, the message concerned collective risks to women and children. Interpersonal skills required for negotiating safer sex with a partner were modeled.

The first experiment revealed that subjects who had received the intervention had greater knowledge, expressed attitudes more accepting of condoms, and cited more strategies to persuade partners to use condoms than did their counterparts who had not received the intervention. The second experiment is one of the few AIDS risk-reduction studies to include an objective measure of behavior. The dependent measure was condom coupon redemption, an objective measure of condom acquisition. Subjects who viewed the AIDS video were subsequently more likely than were the other subjects to redeem coupons for free condoms.

Gilliam and Seltzer (1989) also tested the efficacy of an AIDS film. Students from five classes at a predominantly Black university were assigned randomly to an AIDS prevention condition or a control condition. Students in the AIDS prevention condition saw a film in which a Black doctor and a Hispanic male answered questions about AIDS posed by persons representing various walks of life. Thus, the film addressed source factors. The content of the film included signs, symptoms, transmission of HIV infection, precautionary measures, and myths about AIDS. Most AIDS intervention studies that have employed control groups have used no-treatment control groups. The potential problem is that differences between the intervention group and a no-treatment control condition might reflect nonspecific features of the intervention such as special attention rather than the theoretically important features of the intervention. A strength of the Gilliam and Seltzer (1989) study is that it controlled for special attention by also showing a film on first aid to students in the control condition. Six weeks after the films were shown, subjects in both conditions completed a postintervention questionnaire.

Analyses revealed scant evidence that the AIDS film had a significant impact on AIDS knowledge. Surprisingly, students who saw the film on first aid were significantly more likely than students who saw the film on AIDS to mention condoms and not having sex as ways to avoid contracting AIDS. Students who saw the AIDS film were marginally ($p < .07$) more likely than students who saw the first aid film to mention other forms of safer sex. In addition, students who saw the AIDS film were marginally ($p < .09$) more likely than those who saw the film on first aid to say they were doing something to avoid exposing themselves to AIDS. When asked what were some of the precautions they were taking to avoid contracting AIDS, students who had seen the AIDS film were significantly more likely than were the students who saw the first aid film to say they were using condoms. However, Gilliam and Seltzer also reported that because of a breakdown in the implementation of random assignment to conditions, there was some self-selection into conditions associated with academic major and that controlling for major, the effect of type of film on condom use was nonsignificant.

Studies of Black and Hispanic Adolescents.   Seven studies have been done on adolescents. One of the earliest studies to report the impact of an AIDS intervention was the Lanier and McCarthy (1989) study on adolescents in juvenile corrections facilities in Alabama. Juvenile delinquents are at elevated risk for early sexual activity, sexually transmitted disease, and injection drug use. The AIDS intervention used by Lanier and McCarthy consisted of one hour of instruction for 5 days, focusing on AIDS knowledge and emphasizing abstinence as the preferred means of AIDS prevention. The article did not provide further details of the intervention's content. The adolescents participating in the study, the majority of whom were African-American males, completed an anonymous questionnaire. Several weeks prior to the administration of the questionnaire, adolescents at some institutions received the full 5-day intervention, adolescents at other institutions received 3 days of instruction, and those at other institutions had not received their instruction. Although the study did not examine effects of the intervention on the behavior of these incarcerated youths, there were significant effects on AIDS knowledge and perceived risk of HIV infection. Adolescents who received the 5 days of instruction as compared with other adolescents, were more likely to answer correctly AIDS knowledge questions, to believe that AIDS is a significant problem, and to view themselves as facing high risk of infection and were more willing to tell potential sexual partners if they tested positive for AIDS.

Conclusions that can be drawn from this study are somewhat limited because if did not have a true experimental design, but a nonequivalent groups posttest-only design. The study does not rule out alternative explanations in terms of selection. It is unknown whether there may have been preexisting AIDS knowledge or perceived risk differences among adolescents in the three groups that might account for the significant differences obtained on the questionnaire administered after the intervention. The study also does not rule out explanations in terms of attrition. About 13% of the youths did not complete the questionnaire, and the researchers did not indicate whether the percentage varied by condition. Thus, whether or not the observed differences might reflect differential drop out of persons across conditions is unclear.

Another group of adolescents at high risk of early sexual activity and sexually transmitted disease is runaways. Rotheram-Borus, Koopman, Haignere, and Davies (1991) reported a study that tested the effects of an AIDS prevention program on the sexual risk behavior of runaways, primarily Black and Hispanic adolescents, at two residential shelters in New York City. The study used a nonequivalent groups pretest–posttest design in which one of the shelters was selected as the intervention site, whereas the other served as the nonintervention site. The intervention consisted of 20, 90-to-120-minute sessions rotated in a 3-week sequence, with runaways joining the sequence at various points. The number of intervention sessions attended by adolescents at the intervention site ranged from 3 to 30, with a mean of 12.8 sessions. The intervention addressed four components: (a) general knowledge about AIDS, (b) coping skills training to ameliorate runaways' unrealistic expectations about their emotional and behavioral responses in high-risk situations, (c) access to health care and other resources, and (d) individual barriers to safer sex, including dysfunctional attitudes. The activities included video and art workshops where runaways developed soap opera dramatizations, public service announcements, commercials, raps, about HIV prevention, and viewing commercial HIV/AIDS prevention videos. The activities addressed many factors suggested by social psychological theory. Hedonistic beliefs were addressed by a focus on the use of condoms in a sensuous manner (Rotheram-Borus, Mahler, & Rosario, 1991). Although personal risk of HIV was addressed, a key message was the harm of HIV to babies—as mentioned earlier, an emphasis on family and community is thought to be effective with ethnic minority populations. Activities were used to build over time group norms of safer sex, which might affective salient normative beliefs. The use of role-playing, video workshops, dramatizations of soap operas, and practicing prepared scripts for handling interpersonal problems would seem to strengthen feelings of competence in negotiating with sexual partners safer sex practices and should heighten perceived behavioral control. At the nonintervention site, there was no systematic introduction of AIDS education. The adolescents received the standard education involving individual counseling from staff, educational programs on television, and referrals and treatment by local physicians for health concerns. Occasionally, a 2-hour AIDS prevention workshop was conducted; but no runaway received more than two session of AIDS activities while at this shelter. Runaways at the intervention site did not significantly differ from those at the nonintervention site in age, gender, ethnicity, length of time since living at home, or sexual risk behavior. About 77% of participants took part in 3- or 6-month post-baseline interviews. Although males were significantly more likely than were females to miss their 3- and 6-month interview, no significant differences were found in age, ethnicity, number of days at the shelter, number of sessions attended, or sexual risk behaviors between participants and the runaways who did not receive either the 3- or 6-month post-baseline interviews.

Reasoning that number of intervention sessions attended (irrespective of site) would provide a more sensitive indicator of intervention dosage than would site, Rotheram-Borus, Koopman et al. found that adolescents who attended a greater number of intervention sessions reported more consistent condom use during follow-up interviews, controlling for baseline self-reports. Number of intervention sessions attended also significantly predicted reductions in the high-risk pattern of sexual behavior, defined as infrequent condoms use (<50% of sexual encounters) combined with more than 10 sexual encounters and/or with 3 or more partners, 3 and 6 months post-baseline. Although a greater number of subjects in the intervention site than in the nonintervention site dropped out of the study, evidence against alternative explanations in terms of attrition was presented. Adolescents who dropped out did not differ from those who participated in the 3- or 6-month interviews in number of intervention sessions attended or baseline self-reports of sexual behavior.

Based on inspection of differences among subjects categorized according to number of sessions attended, Rotheram-Borus, Koopman et al. suggested that adolescent HIV/AIDS prevention programs must extend beyond two to three sessions to achieve behavior change. However, inasmuch as the intervention was designed to be 20 sessions long, it may be that subjects who received only 10% to 15% of the full dose of an intervention are unlikely to show behavior change. It would seem that the critical ingredient may not necessarily be the quantity of the intervention or number of sessions, but the content of the intervention. The intervention placed greater emphasis on coping skills and access to health care and resources than did any of the other AIDS interventions. A stronger case could be made for the quantity-of-intervention argument had subjects been assigned randomly to receive differing numbers of sessions. This would have dealt with the possibility that those who were able and willing to attend more sessions were the kind of individuals who would practice safer sex in the absence of intervention. In addition, the correlation between number of sessions and safer sex may not reflect stronger effects of the intervention when adolescents attend more sessions, but apparently stronger effects when the follow-up data are collected within a shorter period of time after the intervention. Follow-up data were collected 3 months and 6 months after the baseline assessment, not 3 and 6 months after the intervention. Consequently, subjects whose intervention continued for a larger number of sessions, which presumably would take a greater number of weeks, may have had a shorter follow-up period than did those whose intervention involved only a few sessions. Clearly, this study raises a number of important questions about the nature of AIDS risk-reduction interventions, questions that must be addressed in future research.

An experiment by Schinke et al. (1990) tested the efficacy of a self-instruction intervention designed to reduce the risk of HIV infection associated with drug use and unsafe sex. The subjects, 60 male and female Black and Hispanic adolescents enrolled in an urban job-training program, were assigned randomly to one of three conditions. Participants in a self-instructional-guide-plus-group-instruction condition received the guide and met with intervention leaders for three 1-hour sessions in which the intervention leaders described the rationale and use of the guide. Subjects in a guide-only condition did not receive these group sessions. Subjects in the control condition did not receive the guide or the group sessions. The guide was written in comic book format and included rap lyrics presented by cartoon characters drawn to mirror participants' age and ethnic-racial background, features that addressed source factors in light of the recipients' age and ethnicity. The characters provided information about AIDS risks, myths, and prevention strategies. Topics included risks associated with injection drug use and sexual contact with partners who inject drugs. To enhance decision-making skills, the guide introduced participants to the steps involved in cognitive problem solving. In a game format, the youths made hypothetical decisions about drug use and AIDS risks.

Data were collected before the intervention and 1 month after it. Although the pattern of means across several dependent measures suggested positive effects of the self-instructional interventions, there were few significant differences. Analyses of covariance revealed no between-condition differences in AIDS knowledge, fear of AIDS, approval of casual drug use, or intentions to use condoms, controlling for preintervention beliefs. There was a significant effect on participants' disapproval of injection drug use, which seemed to indicate that participants who received the self-instructional guide plus small group intervention decreased their permissiveness toward IV drug use as compared with the control subjects.

One weakness of this study was the manner in which the data were analyzed. Although Schinke et al. (1990) used analysis of covariance to examine differences among conditions in postintervention variables with preintervention measures of those variables as the covariate, they did not compare the adjusted postintervention means of the groups. Instead, they used t tests to compare subjects' pre- and postintervention scores within conditions. The trouble is that such comparisons do not address the critically important question of whether the amount of change in a given experimental condition is significantly greater than the amount of change in the control condition. In addition, these within-condition comparisons are subject to the limitations of single sample pretest–posttest designs (e.g., alternative explanations in terms of history). Furthermore, this analysis reduced statistical power because it substantially reduced the number of subjects who were included in the critical analyses, particularly important in light of the study's small sample size ($N = 60$).

Rickert, Gottlieb, and Jay (1990) conducted a study to test the effects of AIDS interventions on Black and White female adolescents who attended an adolescent medicine clinic in a metropolitan area in central Arkansas. The subjects were assigned randomly to one of three conditions: (a) a control condition, in which they were given the opportunity to ask questions about AIDS and were given a booklet on AIDS; (b) an education condition, in which they were given the booklet and a brief lecture on AIDS using guidelines published by the CDC; or (c) an enhanced education condition, in which they received the booklet and the lecture and viewed a humorous videotape demonstrating the purpose and use of condoms. From a social psychological perspective, the video may have reduced anxiety about using condoms and may have heightened specific beliefs about ability to use condoms. Immediately after the intervention, subjects in all conditions completed questionnaire measures and were given a coupon that they could redeem for free condoms at an on-site pharmacy. Although there were no significant differences between groups in attitudes toward practicing preventive behaviors, attitudes toward persons with AIDS, or perceived seriousness of AIDS, subjects in the education and enhanced education conditions scored significantly higher in AIDS knowledge than did those in the control condition. Considering the whole sample, there were no significant between-condition differences in the proportion of adolescents who redeemed coupons for free condoms. In the subsample of adolescents who had reported previously purchasing condoms, however, those who received enhanced education were more likely to redeem the coupons than were those in the other two conditions.

Jemmott et al. (1992) reported a study testing the effects of an AIDS risk-reduction intervention on inner-city Black male adolescents (mean age = 14.6 years) who had volunteered for a study to discover ways to reduce important risks Black youths face. The adolescents were assigned randomly to either an AIDS risk-reduction condition or a control condition. In the AIDS risk-reduction condition, adolescents received a 5-hour intervention involving videotapes, games, and exercises aimed at increasing AIDS-related knowledge and reducing positive attitudes and intentions regarding risky sexual behavior. The intervention addressed source factors. It was implemented by Black facilitators. One video, *The Subject is AIDS,* presented factual information about AIDS and was narrated by a Black woman and had a multiethnic cast. Another video, *Condom Sense,* addressed negative attitudes toward the use of condoms, hedonistic beliefs, and normative beliefs. It attacked the idea that sex is substantially less pleasurable when a condom is used. A major character is a Black man who tries to convince a basketball buddy that his girlfriend's request that they use condoms during sex is reasonable. The intervention also addressed perceived behavioral control, including beliefs about technical skill and negotiation skill. A condom exercise focused on familiarity with condoms and the steps involved in the correct use of them. Participants engaged in role-playing situations depicting potential problems in trying to implement safer sex practices, including abstinence. To control for Hawthorne effects to reduce the likelihood that effects of the AIDS intervention could be attributed to nonspecific features including group interaction and special attention, adolescents randomly assigned to the control condition also received a 5-hour intervention. Structurally similar to the AIDS intervention, it involved videotapes, exercises, and games, but regarding career opportunities. Adolescents in both conditions completed questionnaires before, immediately after the intervention, and 3 months after the intervention. Analyses of covariance, controlling for preintervention measures, revealed that adolescents who received the AIDS risk-reduction intervention subsequently had greater AIDS knowledge, less favorable attitudes toward risky sexual behavior, and reduced intentions for such behavior compared with adolescents in the control condition. Of the original participants, 150 (95.5%) completed follow-up questionnaires 3 months after the intervention. The return rate was not significantly different between conditions. As compared with adolescents in the control condition, those who had received the AIDS risk-reduction intervention reported less risky sexual behavior in the 3 months following the intervention, controlling for preintervention behavior. They reported a lower frequency of coitus, fewer coital partners, greater use of condoms, and a lower incidence of heterosexual anal intercourse. Jemmott et al. also found that social desirability bias as indexed by scores on the Marlow-Crowne scale was unrelated to self-reports of risky sexual behavior at preintervention and the 3-month follow-up or to the amount of changes in self-reports of risky sexual behavior. In addition, there was no evidence of contamination of effects due to cross-talk between conditions. About 18% of the subjects said they discussed the group activities with someone from another group in the study. Subjects in the AIDS condition and career condition were equally likely to talk to someone from another group. Analyses of covariance on AIDS knowledge, attitudes, intentions, and risky sexual behavior at the 3-month follow-up revealed no significant interaction between experimental condition and whether or not the subject reported discussing the study with someone from another group. Thus, the intervention's effects were not significantly weaker among the subsample of participants who talked with participants in other groups.

Two recent studies on intentions to use condoms provide data that are especially relevant to social psychological approaches to AIDS risk reduction among inner-city African-American youths. In the first study, Jemmott, Jemmott, Spears, Hewitt, and Cruz-Collins (1992) compared the effects on intentions of three interventions: (a) a social cognitive intervention designed to increase perceived self-efficacy/ behavioral control to use condoms and hedonistic beliefs favorable to condom use; (b) an information-alone intervention designed to increase general AIDS knowledge and specific prevention beliefs; and (c) a general health promotion intervention designed to provide information about health problems other than AIDS. The subjects were 19 sexually active Black adolescent women from an inner-city family planning clinic. As in the Jemmott et al. (1992) study, all interventions lasted the same amount of time and involved the use of films and small group exercises and games. Analysis of covariance revealed that although participants in both the social cognitive condition and the information-alone condition scored higher in AIDS knowledge and prevention beliefs than did those in the health promotion condition, participants in the social cognitive condition registered greater intentions to use condoms than did those in the other two conditions. In addition, participants in the social cognitive condition, as compared with the other conditions, reported greater perceived self-efficacy/behavioral control and more favorable hedonistic beliefs, the two hypothesized mediators of the effects on condom-use intentions of the intervention. The study was limited by the relatively small sample size. Although significance tests take sample size into account by making it more difficult to achieve statistical significance with small samples, additional studies are needed to demonstrate the generalizability of these findings in larger samples.

The second study evaluated an AIDS prevention program for inner-city adolescent women implemented by a community-based organization, the Urban League of Metropolitan Trenton. The three session, 5-hour AIDS prevention program drew upon the studies by Jemmott et al. (1992) and Jemmott et al. (1992) and used many of the same activities. The intervention, implemented by a Black female facilitator, addressed perceived behavioral control, hedonistic beliefs, and prevention beliefs. The participants scored higher in AIDS knowledge, registered more favorable prevention beliefs and hedonistic beliefs, expressed greater self-efficacy/perceived behavioral control, and scored higher in intentions to use condoms after the intervention, as compared with before it. In addition, increases in perceived self-efficacy/behavioral control and hedonistic beliefs predicted increases in intentions to use condoms, whereas increases in general AIDS knowledge and specific prevention beliefs did not. One weakness of the study is that the changes in intentions might not reflect intervention effects, but history. Jemmott and Jemmott (1992) reasoned that history is an unlikely explanation because the women participated in intervention groups that were run sequentially over a 6-month period. In this view, it is unlikely that events besides the intervention activities could have occurred between preintervention and postintervention and increased scores for these multiple intervention groups. Although history cannot account for the differential predictive power of perceived self-efficacy and hedonistic beliefs as compared with AIDS knowledge and prevention beliefs, the fact that the study did not include a control group that did not receive AIDS interventions limits the ability to draw causal inferences about intervention effects.

Obstacles to Behavior Change Efforts

Our review of the literature clearly suggests that there is a great need for additional research to develop, implement, and test AIDS risk-reduction interventions for Black and Hispanic individuals. Such efforts, however, may encounter substantial obstacles. Because of the legacy of racism, many ethnic minority individuals may distrust researchers who seek to recruit them for studies and government officials and health authorities who provide AIDS-related information and recommendations. Some ethnic minority individuals may believe that researchers are trying to exploit their community rather than to generate research that is useful to their community. They may hold the belief that researchers will use their findings to support insidious stereotypes of ethnic minority individuals or, more generally, that researchers will draw interpretations that disparage ethnic minority individuals. There has been great concern that psychological testing and research has been used inappropriately to label ethnic minority individuals as pathological or intellectually inferior (Marin & Marin, 1991; Williams, 1980).

There is also distrust of medical research. Ethnic minority individuals may believe that they are being used as guinea pigs in experiments to try out procedures that would not be tried on Whites. One often-cited example of medical research that has exploited Blacks is the infamous Tuskegee study. In that study, begun in 1934, treatment for syphilis was withheld from 412 Black male sharecroppers from Tuskegee, 1934, Alabama as a part of a study on the natural course of the disease. For 40 years, researchers observed the men as they suffered and died from the disease, without telling them that they had syphilis or treating them for it. Distrust and feelings of being exploited or used as guinea pigs could discourage participation in AIDS-related studies and negatively affect the quality of the data that are collected (Marin & Marin, 1991). This would have adverse consequences for psychological and medical research to understand the disease and AIDS-related behavior in ethnic minority individuals. Physiological and cultural differences may greatly affect treatment of diseases and risk-reduction efforts, and unless ethnic minority individuals are included in the research, these differences will not be uncovered before the research is applied. For example, drugs to treat AIDS might be differentially effective when used to treat different people depending on their ethnicity, race, or gender.

In addition to distrusting researchers, ethnic minority individuals may distrust AIDS risk-reduction advice provided by government officials and health professionals. There is evidence of distrust among a substantial number of Blacks. A New York Times/CBS telephone poll conducted in New York City in June 1990 found that 10% of Black respondents said that the AIDS virus was deliberately created in a laboratory to infect Black people. Another 19% felt that the theory might possibly be true (DeParle, 1990). Ethnic minority individuals may perceive ulterior motives in behavior change messages. For example, the message that condoms should be used or that HIV-positive pregnant women should have abortions might be seen as an effort by the system to reduce the number of ethnic minority individuals, not to reduce the spread of AIDS. Similarly, ethnic minority individuals also might be skeptical about other recommendations regarding the value of early testing to detect HIV and the use of drugs to treat AIDS.

These possibilities present formidable challenges to those who would seek to understand risk behavior among ethnic minority individuals. Research, education, and intervention strategies must take the whole context of racism and distrust into account. Researchers must be aware of the issues and must be sensitive to the culture of ethnic minority individuals in the development of conceptual models, the design and implementation of research, and the interpretation of findings. This may means seeking community involvement in the planning and implementation for AIDS risk-reduction studies. In addition, there is a need for more ethnic minority scientists who are actively involved in health and behavior research. This might include more training of ethnic minority individuals in behavioral medicine as well as incentives for established ethnic minority researchers to turn their attention to health and behavior, including HIV risk-associated behavior.

CONCLUSIONS

In conclusion, we have seen that there is ample evidence that African-Americans and Latinos are disproportionately burdened by AIDS and that the pattern of HIV exposure in African/Americans and Latinos differs from that in Whites. HIV exposure as a result of injection drug use, heterosexual sexual activity, and perinatal transmission have been far more common in African-Americans and Latinos who have AIDS, whereas exposure associated with male homosexual/bisexual contact has been most important among Whites who have AIDS. Although these risks among African-Americans and Latinos have been well documented, much less progress has been made toward scientific knowledge regarding how to reduce their risks. To be sure, we did find that some studies on ethnic minority individuals have evaluated interventions to change HIV risk-associated behavior, primarily risky sexual behavior. In addition, the subjects in these studies have included injection drug users, STD patients, adolescents in detention centers, runaway youths, and inner-city adolescents—populations thought to be at elevated risk of HIV infection. However, there have been relatively few such studies. Indeed, we are now in the second decade of the AIDS epidemic, yet there have been only 10 published intervention studies on African-Americans and only 2 that include a substantial number of Hispanics. Moreover, making it even more difficult to draw firm conclusions about the social psychology of AIDS among African-Americans and Latinos is the fact that most of the studies were not designed to test social psychological theories. Although we examined the studies and offered assessments of how they dovetail with social psychological theory, these kinds of assessments cannot substitute for a body of research aimed at testing the implications of social psychological theory for HIV risk-related behaviors. Clearly, more research is needed in this area.

Our review of the literature suggests a number of avenues that future studies should pursue. The chief weakness of the available literature from the point of view of causal inference is that few of the studies were true experiments with random assignment to conditions. More such experiments on ethnic minority individuals are needed. Particularly valuable would be experiments that test theory-based interventions. But the use of social psychological theory should not be limited to the design of intervention procedures. Theory should also drive the selection of variables to be assessed. By measuring the putative social psychological mediators of behavior change, a better conceptual understanding of risk behavior will emerge. Thus, statistical analyses might focus on whether the effects of an intervention are mediated by the conceptual variables it was designed to influence. In addition, if a theory-based intervention fails to change behavior, an examination of the putative mediators might shed light on why change did not occur or may suggest that the hypothesized variables are not important mediators. In this way, the key social psychological variables that risk-reduction interventions should target might be identified.

Future research might also attempt to find ways to reduce attrition at follow-up data collections and, in studies with multiple intervention sessions, to increase attendance at intervention sessions so as to maintain the integrity of experimental conditions. Another important issue that might be addressed is the measurement of the key outcome variable—risky sexual behavior. For the most part, the studies have relied on self-reports of behavior. The frequent criticism of self-reports is that they may be inaccurate due to memory problems or social desirability biases. A couple of studies have used condom coupon redemption as an outcome measure. Although this innovative measure is less reactive than are self-reports, a link between condom coupon redemption and condom use has not been established. Unclear is whether people who redeem condoms for coupons actually use them with their sexual partners. Moreover, there is also a potential ambiguity in the meaning of this measure. On the one hand, lower condom coupon redemption may mean more unprotected sexual activity. On the other hand, it may mean less sexual activity and consequently less need for condoms. Another potentially valuable measure for studies of sexual behavior is clinically documented sexually transmitted infections. However, even here the theoretical link with condom use is less than perfect. The absence of an STD does not necessarily mean the absence of risky sexual behavior. The upshot is that although condom procurement and STD incidence are not subject to the same sources of bias as are self-reports, there is no evidence that these measures are more valid than are self-reports. It would be premature to substitute such measures for self-reports, but a reasonable strategy might be to assess both self-reports of sexual behavior and more nonreactive measures such as STD incidence and condom coupon redemption. Although these comments on theory and method are specifically directed at AIDS risk-reduction research on ethnic minority individuals, many of them would characterize aptly AIDS risk-reduction research in general.

A number of issues regarding the specifics of intervention procedures also might be addressed in future studies. One issue that arose in the present review was the number of intervention sessions needed for optimal behavior change. Thus, studies might examine whether, holding content constant, an intervention delivered over a greater number of sessions is more effective than is an intervention delivered in fewer sessions. Another issue that arose was the specificity to AIDS of intervention content. Most studies have used interventions that were highly focused on AIDS. An alternative approach that has not received much attention is to emphasize both specific AIDS content and more general life skills and resources. According to this view, people's concerns about the risk of AIDS may take a back seat to more pressing economic and family problems, and under such circumstances, AIDS interventions may be most effective when they consider the broader context of people's lives. Future studies might test this hypothesis.

It is generally believed that interventions to reduce risky behavior among Blacks and Hispanics should adopt a culturally sensitive approach. We suggested that social psychological theories such as McGuire's model of persuasion and Fishbein and Ajzen's theory of reasoned action and its extension the theory of planned behavior can be used as conceptual frameworks for taking culture into account. However, there were no studies that provided direct tests of whether seemingly culturally sensitive aspects of interventions made a difference on any outcome measures. On the simplest level, no published studies have documented that AIDS risk-reduction interventions for Blacks are more effective when the AIDS educator is Black. More generally, the important unanswered question is whether interventions that are designed to be culturally appropriate for Blacks and Hispanics have a greater impact on HIV risk-associated behavior than do more generic interventions.

In this connection, another issue that must be addressed is how heterogeneity within ethnic minority groups might affect efforts to implement culturally sensitive interventions. It may well be that interventions that are designed to be culturally sensitive will be differentially effective depending on the individual's degree of acculturation or identification with the culture. In other words, there may be interactions between the cultural sensitivity of the intervention and the cultural identification of the recipients. Afro-centric interventions for Blacks might be most effective with Blacks who are more Afro-centric. Culturally sensitive interventions for Hispanics might be most effective with those Hispanics who are less acculturated to Anglo-American culture. Adding to the complexity, Blacks or Latinos may differ not only in identification with African-American or Latino culture, but in their ethnicity within the Black or Latino community. Thus, there are Afro-Caribbean Americans as well as African-Americans who trace their roots to the southern United States; and there are Puerto Ricans and Cuban Americans as well as Mexican Americans. Moreover, there are variations in region of the country, urban versus rural living conditions, gender by race interaction effects, immigration status, and language capability. The implications for intervention strategies of these and many other factors have not been well defined. Research programs have yet to grasp fully the behavioral implications of within-ethnic-group variation, and therefore, change efforts may have missed key features of a subgroup's response to behavior change messages.

Finally, given the paucity of empirical evidence, the conclusions we offer about the social psychology of HIV among African-Americans and Latinos must be seen as tentative—as hypotheses rather than as well-established findings. There is clearly a need for additional research in this area, but there are also potential obstacles having to do with ethnic minority individuals' distrust of researchers and skepticism about behavior change recommendations. In light of the enormity of the health problem that AIDS represents, it is hoped that sensitivity to the culture of the population, coupled with the involvement in the research of members of the population, may make those obstacles surmountable, for a social psychological perspective on HIV among ethnic minority individuals has much to offer.

ACKNOWLEDGMENTS

This research was supported in part by National Institute of Child Health and Human Development Grant R01-HD24921 and National Institute of Mental Health Grant R01-MH45668.

REFERENCES

Abelson, H., Cohen, R., Heaton, E., & Suder, C. (1971). National survey of public attitudes toward and experience with erotic materials. In *Technical report of Commission on Obscenity and Pornography* (Vol. 6, pp. 1–137). Washington, DC: U.S. Government Printing Office.

Ajzen, I. (1985). From intentions to actions: A theory of planned behavior. In J. Kuhl & J. Beckmann (Eds.), *Action-control: From cognition to behavior* (pp. 11–39). Heidelberg: Springer.

Ajzen, I. (1991). The theory of planned behavior. *Organizational Behavior and Human Decision Processes, 50,* 179–211.

Ajzen, I., & Fishbein, M. (1980). *Understanding attitudes and predicting social behavior.* Englewood Cliffs, NJ: Prentice-Hall.

Ajzen, I., & Madden, T. (1986). Prediction of goal-directed behavior: Attitudes, intentions, and perceived behavioral control. *Journal of Experimental Social Psychology, 22,* 453–74.

Baker, S. A., Thalberg, S. P., & Morrison, D. M. (1988). Parents' behavioral norms as predictors of adolescent sexual activity and contraceptive use. *Adolescence, 23,* 265–282.

Baldwin, J., & Baldwin, J. (1988). Factors affecting AIDS-related risk-taking behavior among college students. *Journal of Sex Research, 25,* 181–196

Bandura, A. (1982). Self-efficacy mechanism in human agency. *American Psychologist, 37,* 122–147.

Bandura, A. (1986). *Social foundations of thought and actions: A social cognitive theory.* Englewood Cliffs, NJ: Prentice-Hall.

Bandura, A. (1989). Perceived self-efficacy. In V. M. Mays, G. W. Albee, & S. F. Schneider (Eds.), *Primary prevention of AIDS: Psychological approaches* (pp. 128–141). Newbury Park, CA: Sage.

Belcastro, P. A. (1985). Sexual behavior differences between Black and White students. *Journal of Sex Research, 21,* 56–67.

Bell, T. A., & Holmes, K. K. (1984). Age-specific risks of syphilis, gonorrhea, and hospitalized pelvic inflammatory disease in sexually experienced U.S. women. *Sexually Transmitted Diseases, 7,* 291.

Billy, J., & Udry, J. (1985a). Patterns of adolescent friendship and effects on sexual behavior. *Social Psychology Quarterly, 48,* 27–41.

Billy, J., & Udry, J. (1985b). The influence of male and female best friends on adolescent sexual behavior. *Adolescence, 20,* 21–32.

Catania, J. A., Coates, T. J., Kegeles, S. M., Estrand, M., Guydish, J. R., & Bye, L. L. (1989). Implications of the AIDS risk-reduction model for the gay community: The importance of perceived sexual enjoyment and help-seeking behaviors. In V. M. Mays, G. W. Albee & S. F. Schneider (Eds.), *Primary prevention of AIDS: Psychological approaches* (pp. 242–261). Newbury Park, CA: Sage.

Catania, J. A., Dolcini, M. M., Coates, T. J., Kegeles, S. M., Greenblatt, R. M., Puckett, S., Corman, M., & Miller, J. (1989). Predictors of condom use and multiple partnered sex among sexually-active adolescent women: Implications for AIDS-related health interventions. *Journal of Sex Research, 26,* 514–524.

Cates, W., Jr. (1987). Epidemiology and control of sexually transmitted diseases: Strategic evolution. *Infectious Disease Clinics of North America, 1,* 1–23.

Cauce, A., Felner, R., & Primavera, J. (1982). Social support in high risk adolescents: Structural components and adaptive impact. *Journal of Community Psychology, 10,* 417–428.

Centers for Disease Control. (1990). *National HIV seroprevalence surveys: Summary of results. Data from serosurveillance activities through 1989.* Atlanta, GA: Center for Infectious Disease, Centers for Disease Control.

Centers for Disease Control. (1991a). *HIV/AIDS Surveillance Report, July, 1–18.* Atlanta, GA: Center for Infectious Diseases, Centers for Disease Control.

Centers for Disease Control. (1991b). Premarital sexual experience among adolescent women: United States, 1970–1988. *Morbidity and Mortality Weekly Report, 39,* 929–932.

Clark, M. L. (1989). Friendship and peer relations in Black adolescents. In R. L. Jones (Ed.), *Black adolescents* (pp. 175–204). Berkeley, CA: Cobb & Henry.

Coates, T. J., McKusick, L., Kuno, R., & Stites, D. P. (1989). Stress reduction training changed number of sexual partners but not immune function in men with HIV. *American Journal of Public Health, 79,* 885–887.

Darabi, K. F., Dryfoos, J., & Schwartz, D. (1986). Hispanic adolescent fertility. *Hispanic Journal of Behavioral Sciences, 8,* 157–171.

DeParle, J. (1990 October 29). Talk of government being out to get Blacks falls on more attentive ears. *New York Times,* p. B7.

DiCindio, L., Floyd, H., Wilcox, J., & McSeveny, D. (1983). Race effects in a model of parent-peer orientation. *Adolescence, 18,* 369–379.

DiClemente, R. J., Boyer, C. B., & Morales, E. (1988). Minorities and AIDS: Knowledge, attitudes, and misconceptions among Black and Latino adolescents. *American Journal of Public Health, 78,* 55–57.

DiClemente, R. J., Forrest, K. A., & Mickler, S. (1990). College students' knowledge and attitudes about AIDS and changes in HIV-preventive behaviors. *AIDS Education and Prevention, 2,* 201–212.

DiClemente, R. J., Zorn, J., & Temoshok, L. (1986). Adolescents and AIDS: A survey of knowledge, attitudes and beliefs about AIDS in San Francisco. *American Journal of Public Health, 76,* 1443–1445.

Emmons, C., Joseph, J. G., Kessler, R. C., Wortman, C. B., Montgomery, S. B., & Ostrow, D. G. (1986). Psychosocial predictors of reported behavior change in homosexual men at risk for AIDS. *Health Education Quarterly, 13,* 331–345.

Fishbein, M., & Ajzen, I. (1975). *Belief, attitude, intention and behavior.* Boston: Addison-Wesley.

Fishbein, M., & Middlestadt, S. (1989). Using the theory of reasoned action as a framework for understanding and changing AIDS-related behaviors. In V. Mays, G. Albee, & S. Schneider (Eds.), *Primary prevention of AIDS: Psychological approaches* (pp. 93–110). Newbury Park, CA: Sage.

Fisher, J., & Fisher, W. (1992). Changing AIDS risk behavior. *Psychological Bulletin, 111,* 455–474.

Fox, G. L, & Inazu, J. K. (1980). Patterns and outcomes of mother-daughter communication about sexuality. *Journal of Social Issues, 36,* 7–29.

Furstenberg, F. F. (1971). Birth control experience among pregnant adolescents: The process of unplanned parenthood. *Social Problems, 19,* 192–203.

Gilliam, A., & Seltzer, R. (1989). The efficacy of educational movies on AIDS knowledge and attitudes among college students. *Journal of American College Health, 37,* 261–265.

Handelsman, C. D., Cabral, R. J., & Weisfeld, G. E. (1987). Sources of information and adolescent sexual knowledge and behavior. *Journal of Adolescent Research, 2,* 455–463.

Hatcher, R. A., Stewart, F. H., Trussell, J., Kowal, D., Guest, F., Stewart, G. K., & Cates, W. (1990). *Contraceptive technology 1990–1992.* New York: Irvington.

Hingson, R. W., Strunin, L., Berlin, B., & Heeren, T. (1990). Beliefs about AIDS, use of alcohol and drugs, and unprotected sex among Massachusetts adolescents. *American Journal of Public Health, 80,* 295–299.

Hofferth S., & Hayes, C. (1987). *Risking the future* (Vol. 2). Washington, DC: National Academy Press.

Hofferth, S., Kahn, J., & Baldwin, W. (1987). Premarital sexual activity among U.S. teenage women over the past three decades. *Family Planning Perspectives, 19*(20) 46–53.

Hovland, C., Janis, I., & Kelley, H. H. (1953). *Communication and persuasion.* New Haven, CT: Yale University Press.

Janz, N. K., & Becker, B. H. (1984). The health belief model: A decade later. *Health Education Quarterly, 11,* 1–47.

Jemmott, J. B. III, Jemmott, L. S., & Fong, G. T. (1992). Reductions in HIV risk-associated sexual behaviors among Black male adolescents: Effects of an AIDS prevention intervention. *American Journal of Public Health, 82,* 372–377.

Jemmott, J. B., III, Jemmott, L. S., Spears, H., Hewitt, N., & Cruz-Collins, M. (1992). Self-efficacy, hedonistic expectancies, and condom-use intentions among inner-city Black adolescent women: A social cognitive approach to AIDS risk behavior. *Journal of Adolescent Health, 13,* 512–519.

Jemmott, L. S., & Jemmott, J. B., III. (1990). Sexual knowledge, attitudes, and risky sexual behavior among inner-city Black male adolescents. *Journal of Adolescent Research, 5,* 346–369.

Jemmott, L. S., & Jemmott, J. B., III. (1991). Applying the theory of reasoned action to AIDS risk behavior: Condom use among Black women. *Nursing Research, 40,* 228–234.

Jemmott, L. S., & Jemmott, J. B., III. (1992). Increasing condom-use intentions among sexually active inner-city Black adolescent women: Effects of an AIDS prevention program. *Nursing Research, 41,* 273–279.

Jones, L., Forrest, J. D., Goldman, N., Henshaw, S., Lincoln, R., Rosoff, J. I., Westoff, C. F., & Wulf, D. (Eds.). (1986). *Teenage pregnancy in industrialized countries.* New Haven, CT: Yale University Press.

Jones, J. B., & Philliber, S. (1983). Sexually active but not pregnant: A comparison of teens who risk and teens who plan. *Journal of Youth and Adolescence, 12,* 235–251.

Joseph, J. G., Montgomery, S. B., Emmons, C., Kessler, R. C., Ostrow, D., Wortman, C., O'Brien, K., Eller, M., & Eshleman, S. (1987). Magnitude and determinants of behavioral risk reductions: Longitudinal analysis of a cohort at risk for AIDS. *Psychology and Health, 1,* 73–95.

Kalichman, S. C., Kelly, J. A., & St. Lawrence, J. S. (1990). Factors influencing reduction of sexual risk behaviors for human immunodeficiency virus infection: A review. *Annals of Sex Research, 3,* 129–148.

Kegeles, S. M., Adler, N. A. & Irwin, C. E., Jr. (1988). Sexually active adolescents and condoms: Changes over one year in knowledge, attitudes, and use. *American Journal of Public Health, 78,* 460–461.

Kelly, J. A., & Murphy, D. A. (1992). Psychological interventions with AIDS and HIV: Prevention and treatment. *Journal of Consulting and Clinical Psychology, 60,* 576–585.

Kelly, J. A., St. Lawrence, J. S., Diaz, Y. E., Stevenson, L. Y., Hauth, A. C., Brasfield, T. L., Kalichman, S. C., Smith, J. E., & Andrew, M. E. (1991). HIV risk behavior reduction following intervention with key opinion leaders of population. *American Journal of Public Health, 81,* 168–171.

Kelly, J. A., St. Lawrence, J. S., Hood, H. V., & Brasfield, T. L. (1989). Behavioral intervention to reduce AIDS risk activities. *Journal of Consulting and Clinical Psychology, 57,* 60–67.

Kirscht, J. P., & Joseph, J. G. (1989). The health belief model: Some implications for behavior change with reference to homosexual males, In V. M. Mays, G. W. Albee, & S. F. Schndeider (Eds.), *Primary prevention of AIDS: Psychological approaches* (pp. 111–127). Newbury Park, CA: Sage.

Lanier, M. M., & McCarthy, B. R. (1989). AIDS awareness and the impact of AIDS education in juvenile corrections. *Criminal Justice and Behavior, 16,* 395–411.

LeVine, E., & Franco, J. N. (1981). A reassessment of self-disclosure patterns among Anglo Americans and Hispanics. *Journal of Counseling Psychology, 28,* 522–524.

Lindemann, C., & Scott, W. (1982). The fertility-related behavior of Mexican American adolescents. *Journal of Early Adolescence, 2,* 31–38.

London, K. A. (1991). *Cohabitation, marriage, marital dissolution, and remarriage: United States. 1988. Advance data from vital and health statistics,* (no. 194). Hyattsville, MD: National Center for Health Statistics.

Madden, T. J., Ellen, P. S., & Ajzen, I. (1992). A comparison of the theory of planned behavior and the theory of reasoned action. *Personality and Social Psychology Bulletin, 18,* 3–9.

Marin, B., Marin, G., Juarez, R. (1990). Differences between Hispanics and non-Hispanics in willingness to provide AIDS prevention advice. *Hispanic Journal of Behavioral Sciences, 12,* 153–164.

Marin, G., & Marin, B. V. (1991). *Research with Hispanic populations.* Newbury Park, CA: Sage.

Mays, V. M. (1989). AIDS prevention in Black populations: Methods of a safer kind. In V. M. Mays, G. W. Albee, & S. F. Schneider (Eds.), *Primary prevention of AIDS: Psychological approaches* (pp. 264—279). Newbury Park, CA: Sage.

Mays, V. M., & Cochran, S. D. (1988). Issues in the perception of AIDS risk and risk reduction activities by Black and Hispanic/Latina women. *American Psychologist, 43,* 949–957.

MacDonald, N. E., Wells, G. A., Fisher, W. A., Warren, W. K., King, M., Doherty, J. A., & Bowie, W. R. (1990). High-risk STD/HIV behavior among college students. *Journal of the American Medical Association, 263,* 3155–3159.

McGuire, W. J. (1969). The nature of attitudes and attitude changes. In G. Lindzey & E. Aronson (Eds.), *Handbook of social psychology* (Vol. 3, pp. 136–314). Reading, MA: Addison-Wesley.

McGuire, W. J. (1985) Attitudes and attitude change. In G. Lindzey & E. Aronson (Eds.), *Handbook of social psychology* (pp. 233–346). New York: Random House.

Mosher, W. D., & Pratt, W. F. (1990). *Contraceptive use in the United States, 1973–1988. Advance data from vital and health statistics* (no. 182). Hyattsville, MD: National Center for Health Statistics.

McKusick, L., Coates, T., Morin, S. F., Pollac, M. A., & Hoff, C. (1990). Longitudinal predictors of unprotected anal intercourse among gay men in San Francisco: The AIDS Behavioral Research Project. *American Journal of Public Health, 80,* 978–983.

Namerow, P. B., & Jones, J. E. (1982). Ethnic variation in adolescent use of a contraceptive service. *Journal of Adolescent Health Care, 3,* 165–172.

Nathanson, C. A., & Becker, M. H. (1986). Family and peer influence on obtaining a method of contraception. *Journal of Marriage and the Family, 48,* 513–526.

O'Leary, A. (1985). Self-efficacy and health. *Behavioral Research and Therapy, 23,* 437–451.

O'Leary, A., Goodhart, F., Jemmott, L. S., & Boccher-Lattimore, D. (1992). Predictors of safer sex on the college campus: A social cognitive theory analysis. *Journal of American College Health, 40,* 254–263.

Padilla, E. R., & O'Grady, K. E. (1987). Sexuality among Mexican Americans: A case of sexual stereotyping. *Journal of Personality and Social Psychology, 52,* 5–10.

Peterson, J. L., & Marin, G. (1988). Issues in the prevention of AIDS among Black and Hispanic men. *American Psychologist, 11,* 871–877.

Petty, R., & Cacioppo, J. (1986). The elaboration likelihood model of persuasion. In L. Berkowitz (Ed.), *Advances in experimental social psychology* (Vol. 19, pp. 123–205). New York: Academic Press.

Pleck, J. H. (1989). Correlates of Black adolescent males' condom use. *Journal of Adolescent Research, 4,* 247–253.

Pratt, W., Mosher, W., Bachrach, C., & Horn, M. (1984). Understanding U.S. fertility: Findings from the National Survey of Family Growth, Cycle III. *Population Bulletin, 39,* 1–42.

Price, J. H., Desmond, S., & Kukula, G. (1985). High school students' perceptions and misperceptions of AIDS. *Journal of School Health, 55,* 107–109.

Reinisch, J. M., Sanders, S. A., & Ziemba-Davis, M. (1988). The study of sexual behavior in relation to the transmission of human immunodeficiency virus. *American Psychologist, 43,* 921–927.

Rickert, V. I., Gottlieb, A., & Jay, M. S. (1990). A comparison of three clinic-based AIDS education programs on female adolescents' knowledge, attitudes and behavior. *Journal of Adolescent Health Care, 11,* 298–303.

Rotheram-Borus, M. J., Koopman, C., Haignere, C., & Davies, M. (1991). Reducing HIV sexual risk behaviors among runaway adolescents. *Journal of the American Medical Association, 266,* 1237–1241.

Rotheram-Borus, M. J., Mahler, K. A., & Rosario, M. (1991). *AIDS prevention with adolescents.* Unpublished manuscript, Division of Child Psychiatry, College of Physicians and Surgeons, Columbia University, New York.

Schifter, D. E., & Ajzen, I. (1985). Intention, perceived control, and weight loss: An application of the theory of planned behavior. *Journal of Personality and Social Psychology, 49,* 843–851.

Schinke, S. P., Gordon, A. N., & Weston, R. E. (1990). Self-instruction to prevent HIV infection among African-American and Hispanic-American adolescents. *Journal of Consulting and Clinical Psychology, 58,* 432–436.

Selik, R. M., Castro, K. G., Pappaioanou, M., & Buehler, J. W. (1989). Birthplace and the risk of AIDS among Hispanics in the United States. *American Journal of Public Health, 79,* 836–839.

Solomon, M. Z., & DeJong, W. (1989). Preventing AIDS and other STDs through condom promotion: A patient education intervention. *American Journal of Public Health, 79,* 453–458.

Sonenstein, F. L., Pleck, J. H., & Leighton, C. K. (1989). Sexual activity, condom use and AIDS awareness among adolescent males. *Family Planning Perspectives, 21,* 152–158.

Sorensen, R. (1973). *Adolescent sexuality in contemporary America.* New York: World Publishing.

Stephens, R., Feucht, T., & Roman, S. (1991). Effects of an intervention program on AIDS-related drug and needle behavior among intravenous drug users. *American Journal of Public Health, 81,* 568–571.

Taylor, H., Kagay, M., & Leichenko, S. (1986). *American teens speak: Sex, myths, TV, and birth control.* New York: Planned Parenthood Federation of America, Inc.

Thomas, S. B., Gilliam, A. G., & Iwrey, C. G. (1989). Knowledge about AIDS and reported risk behaviors among Black college students. *Journal of American College Health, 38,* 61–66.

Thompson, L., & Spanier, G. (1978). Influence of parents, peers and partners on the contraceptive use of college men and women. *Journal of Marriage and the Family, 40,* 481–492.

Valdiserri, R. O., Arena, V. C., Proctor, D., & Bonati, F. A. (1989). The relationship between women's attitudes about condoms and their use: implications for condom promotion programs. *American Journal of Public Health, 79,* 499–503.

Valdiserri, R. O., Lyter, D. W., Leviton, L. C., Callahan, C. M., Kingsley, L. A., & Rinaldo, C. R. (1989). AIDS prevention in homosexual and bisexual men: Results of a randomized trial evaluating two risk reduction interventions. *AIDS, 3,* 21–26.

Williams, R. L. (1990). The death of white research in the Black community. In R. L. Jones (Ed.), *Black psychology* (pp. 403–416). New York: Harper & Row.

Wyatt, G. E., Peters, S., & Guthrie, D. (1988a). Kinsey revisited, I: Comparisons of sexual socialization and sexual behavior of White women over 33 years. *Archives of Sexual Behavior, 17,* 201–239.

Wyatt, G. E., Peters, S., & Guthrie, D. (1988b). Kinsey revisited, II: Comparisons of sexual socialization and sexual behavior of Black women over 33 years. *Archives of Sexual Behavior, 17,* 289–332.

Zabin, L., & Clark, S. D., Jr. (1981). Why they delay: A study of teenage family planning clinic patients. *Family Planning Perspectives, 13,* 205–217.

Zelnik, M., & Kantner, J. (1980). Sexual activity, contraceptive use, and pregnancy among metropolitan-area teenagers: 1971–1979. *Family Planning Perspectives, 12,* 230–237.

Zelnik, M., Kantner, J., & Ford, K. (1981). *Sex and pregnancy in adolescence.* Beverly hills, CA: Sage.

II THE DILEMMA OF THE PWA: STIGMA, PROSOCIAL REACTIONS, AND COPING

UNDERSTANDING THE STIGMA OF AIDS

8 Public Attitudes Toward AIDS-Related Issues in the United States

Gregory M. Herek
University of California, Davis

Eric K. Glunt
Graduate Center, City University of New York

During the 1980s, California voters were asked four times to enact sweeping public policies concerning AIDS. The first occasion was in 1986 when Proposition 64 was placed on the state ballot by a group called the Prevent AIDS Now Initiative Committee (PANIC), which was closely linked to Lyndon LaRouche's National Democratic Policy Committee. Proposition 64 would have declared AIDS and HIV infection as "infectious, contagious, and communicable" conditions and would have required that they be placed on the state's list of reportable diseases and conditions. As a consequence, people with AIDS or infected with HIV would be subject to various public health restrictions, including quarantine (California Senate Office of Research, 1986; Petit, 1986). Proposition 64 was eventually defeated by a 2-to-1 margin (see Krieger & Lashof, 1988, for a case study of the campaign). It was revived in 1988 as Proposition 69, but received little attention and ultimately lost by an even greater margin ("Election highlights," 1988; McLeod, 1988).

In November 1988, two new AIDS initiatives appeared on the California ballot. Proposition 102 was sponsored by Orange County Congressman William Dannemeyer. It would have eliminated anonymous HIV testing, required reporting of HIV-infected persons and their sexual partners to health departments, repealed legislation prohibiting employment discrimination on the basis of HIV antibody test results, and permitted use of test results by insurance companies (Coles, 1988a; Olszewski, 1988a). Proposition 102 was defeated on election day by a margin of 66% to 34% (Olszewski, 1988c).

The second 1988 initiative, Proposition 96, was sponsored by the sheriff of Los Angeles County. It required HIV testing (with or without consent) of anyone who was both charged with a crime and accused of having interfered with the

229

official duties of a police officer, firefighter, or emergency medical worker. Testing would be mandatory if requested by the officer and ordered by a judge (Coles, 1988b; "First use of Prop. 96's AIDS test rule," 1988; Olszewski, 1988b). Proposition 96 passed by a margin of 62% to 38% (Hilton, 1988).

The four California initiatives were unusual in that they required voters directly to decide public policy concerning AIDS. More often in the epidemic's first decade, the public's influence was through elected representatives who implemented AIDS policy. Although less direct than the initiative process, the public's choice of elected leaders has had profound consequences for the epidemic. Ronald Reagan, for example, whose presidency included the first 7 years of the epidemic, did not even make explicit public statements about AIDS until 1987—more than 5 years and tens of thousands of deaths after the first cases were diagnosed (Panem, 1987; Shilts, 1987). And, apparently perceiving widespread public antipathy toward gay men, the U.S. Senate twice endorsed an amendment by Jesse Helms (R-NC) that prohibited federal funds for AIDS education materials that "promote or encourage, directly or indirectly, homosexual activities" ("Limit voted on AIDS funds," 1987). During the same period, members of congress (including many of the same senators who voted for the Helms amendments) also appropriated large sums of money for AIDS research and prevention efforts, often in opposition to the wishes of the president (Panem, 1987; Shilts, 1987).

As illustrated by these examples, public opinion has shaped the response of American society to AIDS. In the epidemic's second decade, this influence will become even more important. In addition to being confronted by questions about public health aspects of HIV (e.g., how to prevent transmission), Americans increasingly will be called on to respond individually to persons with AIDS in their schools, neighborhoods, workplaces, and families. They also will have to confront the epidemic's considerable economic costs (Bloom & Carliner, 1988; Hay, Osmond, & Jacobson, 1988; Scitovsky & Rice, 1987). Consequently, understanding public reactions will continue to be critically important for educating the U.S. population about the epidemic, promoting enlightened public policy, and fostering compassion for persons infected with HIV.

Because the epidemic is a complex social phenomenon, individual attitudes concerning AIDS are multifaceted. The rubric of "AIDS-related attitudes" includes: (a) attitudes associated with reducing one's own risk for infection or, if already infected, for slowing disease progression and maintaining the quality of one's life; (b) attitudes toward various strategies for society to prevent HIV transmission and to care for the sick; and (c) attitudes toward persons with AIDS, persons infected with HIV, and their communities.

This chapter addresses the last two categories: the attitudes of U.S. adults— most of them not infected with HIV—toward AIDS-related public policies and toward people with AIDS. Most previous research in this area has been descriptive (Blake & Arkin, 1988; Hardy, 1991; Singer & Rogers, 1986; Singer, Rogers, & Blattner, 1991; Singer, Rogers, & Corcoran, 1987), much of it conducted by mass media organizations in response to current news stories about AIDS (Dearing, 1989). The primary goal of our project, in contrast, is to provide insights into the social psychological origins of AIDS-related attitudes.

In our research, we have paid special attention to the stigma that so closely accompanies HIV disease in the United States. *Stigma* is defined here as a pattern of social prejudice, discounting, and discrediting that an individual experiences as a result of others' judgments about her or his personal characteristics or group membership (Goffman, 1963; Herek, 1990). As discussed elsewhere (Herek, 1990; Herek & Glunt, 1988), AIDS-related stigma results from the properties of AIDS as a disease (e.g., its tendency to disfigure one's appearance and to impair one's ability for social interaction, its communicability, its lethality) and from its characteristics as a social phenomenon (i.e., its prevalence among already stigmatized groups such as gay men, IV-drug users, African-Americans, and Hispanics).

Stigma has had profound consequences for people with AIDS (PWAs). Individuals perceived to be infected with HIV have been fired from their jobs, driven from their homes, and socially isolated (Herek & Glunt, 1988). PWAs are more negatively evaluated than are persons with other diseases (Katz, Hass, Parisi, Astone, & McEvaddy, 1987; Kelly, St. Lawrence, Smith, Hood, & Cook, 1987; Triplet & Sugarman, 1987; Weiner, 1988). Avoidance of PWAs and overestimation of the risks of casual contact have been common, even among medical professionals and caregivers (Blumenfield, Smith, Milazzo, Seropian, & Wormser, 1987; Gerbert, Maguire, Bleecker, Coates, & McPhee, 1991: Kelly et al., 1987; Knox, Dow, & Cotton, 1989; Mejta, Denton, Krems, & Hiatt, 1988; O'Donnell, O'Donnell, Pleck, Snarey, & Rose, 1987; Wallack, 1989; Wertz, Sorenson, Liebling, Kessler, & Heeren, 1987; Wiley, Heath, & Acklin, 1988). Despite repeated explanations by public health officials, a significant minority of the U.S. public has endorsed ineffective and repressive measures such as general quarantine of HIV-infected persons, universal mandatory testing, and even tattooing of infected individuals (e.g., Blendon & Donelan, 1988; Price & Hsu, 1992; Schneider, 1987; Singer & Rogers, 1986; Stipp & Kerr, 1989).

To some extent, such reactions would be expected to accompany any epidemic of a lethal disease (Herek, 1990; McNeill, 1976; Rosenberg, 1987). The specific nature of AIDS-related stigma, however, appears to derive in large part from the high prevalence of AIDS in the United States among society's outgroups. In particular, AIDS seems to have provided many Americans with a vehicle for expressing antigay prejudice. It is a convenient hook upon which they can hang their preexisting hostility toward gay men, lesbians, and anyone who engages in homosexual behavior.[1]

---

[1] Although the proportion of U.S. cases resulting from unprotected male homosexual behavior is decreasing relative to those resulting from injecting drug use and unprotected heterosexual behavior, unprotected male–male sexual behavior continues to be the route of transmission for most reported AIDS cases in this country (Centers for Disease Control, 1992).

During the mid-1980's, for example, approximately one-quarter of the respondents to *Los Angeles Times* polls agreed that "AIDS" is a punishment God has given homosexuals for the way they live"—28% on December 5, 1985; 24% on July 9, 1986; and 27% on July 24, 1987. Nearly half (46%) of the respondents to a CBS poll in September 1988 expressed "a lot" of sympathy for people who have AIDS; only 15% replied "not much" and 5% volunteered "none." But when asked about sympathy for people who get AIDS from homosexual activity, only 17% replied "very much," whereas 42% replied "not much" and 18% volunteered "none"[2] (see also Blendon & Donelan, 1988). Heterosexuals who express negative attitudes toward gay people are more likely than others to be poorly informed and excessively fearful concerning AIDS, and to stigmatize people with AIDS (Bouton et al., 1987; D'Augelli, 1989; Goodwin & Roscoe, 1988; McDevitt, Sheehan, Lennon, & Ambrosio, 1990; Michaels, Gagnon, Laumann, & Michael, 1990; Pryor, Reeder, Vinacco, & Kott, 1989; Sheehan, Lennon, & McDevitt, 1990; Stipp & Kerr, 1989; Young, Gallaher, Belasco, Barr, & Webber, 1991). Further, gay men with AIDS are more likely to be negatively evaluated than are heterosexuals with AIDS (Triplet & Sugarman, 1987; Weiner, 1988).[3]

Clearly, understanding attitudes toward gay people is necessary for understanding AIDS-related attitudes generally and AIDS-related stigma specifically. But how does antigay prejudice combine with other factors to affect public reactions to AIDS? Are AIDS attitudes unidimensional, or do they consist of multiple domains? If so, do AIDS attitudes in different domains have the same social psychological antecedents? Are these relationships similar among different demographic groups?

To answer these questions, we began by conducting focus groups in different cities and towns in the United States. We listened to the language that participants used to discuss AIDS, assessed their reactions to specific attitude items, and developed hypotheses concerning the social psychological bases for reactions to AIDS. The qualitative and quantitative data from the groups then guided us in constructing a survey instrument for administration by telephone with a national sample.

---

[2]The data described in this section were obtained from the Roper Center, University of Connecticut at Storrs. We thank Professor Bliss Siman, Baruch College of the City University of New York, for her assistance in obtaining them.

[3]It is worth noting here the distinction between gay people as a social group and non-gay individuals who engage in homosexual behavior. The former category comprises men and women who belong to a community and for whom being gay or lesbian is an important component of identity (and who may or may not currently engage in sexual activity). The latter consists of people who have in common only the fact that they engage in sexual behavior with others of their own gender; they may think of themselves as bisexual, heterosexual, or even asexual. In epidemiological terms, HIV can infect any man who engages in unprotected homosexual behavior, regardless of whether or not he thinks of himself as gay (HIV transmission through female homosexual behavior appears to be rare). From a social psychological perspective, however, it is important to recognize that public attitudes concerning AIDS are often intertwined with attitudes toward the gay and lesbian community.

STUDY 1: THE 1988 FOCUS GROUP SAMPLE

Method

During the spring and summer of 1988, we conducted 22 focus groups with 155 English-speaking adult participants in five U.S. cities: 3 groups each in Detroit, Michigan ($n = 16$), Houston, Texas ($n = 29$), Atlanta, Georgia ($n = 29$), and Lincoln, Nebraska ($n = 27$), and 10 groups in New York ($n = 54$).[4] Overall, the racial composition of participants was divided nearly equally between Blacks (48% of males, 46% of females) and Whites (42% of males, 50% of females). The remaining 13 participants classified themselves as Hispanic, Asian, or of mixed ancestry.

Before beginning each 90-minute group discussion, we asked participants to complete a preliminary questionnaire that included knowledge and attitude items about AIDS. After the discussion, they completed the short form of the Attitudes Toward Gay Men (ATG) scale (Herek, 1988), some demographic items, and additional scales not pertinent to this chapter. In the remainder of this section, we focus on the quantitative data obtained from respondents' questionnaire responses. Insights from the content of the focus group discussions are mentioned when appropriate.

Questionnaires

Knowledge about AIDS Transmission. Respondents judged the likelihood that each of 12 different behaviors could transmit AIDS, using a 5-point, Likert-type scale ranging from "not at all likely" to "very likely." Only 2 of the 12 behaviors are recognized as capable of transmitting HIV ("sharing a hypodermic needle ['works']" and "during sex, having a man's semen [sperm/cum] enter one's body"). The remaining items represented various types of casual social contact through which HIV cannot be transmitted. Based on the results of a factor analysis, 10 items were selected to constitute two different scales: a 2-item Intimate Contact Knowledge scale, with high scores indicating accurate knowledge about the routes through which HIV can be transmitted (*alpha* = .54), and an 8-item Casual Contact Beliefs scale,[5] with high scores indicating overestima-

---

[4]We thank Jorge Ayala, Cristobal Carambo, Heléne Clark, Marsha Jordan-Wright, Julia Navarez de Jesus, Barbara Tiwald, and David Whittier for their assistance in conducting the focus groups; and Carolyn Block Talar for her invaluable administrative assistance.

[5]The items included in the scale are:

1. eating food in a restaurant
2. using a public telephone
3. using a public toilet
4. being in a place where persons with AIDS gather
5. standing near a person with AIDS who is coughing or sneezing
6. sharing a drinking glass
7. being bitten by a mosquito
8. shaking hands with a person with AIDS.

tion of the risks posed by casual contact (*alpha* = .77). (For details of the factor analysis and other results described in this section, see Herek & Glunt, 1991.)

AIDS Policy Attitudes.   Respondents also indicated their level of agreement with 13 different statements about AIDS, people with AIDS, and AIDS-related policies. A 5-point, Likert-type scale was used, ranging from "strongly disagree" to "strongly agree." A series of exploratory principal components factor analyses were conducted using different rotational techniques and extracting different numbers of factors. A two-factor solution using an oblique rotation emerged as the most interpretable. The first factor, which accounted for 22.5% of the variance, included items advocating government distribution of condoms and clean needles for IV drugs, government sponsorship of AIDS research and education about safer sex techniques, and enactment of AIDS-related civil rights legislation. Informed by the group discussions, we hypothesized that endorsement of these items represented respondents' willingness to suspend moral judgments about sexual behavior and drug use in the interests of preventing AIDS and thereby saving lives. Acceptance for free distribution of clean needles, AIDS-education in public schools, and distribution of free condoms seemed to reflect a sentiment that responding to the AIDS crisis should override concerns about "public morality" that typically have infused debate about sex education and drug abuse prevention programs. Rejection of the items, we hypothesized, represented an unwillingness to "condone" drug use or certain sexual behaviors through government policies. We labeled this the *pragmatism/moralism* factor.

The second factor, accounting for 16.6% of the variance, included items advocating quarantine, mandatory HIV testing, and public identification of people with AIDS. We hypothesized that endorsement of these items indicates a perception of persons with AIDS as dangerous and requiring physical containment, through punitive measures if necessary. Rejection of the items indicated a general view that PWAs are not dangerous and are deserving of compassion. We labeled this the *coercion/compassion* factor.

Two 5-item additive scales were constructed from the items (see Table 8.1). The pragmatism/moralism items were combined into an AIDS Pragmatism scale (*alpha* = .68), with high scores indicating endorsement of nonmoralistic prevention policies. The coercion/compassion items were combined into an AIDS Coercion scale (*alpha* = .66), with high scores indicating endorsement of restrictive and punitive policies. The two measures were not significantly correlated (*r* = .13).

Attitudes Toward Gay Men.   The 5-item short form of the Attitudes Toward Gay Men (ATG) scale (Herek, 1988) was administered, with the same 5-point Likert-type scale as used for the AIDS policy attitudes items. The ATG is a highly reliable measure of heterosexuals' attitudes toward gay men; its validity has been well-documented (Herek, 1984, 1987a, 1987b, 1988). High scores

TABLE 8.1
Factor Loadings for AIDS-Related Policy Attitude Items (Focus Group Sample)

Item	Coercion/Compassion (16.6%)	Pragmatism/Moralism (22.5%)
The government should give away condoms ("rubbers") to stop the spread of AIDS.	—	.7557
The federal government should pay for educational programs to teach people how to have "safer sex."	—	.7431
The federal government should spend more money for reearch on AIDS.	—	.6430
Our country needs civil rights laws to protect people with AIDS from discrimination.	—	.5945
The government should fight AIDS among drug users by giving clean needles to anyone who wants them.	—	.5629
Parents should not have to send their children to a school where another child with AIDS is enrolled.	.7122	—
People with AIDS should be legally quarantined to protect the public health.	.6963	—
More effort should go to testing people for the AIDS virus than should go to public education about AIDS.	.5650	—
The names of people with AIDS should be published in newspapers so that other can avoid them.	.5545	—
All people at high risk for AIDS should be required to take the test for AIDS antibodies.	.4996	—
People who want to quarantine persons with AIDS are just showing their own bigotry.	—	—
I would accept a group home in my neighborhood where people with AIDS could live and get good care.	—	.4534
Scientists who say that AIDS isn't spread by casual contact don't really know as much as they claim.	.5263	—

Note: Loadings less than .45 are omitted. Loadings are for a principal components analysis with varimax rotation (with oblique rotation, interfactor correlation = -.11). Responses are on a 5-point Likert type scale, ranging from "strongly disagree" to strongly agree" (n = 143). The final three items were not used in the AIDS attitude scales.

indicate more negative attitudes. Internal consistency for the ATG scale was acceptably high (*alpha* = .83).[6]

---

[6]Because of time limitations and because the AIDS epidemic has been closely linked to gay men in popular perceptions, the Attitudes Toward Lesbians (ATL) scale was not included in the questionnaire battery.

Demographic Data.   Information was obtained about participants' gender, age, race, frequency of attendance at religious services in the past year ("never," "once or twice," "monthly," or "weekly"), and number of years of formal education.

Results

We explored the social psychological antecedents of AIDS-related attitudes by conducting separate regression analyses with AIDS-Coercion and AIDS-Pragmatism scores as dependent variables. Our overall approach was first to assess the extent to which demographic variables could account for variance in the dependent variables and then to examine whether measures of attitudes, values, and beliefs could explain additional variance.

Accordingly, the variables of gender and race (coded as dummy variables), education and age were entered on the first step of the equation. On the second step, multiplicative interaction terms for these demographic variables (e.g., race X gender) were entered. ATG and Casual Contact Beliefs scores were entered on the third step, along with religious attendance. In preliminary analyses, Intimate Contact Knowledge scores and two-way and three-way multiplicative interaction terms failed to explain a significant amount of variance in AIDS attitudes and so were excluded from the final regression equations.

We obtained different results for the two equations. For AIDS-Coercion attitudes, three variables emerged as significant predictors ($R^2 = .3819, p < .001$): (1) Casual Contact Beliefs (accounting for 10.4% of the variance; $b = 0.2290$, $beta = .3359, t = 3.968, p < .001$); (2) educational level (9.9% of the variance; $b = -0.4317, beta = -.2380, t = -2.957, p < .01$); and (3) ATG scores (7.4% of the variance; $b = 0.2447, beta = .3282, t = 3.680, p < .001$). Respondents were more likely to endorse coercive policies to the extent that they overestimated the risks posed by casual contact, did not have extensive formal education, and expressed negative attitudes toward gay men. For AIDS-Pragmatism attitudes ($R^2 = .1527, p < .05$), only religious attendance emerged as significant (9.3% of the variance; $b = -1.2565, beta = -.3482, t = -3.387, p < .001$), indicating that pragmatic policies were more strongly supported by individuals who were not highly religious.

Discussion

The results from the focus group sample suggested four important hypotheses for follow-up research. First, AIDS-related attitudes appeared to be cognitively organized into two distinct domains, which we tentatively labeled coercion/compassion and pragmatism/moralism. Second, attitudes in the two domains were not strongly intercorrelated. Some people scored high only on AIDS-Coercion attitudes, others only on AIDS-Pragmatism attitudes, others on both, and still others did not score high on either. Third, attitudes in the two domains appeared to have different social psychological antecedents. High AIDS-Coercion scores were associated with misinformation about casual contact, lower educational levels, and hostile attitudes toward gay men. High AIDS-Pragmatism scores, in contrast, were predicted only by infrequent attendance at religious services.

Finally, the content of the focus group discussions suggested to us that Blacks and Whites may have different views of the epidemic. In particular, we noted that the epidemic seemed to be perceived as a more immediate threat by African-Americans, whereas Whites' concerns were less realistic and more abstract. African-American participants also expressed greater distrust of the government and of experts, and were more likely to believe that the AIDS epidemic is being used as an excuse to persecute racial minorities. Because these data were obtained with a convenience sample, we regarded the results as the basis for hypotheses rather than conclusions. We subsequently tested these hypotheses in a national telephone survey, described in the next section.

STUDY 2: 1988 NATIONAL TELEPHONE SURVEY

Between July 5 and August 10, 1988, telephone interviews were conducted by the staff of the New York City Study at the C.U.N.Y. Center for Social Research with a random sample of 1,078 English-speaking U.S. adults. Using random digit dialing (RDD) techniques, the sample was drawn from the universe of all U.S. households with telephones. Eligibility requirements were that the respondent be an English-speaking household resident and at least 18 years of age.

Once a number was reached, a preliminary enumeration of household members was obtained from the person who answered the telephone (or any other available person). After listing the eligible household members, the interviewer randomly selected a respondent. If that person was unavailable, callbacks were attempted until the interview was completed, the respondent was reached and refused to participate, or the study ended. The interview lasted approximately 25 minutes. The response rate was 47%.[7]

Of the completed interviews, 960 contained sufficiently complete data for the analyses relevant to this chapter. Approximately 60% (580) of these interviews were with females and 38% (364) were with males; gender was not coded for 2%

---

[7]Calculation of response rate was based on the formula: R = C/T, where R = response rate, C = number of completed interviews (1,078), and T = total number of eligible numbers sampled (2,302). T is equal to the total number of telephone numbers sampled, minus nonworking numbers, minus nonresidential numbers, minus households without any eligible respondents, minus numbers with no answer after at least 20 calls. We gratefully acknowledge the work of Professor Charles Kadushin and Susanne Tumelty of the CUNY Graduate Center, who designed and supervised the sampling and data collection procedures.

(16). Most of the respondents (784 or 82%) were White. Of the remainder, 82 (9%) were Black, 31 (3%) were Hispanics, 34 (4%) were coded as "other," and 29 (3%) did not indicate their race. Using the U.S. Census Bureau's Current Population Survey for March 1988, the data were post-stratified by gender, race, and age. The post-stratified data are used for the analyses described in this chapter.[8]

Questions Asked.   The types of items used for the analyses presented here were similar to those administered to the focus groups. First, respondents judged whether HIV could be transmitted through each of 12 different routes; the items were modified versions of those administered earlier to focus groups.[9] Second, respondents were asked to indicate whether they agreed, disagreed, or were "in between" for 16 different items assessing AIDS-related attitudes. The set included items administered previously to the focus groups, some with modifications of wording, as well as new items. Third, respondents were asked whether they agreed, disagreed, or were "in the middle" for the five items constituting the short form of the Attitudes Toward Gay Men (ATG) scale. The 5-item ATG scale displayed an acceptable level of internal consistency in this, its first telephone administration to a national sample (*alpha* = .85).

In addition, a new set of items was developed specifically for this survey, based on the functional approach to attitudes (Herek, 1986, 1987a; Katz, 1960; Smith, Bruner, & White, 1956). The various formulations of this approach share the premise that people hold and express particular attitudes because they derive psychological benefit from doing so, and that the type of benefit varies among individuals. Thus, the same attitude can serve different psychological functions for different people.

We identified five psychological attitude functions for AIDS-related attitudes,

---

[8]In our earlier report on the survey (Herek & Glunt, 1991), we did not use weighted data in the regression equations. Consequently, readers will note slight discrepancies between the regression coefficients reported here and those in our earlier article.

[9]The transmission routes were:

1. eating food in a restaurant
2. using a public telephone
3. using a public toilet
4. standing near a person with AIDS who is coughing or sneezing
5. sharing a drinking glass with someone you don't know
6. being bitten by a mosquito
7. shaking hands with a person with AIDS
8. working in the same room as a person with AIDS
9. having sexual intercourse without using a condom
10. having sexual intercourse while using a condom
11. receiving a blood transfusion and
12. giving blood to a blood bank.

The response options were YES (i.e., AIDS could be transmitted through this route), NO (AIDS could not be transmitted), and MAYBE.

fitting into the two broad categories of *evaluative* and *expressive* functions (Herek, 1987a, 1990). Attitudes serving one of the *evaluative functions* are based on actual characteristics of the attitude object (e.g., HIV disease, people with AIDS) and the individual's judgment about how her or his personal well-being has been or will be affected by that object. These attitudes help the individual to organize knowledge and past experience with instances of the attitude object into a more or less coherent personal strategy for behavior that will maximize rewards and minimize costs to the self. Such attitudes, for example, may be based on an individual's personal experiences—pleasant or unpleasant—with people with AIDS. This is an example of the *experiential schematic* function; the attitudes form part of a cognitive schema through which the individual can effectively organize her or his future responses to PWAs (e.g., "From my past experiences with John, my friend with AIDS, I know that people with AIDS do not pose a threat to me, and that friendship with them might be rewarding"). Having such a schema is presumed to be inherently positive for some individuals.

Another evaluative function also entails the development of a cognitive schema, one that reflects expectations about the future rather than past experiences. These attitudes, serving an *anticipatory evaluative* function, help individuals to organize their knowledge about AIDS and their expectations about the future in such a way as to increase their feelings of safety, both for themselves and for their loved ones.

In contrast to the evaluative functions, attitudes serving one of the three *expressive functions* are based on the metaphorical (Sontag, 1988) or symbolic qualities of AIDS and PWAs. Whereas the benefits associated with evaluative functions derive from their utility for guiding interactions with the attitude object, the benefits derived from the expressive functions are realized when the attitude is expressed. This expression may be public or private, verbal or behavioral. The expressive functions include: (a) *value-expression,* through which one's self-esteem is increased by affirming values central to one's self-concept; (b) *social-expression,* through which feelings of social acceptance and support are increased by expressing opinions expected to gain approval from important others; and (c) *defense,* through which anxiety resulting from intrapsychic conflicts is reduced.

The national survey included seven items designed to assess these functions (see Table 8.2). They were adapted from the first author's Attitude Functions Inventory (AFI), a paper-and-pencil questionnaire format developed to assess the functions served by various attitudes (Herek, 1987a).[10] The items were included in the survey both to determine the feasibility of their administration by telephone to a diverse sample of the population, and to provide data that would shed light on the social psychological underpinnings of AIDS attitudes.

---

[10]Because of time limitations, the 15-item AFI had to be condensed into a 7-item version for the telephone survey. Consequently, the results reported here are not directly comparable to those obtained with the instrument described in Herek (1987a).

TABLE 8.2
Attitude Functions Inventory Items and Response Distribution (National Sample)

How much would you say your own opinions about AIDS have been affected by:

	Very Much	Somewhat	Not at all
Evaluative Functions			
Experimental Schematic			
...your own experiences with someone who has AIDS or is a high risk for AIDS?	12.5	13.3	70.8
Anticipatory Evaluative			
...your concern that someone you care about might get AIDS?	40.4	26.9	30.6
Expressive Functions			
Social Expressive			
...the opinions of your friends and family and the people you most respect?	14.6	32.9	50.8
Value Expressive			
...your concern that we protect everyone's civil rights?	48.6	31.9	16.0
...your religious or moral beliefs, or your feelings about right and wrong?	41.8	29.2	27.1
Defensive			
...personal feelings of discomfort or disgust when you think about AIDS?	24.7	31.2	41.4
Some people prefer not to think about AIDS or the people it affects. Do your yourself try not to think about AIDS or the people it affects very much, somewhat, or not at all?	15.4	41.3	42.4

Proportion of responses in each category are weighted by gender, race, and age, based on the U>S> Census Bureau's Current Population Survey for March, 1988. Percentages across rows do not total to 100% because refusals and "don't know" responses were not included in the table. Margin of error due to sampling: +/-3 (n = 960).

Results

Item and Scale Analyses

Factor Analysis of AIDS Knowledge and Attitude Items.   As with the focus group data, a series of principal components analyses was conducted with the knowledge and attitude items using various rotational techniques and extracting

TABLE 8.3
AIDS-Related Attitudes: Factor Loadings and Response Distribution (National Sample)

	% Agree	% Disagree	% Not Sure
Pragmatism/Moralism (11.6% of variance)			
The government should give away condoms to stop the spread of AIDS (.7289)	47.6	47.9	4.2
The government should pay from programs to teach people how to have "safer sex" (.6695)	68.7	25.5	5.7
The government should fight AIDS among drug users by giving clean needles to anyone who wants them (.5828)	31.8	61.8	5.6
The federal government should spend more money for research on AIDS even if it means raising taxes (.5176)	69.6	25.5	5.0
Our country needs laws to protect people with AIDS from discrimination (.5016)	70.5	21.3	7.5
Coercion/Compassion (19% of variance)			
People with AIDS should be legally separated to protect the public health (.7439)	19.5	72.5	7.8
The names of people with AIDS should be published in newspapers (.6453)	9.6	86.7	3.6
People with AIDS are getting what they deserve (.6139)	10.9	80.0	8.5
People with AIDS are a serious risk to the rest of the society (.5713)	51.6	35.0	13.0
People with AIDS have only themselves to blame (.5134)	19.1	67.9	12.5

Numbers in parentheses are factor pattern loadings for a principal components analysis with oblique rotation (n = 925; interfactor correlation = -.17); each item leading highly (> .44) only on the factor under which the item is listed in the table. Five additional items did not load highly on either factor and are omitted from the table. Proportion of responses in each category were poststratified by gender, race, and age, based on the U.S. Census Bureau's Current Population Survey for March, 1988. Margin of error due to sampling: +/- 3.

different numbers of factors. The factors were very similar to those observed with the focus group sample. For the knowledge items, a Casual Contact Beliefs factor accounted for 33.6% of the variance and an Intimate Contact Knowledge factor accounted for an additional 10.4% of the variance. When the items were combined into scales, internal consistency for the Casual Contact Beliefs items was acceptably high (*alpha* = .84). The 2-item Intimate Contact Knowledge scale, however, displayed low internal consistency (*alpha* = .11) and was dropped from the analysis.[11]

For the attitude items, a two-factor oblique solution was again the most interpretable. The coercion/compassion factor accounted for 19% of the variance and the pragmatism/moralism factor accounted for 11.6%. Two newly constructed items assessing attributions of blame to people with AIDS loaded the coercion/compassion factor (see Table 8.3). Separate factor analyses with responses from Blacks and Whites yielded essentially the same factors. As with the focus groups, two 5-item scales were constructed, each of which displayed an acceptably high level of internal consistency: *alpha* = .70 for the AIDS Coercion scale, and .63 for the AIDS Pragmatism scale. The correlation between the two scales ($r = -.25$) was higher than with the focus group sample, but was still sufficiently low to indicate that scores in the two domains were relatively independent.

Attitude Functions Items.   In order to assess the validity of the AFI items, they were cross-tabulated with responses to other theoretically relevant items from the survey.[12] Respondents who scored high on the experiential schematic function also were more likely than others to report that they personally knew someone who had AIDS or someone who was infected with HIV. Among those who said that their own opinions about AIDS had been "very much" affected by their own experiences, 57% of Whites and 60% of Blacks reported knowing a person with AIDS or HIV. Among those whose own opinions were affected "somewhat" or "not at all" by such experiences, 13% of Whites and 18% of Blacks reported knowing someone with AIDS or HIV (for the main effect for function, F [1,845] = 71.59, $p < .001$).

As expected, persons with value expressive attitudes based on concern about

---

[11]Throughout our research, we have observed that most respondents correctly understand the routes through which HIV is transmitted, even if they overestimate the risks posed by casual contact (see also Hardy, 1991). Consequently, they usually obtain perfect or very high scores on measures of knowledge about transmission. Because of its low variance, this measure has proved unsuitable for regression analyses. In our attempt to develop a measure with greater variance for the national sample, we included an item concerning the risks of "receiving a blood transfusion." Examination of responses to this question, however, indicates ambiguity in the minds of respondents concerning whether it was referring to risk before or after 1985 (when reliable blood tests began to be used for mass screening of blood donations). After eliminating this item, we were left only with the item concerning risks from "having sexual intercourse without using a condom." Of all the respondents, 91% believed that HIV could be transmitted in this manner, and another 5% believed that maybe it could be transmitted in this way.

[12]Blacks scored significantly higher than Whites on six of the seven functions; the two groups were similar only on the value-expressive item assessing religious values. Unless otherwise noted, comparisons described in this section were conducted with two-way ANCOVA (race-by-function), using age and education as covariates. For all comparisons, only the responses of Whites and Blacks were included in the analysis.

civil liberties were more politically liberal than others, whereas those with value-expressive attitudes based on moral beliefs were more religious. On a 9-point scale of political ideology, mean scores were significantly lower (more liberal) for those who responded "very much" to the civil liberties item (means = 5.0 for Whites, 4.7 for Blacks) than for those who responded "somewhat" or "not at all" (means = 6.0 for both Whites and Blacks; $F [1,777] = 20.14, p < .001$). On a 3-point scale of attendance at religious services (monthly or less often, several times per month, weekly or more often), 59% of those whose opinions were "very much" affected by their moral beliefs attended religious services at least weekly, whereas only 40% of those who responded "somewhat" or "not at all" did so (*chi-square* = 65.3242, $p < .001$). The pattern was similar for Whites and Blacks.

We expected respondents who scored high on the defensive function also to avoid information about AIDS. We found that respondents whose opinions were "very much" affected by their personal feelings of discomfort or disgust about AIDS were less likely than others to remember receiving the Surgeon General's report on AIDS (Koop, 1988), which was mailed to all U.S. households shortly before the survey was conducted. Among Whites who were "very much" influenced by feelings of discomfort, 59% remembered receiving the report, in contrast to 68% of other Whites. Blacks, who overall were less likely to say they had received the report, manifested a similar pattern (48% vs. 56%). Although the effect for attitude function was in the expected direction, it was only marginally significant ($F = 3.27, p = .07$); it became nonsignificant when education was added as a covariate. Similarly, Whites and Blacks who "very much" tried not to think about AIDS or the people it affects were less likely to remember receiving the report (61% vs. 67% of other Whites; 42% vs. 57% of Blacks). As before, the effect for function was marginally significant ($F = 3.3, p = .07$) in a two-way ANOVA, but became nonsignificant when education was added as a covariate.[13]

These results generally support the validity of the function items described thus far. Comparable support was not obtained for the remaining two items. We expected those who scored high on the social expressive function to be more likely than low scorers to report that their friends or relatives were a source of AIDS information; but only 14 respondents (1% of the sample) mentioned friends or family as a source of information, making a meaningful test of this hypothesis impossible. Finally, although we expected that those whose opinions were "very much" influenced by their concern that someone they care about

---

[13]We noted with interest that education appeared to exert differential effects on Whites and Blacks for the defensive functions. Education was negatively correlated with preferring not to think about AIDS among Whites (those responding "very much" had lower levels of education), whereas the correlation was positive among Blacks. It was negatively correlated with discomfort among Whites, but not correlated with discomfort among Blacks.

might get AIDS (anticipatory evaluative function) would also be more likely than others to perceive themselves to be at high risk, we observed no significant differences on this variable. Those who scored high on the anticipatory evaluative function, however, were more likely than low scorers to report that they knew someone with AIDS (22.7% vs. 16.5%, F [1,858] = 3.71, p = .05) or that they had a close friend or relative who is gay or lesbian (36% vs. 33%, F [1,858] = 6.39, p < .05).

These data support the validity of the items measuring experiential schematic, value-expressive, and defensive functions. Although we included the measures of social expressive and anticipatory evaluative functions in subsequent analyses, we interpret them with caution because their validity has not been established.

Racial Differences in Item Responses

Our observations in the focus groups suggested to us that Black and White Americans would differ in their willingness to trust the government and scientific authorities. This hypothesis was supported in the national sample. African-Americans more often agreed that the government is not telling the whole story about AIDS (67% agreed, compared to 34% of Whites; *chi-square* = 29.84, p < .001). Whites were more likely to state that they believed scientists and doctors who say that AIDS is *not* spread through casual contact (71% agreed, compared to 58% of African-Americans; *chi-square* = 9.84, p < .01). Blacks were somewhat more likely than Whites (51% vs. 41%) to agree that the AIDS epidemic is being used to promote hatred of minority groups, although the difference was not statistically significant (*chi-square* = 2.99).

In addition to these items, we found significant differences between Blacks and Whites on five other variables of interest (comparisons were not made with other racial groups because of their small numbers in the sample).[14] Comparisons using ANOVA revealed that Black respondents were more likely than Whites to: (a) overestimate the risks posed by casual contact, (b) endorse coercive AIDS-related policies, (c) endorse pragmatic AIDS-related policies, (d) express hostile attitudes toward gay men, and (e) attend religious services frequently.

Regression Analyses

Following the same approach as described earlier for the focus groups, separate regression analyses were conducted for AIDS-Coercion and AIDS-Pragmatism attitude scores (see Table 8.4). Once again, different variables emerged

---

[14]On average, Blacks in our sample were significantly younger than Whites (mean ages were 35.7 [*sd* = 13] and 42.3 [*sd* = 15.8], respectively) and had lower educational levels (median educational levels were "high school graduate" and "some college, respectively"). Consequently, we used age and educational level as covariates in interracial comparisons for other variables.

TABLE 8.4
Regression Coefficients for Equations Without Attitude Functions: National Sample, Whites and Blacks Combined

	Coercion/Compassion Attitudes (Races Combined)		
Variable	Unstandardized	Standardized (b)	T (beta)
Gender	-1.40091	-.27210	-3.369[c]
Age	0.03933	.26498	3.107[b]
Race	-0.03812	—	n.s.
Education	-0.04987	—	n.s.
Gender X Race	1.11730	.21655	2.523[a]
Age X Race	-0.02501	—	n.s.
Ed X Race	-0.03909	—	n.s.
Casual contact beliefs	0.26560	.35631	12.114[c]
ATG	0.19439	.27171	8.885[c]
Rel. Attend	0.06707	—	n.s.
Rel. Denomination	0.09371	—	n.s.

For Equation: R^2 (adj) = .3243 F (11,854) = 41.5418[c]

	Pragmatism/Moralism Attitudes (Races Combined)		
Gender	-1.15185	-.20476	-2.300[a]
Age	0.01300	—	n.s.
Race	-1.05134	—	n.s.
Education	-0.29827	-.14735	-2.896[b]
Gender X Race	1.44836	.25691	2.716[b]
Age X Race	-0.03918	-.29912	-2.441[a]
Ed X Race	-0.04341	—	n.s.
Casual contact beliefs	-0.04015	—	n.s.
ATG	-0.25316	-.32385	-9.607[c]
Rel. Attend	-0.07327	—	n.s.
Rel. Denomination	-0.15738	—	n.s.

For Equation: R^2 (adj) = .1789 F (11,854) = 19.4045[c]

[a]$p < .05$; [b]$p < .01$; [c]$p < .001$.
Note. Undtandardized regression coefficients are reproduced for all variables to permit comparison across equations; standardized regression coefficients and T-values are reproduced only when statistically significant. Coefficients reflect final step of the regression equation with all variables included. Mean scores were substituted for missing data in independent variables; listwise deletion of missing data yielded similar results. Data were poststratified by race, gender, and age, according to 1988 census data.

as significant ($p < .05$) predictors of the two dimensions of attitudes. As with the focus group data, coercive policies were more likely to be supported by respondents who overestimated the risks of casual contact, and those who expressed antigay attitudes. Education was not a significant predictor, but age was: Older respondents were more supportive of coercive policies. A significant multiplicative interaction term indicated that White females were more likely than others to reject coercive policies.

Our analyses with the focus group data led us to expect religiosity to be a significant predictor of AIDS-Pragmatism scores. This, however, was not the case. Instead, pragmatism scores were predicted by education, ATG scores, and the race–gender and race–age interactions. Pragmatic policies were most likely to be supported by respondents with lower educational levels, by those who expressed antigay attitudes, and by White females; they were more likely to be rejected by older Whites.

The significant interactions of gender and age with race suggested that attitude scores should be analyzed separately for Blacks and Whites. The utility of this analytic strategy became more apparent when we added interaction terms to the regression equations described earlier in order to assess the joint effects of race with religiosity, attitudes toward gay men, casual contact beliefs, and religious denomination. In that analysis, the interaction of race with attitudes toward gay men accounted for an additional 0.5% of the variance in AIDS-Coercion scores ($p = .01$), and the interaction of race with the religious attendance accounted for an additional 0.4% ($p < .05$).

Accordingly, we recalculated the regression equations separately for Blacks and Whites (see Table 8.5). On the first step, we entered the variables of gender, age, attitudes toward gay men, religious attendance, and beliefs about casual contact. On the second step, we entered scores for the seven survey items assessing attitude functions, each scored dichotomously (with a response of "very much" coded as 1 and other responses as 0). The functional variables were entered in order to obtain a better understanding of the social psychological underpinnings of AIDS-related attitudes.

Examining the first step of the equations in Table 8.5, it is clear that over-estimating the risks of casual contact was the principal predictor of support for coercive policies among both Whites and Blacks. Age also was correlated with support for coercive policies. For Whites, antigay attitudes were another important predictor. For African-Americans, in contrast, religious attendance and gender were additional predictors: Blacks who attended church frequently were more likely than nonreligious Blacks to support coercive policies, and African-American men were more likely than African-American women to support such policies.

For AIDS-Pragmatism attitudes among Blacks, gender was the only significant predictor on the equation's first step; females were more likely than males to reject pragmatic policies. For Whites, the predictors were the same as for AIDS-Coercion scores except that the directionality was reversed: rejection of pragmatic policies was associated with the same variables that predicted support for coercive policies.

The expressive functional items, entered on the second step, explained additional variance for both types of attitudes and for both racial groups. In general terms, the results in Table 8.5 can be summarized as follows: High scores on the social expressive function predicted support for both types of policies; high

TABLE 8.5
Regression Coefficients for Equations With Attitude Function: Separate Equations for Blacks'
and Whites' AIDS Attitudes (National Sample)

AIDS-Coercion Attitudes

Variable	Whites			Blacks		
	b	beta	T	b	beta	T
Age	0.0131	.0912	3.11[b]	0.0335	.1911	2.129[a]
Gender	-0.2406	—	n.s.	-1.6915	-.2888	-3.171[b]
Education	-0.0399	—	n.s.	-0.2704	—	n.s.
Casual contact	0.2634	.3385	11.614[c]	0.2789	.4302	4.673[c]
ATG	0.1532	.2251	6.997[c]	-0.1155	—	n.s.
Rel Attendance	-0.0349	—	n.s	0.6854	.2060	2.321[a]
Rel Denomination	0.0362	—	n.s.	0.9084	—	n.s.
Social Express	0.4937	.0648	2.243[a]	0.0786	—	n.s.
Value (secular)	-0.9047	-.1782	-6.031[c]	-1.0963	—	n.s.
Value (relig)	0.3304	.0649	2.162[a]	-0.1552	—	n.s.
Defens. (discom)	1.2055	.2011	6.677[c]	0.6162	—	n.s.
Defens. (avoid)	0.4993	.0692	2.463[a]	1.2899	.1991	2.432[a]
Experiential	-0.0935	—	n.s.	-0.8360	—	n.s.
Anticipatory	0.0529	—	n.s.	-0.4939	—	n.s.
Adj. R^2 for Equation:	.3892			.3851		
F	.38.5230[c]			5.6362[c]		
Age	-.0210	-.1295	-4.014[c]	0.0006	—	n.s.
Gender	.1961	—	n.s.	-1.7558	-.3340	-3.291[b]
Education	-.1881	—	n.s.	-.1457	—	n.s.
Casual contact	-.0777	-.0881	-2.747[b]	.0223	—	n.s.
ATG	-.2273	-.2947	-8.332[c]	-.1433	—	n.s.
Rel Attendance	-.0006	—	n.s.	.1195	—	n.s.
Rel Denomination	-.2558	—	n.s.	1.2738	—	n.s.
Social Express	.6730	.0780	2.452[b]	1.7380	.3120	2.396[a]
Value (secular)	1.2718	.2211	6.799[c]	-1.4353	-.2587	-2.501[a]
Value (relig)	-.4538	-.0787	-2.382[a]	-1.2666	-.2377	-2.513[a]
Defens. (discom)	-.1311	—	n.s.	.6819	—	n.s.
Defens. (avoid)	.2728	—	n.s.	-1.8962	-.3260	-3.574[c]
Experiential	.2092	—	n.s.	-.6573	—	n.s.
Anticipatory	.3258	—	n.s.	.3723	—	n.s.
Adj. R^2 For Equation:	.2596			.2370		
F	21.6523[c]			3.2989[c]		

[a] $p < .05$; [b] $p < .01$; [c] $p < .001$.

Note. Coefficients reflect final step of the regression equation with all variables included. Mean scores were substituted for missing data in independent variables. Data were weghted by race, gender, and age, according to 1988 consus data.

scores on the defensive and religious value-expressive functions predicted support for coercive policies and rejection of pragmatic policies; and high scores on the secular value-expressive function (civil liberties) predicted rejection of coercive attitudes and support for pragmatic policies among Whites but rejection of pragmatic policies among Blacks.

GENERAL DISCUSSION

The data from the national sample supported our earlier conclusion that public attitudes concerning AIDS-related policies are cognitively organized into at least two domains. In one domain are attitudes concerning restrictive and stigmatizing policies. In the other are attitudes concerning policies to prevent HIV transmission among individuals who engage in potentially high-risk behavior. The two types of attitudes are largely uncorrelated. Attitudes of Whites and Blacks alike appear to differ in both domains. The data also suggest that, for many Americans, AIDS-related attitudes serve as a vehicle for meeting psychological needs and that a variety of factors may affect beliefs about how HIV is transmitted. We discuss each of these points here.

AIDS Policy Attitudes are Cognitively Organized into Two Separate and Largely Uncorrelated Domains

In the United States, public attitudes associated with AIDS are not monolithic. Rather, by the late 1980s, they comprised at least two separate domains. The pragmatism/moralism domain encompassed attitudes concerning how society should respond to behaviors through which HIV can be transmitted (i.e., sexual behavior and drug use). Opposing views in this arena represented a clash between conflicting priorities: preventing disease by any means necessary (the pragmatism end of the dimension) versus promoting a particular set of moral standards concerning behavior (the moralism end). At the risk of oversimplifying, it might be said that the former position's primary emphasis is saving lives, whereas the latter's is saving souls.

Similar conflicts between moralism and pragmatism have been documented in public reactions to earlier health problems. In a detailed history of societal response to venereal diseases in the United States, for example, Brandt (1987) described the historical antagonism between secular rationalists and moralists. Advocates of a secular rationalist approach generally recognized and accepted the inevitability of sexual behavior outside of marriage; they sought to reduce the incidence of venereal disease through distribution of prophylactics and, when effective antibiotics became available, through nonjudgmental treatment of infected individuals. Moralists in contrast, considered venereal disease to be symptomatic of deeper social and moral disorder; they advocated abstinence and encouraged it by appealing to moral values and fear of disease.

Similar clashes of worldviews occurred during the 19th-century cholera epidemics in the United States (Rosenberg, 1987). Many viewed cholera as a punishment inflicted on sinners; they prescribed virtuous behavior (such as a temperance and abstinence from excessive sexual activity) as the proper prevention. Others took a less moralistic perspective and located the sources of cholera in the unsanitary living conditions of its victims. The latter view eventually prevailed, laying the groundwork for such modern public health practices as garbage removal and maintenance of sanitary water supplies (for further discussion of the parallels between cholera and AIDS, see Herek, 1990).

We might have labeled the coercion/compassion domain of AIDS-related attitudes as the stigma factor. At one extreme, these attitudes reflect perceptions of people with HIV as blameful and menacing, as paying the price for their own behavior and posing a threat to the "innocent." Punitive measures such as quarantine are justified not only by fears of contagion but also by the belief that AIDS is itself a punishment from God or from Nature. Agreement with some items on this factor (e.g., that people with AIDS deserve their disease) may reflect a general ideology that the world is just (e.g., Lerner, 1970; but see Ambrosio & Sheehan, 1991; Connors & Heaven, 1990; Witt, 1990) or may simply be a symbolic expression of hostility toward gay men or other outgroups. At the dimension's other extreme, punitive measures against people with AIDS are rejected; instead, the sick and infected are regarded not as dangerous but as deserving of help, compassion, and respect.

As with the pragmatism/moralism domain, the conflict between coercion and compassion has historical precedents. Persons with cholera, for example, were stigmatized during the 1832 epidemic in the United States. Many healthy individuals ignored physicians' (inaccurate) assertions that cholera was not contagious and they avoided all contact with the sick (Rosenberg, 1987). Neighbors opposed the establishment of cholera hospitals in their communities. People with cholera were physically assaulted, even murdered. Additionally, fear and blame of "risk groups" were widespread and often combined with longstanding prior prejudices. For example, newly arrived European immigrants, most of whom were Catholic, were feared; many were kept out of the country and left to wander "starved and half-naked along the Canadian border" (p. 62). Similarly, many White Americans believed that "the Negro's innate character invited cholera. He was, with few exceptions, filthy and careless in his personal habits, lazy and ignorant by temperament. A natural fatalist, moreover, he took no steps to protect himself from disease" (Rosenberg, 1987, pp. 59–60).

Cholera-related stigma resulted from both the characteristics of the disease and preexisting hostility toward the groups most affected by it. We believe that AIDS-related stigma follows a similar pattern, and that these two aspects of it might be empirically distinguishable. Stigma associated with the physical disease might result primarily from fears for one's personal safety, whereas stigma associated with social groups at greatest risk might be motivated largely by negative feelings toward those groups. Recent survey data suggest that the former pattern of stigma may be prevalent among African-Americans, whereas the latter pattern is prevalent among Whites. Data collected in 1991–1992 replicated the finding reported here that Black Americans were more supportive of coercive policies and more likely to overestimate the risks of casual contact than were Whites (Herek & Capitanio, 1992a, 1992b, 1992c). But when we separately analyzed the items concerning blame for persons with AIDS, we found that Blacks were *less* likely than Whites to feel that PWAs deserved their illness. And Whites reported greater feelings of anger, disgust, and fear toward persons with AIDS.

The extremes of the pragmatism/moralism and coercion/compassion dimensions can be combined into four categories that correspond to four societal responses to the AIDS epidemic in the United States. First, the combination of pragmatism (e.g., support for free distribution of condoms) and compassion (e.g., opposition to quarantine) might be labeled *compassionate secularism*. This pattern matches the general stance taken toward AIDS by the U.S. public health profession and the lesbian and gay community (e.g., Koop, 1988). Second, a pattern of *compassionate moralism* is characterized by compassion for people with AIDS but opposition to prevention programs that are not based on abstinence from sex and drug use. This combination of moralism and compassion is reflected in the official pronouncements of the National Conference of Catholic Bishops (e.g., Lattin, 1989). Third, *punitive moralism*, endorsement of coercive measures and rejection of nonmoralistic risk-reduction programs, is perhaps best exemplified in the United States by spokespersons of conservative political and religious groups, including the Religious Right (e.g., Buchanan, 1987; Cohen, 1987).

Finally, the combination of pragmatism and coercion might be labeled *indiscriminate action*. This tendency to agree with all proposed actions—pragmatic and coercive alike—may reflect a "do-something" mentality, a willingness to endorse any policy that appears to respond to AIDS, regardless of its likely costs, consequences, or effectiveness (Schneider, 1987). Such attitudes may result from what Janis and Mann (1977) termed *hypervigilance,* a coping pattern characteristic of decision makers who experience intense stress due to their perception that: (a) severe losses are imminent, whether or not current practices are changed; (b) a satisfactory solution is possible; but (c) insufficient time is available to search for it carefully. Janis (1989) summarized this pattern as "Try anything that looks promising to get the hell out of this agonizing dilemma as fast as you can. Never mind any other consequences" (p. 80). The indiscriminate action pattern also might reflect considerable ambivalence concerning AIDS (e.g., views of people with AIDS as a dangerous source of infection and yet deserving of compassion). Alternatively, the pattern may simply reflect an acquiescent response set, although more recent research with new survey items (Herek & Capitanio, 1992a, 1992b, 1992c) casts doubt on this explanation.

We found that 81% of Whites and 90% of Blacks manifested one of the four patterns (using a criterion of agreement or disagreement, as appropriate, with the majority of items on the two scales). Most Whites (51%) and a plurality of Blacks (41%) fit the compassionate secularism pattern (i.e., they agreed with at least three AIDS-Pragmatism items and disagreed with at least three AIDS-Coercion items). Respondents in this category tended to be younger, more highly educated, and more politically liberal than others. Whites in this category were more likely than other Whites to say that their attitudes were strongly motivated by concerns about civil liberties. They also were more likely to know a person with AIDS, to express positive attitudes toward gay men, and to know gay people personally.

About one fifth of the sample (19% of Whites and 20% of Blacks) displayed the compassionate moralism pattern. Blacks in this category somewhat resembled Whites in the previously described compassionate secularism category. They were more likely than other Blacks to know a person with AIDS and to express positive attitudes toward gay men. They also were likely to say that their attitudes were based both on concerns about civil rights and on moral values. Their moralism, however, was not necessarily linked with political conservatism; they tended to be liberal and they were less likely than other Blacks to belong to a conservative religious denomination.

Only 7% of Whites and 5% of Blacks displayed the punitive moralism pattern. Such small numbers obviously place limits on our ability to generalize about people within the category. Nevertheless, it appears that many of them manifested a defensive attitude function: They were more likely than others to avoid thinking about AIDS. Additionally, Whites in this group were older than other Whites in the sample.

Finally, 4% of Whites and 25% of Blacks fit the indiscriminate action pattern. Respondents in this group appeared generally to lack personal experience with the epidemic. They were least likely to know a person with AIDS and the most likely to overestimate the risks of casual contact. Additionally, Whites in this group were more likely than others to hold AIDS attitudes serving a social-expressive function. Blacks in this group were older than others and attended religious services more frequently; they also were the least likely to have value-expressive attitudes, either secular or moral.

White and Black Americans Differ in Their Attitudes Concerning AIDS

Quantitative and qualitative differences in AIDS-related attitudes exist between White and Black Americans. Blacks are more likely to support coercive policies, overestimate the risks posed by casual contact, and support prevention programs such as safer sex education and condom distribution. As noted earlier, more recent research (Herek & Capitanio, 1992a, 1992b, 1992c) has replicated these findings, and also indicates that Whites are more likely than Blacks to hold negative attitudes toward people with AIDS.

These patterns may reflect fundamental racial differences in how individuals define their own relationship in AIDS. In the focus groups,[15] we noticed that Whites often seemed personally removed from the epidemic. Many seemed motivated to find some way in which they could be at risk, even though doing so often required imaginative thinking. One participant, for example, described an unlikely scenario in which he would be at risk from shaking hands with a person with AIDS if both he and the other individual had extensive open sores on their hands. Another White participant (who had not engaged in any high-risk behaviors) stated with conviction that 20% of AIDS cases in the United States have been caused by contaminated blood transfusions (according to the Centers for Disease Control, 1992, the true proportion of transfusion-related cases is approximately 2%). This misstatement substantially inflated the participant's own personal risk for HIV infection.

African-Americans, in contrast, more often described AIDS as an immediate problem in their own community—among their family members, friends, and neighbors. This fits with a recent finding that African-Americans are more likely than Whites to know a person infected with HIV (Herek & Capitanio, 1992a, 1992b, 1992c). Blacks in the focus groups frequently placed AIDS in the context of other community problems—poverty, discrimination, crime, and drug addiction. Although they typically expressed the philosophy that everything necessary should be done to stop the spread of HIV, many also voiced unwillingness to trust White-identified government officials and scientific experts concerning AIDS. Many were deeply suspicious about the origins of AIDS and about its political uses to promote racism.

A frequent theme in focus groups with Blacks, for example, was discussion of "conspiracy theories" concerning the origins of AIDS (e.g., that it is a result of CIA experiments in germ warfare). Several participants likened AIDS to the Tuskegee syphilis experiments (see Thomas & Quinn, 1991). To some extent, such comparisons probably reflect the common tendency to utilize readily available information from past experiences when making judgments under conditions of uncertainty, even if that information is irrelevant to the current situation (Gilovich, 1981). Given the history of government antipathy toward minority

---

[15]This discussion draws on the 1988 focus groups, as well as a more recent series of 18 groups conducted during the fall of 1989 and the early winter of 1990 with 157 English-speaking adult participants in five U.S. cities: two groups in Marion, Ohio ($n = 18$); three groups each in Minneapolis, Minnesota ($n = 30$) and Denver, Colorado ($n = 38$); four groups in Houston, Texas ($n = 32$); and six groups in New York ($n = 39$). The groups consisted largely of Blacks (30 males, 27 females) and Whites (29 males, 56 females). The remaining 15 participants classified themselves as Hispanic or Asian. Roughly equal numbers of groups were all or predominantly Black, all or predominantly White, or racially mixed. All but two groups included both men and women. Procedures were similar to those described previously, except that 11 of the groups comprised individuals recruited through a local church or a community organization; the remaining seven groups were made up of individuals with no common organizational or group membership.

group members, however, it would be naive to explain mistrust about AIDS as resulting solely from the inappropriate use of cognitive heuristics. African-Americans have historical reasons for questioning the motives of government officials and scientists, and that distrust is likely to affect their receptivity to government-sponsored AIDS prevention efforts.

In contrast, many Whites in the focus groups (and in the national sample) seemed to perceive AIDS as largely a disease of the "other"—an abstract, symbolic issue. Because AIDS was remote from their daily lives, their responses to the epidemic were framed largely in symbolic or ideological terms, such as support for or opposition to gay rights. Consequently, their attitudes toward gay men were a primary predictor of their attitudes toward AIDS-related policies (this finding was replicated by Price & Hsu, 1992). Attitudes toward gay men may have been relatively unimportant to Blacks' AIDS-related attitudes because "gay" was usually equated with "White."[16] Consequently, gay men were not perceived to be particularly relevant to AIDS in the African-American community (despite the fact that a plurality of Black men who have AIDS were infected through homosexual contact [Centers for Disease Control, 1992]).

AIDS Attitudes Serve Expressive Psychological Functions

Attitudes concerning AIDS policies are not simply motivated by a desire to prevent the spread of HIV or to reduce one's own risk for infection. In addition, such attitudes often serve an expressive function, especially for White Americans. Agreement or disagreement with an AIDS policy may result from the need to enhance one's self esteem or to reduce anxiety more than from reasoned consideration about that policy's likely effect on the epidemic.

In the national sample, AIDS attitudes were strongly linked to personal values, either religious or secular (see Table 8.2). Here again, we observed racial differences. Whites whose attitudes were based on their concerns about civil liberties were more likely than others to endorse pragmatic prevention policies, whereas those whose attitudes derived from religious values tended to reject such policies. But Blacks with either type of value-expressive motivation (secular or religious) tended to reject pragmatic prevention policies.

This difference further illustrates how AIDS policies can be perceived differently in Black and White communities. Whites whose attitudes are motivated by concerns about civil liberties, for example, may support needle exchange pro-

---

[16]In a 1990-1991 survey (Herek & Capitanio, 1992a), 34% of the 607 African-American respondents "never" or "rarely" thought of Black men when they heard the term *male homosexual* or *gay man*. Only 23% said they "usually" thought of Black men in this context, or said that Blacks came to mind first. Among the 436 White respondents, only 15% "usually" included Blacks in this category (or thought of them first), whereas 47% "never" or "rarely" did so.

grams as an enlightened, nonjudgmental approach to preventing HIV transmission among injecting drug users. African-Americans whose attitudes are motivated by the same concerns, however, may oppose needle exchange programs because they feel that such programs represent society's abandonment of the goal of ending drug addiction, which they perceive to be destructive to the entire Black community (Dalton, 1989).

AIDS-Related Beliefs are not Determined Solely by Access to Information

Beliefs about the risks posed by casual contact affected the AIDS-Coercion attitudes of both Blacks and Whites, and the AIDS-Pragmatism attitudes of Whites. To the extent that respondents overestimated the risks of casual contact, they also supported punitive policies and, if they were White, rejected pragmatic policies.

We do not believe that participants who overestimate HIV risks should be assumed simply to lack correct information about AIDS. Most American adults know that AIDS is spread through unprotected sexual intercourse and through sharing contaminated needles (Albrecht, Levy, Sugrue, Prohaska, & Ostrow, 1989; Hardy, 1991). Consequently, we believe that incorrect beliefs about casual contact often result from how people use the knowledge that they have.

As already discussed, some people who overestimate the risks posed by casual contact simply do not believe public health authorities who say that HIV cannot be transmitted through these routes. In the national sample, both Blacks and Whites were more likely to believe that casual contact poses a transmission risk if they distrusted governmental and health authorities. For Blacks, a secondary predictor was the belief that the government is not telling the whole story about AIDS (Herek & Glunt, 1991).

Beliefs about casual contact also may have a symbolic component just as AIDS policy attitudes do. A heterosexual whose response to the AIDS epidemic is based primarily on ideological opposition to the gay community, for example, may transfer previously held fears about contagion and pollution from homosexuality to AIDS (see Price & Hsu, 1992; Stipp & Kerr, 1989). Relevant to this explanation, we found that AIDS-Coercion scores (but not AIDS-Pragmatism scores) were predictive of Casual Contact Beliefs (Herek & Glunt, 1991).

Overestimation of transmission risks probably also reflects faulty reasoning about AIDS, which is fostered by the anxiety created by a lethal illness. We noted several manifestations of such faulty reasoning in the focus groups. For example, in their hunger for information about AIDS, many discussants gave equal credence to information from all sources without critical evaluation of the source's expertise. Statements by a telephone caller to a radio talk show were assigned the same credibility as those made by a scientist or health official. Focus group participants also displayed a willingness to believe any accounts of first-hand experience with AIDS, without any attempt to assess the veracity of the story. Special credibility also seemed to be attached to the comments of anyone with even a remote connection to the health-care system. We frequently observed group members accept as factual the inaccurate statements of a part-time nurse or hospital worker.

Another contributing factor to overestimation of HIV transmission is selective willingness to accept risks. Health experts often have discussed transmission in probabilistic terms, typically referring to the extremely low likelihood of contracting HIV through casual contact. Unfortunately, many members of the public have misconstrued those statements to mean that casual contact does indeed pose some risk, albeit small. In the focus groups, for example, a frequent justification for coercive policies was that casual contact has not been proved to be free from risk. As one participant expressed it, "If the odds are a thousand-to-one, who wants to be the one?" Many people who routinely ignore the risks posed by activities such as riding in an automobile are unwilling to accept much more remote risks associated with HIV. Paradoxically, some people who express concerns about low-risk events (e.g., having an AIDS treatment facility in one's neighborhood) do not change their own sexual behaviors (which might actually put them at risk for infection). Weinstein (1989) offered several possible explanations for such contradictory behaviors, including that people may demand action from others but are reluctant to make efforts themselves to reduce risk and that people accept current risks to which they are accustomed but avoid incurring new risks. To these we add another possibility: Expressing concerns about HIV infection may be a strategy for symbolically expressing fear or hostility toward people with AIDS or outgroups associated with the AIDS epidemic (e.g., gay men).

IMPLICATIONS FOR PREVENTION AND RESEARCH

The data reported here have important implications for AIDS prevention programs. First, they indicate that public education about AIDS should explicitly address issues of stigma as well as primary prevention. Attitudes in these two domains appear to be distinct and largely uncorrelated. Given the pervasiveness of stigma and its destructive consequences for individuals and society, prevention programs should stress not only personal protection from HIV but also the need to treat PWAs with compassion and respect.

Second, the data underscore the importance of understanding public attitudes about AIDS within their cultural context. Clearly, Blacks and Whites in the United States perceive HIV in different ways. Although not assessed in the present research, it seems likely that AIDS-related attitudes also will differ among Hispanic Americans, Asian Americans, Native American Indians, and other racial and ethnic groups. Thus, each AIDS-related education program should be individually designed for its target community. Based on the qualitative and quantitative differences in attitudes reported here, it should be clear that targeting information and advocacy appeals involves much more than simply varying the race of the person communicating them. Rather, the content of each message should be evaluated in terms of how AIDS is perceived within its target community. In many communities, AIDS education programs will have to be designed with special attention to gaining the trust of community members who are highly suspicious of the government and scientists. Among African Americans, one promising approach to this problem may be to develop AIDS programs within community institutions such as churches and mosques (Dalton, 1989; Lambert, 1989; Shipp & Navarro, 1991). The potential value of programs in these sites is indicated by our finding that religious attendance exerted a greater influence on attitudes toward coercive policies among Blacks than among Whites.[17]

Third, public education about AIDS should confront symbolic issues as well as providing factual information. Religious values, concerns about civil liberties, feelings of anxiety, the desire to be accepted by others—all are likely to influence attitudes concerning AIDS policies. Consequently, AIDS education programs are likely to be more effective to the extent that they directly address these concerns. Given the strong relationship between AIDS-related attitudes and attitudes toward gay men, especially among Whites, AIDS education programs are more likely to be successful to the extent that they reduce antigay prejudice and hostility (see Herek, 1991, for further discussion of such prejudice).

The importance of understanding the symbolic functions of AIDS-related attitudes is illustrated by the successful campaigns to defeat Propositions 64, 69, and 102, described at the beginning of this chapter. Although considerable energy during the campaigns was devoted to explaining why the propositions would not prevent the spread of HIV, much effort also was devoted to linking the initiatives to unpopular political ideas and concerns about civil rights. One of the principal strategies taken by opponents to Propositions 64 and 69 was to publicize their connection to Lyndon LaRouche, an unpopular figure in California in the 1980s whose political views were widely regarded as extremist. Proposition 102 was sponsored not by LaRouche but by Representative Wiliam Dannemeyer. Nevertheless, the initiative's opponents successfully portrayed it as "Son of LaRouche," emphasizing its similarities to the earlier initiatives and evoking many of the concerns about political extremism raised by them (Chung, 1988).

---

[17]Because the Black respondents were more likely than Whites to belong to a conservative religious denomination, we wondered whether race might actually have served as a proxy variable for religious conservatism in our sample. To test this hypothesis, supplementary regression analyses were conducted for the entire sample for both AIDS attitude scales with three independent variables: race, religious denomination, and the multiplicative interaction between the two (see Herek & Glunt, 1991). For AIDS-Pragmatism scores, race accounted for 0.3% of the variance whereas religious denomination accounted for 1.3%. For AIDS-Coercion attitudes, race accounted for 1.6% of the variance and religious denomination for 0.5%. Thus, religious background appears to explain much of the racial difference in AIDS-Pragmatism attitudes, but not in AIDS-Coercion attitudes.

Some who worked to defeat Proposition 102 felt that this tactic tipped the balance of public opinion against the measure.

Because the research described in this chapter was primarily exploratory, we emphasize the need for caution in generalizing from it. Not only was the number of African-American respondents small ($n = 81$), the overall response rate for the national survey also was low (47%). This occurred largely because resources were lacking for extensive follow-up calls to "convert" respondents who initially declined to be interviewed. Another shortcoming is that response options for several scales included in the survey were limited to "agree," "disagree," or "in the middle"; a 5-item or 7-item Likert-type response scale would have permitted greater response variation which, in turn, would have increased our confidence in the factor analyses and multiple regressions. We also recognize limitations in the strategy used for assessing attitude functions. The item wording in some cases (especially for the anticipatory function) appears to have been less than optimal.

Herek is currently conducting a longitudinal study of public opinion in which many of these problems have been resolved. African-Americans have been over-sampled sufficiently to permit meaningful analyses, a higher response rate has been obtained, and the attitude function items have been revised. As already mentioned, preliminary analyses of data from the 1990-1991 national telephone survey generally support the findings reported here (Herek & Capitanio, 1992a, 1992b, 1992c).

Because of the continually changing nature of the AIDS epidemic, we expect the new data to reveal emerging trends in public opinion. The studies described in this chapter, therefore, represent work in progress and should be understood as providing merely a few snapshots of an evolving phenomenon. We believe that these snapshots are tremendously important, however, if they improve our ability to foster compassion for people with AIDS and to promote a rational response to the HIV epidemic.

ACKNOWLEDGMENTS

Preparation of this chapter was supported by a grant to the first author from the National Institute of Mental Health (#RO1-MH43253) and additional funds provided by the late Harold Proshansky, president of the Graduate Center of the City University of New York.

REFERENCES

Albrecht, G. L., Levy, J. A., Sugrue, N. M., Prohaska, T. R., & Ostrow, D. G. (1989). Who hasn't heard about AIDS? *AIDS Education and Prevention, 1,* 261–267.

Ambrosio, A. L., & Sheehan, E. P. (1991). The just world belief and the AIDS epidemic. *Journal of Social Behavior and Personality, 6,* 163–170.

Blake, S. M., & Arkin, E. B. (1988). *AIDS information monitor: A summary of national public opinion surveys on AIDS, 1983 through 1986*. Washington, DC: American Red Cross.

Blendon, R. J., & Donelan, K. (1988). Discrimination against people with AIDS: The public's perspective. *New England Journal of Medicine, 319*(15), 1022–1026.

Bloom, D. E., & Carliner, G. (1988). The economic impact of AIDS in the United States. *Science, 239*, 604–610.

Blumenfield, M., Smith, P. J., Milazzo, J., Seropian, S., & Wormser, G. P. (1987). Survey of attitudes of nurses working with AIDS patients. *General Hospital Psychiatry, 9*, 58–63.

Bouton, R. A., Gallagher, P. E., Garlinghouse, P. A., Leal, T., Rosenstein, L. D., & Young, R. K. (1987). Scales for measuring fear of AIDS and homophobia. *Journal of Personality Assessment, 51*, 606–614.

Brandt, A. M. (1987). *No magic bullet: A social history of venereal disease in the United States since 1880* (expanded edition). New York: Oxford University Press.

Buchanan, P. J. (1987, December 2). Aids and moral bankruptcy. *The New York Post*, p. 23.

California Senate Office of Research. (1986, September). *Proposition 64: The AIDS Initiative in California*. Sacramento, CA: Author.

Centers for Disease Control. (1992, January). *HIV/AIDS Surveillance Report*, 1–18.

Chung, L. A. (1988, August 24). Support for AIDS initiative stirs its foes. *San Francisco Chronicle*. p. A–10.

Cohen, R. (1987, May 1). Falwell's hate mailing. *Washington Post*, p. A23.

Coles, M. (1988a, August 18). *The Dannemeyer AIDS initiative (Proposition 102)*. Legislative analysis prepared by the American Civil Liberties Union of Northern California, 1663 Mission Street, San Francisco, CA.

Coles, M. (1988b). *The "Block" initiative (Proposition 96)*. Legislative analysis prepared by the American Civil Liberties Union of Northern California, 1663 Mission Street, San Francisco, CA.

Connors, J., & Heaven, P. C. L. (1990). Belief in a just world and attitudes toward AIDS sufferers. *Journal of Social Psychology, 130*, 559–560.

Dalton, H. L. (1989). AIDS in blackface. *Daedelus, 118*(3), 205–227.

D'Augelli, A. R. (1989). AIDS fears and homophobia among rural nursing personnel. *AIDS Education and Prevention, 1*, 277–284.

Dearing, J. W. (1989). Setting the polling agenda for the issue of AIDS. *Public Opinion Quarterly, 53*, 309–329.

Election highlights. (1988, June 8). *San Francisco Chronicle*, p. A–1.

First use of Prop. 96's AIDS test rule. (1988, November 11). *San Francisco Chronicle*, p. A9.

Gerbert, B., Maguire, B. T., Bleecker, T., Coates, T. J., & McPhee, S. J. (1991). Primary care physicians and AIDS: Attitudinal and structural barriers to care. *Journal of the American Medical Association, 266*(20), 2837–2842.

Gilovich, T. (1981). Seeing the past in the present: The effect of associations to familiar events on judgments and decisions. *Journal of Personality and Social Psychology, 40*, 797–808.

Goffman, E. (1963). *Stigma: Notes on the management of spoiled identity*. Englewood Cliffs, NJ: Prentice-Hall.

Goodwin, M. P., & Roscoe, B. (1988). AIDS: Students' knowledge and attitudes at a Midwestern university. *Journal of American College Health, 36*(4), 214–222.

Hardy, A. M. (1991, July 1). AIDS knowledge and attitudes for October–December 1990: Provisional data from the National Health Interview Survey. In *Advance data from vital and health statistics* (No. 204). Hyattsville, MD: National Center for Health Statistics (DHHS Publication No. 91–1250).

Hay, J. W., Osmond, D. H., & Jacobson, M. A. (1988). Projecting the medical costs of AIDS and ARC in the United States. *Journal of Acquired Immune Deficiency Syndromes, 1*, 466–485.

Herek, G. M. (1984). Attitudes toward lesbians and gay men: A factor-analytic study. *Journal of Homosexuality, 10*(1/2), 39–51.

Herek, G. M. (1986). The instrumentality of attitudes: Toward a neofunctional theory. *Journal of Social Issues, 42*(2), 99–114.

Herek, G. M. (1987a). Can functions be measured? A new perspective on the functional approach to attitudes. *Social Psychology Quarterly, 50*(4), 285–303.

Herek, G. M. (1987b). Religious orientation and prejudice: A comparison of racial and sexual attitudes. *Personality and Social Psychology Bulletin, 13,* 34–44.

Herek, G. M. (1988). Heterosexuals' attitudes toward lesbians and gay men: Correlates and gender differences. *Journal of Sex Research, 25*(4), 451–477.

Herek, G. M. (1990). Illness, stigma, and AIDS. In P. Costa & G. R. VandenBos (Eds.), *Psychological aspects of serious illness* (pp. 103–150). Washington DC: American Psychological Association.

Herek, G. M. (1991). Stigma, prejudice, and violence against lesbians and gay men. In J. Gonsiorek & J. Weinrich (Eds.), *Homosexuality: Research implications for public policy* (pp. 60–80). Newbury Park, CA: Sage.

Herek, G. M., & Capitanio, J. P. (1992a, March). *AIDS-related attitudes and beliefs among African Americans in California.* Paper presented at the annual investigators' conference of the Universitywide AIDS Research Program, San Francisco, CA.

Herek, G. M., & Capitanio, J. P. (1992b, July). *AIDS-related stigma persists in the United States.* Paper presented at the VIII International Conference on AIDS, Amsterdam, The Netherlands.

Herek, G. M., & Capitanio, J. P. (1992c). *Public reactions to AIDS in the United States: A second decade of stigma.* Unpublished manuscript, Department of Psychology, University of California, Davis.

Herek, G. M., & Glunt, E. K. (1988). An epidemic of stigma: Public reactions to AIDS. *American Psychologist, 43*(11), 886–891.

Herek, G. M., & Glunt, E. K. (1991). AIDS-related attitudes in the United States: A preliminary conceptualization. *Journal of Sex Research, 28*(1), 99–123.

Hilton, B. (1988, November 13). AIDSWEEK. *San Francisco Examiner,* p. A–8.

Janis, I. L. (1989). *Crucial decisions: Leadership in policymaking and crisis management.* New York: The Free Press.

Janis, I. L., & Mann, L. (1977). *Decision making: A psychological analysis of conflict, choice, and commitment.* New York: The Free Press.

Katz, D. (1960). The functional approach to the study of attitudes. *Public Opinion Quarterly, 24,* 163–204.

Katz, I., Hass, R. G., Parisi, N., Astone, J., & McEvaddy, D. (1987). Lay people's and health care personnel's perceptions of cancer, AIDS, cardiac, and diabetic patients. *Psychological Reports, 60,* 615–629.

Kelly, J. A., St. Lawrence, J. S., Smith, S., Hood, H., & Cook, D. J., (1987). Stigmatization of AIDS patients by physicians. *American Journal of Public Health, 77,* 789–791.

Knox, M. D., Dow, M. G., & Cotton, D. A. (1989). Mental health care providers: The need for AIDS education. *AIDS Education and Prevention, 1,* 285–290.

Koop, C. E. (1988). *Understanding AIDS: A message from the Surgeon General.* Washington, DC: U.S. Dept. of Health & Human Services (#HHS–88–8404).

Krieger, N., & Lashof, J. C. (1988). AIDS, policy analysis,and the electorate: The role of schools of public health. *American Journal of Public Health, 78,* 411–415.

Lambert, B. (1989, June 10). Black clergy set to preach about AIDS. *New York Times,* p. 29.

Lattin, D. (1989, November 10). Bishops reject condom use in AIDS education. *San Francisco Chronicle,* pp. A1,A12.

Lerner, M. J. (1970). The desire for justice and reactions to victims. In J. Macauley & L. Berkowitz (Eds.), *Altruism and helping behavior.* (pp. 205–229). New York: Academic Press.

Limit voted on AIDS funds. (1987, October 15). *The New York Times,* p. B12.

McDevitt, T. M., Sheehan, E. P., Lennon, R., & Ambrosio, A. L. (1990). Correlates of attitudes toward AIDS. *Journal of Social Psychology, 130,* 699–701.

McLeod, R. G. (1988, June 1). Low profile for LaRouche's AIDS initiative. *San Francisco Chronicle*, p. A-7.

McNeill, W. H. (1976). *Plagues and peoples*. Garden City, NY: Anchor.

Mejta, C. L., Denton, E., Krems, M. E., & Hiatt, R. A. (1988). Acquired immunodeficiency syndrome (AIDS): A survey of substance abuse clinic directors' and counselors' perceived knowledge, attitudes and reactions. *Journal of Drug Issues, 18*, 403–419.

Michaels, S., Gagnon, J. H., Laumann, E. O., & Michael, R. T. (1990, June). *Anti-gay attitudes, knowing persons with AIDS, and AIDS policy attitudes*. Paper presented at the VI International Conference on AIDS, San Francisco, CA.

O'Donnell, L., O'Donnell, C. R., Pleck, J. H., Snarey, J., & Rose, R. M. (1987). Psychosocial responses of hospital workers to Acquired Immune Deficiency Syndrome (AIDS). *Journal of Applied Social Psychology, 17*(3), 269–285.

Olszewski, L. (1988a, September 22). Economic warning on AIDS initiative. *San Francisco Chronicle*, p. A14.

Olszewski, L. (1988b, November 9). Voters split over 2 AIDS propositions. Prop. *San Francisco Chronicle*, Election Supp., p. B.

Olszewski, L. (1988c, November 10). Prop. 102 backer says AIDS reporting battle not over. *San Francisco Chronicle*, p. A-9.

Panem, S. (1987). *The AIDS bureaucracy*. Cambridge, MA: Harvard University Press.

Petit, C. (1986, October 17). California to vote on AIDS proposition. *Science, 234*, 277–278.

Price, V., & Hsu, M. (1992). Public opinion about AIDS policies: The role of misinformation and attitudes toward homosexuals. *Public Opinion Quarterly, 56*, 29–52.

Pryor, J. B., Reeder, G. D., Vinacco, R., & Kott, T. (1989). The instrumental and symbolic functions of attitudes toward persons with AIDS. *Journal of Applied Social Psychology, 19*, 377–404.

Rosenberg, C. E. (1987). *The cholera years: The United States in 1832, 1849, and 1866* (2nd ed.). Chicago: University of Chicago Press.

Schneider, W. (1987, July/August). Homosexuals: Is AIDS changing attitudes? *Public Opinion, 10* (2), 6–7, 59.

Scitovsky, A. A., & Rice, D. P. (1987). Estimates of the direct and indirect costs of Acquired Immunodeficiency Syndrome in the United States, 1985, 1986, and 1991. *Public Health Reports, 102*, 5–17.

Sheehan, E. P., Lennon, R., & McDevitt, T. (1990). Reactions to AIDS and other illnesses: Reported interactions in the workplace. *Journal of Psychology, 123*, 526–536.

Shilts, R. (1987). *And the band played on: Politics, people, and the AIDS epidemic*. New York: St. Martin's.

Shipp, E. R., & Navarro, M. (1991, November 18). Reluctantly, Black churches confront AIDS. *New York Times*, pp. A-1, A-6.

Singer, E., & Rogers, T. F. (1986). Public opinion and AIDS. *AIDS and Public Policy Journal, 1*, 1–13.

Singer, E., Rogers, T. F., & Blattner, C. (1991, May). *Trends in public opinion about AIDS*. Paper presented at the anual meeting of the American Association for Public Opinion Research, Phoenix, AZ.

Singer, E., Rogers, T. F., & Corcoran, M. (1987). The polls: AIDS. *Public Opinion Quarterly, 51*, 580–595.

Smith, M. B., Bruner, J. S., & White, R. W. (1956). *Opinions and personality*. New York: Wiley.

Sontag, S. (1988). *AIDS and its metaphors*. New York: Farrar, Straus & Giroux.

Stipp, H., & Kerr, D. (1989). Determinants of public opinion about AIDS. *Public Opinion Quarterly, 53*, 98–106.

Thomas, S. B., & Quinn, S. C. (1991). The Tuskegee Syphilis Study, 1932 to 1972: Implications for HIV education and AIDS risk reduction programs in the Black community. *American Journal of Public Health, 11*, 1498–1505.

Triplet, R. G., & Sugarman, D. B. (1987). Reactions to AIDS victims: Ambiguity breeds contempt. *Personality and Social Psychology Bulletin, 13*(2), 265–274.

Wallack, J. J. (1989). AIDS anxiety among health care professionals. *Hospital and Community Psychiatry, 40,* 507–510.

Weiner, B. (1988). An attributional analysis of changing reactions to persons with AIDS. In R. A. Berk (Ed.), *The social impact of AIDS in the U.S.* (pp. 123–132). Cambridge, MA: Abt Books.

Weinstein, N. D. (1989). Personal susceptibility to harm. In V. M. Mays, G. W. Albee, & S. F. Schneider (Eds.), *Primary prevention of AIDS: Psychological approaches* (pp. 142–167). Newbury Park, CA: Sage.

Wertz, D. C., Sorenson, J. R., Liebling, L., Kessler, L., & Heeren, T. C. (1987). Knowledge and attitudes of AIDS health-care providers before and after education programs. *Public Health Reports, 102,* 248–254.

Wiley, K., Heath, L., & Acklin, M. (1988). Care of AIDS patients: Student attitudes. *Nursing Outlook, 36,* 244–245.

Witt, L. A. (1990). Factors affecting attitudes toward persons with AIDS. *Journal of Social Psychology, 130,* 127–129.

Young, R. K., Gallaher, P., Belasco, J., Barr, A., & Webber, A. W. (1991). Changes in fear of AIDS and homophobia in a university population. *Journal of Applied Social Psychology, 21,* 1848–1858.

9 Collective and Individual Representations of HIV/AIDS Stigma

John B. Pryor
Glenn D. Reeder
Illinois State University

> *On March 25, 1987, Jane Doe, her husband John, and a male friend were traveling in the Doe's pickup truck through Barrington, New Jersey. The trio was pulled over by Barrington police as part of a general vehicle stop. After a computer search, John Doe was arrested on a burglary warrant and for unlawful possession of a hypodermic needle. His truck was impounded. During the initial arrest, John Doe warned the police that he had tested positive for HIV and that they should be careful while searching him because he had "weeping lesions." Jane Doe and the friend were released and later that day drove* the friend's car *to the Doe's residence in nearby Runnemead. They left the car running and apparently it slipped out of gear, rolling down the driveway into a neighbor's fence. Runnemead police and a detective from Barrington arrived at the scene of the accident simultaneously. The Barrington detective told the Runnemead police that John Doe had been arrested earlier and had admitted that he had AIDS. The Runnemead police told the neighbor that Jane Doe's husband had AIDS and that, to protect herself, she should wash with a disinfectant. There is no evidence that Jane Doe had any physical contact with the neighbor. John Doe, of course, was in the Barrington jail at the time of the accident. The neighbor had a child who attended the same school as the four Doe children. She called several people whose children also attended that school. In addition, the neighbor also contacted the media. The next day, 11 parents removed 19 children from the school with coverage from local newspapers and television stations*
>
> (Doe v. Borough of Barrington, 1990).

This example illustrates some of the complex issues surrounding HIV/AIDS stigma. It vividly portrays the sense of contamination and peril evoked by the stigma. It also shows how this stigma may not only affect the person afflicted with HIV/AIDS, but the lives of friends and family as well. The dynamics of any stigma entail both psychological and social dimensions. The feelings of contamination and peril shared by the police and the neighbor in this case are rooted in a shared social meaning of HIV/AIDS. A complete understanding of HIV/AIDS stigma must examine both an individual and social level of analysis.

The goal of this chapter is to outline an integrative social psychological theory of how people react to HIV/AIDS stigma. In the first section, HIV/AIDS stigma is framed in the context of general theories of stigma derived from the sociological and psychological literatures. Here the concept of HIV/AIDS stigma as a *social contaminant* is developed. In the second section, reasons why people experience a sense of *peril* from contact with HIV/AIDS stigma are examined. Does peril derive from a fear of actually contracting HIV or from other psychological factors? In the third section, factors that have contributed to the *social construction* of HIV/AIDS stigma are analyzed. Because of the relatively recent emergence of HIV/AIDS, tracing the development of the social meaning of HIV/AIDS seems more tractable than for many other diseases. In the fourth section, a theory of how HIV/AIDS stigma influences the thoughts and feelings of individuals is proposed. This theory incorporates research from the social cognition literature and attempts to describe how the social representations of HIV/AIDS stigma function on an individual psychological level. In the fifth section, alternative theories of how HIV/AIDS stigma might function are discussed. Finally, in the last section, social interventions to combat HIV/AIDS stigma are discussed.

STIGMA AS A SOCIAL CONTAMINANT

To the ancient Greeks the term *stigma* referred to a bodily mark or brand that exposed its bearers as people to be avoided (e.g., criminals, slaves, etc., Goffman, 1963). Contemporary usage of the term implies an undesirable or discrediting differentness (Jones et al., 1984). A stigma is like a contaminant, it spoils the identity of its bearer and labels the person as inferior, dangerous, or bad. For the individual who bears the mark, the stigma may become a "master status" attribute that contaminates the perception of all other aspects of the person's abilities and character (Fraeble, Blackstone, & Scherbaum, 1990).

The early work of Goffman (1963) delineated three major types of stigma: an abomination of the body (e.g., obvious physical deformities), a character flaw, and a tribal stigma (i.e., a mark or fault afflicting the members of a social group). Persons with HIV infection potentially have all three types of stigma. The physical manifestations of HIV infection during the later stages of the disease are devastating and often include massive weight loss. Societal views of homosexuality and IV drug use, two behaviors commonly associated with HIV infection, suggest that those involved in these pursuits are immoral and disgusting (Conrad, 1986; Pryor, Reeder, Vinacco, and Kott, 1989). Finally, the association of HIV/AIDS with previously stigmatized social groups such as gay men or racial/ethnic minorities provides a convenient social categorization for persons infected with HIV.

Similar in some ways to the tribal stigma concept, Goffman also recognized a fourth type he described as a "courtesy stigma." A courtesy stigma is shared by those closely associated with the stigmatized. For example, Goffman (1963) suggested that the stigma of being labeled a *criminal* can spoil the identity of not only the person who bears this mark, but that of his or her offspring as well. So, there is a stigma to being the son or daughter of a murderer. As people are often judged by the company they keep, Goffman asserted that this stigma might be shared by friends of the offsprings of murderers. The New Jersey case described earlier illustrates how the children of an HIV-infected person can share the stigma of HIV/AIDS.

A study conducted by the American Civil Liberties Union (Hunter, 1990) examined over 13,000 cases of AIDS or HIV-related discrimination reported by 260 legal and advocacy groups across the United States. Thirty percent of the individuals reporting discrimination were not HIV positive. Of these, 21% felt that they were targeted because of the risks associated with their lifestyles (e.g., gay men), jobs (e.g., health-care workers), or other factors. The remaining 9% felt that they were targeted for discrimination because of their close association with someone who is HIV positive. That association was through family relationships in some cases or by providing care for an infected person in others (see Omoto, Snyder, & Berghuis, this volume, for related examples).

The social contamination of a stigma may even spread to objects that are somehow associated with the stigmatized so that the physical possessions of marked individuals also may be viewed as tainted. In recent research, Rozin and his colleagues (Rozin, Markwith, & McCauley, 1991; Rozin, Nemeroff, & Markwith, 1991) found the stigma of being a murderer, being homosexual, having a serious accident, having tuberculosis, or having AIDS can be transmitted to objects once associated with the stigma bearers. So, people display aversions to laundered sweaters if they were once worn by someone with any of these stigmatizing conditions. Rozin also has found negative reactions to sleeping in a hotel bed or owning a car if these things recently came into contact with a stigmatized person.

The spread of contamination to possessions is also illustrated in *Doe v. the Borough of Barrington*. The stigma of HIV/AIDS spread from John Doe to his wife to the friend's car that crashed into the neighbor's fence. The neighbor was "warned" to disinfect herself. Because there was no driver when the car crashed and there were no reported injuries, exactly what was the meaning of the warning? Although the HIV virus can only infect living creatures, *AIDS stigma* can infect or contaminate virtually anything associated with an HIV-infected person.

Thus, hotel beds, sweaters, and even cars can become contaminated once they have come into contact with a person with AIDS (PWA).

In summary, the major routes of HIV transmission seem well established in the scientific literature and few in number (Francis & Chin, 1987; Sande, 1986). Sexual intercourse with an HIV-infected person and injection of HIV-contaminated blood or blood products account for the overwhelming majority of the known cases of HIV infection in the United States (Centers for Disease Control [CDC], 1992). However, although the routes of *stigma* transmission also are well established in the scientific literature, they seem much larger in number. As documented earlier, almost any association to HIV seems potentially sufficient to result in some transmission of HIV/AIDS stigma. Why do people fear the stigmatized and even objects associated with the stigmatized?

SOURCES UNDERLYING THE PERIL OF HIV/AIDS

According to Jones et al. (1984), an essential feature of any stigma is a sense of peril that is evoked by the mark. Bearers of a stigma are perceived by others as dangerous. Jones and his colleagues outlined four possible sources of peril or reasons that the stigmatized are feared. First, the stigma bearer may remind people of their own personal vulnerability. Second, people may fear acquiring a courtesy stigma in the minds of others. Third, the stigmatized may tempt people to engage in stigmatizing behaviors (i.e., to indulge in forbidden fruit). Fourth, people may fear being obligated to help the stigmatized. All of these reasons could potentially apply to HIV/AIDS stigma or to some of the other stigmata associated with HIV/AIDS. All represent perceived costs of interacting with the stigmatized. In many ways, such a subjective cost analysis is similar to what Pryor, Reeder, Vinacco, and Kott (1989) described as an *expectancy-value* analysis. In specific situations, there could be both perceived costs and benefits from interacting with someone infected with HIV.

Of course, a major cost that people often perceive from interacting with PWAs is possible transmission. After all, HIV infection is contagious under some circumstances and the likely consequence of infection is death. Even though the CDC has repeatedly proclaimed that HIV cannot be contracted from casual contact, the popular media is loaded with those who question the safety of interacting with PWAs. A mistrust of medical information on HIV transmission certainly intensifies fear of HIV/AIDS even if it is not the origin of this fear (Herek & Glunt, 1988). Using an expectancy-value analysis, Pryor, Reeder, Vinacco, and Kott (1989) found that beliefs about potential contagiousness often contribute to a desire to avoid PWAs. So, those who shun and avoid PWAs could be responding to what they perceive as a real danger of infection. When an employer fires a PWA, is it because of a reaction to the stigma or a fear of transmission or both?

Whether real or imagined, concerns about HIV transmission can be legitimate sources of fear about HIV/AIDS. Some populations may not distinguish between scientific routes of HIV/AIDS transmission and superstitious routes. For example, young children's concepts of illness seem primarily based on the idea that proximity (e.g., simply being around someone who is ill) is sufficient for transmission (Bibace & Walsh, 1980; Siegal, 1988). Landau, Pryor, Patterson, and Belfield (1992) found that, compared to older age groups, kindergarten-aged children are especially fearful of other children who have HIV/AIDS. Kindergartners show aversions to children with a variety of other illnesses as well.

Also, the distinction between social contamination and illness transmission often seems lost in the traditional belief systems of some "primitive" cultures (Frazer, 1890/1959; Rozin, Millman, & Nemeroff, 1986). A common explanation for illness in many societies is retribution for moral transgression (Murdock, 1980). So, social contamination, moral taint, and illness are often highly interrelated concepts (Rozin, Markwith, & McCauley, 1991). Some anthropologists even have argued that modern lay germ theories of disease may be merely rationalizations of the disgust at unwanted social contamination by others (Douglas, 1966).

On a basic psychological level, people may fear the stigmatized simply because they bring to mind negative affect. The more obvious the stigma, the more inescapable the potential negative affect. With a stigma like HIV/AIDS that is so intricately connected with a variety of other stigmata, many negative feelings may be evoked.

To some extent, the fear of objects which have come in contact with stigmatized persons also could be rooted in a desire to avoid negative affect. An anecdotal example seems to illustrate this process. In Los Angeles, a hospital administrator spoke with a man known to be infected with HIV. Throughout their conversation, the man continually played with a pencil lying on the administrator's desk. Afterward the administrator was reluctant to use this pencil and finally threw it away. She admitted that the pencil evoked negative feelings despite her realization that there was no possible danger of contracting HIV/AIDS from it. Why did she throw away the pencil? Perhaps she was afraid of being reminded of HIV/AIDS and the negative affect it evoked. The work of Rozin and his colleagues described earlier seems to illustrate that almost any object once associated with HIV/AIDS has the power to evoke such fears.

In summary, the sense of peril experienced by those in contact with PWAs may emanate from a variety of sources. Sometimes peril may reflect concerns about contracting HIV/AIDS or encountering other costs. Other times, people seem to fear "fear itself." In other words, they fear being reminded of the negative feelings evoked by HIV/AIDS. The underlying threat of any stigma lies in its power to activate negative affect, whatever the source. Like other illness stigmata, HIV/AIDS has acquired a unique set of social connotations that contribute to the sense of peril it evokes. In the next section, an analysis of the evolving social meaning of HIV/AIDS is offered.

THE SOCIAL CONSTRUCTION OF HIV/AIDS STIGMA

Among his many contributions to our theoretical understanding, Goffman (1963) recognized the central role of culture in defining stigma. To a great extent, a stigma is defined by a deviation from what is culturally accepted as "normal." Central to the experience of stigmatized persons is the negotiation of status with the "normal group." What is stigmatizing in some groups may be normal in others. For example, injecting intravenous drugs might be a stigmatizing behavior among a group of rural junior high school students and a rite of passage among a group of inner-city youth. Thus, "stigma is a social construct—a reflection of culture itself, not a property of individuals" (Ainlay, Coleman, & Becker, 1986, p. 4).

To some extent, negative social reactions to persons infected with HIV could reflect a general rejection of deviance (Albert, 1986). By definition, a deviant is anyone who differs in some significant way from the normal group. The extremity of social reactions to deviance varies widely across individuals. Pryor, Reeder, and McManus (1991) explored some of the personality and attitudinal correlates of socially rejecting persons infected with HIV. They found that college students' rejection of HIV-infected co-workers in student jobs was correlated with a general measure of authoritarianism (Berkowitz & Wolkon, 1964). Similar findings have been reported by Larsen, Elder, Bader, and Dougard (1990) and Witt (1989). People who are high in authoritarianism tend to reject all deviants, no matter what the basis of the deviance. From this perspective, those with any chronic illness may be the targets of social rejection, at least from those high in authoritarianism. However, Pryor et al. (1991) also found that specific attitudes toward homosexuality uniquely contributed to the social rejection of HIV-infected persons even when the relationship with authoritarianism was partialled out. One interesting aspect of this research is that the persons who were said to be infected with HIV were described as having contracted the illness through blood transfusions. They were not described as homosexuals. This point is discussed further in a later section. The essential point here is that the social rejection of those infected with HIV seems to be more than just a general reaction to social deviance. It seems tied to the unique associations that HIV has acquired in contemporary society. Rejection is tied to the social meaning of HIV/AIDS.

The social meaning of HIV/AIDS is strongly linked to the social history of the disease. Excellent accounts of the confluence of the political, ethical, and scientific forces in this evolving meaning are found in Conrad (1986), Frankenberg (1989), Horton (1989), Shilts (1987), and Valdiserri (1987). Also, Brandt (1986) provided a longer range view of the historical forces that have shaped contemporary views of sexually transmitted disease (STD) in Western culture. (Some of these issues are discussed in Herek and Glunt's chapter in this volume.) Here, the focus is on developments in public health that have helped mold the meaning of HIV/AIDS in the United States.

268

As Siegfried (1960/1965) pointed out: "There is a striking parallel between the spreading of germs and the spreading of ideas or propaganda" (p. 84). Although there are various theories about the origin of the HIV virus, the idea of HIV/AIDS seems to have origins in the public health and medical communities of the United States. In 1981, physicians in California and New York began reporting the occurrence of two rare diseases: a form of cancer called Kaposi's Sarcoma and a form of pneumonia caused by the pneumocystis carnii organism. The victims of these opportunistic diseases were gay men who had mysteriously compromised immune systems. In the July 4th, 1981 edition of the *Mortality and Morbidity Weekly Report* (*MMWR*), the National Centers of Disease Control published an article entitled "Karposi's Sarcoma and Pneumocystis Pneumonia Among Homosexual Men—New York City and California." An early acronym for HIV/AIDS was GRID, which stood for Gay Related Immune Deficiency Syndrome (Shilts, 1987). These initial connections of HIV/AIDS to homosexuality set the stage for AIDS to be dubbed the *gay plague* (Krauthammer, 1983). Throughout the 1980s into the 1990s, this conception of HIV/AIDS has been reinforced by epidemiology statistics revealing that the majority of persons infected with HIV in the United States have been homosexual and bisexual men. As of December 31, 1991, 58% of the adult AIDS cases in the United States involved men who had sex with men (CDC, 1992).

The social meaning of HIV/AIDS also has been influenced by the large proportions of minorities and intravenous drug users who have been infected with the virus. Through the end of 1991, Blacks made up about 29% of the reported AIDS cases in the United States (adult and pediatric). Hispanics accounted for approximately 16% (adult and pediatric; CDC, 1992). Census data indicate that Blacks and Hispanics make up only about 12% and 7% of the total population of the United States. During this time period, intravenous drug users made up about 23% of the reported cases of AIDS among adults.

A final epidemiology statistic adds yet another dimension to the social meaning of HIV/AIDS. Sixty-five percent of the adults and 53% of the children diagnosed with AIDS since CDC began to track HIV/AIDS 10 years ago are dead (CDC, 1992). As of early 1992, there is no known cure.

The early 1990s hold the possibility for additional inputs to the evolving social meaning of HIV/AIDS. Recent reports have linked HIV/AIDS to yet another source of stigma: tuberculosis (Altman, 1992). Once again, this dimension of social meaning is spawned from the medical and public health sectors. People with HIV/AIDS seem to be vulnerable to new drug-resistant strains of tuberculosis.

In summary, one reason that the stigma of HIV/AIDS is so severe may be that it is linked to other stigma (Crandall, 1991). These links are traced in the public health statistics cited earlier. The statistics provide the grist for the media mills churning out an image of HIV/AIDS as the nexus in a web of ostracized groups and threatening images. These same links can also be traced in numerous surveys across diverse samples. Prejudice against homosexuals, intolerance of drug use, hostility toward minorities, and fear of death all have been shown to contribute to feelings about HIV/AIDS (Ficarroto, Grade, Bliwise, & Irish, 1990; Henry, Campbell, & Willenbring, 1990; Larsen, Serra, & Long, 1990; O'Donnell, O'Donnell, Pleck, Snarey, & Rose, 1987; Ross, 1988; Royse & Birge, 1987; Stipp & Kerr, 1989; Wiener & Siegel, 1990). A final link in the web of social meaning is to feelings about sexuality. As with the other issues connected to HIV/AIDS, personal feelings about sexuality vary widely across people. Pryor, et al. (1991) and Larsen, Serra, & Long (1990) found connections between general sexual attitudes and feelings about HIV/AIDS. The power of HIV/AIDS stigma to contaminate may reflect the culminating contamination potential of all the social meanings associated with it.

THE INDIVIDUAL PERSPECTIVE: HIV/AIDS STIGMA IN SOCIAL COGNITION PROCESSES

The social meaning of any phenomena has both collective and individual representations (Markova & Wilkie, 1987). The individual cognitive representations possessed by specific persons may be fragmented, containing only part of the collective representation, or idiosyncratic, containing unique parts or properties. However, mass communication is based on and promulgates shared meaning. So, one may expect that the cognitive representations of HIV/AIDS held by individuals in the United States will have some typical elements as well as some idiosyncratic ones. In the previous section, some of the typical elements of the social meaning of HIV/AIDS stigma were discussed. In this section, attention is turned to how individuals cognitively represent and process information about persons with HIV/AIDS stigma.

According to Pryor and Ostrom (1987), all social behaviors are, at least in part, *memory driven*. Thus, discriminatory behaviors, avoidance, and hostility directed at PWAs can be traced to individual cognitive representations of these persons. One theoretical approach often applied to the cognitive representation of person information depicts human memory as an associative network (Anderson, 1983). In this model, a PWA is cognitively represented as a person node within an associative network of related concept nodes (Pryor & Ostrom, 1987). AIDS (or HIV infection) is an attribute associated with this person node. Like other stigmatizing attributes, HIV/AIDS may be associatively linked to a rich network of other concepts. Figure 9.1 depicts a possible cognitive representation of a PWA within such an associative network.

As shown in Fig. 9.1, affective as well as propositional information can be contained within the network (Isen & Diamond, 1989). Affective responses to a PWA may emanate simultaneously from several sources in the network. As with other associative network models, the probability of activation spreading along

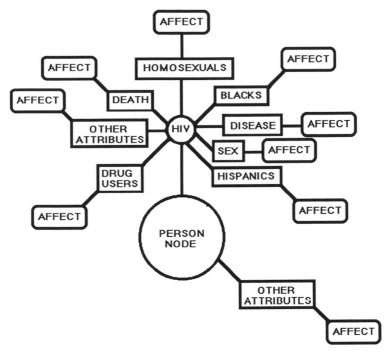

FIG. 9.1. Associative network representation of a person with HIV infection.

some associative juncture is thought to be a function of the recency and frequency of activation (Wyer & Carlston, 1979; Srull & Wyer, 1989). Thus, recent experiences (priming) and the chronic accessibility of certain concepts may be important in an individual's reaction to a PWA. A chain of information nodes that is repeatedly accessed in the network may take on a *procedural property* (Smith, 1984; Smith & Lerner, 1987). By this, it is meant that these associated concepts come to mind as a unit. For example, if someone repeatedly thinks of HIV as a disease associated with homosexuals and then how much one loathes homosexuals, over time HIV, homosexuals, and negative affect will become a single thought rather than three separate thoughts. When one of these thoughts comes to mind, the others follow in a relatively automatic fashion.

As described earlier, one factor that may contribute to the often powerful negative reactions to PWAs is the connection of HIV to other stigmatizing attributes, most notably, to homosexuality and drug use. Each of these attributes is linked to its own affect. The specific links and their associative strength in any individual's cognitive representation are the products of both cultural and idiosyncratic experiences. For example, although the connection between gay men and HIV/AIDS seems especially strong in the United States owing to the course of the epidemic in this country, this connection might be weaker in African countries like Ghana where most of those infected are heterosexual women (Bourne, 1990). Also, the valence of the affect that is associated with homosexuality, drug use, or other HIV-related attributes varies widely across individuals in our own culture.

Two additional points depicted in Fig. 9.1 also seem worthy of mention. For some people, HIV may have very specific connotations (note the "other attributes" link). Personal experiences, like having a family member who has died from HIV disease, may add significantly to an individual's representation. Also, the other attributes link to the person node suggests that other information about this person could enter into affective reactions. When someone encounters a PWA, activation spreads from the person node across the various pathways to related attributes and then to their related affect. The resulting affective experience represents the culmination of affect activated throughout the network.

Figure 9.1 depicts some of the rudimentary associative links connected to a person with HIV/AIDS. However, HIV/AIDS stigma can also afflict those without HIV infection, but who are somehow associated with HIV/AIDS. For example, prejudicial reactions toward gay men could stem from the connection between HIV/AIDS and homosexuality as well as other sources. Also, family members associated with PWAs could bear the burden of HIV/AIDS stigma. In these cases the structure of the networks may be different from that depicted in Fig. 9.1, but the nature of the process is essentially the same.

A fundamental quality of the associative network account of HIV/AIDS stigma is that the connections within the network may have less to do with logic than with arbitrary associations. For example, the hemophiliac who contracts HIV through the use of contaminated blood products has a disease associated with homosexuals and drug users, but may have no other connection with these groups. That arbitrary or coincidental connections with a stigma are sufficient for social contamination seems evident in many of the examples presented throughout this chapter. This issue was addressed in several original studies presented here.

Empirical Evidence for the Model.   In a series of studies, Pryor, Reeder, and their colleagues examined how the affect associated with homosexuality influences social judgments made about PWAs. Thus, these studies examined the basic process of affect spreading from a single node in the network to related nodes. In an early study, Pryor, Reeder, and Lavalle (1989) asked 139 members of business/professional organizations from a mid-size midwestern city to rate the likelihood of their hiring a trainee for a permanent staff position. The trainee was described as either (a) in the early stages of HIV infection (i.e., no symptoms), (b) in a later stage of HIV infection (minor symptoms, but no serious opportunistic infections), or (c) without any mention of HIV. In all cases, the trainee was described as competent and qualified for the job. In no case was the trainee described as a homosexual. Results showed that prospective employers who held negative attitudes toward homosexuality were less likely to hire either of the two trainees with HIV than the trainee without HIV. In contrast, employers without negative attitudes toward homosexuality were equally likely to hire all the trainees. These findings are depicted in Table 9.1.

Although no mention was made of the trainees' being homosexual in the Pryor, Reeder, and Lavalle study, one might speculate that the subjects inferred that those with HIV were homosexual. Thus, the attribute of homosexuality and its associated affect could have influenced people's reactions to the trainees with HIV for at least two reasons. First, subjects may have been responding to a trainee who they perceived to be homosexual (a direct link of the attribute "homosexual" to the person node). Second, people could have been responding to a trainee who had a disease associated with homosexuality (an indirect link or chain of associations to the person node). Of course, these two possibilities are not mutually exclusive. The next studies established that the indirect link is sufficient for affect about homosexuality to influence reactions to a PWA.

Pryor, Reeder, Vinacco, and Kott (1989) examined the correlates of reactions to children infected with HIV. These studies found that people who held negative attitudes toward homosexuality tended to hold negative attitudes toward having a child in class with an HIV-infected child. Multiple regression procedures established that these relationships were independent of beliefs about contagiousness. These same results have been replicated in several subsequent studies with different populations. For example, in an ongoing longitudinal study of reactions to PWAs in public schools, Pryor and Landau (1992) studied fathers' and mothers' attitudes toward their children interacting with HIV-infected children in school

TABLE 9.1
Liklihood of Hiring an Employee as a Function of Attitudes Toward Homosexuality
and HIV/AIDS Condition

	Attitudes Toward Homosexuality	
HIV/AIDS Condition	*Anti*	*Pro*
HIV/AIDS asympotomatic	2.28[a] $N = 25$	3.70[b] $N = 26$
HIV/AIDS symptomatic	1.59[a] $N = 22$	3.26[b] $N = 23$
Control	3.88[b] $N = 17$	3.58[b] $N = 26$

Note. The means with different superscripts within each row or column are significantly different from one another ($ps < .05$). Those sharing the same superscripts are not significantly different. Higher numbers indicate a higher likelihood of hiring. The likelihood scale ranged from 1 to 7 with 1 labeled "not at all likely" and 7, "very likely." ANTI and PRO designations refer to groups that were below and above the median, respectively, on a 3-item measure of attitudes toward homosexuality.

settings. They found that attitudes toward homosexuality consistently correlated with reactions to a variety of different possible school-related interactions. These ranged from their children playing with the HIV-infected child at recess to their children eating cookies that the HIV-infected child's mother sent to school. In general, attitudes toward homosexuality have been found to contribute importantly to reactions toward *nonhomosexual* PWAs. This relationship still holds when a variety of possible "third variables" are partialled out (Pryor, et al., 1991).

The cognitive account of these findings reflects the process of spreading activation. HIV infection, as an attribute, brings to mind homosexuals. This, in turn, brings to mind whatever affective responses an individual has toward homosexuals. These affective responses are subject to wide individual differences. For those who hold extremely negative attitudes toward homosexuality, there is the experience of negative affect. Thus, part of the negative affect evoked by an HIV-infected child is related to the feelings about homosexuality the child brings to mind by having a disease strongly associated with homosexuals. This happens even though the child is not a homosexual. An important point about these findings is that the connection between the HIV-infected child and affect toward homosexuals represents a chain of arbitrary associations.

If this analysis is correct, then other illnesses associatively linked to stigmatized groups, like homosexuals, also may be expected to evoke similar negative affect. Pryor and Reeder (1990) tested this idea by creating associative links between a hypothetical disease and homosexuality, and then assessing subjects' reactions to persons afflicted with this disease. Subjects were asked to read one of two fabricated news stories describing the outbreak of a disease called "suproxiosis." In both stories suproxiosis was described as commonly contracted from eating shellfish. However, one news story portrayed suproxiosis as a disease that also could be sexually transmitted and that had begun infecting homosexual men. In the other story, no mention was made of sexual transmission or the occurrence among homosexual men. The prediction was that people who held negative attitudes toward homosexuality would be especially likely to socially reject the suproxiosis victim when the disease was associated with homosexuality. These results were expected even though the suproxiosis victim was described as having contracted the disease from eating shellfish.

Results from this study are shown in Fig. 9.2. The figure shows that anti-homosexual subjects who read stories linking suproxiosis to homosexuals were most likely to reject the suproxiosis victim as a potential lab partner. Thus, arbitrary associations to a stigmatized group can contribute to the rejection a person infected with a novel disease. In effect, the suproxiosis victim became contaminated by virtue of the association.

According to the current theoretical model, the critical feature of this process is bringing the affect associated with the stigmatized group to consciousness. Spreading activation along established associative pathways is one way in which

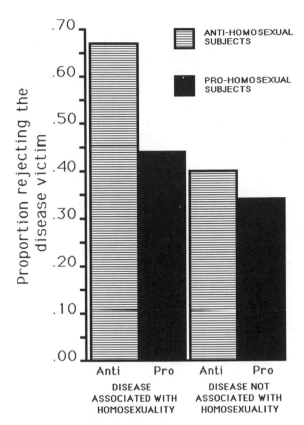

FIG. 9.2.   Rejection of a potential roommate infected with suproxiosis as a function of the association of suproxiosis with homosexuality and subjects' attitudes toward homosexuality.

this commonly is accomplished. However, in controlled laboratory conditions, other means are also possible. A subsequent study (Pryor & Reeder, 1990) sought to establish that simply bringing the affect of the stigma to mind while a subject contemplated an interaction with a stimulus person is enough for a contamination reaction. The study utilized a subliminal priming procedure to evoke affective responses people held about homosexuals and then assessed their reactions to a person afflicted with a novel illness. The priming procedure was adapted from work by Bargh (1989).

In one condition, subjects were exposed to 20 words associated with the stereotype of homosexual men. Each word was presented four times for a total of 80 stereotype-relevant exposures. The order was randomized and randomly interspersed were 20 neutral words. In a second condition, subjects were given only one exposure to the stereotype-relevant words and 4 exposures each for the neutral words. In both conditions, the exposure duration was 100 milliseconds.

The words were flashed on a computer screen as the subjects engaged in a vigilance task in which they monitored the location of the flashes on the screen. Research by Bargh and Petromonaco (1982) found that subjects are unable to recognize words presented using this methodology even though the content of such words influences subsequent impression judgments. Immediately following the presentation of the priming words in the current study, subjects were asked to rate their reactions to having a roommate infected with a noncontagious, but unusual disease (suproxiosis).

In brief, the results of this study revealed that reactions of subjects to the suproxiosis-infected roommate were significantly correlated with their attitudes toward homosexuality if they had just been exposed to 80 homosexual stereotype primes. In this condition, those with negative attitudes toward homosexuality tended to reject the suproxiosis victim as a roommate. Presumably, the affect associated with the concept "homosexuality" was brought to mind for these subjects. In the other priming condition, where only 20 of the priming words were related to homosexual stereotypes, there was no relationship between attitudes toward homosexuality and subjects' reactions to the suproxiosis-infected roommate. In a pair of companion conditions, the roommate-rating task was replaced with a recognition task. Results from these conditions revealed that subjects did not recognize the presented primes at a level greater than chance, nor was there any difference between recognition rates of the various primes across the two priming conditions.

This study suggests that affect may be automatically activated by stigmatized concepts like *homosexuality*. For some people, subliminal exposure to the stereotypic concept *homosexuality* brought to mind aversive affect and it was this affect that provoked negative reactions to the stimulus person. Subjects were not even aware of the source of their feelings and yet this contamination reaction took place (Krosnick, Betz, Jussim, & Lynn, 1992).

The focus of this research has been on the affect associated with homosexuality. The research demonstrates that arbitrary and even nonconscious links to homosexuality can serve to stigmatize. Obviously, the associative links of HIV to other affect-laden concepts also could serve as conduits for stigma in a similar manner. Using a procedure similar to that of the Pryor and Reeder (1990) subliminal priming study, Devine (1989) showed that negative affect toward Blacks can influence how people react toward neutral stimulus persons. One difference between Devine's findings and those in the Pryor and Reeder (1990) study was that the negative affect emanating from Black stereotypes was not mediated by a questionnaire measure of racial prejudice. That is, subjects were biased by exposure to Black stereotype words regardless of their level of self-reported prejudice. Because HIV also is associated with minorities, Devine's research implies that (nonconscious) negative affect from this source may contribute to HIV/AIDS stigma as well.

ALTERNATIVE THEORIES OF STIGMA

As the research of Pryor, Reeder, and their associates illustrates, the connection of HIV/AIDS to homosexuality influences how people react to PWAs even when the PWA is not homosexual. The spreading affect model described previously implies that any associated negative attribute can contribute to the contamination power of a stigma. Three alternative theoretical perspectives of stigma are discussed here. Each provides a different account for how stigmata may result in negative social reactions.

Sympathetic Magic. An alternative conceptualization of the social contamination properties of stigma comes from the work of Rozin and his colleagues (e.g., Rozin & Fallon, 1987). Rozin suggested that social contamination reactions derive from the application of the laws of sympathetic magic (Frazer, 1890/1959; Mauss, 1902/1972). These laws first were formulated to account for a variety of magical practices and beliefs in traditional cultures. The first law is *contiguity*. This principle suggests that things that once come into contact with each other will continue ever afterward to influence one another. The second law is *similarity*. This principle assumes that "like produces like" (Frazer, 1890/1959, p. 35) or that if two things are similar, then action against one will influence the other. Rozin, Millman, and Nemeroff (1986) found evidence for these laws in studies of college students' contamination reactions in the domain of food aversions (e.g., displaying disgust toward food that has come in contact with some disgusting stimulus). So, the laws of sympathetic magic are thought to govern everyday contamination reactions in modern societies as well as in traditional cultures. Relevant to the current focus on stigma, Rozin's work on how HIV/AIDS stigma may contaminate objects could be interpreted as evidence for the law of contiguity. For example, a sweater once worn by a PWA becomes contaminated (Rozin, Markwith, & McCauley, 1991; Rozin, Nemeroff, & Markwith, 1991).

Although the sympathetic magic account of contamination effects seems to have generated some interesting research, it is difficult to see how this account is really different from the associative network account. Similar predictions can be made from both models. Rozin and Fallon (1987) contended that the laws of sympathetic magic are different from *laws of association* (Hume, 1748/1959; J. S. Mill, 1843/1963) in that they represent "not only statements about thought but statements about causation in the world" (p. 30). However, on a rudimentary level much of what is inferred about causation is based on associations formed on the basis of spatiotemporal contiguity (Duncker, 1945; Kassin & Pryor, 1985; Michotte, 1946/1963). Furthermore, many theorists have postulated that inferences about causation play a key role in the formulation of associations (Hilton, 1988). So, it is difficult to argue that causal significance somehow plays a role in distinguishing the laws of sympathetic magic as separate from general associative learning principles. On the other hand, by incorporating general principles of associative learning, the associative network account of stigma seems more general and more parsimonious than the sympathetic magic account.

Attribution of Control.   Another theoretical view of stigma is offered by Weiner (this volume). Weiner argues that causal attributions may be important in reactions to the stigmatized. For example, people may attribute more blame for HIV infection to a homosexual who became infected through sexual intercourse than to a child who became infected through a blood transfusion. Because of this difference in blame, people have more negative reactions to the homosexual than the child. Central to Weiner's analysis is the attribution of control. In the example, homosexuals may be blamed more because the behavior that resulted in their being infected with HIV is perceived as more under their volitional control than the behavior that infected the child.

This analysis is derived from Weiner's (1986) general attributional theory of emotions. Research supports the claim that reactions to those who have experienced some malady are mediated by the attributions people make about the cause of the malady (e.g., Schmidt & Weiner, 1988). If victims are believed to have brought on their maladies through their own actions, then reactions are less sympathetic. Also, attitudes toward persons with other illnesses like cancer seem to be influenced by perceptions of controllability (Meyerowitz, Williams, & Gessner, 1987).

Such an attributional analysis has problems in explaining negative reactions to so-called "innocent victims" or those who are perceived to have acquired a stigma through no action of their own. As documented throughout this chapter, HIV/AIDS stigma can "infect" children who contracted HIV through contaminated blood products or even people and objects simply associated with HIV.

Moreover, the spreading affect account of stigma offered in this chapter could be extended to integrate certain types of attributional reasoning. There are several possible ways in which attributional information about control might be represented in an associative network model. First, "transmission mode" might take on the status of a separate attribute connected to either the person node or the HIV node in a representation like the one depicted in Fig. 9.1. As such, this attribute might be related to specific affect. Thus, attributional information could become a distinct set of links and nodes.

Another way in which attributional information could be represented within an associative network concerns the specific associative links connecting the nodes. Weiner, Perry, and Magnusson (1988) depicted stigmata as *unexpected negative outcomes*. If a person is connected to such a negative outcome through a volitional act, then the associative link between the outcome and the person node could be stronger. Thus, the probability of the stigma and its associated affect coming to mind would be higher. This could help explain why stigmata believed to be brought on by volitional actions are more powerful determinants of negative affect.

A third possibility for integrating attributional findings with the current associative network perspective involves a two-stage process. In the first stage of thinking about a person with HIV, activation spreads through an associative network like that portrayed in Fig. 9.1, thus producing affect. This is similar to a characterization phase of person perception described in Gilbert (1989; see also Reeder, Damashek, & Bartman, 1992; and Trope, 1986). In a second phase, attributional information (i.e., information about how the person was infected) may be used to adjust this initial impression. The end result is a less negative impression if the person with HIV is not perceived as being responsible for the infection. Obviously, these ideas present some interesting possibilities for future research.

AIDS as a Symbol.   Pryor, Reeder, Vinacco, and Kott (1989) presented a third theoretical perspective for understanding HIV/AIDS stigma: the symbolic approach. Building on ideas developed by Sontag (1978), Pryor et al. suggested that HIV/AIDS may have acquired a symbolic meaning in our culture. As a symbol or a metaphor, it represents things like homosexual promiscuity, moral decadence, and the wrath of God for moral transgressions (Conrad, 1986; Krauthammer, 1983). So, when people react negatively to someone with AIDS (or HIV), they may be expressing their feelings about the symbol. This analysis could explain why those strongly opposed to homosexuality react negatively to nonhomosexuals with HIV. Even the infected child bears the symbol of homosexual promiscuity. The idea that people respond to HIV/AIDS on a symbolic or metaphoric level has since emerged in other studies as well. For example, Norton, Schwartzbaum, and Wheat (1990) found that physicians who completed the thought "AIDS is like. . . " often tended to mention derogatory metaphors such as "the wrath of God," a "plague brought to us by a minority of aberrant individuals," and "poetic justice, almost." (See also Valdiserri, 1987.)

The symbolic approach has several advantages. Perhaps the most distinct of which is an integration of stigma with the functional approach to attitudes (Herek, 1986). However, this approach has little to say about the individual cognitive representations of HIV. Ultimately, the essential distinction between the symbolic approach and the associative network approach is in the level of analysis: The symbolic approach focuses more on the social level, whereas the network approach is located at the individual level. In this respect, the associative network account seems more integrative in that it provides an analysis of how collective social meanings may be represented on an individual cognitive level.

In summary, the HIV epidemic has forced psychologists to take a fresh look at stigma and to try to integrate the concept of stigma into mainstream theory and research in social cognition. The associative network model outlined in this chapter is obviously in its beginning stages and many of its assumptions need further study. However, such a model holds the promise of integrating a wide array of literature on the topic of stigma.

CONCLUSIONS: COMBATING THE STIGMA

AIDS stigma is as much an epidemic as the spread of the virus (Herek & Glunt, 1988). In addition to the cost in human misery to the stigmatized (Zich & Temoshok, 1987), the stigma of HIV/AIDS also may enact an awful cost to society. In a press conference in 1988, retired Admiral James D. Watkins, chairman of the President's Commission on AIDS, stated that discrimination is the "most significant threat to progress" against the epidemic (Boffey, 1988). Watkins contended that the fear of discrimination discouraged many of those who suspect they have HIV from being tested or cooperating with public health initiatives. The two major weapons in battling this epidemic of stigma are litigation and education.

In a review of 469 HIV/AIDS-related legal cases in the United States, Gostin (1990a) categorized 32% as *discrimination cases*. Up until the present, the basis for legal action in many AIDS discrimination cases is that having AIDS can be considered a handicap and that PWAs are protected under the Rehabilitation Act of 1973 as well as many state statutes (Wing, 1988). For example, the case of *Thomas v. Atascadero Unified School District* (1987) involved an HIV-infected child who was barred from kindergarten after he bit a classmate. The federal court ruled that the child's condition was a protected handicap and ordered that the child be readmitted to school. The court contended that the school had not shown that the child's presence in the classroom presented a significant risk for transmission.

Although this case set some important legal precedents for considering AIDS a handicap, the courts vacillated on whether simply being infected with HIV without any obvious symptoms also might be considered a handicap (see e.g., *School Board of Nassau County, Florida v. Arline*, 1987). Fortunately, the Americans with Disabilities Act (ADA) of 1990 extended the definition of disability offered in the Rehabilitation Act to explicitly cover both persons with symptomatic AIDS and asymptomatic carriers of HIV (Pyle, 1992). The ADA also prohibited employers from discriminating against nondisabled persons because of any association or relationship with a disabled person. The major employment discrimination provisions of the ADA became effective in 1992.

Both the ADA and the Rehabilitation Act included in the definition of a "handicapped person" someone who is *regarded* as having a handicap. In *Arline*, the Supreme Court asserted that by including those who are simply regarded as handicapped, "Congress acknowledged that society's accumulated myths and fears about disability and disease are as handicapping as are the physical limitations that flow from actual impairment" (p. 1129). Gostin (1990b) argued that ADA protection against employment discrimination could extend to homosexuals and other groups who are often *regarded* as having HIV/AIDS because of their lifestyles or high-risk behaviors. The full extent of this kind of protection under the ADA has yet to see litigation.

The ADA was built primarily on two pieces of previous legislation: the Rehabilitation Act of 1973 and the Civil Rights Acts of 1964. In the ADA, the U.S. Congress recognized the power of stigma emitting from HIV/AIDS and other disabilities, and the importance of protecting the disabled from discriminatory practices. The Civil Rights Act had a similar intent in protecting women and minorities from discriminatory practices. However, legal protections against discrimination do not eliminate stigma, prejudice, or discrimination. They simply make their overt manifestations more difficult. With regard to racism, Sears and his colleagues (Kinder & Sears, 1981; Sears & Kinder, 1985) argued that contemporary racism in the United States is still just as ubiquitous as old fashioned racism, it is simply more subtle. Contemporary people do not wish to *appear* racist. Similarly, people do not wish to appear to discriminate against persons with handicaps, but often do so when their motives can be conveniently disguised (Snyder, Kleck, Strenta, & Mentzer, 1979). Still, some studies indicate that legal sanctions can help stem the tide of discriminatory behaviors even when discriminatory attitudes still persist (Gross & Niman, 1975).

Traditionally, education has been the weapon of choice in the battle against prejudice and discrimination. Unfortunately, most HIV education attempts on a mass scale seem to be limited largely to conveying medical information about transmission (Koop, 1986; U.S. Department of Education, 1987). There are many indications that such educational strategies do not eliminate HIV/AIDS stigma. First, national surveys have shown that improved knowledge about HIV/AIDS transmission does not necessarily mitigate discriminatory attitudes. For example, Blendon and Donelan (1988) found that although only 1 in 10 U.S. parents reported believing that children can contract HIV/AIDS from sitting in a classroom with someone who has the disease, 1 in 3 reported that they would withdraw their children from such a class. Second, several studies have found that physicians and other medical personnel, representing groups with very specific training and education about infectious diseases, manifest many of the same prejudices about persons with HIV/AIDS as the general public (Kelly, St. Lawrence, Smith, Hood & Cook, 1987; O'Donnell et al., 1987). Also, Morton and McManus (1986) found that prejudicial attitudes manifested by medical students were not related to knowledge about HIV/AIDS, but to anti-homosexual feelings. Finally, Pryor, Reeder, and McManus (1991) found that people whose negative reactions to HIV-infected co-workers are rooted in anti-homosexual feelings may be resistant to HIV education programs, particularly those programs that focus solely on knowledge about transmission.

A major reason why HIV/AIDS education programs have not reduced stigma is that they often contain obvious or subtle anti-homosexual or prejudicial messages (Croteau & Morgan, 1989). For example, many educational messages seem to emphasize an "us–them" perspective.

Still, education programs may offer some hope for altering HIV/AIDS stigma. According to the associative network model proposed here, if educational efforts are to succeed, they must target the associations and affect connected with HIV/AIDS. In order to accomplish this, it may be necessary to depart from conventional pedogogical formulas and embrace a more experiencial view of HIV/AIDS education. Research by Hancock (1986) and Herek (1984) showed that personal experiences such as having a friend or relative who is gay predict more positive attitudes toward homosexuality. Also, Grieger and Ponterotto (1988) found that positive attitudes toward PWAs are predicted by closeness with a gay person. Finally, Pleck, O'Donnell, O'Donnell, and Snarey (1988) found that hospital workers who actually came in contact with HIV/AIDS patients manifested less fear about HIV/AIDS than those who did not. Consistent with these findings, research on the contact hypothesis suggests that positive one-on-one interactions with an outgroup member can reduce prejudice (Miller & Brewer, 1984; Desforges, Lord, Ramsey, Mason, Van Leeuwen, West, & Lepper, 1991). Recent work by Werth and Lord (1992) has shown that positive contact with a PWA in a classroom setting can help change students' general attitudes toward PWAs through altering their conceptions of what constitutes a "typical" group member. Systematic evaluation of educational programs that reduce HIV/AIDS stigma may offer insights into the reduction of other prejudices as well.

ACKNOWLEDGMENTS

Preparation of this chapter was facilitated by grants from Ronald McDonald Children's Charities and the Illinois State University Research Office to John B. Pryor.

REFERENCES

Ainlay, S., Coleman, L., & Becker, G. (1986). Stigma reconsidered. In S. Ainlay, L. Coleman, & G. Becker (Eds.), *The dilemma of difference: A multidisciplinary view of stigma.* (pp. 1–13). New York: Anchor/Press Doubleday.

Albert, J. (1986). Illness and deviance: The response of the press to AIDS. In D. A. Feldman & T. M. Johnson (Eds.), *The social dimensions of AIDS: Method and theory,* (pp. 163–178). New York: Praeger.

Altman, L. K. (1992, January 24). Deadly strain of tuberculosis is spreading fast, U. S. finds. *New York Times,* pp. A1, A10.

Anderson, J. (1983). *The architecture of cognition.* Cambridge, MA: Harvard University Press.

Bargh, J. A. (1989). Conditional automaticity: Varieties of automatic influence in social perception and cognition. In J. S. Uleman & J. A. Bargh (Eds.) *Unintended thought.* (pp. 3–51). New York: Guilford.

Bargh, J. A., & Petromonaco, P. (1982). Automatic information processing and social perception: The influence of trait information presented outside of conscious awareness on impression formation. *Journal of Personality and Social Psychology, 43,* 437–439.

Berkowitz, N. H., & Wolkon, G. H. (1964). A forced choice form of the F scale—Free of acquiescent response set. *Sociometry, 27,* 54–65.

Bibace, R., & Walsh, M. E. (1980). Development of children's concepts of illness. *Pediatrics, 66,* 912–917.

Blendon, R. J., & Donelan, K. (1988). Discrimination against people with AIDS: The public's perspective. *The New England Journal of Medicine, 319,* 1022–1026.

Boffey, P. M. (1988, June). AIDS panelists vote to expand anti-bias law. *New York Times, 137,* 6.

Bourne. (1990). The behavioral aspects of AIDS: An international perspective. In L. Temoshok & A. Baum (Eds.), *Psychosocial perspectives on AIDS: Etiology, prevention and treatment* (pp. 167–172). Hillsdale, NJ: Laurence Erlbaum Associates.

Brandt, A. (1986). *No magic bullet.* New York: Oxford University Press.

Centers for Disease Control. (1992, January). *HIV/AIDS surveillance report.* Rockville, MD: National AIDS Information Clearinghouse.

Conrad, P. (1986). The social meaning of AIDS. *Social Policy, 17*(1), 51–56.

Crandall, C. (1991). *Multiple stigma and AIDS: Medical stigma and attitudes toward homosexuals and IV drug users in AIDS-related stigmatization.* Unpublished manuscript, University of Florida, Gainsville.

Croteau, J. M., & Morgan, S. (1989). Combating homophobia in AIDS education. *Journal of Counseling and Development, 68,* 86–91.

Desforges, J. G., Lord, C. G., Ramsey, S. L., Mason, J. A., Van Leeuwen, M. D., West, S. C., & Lepper, M. R. (1991). Effects of structured cooperative contact on changing negative attitudes towards stigmatized social groups. *Journal of Personality and Social Psychology, 60,* 531–544.

Devine, P. (1989). Stereotypes and prejudice: Their automatic and controlled components. *Journal of Personality and Social Psychology, 56,* 5–18.

Doe v. Borough of Barrington. (1990). 729 F. Supp. 376 (D.N.J. 1990).

Douglas, M. (1966). *Purity and danger.* London: Rutledge & Kegan Paul.

Duncker, K. (1945). On problem solving. *Psychological Monographs, 58* (Whole No. 270).

Fraeble, D. E. S., Blackstone, T., & Scherbaum, C. (1990). Marginal and mindful: Deviants in social interaction. *Journal of Personality and Social Psychology, 59,* 140–149.

Ficarrotto, T. J., Grade, M., Bliwise, N., & Irish, T. (1990). Predictors of medical and nursing students' levels of HIV/AIDS knowledge and their resistance to working with AIDS patients. *Academic Medicine, 65,* 470–471.

Francis, D. P., & Chin, J. (1987). The prevention of Acquired Immunodeficiency Syndrome in the United States. *Journal of the American Medical Association, 257,* 1357–1376.

Frankenberg, R. (1989). One epidemic or three? Cultural, social, and historical aspects of the AIDS Pandemic. In P. Aggleton, G. Hart, & P. Davies (Eds.), *AIDS: Social representations, social practices.* (pp. 21–38). New York: Falmer Press.

Frazer, J. G. (1959). *The new golden bough: A study of magic and religion* (abridged ed., T. H. Gaster, Ed.). New York: Macmillan. (Original work published 1890)

Gilbert, D. T. (1989). Thinking lightly about others: Automatic components of the social inference process. In J. S. Uleman & J. A. Bargh (Eds.) *Unintended thought.* (pp. 189–211). New York: Guilford.

Goffman, E. (1963). *Stigma: Notes of the management of spoiled identity.* Englewood Cliffs, NJ: Prentice-Hall.

Gostin, L. O. (1990a). The AIDS litigation project, A national review of court and human rights commission decisions, Part I: The social impact of AIDS. *Journal of the American Medical Association, 263,* 1961–1970.

Gostin, L. O. (1990b). The AIDS litigation project, A national review of court and human rights commission decisions, Part II: Discrimination. *Journal of the American Medical Association, 263*, 2086–2093.

Grieger, I., & Ponterotto, J. G. (1988). Students' knowledge of AIDS and their attitudes toward gay men and lesbian women. *Journal of College Student Personnel, 29*, 415–422.

Gross, S. J., & Niman, C. M. (1975). Attitude-behavior-consistency: A review. *Public Opinion Quarterly, 39*, 358–368.

Hancock, K. A. (1986). *Homophobia* (part of the Lesbian and Gay Issues in Psychology Series of the Committee on Lesbian and Gay Concerns). Washington, DC: American Psychological Association.

Henry, K., Campbell, S., & Willenbring, K. (1990). A cross-sectional analysis of variables impacting on AIDS-related knowledge, attitudes, and behaviors among employees of a Minnesota teaching hospital. *AIDS Education and Prevention, 2*, 36–47.

Herek, G. (1984). Beyond "homophobia": A social psychological perspective on attitudes toward lesbians and gay men. In J. P. DeCecco (Ed.), *Homophobia in American society: Bashers, baiters, & bigots* (pp. 1–21). New York: Harrington Park Press.

Herek, G. M. (1986). The instrumentality of attitudes: Toward a neofunctional theory. *Journal of Social Issues, 42*, 99–114.

Herek, G. M., & Glunt, E. K. (1988). An epidemic of stigma: Public reactions to AIDS. *American Psychologist, 43*, 886–891.

Hilton, D. J. (1988). *Contemporary science and natural explanation: Commonsense conceptions of causality*. Oxford: Oxford University Press.

Horton, M., with Aggleton, P. (1989). Perverts, inverts, and experts: The cultural production of an AIDS research paradigm. In P. Aggleton, G. Hart, & P. Davies (Eds.) *AIDS: Social representations, social practices*. (pp. 74–100). New York: Falmer Press.

Hume, D. (1959). *Enquiry concerning human understanding*. New York: Dover. (Original work published 1748)

Hunter, N. D. (1990). *Epidemic of fear*. New York: ACLU AIDS Project.

Isen, A. M., & Diamond, G. A. (1989). Affect and automaticity. In J. S. Uleman & J. A. Bargh (Eds.) *Unintended thought*. (pp. 124–154). New York: Guilford.

Jones, E. E., Farina, A., Hastorf, A. H., Markus, H., Miller, D. T., & Scott, R. A. (1984). *Stigma: The psychology of marked relationships*. New York: Freeman.

Kassin, S. M., & Pryor, J. B. (1985). The development of attribution processes. In J. B. Pryor & J. D. Day (Eds.), *The development of social cognition*. (pp. 3–34). New York: Springer-Verlag.

Kelly, J. A., St. Lawrence, J. S., Smith, S., Hood, H. V., & Cook, D. J. (1987). Stigmatization of AIDS patients by physicians. *American Journal of Public Health, 78*, 789–791.

Kinder, D. R., & Sears, D. O. (1981). Prejudice and politics: Symbolic racism versus racial threats to the good life. *Journal of Personality and Social Psychology, 40*, 414–431.

Koop, C. E. (1986, December 7). The surgeon general's report on acquired immune deficiency syndrome. *Los Angeles Times*, pp. 1–8.

Krosnick, J. A., Betz, A. L., Jussim, L., & Lynn, A. R. (1992). Subliminal conditioning of attitudes. *Personality and Social Psychology Bulletin, 18*, 152–162.

Krauthammer, C. (1983). The politics of a plague. *The New Republic, 189*, 18–21.

Landau, S., Pryor, J. B., Patterson, C., & Belfield, J. (1992). *AIDS-infected children in the classroom: A study of child and parent attitude*. Paper presented at the convention of the National Association of School Psychologists, Nashville, TN.

Larsen, K. S., Elder, R., Bader, M., & Dougard, C. (1990). Authoritarianism and attitudes toward AIDS victims. *Journal of Psychology, 130*, 77–80.

Larsen, K. S., Serra, M., & Long, E. (1990). AIDS victims and heterosexual attitudes. *Journal of Homosexuality, 19*, 103–116.

Markova, I., & Wilkie, P. (1987). Representations, concepts, and social change: The phenomenon of AIDS. *Journal for the Theory of Social Behaviour, 17*, 389–409.

Mauss, M. (1972). *A general theory of magic* (R. Braun, Trans.). New York: Norton. (Original work published 1902)

Meyerowitz, B. E., Williams, J. G., & Gessner, J. (1987). Perceptions of controllability and attitudes toward cancer and cancer patients. *Journal of Applied Social Psychology, 17,* 471–492.

Michotte, A. (1963). *The perception of casuality.* London: Metheum. (Original work published in 1946)

Mill, J. S. (1963). *A system of logic.* In *Collected works of John Stuart Mill,* (Vol. 2). Toronto: University of Toronto Press. (Original work published in 1843)

Miller, N., & Brewer, M. B. (1984). *Groups in contact: The psychology of desegregation.* New York: Academic Press.

Morton, A. D., & McManus, I. C. (1986). Attitudes to and knowledge about acquired immune deficiency syndrome: Lack of a correlation. *British Medical Journal, 293,* 1212.

Murdock, G. P. (1980). *Theories of illness: a world survey.* Pittsburgh, PA: University of Pittsburgh Press.

Norton, R., Schwartzbaum, J., & Wheat, J. (1990). Language discrimination of general physicians: AIDS metaphors used in the AIDS crisis. *Communication Research, 17,* 809–826.

O'Donnell, L. O., O'Donnell, P. R., Pleck, J. H., Snarey, J., & Rose, R. M. (1987). Psychosocial responses of hospital workers to acquired immune deficiency syndrome (AIDS). *Journal of Applied Social Psychology, 17,* 269–285.

Pleck, J. H., O'Donnell, L., O'Donnell, C., & Snarey, J. (1988). AIDS-Phobia, Contact with AIDS, and AIDS-related job stress in hospital workers. *Journal of Homosexuality, 15,* 41–54.

Pryor, J. B., & Landau, S. (1992). [Unpublished data], Illinois State University, Normal, IL.

Pryor, J. B., & Ostrom, T. M. (1987). Social cognition theory of group processes. In B. Mullen & G. R. Goethals (Eds.), *Theories of group behavior.* (pp. 149–183). New York: Springer-Verlag.

Pryor, J. B., & Reeder, G. D. (1990). *AIDS stigma: A cognitive conceptualization.* Paper presented at the convention of American Psychological Association, Boston, MA.

Pryor, J. B., Reeder, G. D., & Lavalle, T. (1989). *Employment discrimination against AIDS-infected workers.* Unpublished manuscript, Illinois State University, Normal, IL.

Pryor, J. B., Reeder, G. D., & McManus, J. (1991). Fear and loathing in the workplace: Reactions to AIDS-infected co-workers. *Personality and Social Psychology Bulletin, 17,* 133–139.

Pryor, J. B., Reeder, G. D., Vinacco, R., & Kott, T. (1989). The instrumental and symbolic functions of attitudes toward persons with AIDS. *Journal of Applied Social Psychology, 19,* 377–404.

Pyle, C. R. (1992). *AIDS and government responsibility and/or liability.* Paper presented at the National College of District Attorneys, San Francisco, CA.

Reeder, G. D., Damashek, S., & Bartman, A. (1992). *The correction stage of dispositional inference: Content and process.* Unpublished manuscript, Illinois State University, Normal, IL.

Ross, M. W. (1988). Components and structure of attitudes toward AIDS. *Hospital and Community Psychiatry, 39,* 1306–1308.

Royce, D., & Birge, B. (1987). Homophobia and attitudes towards AIDS patients among medical, nursing and paramedic students. *Psychological Reports, 61,* 867–870.

Rozin, P., & Fallon, A. E. (1987). A perspective on disgust. *Psychological Review, 94,* 23–41.

Rozin, P., Markwith, M., & McCauley, C. (1991). *Aversion to indirect contact with AIDS: A composite of aversion to strangers, infection, moral taint, and misfortune.* Unpublished manuscript, University of Pennsylvania, University Park.

Rozin, P., Millman, L., & Nemeroff, C. (1986). Evidence for the operation of the laws of sympathetic magic in disgust and other domains. *Journal of Personality and Social Psychology, 51,* 703–712.

Rozin, P., Nemeroff, C., & Markwith, M. (1991). *Magical contagion beliefs and fear of AIDS.* Unpublished manuscript, University of Pennsylvania, University Park.

Sande, M. A. (1986). The transmission of AIDS: The case against casual contagion. *New England Journal of Medicine, 314,* 380–382.

Schmidt, G., & Weiner, B. (1988). An attribution-affect-action theory of behavior: Replication of judgments of help-giving. *Personality and Social Psychology Bulletin, 14*, 610–621.

School Board of Nassau County, Florida v. Arline. 43 FEP Cases 81 (U.S. Sup. Ct. 1987).

Sears, D. O., & Kinder, D. R. (1985). Whites' opposition to bussing: On conceptualizing and operationbalizing group conflict. *Journal of Personality and Social Psychology, 48*, 1141–1147.

Shilts, R. (1987). *And the band played on.* New York: St. Martin's Press.

Siegal, M. (1988). Children's knowledge of contagion and contamination as causes of disease. *Child Development, 59*, 1353–1359.

Siegfried, A. (1965). *Routes of contagion.* New York: Harcourt, Brace & World. (Original work published 1960)

Smith, E. (1984). Model of social inference processes. *Psychological Review, 91*, 392–413.

Smith, E., & Lerner, M. (1987). Development of automatism of social judgments. *Journal of Personality and Social Psychology, 50*, 246–259.

Snyder, M. L., Kleck, R., Strenta, A., & Mentzer, S. (1979). Avoidance of the handicapped: An attributional ambiguity analysis. *Journal of Personality and Social Psychology, 37*, 2297–2306.

Sontag, S. (1978). *Illness as metaphor.* New York: Farrar, Straus and Giroux.

Srull, T. K., & Wyer, R. S., Jr. (1989). Person memory and judgment. *Psychological Review, 96*, 58–83.

Stipp, H., & Kerr, D. (1989). Determinents of public opinion about AIDS. *Public Opinion Quarterly, 53*, 98–106.

Thomas v. Atascadero Unified School District. No. 886–609 AHS (BY) (C. D. Cal. 1987).

Trope, Y. (1986). Identification and inferential processes in dispositional attribution. *Psychological Review, 93*, 239–257.

U.S. Department of Education. (1987). *AIDS and the education of our children.* Pueblo, CO: Consumer Information Center.

Valdiserri, R. O. (1987). Epidemics in perspective. *Journal of Medical Humanities and Bioethics, 8*, 95–100.

Weiner, B. (1986). *An attributional theory of motivation and emotion.* New York: Springer-Verlag.

Weiner, B., Perry, R., & Magnusson, J. (1988). An attributional analysis of stigmas. *Journal of Personality and Social Psychology, 55*, 245–271.

Werth, J. L., & Lord, C. G. (1992). Previous conceptions of the typical group member and the contact hypothesis. *Basic and Applied Social Psychology, 13*, 351–369.

Wiener, L., & Siegel, K. (1990). Social workers' comfort in providing services to AIDS patients. *Social Work, 35*, 18–25.

Wing, D. L. (1988). *AIDS: Legal issues in employment.* Kansas City, MO: Spencer, Fain, Britt & Browne.

Wyer, R. S., & Carlston, D. (1979). *Social cognition, inference, and attribution.* Hillsdale, NJ: Laurence Erlbaum Associates.

Witt, L. A. (1989). Authoritarianism, knowledge of AIDS, and affect toward persons with AIDS: Implications for health education. *Journal of Applied Social Psychology, 19*, 599–607.

Zich, J., & Temoshok, L. (1987). Perceptions of social support in men with AIDS and ARC: Relationships with distress and hardiness. *Journal of Applied Social Psychology, 17*, 193–215.

10 AIDS From an Attributional Perspective

Bernard Weiner
University of California, Los Angeles

Textbook writers often face the choice of organizing their scientific fields with a theory- or with a problem-focused orientation. Each approach has advantages and disadvantages. For example, one might write a personality book with a theory focus and within it include Freud's conception of human behavior. It is quite likely that this chapter would contain a discussion of aggression. Aggression therefore would be examined within a specific theoretical framework and its relation to wit, or to slips of the tongue, or even to love could be pointed out. In so doing, the topic of aggression would be parsimoniously addressed and unexpected insights might be communicated. The disadvantage of this strategy, however, is that the many determinants of aggression that fall outside the range of psychoanalytic theory or, for that matter, outside the conceptual reach of other theories of personality, would be ignored. It is unlikely that the discussion of aggression within a chapter on Freud or any of the remaining theories of personality would consider, for example, weather conditions and temperature, social hierarchy and social norms, perceived intentionality and responsibility, and so on, although all these have been documented to affect hostile behaviors.

The alternative approach when writing a personality book is to include chapters on problems or topics. A chapter on aggression certainly would be reasonable to have within this book. It could then be indicated that aggression is influenced by a multiplicity of factors, such as temperature, social roles, and perceived responsibility, as well as by the unconscious forces stressed by Freud. But it is likely that this analysis will not be theoretically satisfying, as determinants with little conceptual coherence are merely listed and catalogued. And the insights that often are provided only by an accompanying and encompassing theoretical framework will be missing. That is, there is liable to be prediction without understanding, and making sense without making deep discoveries that link aggression to other aspects of the structure and the dynamics of personality.

This introduction is pertinent to the present chapter, for this book examines what can be considered an issue, or a disease, or a social problem—AIDS.[1] However, rather than focusing on this problem I am centered on a conception, namely, attribution theory, and how this theory sheds light on reactions to persons with AIDS (PWAs). Therefore I am able to relate attitudes and actions regarding AIDS to more general principles and to other phenomena considered by attribution theorists. I believe that this approach provides interpretation, meaning, and generality to a set of AIDS-related observations. At the same time, however, this theory focus results in a grievous neglect of many pertinent factors that fall outside the sweep of an attributional analysis. In addition, a myriad of topics that lie at the very heart of applied questions related to reducing the risk of contracting HIV, such as condom use, risk perception, and education, are ignored.

ATTRIBUTIONAL PRINCIPLES AND AIDS

Attribution theory is based on the belief that perceptions of causality play an important role in determining affective reactions to an event as well as subsequent behavior. That is, perceptions of "why" are crucial in the analysis of human action. It is presumed that humans seek mastery and understanding, not only because it is functional to know what caused an outcome, but also because the basic nature of the organism is to seek to make sense out of one's environment and oneself (Heider, 1958).

Perceived Causes of AIDS

It is known that negative and unexpected events particularly engage thoughts about causality and elicit search processes to enhance understanding (Weiner, 1986). Hence, AIDS, which certainly is negative as well as atypical, will give rise to questions regarding why this condition has arisen. There is sufficient scientific comprehension and knowledge dissemination to the public so that the person on the street, just as the scientist, now realizes that HIV is a type of virus that is transmitted via blood and bodily fluid exchange. This, in turn, transpires by means of sharing contaminated needles during drug use, blood transfusions, exchange from the parent to the unborn infant, and sexual behavior. Furthermore, the likelihood of sexual transmission is greater from the male to a sexual partner, and frequently is from one male to another while engaged in a homosexual activity. Again this is public knowledge. Inasmuch as the blood supply available

---

[1]For ease of communication, and to be consistent with the terms used in the research, the label of *AIDS* is used throughout except when specifically referring to the virus, although at times AIDS may connote HIV or HIV/AIDS.

for transfusions is now relatively well-monitored, by far the main causes of AIDS are recognized as being drug use and sexual behavior. Hence, the question of causality in the case of AIDS requires little cognitive activity. Rather, the lay person associates AIDS primarily with homosexuality and drug use (although there is a large amount of attention and educational emphasis given to safe sex during heterosexual encounters).

Causal Organization

Humans tend to think in broad categories. In so doing, cognitive strain is minimized and we are able to readily classify events and reach conclusions regarding their similarity and difference.

Attributions also are grouped or categorized, based on their underlying properties. Three characteristics or dimensions of causality have been identified. They are locus (does the cause lie within or outside of the person?), stability (is the cause temporary or permanent?), and controllability (is or is not the cause subject to volitional change?). The latter concept is closely related to the notion of responsibility, for if a cause is perceived as controllable, then the agent may be held responsible. Considering for the moment an achievement setting, low aptitude as the perceived cause of failure would be construed as internal to the failing student, stable over time, and uncontrollable (the student would not be held responsible). On the other hand, lack of effort as a cause of failure also would be considered internal to the student, it might or might not be thought of as stable, but it surely would be construed as controllable (i.e., the failing student would be held responsible, or able-to-respond; see Weiner, 1986).

The study of AIDS from an attributional perspective has particularly focused on causal controllability and examined whether AIDS patients are held personally responsible for their plights. Weiner, Perry, and Magnusson (1988) asked college students in both the United States and Canada the extent to which individuals are personally responsible for various stigmas (Alzheimer's disease, blindness, cancer, heart disease, paraplegia, Vietnam War syndrome, AIDS, child abuser, drug abuse, and obesity). The ratings from two experiments are reported in Table 10.1. As can be seen in the table, AIDS was perceived as similar to the other behavioral stigmas (child abuser, drug abuse, and obesity) in terms of assigned responsibility, and different from the other somatic stigmas including blindness, cancer, and so on, which elicited much weaker perceptions of personal responsibility. Inasmuch as personal responsibility for negative events connotes "sin," AIDS is considered a sin rather than (in addition to) a sickness.

Does this mean that our college student respondents tend to "blame the victim," a phrase psychologists too often use? Not in general, for those with Alzheimer's disease, blindness, and so on, are not blamed. Rather, blamed victims are held accountable in the sense that controllable responses are perceived to have resulted in their problems. It is true that we sometimes hold others

TABLE 10.1
Perceptions of Responsibility for Various Stigmas

Stigma	Responsibility Ratings	
	Exp. 1	Exp. 2
Alzheimer's disease	0.8	1.2
Blindness	0.9	1.5
Cancer	1.6	2.7
Heart disease	2.5	3.4
Paraplegia	1.6	2.1
Vietnam War snydrome	1.7	1.2
AIDS	4.4	5.2
Child abuser	5.2	5.4
Drug abuse	6.5	6.4
Obesity	5.3	5.2

Data from Weiner, Perry, and Magnusson (1988).

responsible for their plights, but only given certain conditions. We do, however, judge the victim.

A related question worth raising is whether perceptions of responsibility for AIDS can be altered. The answer to this question is an unequivocal "yes." In Experiment 2 by Weiner et al. (1988), AIDS was described as either due to a blood transfusion (a priori considered by the experimenters to be uncontrollable by the recipient of the transfusion) or due to leading a promiscuous sex life (a priori considered by the experimenters to be perceived as controllable by persons with AIDS). A similar manipulation was made by Strasser and Damrosch (1989), who contrasted ratings of responsibility for AIDS given a blood transfusion versus homosexual activity as the causes (see also Chapman & Levin, 1989). In the Weiner et al. (1988) research, responsibility in the transfusion condition was rated 0.6, whereas in the promiscuous sex condition it was 6.7 (on a scale ranging from 0 or not at all responsible to 8 or totally responsible). Similar findings were reported by Strasser and Damrosch (1989). Thus, beliefs about responsibility for AIDS can be readily altered.

As shown in Table 10.1, ratings of responsibility for AIDS given no information in Experiment 2 of Weiner et al. (1988) was 5.2. Hence, the label of "AIDS" activates causal beliefs much closer to "promiscuous sex life" ($\bar{x} = 6.7$) than to "blood transfusion" ($\bar{x} = 0.6$). Interestingly, two historical causes of AIDS, blood transfusions and transmission to a fetus, have been or are being reduced. Hence, primarily controllable causes of AIDS remain extant; one might therefore anticipate that responsibility ratings will increase even further in time. At least for the present, however, perceptions of responsibility may be dramatically altered with the communication of new information. This is true for many, but not for all stigmas. For example, heart disease due to smoking evokes quite higher beliefs about personal responsibility than does heart disease due to hereditary factors (Weiner et al., 1988). However, we have found it quite difficult to absolve child abusers of responsibility, in spite of information about their own unfortunate upbringing, and it is not possible to increase judgments of responsibility for some illnesses, such as Alzheimer's disease.

Affective Reactions

Attribution theory specifies a set of relations between causal ascriptions and affective reactions (see reviews in Weiner, 1985, 1986). Most pertinent to this discussion are the linkages between perceptions of controllability and the emotions of anger and sympathy. To illustrate these associations, consider an investigation by Weiner, Graham, and Chandler (1982) that involved the recall of life incidents. Weiner et al. (1982) asked college students to describe occasions in their lives in which the emotions of anger or pity were experienced. After recounting experiences of each emotion, the subjects rated the controllability of the events instigating these emotional reactions. For anger, almost 90% of the situations involved a cause or a reason that was appraised as under the control of the transgressor. Two typical anger-arousing events were:

1. My roommate brought her dog into our no-pets apartment without asking me first. When I got home, she wasn't there, but the barking dog was. . . . As well, the dog relieved itself in the middle of the entry.
2. I felt angry toward my boyfriend for lying to me about something he did. (Weiner et al., 1982, p. 228)

The violation of an "ought" or "should" and anger has been noted by many prior investigators. For example, in one of the very early investigations pertinent to the cognitive antecedents of anger, Pastore (1952) demonstrated that the relation between frustration, anger, and aggression is mediated by perceptions of responsibility and control. His data suggest that anger is not merely the product of nonattainment of a desired goal, but rather follows only when a barrier imposed by others is "arbitrary" (e.g., "Your date phones at the last minute and breaks an appointment without adequate explanation"), and not when the barrier is "nonarbitrary" (e.g., "Your date . . . breaks an appointment because of suddenly becoming ill"). More recently, a thorough analysis of anger has been presented by Averill (1983). In describing his own research that also made use of the recall of critical incidents, Averill concluded:

> Over 85% of the episodes described by angry persons involved either an act that they considered voluntary and unjustified or else a potentially avoidable accident (e.g., due to negligence or lack of foresight) . . . More than anything else, anger is an attribution of blame. (p. 1150)

In contrast to the linkage between controllability and anger, uncontrollable causes are associated with sympathy and the related affect of pity. In the research by Weiner et al. (1982), approximately 75% of the sympathy stories involved an uncontrollable cause. Two typical reports were:

1. A guy on campus is terribly deformed. I pity him because it would be hard to look so different and have people stare at you.
2. My great grandmother lives in a rest home, and every time I go there I see these poor old half-senile men and women. . . . I feel pity when I go there. (Weiner et al., 1982, p. 228)

Turning attention back to AIDS, one can now ask whether people with AIDS elicit anger and/or pity, and in what relative magnitudes. To examine this question, in the studies reported by Weiner et al. (1988) we also asked respondents how much anger and pity they experience toward individuals with various stigmas. These data are reported in Table 10.2. Table 10.2 indicates that AIDS elicits more anger and less pity than the other somatic stigmas, such as paraplegia and blindness, although it does evoke more positive reactions than the child and drug abuser.

Are these affective reactions changed as a function of information about responsibility? In Weiner et al. (1988, Experiment 2), affective ratings were obtained when subjects believed that AIDS was either due to a blood transfusion or to promiscuous sexual behavior. Table 10.3 shows that, regardless of the cause, the absolute ratings of pity exceed those of anger. However, this is particularly the case when AIDS was described as due to a blood transfusion. And again, ratings made just on the basis of the AIDS label more closely resemble the judgments given controllable than uncontrollable causal information, demonstrating that the label itself connotes controllability.

Additional Complexities.   The prior review and Tables 10.2 and 10.3 imply that negative affective responses toward PWAs are guided by the identical rules as negative affects toward others responsible for their plights or needs. That is, emotional reactions to PWAs can be interpreted with the same laws that explain emotional responses to other stigmas. Before accepting this conclusion, however, several complexities need to be considered.

First of all, homosexuality and drug use, the two perceived causes of AIDS, are considered by many to be threats to society and to the "moral order." It may therefore be that one is angry at drug users and persons with homosexual preferences, independent of perceptions of personal responsibility. Given the data presented thus far, it is not possible to determine if the negative emotions toward those with AIDS are due to homophobia, for example, or because of appraisals regarding responsibility for sexual behavior. Indeed, it has been documented that negative feelings about homosexuals are related to descriptions of AIDS as "disgusting" and "dirty" (Pryor, Reeder, Vinacco, & Kott, 1989).

Furthermore, AIDS, in distinction to most stigmas, can be transmitted to others. Therefore, it presents a personal threat. This perceived danger may arouse fear as well as anger toward the source of the fear (see Bouton et al., 1989). Finally, also in contrast to the vast majority of stigmas, AIDS is terminal.

TABLE 10.2
Ratings of Anger and Pity Toward Various Stigmas

Stigmas	Anger Exp. 1	Anger Exp. 2	Pity Exp. 1	Pity Exp. 2
Alzheimer's disease	1.4	2.4	7.9	7.1
Blindness	1.7	1.9	7.4	6.7
Cancer	1.6	2.2	8.0	6.9
Heart disease	1.6	2.1	7.4	6.3
Paraplegia	1.4	2.0	7.6	7.1
Vietnam War syndrome	2.1	2.2	7.1	6.8
AIDS	4.0	3.6	6.2	6.0
Child abuser	7.9	6.7	3.3	4.4
Drug abuse	6.4	5.2	4.0	4.7
Obesity	3.3	2.7	5.1	5.5

Data from Weiner, Perry, and Magnusson (1988).

TABLE 10.3
Reactions of Anger and Pity Toward People With AIDS as a Function of the Cause of the AIDS

Cause	Anger	Pity
Uncontrollable (blood transfusion)	1.8	8.2
Controllable (promiscuous sexual behavior)	4.2	4.9
Unspecified (AIDS label only)	3.6	6.0

Data from Weiner, Perry, and Magnusson (1988, Exp. 2).

It has more serious consequences than most other illnesses and therefore elicits empathic concerns. The hypothesized cognition–affect linkages in the case of persons with perceived controllable AIDS (drug use and homosexuality) are shown in Table 10.4 (which surely is not the complete story).

In an attempt to separate and disconfound affective reactions of anger and pity due to responsibility versus homophobia, Mallery (1990) created vignettes that

TABLE 10.4
Cognition-Affective Sequence Concerning Persons With Perceived Controllable AIDS

Causal Perceptions	Cognitive Connections	Affective Consequences
Homosexuality Drug Use ———————>	Controllable (person is —————————>Anger; no pity responsible)	
	can be transmitted ——————> Anger and fear	
	morally repugnant ——————> Anger and disgust	
	terminal ———————————> Sympathy and pity	

TABLE 10.5
Ratings of Anger and Pity Toward People With AIDS as a Function of the Controllability of
the Cause and Sexual Orientation of the Victim

Causal Condition and Sexual Orientation	Anger	Pity
Controllable - Homosexual	4.10	4.36
Controllable - Heterosexual	3.45	5.14
Uncontrollable - Homosexual	1.67	6.17
Uncontrollable - Heterosexual	1.10	6.70

From Mallery (1990).

independently varied and factorially combined two levels of responsibility information (controllable and uncontrollable) with two types of sexual preference
(heterosexual and homosexual). The two vignettes in which the person was held
responsible, while sexual orientation varied, read as follows:

> Lately, you have noticed that your friend has been losing weight. When you ask
> him what is wrong, he confides in you that he caught AIDS because he didn't use a
> condom while he was having sex with a man he met in a gay bar (Alternate form: he
> caught AIDS because he didn't use a condom while having sex with a woman he
> met in a bar. You know that your friend is not gay).

In the remaining two vignettes, the cause of AIDS for both a homosexual as well
as a heterosexual person was described as uncontrollable:

> Lately, you have noticed that your friend has been losing weight. When you ask
> him what is wrong, he confides in you that he has AIDS. The doctor's report,
> which certainly is correct, says that he caught AIDS during a blood transfusion he
> received after a ski accident. You know that your friend is (is not) gay.

Subjects then made a number of attributional ratings, as well as indicating
their feelings of anger and pity. These ratings are given in Table 10.5. Table 10.5
reveals that controllable causes elicit more anger and less pity than do uncontrollable causes. Furthermore, a homosexual person with AIDS elicits more anger
and less pity than does a heterosexual. It also is evident from Table 10.5 that
these two factors do not interact, and that perceptions of responsibility are far
more dominant or influential in determining the disparate ratings than is sexual
orientation. Hence, attributional thoughts more than homophobia directed the
affective responses in this experiment.

Going Toward (Prosocial Behavior) and
Going Away From (Neglect)

Attribution theorists have postulated that causal attributions influence what one
feels, and those feelings in turn determine what one does. That is, a motivational
episode proceeds through the stages of thinking, feeling, and acting (see Weiner,

1985, 1986). Inasmuch as AIDS evokes particular feelings in regards to anger and pity, it follows that specific action tendencies also will be aroused.

Two thinking–feeling–acting motivational sequences have been documented in help-giving settings:

1. Attributions of controllability → anger → neglect and
2. Attributions of uncontrollability → sympathy (pity) → help

Consider, for example, an investigation by Schmidt and Weiner (1988). In that study, subjects read the following scenarios:

> At about 1:00 in the afternoon you are walking through campus and a student comes up to you. He says that you do not know him, but you are both enrolled in the same class and he has happened to notice you. He asks if you would lend him the class notes from the meetings last week. He indicates that he needs the notes because he was having difficulty with his eyes, a change in type of glasses was required, and during the week he had difficulty seeing because of eye drops and other treatments. You notice that he is wearing especially dark glasses and has a patch covering one eye. (Alternate condition: He says he needs the notes because he went to the beach instead of class). (Schmidt & Weiner, 1988, p. 615)

In addition, subjects read these scenarios with instructions to primarily consider the other person or the self, and to focus on the objective circumstances or the emotions involved. The dependent variables included ratings of causal controllability, sympathy, anger, and the certainty and likelihood of help-giving.

The various instructional conditions had little influence over the attribution–emotion–helping associations. A multicondition path analysis, combining the data from the various instructional conditions, is shown in Fig. 10.1. It is quite evident from this figure that controllability relates positively to anger and nega-

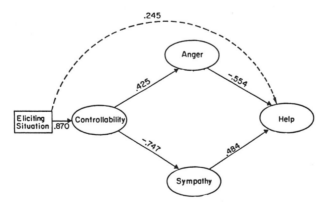

FIG. 10.1. Structural model of relations between attributions, affect, and helping. Adapted from Schmidt and Weiner (1988).

tively to sympathy, as already has been discussed. Anger, in turn, inhibits helping, whereas sympathy promotes judgments to help. Note that in Fig. 10.1 there is no path between thoughts (controllability) and behavior; action is directly tied to feelings and to a small extent to the particular features of the situation.

This general model of helping is quite applicable to issues related to AIDS. One question to be raised is what determines social support and other prosocial actions directed to persons with AIDS. Of course, support, personal assistance, and charity donations are determined by numerous factors, including type and length of the relationship with the ill person, availability of resources, personal role, and so on. However, as stated in the earlier discussion of aggression, such an amalgam often does not deeply add to our theoretical understanding, for the listed factors have little conceptual coherence. Attribution theory, on the other hand, ignores many determinants of help-giving, but places altruism and social support within a larger theoretical framework.

Guided by attributional principles, it can be derived that AIDS will elicit more anger and less pity than the other somatic illnesses, inasmuch as it is perceived as controllable. Hence, those with AIDS should receive less support and help than individuals with perceived uncontrollable stigmas. Helping judgments regarding persons with various stigmas also were collected by Weiner et al. (1988) in their two experiments. These judgments of personal assistance and charity donations are shown in Table 10.6. It is evident in Table 10.6 that, in accord with attributional predictions, both judgments regarding prosocial behaviors toward persons with AIDS are less than those toward individuals with cancer, heart disease, blindness, and so on. And, as would be expected based on the prior discussion, helping judgments are much more positive when AIDS is ascribed to a blood transfusion rather than to sexual behavior.

TABLE 10.6
Ratings of Two Types of Help-Giving Toward Various Stigmatized Groups

Stigmas	Personal Assistance		Charity Donations	
	Exp. 1	Exp. 2	Exp. 1	Exp. 2
Alzheimer's disease	7.3	8.0	6.3	6.9
Blindness	7.9	8.5	6.7	7.2
Cancer	7.5	8.4	6.9	8.1
Heart disease	7.3	8.0	6.1	7.5
Paraplegia	7.7	8.1	6.7	7.1
Vietnam War syndrome	7.4	7.0	6.5	6.2
AIDS	5.2	5.8	5.5	6.5
Child abuser	4.9	4.6	3.7	4.0
Drug abuse	4.9	5.3	4.0	5.0
Obesity	6.3	5.8	4.0	4.0
AIDS (blood transfusion)		7.1		6.9
AIDS (promiscuous sex)		4.8		4.2

Data from Weiner, Perry, and Magnusson (1988).

TABLE 10.7
Cognitive and Affective Determinants of Helping Behavior Toward Persons With AIDS

Cognition	Affective Reactions	Behavior Tendency
Controllable	Anger	Neglect
Homosexuals and drug users	Anger	Neglect
Communicable	Anger/Fear	Neglect/Nonaltruistic help
Terminal	Pity	Altruistic help
Uncontrollable	Pity	Altruistic help

Additional Complexities and Historical Change.   In contrast to the parsimony suggested in Table 10.6 and Fig. 10.1, Table 10.4 revealed that there are a variety of cognitive associates of controllable AIDS, each giving rise to affective experiences. Hence, many possible conceptions of help-giving can be proposed, attempting to incorporate some of the complexity shown in Table 10.4. Consider, for example, the determinants of helping as outlined in Table 10.7. Table 10.7 reveals that there are three sources of anger, and in turn neglect, elicited by AIDS. First, AIDS is perceived as controllable; second, it is morally repugnant because of an association with homosexuality and drug use; and third, anger is aroused because people associate AIDS with personal danger. On the other hand, Table 10.7 shows that approach behavior and altruism also may be elicited because AIDS is a terminal disease and, at times, perceived as being caused by uncontrollable factors. In addition, help may be offered to cure the disease because of personal fear.

Table 10.7 depicts the competing approach and avoidance tendencies that are aroused because of the complex cognitive associates and affective reactions generated by AIDS. This model also suggests that help may or may not be altruistically motivated. Individuals driven by nonaltruistic (personal) concerns might be expected to provide money for research and for other endeavors that directly or indirectly abet personal survival, rather than the survival of those already with AIDS. On the other hand, for those altruistically motivated, it is contended that helping is just as likely to take the form of personal assistance to those infected.

Finally, it might be the case that different cognitive and affective components have disparate activation likelihoods as a function of scientific knowledge and the dissemination of this knowledge to the lay public. This hypothesis is explored in Table 10.8, which considers affective reactions to those with AIDS in four different historical periods. The table reflects public perceptions rather than the actual state of the world.

The possibility of heterosexual transmission, and its evocation of aggression and fear, did not enter into the determinants of emotion and action until Stage 2 (1985-1987). Further, the knowledge that AIDS could be caught via blood trans-

TABLE 10.8
Historical Analysis of Reactions to Persons With AIDS

Stage 1 (1981-1984):

---

[a] AIDS onset controllable--little pity, some anger--neglect
[b] AIDS contracted by gay males--sexual hostility (homophobia)--little pity, anger--neglect

---

Stage 2 (1985-1987):

---

[a] AIDS onset controllable--little pity, some anger--neglect
[b] AIDS contracted by gay males and drug users--sexual hostility and/or moral condemnation--little
pity, anger--neglect
[b] AIDS perception of communicability--anger--aggression
[b] AIDS perceptions of communicability--fear--nonaltruistic help

---

Stage 3 (1987-1989):

---

[a] AIDS onset controllable--little pity, some anger--neglect
[a] AIDS onset uncontrollable--pity, no anger--altruistic help
[b] AIDS contracted by gay males and drug users--sexual hostility and/or moral condemnation--little
pity, anger--neglect
[b] AIDS perceptions of communicability--anger--aggression
[b] AIDS perceptions of communicability--fear--nonaltruistic help

---

Stage 4 (1990-   ):   See Stage 2

Note. [a] Attributionally mediated reactions; [b] Nonattributionally mediated reactions.

---

fusions (onset uncontrollable) was not fully recognized until Stage 3 (1987–1989). In Stage 4, which we are now in, uncontrollable sources of AIDS are diminishing. We might then anticipate that AIDS will generate less sympathy and help than in the period that just passed, considering only the source of motivation produced by perceptions of uncontrollability.

And Still More Complications: Individual Differences as Antecedents.   The apparent complexities shown in Tables 10.7 and 10.8 are still far from sufficient to capture the overdetermination of the affective and behavioral reactions to those with AIDS. For example, the role of individual differences in beliefs has not been addressed. Consider, for example, how general conservatism might influence the sequences that have been proposed. It is known that conservatism, homophobia, and fear of AIDS are linked (Bouton et al., 1989). In addition, conservatives tend to perceive the causes of personal difficulties as more controllable than do liberals (Zucker, 1990). That is, they tend to blame the individual and exonerate the situational determinants of behavior, such as the larger social system. These relations can be depicted as follows:

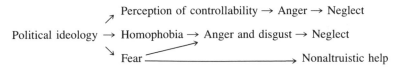

Perception of controllability → Anger → Neglect

Political ideology → Homophobia → Anger and disgust → Neglect

Fear ——————————————→ Nonaltruistic help

But it also may be the case that ideology has a direct as well as an indirect influence on affect and behavior, so that the associations might best be represented as follows, considering now just those determinants involving perceptions of controllability:

Political ideology → Perceptions of controllability → Anger → Neglect

In summary, a variety of specific models can be hypothesized regarding attitudes and behaviors toward PWAs, although these all remain consistent with the general theoretical framework advocated by attribution theorists.

Onset Versus Offset Responsibility

Stigma onset may not be the sole generator of causal inferences and their associated consequences. Prior or even current drug use and smoking, for example, might be weak predictors of the emotions and behaviors of observers when compared with the present efforts of the target person to cope with and alter these stigmas. Indeed, in the achievement domain it is known that even after failure at an important task, present expenditure of effort generates positive affects and rewards for a student who previously failed because he or she did not try (Karasawa, 1991). When generalized to the health domain and to AIDS, this finding suggests that positive coping attempts with a serious health condition (i.e., the exercise of personal control), could play an important role in affecting the emotional and behavioral reactions of others. Thus, even though homosexuality or drug use was the cause of AIDS, presently leading an "exemplary life" to counteract the course of the illness may diffuse anger and increase sympathy. Stated somewhat differently, both the origin of a problem and its solution may be taken into account by others when evaluating a stigmatized person (Brickman et al., 1982). This important distinction has been overlooked in the studies that have thus far been examined.

To address this issue, Schwarzer and Weiner (1991) created vignettes that independently varied both onset responsibility and offset coping for eight stigmas (AIDS, anorexia, cancer, child abuser, depression, drug abuse, heart disease, and obesity). In the case of AIDS, the two offset vignettes given that the person was responsible for the onset of the illness were as follows:

> Your roommate has contracted AIDS from leading a promiscuous sex life. Despite many warnings, sex partners have not been chosen carefully. This roommate declines to take any medication, sticks to a lifestyle that does not strengthen the

immune system, and refuses to take new medication which has been found to be helpful. (Alternate form: . . . After learning about this infection, the lifestyle immediately changed. This roommate is sticking to a healthy diet and adheres to medication prescribed by doctors to strengthen the immune system.)

The two vignettes in which onset was uncontrollable indicated that the roommate was infected with AIDS from a blood transfusion during surgery. This was followed by the no-coping or coping information just given. The subjects then rated how much they would blame the individual, as well as their feelings of pity.

Concerning just AIDS, Fig. 10.2 (left panel) shows the effects of onset responsibility and coping efforts on judgments of blame. It can be seen in Fig. 10.2 that if the person is responsible for the onset of AIDS, then blame is high and is not altered by good or poor coping. However, if the PWA was not responsible for the onset of the illness, then coping processes do influence blame, with less blame given to the person attempting to cope with the disease. For the pity ratings, shown in the right panel of Fig. 10.2, both onset responsibility and maintenance behavior equally contribute to the judgments, with most pity directed toward the person not responsible for AIDS onset who is attempting to cope. Very similar relations capture the social support data.

One implication of these data is that feelings toward individuals at the onset of an illness may be different from the feelings experienced with the passage of time. Given that AIDS patients decline in health, and that there is no control over the offset of this illness, it is quite reasonable to propose that initial anger will change to pity over time, as the onset information is less salient.

The Responsibility Dilemma

The metaphor guiding attribution theory is "the person is a scientist," gathering data, formulating hypotheses, and acting on the basis of the processed information. But another metaphor also is valid, one that has not received as much attention. This is "the person is a judge," determining if the other is responsible, holding others accountable, monitoring the behaviors of others under the as-

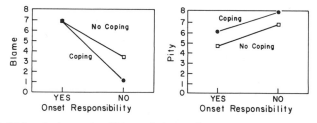

FIG. 10.2.   Judgments of blame (left panel) and pity (right panel) as a function of responsibility for the onset of AIDS and coping behavior. Data from Schwarzer and Weiner (1991).

sumption that social transgressions should be punished, and passing out sentences (see Fincham & Jaspers, 1980).

One manifestation of the "person is a judge" characterization is the prevalence of responsibility judgments. It has been argued that one of the main dimensions along which we construe the world is "controllability," or agent responsibility. Thus, students are held responsible and accountable for not trying in school, just as stigmatized others are held responsible if the stigma is traceable to some behavioral act.

In one sense, these judgments of responsibility and blame are unfortunate, for blame of those with AIDS and others stigmas results in anger and neglect, when help is badly needed. The fact that most onset-controllable stigmas can be altered in the direction of uncontrollability with the receipt of additional information, and that perceptions of uncontrollability are likely to become more salient over time, offers promise that the negative responses to some stigmas can be overcome. What in part appears to be needed are procedures and methods of education that point out the array of determinants of the onsets of stigmas. This could lessen perceived responsibility and increase altruism. However, this creates a dilemma, pitting the positive and negative benefits of reducing personal responsibility for stigma onset. On the one hand, individuals must accept responsibility for their actions. This promotes personal change and is the basis of educational programs to protect those not yet infected. However, altruistic actions from others are augmented by perceptions of uncontrollability.

This is a quandary not only for AIDS, but for many other stigmas as well. I see no solution to this dilemma, given the nature of humans and the attribution–affect–action sequences that have been reviewed in this chapter. At best, one might proclaim a moral imperative: "Yes, they are responsible for what they did. Yes, we are angry. Nonetheless, the needy must be helped."

REFERENCES

Averill, J. R. (1983). Studies on anger and aggression. *American Psychologist, 38,* 1145–1160.

Bouton, R. A., Gallaher, P. E., Garlinghouse, P. A., Leal, T., Rosenstein, L. D., & Young, R. K. (1989). Demographic variables associated with fear of AIDS and homophobia. *Journal of Applied Social Psychology, 19,* 885–901.

Brickman, P., Rabinowitz, P. C., Karuza, J. Jr., Coates, D., Cohn, E., & Kidder, M. (1982). Models of helping and coping. *American Psychologist, 37,* 368–384.

Chapman, D. P., & Levin, I. P. (1989). *Attribution in AIDS victimization: Experimental paradigm and theoretical model.* Paper presented at the 97th annual convention of the American Psychological Association, New Orleans, LA.

Fincham, F. D., & Jaspers, J. M. (1980). Attribution of responsibility: From man the scientist to man as lawyer. In L. Berkowitz (Ed.), *Advances in experimental social psychology* (Vol. 13, pp. 82–139). New York: Academic Press.

Heider, F. (1958). *The psychology of interpersonal relations.* New York: Wiley.

Karasawa, K. (1991). The effects of onset and offset responsibility on affects and helping judgments. *Journal of Applied Social Psychology, 21,* 482–499.

Mallery, P. (1990). *Attributions and attitudes towards AIDS*. Unpublished manuscript, University of California, Los Angeles.

Pastore, N. (1952). The role of arbitrariness in the frustration-aggression hypothesis. *Journal of Abnormal and Social Psychology, 47,* 728–732.

Pryor, J. B., Reeder, G. D., Vinacco, R., Jr., & Kott, T. L. (1989). The instrumental and symbolic functions of attitudes toward persons with AIDS. *Journal of Applied Social Psychology, 19,* 377–404.

Schmidt, G., & Weiner, B. (1988). An attribution-affect-action theory of motivated behavior: Replications examining judgments of help-giving. *Personality and Social Psychology Bulletin, 14,* 610–621.

Schwarzer, R., & Weiner, B. (1991). Stigma controllability and coping as predictors of emotions and social support. *Journal of Social and Personality Relationships, 8,* 133–140.

Strasser, J. A., & Damrosch, S. (1989). *Nurses' attitudes toward gay and hemophiliac patients with AIDS*. Paper presented at the 97th annual convention of the American Psychological Association, New Orleans, LA.

Weiner, B. (1985). An attributional theory of achievement motivation and emotion. *Psychological Review, 92,* 548–573.

Weiner, B. (1986). *An attributional theory of motivation and emotion*. New York: Springer-Verlag.

Weiner, B., Graham, S., & Chandler, C. C. (1982). Pity, anger, and guilt: An attributional analysis. *Personality and Social Psychology Bulletin, 8,* 226–232.

Weiner, B., Perry, R. B., & Magnusson, J. (1988). An attributional analysis of reactions to stigmas. *Journal of Personality and Social Psychology, 55,* 738–748.

Zucker, G. S. (1990). *Conservatism and perceptions of the causes of poverty*. Unpublished manuscript, University of California, Los Angeles.

COPING WITH HIV
INFECTION AND
SOCIAL SUPPORT

11

Coping With the Threat of AIDS

Shelley E. Taylor
Margaret E. Kemeny
Stephen G. Schneider
Lisa G. Aspinwall
University of California, Los Angeles

The AIDS epidemic has presented gay and bisexual men with a set of stressors of unprecedented magnitude. Relatively young men whose major life tasks should be settling into a career and evolving a satisfying personal life are instead facing the demands of debilitating illness, symptoms usually associated with aging, and death. In addition, this population is experiencing the death of a lifestyle and bereavement, often of large numbers of friends, acquaintances, and former lovers. The demands of this multifaceted crisis evoke needs for coping that may also be unprecedented.

Men who currently test seronegative for the AIDS virus must manage their risk through appropriate health behaviors, cope with the threat the crisis poses to their lifestyle and friendship networks, and manage the often substantial guilt that may come from not having been exposed thus far to the ravages of this disease (Wayment, Silver, & Kemeny, 1990). Men who have tested seropositive for the AIDS virus must develop ways to manage their anxiety over their risk status and to continue to function effectively in the face of potential deterioration of health and risk for death. Both seropositive and seronegative men are being asked to undertake behavioral changes in their lives in order to avoid becoming infected themselves or passing the human immunodeficiency virus (HIV) on to others. Often these changes require major modification of sexual behavior.

In this chapter, we consider three aspects of the extensive process of coping with the threat of AIDS. First, we examine determinants of changes in sexual practices in a large cohort of HIV seropositive and HIV seronegative men, focusing on the factors that appear to promote or to undermine health behavior change. Next, we turn to the issue of how gay and bisexual men cope with the threat of developing AIDS. We compare the coping strategies used by HIV

305

seropositive and HIV seronegative men to deal with their risk of developing AIDS. We focus on specific coping strategies used and whether or not they promote or undermine psychological well-being in the face of this threat. Finally, we focus on suicidal ideation. Research suggests that the AIDS crisis has lead to a high level of suicide among men with AIDS, as high as 36 times that experienced in the male heterosexual population of the same age range (Mazurk et al., 1988). In the third section of this chapter, we consider suicidal ideation, its predictors, and the question of whether such ideation may, at least under some circumstances, function as a coping strategy.

THE SAMPLE

Our sample is recruited from the existing cohort of gay and bisexual men participating in the Multi-Center AIDS Cohort Study (MACS) in Los Angeles. The MACS is a multisite collaborative longitudinal research investigation of the epidemiology and natural history of AIDS. It is designed to identify the factors associated with the risk of HIV infection and the factors affecting the course of HIV infection among HIV seropositive individuals.

Between April 1984 and December 1985, 1,637 participants were enrolled in the Los Angeles MACS cohort. Inclusion criteria were: 18 years of age or older, no diagnosis of AIDS or cancer except skin cancer, and no radiation therapy. In addition, 122 subjects were recruited in 1986 if they were current intimate partners of MACS participants. Initially, participants ranged in age from 18 to 50 with a mean age of 32. Ninety-five percent were White, including White Hispanic. The majority of subjects had at least a college education (55%) and were employed in professional or managerial positions (51%). At the start of the study in 1984, 49.5% were HIV seropositive.

Beginning in August 1987, active MACS participants, except those diagnosed with AIDS, were invited to participate in our investigation, the Natural History of AIDS—Psychosocial Study (NHAPS). The goals of this study are to identify current psychological appraisals of, emotional responses to, and methods of coping with the risk of developing AIDS, and the impact of these processes on behavior and health. Between August 1987 and October 1988, 798 men were recruited into the NHAPS. Over this same time period, approximately 1,330 MACS participants without AIDS visited the MACS study for their exam (and thus were active MACS participants), yielding a participation rate in our study of 60%. Our NHAPS sample is very similar demographically to the overall MACS sample. More than 90% are White and have at least a college education (66.6%). Our participants range in age from 22 to 60, with a median age of 36 (as of 1987), which is identical to the 1987 median age of the Los Angeles MACS study.   The data presented here draw on this sample of 798,   although the sample sizes vary according to the inclusion criteria for individual analyses, described later.

As part of our psychosocial study, participants are mailed a questionnaire packet just prior to their MACS examination and asked to fill it out the day before the exam and return it to the MACS exam site or by mail. The questionnaire packet consists of a number of standardized psychological scales, as well as our own AIDS-related questionnaires, which is described in the following sections.

As part of the MACS study, participants are assessed at 6-month intervals. Assessment procedures include a physical examination to detect signs and symptoms of AIDS, collection of blood and other specimens for virological and immunological studies, and an interview assessing behavioral practices (e.g., sexual behaviors, drug use) that may contribute to seroconversion and/or the development of AIDS. HIV antibody status and the absolute number of CD4 helper/inducer and CD8 suppressor/cytotoxic T cells are assessed every 6 months on the basis of blood samples drawn at these visits.

AIDS RISK-REDUCTION BEHAVIORS

Considerable research has now elucidated the behavioral factors involved in the transmission of HIV. Avoiding or modifying anal-receptive intercourse, avoiding anonymous sexual partners, and reducing the number of sexual partners overall have been identified as behaviors that reduce AIDS risk (Chmiel et al., 1987; Darrow et al., 1987; Detels et al., 1989). An emerging literature suggests that gay men have substantially modified these behaviors in response to AIDS (Martin, 1986; McKusick, Horstman, & Coates, 1985; McKusick, Wiley et al., 1985; Reisenberg, 1986; see Becker & Joseph, 1988, and Stall, Coates, & Hoff, 1988, for reviews). Most frequently reported are a decrease in the number of sexual partners, a reduction in the number of anonymous sexual partners, and a decreased use of bathhouses for sex. Despite these promising trends, many men have not changed their sexual behaviors (Martin, 1986, 1987) and others have relapsed, returning to high-risk patterns. Such trends underscore the need to examine why some men adopt and maintain risk-reduction behaviors, whereas others do not. The problem does not appear to be simply one of AIDS education, inasmuch as studies find that gay men are extremely knowledgeable about AIDS transmission and that such knowledge shows little or no relation to risk-reduction behavior (e.g., Joseph et al., 1987; McKusick, Horstman, & Coates, 1985).

Drawing on the health belief model (Rosenstock, 1974), self-efficacy theory (Bandura, 1977, 1986), and protection motivation theory (Rogers, 1975, 1984), we examined the potential contributing role of several psychological variables to the practice of risk-reduction behaviors. The variables on which we focused included perceived risk (one's personal risk of developing AIDS), perceived response efficacy (the effectiveness of a particular risk-reduction behavior for reducing the risk of developing AIDS), self-efficacy (the perception that one is able to perform the activity involved in undertaking safer sexual behavior), and perceived barriers to AIDS-related risk-reduction behaviors, such as personal difficulty controlling sexual impulses or the importance of a particular behavior to self-image. We also examined the impact of AIDS-related bereavement and social norms favoring high-risk sexual behavior. Perceived severity of the disease, a variable usually included in tests of attitudinal models of risk-related behaviors, could not be examined in the present research, because there was a ceiling effect on this particular variable. That is, virtually everyone in the sample recognized AIDS to be an intensely severe threat.

In addition to these psychological variables, we examined two factors that may play an important role in AIDS risk-reduction behavior. The first is partner status, or whether respondents had a primary romantic or intimate partner. There is some evidence to suggest that men in primary relationships are more likely to have reduced their number of sexual partners than are single men (Klein et al., 1987). The second factor is HIV antibody status. The few studies examining the impact of learning one's serostatus on subsequent sexual behavior have yielded mixed results. For example, one study found that gay men who learned they were seropositive subsequently reduced some high-risk behaviors, such as insertive anal intercourse, but increased other risk behaviors, such as receptive anal intercourse (McCusker, Zapka, Stoddard, & Mayer, 1989). Studies of gay men who learned they were seronegative find that these men may not reduce high-risk behaviors, such as unprotected anal receptive intercourse (McKusick, Coates, Morin, Pollack, & Hoff, 1989), or may do so to a lesser extent than do men who learned they were seropositive (Fox, Odaka, Brookmeyer, & Polk, 1987). More recently, another study found no relation between knowledge of serostatus and subsequent sexual behavior (Doll et al., 1990). As more gay men choose to learn their antibody status, it will be critical to understand the impact this information may have on risk-reduction behavior. The present study was designed to address this issue and also to determine whether the relations of the psychological variables described above to risk-reduction behavior are different for men who have a primary partner versus men who are single and for men who are HIV seropositive versus men who are HIV seronegative.[1]

Drawn from the overall study sample, the sample for these analyses consisted of 389 exclusively homosexual men with no history of prostitution, no diagnosis of ARC, who knew their antibody status, and who had completed two waves of data collection. The demographic attributes of this subset of the sample were not significantly different from those of the MACS cohort overall. Health beliefs, HIV status, partner status, and sexual practices were assessed and used to predict sexual practices 6 months later. Two high-risk sexual behaviors were assessed by

---

[1]On the surface, it might seem odd to be asking who are HIV seropositive to estimate their risk of getting AIDS. Presumably, most of these men would recognize it to be extremely high as a result of having tested positive for the virus. This is not the case, however. Among the HIV seropositive men in our sample, perceived risk of getting AIDS is only 4.53 out of 7. Most of these men distinguish between being exposed to HIV and getting AIDS, with some assuming that a combination of a strong immune system and good health habits will be able to forestall the adverse effects of the virus (see, e.g., Taylor et al., 1992).

TABLE 11.1
Psychosocial Predictors of the Number of Male Sexual Partners Over a 6-Month Interval
Controlling for Prior Behavior by Subgroup of Gay Men

	HIV Seropositive		HIV Seronegative	
	Has Partner	No Partner	Has Partner	No Partner
Health Belief				
Self-efficacy	-	0	-	-
Perceived risk	0	+	0	-
Response efficacy	0	+	0	0

Note. + indicates an increase in the number of male sexual partners; -, a decrease in the number of partners.
0 indicates the variable had no effect on the number of partners. The health beliefs were scored so that
higher numbers indicate higher levels of the belief.

structured interview. The first was the number of male sexual partners for either oral or anal intercourse; the second was the number of anonymous sexual partners for these activities. A third high-risk behavior, anal-receptive intercourse without a condom, was practiced by only 12% of the sample, and so we do not report determinants of this behavior.

Hierarchical regression analyses were used to predict the number of partners over time and the number of anonymous sexual partners. We describe only the results for number of sexual partners, inasmuch as the results are virtually identical for number of anonymous partners.[2] Past sexual behavior was the strongest predictor, accounting for 51% of the variance. Those men who had more partners in the past continued to have more partners over the 6-month duration of the study. Controlling for prior sexual behavior, three psychological variables—self-efficacy, perceived risk, and response efficacy—predicted an additional 15% of the variance in the number of sexual partners over the 6-month interval. First, self-efficacy—the belief that one is capable of reducing one's number of partners—predicted successful risk-reduction behavior over time. Interestingly, although neither HIV status nor partner status alone had an impact on risk-reduction behavior, these two factors moderated the impact of perceived risk and response efficacy on subsequent risk-reduction behavior. The pattern of results for each of these variables is summarized in Table 11.1.

Perceived Risk. The relation of perceived risk to subsequent risk-reduction behavior depended on the respondents' HIV and partner status. Specifically, among seronegative men who did not have a primary partner, those who perceived themselves to be at greater risk of getting AIDS subsequently reduced their number of sexual partners. However, perceived risk showed the opposite relation of risk-reduction behavior among HIV seropositive men without primary

---

[2]For additional details regarding the methods and results of this study, the reader is referred to Aspinwall, Kemeny, Taylor, Schneider, and Dudley (1991).

partners; that is, men in this group who perceived themselves to be at greater risk for developing AIDS reported *increases* in high-risk sexual behavior over the 6-month interval.

Response Efficacy. Another factor that predicted an increased number of sexual partners among HIV seropositive men without primary partners was response efficacy, or the belief that reducing one's number of partners would reduce one's risk of getting AIDS. Men who did not believe that reducing their number of partners would reduce their risk of getting AIDS reported sharp increases in the number of sexual partners over the 6 months of the study. Men in this group whose perceptions of response efficacy were high reported no such increases. Response efficacy was unrelated to risk-reduction behavior in the other groups.

The results of this prospective study provide strong support for the importance of health-related beliefs in predicting AIDS risk-reduction behavior in gay men. Controlling for the influence of prior sexual behavior, variables identified by the health belief model, protection motivation theory, and Bandura's self-efficacy theory predicted numbers of sexual partners and numbers of anonymous sexual partners 6 months later, largely in the expected directions. Self-efficacy, response efficacy, and perceived risk were strong predictors of these behaviors, whereas AIDS-related bereavement, barriers to change, and social norms did not predict high-risk sexual behavior over time.

That prior sexual behavior predicted half of the variance in number of sexual partners 6 months later may illustrate, in part, the importance of habit in determining AIDS-related behaviors. Indeed, one reason barriers to change may not have emerged as a significant predictor of number of sexual partners in this analysis is that barriers, or the extent to which it is hard to refrain from a behavior, may overlap substantially with habit, such that controlling for prior behavior may remove the variance that could be explained by difficulties in controlling sexual impulses or the importance of a particular behavior to self-image. This overlap may explain why studies that do not control for prior sexual behavior find a substantial negative correlation between barriers to change and AIDS risk-reduction behavior. An examination of the correlation between barriers to change and the number of sexual partners predicted by the regression equation reveals that the higher scores on the barriers index were significantly related to higher predicted scores for the number of sexual partners over the 6-month interval. This result suggests that barriers to change are reliably associated with increased risk behavior over time, although prior sexual behavior, self-efficacy, response efficacy, and risk seem to account for the bulk of the variance.

The inclusion of HIV status and partner status as potential moderators of the relation between psychological variables and risk-reduction behavior allowed the present study to pinpoint several targets for intervention and future study. Specifically, the finding that HIV seropositive men without primary partners who report particular health-related beliefs show increases in potentially risky sexual behavior suggests a need to develop interventions to assist this group in modifying their behavior.

In interpreting these results, it is important to note that it is impossible to determine whether the increased sexual behavior reported by these men confers risk to their partners. Although these men might be spreading HIV, it is impossible to draw this conclusion from the present study for two reasons. First, the data presented for the number of sexual partners do not allow us to determine the particular form of intercourse and its corresponding risk of transmitting the virus. For example, HIV seropositive men may increase their frequency of intercourse behaviors that may not spread the virus, such as receptive oral sex or sex with a condom. Second, the data do not allow us to determine the HIV status of the respondents' partners. It is possible—and anecdotal evidence from our interviews suggests—that HIV seropositive men may seek out other HIV seropositive men as sexual partners. Although safer sexual practices between seropositive partners are still important so as to avoid further compromise of the immune system and to prevent exposure to other strains of HIV, the HIV seropositive men in our study may have engaged in activities that avoided these risks. For these reasons, it would be inaccurate to conclude from this study that HIV seropositive men without primary partners who endorse particular health-related beliefs are spreading HIV.

Nonetheless, it will be critical to prevention efforts to understand why increased perceptions of the risk of getting AIDS predict increased sexual activity among HIV seropositive men without primary partners. For example, it is possible that the distress accompanying increased risk perceptions may lead people to engage in increased sexual activity as a way to relieve tension or to obtain intimate contact. If this line of reasoning is correct, it may be important to target men as they become symptomatic, because the appearance of AIDS-related symptoms may increase perceptions of risk.

It will also be important to explore the potential protective benefits of having a primary partner in coping with increasing perceptions of AIDS risk, because the relation between increased perceptions of risk and increased numbers of sexual partners does not hold for HIV seropositive men who have primary partners. It may be simply that having a steady partner may provide an outlet for sexual energy, but it is also possible that a primary partner may assist one in coping with increasing perceptions of risk, as well as with other stressors. It is also possible, of course, that men who have primary partners may differ in other ways from men who do not, and it will be important to explore such differences and their potential link to high-risk behavior.

Importantly, the finding that the effects of some psychological variables on risk behavior depend on HIV status and partner status may explain the inconsistent results of previous studies. In the case of perceived risk, studies have found that increased risk sometimes predicts decreases in risky behavior (Klein et al., 1987), sometimes predicts increases in risky behavior (Joseph et al., 1987), and sometimes is unrelated to risk behavior (Siegel, Mesagno, Chen, & Crist, 1989).

In the present study, perceived risk predicted *decreases* in high-risk behavior among single men who are HIV seronegative and *increases* among single men who are HIV seropositive.

The finding that HIV seropositive men without primary partners who believe that reducing their number of partners would not reduce their risk of getting AIDS actually increase their level of potentially risky sexual behavior suggests that it is important to study gay men's beliefs about the efficacy of various risk-reduction measures. It will be important to distinguish beliefs that a change in a specific behavior will reduce the likelihood of HIV infection from beliefs that behavior change will reduce the likelihood of developing AIDS. For example, men who know they are already HIV seropositive may believe that subsequent risk reduction is futile. Conversely, believing in a dose-response relationship between the number of exposures to HIV and developing AIDS or believing that one can be exposed to different strains of the virus may contribute to increased perceptions of response efficacy among HIV seropositive men. Similarly, men who are aware that exposure to other sexually transmitted diseases (STDs) may increase their risk of developing AIDS may believe in the efficacy of reducing their number of sexual partners. The extent to which gay men are aware of the possibility of increased risk of developing AIDS among people who are HIV seropositive as a result of exposure to different strains of the virus or exposure to other infections is currently unknown. To date, the vast majority of education efforts have focused on primary prevention. Less attention has been paid to developing and publicizing risk-reduction measures for people who are already HIV seropositive. The results of this study suggest that this information may be a particularly important target for intervention.

Prospective studies that take into account the HIV status and partner status of respondents may be able to provide a more fine-grained account of the impact of health-related beliefs on subsequent risk-reduction behavior and may also aid in the design of interventions to assist specific subgroups of gay men. Along these lines, an 8-week stress-reduction program has been found to help HIV seropositive men to reduce their number of sexual partners (Coates, McKusick, Kuno, & Stites, 1989). Interventions have also begun to focus on fostering perceived self-efficacy in managing the interpersonal aspects of sexuality (Bandura, in press; Kelly, St. Lawrence, Hood, & Brasfield, 1989). Such programs, supplemented by information that stresses the effectiveness of risk-reduction measures even for men who are HIV seropositive, may help men maintain risk-reduction behaviors over time and may ultimately prove useful in combatting the spread of the AIDS virus in the gay male population.

COPING WITH THE THREAT OF AIDS

The threat of developing AIDS places significant demands on the psychological resources of gay and bisexual men. Consequently, it is important to identify the coping strategies that are employed for dealing with this chronic stressor and to determine which of those coping strategies may be most effective in maintaining feelings of well-being and preventing feelings of hopelessness and heightened AIDS-related fears.

Coping is "the process of managing demands (external or internal) that are appraised as taxing or exceeding the resources of the person" (Lazarus & Folkman, in press). Coping consists of "efforts, both action-oriented and intra-psychic, to manage (that is, master, tolerate, reduce, minimize) environmental and internal demands and conflicts among them which tax or exceed a person's resources" (Cohen & Lazarus, 1979, p. 219). Generally, two types of coping efforts have been distinguished: problem-solving efforts and efforts at emotional regulation (cf. Folkman, Schaefer, & Lazarus, 1979; Lazarus & Folkman, 1984; Leventhal & Nerenz, 1982; Pearlin & Schooler, 1978). Problem-focused efforts are attempts to do something active concerning stressful conditions, whereas emotion-focused coping involves efforts to regulate the emotional consequences of the stressful event.

The effectiveness of particular strategies used to cope with chronic illness has been investigated by a number of research groups. A chief focus has been on avoidant versus confrontative strategies. Neither style has been found to be necessarily more effective in managing stress, inasmuch as each seems to have its advantages and liabilities for different situations. People who cope with stress by minimizing or avoiding threatening events seem to cope effectively with short-term threats (e.g., Kaloupek & Stoupakis, 1985; Kaloupek, White, & Wong, 1984; Kiyak, Vitaliano, & Crinean, 1988; Wong & Kaloupek, 1986). However, if the threat persists over time, the strategy of avoidance is not so successful. There is evidence in the literature on coping and chronic illness, for example, that avoidant coping is associated with increased psychological distress and may thereby be a risk factor for adverse reactions to stressful circumstances (Felton, Revenson, & Hinrichsen, 1984; Holahan & Moos, 1986, 1987). Similarly, Weisman and Worden (1976–1977) found efforts to forget the disease, fatalism, passive acceptance, withdrawal from others, blaming of others, and self-blame to be associated with poor adjustment to cancer.

There is some evidence that those who employ more than one coping strategy may cope better with a stressful event than those who engage in a predominant style. Collins, Taylor, and Skokan (1990) found that patients who coped with cancer using a variety of coping strategies were better adjusted than those who used a predominant style. They argued that coping strategies may be most effective when they are matched to the particular problem for which they are most helpful. Those people who have multiple coping strategies available to them may be more able to engage in this matching process than those who have a predominant coping style.

Although some of the psychological reactions of gay men at risk for AIDS have been documented, there have been few studies of the methods of coping used to deal with the threat of AIDS and the nature of the strategies most closely tied to psychological adjustment. We were particularly interested in whether HIV seropositive and HIV seronegative men would cope differently with thoughts of developing AIDS, because the threat to these two groups is quite different.

Certainly, the magnitude of the threat of developing AIDS is greater in men who know they have already been infected with HIV. In addition, the nature of the threat is different in these two groups. For HIV seronegative men, the immediate threat is infection with HIV. It is well known that this threat can be dramatically reduced, if not eliminated, by changes in sexual practices. For HIV seropositive men, however, infection has already taken place and the threat is the development of AIDS. The extent to which this threat can be reduced is unknown. Consequently, we examined whether these two groups of men cope differently with thoughts of developing AIDS, given the very different degree of control each has over the threat. Thus, we examined differences in coping by HIV seropositive and HIV seronegative men and the relationship between coping strategies and adjustment in both groups (Kemeny et al., 1990).

On the basis of the coping literature, we predicted that individuals who know they are HIV seropositive will initiate more coping efforts to deal with distressing thoughts of AIDS than individuals who know they are HIV seronegative. This prediction is based on the assumption that more intensely stressful events evoke more coping efforts than less stressful events. Second, we hypothesized that psychological adjustment to the threat of AIDS will be positively associated with the extent of coping efforts initiated and the breadth of coping strategies used; that is, multiple coping efforts should be associated with better adjustment. Finally, we hypothesized that more active coping strategies, aimed at reducing the threat and its associated distress, would be positively associated with psychological adjustment, whereas more passive and avoidant forms of coping would be negatively associated with adjustment. This may be considered a strong test of the relation of active coping strategies to psychosocial adjustment. Previous research has indicated the advantages of active coping strategies primarily with stressful events that were at least somewhat amenable to personal control. In the case of the HIV seropositive individuals especially, this is a somewhat counterintuitive prediction; previous research documenting the adjustment benefits of active coping strategies have typically explored stressful events that were at least somewhat amenable to personal control, and the likelihood of developing AIDS after having tested HIV seropositive may be, to a greater degree, an uncontrollable stressor.

To address these issues, we analyzed data from the 550 NHAPS subjects who knew their HIV antibody status: 238 of these subjects were HIV seropositive, and 312 were HIV seronegative. (The 248 men who had chosen not to know their antibody status were excluded from the study.) The demographics of the sample were virtually identical to those of the larger study.

Pilot testing had identified "thoughts of developing AIDS" as the major AIDS-related stressful event experienced by both the HIV seropositive and HIV seronegative men in this sample. Therefore, a 48-item scale, Coping With Thoughts of Developing AIDS, was developed based on the Ways of Coping instrument (Folkman & Lazarus, 1980). Coping items from the Ways of Coping instrument were excluded if they could not be used to deal with thoughts of AIDS. In addition, some AIDS-related coping strategies suggested by pilot subjects were added, and some original scale items were reworded slightly to make them specific to coping with thoughts of AIDS. Respondents indicated on 4-point scales, ranging from "regularly" to "not at all," the extent to which they had used each method to cope with the threat of AIDS.

Psychosocial adjustment was assessed via the Hopelessness Scale and the Profile of Mood States (POMS). The Hopelessness Scale (Beck, Weissman, Lester, & Trexler, 1974) measures negative expectations about the future and includes 20 true–false items. The POMS (McNair, Lorr, & Droppleman, 1971) is a measure of current mood state. Respondents rate how much they have been feeling each of 65 affects over the past week on a 5-point scale. A Negative Affect score was developed that included the score from the Hopelessness Scale and the depression–dejection, tension–anxiety, and anger–hostility subscale scores from the Profile of Mood States.[3] These four scores were standardized and then summed to form the Negative Affect score.

A second dependent measure assessed AIDS-related worries and concerns. Respondents were asked to rate the degree to which they had felt a number of emotions over the past month concerning their risk of developing AIDS, such as anxious, fearful, or worried. They were also asked how often the thought of developing AIDS intruded into their day-to-day thoughts and how often they found themselves thinking that a physical symptom might be the first symptoms of AIDS. These items were combined into a single index.

Coping With Thoughts of Developing AIDS.   A factor analysis of the Coping With Thoughts of Developing AIDS items yielded five interpretable factors with eigenvalues greater than 1. The first factor (10 items) contains items representing the process of maintaining *Positive Attitudes* (e.g., try to keep a positive outlook in life; try to keep myself from worrying about getting AIDS, since there is no use in worrying). The second factor (8 items) represents personal growth, involving spiritual activities or developing oneself as a person (e.g., finding new faith), and helping others (e.g., do nice things for people to feel better). This factor is called *Personal Growth/Helping Others.* The third factor (7 items) includes items primarily involved with *Seeking Social Support* of various forms, including emotional support, as well as advice and informational support. This factor also includes two items that focus on thinking about or analyzing the problem. The

---

[3]The confusion-bewilderment, fatigue-inertia, and vigor-activity subscales of the POMS were not included because of the possibility that responses to these scales might be confounded by the physical health status of the respondents.

fourth factor (9 items) includes three components, fatalism (e.g., prepare myself for the worst), self-blame (e.g., realize I brought this risk on myself), and escape/avoidance, including both cognitive and behavioral methods of avoidance (e.g., daydream or imagine a better time or place than the one I am in; try to make myself feel better by overeating, drinking, smoking, using drugs or medications). This factor is called *Fatalism/Self-Blame/Escape-Avoidance*. The fifth factor (3 items) involves avoidance of information or thought concerning AIDS (e.g., keep myself from thinking too much about AIDS). This factor is called *Avoidance of AIDS*.

Coping and HIV Serostatus.   We next related these coping strategies to negative affect and AIDS-related concerns and worries. It should first be noted there were no significant differences between the HIV seropositive and the HIV seronegative men on Negative Affect. However, the HIV seropositive subjects reported more AIDS-related concerns and worries.

When controlling for age and the presence of an intimate partner,[4] the HIV seropositive respondents reported that they used significantly more Positive Attitudes and more Avoidance of AIDS to cope with the thoughts of developing AIDS than did the HIV seronegative subjects. There was a nonsignificant trend for HIV seropositive men to seek more social support as a coping strategy than HIV seronegative men. The two groups did not differ significantly in their use of Personal Growth/Helping Others of Fatalism/Self-Blame/Escape-Avoidance (see Table 11.2).

The two HIV status groups were compared to see if they differed in the number of coping strategies they used. We assessed multiple coping as the number of coping factors that constitute 15% or more of the person's total coping effort. There was a significant difference between the two groups, such that the HIV seropositive group used more coping strategies than the HIV seronegative group.

Were any coping strategies especially associated with good or poor adjustment? To answer these questions, we analyzed the data of the HIV seropositive and seronegative men separately, inasmuch as they are coping with qualitatively different stressors. Among HIV seropositive men, age was significantly associated with Negative Affect and AIDS-Related Concerns, with older men (over 35 years-of-age) reporting higher levels of negative psychological states. Partner status was unrelated to psychological state. Positive Attitude was associated with lower levels of Negative Affect and AIDS-Related Concerns. Greater use of Fatalism/Self-Blame/Escape-Avoidance was associated with higher levels of Negative Affect and AIDS-Related Concerns. Personal Growth/Helping Others, Seeking Social Support, and Avoidance of AIDS were not associated with Negative Affect or AIDS-Related Concerns.

---

[4]We controlled for age and partner status, because preliminary results suggested that they made some differences in the patterns of coping obtained.

TABLE 11.2
Adjusted Means for Psychological States and Coping Factors: Comparison of HIV+ and HIV- Men

	Adjusted Mean		F*	p
	HIV+	HIV-		
Psychological State				
Negative mood	-.07	.11	.32	.57
AIDS-related concerns	.73	-.72	61.94	.0001
Coping With Thoughts of AIDS				
Positive attitudes	1.68	1.45	20.31	.0001
Personal growth/helping others	.73	.65	2.53	.11
Seeking social support	1.26	1.16	3.36	.07
Fatalism/self-blame/escape avoidance	.77	.72	1.49	.22
Avoidance of AIDS	.55	.39	16.33	.0001

*ANCOVA analyses were conducted controlling for Age and Partner Status. Table entries are standardized scores.

The relation between coping and psychological state among HIV seropositive men also depended on age. The older men who reported using Personal Growth/Helping Others had lower levels of Negative Affect and AIDS-related concerns, but these variables were not significantly related in the younger men. Similar trends emerged for the Positive Attitudes factor. Finally and unexpectedly, the relation between the use of multiple coping strategies and psychological state was significantly negative, rather than positive. That is, individuals who used multiple coping strategies had higher levels of Negative Affect and AIDS-Related Concerns.

Age and partner status were unrelated to Negative Affect or AIDS-Related Concerns among the HIV seronegative men. As was seen with the HIV seropositive men, the Positive Attitudes factor was associated with a lower level of Negative Affect. Higher levels of Fatalism/Self-Blame/Escape-Avoidance were associated with a higher level of Negative Affect and AIDS-Related Concerns. Also, as was true for the HIV seropositive men, use of multiple coping strategies was associated with higher levels of Negative Affect and AIDS-Related Concerns.

Implications of Coping Patterns. The gay and bisexual men in this study who knew they were HIV seropositive were more worried about developing AIDS than individuals who know they are HIV seronegative. However, they were not responding to this threat with heightened negative affect and hopelessness. This relatively low level of negative affect in the face of a severe threat to mortality may be a result of the coping strategies that HIV seropositive individuals report using. In comparison to HIV seronegative men, HIV seropositive men used more of the emotion-regulating strategies, such as maintaining a positive attitude and also avoidance of AIDS. HIV seropositive men were also using more different coping strategies than the seronegative men.

These differences in coping strategies used by HIV seropositive versus seronegative men may be due not only to the quantitative differences in the nature of the stressor to which they are exposed (i.e., degree of threat), but also to qualitative differences in the nature of the stressor. HIV seropositive men are faced with the fact that they may develop AIDS at any time and that there is, as yet, no way to ensure their health will not deteriorate. Maintaining a positive attitude and not thinking too much about AIDS may be a common response to this type of uncontrollable stressor. The stressor for HIV seronegative men—becoming infected with HIV—is ultimately under their own control. For these men, failing to think about AIDS may be less common, partly because more active strategies are available for use and because it may not be as distressing to think about a threat that can be prevented.

Escape/avoidance strategies, which involve behaviors such as overeating or drinking to feel better, social isolation, or daydreaming, comprised a factor that was associated with higher levels of negative mood and hopelessness. These findings are consistent with the previous literature indicating that avoidant coping strategies are generally ineffective in dealing with chronic stressors (see, e.g., Suls & Fletcher, 1985), and may actually increase risk for psychological distress (Aspinwall & Taylor, in press; Cronkite & Moos, 1984; Felton et al., 1984; Holahan & Moos, 1984; Quinn, Fontana, & Reznikoff, 1987). It may be that such strategies prevent individuals from receiving social support or achieving their goals, or that they preclude more active, problem-oriented efforts and, consequently, are associated with hopelessness and negative mood.[5]

Contrary to prediction, the use of multiple coping strategies was associated with more rather than less psychological distress. A previous investigation with cancer patients (Collins et al., 1990) found the opposite relation, namely that the use of multiple coping strategies was associated with more positive affect. It may be that psychological distress prompts people to engage in more different kinds of coping that, over time, may improve psychological state. Thus, the relation between psychological state and the use of multiple coping efforts would change over time, being negative when the multiple coping efforts are first initiated, but positive over the long term. The cancer sample in the Collins et al. study had

---

[5]It should be noted, however, that the items indicating the avoidance of thoughts or reading about AIDS or of having contacts with AIDS-related organizations did not load on the same factor with the other avoidance strategies and were not associated with good or bad adjustment. This form of avoidance may not be maladaptive and may even be necessary when an individual is faced with a crisis that involves constant reminders of one's risk of mortality. It is also possible that this form of avoidance may be part of a more general adaptive response to a variety of stressors, particularly those that are anticipated rather than current, and over which the individual may not have much control. Thus, it would appear that when escape-avoidance is employed as a general coping strategy for dealing with a threatening event, it may be part of a maladaptive response, but that the specific strategy of avoiding thoughts about a future threat (in this case, AIDS) may not be. The potential differential adaptiveness of these forms of avoidance merits future study.

been diagnosed with cancer, on average, at least 3 years earlier; consequently, these people would have had several years to adjust to their cancer. Moreover, most of them were in remission at the time of the study and, consequently, may not have been dealing with a very active threat. The use of multiple coping strategies may have served them well earlier and contributed to the low levels of distress observed in the sample. In contrast, the AIDS crisis and the problems it poses were very much a current issue for the men in the present study, and some of them had experienced renewed threats with respect to AIDS, such as bereavements, physical symptoms, or immune system changes. Consequently, they may have been at a stage where multiple coping strategies were being enlisted to combat a continuing series of highly distressing events; thus, a negative relation between the use of multiple coping strategies and distress would be observed, which might shift to a positive relation over time. Only longitudinal data can address this question definitively.

In summary, our data indicate that the gay men in our sample were engaged in efforts to alleviate AIDS-related distress. Men who know they are HIV seropositive use more active coping strategies than men who know they are HIV seronegative, and their greater use of this coping strategy may contribute to the fact that HIV seropositive men do not report higher levels of negative mood than HIV seronegative men. The greater degree of active coping reported by HIV seropositive men may be due to the increased threat to mortality they experience. However, the differences in coping strategies reported by the two groups may also be due to qualitative differences in the nature of the stressors they face, such as the extent to which the outcomes are controllable. Thus, controllability of stress may be an important domain to evaluate in coping research, given that different coping strategies may be adopted depending on the controllability of the stressor or threat.

In both groups, reported use of more positive attitudes and less fatalism, self-blame, and escape-avoidant strategies was associated with a more positive mood and greater hopefulness. Future studies are required to assess prospectively the relationship between coping strategies and psychological adjustment to confirm and to extend these findings. Such data may be useful for identifying those at risk for psychological distress in response to the threat of AIDS. Ultimately, they may also be valuable in constructing interventions aimed at enhancing effective methods for dealing with the AIDS crisis.

SUICIDAL RESPONSES TO AIDS THREAT

The threat of a currently fatal disease like AIDS raises the spectre of a lingering and painful death, especially among men who have already tested positive for the AIDS virus. Moreover, living in a community with such a high concentration of illness, death, and loss makes this spectre even more concrete. A number of men facing the threat of AIDS respond to the threat with some degree of suicidal ideation, and some go on to commit suicide. Mazurk et al. (1988), for example, reported that in New York City, for gay men ages 20 to 59, the relative risk of suicide was 36 times greater than that of age-matched men in the general population. The California Department of Health Services reported that the relative risk of suicide among men with AIDS in 1986 was 17 times that of men without AIDS (Kizer, Green, Perkins, Doebbert, & Hughes, 1988). Suicide is known to be a response to other life-threatening illnesses, such as cancer (Louhivuori & Hakama, 1979; Marshall, Burnett, & Brashure, 1983), Huntington's disease (Farrer, 1985; Schoenfeld et al., 1984), and chronic renal dialysis (Haenel, Brunner, & Battegay, 1980), yet little research has examined which specific aspects of illness or the threat of illness contribute to suicidal ideation and suicide. Because of the apparent prevalence of suicidal ideation and suicide in this population, we examined factors that contribute to suicidal intent.[6]

In keeping with psychosocial models that have explored adverse psychological outcomes, we examined *precipitating factors,* or proximate causes of the onset of an adverse response. Specifically, we assessed AIDS-related stressors in two ways: biological risk of developing AIDS and AIDS-related life events, namely illnesses befalling one's self and others and deaths among one's community of close relationships. Such loss events and severe threats have been found to predict suicide-related outcomes in the past (Paykel, Prusoff, & Meyers, 1975; Slater & Depue, 1981). We also assessed *resistance factors,* in particular current confidant support, a factor assumed to help individuals withstand the adverse effects of stressful events (e.g., Cohen & Wills, 1985). In this context, we expected that the presence of fewer confidants would relate to greater suicide intent (e.g., Slater & Depue, 1981).

We examined *cognitive appraisals* of both AIDS-related stress and available social resources. In this context, perceived risk of developing AIDS was assessed, as was loneliness. Subjective appraisal of loneliness may mediate the effects of AIDS-related stressors that lead to suicidal ideation by way of the perceived and real isolation accompanying illness and loss events. Subjective appraisals of loneliness (or the lack thereof) may at the same time mediate the effects of adequate confidant support.

We also assessed *predisposing factors,* past psychosocial resources and individual difference factors that may render a person more prone to a particular adverse psychological outcome when exposed to an extremely stressful event. These included past measures of confidant support, the lack of which (e.g., social isolation, lack of social integration) has been posited as an important factor predisposing individuals to suicidal behavior (e.g.,Durkheim, 1952; Trout, 1980). Past depression, another factor documented as predisposing individuals to suicidal behavior (Francis, Fyre, & Clarkin, 1986), was also assessed.

As in the study of ways of coping with the threat of AIDS, we developed

---

[6]For additional details regarding the methods and results of this study, the reader is referred to Schneider, Taylor, Kemeny, Hammen, and Dudley (1991).

separate models for HIV seropositive and HIV seronegative men, HIV seropositive men are already facing a severe stressor (being HIV seropositive) that should highly tax their psychosocial resources; men who are currently HIV seronegative are facing a significant but less immediate threat. We expected that predisposing factors would more powerfully predict suicidal intent among the HIV seropositive men, given the higher adaptational demands that being HIV seropositive poses. We also expected that AIDS-related stressors would be a primary focus around which distress may be organized for the HIV seropositive sample, which might not be as true for the HIV seronegative men who are at less immediate risk.

We were also interested in identifying factors that specifically predict suicide intent, as compared with general distress symptoms, among HIV seropositive men. Unique predictors of suicidal thinking might define factors that determine the bend toward suicidal thinking within distressed individuals. Alternatively, unique predictors of suicide intent may define factors or situations that give rise to suicidal thinking in the absence of extreme distress. Such suicidal thoughts may reflect successful efforts at mastering otherwise uncontrollable existential threats, such as the threat of developing AIDS. As Neitzche observed, "The thought of suicide is a great consolation, by means of it, one gets successfully through many a bad night." Suicidal thoughts may help some HIV seropositive men continue to function in the face of severe threat with less distress than would otherwise be true. If this is true, suicidal thoughts may be a coping-related, as opposed to a distress-related, response for at least some HIV seropositive men. As such, we expected that AIDS-related stressors might predict suicide intent more strongly than current distress symptoms in HIV seropositive men.

Our analyses centered on the 212 NHAPS participants (27% of the NHAPS sample of 798) who reported suicidal ideation over the past 6 months. The sample was similar demographically to the MACS sample from which they were recruited. The mean age of the subjects experiencing suicidal ideation was 36.5 years, 93% were White, 58% had a college education, and approximately 50% were HIV seropositive. Levels of suicide intent provided a continuous dependent measure that represents the degree of seriousness in contemplated action aimed at ending one's own life (Beck et al., 1973). This continuous dependent measure allowed us to employ causal modeling. A dichotomous dependent measure of presence versus absence of suicidal ideation would not have afforded us the opportunity. Thus, nonideators were eliminated from the models, as their inclusion would have greatly disturbed the distribution of the suicide intent measure, because most subjects (73%) scored "0."

Variables included in the models were operationalized as follows. *AIDS-Related Events* included receipt of a positive HIV antibody test result or an ARC diagnosis; current illness of a long-term committed partner with AIDS or ARC; number of close friends who have an AIDS or ARC diagnosis; death of a long-term committed partner; and number of deaths among close friends. *Biologic AIDS Risk* was assessed by the percent of CD4 helper/inducer and CD8 suppressor/cytotoxic T cells, HIV antibody test status, and slope reflecting declines in absolute numbers of CD4 T cells. Low numbers of CD4 cells as well as steeper slopes of declining CD4 cells are established predictors of AIDS (Detels et al., 1987; Fahey et al., 1987). High CD8 cell counts are predictive of more steeply declining CD4 cell levels (Munoz et al., 1988). *Loneliness* was measured via the UCLA Loneliness Scale, and *Perceived AIDS Risk* was assessed by three questions assessing personal risk of developing AIDS. *Current Confidant Support* was assessed by a single question. *Past Depressive Symptoms* were assessed by three earlier administrations (each 6 months apart and beginning as early as 4 years prior to current measures) of the Center for Epidemiologic Studies Depression Scale (CES-D; Radloff, 1977) and *Past Confidant Support* was assessed similarly by three earlier administrations of the confidant question. *Current Distress Symptoms* were assessed by the CES-D (Radloff, 1977), the Hope-

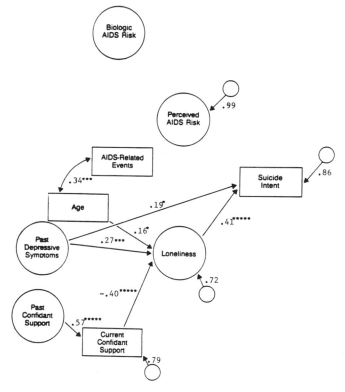

FIG. 11.1. Significant ($p < .05$) regression paths and correlations from HIV–suicide ideators. Regression paths are represented by a single-headed arrow. A double-headed arrow represents a correlation or covariance. By convention, latent factors are represented by circles (as are error terms), and manifest variables are represented by rectangles. Significance levels: *$p < .05$; ***$p < .001$; *****$p < .00001$. Pathways predicting Current Distress Symptoms are not shown.

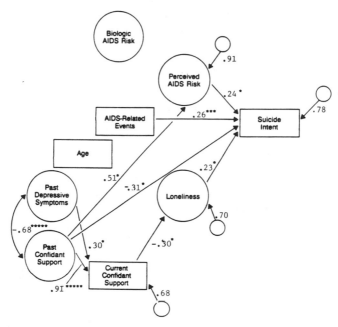

FIG. 11.2. Significant ($p < .05$) regression paths and correlations from HIV+ suicide ideators. Regression paths are represented by a single-headed arrow. A double-headed arrow represents a correlation or covariance. By convention, latent factors are represented by circles (as are error terms), and manifest variables are represented by rectangles. Significance levels: *$p < .05$; ***$p < .001$; *****$p < .00001$. Pathways predicting Current Distress Symptoms are not shown.

lessness Scale (Beck et al., 1974), and the Profile of Mood States (McNair et al., 1971). *Suicide Intent* was measured by a self-report inventory based on the Scale for Suicide Ideation (Beck, Kovacs, & Weissman, 1979; see Schneider, 1989, for validity and reliability information on this measure).

Separate models were constructed for the HIV seropositive and HIV seronegative suicidal ideator subgroups. A best-fit group solution was obtained by dropping regression paths and correlations that were very weak in either group.[7] The chi square for this two-group solution strongly supported the model: $X^2(373, n = 112, \text{HIV}-; n = 100, \text{HIV}+) = 363.37, p = .63$. The Bentler-Bonnet Normed Fit Index was adequate: NFI = .88. The relation of the predictor variables to suicide intent are represented diagrammatically in Fig. 11.1 (HIV seronegative men) and Fig. 11.2 (HIV seropositive men). Only significant path-

---

[7]To improve fit, significant correlations among 10 pairs of error terms were added to the HIV– model, and an inequality constraint was imposed on one error term; significant correlations among 13 pairs of error terms were added to the HIV+ model, and the variances of one pair of error terms were constrained to be equal.

ways ($p < .05$) are shown. Neither Current Distress nor pathways predicting to that construct are shown, as our focus is on the prediction of Suicide Intent.

HIV Seronegative Men. As can be seen in Fig. 11.1, among the HIV seronegative subjects, Past Depressive Symptoms ($r = .19$, $p < .05$) and Loneliness (.41, $p < .00001$) alone predict Suicide Intent directly. AIDS-Related Events, Perceived AIDS Risk, and Biologic AIDS Risk did not predict Suicide Intent either directly or indirectly through a mediating factor.

Loneliness is significantly predicted by higher Age (.16, $p < .05$), Past Depressive Symptoms (.27, $p < .001$), and Current Confidant Support ($-.40$, $p < .00001$). Current Confidant Support is predicted mostly by Past Confidant Support (.57, $p > .00001$). Finally, there is a significant correlation between Age and AIDS-Related Events (.34, $p < .001$).

HIV Seropositive Men. In contrast to the HIV seronegative subjects, among whom AIDS-Related Events and Perceived AIDS Risk explained little variance, both AIDS-Related Events (.26, $p < .001$) and Perceived AIDS Risk (.24, $p < .05$) are significant predictors of Suicide Intent (see Fig. 11.2). Surprisingly, as in the model for HIV seronegative men, Biologic AIDS Risk does not predict Suicide Intent. Past Confidant Support ($-.31$, $p < .05$) and Loneliness (.23, $p < .05$) are additional significant predictors of Suicide Intent. A larger percentage of the variance in Suicide Intent is accounted for among these HIV seropositive (39%) compared to the HIV seronegative (26%) subjects.

Loneliness is significantly predicted by Current Confidant Support ($-.30$, $p < .05$), and Perceived AIDS Risk is significantly predicted by Past Confidant Support ($-.51$, $p < .01$). Contrary to expectations, however, Perceived AIDS Risk is not predicted by Biologic AIDS Risk in either model. Current Confidant Support is predicted by both Past Confidant Support (.91, $p < .000001$) and Past Depressive Symptoms (.30, $p < .05$). Finally, there is a significant correlation between Past Depressive Symptoms and Past Confidant Support ($-.68$, $p < .00001$).

Comparison Between HIV Seropositive and HIV Seronegative Models. Direct comparisons of the paths in the two models indicated that Perceived AIDS Risk and AIDS-Related Events were significantly more powerful predictors of Suicidal Intent among HIV seropositive than HIV seronegative ideators. We had also predicted that current psychological functioning and adaptation among HIV seropositive ideators would be more highly predicted by predisposing factors than would be true for HIV seronegative ideators. Consistent with this hypothesis, Past Confidant Support was a significantly more powerful predictor of Suicidal Intent among the HIV seropositive than the HIV seronegative ideators, and a significantly more powerful predictor of Perceived AIDS Risk and Current Confidant Support. In addition, Past Depressive Symptoms were more strongly correlated with Past Confidant Support and were a more powerful predictor of Current Confidant Support among the HIV seropositive than among the HIV seronegative ideators.

DISTINGUISHING SUICIDE INTENT FROM GENERAL DISTRESS

To explore factors specifically predictive of suicide intent as opposed to current general distress, all pathways predicting Suicide Intent were compared to all pathways predicting Current Distress (not shown in Fig. 11.2) among the HIV seropositive suicide ideators. We had predicted that AIDS-Related Stressors would be more powerfully predictive of suicide intent than Current Distress. Chi-square difference tests were employed to examine this hypothesis. Overall goodness of fit for the best-fitting, one group, HIV seropositive model was adequate: X^2 (179, $n = 100$) = 2.0854, $p < .07$, NFI = 87.4). In terms of specific predictors, AIDS-Related Events was a significantly stronger predictor of suicide intent than Current Distress ($p < .005$), as was Past Confidant Support ($p < .03$). Perceived AIDS Risk, Loneliness, and Past Depressive Symptoms did not discriminate between the two outcome variables. Biologic AIDS Risk unexpectedly predicted neither outcome. In summary, then, as predicted, AIDS-related stressors were more powerfully predictive of suicide intent than current distress among the HIV seropositive men.

Overall, the results indicate that suicide intent is predicted by different factors, depending on whether one tests positive or negative for the antibodies to AIDS virus. Among HIV seronegative ideators, traditional predictors, such as past depression and loneliness, predicted suicide intent. Among HIV seropositive ideators, these traditional predictors were related to suicidal intent, but long-standing, stable, possibly depression-linked patterns of social isolation were more powerful predictors of suicide intent, as were current AIDS-related stressors. Biological indices of AIDS risk were not predictive of suicide intent, indicating, along with other studies (e.g., Kessler et al., 1988), the primacy of psychological, rather than biological, pathways to social and emotional impairment among HIV seropositive, asymptomatic men. That lack of past confidant support emerges as a specific predictor of suicide supports the strong role of long-standing social isolation in determining the bent toward suicide (e.g., Durkheim, 1952; Trout, 1980). That AIDS-related events predicted suicide intent, but not distress symptoms, indicates that such suicidal thoughts in reaction to these events may have constituted some form of cognitive coping. That is, they may have served to alleviate, rather than reflect, substantial distress.

Theoretically, such a view is possible. In view of severe and uncontrollable threats posed by AIDS, suicidal thoughts may serve the function of mastery (e.g., Taylor, 1983). In asymptomatic HIV seropositive persons, considering the option of suicide in the relative absence of distress and hopelessness may assist an individual in continuing to function with a greater sense of control in the face of such a severe threat. The following comments by one suicidal participant illustrates such coping:

> My suicidal thoughts were centered around what I would do if I developed AIDS. Suicide would be an option. A close friend of 32 years (he is now 35) is dying of KS (Kaposi's sarcoma). I try to imagine what I would do in his circumstances. This leads me to suicidal thoughts. . . . I guess I would do it if there was no other option and I was in a lot of pain. . . . I think that thinking about suicide alternatives is a way for me to cope, or deal with the "what I would do" question, if I were to develop AIDS.

The idea that suicidal thoughts can serve an adaptive or coping function has been relatively unexplored in the research literature. In suggesting that suicidal thoughts can sometimes be coping related, we are not advocating this as a coping strategy, nor are we suggesting that it is necessarily more effective than other ways of coping. Do suicidal thoughts offer greater benefit than social support, joining a church, taking drugs, mobilizing positive illusions, or denying threatening events? This is unlikely to be the case, at least under all conditions. For certain types of individuals who hold certain beliefs or construe the world in certain ways, and under certain compelling circumstances (e.g., the presence of a severe future threat that seems inevitable, uncontrollable, and unacceptable), suicidal thoughts may assist coping. However, such thoughts may not assist coping in other types of people or under other circumstances. Our point is merely that suicidal thoughts are not always a cry for help or a desperate move toward surcease. Sometimes, they may be an effort to make the present more liveable and more bearable. They may allow one to live more fully in the face of a future threat that one feels unable to face. Persons entertaining suicidal thoughts may not, on the whole, be less distressed or be coping better than those who do not entertain suicidal thoughts. However, not all suicidal thoughts need be distress-linked. Not all call for intervention. In fact, some may serve as the intervention. The relationship between coping and distress-related suicidal thoughts is, thus, complex and demands further investigation.

What are the treatment implications of such findings? Clearly, clinical interventions need to address long-standing social isolation or depression that may fuel both high perceived AIDS risk and high levels of suicide intent, particularly in HIV seropositive men. That is, interventions should focus not only on current AIDS-related psychosocial circumstances, but also on more long-standing, perhaps personality-related propensities to isolate the self or to become depressed in the face of such a highly stressful event. Second, the assumption that distress symptoms and suicide intent are linked to biological AIDS risk and are entirely reliant on a rational assessment of AIDS risk is unwarranted in view of these data. Psychological adaptation to HIV infection is complex and may be determined by past social isolation and depression, AIDS-related events, perceived AIDS risk, and loneliness. Psychosocial interventions, accordingly, must also be complex, based on a thorough understanding of the factors that may contribute to the current state of distress. Finally, suicidal ideation should not be taken as an unambiguous sign of psychological distress that warrants intervention. Non-distress-related suicidal ideation among the HIV seropositive men may be instead coping-related, reflecting efforts at gaining cognitive mastery over an otherwise uncontrollable threat.

GENERAL CONCLUSIONS

The AIDS crisis has created an intensely stressful situation for gay men, challenging them in virtually every aspect of life. These men face the death of a lifestyle, multiple bereavements, fear, and anxiety over their own health status, and often debilitating disease and the likelihood of premature death. Such intensely stressful events clearly evoke a multitude of coping strategies to deal with different aspects of the AIDS spectre.

Among the foremost accommodations these men must make are changes in health practices, especially risk-related sexual behaviors. Our results suggest that many men have successfully modified their behavior and that their behavior is responsive to the perceptions that guide the practice of other health behaviors, namely perceived risk, perceived response efficacy, and perceived self-efficacy. However, there is a small subpopulation of HIV seropositive men without partners who have either high perceived risk or little sense of response efficacy and, consequently, appear to have increased their practice of potentially risky sexual behavior. Whether these behaviors are undertaken primarily with other HIV seropositive men is currently unknown. Helping these men manage their perceptions of risk and stressing the importance of risk reduction among people who are already HIV seropositive may be important areas for intervention.

Clearly, being HIV seropositive is a more stressful event than being HIV seronegative. Consistent with this fact, HIV seropositive men reported using a broader range of coping strategies than seronegative men. The relation of multiple coping strategies to psychological distress, however, was unexpectedly positive. This suggests that, although the use of multiple coping strategies may be an effort to control distress, it may not yet have been a successful means of so doing.

The HIV seropositive men reported a greater use of positive attitudes and avoidance of thoughts of AIDS. These strategies may be particularly common in the context of uncontrollable stressors such as the development of AIDS in a person who is HIV seropositive. Relations between the coping strategies used and psychological distress were also found. Those who used active cognitive coping strategies showed less psychological distress than those who coped using fatalistic and avoidant strategies. These findings are consistent with the previous literature documenting the importance of active coping for managing the demands of a chronic stressor. The use of these active coping strategies would seem to be at least somewhat successful, inasmuch as the seropositive men do not differ from the seronegative men in terms of degree of distress experienced.

Finally, we considered suicidal intent, which was predicted by divergent processes in HIV seropositive and HIV seronegative suicide ideators. In the face of the great adaptive demands of being HIV seropositive, it appears as though overall adaptation is more strongly determined by long-standing propensities to self-isolate or to become depressed in the face of stress. In addition, among HIV seropositive men, suicide intent was more strongly organized around AIDS-related stressors. Finally, among HIV seropositive men, suicidal thoughts in response to AIDS-related stress were not distress-linked. This suggests that suicidal ideation may have served as a coping strategy. Thus, among the arsenal of coping strategies these men use to manage the otherwise uncontrollable, severe future threat of AIDS, the thought that one may end one's suffering at a time of one's choice may enhance one's successful adaptation to the future.

A few cautions should be introduced when interpreting the results of these studies. First, these relationships were uncovered in a large sample of urban gay men, and may not generalize to other populations at risk for AIDS, such as IV drug users or sexually active heterosexual adults. It should also be noted that findings from this and any other study of AIDS-related behaviors may not generalize to risk-reduction behavior for other illnesses, because of the high levels of perceived illness severity reported by the sample. Despite these cautions, the results suggest a number of theoretical points, as well as bases for intervention that may be undertaken in order to ameliorate the risk and stressfulness of HIV infection and the concomittant likelihood of AIDS.

ACKNOWLEDGMENTS

The research described in this chapter and preparation of the chapter were supported by a grant from the National Institute of Mental Health to the first and second authors (MH 42918) and by a grant from the National Institute of Allergy and Infectious Diseases (NO1-A1-72631). The first and second authors were supported by NIMH Research Scientist Development Awards (MH 00311 and MH 00820, respectively). The third author was partially supported by an NIMH Training Grant (MH 15750). The fourth author was supported alternately by a National Science Foundation Graduate Fellowship and by an NIMH Training Grant (MH 15750).

REFERENCES

Aspinwall, L. G., Kemeny, M. E., Taylor, S. E., Schneider, S. G., & Dudley, J. P. (1991). Psychosocial predictors of gay men's AIDS risk-reduction behavior. *Health Psychology, 10*, 432–444.

Aspinwall, L. G., & Taylor, S. E. (in press). Modeling cognitive adaptation: A longitudinal investigation of the impact of individual differences and coping on college adjustment and performance. *Journal of Personality and Social Psychology.*

Bandura, A. (1977). Self-efficacy: Toward a unifying theory of behavioral change. *Psychological Review, 84*, 191–215.

Bandura, A. (1986). *Social foundations of thought and action: A social cognitive theory.* Englewood Cliffs, NJ: Prentice-Hall.

Bandura, A. (in press). Perceived self-efficacy in the exercise of control over AIDS infection. In S. J. Blumenthal, A. Eichler, & G. Weissman (Eds.), *Women and AIDS.* Washington, DC: American Psychiatric Press.

Beck, A. T., Davis, J. H., Frederick, C. J., Perlin, S., Pokorny, A., Schulman, R. E., Seiden, R. H., & Wittlin, B. J. (1973). Classification and nomenclature. In H. L. P. Resnick & B. C. Hathorne (Eds.), *Suicide prevention in the seventies* (pp. 7–12). Washington, DC: Department of Health, Education, and Welfare.

Beck, A. T., Kovacs, M., & Weissman, A. (1979). Assessment of suicidal intention: The scale for suicide ideation. *Journal of Consulting and Clinical Psychology*, 343–352.

Beck, A. T., Weissman, A., Lester, D., & Trexler, L. (1974). The measurement of pessimism: The hopelessness scale. *Journal of Consulting and Clinical Psychology, 42*, 861–865.

Becker, M. H., & Joseph, J. G. (1988). AIDS and behavioral change to reduce risk: A review. *American Journal of Public Health, 78*, 394–410.

Chmiel, J. S., Detels, R., Kaslow, R. A., van Raden, M., Kingsley, L. A., Brookmeyer, R., & The Multicenter AIDS Cohort Study Group. (1987). Factors associated with prevalent Human Immunodeficiency Virus (HIV) infection in the Multicenter AIDS Cohort Study. *American Journal of Epidemiology, 126*, 568–577.

Coates, T. J., McKusick, L., Kuno, R., & Stites, D. P. (1989). Stress reduction training changed number of sexual partners but not immune function in men with HIV. *American Journal of Public Health, 79*, 885–887.

Cohen, F., & Lazarus, R. (1979). Coping with the stresses of illness. In G. C. Stone, F. Cohen, & N. E. Adler (Eds.), *Health psychology: A handbook* (pp. 77–112). San Francisco: Jossey-Bass.

Cohen, S., & Wills, T. A. (1985). Stress, social support, and the buffering hypothesis. *Psychological Bulletin, 98*, 310–357.

Collins, R. L., Taylor, S. E., & Skokan, L. A. (1990). A better world or a shattered vision? Changes in perspectives following victimization. *Social Cognition 8*, 263–285.

Cronkite, R. C., & Moos, R. H. (1984). The role of predisposing and moderating factors in the stress-illness relationship. *Journal of Health and Social Behavior, 25*, 372–393.

Darrow, W. W., Echenberg, D. F., Jaffe, H. W., O'Malley, P. M., Byers, R. H., Getchell, J. P., & Curran, J. W. (1987). Risk factors for Human Immunodeficiency Virus (HIV) infections in homosexual men. *American Journal of Public Health, 77*, 479–483.

Detels, R., English, P., Visscher, B. R., Jacobson, L., Kingsley, L. A., Chmiel, J. S., Dudley, J. P., Eldred, L. J., & Ginzburg, H. (1989). Seroconversion, sexual activity, and condom use among 2915 HIV seronegative men followed for up to two years. *Journal of AIDS, 2*, 77–83.

Detels, R., Visscher, B. R., Fahey, J. L., Sever, J. L., Gravell, M., Madden, D. L., Schwartz, K., Dudley, J. P., English, P. A., & Powers, H. (1987). Predictors of clinical AIDS in young homosexual men in a high risk area. *International Journal of Epidemiology, 16*, 271–276.

Doll, L. S., O'Malley, P. M., Pershing, A. L., Darrow, W. W., Hessol, N. A., & Lifson, A. R. (1990). High-risk behavior and knowledge of HIV antibody status in the San Francisco City Clinic Cohort. *Health Psychology, 9*, 253–265.

Durkheim, E. (1952). *Suicide*. London: Routledge & Kegan Paul.

Fahey, J. L., Giorgi, J., Martinez-Maza, O., Detels, R., Mitsuyasu, R., & Or, J. (1987). Immune pathogenesis of AIDS and related syndromes. *Annals Institute Pasteur/Immunology, 138*, 245–252.

Farrer, L. A. (1985). Suicide and attempted suicide in Huntington's disease: Implications for preclinical testing of persons at risk. *American Journal of Medicine and Genetics, 24*, 305–311.

Felton, B. J. Revenson, T. A., & Hinrichsen, G. A. (1984). Stress and coping in the explanation of psychological adjustment among chronically ill adults. *Social Science and Medicine, 18*, 889–898.

Folkman, S., & Lazarus, R. S. (1980). An analysis of coping in a middle-aged community sample. *Journal of Health and Social Behavior, 21*, 219–239.

Folkman, S., Schaefer, C., & Lazarus, R. S. (1979). Cognitive processes as mediators of stress and coping. In V. Hamilton & D. M. Warburton (Eds.), *Human stress and cognition: An information processing approach* (pp. 265–298). London, England: Wiley.

Fox, R., Odaka, N., Brookmeyer, R., & Polk, B. F. (1987). Effect of HIV antibody disclosure on subsequent sexual activity in homosexual men. *AIDS, 1*, 241–246.

Francis, A., Fyre, M., & Clarkin, J. (1986). Personality and suicide. *Annals of the New York Academy of Sciences, 487*, 281–293.

Haenel, T. H., Brunner, F., & Battegay, R. (1980). Renal dialysis and suicide: Occurrence in Switzerland and in Europe. *Comparative Psychiatry, 21*, 140–145.

Holahan, C. J., & Moos, R. H. (1986). Personality, coping, and family resources in stress resistance: A longitudinal analysis. *Journal of Personality and Social Psychology, 51*, 389–395.

Holahan, C. J., & Moos, R. H. (1987). Risk, resistance, and psychological distress: A longitudinal analysis with adults and children. *Journal of Abnormal Psychology, 96*, 3–13.

Joseph, J. G., Montgomery, S. B., Emmons, C. -A., Kirscht, J. P., Kessler, R. C., Ostrow, D. G., Wortman, C. B., O'Brien, K., Eller, M., & Eschleman, S. (1987). Perceived risk of AIDS: Assessing the behavioral and psychological consequences in a cohort of gay men. *Journal of Applied Social Psychology, 17*, 231–250.

Kaloupek, D. G., & Stoupakis, T. (1985). Coping with a stressful medical procedure: Further investigation with volunteer blood donors. *Journal of Behavioral Medicine, 8*, 131–148.

Kaloupek, D. G., White, H., & Wong, M. (1984). Multiple assessment of coping strategies used by volunteer blood donors: Implications for preparatory training. *Journal of Behavioral Medicine, 7*, 35–60.

Kelly, J. A., St. Lawrence, J. S., Hood, H. V., & Brasfield, T. L. (1989). Behavioral intervention to reduce AIDS risk activities. *Journal of Consulting and Clinical Psychology, 57*, 60–67.

Kemeny, M. E., Taylor, S. E., Schneider, S. G., Rodriguez, R., Herbert, M., & Dudley, J. (1990). *Threat, coping, and psychological state among men at risk for AIDS*. Manuscript submitted for publication.

Kessler, R. C., O'Brien, K., Joseph, J. G., Ostrow, D. G., Phair, J. P., Chmiel, J. S., Wortman, C. B., & Emmons, C. (1988). Effects of HIV infection, perceived health and clinical status on a cohort at risk for AIDS. *Social Science and Medicine, 27*, 569–578.

Kiyak, H. A., Vitaliano, P. P., & Crinean, J. (1988). Patients' expectations as predictors of orthognathic surgery outcomes. *Health Psychology, 7*, 251–268.

Kizer, K. W., Green, M., Perkins, C. I., Doebbert, G., & Hughes, M. J. (1988). AIDS and suicide in California [letter]. *Journal of the American Medical Association, 260*, 1881.

Klein, D. E., Sullivan, G., Wolcott, D. L., Landsverk, J., Namir, S., & Fawzy, F. I. (1987). Changes in AIDS risk behaviors among homosexual male physicians and university students. *American Journal of Psychiatry, 144*, 742–747.

Lazarus, R. S., & Folkman, S. (1984). *Stress, appraisal, and coping*. New York: Springer.

Lazarus, R. S., & Folkman, S. (in press). Coping and adaptation. In W. D. Gentry (Ed.), *The handbook of behavioral medicine*. New York: Guilford.

Leventhal, H., & Nerenz, D. R. (1982). A model for stress research and some implications for the control of stress disorders. In D. Meichenbaum & M. Jaremko (Eds.), *Stress prevention and management: A cognitive behavioral approach.* (pp. 5–38). New York: Plenum.

Louhivuori, K. A., & Hakama, M. (1979). Risk of suicide among cancer patients. *American Journal of Epidemiology, 109,* 59–65.

Marshall, J., Burnett, W., & Brashure, J. (1983). On precipitating factors: Cancer as a cause of suicide. *Suicide and Life-Threatening Behavior, 13,* 15–27.

Martin, J. L. (1986). AIDS risk reduction recommendations and sexual behavior patterns among gay men: A multifactorial categorical approach to assessing change. *Health Education Quarterly, 13,* 347–358.

Martin, J. L. (1987). The impact of AIDS on gay male sexual behavior patterns in New York City. *American Journal of Public Health, 77,* 578–581.

Mazurk, P. M., Tierney, H., Tarfidd, K., Gross, E. M., Morgan, E. B., Hsu, M. A., & Mann, J. G. (1988). Increased risk of suicide in persons with AIDS. *Journal of the American Medical Association, 259,* 1332–1333.

McCusker, J., Zapka, J. G., Stoddard, A. M., & Mayer, K. H. (1989). Responses to the AIDS epidemic among homosexually active men: Factors associated with preventive behavior. *Patient Education and Counseling, 13,* 15–30.

McKusick, L., Coates, T. J., Morin, S. F., Pollack, L., & Hoff, C. (1989). *Longitudinal predictors of reductions in unprotected anal intercourse among gay men in San Francisco: The AIDS Behavioral Research Project.* Manuscript submitted for publication.

McKusick, L., Horstman, W., & Coates, T. J. (1985). AIDS and sexual behavior reported by gay men in San Francisco. *American Journal of Public Health, 75,* 493–496.

McKusick, L., Wiley, J. A., Coates, T. J., Stall, R., Saika, G., Morin, S., Charles, K., Horstman, W., & Conant, M. A. (1985). Reported changes in the sexual behavior of men at risk for AIDS, San Francisco, 1982–84—the AIDS Behavioral Research Project. *Public Health Reports, 100,* 622–629.

McNair, D. M., Lorr, M., & Droppleman, L. F. (1971). *Profile of mood states.* San Diego: Educational and Industrial Testing Service.

Munoz, A., Carey, V., Saah, A. J., Phair, J. P., Kingsley, L. A., Fahey, J. L., Ginzburg, H. M., & Polk, B. F. (1988). Predictors of decline in CH4 lymphocytes in a cohort of homosexual men infected with human immuno deficiency virus. *Journal of Acquired Immune Deficiency Syndromes, 1,* 396–404.

Paykel, E. S., Prusoff, B. A., & Myers, J. K. (1975). Suicide attempts and recent life events. *Archives of General Psychiatry, 32,* 327–333.

Pearlin, L. I., & Schooler, C. (1978). The structure of coping. *Journal of Health and Social Behavior, 19,* 2–21.

Quinn, M. E., Fontana, A. F., & Reznikoff, M. (1987). Psychological distress in reaction to lung cancer as a function of spousal support and coping strategy. *Journal of Psychosocial Oncology, 4,* 79–90.

Radloff, L. S. (1977). The CES-D scale: A self-report depression scale for research in the general population. *Journal of Applied Psychological Measurement, 1,* 385–401.

Reisenberg, D. E. (1986). AIDS-prompted behavior changes reported. *Journal of the American Medical Association, 255,* 171–176.

Rogers, R. W. (1975). A protection motivation theory of fear appeals and attitude change. *The Journal of Psychology, 91,* 93–114.

Rogers, R. W. (1984). Changing health-related attitudes and behavior: The role of preventive health psychology. In J. H. Harvey, J. E. Maddux, R. P. McGlynn, & C. D. Stoltenberg (Eds.), *Social perception in clinical and counseling psychology* (Vol. 2, pp. 91–112). Lubbock, TX: Texas Tech University Press.

Rosenstock, I. M. (1974). Historical origins of the health belief model. *Health Education Monographs, 2,* 1–8.

Schneider, S. G. (1989). *Suicidal ideation in gay and bisexual men as predicted by AIDS-related life stressors, social support, and pre-existing chronic depression*. Los Angeles: University of California.

Schneider, S. G., Taylor, S. E., Kemeny, M., Hammen, C., & Dudley, J. (1991). Factors influencing suicide intent in gay and bisexual suicide ideators: Differing models for HIV+ and HIV− men. *Journal of Personality and Social Psychology, 16*, 776–788.

Schoenfeld, M., Myers, R. H., Cupples, L. A., Berkman, B., Sax, D. S., & Clark, E. (1984). Increased rate of suicide among patients with Huntington's disease. *Journal of Neurology, Neurosurgery, and Psychiatry, 47*, 1283–1287.

Siegel, K., Mesagno, F. P., Chen, J. -Y., & Crist, G. (1989). Factors distinguishing homosexual males practicing risky and safer sex. *Social Science and Medicine, 28*, 561–569.

Slater, J., & Depue, R. A. (1981). The contribution of environmental events and social support to serious suicide attempts in primary depressive disorder. *Journal of Abnormal Psychology, 90*, 275–285.

Stall, R. D., Coates, T. J., & Hoff, C. (1988). Behavioral risk reduction for HIV infection among gay and bisexual men: A review of results from the United States. *American Psychologist, 43*, 878–885.

Suls, J., & Fletcher, B. (1985). The relative efficacy of avoidant and nonavoidant coping strategies: A meta-analysis. *Health Psychology, 4*, 249–288.

Taylor, S. E. (1983). Adjustment to threatening events: A theory of cognitive adaptation. *American Psychologist, 41*, 1161–1173.

Taylor, S. E., Kemeny, M., Aspinwall, L. G., Schneider, S. C., Rodriguez, R., & Herbert, M. (1992). Optimism, coping, psychological distress, and high-risk sexual behavior among men at risk for AIDS. *Journal of Personality and Social Psychology, 63*, 460–473.

Trout, D. (1980). The role of social isolation in suicide. *Suicide and Life-Threatening Behavior, 10*, 10–23.

Wayment, H. A., Silver, R. C., & Kemeny, M. E. (1990). *Spared at random: Survivor reactions in the gay community*. Manuscript submitted for publication.

Weisman, A. D., & Worden, J. W. (1976–1977). The existential plight in cancer: Significance of the first 100 days. *International Journal of Psychiatry Medicine, 7*, 1–15.

Wong, M., & Kaloupek, D. G. (1986). Coping with dental treatment: The potential impact of situational demands. *Journal of Behavioral Medicine, 9*, 579–598.

12

The Psychology of Volunteerism: A Conceptual Analysis and a Program of Action Research

Allen M. Omoto
University of Kansas

Mark Snyder
University of Minnesota

James P. Berghuis
University of Kansas

> *A society is judged by how well it responds in times of greatest need.*
> —Admiral James D. Watkins (1988), Chair, Presidential Commission on the Human Immunodeficiency Virus Epidemic

> *There is nothing so practical as a good theory.*
> —Kurt Lewin (1951)

These two assertions highlight what we believe to be critical considerations for basic and applied research on the social and psychological aspects of the HIV (i.e., the human immunodeficiency virus that causes AIDS) epidemic. The HIV epidemic presents numerous challenges, both to individuals and to society at large, the responses to which have implications not only for how judgment will be passed on society and its responses to these challenges, but also for the long-term effects of HIV on U.S. society and all of its members. In this chapter, we examine one of society's most creative and important responses to the HIV epidemic—the phenomenon of *AIDS volunteerism*—and do so in ways that illustrate the potential contributions of basic theory and research in personality and social psychology to addressing the practical problems of society.

To set the stage for our discussion, let us introduce you to Oscar and Monika:

> Oscar, a 39-year-old Costa Rican emigré and former airline purser, thought he would share little in common with Monika, an entrepreneur and Bavarian native, when they were introduced . . . .
>
> But after several lengthy phone conversations and a couple of informal lunches, the two quickly formed a close friendship—strangers who were brought together by the most unlikely of matchmakers. AIDS.

Oscar, who was diagnosed with acquired immunodeficiency syndrome in 1986, was introduced to Monika, a volunteer with the San Diego AIDS Project, through the project's Buddy System. The buddy program matches volunteers with AIDS patients in hopes of providing the patient with a companion who will help fill the loneliness associated with the terminal disease.

For Oscar, the new-found friendship ended four years of excruciating seclusion . . . .

Abandoned by some of his friends, and scorned and pitied by others . . . [Oscar found that] "Monika has really changed my life,". . . "[she] has filled out the empty space and I no longer feel lonely. . . . We solve our problems together and I know she's there."

And the relationship is far from one-sided . . . .

[Monika has discovered that] "this really works both ways. When something happens, Oscar is so positive. He really picks me up . . . .

I've led a full and interesting life, but I felt like I hadn't done much to give back what I had received. I wanted to find something where I could make a difference in someone's life, so I volunteered." ("Friends indeed," 1990, pp. B1–B2)

Although Oscar and Monika may seem to be an unlikely pair to have become friends, and such close friends at that, their relationship is hardly an isolated curiosity. Increasingly, a critical component of society's response to the HIV epidemic has been the development of community-based grass-roots organizations of *volunteers* involved in caring for persons living with AIDS (PWAs) and in educating the public about HIV, AIDS, and PWAs. For example, some volunteers (like Monika), provide emotional and social support as "buddies" to PWAs (like Oscar), whereas other volunteers may provide direct services to PWAs in the form of help with household chores or transportation needs. Among the educational services provided by volunteers are the staffing of AIDS information, counseling, and referral hotlines, as well as volunteer assignments that involve public speaking, informational presentations, fund raising, and legal advocacy. In the face of a profound public health crisis, then, groups of ordinary citizens have organized and banded together to begin to meet the great needs and extraordinary challenges posed by HIV. In the United States, AIDS volunteer programs have emerged in every state, in cities large and small, and in rural areas as well. Indeed, it has been observed that "one of the most remarkable and heartening byproducts of the HIV epidemic . . . has been the development of grass-roots organizations [of volunteers] dedicated to serving the needs of people with AIDS" (Fineberg, 1989, p. 117). With neither a vaccine or a cure for AIDS in sight, and with AIDS no longer a disease restricted to certain so-called "high-risk" groups, it is clear that the full impact of HIV, as devastating and profound as it already has been, has yet to be felt, and will touch all segments of the population. It is also clear that volunteers and volunteer organizations will continue to play integral roles in society's response to the HIV epidemic.

As striking as the emergence of AIDS volunteerism is, the fact is that these volunteers are part of a much larger and a much more pervasive social phenomenon in U.S. society. A recent Gallup Poll on the prevalence of volunteerism estimated that, in 1989, 98.4 million American adults engaged in some form of volunteerism, with 25.6 million giving 5 or more hours per week to volunteer work (Independent Sector, 1990). Volunteerism, by its very nature, is prosocial action, involving people devoting substantial amounts of their time and energy to aiding and comforting others, often doing so for extended periods of time and at considerable personal cost.

The tradition of people offering assistance to others, in fact, is an enduring fixture of American culture (Chambré, 1989). From settlers on the prairie who helped one another to clear land, build roads, raise barns, and construct houses to organizations formed in response to community needs, such as orphaned children, isolated elderly, the mentally ill, fire protection, and health epidemics, United States citizens have long committed themselves to self-help and citizen involvement. In many ways, volunteers have been innovators and risk-takers, and countless new programs have been developed in response to changing community needs. And, indeed, even the political landscape of the United States has been shaped by volunteer movements aimed at issues such as abolishing slavery, establishing civil liberties and women's rights, and advocating for peace and the preservation of natural resources. Today's volunteers—whether they provide tutoring to the illiterate, home services to the shut in, companionship to the lonely, or support services to PWAs—carry on the tradition of citizens in service to others. Finally, the tradition of volunteer involvement and civic participation is very much a part of the political ideology of this country, or at least of its rhetoric. Every president from Kennedy to Bush, in accepting the nomination of his party or in his inaugural address to the nation, stressed the importance of citizen involvement and of doing good deeds and good works (Chambré, 1989), albeit from the vantage point of differing political perspectives.

Not only is the spirit of volunteer involvement woven into the psychological and ideological fabric of the U.S. culture, but volunteerism also provides direct and tangible benefits to society. Volunteers, after all, donate potentially valuable services. In economic terms, volunteers are workers in all but salary, producing goods and services that contribute to the functioning of society. In 1989, it is estimated that adults in the United States contributed volunteer services worth approximately $170 billion, teen-agers another $4.4 billion, and senior citizens an additional $35 billion (Independent Sector, 1990). When it comes to volunteers providing services related to the HIV epidemic, it is estimated that AIDS volunteers in Seattle alone provided over 70,000 hours of services just in the year 1987 (General Accounting Office, 1989). And, in fact, the costs of care for PWAs are greatly reduced in areas with active volunteer and service programs (Hellinger, 1988). Thus, volunteerism not only directly benefits its recipients, but also the society in which it is embedded.

Not incidentally, volunteer work also may provide important social and psychological benefits to those who volunteer. For one, volunteerism promotes a sense of community spirit and civic solidarity. Volunteerism offers concrete evidence to people that they live in a kind and gentle world in which people often choose to "give something back" to society. Volunteer work may also change the self-image of the giver as well as people's perspectives on their own successes, failures, and lives in general. In fact, narrative accounts of the first-hand experiences of AIDS volunteers indicate that their work often proves to be psychologically moving and powerful, and is something that many claim has substantially and irrevocably changed their lives (Omoto & Snyder, 1989a). As a result of her work with Oscar, for example, Monika also seemed to experience feelings of personal fulfillment and to have developed a more optimistic outlook on her life and problems. Increased feelings of helpfulness, heightened self-esteem, and newly formed friendships are other benefits that volunteer work may offer to those who do it (see King, Walder, & Pavey, 1970; Scheibe, 1965).

Ironically, however, in the specific case of AIDS, volunteers may also find themselves punished for their good deeds. That is, they may find themselves "judged by the company they keep" and stigmatized because of the stereotyped beliefs and prejudicial attitudes associated with AIDS and PWAs (Herek & Glunt, 1988; Katz et al., 1987; Pryor, Reeder, Vinacco, & Kott, 1989). Although we do not know whether Monika actually experienced such stigmatizing reactions, others who participated in her volunteer program did, including Koosed, who had to overcome her husband's initial resistance to her participation in the buddy program, and Beth, who hid her volunteer work from some of her longtime friends because she thought they would disapprove of her friendship with a PWA ("Friends indeed," 1990). Thus, when it comes to AIDS volunteerism, it is important to recognize that, although it provides numerous opportunities for reward, it also presents real and potentially injurious costs to those who make the commitment to offer their time, assistance, and expertise.

As we have outlined, then, volunteerism has a rich and storied tradition in U.S. ideology and culture. Moreover, the practical benefits of volunteerism are considerable, whether those benefits accrue to volunteers, to the recipients of their services, or to society at large. Over and above these practical matters, however, the study of volunteerism has strong links to many of the questions traditionally asked by personality and social psychologists. Indeed, the study of helping has long been a mainstay of theory and research for personologists and social psychologists. Its attraction to researchers most likely stems from its obvious practical relevance and its promise of revealing whether or not there is a truly altruistic side of human nature. The HIV epidemic, and the volunteers in service to PWAs it has spawned, present a particularly intriguing and relevant context for investigating individual and collective helping behavior (with especial emphasis on the processes of helping and being helped in the real world) and, more generally, the nature of human relationships.

In the context of these theoretical concerns, we should note that much of the psychological literature on helping behavior has focused on situations in which potential helpers are exposed to unexpected opportunities to help and are required to quickly and immediately decide whether to offer assistance to a stranger (the classic example being the much studied "bystander intervention" situation; Latané & Darley, 1970). The helping that occurs in such situations is typically confined to relatively brief and limited periods of time, may or may not be particularly costly or risky, and generally entails no future contact between helper and recipient.

In contrast, many volunteer activities invoke different and additional considerations. In volunteerism, rather than spontaneously reacting to situations that confront them, people typically have actively sought out their opportunities to help. Rather than being pressed to make quick decisions about offering assistance, volunteers may have deliberated long and hard about whether or not to get involved, about the extent of their involvement, and about the degree to which different volunteer opportunities fit with their own personal constellation of needs, goals, and motivations. And, rather than limited, low-cost, and brief assistance, certain forms of volunteerism entail commitments to ongoing helping relationships that may extend over considerable periods of time and that may encompass sizable personal costs in terms of time, energy, expense, and social regard (see Clary & Snyder, 1991, for a review of psychological research on volunteer activity).

In so many ways, AIDS volunteers embody precisely these defining and characteristic features of volunteerism. In one survey (Omoto & Snyder, 1990), AIDS volunteers reported that they had actively sought out opportunities to be a volunteer (over 80% indicated that they had approached their AIDS organization on their own initiative in search of such opportunities); moreover, their involvement represents a substantial and recurring time commitment (on average, 4 hours per week) and one that extends over a considerable length of time (1½ years, on average, and often extending over several years); finally, they give of themselves in trying and stressful circumstances (spending time with PWAs involving direct confrontation with the tragic realities of serious illness and death) and doing so at some personal cost (with many reporting that they have been made to feel stigmatized as a result of their work as AIDS volunteers).

We note, too, that volunteerism is, at one and the same time, an individual and a collective phenomenon. It involves the activities of individual volunteers (with their own values, motivations, and experiences) and the collective context in which these efforts occur. That is, much volunteerism occurs in the context of organizations that recruit, train, and place volunteers—organizations that range in size and structure from informal social support networks and self-help groups, to local "grass-roots" community associations such as many AIDS projects, to national advocacy groups such as the Sierra Club, to international providers of social services such as the Red Cross.

For these reasons, voluntary helping relationships provide opportunities for studying the personal and social motivations that initially draw people to involve themselves in helping activities as well as the factors that influence their continuing involvement, commitment, and effectiveness. Volunteerism also provides an opportunity to study the organizational structures and processes that are involved when individuals take collective action in response to social problems and societal needs.

Perhaps because of the relatively recent emergence of AIDS volunteerism, there is very little in the way of a published literature, with what little of it there is tending to focus on reports of the development of volunteer programs and organizations (e.g., Arno, 1988; Dumont, 1989; Kayal, 1991; Lopez & Getzel, 1987; Williams, 1988), including a special issue of the journal *Nonprofit and Voluntary Sector Quarterly* (Vol. 20, No. 3, Fall 1991) devoted to "The Response of the Voluntary Sector to the AIDS Pandemic." Nevertheless, we believe that, in studying AIDS volunteerism, we have isolated a socially significant "real-world" laboratory in which psychological theories of individual and social behavior can be tested and refined. In our work, then, we aim to test hypotheses derived from basic theory in a naturally occurring context or, as suggested by others (e.g., McGuire, 1969), to make the best of both worlds, the theoretical and applied.

With a dual focus on applied and theoretical concerns, we believe that our program of research embodies the essential components of *action research* (Lewin, 1947), in which basic and applied research mutually and reciprocally inform and enrich one another. Although action research can take many forms, its very essence is the commitment to research as an integral component of social action (Chein, Cook, & Harding, 1948). As alluded to by Lewin (1951), psychological theories, if they are to be regarded as "good" ones, should ideally have practical value that can help them to illuminate problems of concern to society and to point the way toward solutions to these problems.

It is our conviction that psychological research guided by basic theories can help meet the challenges and needs presented by the HIV epidemic. With this faith, we have developed a conceptual model for understanding AIDS volunteerism, and have embarked on a program of action research guided by this conceptual framework. In the remainder of this chapter, then, we more fully detail the multistage, multilevel framework that guides our research. In addition, we provide illustrative data from our program of research on AIDS volunteerism that are relevant to particular facets of this conceptual model. In particular, we draw upon data from surveys that we have administered to samples of currently active volunteers working with community-based AIDS volunteer organizations. We also describe data from a 1-year follow-up of a subset of these volunteers in attempts to provide empirical illustrations of our conceptual analysis and our strategy of action research (see also, Omoto & Snyder, 1990; Snyder & Omoto, 1991b). We wish to emphasize at the outset, however, that this chapter reflects but one possible contribution of basic and applied research in personality and social psychology to understanding and coping with the HIV epidemic. As the other chapters in this volume illustrate, in fact, there are many other viable and valuable contributions to be made by psychological researchers and practitioners to issues related to HIV.

THREE STAGES OF THE VOLUNTEER PROCESS

In recognition of the potentially unique properties that define volunteerism as sustained, ongoing, and potentially costly helping behavior, we have developed a conceptual model that identifies three stages of what we refer to as the *volunteer process* (see Omoto & Snyder, 1990; Snyder & Omoto, 1992). This model, which is depicted in Fig. 12.1, specifies the psychological and behavioral features associated with each stage, and speaks to activity at three different levels of analysis: the organization, the individual volunteer, and the broader social system. Furthermore, this conceptual model outlines a process that we believe to be characteristic of volunteerism in general, and that is illustrated by our research that has focused on the specific case of AIDS volunteerism as exemplary of voluntary helping relationships.

In our conceptualization, the first stage of the volunteer process involves *antecedents* of volunteerism, and addresses the broad questions of "Who volunteers to do AIDS volunteer work and why do they volunteer?" The second stage concerns *experiences* of volunteers and the PWAs they work with, and the effects of AIDS volunteerism on the general treatment and coping processes. The third

LEVEL OF ANALYSIS	STAGES OF THE VOLUNTEER PROCESS			
	ANTECEDENTS	EXPERIENCES	CONSEQUENCES	
ORGANIZATION OR AGENCY	Recruitment of Volunteers Training	Job Assignment Volunteer Service	Length of Service	Reenlistment
INDIVIDUAL VOLUNTEER	Personality Demographics Personal History Motivations Psychological Functions	Relationship Development	Satisfaction Commitment Increased Knowledge Attitude Change	Motivations Psychological Functions
BROADER SOCIAL INFLUENCES	Recruitment of Volunteers	Effects of PWAs Treatment Process	Social Diffusion	Public Education AIDS Prevention

FIG. 12.1. Conceptual model of the volunteer process.

stage focuses on *consequences* of volunteerism, and is concerned with changes in attitudes, knowledge, and behavior that occur as a result of volunteer work in volunteers themselves, in the members of their immediate social networks, and in society at large. At each stage, relevant psychological theories and the evidence of basic research are helping us to frame our research questions. We hope that the answers to these questions, in turn, will have implications for addressing practical issues related to HIV, as well as for building bridges between basic research and practical application.

Stage I: Antecedents of AIDS Volunteerism

AIDS volunteerism usually occurs, first and foremost, in the context of community-based organizations. For these organizations, the antecedents stage of the volunteer process involves the recruitment of potential volunteers and their subsequent training. AIDS volunteerism entails many costs and presents formidable barriers (e.g., limits of time and energy, fear of AIDS and death, concerns about stigmatization), however, all of which may keep people from getting involved in it. The general questions at the antecedents stage are what motivates some people to volunteer to staff AIDS hotlines, be a "buddy" for a PWA, or serve as an advocate for AIDS-related issues, and what incentives are most effective in recruiting new volunteers?

Our conceptualization of the volunteer process suggests that answers to these questions can be found in the systematic consideration of the personality, experiential, and motivational characteristics of AIDS volunteers. Specifically, in our considerations of the antecedents stage of the volunteer process, we focus on individual differences between volunteers (including attitudes, values, and personality processes) and the personal and social needs that AIDS volunteer work may fulfill for individuals. In Monika's case, for example, AIDS volunteer work provided her with an opportunity to give something back to society and to "make a difference." Other volunteers may act in the service of other forms of motivation, and other sorts of volunteer work (e.g., volunteer work unrelated to AIDS) may require different personal characteristics and motivations to dispose people to get involved in them. In fact, in a survey of volunteers active in non-AIDS organizations, for instance, we found that rather pragmatic and *selfish* reasons (such as resumé building, feeling good about oneself, and gaining experience) were often cited as motivating their current work (Omoto & Snyder, 1989b). But, when asked to speculate on potential reasons for doing AIDS volunteer work, these same volunteers claimed *different* and distinctly altruistic and *self-less* reasons (such as a humanitarian obligation to help others in need) as critical in personal decisions to help. These findings suggest the presence of unique features specific to AIDS volunteer work that distinguish it from other forms of volunteer activity. Importantly, however, the findings also point to the potential value of considering the underlying needs and motivations for volunteer activity and how these may differ between people and among volunteer tasks.

In the antecedents stage of our conceptual model, therefore, we seek to identify the social and psychological *functions* being served by the activities of people who engage in AIDS volunteer work. In so doing, we are attempting to extend psychological theories that suggest that people may hold the same attitudes or engage in similar behaviors for very different motivational reasons and to serve quite different psychological functions (e.g., Herek, 1987; Katz, 1960; Smith, Bruner, & White, 1956; Snyder & DeBono, 1989). The practical value of this *functional approach,* we believe, is that it offers the promise of helping to unravel the complex personal and social motivational foundations of volunteer activity, and for understanding how acts of volunteerism that appear to be quite similar on the surface may reflect markedly different underlying motivational processes. For example, in functional terms (drawing on the set of functions traditionally associated with the functional approach; Snyder, 1988), the act of volunteering may for one person serve a *social adjustive* function, reflecting the normative influences of friends and significant others who are AIDS volunteers or the desire to make friends and solidify social ties through volunteer work. For another person, the same act of volunteering may flow from underlying values that prescribe altruistic contributions to society, thereby serving what may be termed a *value-expressive* function. For yet another person, volunteering may serve a *knowledge* function, providing a sense of understanding and information about AIDS and what it does to people. And, in still other cases, volunteering may serve an *ego defensive* or protective function, helping people to cope with personal fears of AIDS, illness, and death.

Of course, it is also possible that these same functions, just as they may motivate and sustain volunteerism, may also serve as powerful deterrents to AIDS volunteer work for some people and in some circumstances. Personal fears of AIDS, for example, may cause some people to not pursue any AIDS volunteer involvement despite strongly held values that would otherwise move them to help and nurture others. Consequently, it is plausible that the decision to avoid AIDS volunteer work may itself serve certain psychological functions for people or result from the conflict of multiple competing motivations. Thus, it seems particularly important to examine the motivations of people actually working as AIDS volunteers and the psychological functions served by their decisions to begin AIDS volunteer involvement and their continued service in such capacities.

In our research, this theory-based set of functions serves as a heuristic device for considering the diversity of motivations for AIDS volunteer work. We make no claim that these functions are the only ones relevant to AIDS volunteerism, or that volunteering serves one and only one function for any particular volunteer. However, our research has permitted us to make some empirically grounded assertions about the motivational functions served by volunteerism. As part of our research (e.g., Snyder & Omoto, 1991b), in fact, we have asked currently active AIDS volunteers to rate the importance of a set of potential reasons and motivations for their volunteer work. Based on factor analyses of these ratings, we have constructed an inventory that identifies five primary motivational functions served by AIDS volunteer work, some of which overlap with those specified by prior theorizing on psychological functions and some of which do not.

One set of motivations for doing AIDS volunteer work is labeled *community concern;* these motivations reflect people's sense of obligation to or concern about a community or social grouping (e.g., "to help members of certain communities [e.g., the gay community]," and "because of my concern and worry about certain communities [e.g., the gay community]"). A second set of motivations invokes considerations related to personal *values* (e.g., "because of my humanitarian obligation to help others" and "because people should do something about issues that are important to them"). A third set of motivations can be characterized as relevant to concerns about *understanding* (e.g., "to learn about how people cope with AIDS" and "to deal with my personal fears and anxiety about AIDS"). The fourth set of motivations is referred to as *personal development* (e.g., "to challenge myself and test my skills" and "to gain experience dealing with emotionally difficult topics"), whereas the fifth category of reasons concerns *esteem enhancement* (e.g., "to feel better about myself" and "to feel less lonely"). Similar sets of motivations, it should be noted, have also emerged from other attempts to measure the motives of AIDS volunteers (Wong, Ouellette-Kobasa, Cassel, & Platt, 1991) and the motivational functions served by volunteerism in general (e.g., Clary, Snyder, & Ridge, 1992).

Although the motivational inventory that we use in our research is self-report in nature, the pattern of correlations between its scales and relevant personality measures provides some validity evidence for our measures of these five functions and for the distinctions among them. For instance, AIDS volunteer work, by its very nature, should provide excellent opportunities for expressing values central to nurturing, empathic, and socially responsible personalities. In our survey of AIDS volunteers, in fact, stronger endorsement of motivations associated with personal values was only related to relatively high scores on individual difference measures of nurturance (scale from Jackson, 1976), empathic concern (measure from Davis, 1980), and social responsibility (using Berkowitz & Lutterman, 1968, measure), all $rs > .41$, $ps < .001$. To the extent that AIDS volunteers have nurturing dispositions, easily and often feel empathy for others, and think that people should take action on social issues, their work seemed to allow them to express these important aspects of themselves. Similarly, the validity of other motivations identified by this inventory is suggested by appropriate networks of associations (see Omoto & Snyder, 1990; Snyder & Omoto, 1991b).

Extending this functional approach to organizational concerns, it seems likely that attempts to recruit new volunteers will be most successful when they are targeted at and engage the motivations of selected sets of potential volunteers. For example, people struggling with their own fears, anxieties, and uncertainties about AIDS may be indifferent to recruitment appeals that stress societal obligations to help PWAs, but may instead be stirred to action if they learn about the many ways that AIDS volunteer work will provide them with safe opportunities to work through their fears and doubts. At an organizational level, then, the ability to target different motivations in the recruitment of new volunteers is a practical problem that is illuminated with the aid of basic theory.

At an organizational level, furthermore, the antecedents stage involves not only the identification and enlistment of a volunteer work force, but also its education with respect to HIV, the specific procedures of the volunteer organization, and different volunteer job responsibilities. Information about the motivations of prospective volunteers should help volunteer organizations better coordinate and manage their entire programs, thereby better meeting the needs of both volunteers and clients. Specific components of training, for example, could be tailored to emphasize relevant psychological functions and volunteer assignments could be made in ways that would be consonant with an individual's prevailing needs and goals. As one illustration, consider people who volunteer for knowledge reasons. These prospective volunteers may benefit most from a specialized training that focuses on factual information about HIV transmission (rather than, say, issues related to death and dying) and may be maximally effective when assigned to the roles of "HIV educators" with responsibilities for informing others about HIV and its prevention.

There is also the (as-yet untested, but likely, we think) possibility that functions and motivations may change with time and experience. If this is true, then volunteer organizations may do well to periodically emphasize the multiple psychological functions that AIDS volunteer work and volunteer jobs can fulfill. In this way, volunteers would remain cognizant of alternative and potentially satisfying volunteer options should they become dissatisfied with their current positions. Thus, volunteer attrition rates could potentially be lowered and volunteer to volunteer job matches fine-tuned. Although these possibilities await empirical investigation, the simple point here is that organizational attention to and emphasis on the particular psychological functions served by various volunteer roles (e.g., buddy or speakers' bureau) may facilitate volunteer recruitment, assignment, and satisfaction. As this analysis suggests, furthermore, attention to the psychological functions of AIDS volunteer work is not only relevant to the antecedents stage of the volunteer process, but may also carry important implications for critical issues at later stages as well. For elaboration of the particular implications for organizational practice and management of volunteer programs, see Snyder and Omoto (1991a, 1992).

To summarize, then, the major goals of theory, research, and application at the antecedents stage of the volunteer process are to: (a) identify personality, attitudinal, and motivational characteristics of AIDS volunteers; (b) build on this knowledge to develop maximally effective strategies for recruiting and training volunteers; and (c) discover antecedent factors that predict who successfully completes volunteer programs and who becomes an effective and satisfied volunteer. As we have outlined, these goals are being addressed in our research with the aid of social psychological theory and link the concerns of individual volunteers to the broader organizational agenda.

Stage II: The AIDS Volunteer Experience

The second stage in our conceptual model of the volunteer process is the post-training service experiences of volunteers. According to our framework, and as we suggested earlier, it seems likely that the influence of psychological and motivational functions may extend well beyond considerations of the antecedents of volunteerism and into later stages of the volunteer process. In fact, the particular motivations that lead people to become volunteers may subsequently interact with their experiences so as to influence their ultimate effectiveness as volunteers, their satisfaction with their work, or even the length of time that they remain active. The volunteer who enlisted for community concern reasons, for example, may derive little satisfaction from being assigned the solitary task of stuffing and stamping envelopes, and decide to quit the organization as soon as social convention permits. Or for that matter, people may develop different motivations for *staying involved* in AIDS volunteer work than they had for getting started with it in the first place. Thus, AIDS volunteer work initiated primarily in search of knowledge or understanding may wear thin fairly quickly, as volunteers typically become well-informed about HIV relatively early on, often during the course of their preservice training. Rather than continuing in the organization, then, these volunteers may turn their attention and energies to other challenges and causes. Alternatively, they may decide to remain active in the organization not in search of additional knowledge but in order to fulfill different motivations (e.g., value-oriented ones) that have become salient.

As volunteers move through training and the early stages of their work, then, their expectations, knowledge bases, skills, and attitudes may change. These early changes and developments are some of the focal points of the experiences stage of the volunteer process. We have more to say about such changes when we turn our attention to the consequences stage. But, before doing so, we discuss a different and particularly important aspect of the experiences stage, namely the developing *relationships* between volunteers and clients and the implications of these relationships for those involved in them. In our conceptual model and in our research program, we are examining the relationships that develop between client PWAs and the volunteers who work in direct service one-on-one capacities (e.g., buddies, home health-care providers, etc.).

Individuals who are diagnosed with AIDS often lose much of their social support as friends, families, and lovers shun and desert them (Ferrara, 1984; Triplet & Sugarman, 1987). This abandonment and scorn, as in the case of Oscar, can lead to profound feelings of seclusion and loneliness as well as actual isolation. Furthermore, HIV infection can result in prolonged periods of intermittent and serious illness. The severity and chronicity of these bouts of poor health can also extract great tolls from potential caregivers and providers of social support. That is, even if an AIDS diagnosis does not produce rejection by others (due to fear, prejudice, or self-protection), the course of an individual's illness can exhaust and drain friends and families and result *de facto* in isolation. Ironically, however, social support may actually help insulate people against the effects of many stressors and diseases (e.g., Cohen & Wills, 1985; Suls, 1982). One of the important roles some volunteers can and do serve, then, is as significant sources of social support for PWAs. In the experiences stage, then, our conceptual model addresses volunteer/PWA relationships, the forms that these relationships can and do take, and the effects of these relationships on the general treatment and coping processes.

In investigating this stage of the volunteer process, we have again turned to basic theory and research in personality and social psychology to guide us in our explorations. Specifically, we have drawn on the extensive literature on interpersonal relationships (e.g., Clark & Reis, 1988) which, among other things, suggests dimensions along which volunteer/PWA relationships can be studied, as well as the stages through which they may be expected to progress (Altman & Taylor, 1973; Berscheid, Snyder, & Omoto, 1989a, 1989b; Kelley et al., 1983). For example, basic theory (Kelley et al., 1983) has proposed that closeness in relationships can be conceptualized as residing in properties of the interaction patterns between participants in relationships. From this starting point, moreover, basic research has provided a means of assessing closeness in terms of the frequency with which relationship partners interact, the diversity of their shared activities, and the strength of influence they have on one another (Berscheid et al., 1989b).

Beginning with basic theory and research on closeness in personal relationships, we are attempting (in longitudinal research) to quantify and track the patterns of interdependence between AIDS volunteers and PWAs, and to meaningfully analyze the special features and development of these relationships. This type of research, moreover, should make it possible to link features of volunteer/PWA relationships to affective and evaluative experiences of volunteers and the psychological functioning of PWAs. Both of these sets of linkages are central to the experiences stage of the volunteer process. Of particular interest, we suggest, is the extent to which relationship closeness and emotional dependency are related to psychological and physical health outcomes for PWAs, or for that matter, the frequency and types of contacts that are most beneficial to client PWAs. As suggested by anecdote, and by narrative accounts provided by volunteers, very close relationships between volunteers and PWAs are not wholly positive but may be stressful and psychologically draining for both participants. Rather than feeling helpful and intrinsically interested in his or her relationship, the volunteer in this situation may feel smothered and obligated to the client. Similarly, some clients with volunteers report an inability to be themselves or to postpone scheduled visits and activities for fear of offending their volunteer or violating expectations about the behavior of people in close helping relationships. Moreover, conflict and negative emotion may be more likely to occur in close, intense relationships (see Berscheid, 1983; Braiker & Kelley, 1979) as might be expected to occur between volunteers and PWAs.

On the other hand, PWAs without vast reservoirs of social support may especially benefit from close relationships with their volunteers. PWAs who obtain sufficient emotional support from friends and family, moreover, may still have practical and instrumental needs that a volunteer could perform (e.g., driving, shopping, cleaning). In this case, clients may not desire psychologically close relationships with their volunteers, and should closeness develop or be "pushed" on them, it may contribute to feelings of stress, uneasiness, and helplessness. Consequently, one practical goal at this stage is the development of (what we refer to as) *relationship templates* in which the positive effects of volunteer/PWA relationships can be maximized and the negative effects minimized. That is, it should be theoretically possible to assess the needs of volunteers and clients, and then arrange appropriate pairings of the individuals so as to maximize the likelihood of achieving a close match to a beneficial template. Alternatively, volunteers and clients could be made aware of the types of relationships that have proven especially beneficial to people in the past and they could be instructed to try to "reconstruct" such relationships in their own interactions. Although still speculative, then, an understanding of volunteer/PWA relationships and their implications would seem to have tremendous potential for practical benefit. Specifically, the understanding could be put to use in structuring emerging volunteer/PWA relationships in attempts to insure positive outcomes and therapeutic benefit.

Once again, our analysis also suggests that, just as the societally significant phenomenon of AIDS volunteerism may be illuminated with basic psychological theory and research, so too could the state of basic theory be advanced by research on volunteer/PWA relationships. These relationships take place against a backdrop of stigma and chronic illness, and until a cure for AIDS is found, both participants have a good idea from the outset how the relationship will likely end. In addition, volunteer/PWA relationships tend to be asymmetrical in terms of physical capabilities and the expectations of the psychological investments to be made. (Many of the special features of volunteer/PWA relationships, it should be pointed out, also occur in other contexts, such as hospice care and in some foster homes.) Owing to these unique features, theories about the stages of relationship development and evolution may need extension, qualification, or even revision to account for "nontraditional" relationships such as those between volunteers and PWAs.

To illustrate a possible extension of basic theory and research, consider some preliminary data on the connections between perceptions of equity and satisfaction in ongoing volunteer/PWA relationships (Omoto & Snyder, 1992). Specifically, research on romantic relationships and on work associations indicates that the perception of equity between partners is generally related to higher levels of satisfaction and greater longevity (e.g., Adams, 1965; Hatfield, Traupmann, Sprecher, Utne, & Hay, 1985). Perceptions of equity may not be critical in satisfaction with volunteer/PWA relationships, however, as the *expectation* of equity may be tenuous in these relationships to begin with. In our research, we have asked volunteers who have worked as buddies for approximately 3 months to report on their perceptions of equity (see Hatfield, Walster, & Traupmann, 1978) and also to rate their satisfaction with their relationship with a client. These data reveal that most volunteers view their relationships as equitable (59%) and moderately satisfying (mean of 4.5 on a 7-point scale). There appears, however, to be no relationship between perceptions of equity and relationship satisfaction. Volunteers who felt underbenefited relative to clients reported levels of satisfaction comparable to those who claimed that their relationships were equitable or who felt overbenefited. This lack of association between equity and satisfaction contrasts with previous findings on equity and, we believe, suggests an important moderating role of specific relationship expectations in global satisfaction. Alternatively, the lack of association between equity and satisfaction may be explained by the numerous other factors (besides equity concerns) that may be salient in volunteer/PWA relationships. Thus, rather than necessarily expecting *inequitable* relationships, volunteers may gauge their satisfaction by other cues, such as how helpful they feel they are to their clients. Whatever the interpretation, however, the point remains that investigating volunteer/PWA relationships may serve to develop and refine basic theories of interpersonal relationships and relationship processes. Such a focus, moreover, should prove to be particularly informative about the dynamics of relationships that occur under stress.

In terms of the broader organization, the experiences stage involves the assignment of volunteers to appropriate positions and the monitoring of their work performance, presumably after having assessed their individual motivations, strengths, and weaknesses. Organizations must also assess the needs of individual clients so that they can receive appropriate services and/or referrals. Attention to the needs and motivations of both volunteers and clients should facilitate the achievement of favorable "fits" between volunteers and those with whom they work, and thus enhance the positive therapeutic outcome that may be intended in these relationships. Organizations may also play a major role in structuring the contact that occurs between volunteers and clients. For example, organizations may promote close relationships by assigning only one or two volunteers to each client PWA. If, however, less close relationships are likely to be more beneficial to some PWAs and volunteers, the organization may assign a greater number of volunteers to work with individual clients and in more specialized capacities. Hence, organizations may limit the frequency and diversity of volunteer/PWA interactions, potentially constraining the ultimate closeness of those relationships.

Stage III: Consequences of AIDS Volunteerism

What are the consequences of volunteerism, for AIDS volunteers and their social networks, for AIDS volunteer organizations and their programs, and for society at large? With respect to volunteers themselves, the consequences stage of the volunteer process includes several key psychological components. At this stage, for example, we focus on the benefits and stresses that result from volunteer service. We also are interested in volunteers' commitment to their organizations and their concomitant or subsequent involvement in other forms of activism and community affairs. Importantly, we are concerned with the changes that volunteer work inspires in volunteers' attitudes, knowledge, and skills. Volunteers may be shaped by their work experiences and the detailing of these changes are important consequences of voluntary activity. Furthermore, consideration of the organizational concerns of volunteer retention and reenlistment bring renewed interest in volunteer motivations and the psychological needs that new or continuing service could fulfill.

A key focus at this stage, to which we alluded earlier and which occupies a prominent place on our research agenda, is an in-depth examination of how AIDS volunteerism affects the personal attitudes, fears, knowledge, and actions of individual volunteers. Social psychological theories of how new behaviors change old attitudes and subsequent actions (e.g., Bem, 1967; Festinger, 1957) provide every reason to expect that, as a result of working in AIDS organizations, volunteers should develop more favorable attitudes toward PWAs, have decreased fear and increased knowledge about AIDS, become more likely to practice safer sex behaviors, and be more likely to engage in AIDS-related activism (e.g., monetary donations, lobbying). We also expect experienced volunteers to have increased self-esteem and greater feelings of self-efficacy (Bandura, 1986) relative to new volunteers, especially to the extent that their volunteer experiences have been satisfying ones.

The consequences stage of the volunteer process also includes organizational components, in that the organization has recruited, trained, and assigned volunteers to certain jobs or roles in the organization. The issues that must be confronted at this point, then, revolve around retention and reenlistment of trained volunteers. Most organizations ask volunteers to make minimal commitments to their initial positions (generally 6 months), after which time they can reenlist for another 6 months, change job assignments, or quit the organization. In short, at the consequences stage, the organization is focused on how long its volunteers will stay active and the means by which to keep them involved. As such, organizations would benefit from being able to identify the volunteers most at risk for "burnout" (Maslach, 1982; Pines & Aronson, 1981) and attrition and to devise ways to combat these tendencies. This concern is particularly salient as the HIV epidemic enters its second decade, as many AIDS volunteer organizations are now facing dwindling supplies of new volunteers and the formidable task of retaining experienced ones (e.g., "Noble experiment," 1990). Thus, the reduction of volunteer burnout and an understanding of the motivational foundations of continuing and sustained involvement is a critical issue facing organizations, and one that we are addressing in conceptual and empirical considerations relevant to the consequences stage of the volunteer process.

To illustrate some of these matters, let us focus on findings concerning the motivations of AIDS volunteers (Omoto & Snyder, 1990) and the linkages between these motivations and information yielded in a 1-year follow-up of these same volunteers (Snyder & Omoto, 1991b). Specifically, it seems likely that AIDS volunteer work may provide numerous opportunities for people to work on unresolved internal conflicts about their self-worth, their social regard, and their mortality. To the extent that an individual is grappling with such issues, AIDS volunteer work may be an ideal and relatively "safe" context in which to address them and may be performed for ego defensive or, what we refer to in our scheme as esteem enhancement or personal development motivations. This is precisely the pattern of association that we have observed among active AIDS volunteers (e.g., Omoto & Snyder, 1990).Endorsement of esteem enhancement motivations is correlated with perceptions of little social support and with relatively low self-esteem (using the Rosenberg, 1979, measure), high need for social recognition (scale from Jackson, 1976), and high death anxiety (measured with items from Collett & Lester, 1969, and Gesser, Wong, & Reker, 1987), all $rs > .19$, $ps < .05$. AIDS volunteer work, then, seems to allow some people to feel less lonely, better about themselves, and affords them a chance to address their personal fears and anxieties about AIDS and death. A consequence of volunteer service for these people, then, is that it provided them opportunities to help themselves while also helping others.

Turning to the 1-year follow-up of AIDS volunteers, we have explored their reports about their service and the predictors of their active involvement. A year after our initial contact with them, we found that approximately half of the AIDS volunteers we had surveyed had suspended active service with the organization. In asking both those former and continuing volunteers to rate their experiences, however, an interesting picture emerged. Specifically, those volunteers who were still active and those who had discontinued their service did not differ in the satisfaction they found in their work or in how committed they were to the purposes and philosophy of their AIDS organization. Rather, the two groups differed in the perceived *costs* or negative repercussions that they incurred as a result of their volunteer work. That is, quitters claimed that their AIDS volunteer work had been just as satisfying and rewarding as those who stayed involved claimed theirs to have been ($ts < 1.5$, ns), but they also claimed that volunteering had taken up too much of their time, and importantly, had caused them to feel embarrassed, stigmatized, or uncomfortable in other ways ($ts > 2.3$, $ps < .05$). Based on this particular sample, therefore, it would seem that negative more so than positive consequences of AIDS volunteerism are important to consider in combating volunteer attrition. At the very least, recognition of such differences may help AIDS volunteer organizations better prepare their volunteers for the likely (positive and negative) outcomes of their service, and ultimately to reduce rates of attrition.

Furthermore, and as suggested by our model of the volunteer process, it is also possible to link the consequences of volunteerism to previous stages in the process. With respect to predicting volunteer attrition and longevity of service 1 year later, for example, we have found that (even after controlling for subject sex and volunteer assignment) the initial measures of psychological functions were of considerable value (Snyder & Omoto, 1991b). In particular, in a series of regression analyses, continuing volunteers could be distinguished from quitters not so much by their community concern and humanitarian values, as one might expect, but by their greater "selfish" desires to feel good about themselves and to learn about AIDS (i.e., esteem enhancement and personal development functions). The good, and perhaps romantic, intentions related to humanitarian concern may simply not have been strong enough to sustain volunteers faced with the tough realities and costs of working with PWAs. Selfish reasons, as noted previously, are also characteristic of volunteers active in non-AIDS causes (Omoto & Snyder, 1989b). Thus, these findings reinforce the notion that volunteer organizations may want to attend to the psychological benefits that volunteers themselves derive from their work as one key to promoting the enlistment and continuing service of volunteers.

Finally, we should point out a few of the broader *societal* consequences that flow from the volunteer process. Specifically, we propose that experienced AIDS volunteers can be effectively utilized to educate nonvolunteers and also fight "AIDS hysteria" (i.e., negative, fearful, prejudicial attitudes based on scant or incorrect information in the general public; Herek & Glunt, 1988; Omoto & Morier, 1988). The theoretical basis for this contention comes from psychological research on "social diffusion" (Costanzo, Archer, Aronson, & Pettigrew, 1986; Darley & Beniger, 1981). In particular, this research suggests that hearing acquaintances talk about first-hand experiences can be a very effective method of information dissemination and persuasion. We expect, therefore, that as AIDS volunteers become better informed and less fearful about AIDS and PWAs, they may talk about their experiences in ways that encourage others to reassess their own beliefs, attitudes, and behaviors. Changes in the attitudes and behaviors of volunteers may produce similar changes in the attitudes and behaviors of their social networks, and by implication, the broader social system. Relatedly, it may be that AIDS volunteers, by virtue of their experiences, are particularly credible sources of HIV related information. Thus, experienced volunteers could be utilized beyond their work as buddies in direct attempts to educate people about the transmission of HIV and to effect change in social attitudes and behaviors. Extending this analysis still further, experienced volunteers may thus help to lay the groundwork for some of the antecedent conditions that may motivate others to pursue AIDS volunteer work in the future.

Summary

We have provided a description of the conceptual model that guides our program of research on AIDS volunteerism and reported selected illustrative findings in an attempt to explicate some of the issues at each stage of the volunteer process (see also Omoto & Snyder, 1990; Snyder & Omoto, 1991b, 1992). We have not attempted to provide completely detailed descriptions of research findings or, for that matter, to exhaustively address all of the issues potentially pertinent to the volunteer process. Rather, our attempt has been to provide a rough outline of the three general stages of the volunteer process (antecedents, experiences, consequences) and to show how we are incorporating diverse psychological theories in a concerted effort to speak to activity at three different levels (the organization, the individual volunteer, and the broader social system).

Furthermore, although we have endeavored to delineate the different sets of variables and issues of particular relevance at each stage of the volunteer process, we have also attempted to illustrate how the stages can be linked in conceptually meaningful ways. For example, our analysis links the distal causes of volunteer work (personality differences) to more proximal and direct causes (motivations and expectations). In addition, the framework details how volunteer experiences may interact with initial patterns of motivation and expectation so as to promote satisfaction, attitude change, knowledge acquisition, and even new construals of one's work and reasons for continuing it. Thus, contrary to the "linear" appearance of the model depicted in Fig. 12.1, we actually envision the volunteer process to be a dynamic and interactive set of stages that includes feedback and interplay between the stages and the levels of analysis.

Finally, we have attempted to trace at least one theme across all of the stages of the volunteer process: the importance of attending to the personal and social motivations of individual volunteers, that is, the psychological functions served by their involvement in volunteer activities. Clearly, volunteer motivation is multifaceted and complex, with diverse sets of reasons compelling people toward and repelling them away from volunteer involvement. As we have attempted to show, however, attention to the psychological motivations of volunteers has many practical implications for organizations interested in the recruitment, training, and assignment of volunteers. In terms of the broader social system, our research identifies ways that current or past volunteers can be effectively utilized not only in the care and treatment of PWAs, but also in recruitment efforts for new volunteers, public education about AIDS, and ultimately in the prevention of new HIV infection.

BASIC RESEARCH AND PRACTICAL PROBLEMS

It has been suggested that the professional skills and expertise of psychologists can be tapped on at least three fronts as society responds to AIDS: (a) providing psychological support services for PWAs, (b) designing appropriate behavior change campaigns to break the chain of HIV transmission, and (c) developing public education programs to address the social and political fallout resulting from prejudicial reactions to AIDS and PWAs (Morin, 1988). Our program of research on AIDS volunteerism has important implications for each of these concerns. Not only have we focused on understanding the role of AIDS volunteers in caring for PWAs, but also we are examining the roles that volunteers can play in AIDS prevention and public education efforts.

By all accounts, the number of AIDS cases will only increase in the years ahead and, as medical advances extend the life expectancy of PWAs, more and more people will be living with AIDS and living *longer* with AIDS (Lemp, Payne, Neal, Temelso, & Rutherford, 1990). Highly likely, then, is an escalating demand for the benefits and services provided by volunteers and volunteer organizations. As we have outlined, we believe that answers to fundamental questions about the roles of volunteers in society's response to HIV can profitably be built on foundations provided by basic research in personality and social psychology. In addition, we believe that the road we are traveling is a two-way street, such that psychological theory will also benefit from research on volunteerism. As we have attempted to illustrate, research in this applied context can be used to elaborate, extend, or delimit the conclusions of basic research and to contribute to the evolution of psychological theory. Hypotheses derived from basic theory and previously tested in the laboratory can be systematically examined in naturalistic contexts and as they bear on socially significant phenomena.

By focusing on volunteerism, we have begun to empirically address what seems to be an enduring and fundamental component of U.S. social behavior and ideology. In the interests of elaborating basic theory on volunteerism, however, we recognize that it will also be necessary to conduct additional studies of people who volunteer for non-AIDS causes, thereby permitting a delineation of both shared and distinctive features of diverse forms of volunteerism. Nevertheless, we believe that our conceptual model describes a general volunteer process and that our research on AIDS volunteerism will at least provide important points of comparison, or perhaps even a grounding, for such future research.

The conceptual model that we have presented also "borrows" heavily from basic theory and research in personality and social psychology. We have done so with the faith that, in accord with the Lewinian (1946, 1947) strategy of action research, there are many practical benefits of sound theory. Across the many forms of action research is the commitment to research as an integral component of social action (Chein et al., 1948). Of paramount importance, in addition, are the permeable boundaries between theory and research as they join forces to solve practical problems. As a result of the reciprocities that exist between basic and applied research and between theory and application, moreover, basic theory can be developed and advanced by research on practical problems conducted in applied contexts. Thus, in action research strategies, basic theory and applied research are tied together in cooperative and mutually enhancing ways; under optimal circumstances, basic research is advanced and effective social action is undertaken.

In closing, we wish to underscore the fact that the HIV epidemic represents not only a medical crisis, but also a broader challenge to individuals and to society. Among those challenges are those to researchers in the social and behavioral sciences to contribute to society's collective response to the epidemic. Earlier, we affirmed our belief that there is nothing so practical as a good theory. When it comes to confronting AIDS, the practical benefits of not just one, but a host of good theories are sorely needed. As the HIV epidemic continues and intensifies, as all indications are that it surely will, so too will the importance of the contributions of theory-based research relevant to all facets of AIDS. This volume is but one testimonial to the many potential contributions of personality and social psychology to this effort. Ultimately, when the definitive social history of the HIV epidemic is written, we believe that basic and applied research in the psychological sciences will have proven itself to be an integral part of society's collective response to AIDS.

ACKNOWLEDGMENTS

This research and the preparation of this chapter have been supported by grants from the American Foundation for AIDS Research and the National Institute of Mental Health to Mark Snyder and Allen M. Omoto. We are grateful to the volunteers and staff of the Minnesota AIDS Project in Minneapolis and the Good Samaritan Project in Kansas City for their cooperation, and to Stephen Asche for his substantial contributions to this program of research. We thank Stephen Asche, Gil Clary, John Pryor, and Glenn Reeder for their helpful comments on the manuscript.

REFERENCES

Adams, J. S. (1965). Inequity in social exchange. In L. Berkowitz (Ed.), *Advances in experimental social psychology* (Vol. 2, pp. 267–299). New York: Academic Press.

Altman, I., & Taylor, D. A. (1973). *Social penetration: The development of interpersonal relationships.* New York: Holt, Rinehart & Winston.

Arno, P. S. (1988). The nonprofit sector's response to the AIDS epidemic: Community-based services in San Francisco. *American Journal of Public Health, 76,* 1325–1330.

Bandura, A. (1986). *Social foundations of thought and action: A social cognitive theory.* Englewood Cliffs, NJ: Prentice-Hall.

Bem, D. J. (1967). Self-perception: An alternative interpretation of cognitive dissonance phenomena. *Psychological Review, 74,* 183–200.

Berkowitz, L., & Lutterman, K. (1968). The traditionally socially responsible personality. *Public Opinion Quarterly, 32,* 169–185.

Berscheid, E. (1983). Emotion. In H. H. Kelley, E. Berscheid, A. Christensen, J. H. Harvey, T. L.

Huston, E. McClintock, L. A. Peplau, & D. R. Peterson, *Close relationships* (pp. 110–168). New York: Freeman.

Berscheid, E., Snyder, M., & Omoto, A. M. (1989a). Issues in studying close relationships: Conceptualizing and measuring closeness. In C. Hendrick (Ed.), *Review of personality and social psychology* (Vol. 10, pp. 63–91). Newbury Park, CA: Sage.

Berscheid, E., Snyder, M., & Omoto, A. M. (1989b). The Relationship Closeness Inventory: Assessing the closeness of interpersonal relationships. *Journal of Personality and Social Psychology, 57,* 792–807.

Braiker, H. B., & Kelley, H. H. (1979). Conflict in the development of close relationships. In R. L. Burgess & T. L. Huston (Eds.), *Social exchange in developing relationships* (pp. 135–168). New York: Academic Press.

Chambré, S. M. (1989). Kindling points of light: Volunteering as public policy. *Nonprofit and Voluntary Sector Quarterly, 18,* 249–268.

Chein, I., Cook, S. W., & Harding, J. (1948). The field of action research. *American Psychologist, 3,* 43–50.

Clark, M. S., & Reis, H. T. (1988). Interpersonal processes in close relationships. *Annual Review of Psychology, 39,* 609–672.

Clary, E. G., & Snyder, M. (1991). A functional analysis of altruism and prosocial behavior: The case of volunteerism. In M. S. Clark (Ed.), *Review of personality and social psychology* (Vol. 12, pp. 119–148). Newbury Park, CA: Sage.

Clary, E. G., Snyder, M., & Ridge, R. D. (1992). Volunteers' motivations: A functional strategy for the recruitment, placement, and retention of volunteers. *Nonprofit Management and Leadership, 3,* 333–350.

Cohen, S., & Wills, T. A. (1985). Stress, social support, and the buffering hypothesis. *Psychological Bulletin, 98,* 310–357.

Collett, L. J., & Lester, D. (1969). The fear of death and the fear of dying. *Journal of Psychology, 72,* 179–181.

Costanzo, M., Archer, D., Aronson, E. & Pettigrew, T. (1986). Energy conservation behavior: The difficult path from information to action. *American Psychologist, 41,* 521–528.

Darley, J. M., & Beniger, J. R. (1981). Diffusion of energy-conserving innovation. *Journal of Social Issues, 37,* 150–171.

Davis, M. (1980). A multidimensional approach to individual differences in empathy. *JSAS Catalog of Selected Documents, 10,* 85.

Dumont, J. A. (1989). Volunteer visitors for patients with AIDS. *The Journal of Volunteer Administration, 8,* 3–8.

Ferrara, A. J. (1984). My personal experience with AIDS. *American Psychologist, 39,* 1285–1287.

Festinger, L. (1957). *A theory of cognitive dissonance.* Stanford, CA: Stanford University Press.

Fineberg, H. V. (1989). The social dimensions of AIDS. In J. Piel (Ed.), *The science of AIDS: Readings from Scientific American* (pp. 111–121). New York: Freeman.

Friends indeed: Buddies break isolation of AIDS. (1990, July 6). *Times Advocate North County Report,* p. B1–B2.

General Accounting Office. (1989). *AIDS: Delivering and financing health services in five communities* (Report to Congressional Committees, Human Resources Division, #89–120). Washington, DC: Author.

Gesser, G., Wong, P. T. P., & Reker, G. T. (1987). Death attitudes across the life-span: The development and validation of the Death Attitude Profile (DAP). *Omega, 18,* 113–128.

Hatfield, E., Traupmann, J., Sprecher, S., Utne, M., & Hay, J. (1985). Equity and intimate relations: Recent research. In W. Ickes (Ed.), *Compatible and incompatible relationships* (pp. 91–117). New York: Springer-Verlag.

Hatfield, E., Walster, G. W., & Traupmann, J. (1978). Equity and premarital sex. *Journal of Personality and Social Psychology, 36,* 82–92.

Hellinger, F. J. (1988). National forecasts of the medical care costs of AIDS: 1988–1992. *Inquiry, 25,* 469–484.

Herek, G. M. (1987). Can functions be measured?: A new perspective on the functional approach to attitudes. *Social Psychology Quarterly, 50,* 285–303.

Herek, G. M., & Glunt, E. K. (1988). An epidemic of stigma: Public reaction to AIDS. *American Psychologist, 43,* 886–891.

Independent Sector. (1990). *Giving and volunteering in the United States.* Washington, DC: The Gallup Organization for Independent Sector.

Jackson, D. N. (1976). *Jackson Personality Inventory Manual.* Goshen, NY: Research Psychologists Press.

Katz, D. (1960). The functional approach to the study of attitudes. *Public Opinion Quarterly, 24,* 163–204.

Katz, I., Hass, R. G., Parisi, N., Astone, J., McEvaddy, D., & Cucido, D. J. (1987). Lay people's and health care personnel's perceptions of cancer, AIDS, cardiac, and diabetic patients. *Psychological Reports, 60,* 615–629.

Kayal, P. M. (1991). Gay AIDS voluntarism as political activity. *Nonprofit and Voluntary Sector Quarterly, 20,* 289–331.

Kelley, H. H., Berscheid, E., Christensen, A., Harvey, J. H., Huston, T. L., Levinger, G., McClintock, E., Peplau, L. A., & Peterson, D. R. (1983). *Close relationships.* New York: Freeman.

King, M., Walder, L., & Pavey, S. (1970). Personality change as a function of volunteer experience in a psychiatric hospital. *Journal of Consulting and Clinical Psychology, 35,* 423–425.

Latané, B., & Darley, J. M. (1970). *The unresponsive bystander: Why doesn't he help?* New York: Appleton-Century-Crofts.

Lemp, G. F., Payne, S. F., Neal, D., Temelso, T., & Rutherford, G. W. (1990). Survival trends for patients with AIDS. *Journal of the American Medical Association, 263,* 402–406.

Lewin, K. (1946). Action research and minority problems. *Journal of Social Issues, 2,* 34–46.

Lewin, K. (1947). Group decision and social change. In T. M. Newcomb & E. L. Hartley (Eds.), *Readings in social psychology* (pp. 459–473). New York: Holt.

Lewin, K. (1951). *Field theory in social science* (D. Cartwright, Ed.). New York: Harper. (Original work published 1944)

Lopez, D., & Getzel, G. S. (1987). Strategies for volunteers caring for persons with AIDS. *Social Casework, 68,* 47–53.

Maslach, C. (1982). *Burnout, the cost of caring.* Englewood Cliffs, NJ: Prentice-Hall.

McGuire, W. J. (1969). Theory-oriented research in natural settings: The best of both worlds for social psychology. In M. Sherif & C. W. Sherif (Eds.), *Interdisciplinary relationships in the social sciences* (pp. 21–51). Hawthorne, NY: Aldine.

Morin, S. F. (1988). AIDS: The challenge to psychology. *American Psychologist, 43,* 838–842.

Noble experiment: Volunteers' distress cripples huge effort to provide AIDS care. (1990, March 12). *Wall Street Journal,* p. A1.

Omoto, A. M., & Morier, D. (1988). *Fear as a source of information: Perceptions of AIDS.* Unpublished manuscript, University of Kansas, Lawrence, KS

Omoto, A. M., & Snyder, M. (1989a). *AIDS volunteers narrative accounts of their experiences.* Unpublished research, University of Kansas, Lawrence, KS and University of Minnesota, Minneapolis, MN.

Omoto, A. M., & Snyder, M. (1989b, May). *Volunteering to work with people with cancer or AIDS: Differences between me and you.* Paper presented at the annual meetings of the Midwestern Psychological Association, Chicago, IL.

Omoto, A. M., & Snyder, M. (1990). Basic research in action: Volunteerism and society's response to AIDS. *Personality and Social Psychology Bulletin, 16,* 152–165.

Omoto, A. M., & Snyder, M. (1992). Features of relationships between AIDS volunteers and PWAs. Unpublished research, University of Kansas, Lawrence, KS and University of Minnesota, Minneapolis, MN.

Pines, A. M., & Aronson, E. (1981). *Burnout: From tedium to personal growth.* New York: The Free Press.

Pryor, J. B., Reeder, G. D., Vinacco, R., & Kott, T. L. (1989). The instrumental and symbolic functions of attitudes toward persons with AIDS. *Journal of Applied Social Psychology, 19,* 377–404.

Rosenberg, M. (1979). *Conceiving the self.* New York: Basic Books.

Scheibe, K. E. (1965). College students spend eight weeks in mental hospital: A case report. *Psychotherapy: Theory, research, and practice, 2,* 117–120.

Smith, M. B., Bruner, J. S., & White, R. W. (1956). *Opinions and personality.* New York: Wiley.

Snyder, M. (1988, August). *Needs and goals, plans and motives: The new "new look" in personality and social psychology.* Invited "state of the art" address presented at the annual meetings of the American Psychological Association, Atlanta, GA.

Snyder, M., & DeBono, K. G. (1989). Understanding the functions of attitudes: Lessons from personality and social behavior. In A. R. Pratkanis, S. J. Breckler, & A. G. Greenwald (Eds.), *Attitude structure and function* (pp. 339–359). Hillsdale, NJ: Lawrence Erlbaum Associates.

Snyder, M., & Omoto, A. M. (1991a). AIDS volunteers: Who volunteers and why do they volunteer. In V. A. Hodgkinson & R. D. Sumariwalla (Eds.), *Leadership and Management* (pp. 15–26). Washington, DC: Independent Sector.

Snyder, M., & Omoto, A. M. (1991b). Who helps and why? The psychology of AIDS volunteerism. In S. Spacapan & S. Oskamp (Eds.), *Helping and being helped: Naturalistic Studies* (pp. 213–239). Newbury Park, CA: Sage.

Snyder, M., & Omoto, A. M. (1992). Volunteerism and society's response to the HIV epidemic. *Current Directions in Psychological Science, 1,* 113–116.

Suls, J. (1982). Social support, interpersonal relations, and health: Benefits and liabilities. In G. S. Saunders & J. Suls (Eds.), *Social psychology of health and illness* (pp. 255–277). Hillsdale, NJ: Lawrence Erlbaum Associates.

Triplet, R. G., & Sugarman, D. B. (1987). Reactions to AIDS victims: Ambiguity breeds contempt. *Personality and Social Psychology Bulletin, 13,* 265–274.

Watkins, J. D. (1988). Responding to the HIV epidemic: A national strategy. *American Psychologist, 43,* 849–851.

Williams, M. J. (1988). Gay men as "buddies" to persons living with AIDS and ARC. *Smith College Studies in Social Work, 59,* 38–52.

Wong, L. M., Ouellette–Kobasa, S. C., Cassel, J. B., & Platt, L. P. (1991, June). *A new scale identifies 6 motives for AIDS volunteers.* Poster presented at the annual meetings of the American Psychological Society, Washington, DC.

Author Index

A

Abelson, H., 199, 219
Abelson, R. P., 97, 100, 113, 120, 123
Acklin, 231, 261
Adams, J. S., 347, 353
Adelman, M. B., 97, 120
Adler, N. E., 128, 151, 200, 222
Aggleton, P., 268, 284
Ainlay, S., 268, 282
Ajzen, I., 77, 81, 131, 132, 135, 136,
    140, 145, 149, 150, 151, 172, 173,
    175, 178, 179, 195, 196, 220, 221,
    222, 223
Albee, G. W., 128, 150
Albert, J., 268, 282
Albrecht, G. L., 254, 257
Altman, D. G., 129, 153
Altman, I., 345, 353
Altman, L. K., 269, 282
Ambrosio, A. L., 232, 249, 257, 259
Amidei, T., 65, 67, 83, 127, 135, 151
Anderson, J., 270, 282
Andrew, M. E., 202, 222
Archer, D., 350, 354
Arena, V. C., 200, 224
Arkin, E. B., 230, 258
Armstrong, J. S., 32, 36
Arno, P. S., 338, 353
Aronson, E., 348, 350, 354, 356
Aspinwall, L. G., 66, 71, 72, 77, 80, 81,
    84, 163, 178, 308, 309, 318, 329,
    332
Astone, J., 231, 336, 355, 259
Averill, J. R., 291, 301

B

Bachrach, C., 186, 223
Bader, M., 268, 284
Bahr, G. R., 128, 145, 152
Baker, E., 165, 178
Baker, S., 170, 181
Baker, S. A., 198, 220
Baldwin, J. I. , 65, 67, 72, 81, 86, 120,
    200, 220
Baldwin, J., D., 65, 67, 72, 81, 86, 120,
    200, 220
Baldwin, W., 186, 221
Bandura, A., 53, 56, 135, 150, 174,
    175, 178, 196, 201, 220, 307, 312,
    329, 348, 353
Bar-Hillel, M., 15, 16, 36
Bargh, J. A., 275, 276, 282, 283
Barr, A., 232, 261
Bartelme, S., 127, 150
Bartman, A., 279, 285
Battegay, R., 320, 330
Bauman, L. J., 39, 41, 42, 44, 47, 48,
    52, 55, 56
Baumeister, R. F., 49, 56
Baumgardner, M. H., 165, 181
Beck, A. T., 315, 321, 323, 329
Becker, B. H., 201, 221
Becker, G., 268, 282
Becker, M. H., 40, 52, 56, 57, 59, 60,
    61, 66, 70, 72, 74, 75, 76, 77, 81,
    83, 156, 178, 167, 168, 173, 175,
    180, 181, 182, 199, 223, 307, 329
Belasco, J., 232, 261
Belcastro, P. A., 188, 220

Bell, T. A., 186, 220
Bellfield, J., 267, 284
Bem, D. J., 348, 353
Beniger, J. R., 350, 354
Berg, J. H., 87, 120
Berkman, B., 320, 332
Berkowitz, L., 342, 353
Berkowitz, N. H., 268, 283
Berlin, B. M., 65, 83, 200, 201, 221
Bernoulli, D., 11, 36
Berscheid, E., 345, 346, 353, 354, 355
Bertalanffy, L., 89, 120
Bettencourt, B. A., 93, 94, 122
Betts, R., 136, 151
Betz, A. L., 276, 284
Beyth-Marom, R., 32, 36
Bibace, R., 267, 283
Billy, J., 198, 220
Blackstone, T., 264, 283
Blake, S. M., 230, 258
Blalock, H. M., 77, 81
Blattner, C., 230, 260
Bleecker, T., 231, 258
Blendon, R. J., 231, 232, 258, 281, 283
Bliwise, N., 270, 283
Bloom, D. E., 230, 258
Blumenfield, M., 231, 258
Blythe, B. J., 146, 153
Boccher-Lattimore, D., 201, 223
Boffey, P. M., 280, 283
Bonati, F. A., 200, 224
Booraem, C., 127, 152
Botvin, E. N., 165, 178
Botvin, G. J., 165, 178
Bourne, ., 272, 283
Bouton, R. A., 232, 258, 298, 301
Bowen, S., 110, 120
Bowie, W. R., 128, 152, 200, 223
Boyer, C. B., 199, 221
Bradburn, N. M., 32, 37
Bradford, J. B., 66, 69, 83
Bradley, B. G., 128, 145, 152
Braiker, H. B., 346, 354
Brandt, A. M., 248, 258, 268, 283

Brasfield, T. L., 65, 67, 83, 127, 128, 131, 132, 135, 136, 139, 143, 145, 148, 151, 152, 153, 165, 180, 202, 222, 312, 330
Brashure, J., 320, 331
Breda, C., 74, 82
Brehovsky, M., 42, 51, 57
Brewer, M. B., 282, 285
Brickman, P., 299, 301
Brock, B. M., 52, 56
Brock, T. C., 161, 181
Brookmeyer, R., 307, 308, 329, 330
Brown, J. D., 47, 49, 55, 57
Brundage, J. F., 127, 150
Bruner, J. S., 238, 341, 356, 260
Brunner, F., 320, 330
Buchanan, P. J., 250, 258
Budescu, D. V., 32, 37, 38
Buehler, J. W., 189, 224
Burke, D. S., 127, 150
Burnett, W., 320, 331
Burnkrant, R., 168, 178
Burns, D., 93, 94, 99, 120, 122
Bye, L. L., 159, 178, 200, 220
Byers, R. H., 307, 329
Byrne, D., 63, 73, 82, 84

C

Cabral, R. J., 198, 221
Cacioppo, J. T., 145, 152, 156, 161, 164, 167, 170, 171, 178, 180, 181, 191, 192, 223
Callahan, C. M., 65, 67, 84, 128, 136, 153, 202, 224
Calzavara, L. M., 73, 82
Campbell, S. M., 65, 67, 81, 96, 104, 121, 270, 284
Capitanio, J. P., 231, 234, 238, 250, 252, 253, 254, 256, 257, 259
Carballo, M., 128, 150
Carey, V., 322, 331
Carliner, G., 230, 258
Carlsmith, J. M., 145, 150
Carlston, D., 271, 286

Carpenter, K. M., 168, 179
Carroll, J. S., 168, 178
Casriel, C., 127, 150
Cassel, J. B., 342, 356
Castro, K. G., 189, 224
Catania, J. A., 39, 56, 65, 67, 73, 74,
    81, 82, 131, 132, 135, 150, 159,
    168, 178, 200, 220
Cates, W., 185, 186, 220, 221
Cause, A., 199, 220
Cesa, I. L., 115, 122
Chaiken, S., 164, 165, 178
Chambre, S. M., 335, 354
Chandarana, P. C., 66, 69, 82
Chandler, C. C., 291, 302
Chapman, D. P., 290, 301
Charles, K., 307, 311
Chein, I., 338, 352, 354
Chen, J. -Y., 311, 332
Chin, J., 270, 283
Chitwood, D. D., 39, 56, 73, 74, 81, 82
Chmiel, J. S., 307, 325, 329, 330
Christensen, A., 345, 355
Chu, L., 135, 151
Chung, L. A., 256, 258
Cialdini, R. B., 168, 179, 181
Clark, E., 320, 332
Clark, M. L., 199, 220
Clark, M. S., 96, 120, 345, 354
Clark, S. D., Jr., 198, 224
Clarkin, Jr., 320, 330
Clary, E. G., 337, 342, 354
Cleary, P., 59, 82
Clemen, R. T., 5, 13, 36
Clemow, L. P., 128, 150
Cline, R. J., 111, 120, 121
Coates, D., 299, 301
Coates, T. J., 39, 56, 60, 65, 67, 72, 73,
    81, 82, 83, 127, 128, 129, 131, 132,
    135, 150, 151, 152, 153, 156, 159,
    168, 180, 182, 200, 201, 220, 221,
    223, 231, 258, 307, 308, 312, 329,
    331, 332
Cochran, S. D., 39, 56, 127, 135, 152,
    189, 194, 223

Cohen, F., 313, 329
Cohen, R., 199, 250, 258, 219
Cohen, S., 345, 354
Cohn, E., 299, 301
Coleman, L., 268, 282
Coles, M., 229, 230, 258
Collett, L. J., 349, 354
Collins, B., 112, 121
Collins, N., 102, 121
Collins, R. L., 313, 318, 329
Combs, B., 32, 37
Conant, M. A., 168, 180, 307, 331
Conlon, P., 66, 69, 82
Connors, J., 249, 258
Conrad, P., 265, 268, 279, 283
Cook, D. J., 231, 259, 281, 284
Cook, S. W., 338, 352, 354
Cooper, D. A., 73, 83
Corcoran, M., 230, 260
Corman, M., 65, 67, 81, 200, 220
Costanzo, M., 350, 354
Cotton, D. A., 231, 259
Coutinho, R., 42, 56
Coxon, A. P. M., 128, 150
Crandall, C., 269, 283
Crinean, J., 313, 330
Crist, G., 311, 332
Cronen, V. E., 87, 122
Cronkite, R. C., 318, 329
Croteau, J. M., 282, 283
Cruz-Collins, M., 204, 205, 222
Cucido, D. J., 336, 355
Cummings, K. M., 52, 56
Cupples, L. A., 320, 332
Curran, J. W., 12, 26, 27, 36, 307, 329
Cushman, D. P., 87, 121

D

D'Augelli, A. R., 232, 258
Daives, M., 128, 152
Dalton, H. L., 254, 256, 258
Damashek, S., 279, 285
Damrosch, S., 290, 302
Danaher, B., 41, 57

Darabi, K. F., 186, 189, 221
Darkheim, E., 3420, 325, 329
Darley, J. M., 337, 350, 354, 355
Darrow, W. W., 307, 308, 329
Davidson, A. R., 59, 84
Davies, M., 194, 209, 223
Davis, J. H., 321, 329
Davis, M., 342, 354
De Bro, G. C., 65, 67, 81
De Bro, S. C., 95, 96, 104, 121
de Gilder, D., 42, 51, 57
Dearing, J. W., 231, 258
DeBono, K. G., 341, 356
DeJong, W., 159, 165, 179, 182, 193,
    194, 206, 207, 224
Delia, J. G., 87, 121
Denton, E., 231, 260
DeParle, J., 216, 221
Depue, R. A., 320, 332
DesJarlais, D. C., 127, 150, 168, 179
Desforges, J. G., 282, 283
Desmond, S., 199, 223
Detels, R., 307, 322, 329, 330
DeVellis, B. M., 175, 182
Devine, P., 276, 283
Diamond, G. A., 270, 284
Diaz, Y. E., 202, 222
Diaz, Y. Y., 128, 132, 145, 151, 152
DiCindio, L., 199, 221
DiClemente, R. J., 128, 131, 132, 150,
    199, 200, 221
Dielman, T. E., 167, 181
Dietrich, D., 87, 121
Dilova, M., 42, 51, 57
Doebbert, G., 320, 330
Doherty, J. A., 128, 152, 200, 223
Dolcini, M. M., 65, 67, 81, 132, 135,
    150, 200, 220
Doll, L. S., 308, 329
Donelan, K., 231, 232, 258, 281, 283
Donohew, L., 163, 179
Dougard, C., 268, 284
Douglas, M., 276, 283
Dow, M. G., 231, 259
Drems, M. E., 231, 260

Droppleman, L. F., 323, 331
Dryfoos, J., 186, 189, 221
Duck, S., 87, 121
Dudley, J. P., 66, 71, 72, 80, 81, 163,
    178, 307, 309, 314, 320, 322, 329,
    330, 332
Dumont, J. A., 338, 354
Dunker, K., 277, 283

E

Eagly, A., 164, 178, 179
Echenberg, D. F., 307, 329
Edgar, T., 86, 121
Edmunds, M., 63, 82
Edwards, B. K., 27, 37
Edwards, W., 5, 8, 11, 32, 38
Eisele, J., 128, 150
Ekstrand, M., 159, 178
Elder, R., 268, 284
Eldred, L. J., 307, 329
Ellen, P. S., 196, 222
Eller, M., 48, 52, 53, 55, 57, 70, 72, 77,
    83, 163, 168, 180, 200, 222, 307,
    311, 330
Emmons, C. A., 48, 52, 53, 55, 57, 66,
    68, 69, 70, 72, 74, 77, 82, 83, 131,
    150, 163, 168, 180, 200, 201, 221,
    222, 307, 311, 325, 330
Emmons, R. A., 93, 121
Endler, N. S., 87, 121
English, P., 307, 322, 329
Ensminger, M., 65, 72, 84
Eshleman, S., 48, 52, 53, 55, 57, 70, 72,
    77, 83, 163, 168, 180, 200, 222,
    307, 311, 330
Estrand, M., 200, 220
Evatt, B. L., 127, 153

F

Fahey, J. L., 322, 329, 330, 331, 332
Fallon, A. E., 277, 285
Fanning, M. M., 73, 82
Farbisz, R., 41, 57

Farina, A., 264, 266, 284
Farrer, L. A., 320, 330
Fawzy, F., 66, 68, 83, 163, 180, 308, 311, 330
Fazio, R. H., 68, 82, 71, 172, 174, 177, 179
Felner, R., 199, 220
Felton, B. J., 313, 318, 330
Ferrara, A. J., 344, 354
Festinger, L., 145, 150, 348, 354
Fetzer, B. K., 51, 57, 75, 84, 176, 180
Feucht, T., 202, 206, 224
Ficarrotto, T. J., 270, 283
Field, V. A., 66, 69, 82
Filazzola, A. D., 165, 178
Fincham, F. D., 301
Fineberg, H. V., 15, 16, 20, 29, 36, 334, 354
Fischer, G. W., 16, 17, 18, 19, 24, 28, 29, 30, 32, 37
Fischhoff, B., 6, 7, 14, 15, 16, 17, 18, 19, 21, 24, 28, 29, 30, 32, 33, 37, 41, 45, 57
Fishbein, M., 68, 77, 81, 131, 132, 136, 140, 145, 149, 150, 163, 173, 179, 195, 196, 198, 220, 221
Fisher, J. D., 63, 76, 82, 128, 129, 130, 131, 132, 133, 134, 135, 136, 142, 143, 144, 149, 151, 156, 168, 179, 190, 200, 221
Fisher, W. A., 63, 73, 82, 84, 128, 129, 130, 131, 132, 133, 134, 135, 136, 142, 143, 144, 146, 149, 151, 152, 156, 179, 190, 200, 221, 223
Fletcher, B., 318, 332
Flowers, J. V., 127, 152
Floyd, H., 199, 221
Folkman, S., 313, 315, 330
Fong, G. T., 128, 136, 151, 193, 194, 203, 213, 215, 221
Fontana, A. F., 318, 331
Ford, K., 186, 187, 188, 224
Forrest, J. D., 186, 222
Forrest, K. A., 128, 132, 150, 200, 221
Forsyth, B., 32, 38

Fox, G. L., 198, 221
Fox, R., 308, 330
Fraeble, D. E. S., 264, 283
Francis, A., 320, 330
Francis, D. P., 270, 283
Franco, J. N., 193, 222
Frankenberg, R., 268, 283
Frazer, J. G., 267, 277, 283
Frederick, C. J., 321, 329
Freeman, H. E., 159, 180
Freimuth, V. S., 86, 121
Friedman, S. R., 127, 150, 152, 168, 179
Fullilove, M., 65, 67, 81, 140, 151
Fullilove, R. E., 140, 151
Furgeson, J., 135, 151
Furstenberg, F. F., 198, 221
Fyre, M., 320, 330

G

Gaeddert, W. S., 96, 122
Gagnon, J. H., 97, 123, 232, 260
Gallaher, P. E., 232, 258, 261, 298, 301
Gantz, W., 156, 179
Garcia-Tunon, M., 12, 26, 27, 36
Gardner, L. I., 127, 150
Garlinghouse, P. A., 232, 258, 298, 301
Gayle, H. D., 12, 26, 27, 36
Geis, B. D., 63, 82
Georgiewa, P., 42, 51, 57
Gerbert, B., 231, 258
Gerrard, M., 42, 56, 63, 64, 65, 67, 73, 74, 75, 82
Gesser, G., 349, 354
Gessner, J., 278, 285
Getchell, J. P., 307, 329
Getzel, G. S., 338, 355
Gibbons, F. X., 73, 74, 82, 83
Gibert, C., 127, 151
Gibson, D. R., 39, 56, 73, 74, 81, 82, 135, 151
Gilbert, D. T., 279, 283
Gilchrist, L. D., 146, 153

Gilliam, A. G., 188, 193, 194, 203, 208, 221, 224
Gilovich, T., 252, 258
Ginzburg, H. M., 307, 329, 322, 331
Giorgi, J., 322, 330
Glassman, M. B., 159, 160, 181, 182
Gleicher, F., 169, 170, 179, 181
Glunt, E. K., 231, 234, 238, 254, 256, 259, 266, 280, 284, 336, 350, 355
Goffman, E., 231, 258, 264, 265, 268, 283
Goldenbaum, M., 127, 150
Goldman, N., 186, 222
Goldman, R., 161, 181
Goodhart, F., 135, 152, 201, 223
Goodwin, M. P., 232, 258
Gordin, F. M., 127, 151
Gordon, A. N., 194, 205, 211, 212, 224
Gostin, L. O., 280, 281, 283, 284
Gottlieb, A., 205, 212, 223
Grade, M., 270, 283
Graham, S., 291, 302
Graven, M., 322, 329
Gray, L., 163, 179
Green, M., 320, 330
Greenberg, B. S., 156, 179
Greenblatt, R. M., 65, 67, 81, 132, 135, 150, 200, 220
Greenwald, A. G., 161, 165, 179, 181
Gregory, L. W., 168, 179
Gregory, W. L., 135, 151
Grieger, I., 282, 284
Gross, E. M., 306, 320, 331
Gross, S. J., 140, 151, 281, 284
Guest, F., 185, 186, 221
Guten, S., 41, 56
Guthrie, D., 188, 189, 224
Guydish, J. R., 159, 178, 200, 220

H

Haas, R. G., 231, 259
Haefner, D. P., 52, 56
Haenel, T. H., 320, 330
Haignere, C., 128, 152, 194, 209, 223

Hakama, M., 320, 331
Ham, J., 135, 151
Hamilton, M. C., 46, 56
Hammen, C., 320, 332
Hammond, L., 86, 121
Hancock, K. A., 282, 284
Handelsman, C. D., 198, 221
Hankey, B. F., 27, 37
Harding, J., 338, 352, 354
Hardy, A. M., 230, 242, 254, 258
Harkins, S. G., 168, 179
Harre, R., 87, 121
Harris, D. M., 41, 56
Harvey, J., 345, 355
Hass, R. G., 336, 355
Hastorf, A. H., 264, 266, 284
Hatcher, R. A., 185, 186, 221
Hatfield, E., 347, 354
Haugtvedt, C., 164, 167, 171, 179, 181
Hauth, A. C., 128, 132, 145, 151, 152, 202, 222
Hawley, H. P., 127, 151
Hay, J. W., 230, 258, 347, 354
Hayes, C., 186, 221
Haynes, K., 140, 151
Hays, R. B., 127, 151
Hearst, N., 12, 19, 20, 21, 29, 36
Heath, L., 231, 261
Heaton, E., 199, 219
Heaven, P. C. L., 249, 258
Heeren, T. C., 65, 83, 200, 201, 221, 231, 261
Heesacker, M., 168, 181
Heider, F., 163, 179, 288, 301
Heider, G. M., 168, 179
Hellinger, F. J., 335, 355
Henry, K., 270, 284
Henshaw, S., 186, 222
Herbert, M., 77, 84, 308, 314, 330, 332
Herek, G. M., 231, 233, 234, 238, 239, 249, 250, 252, 253, 254, 256, 257, 258, 259, 266, 279, 280, 282, 284, 336, 341, 350, 355
Hessol, N. A., 308, 329
Hewitt, N., 204, 205, 222

Hiatt, R. A., 231, 260
Hilton, B., 230, 259
Hilton, D. J., 272, 284
Hingson, R. W., 65, 83, 200, 201, 221
Hinrichsen, G. A., 313, 318, 330
Hoff, C., 127, 153, 156, 182, 201, 223, 307, 308, 331, 332
Hofferth, S., 186, 221
Hoffman, V., 97, 99, 121
Hogarth, R., 21, 36
Holahan, C. J., 313, 330
Holman, R. C., 127, 153
Holmes, K. K., 186, 220
Hood, H. V., 65, 67, 83, 131, 135, 136, 139, 143, 148, 151, 153, 165, 180, 202, 222, 281, 284, 312, 330, 231, 259
Hooijkaas, C., 42, 43, 44, 48, 53, 56, 58
Hopkins, J. R., 99, 121
Horn, M., 186, 223
Horstman, W., 72, 83, 307, 331
Horton, M., 268, 284
Horvath, W. J., 167, 181
Hoverstad, R., 171, 179
Hovland, C. I., 100, 121, 191, 221
Howard-Pitney, B., 171, 179
Hsu, M. A., 231, 253, 254, 260, 306, 320, 331
Hughes, M. J., 320, 330
Hulley, B. S., 12, 19, 20, 21, 29, 36
Hulley, S., 65, 67, 81
Hume, D., 277, 284
Hunter, N. D., 265, 284
Huston, T. L., 345, 355

I

Inazu, J. K., 198, 221
Ingram, F. R., 12, 26, 27, 36
Irish, T., 270, 283
Irwin, C. E., Jr., 128, 151, 200, 222
Isen, A. M., 270, 282
Iverson, A. E., 127, 152
Iwrey, C. G., 188, 224

J

Jackson, D. N., 342, 349, 355
Jacobson, L., 307, 329
Jacobson, M. A., 230, 258
Jaffe, H. W., 307, 329
Janis, I. L., 40, 48, 53, 168, 180, 191, 221, 250, 259
Janz, N. K., 40, 57, 60, 61, 77, 83, 173, 180, 201, 221
Jason, J. M., 127, 153
Jaspers, J. M., 301
Jay, M. S., 205, 212, 223
Jemmott, J. B., 128, 132, 136, 151, 187, 188, 193, 194, 197, 200, 201, 203, 204, 205, 213, 215, 221, 222
Jemmott, L. S., 128, 132, 135, 136, 151, 152, 187, 188, 193, 194, 197, 200, 201, 203, 204, 205, 213, 215, 221, 222, 223
Jette, A. M., 52, 56
Johnson, A., 127, 153
Johnson, J. K., 73, 82
Jones, E. E., 264, 266, 284
Jones, J. B., 198, 222
Jones, J. E., 187, 223
Jones, L., 186, 222
Jordheim, A. E., 172, 180
Joreskog, K. G., 149, 151
Joseph, J. G., 48, 52, 53, 55, 57, 60, 66, 68, 69, 70, 72, 75, 76, 77, 81, 82, 83, 131, 150, 156, 163, 168, 178, 180, 200, 201, 221, 222, 307, 311, 325, 329, 330
Juarbe, M., 93, 94, 122
Juarez, R., 199, 222
Jussim, L., 276, 284

K

Kagay, M., 186, 198, 224
Kahn, J., 186, 221
Kahneman, D., 6, 13, 14, 15, 21, 28, 36, 37

Kalichman, S. C., 190, 202, 222
Kaloupek, D. G., 313, 330, 332
Kantner, J., 186, 187, 188, 224
Karasawa, K., 299, 301
Karuza, Jr., Jr., 299, 301
Kasl, S. V., 52, 56, 57
Kaslow, R. A., 307, 329
Kassin, S. M., 277, 284
Katz, D., 238, 259, 342, 344
Katz, I., 231, 259, 336, 355
Katzman, E. M., 86, 121
Kayal, P. M., 338, 355
Keeling, R. P., 12, 26, 27, 36
Keeney, R. L., 5, 11, 13, 37
Keeter, S., 66, 69, 83
Kegeles, S. M., 60, 65, 67, 81, 82, 127,
128, 131, 132, 135, 150, 151, 158,
169, 178, 200, 220, 222
Kelley, H. H., 87, 121, 201, 221, 345,
346, 354, 355
Kelley, K., 63, 82
Kelly, J. A., 65, 67, 83, 127, 128, 131,
132, 134, 135, 136, 139, 143, 145,
146, 148, 151, 152, 153, 165, 180,
190, 202, 222, 231, 259, 281, 284,
312, 330
Kemeny, M. E., 66, 71, 72, 77, 80, 81,
84, 163, 178, 305, 308, 309, 320,
325, 314, 320, 330, 332
Kennky, D. A., 87, 121
Kerr, D., 231, 232, 254, 260
Kessler, L., 231, 261
Kessler, R. C., 48, 52, 53, 55, 57, 60,
66, 68, 69, 70, 72, 74, 75, 77, 82, 83,
131, 150, 163, 168, 180, 200, 201,
221, 222, 307, 311, 325, 330
Kidder, M., 299, 301
Kilbourne, B. W., 12, 26, 27, 36
Kilgore, H., 65, 67, 83
Kim, H. C., 128, 150
Kinder, D. R., 281, 284, 286
King, A. C., 129, 153
King, M. A., 128, 152, 200, 223, 336,
355
Kingma, R., 63, 73, 84

Kingsley, L. A., 65, 67, 84, 128, 136,
153, 202, 224, 307, 329, 322, 331
Kintsch, W., 104, 121, 122
Kirscht, J. P., 40, 48, 52, 53, 55, 56, 57,
60, 66, 70, 72, 74, 75, 83, 163, 168,
180, 201, 222, 307, 311, 330
Kiyak, H. A., 313, 330
Kizer, K. W., 320, 330
Kleck, R., 281, 286
Klein, D. E., 66, 68, 69, 72, 83, 84,
163, 180, 308, 311, 330
Klein, M. M., 73, 82
Knopf, A., 41, 57
Knox, M. D., 231, 259
Koop, C. E., 243, 250, 259, 281, 284
Koopman, C., 128, 152, 194, 209, 223
Kott, T., 265, 266, 273, 279, 285, 292,
302, 336, 356
Kovacs, M., 323, 329
Kowal, D., 185, 186, 221
Krauthammer, C., 279, 284
Kreek, M. J., 127, 150
Krieger, N., 229, 259
Krosnick, J. A., 276, 284
Krueger, R. A., 139, 152
Ku, L. C., 65, 67, 84, 132, 152
Kuhn, T. S., 87, 121
Kukula, G., 199, 223
Kuno, R., 202, 220, 221, 312, 329
Kunreuther, H., 41, 57

L

Lambert, B., 256, 259
Landau, S., 267, 273, 284, 285
Lando, H. A., 74, 83
Landsverk, J., 66, 68, 83, 163, 180,
308, 311, 330
Lanier, M. M., 204, 209, 222
Larsen, K. S., 268, 270, 284
Lashof, J. C., 229, 259
Latane, B., 337, 355
Lattin, D., 250, 259
Laumann, E. O., 232, 260

Lavalle, T., 272, 285
Lawrence, J. S., 281, 284
Layman, M., 32, 37
Lazarus, R. S., 313, 315, 329, 330
Leal, T., 232, 258, 298, 301
Lee, C., 52, 57
Leichenko, S., 186, 198, 224
Leighton, C. K., 186, 187, 199, 224
Leippe, M. R., 165, 181
Lemke, A., 65, 67, 83, 127, 135, 151
Lemp, G. F., 353, 355
Lennon, R., 232, 259
Lepper, M. R., 282, 283
Lerner, A., 128, 150
Lerner, M. J., 249, 259, 271, 286
Leslie, C., 86, 121
Lester, D., 315, 323, 329, 349, 354
Leventhal, H., 40, 57, 168, 180, 313,
    330, 331
Levin, I. P., 290, 301
LeVine, E., 193, 222
Levinger, G., 345, 355
Leviton, L. C., 65, 67, 84, 202, 224
Levy, J. A., 254, 257
Lewin, K., 120, 121, 333, 338, 352,
    355
Lewis, C. E., 159, 180
Liberman, A., 164, 178, 179
Lichtenstein, S., 14, 15, 16, 21, 32, 36,
    37, 41, 57
Lichtman, R. R., 47, 49, 55, 57
Liebling, L., 231, 261
Lifson, A. R., 308, 329
Lincoln, R., 186, 222
Lindemann, C., 187, 222
Linville, P. W., 16, 17, 18, 19, 24, 28,
    29, 30, 33, 37
London, K. A., 187, 222
Long, E., 270, 284
Lopez, D., 338, 335
Lorch, E., 163, 179
Lord, C. G., 282, 283, 286
Lorr, M., 323, 331
Louhivouri, K. A., 320, 331
Lovelle-Drache, J., 135, 151

Lutterman, K., 342, 353
Luus, A. E. L., 63, 82
Lynn, A. R., 276, 284
Lyter, D. W., 65, 67, 84, 128, 136, 153,
    202, 224

M

MacDonald, N. E., 128, 152, 200, 223
MacGregor, D., 6, 32, 36
Madden, D. L., 322, 329
Madden, T. J., 135, 149, 196, 220, 222
Maddux, J. E., 61, 83
Magnusson, D., 87, 121
Magnusson, J., 278, 286, 289, 290, 292,
    293, 296, 302
Maguire, B. T., 231, 258
Mahler, K. A., 205, 210, 223
Maiman, L. A., 52, 56, 59, 81
Mallery, P., 293, 294, 302
Malloy, T. E., 132, 135, 136, 142, 143,
    149, 151
Mann, J. G., 306, 320, 331
Mann, L., 40, 48, 53, 250, 259
Mannes, S. M., 104, 122
Marcus-Newhall, A., 115, 122
Marin, B., 65, 67, 81, 194, 195, 199,
    215, 222
Marin, G., 135, 152, 193, 194, 195,
    199, 215, 222, 223
Markova, I., 270, 284
Markus, H., 264, 266, 284
Markwith, M., 265, 267, 285
Marmor, M., 127, 150
Marshall, J., 320, 331
Martin, J. L., 72, 83, 307, 331
Martinez-Maza, O., 322, 330
Maslach, C., 348, 355
Maslansky, R., 127, 150
Mason, J. A., 282, 283
Matts, L., 128, 150
Mayer, K. H., 308, 331
Mays, V. M., 39, 56, 127, 135, 152,
    189, 194, 222, 223
Mazurk, P. M., 306, 320, 331

McCarthy, B. R., 204, 209, 222
McCauley, C., 265, 267, 285
McClelland, J. L., 104, 123
McClintock, E., 345, 355
McCombs, M. S., 127, 152
McCormick, N. B., 95, 96, 122
McCusker, J., 308, 331
McDevitt, T. M., 232, 259
McEvaddy, D., 231, 259, 336, 355
McGovern, P. G., 74, 83
McGuire, W. J., 156, 160, 161, 164,
    180, 192, 193, 223, 338, 355
McKusick, L., 72, 83, 135, 152, 168,
    180, 201, 220, 221, 223, 307, 308,
    312, 329, 331
McLaws, M., 73, 83
McLeod, R. G., 229, 260
McManus, I. C., 281, 285
McManus, J., 268, 274, 281, 285
McNair, D. M., 323, 331
McNeil, B. J., 21, 37
McNeill, C., 65, 67, 83
McNeill, W. H., 231, 260
McPhee, S. J., 231, 258
McSeveny, D., 199, 221
Medin, D. L., 113, 122
Mejta, C. L., 231, 250
Mendelsohn, M. J., 63, 83
Mentzer, S., 281, 286
Merluzzi, T. V., 97, 122
Mesagno, F. P., 311, 332
Meyerowitz, B. E., 278, 285
Michael, R. T., 232, 260
Michael-Johnson, P., 110, 120
Michaels, S., 232, 260
Michotte, A., 277, 285
Mickler, S., 128, 132, 150, 200, 221
Middlestadt, S. E., 132, 150, 151, 163,
    179, 196, 198, 221
Milazzo, J., 231, 258
Mildvan, D., 127, 150
Mill, J. S., 277, 285
Miller, C. T., 63, 82
Miller, D. T., 264, 266, 284
Miller, G. R., 87, 90, 122

Miller, H. G., 129, 152
Miller, J., 65, 67, 81, 200, 220
Miller, L. C., 87, 92, 93, 94, 95, 97,
    99, 102, 104, 112, 113, 115, 116,
    120, 122, 123
Miller, N., 282, 285
Miller, T. E., 127, 152
Millman, L., 267, 277, 285
Mills, J., 96, 120
Misovich, S. J., 76, 82, 128, 132, 144,
    151, 159, 168, 179
Mitsuyasu, R., 322, 330
Montgomery, K., 159, 180
Montgomery, S. B., 48, 52, 53, 55,
    57, 60, 66, 68, 69, 70, 72, 74, 75,
    77, 82, 83, 131, 150, 163, 168,
    180, 200, 201, 221, 222, 307, 311,
    330
Moos, R. H., 313, 329, 330
Morales, E., 199, 221
Morgan, E. B., 306, 320, 331
Morgan, S., 282, 283
Morin, S. F., 135, 152, 201, 223, 308,
    331, 352, 355
Morris, K., 170, 178
Morrison, D. M., 198, 220
Morton, A. D., 281, 285
Moses, L. E., 129, 152
Mosher, W. D., 186, 187, 223
Mosher, D. L., 63, 73, 83
Mulholland, M., 86, 121
Munoz, A., 322, 331
Murdock, G. P., 267, 285
Murphy, A., 32, 37
Murphy, D. A., 190, 222
Murphy, G. L., 113, 122
Myers, J. K., 320, 331
Myers, R. H., 320, 332

N

Naatanen, R., 23, 37
Namerow, P. B., 187, 223
Namir, S., 66, 68, 83, 163, 180, 308,
    311, 330

Narkunas, J. P., 12, 26, 27, 36
Nathanson, C. A., 65, 72, 84, 199, 223
Navarro, M., 256, 260
Neal, D., 352, 355
Nemeroff, C., 265, 267, 277, 285
Nerenz, D. R., 313, 330, 331
Newell, A., 14, 37
Niman, C. M., 281, 284
Noh, 66, 69, 82
Norton, R., 279, 285
Novick, D. M., 127, 150

O

O'Brien, K., 48, 52, 53, 55, 57, 66, 70,
    72, 74, 77, 83, 163, 168, 180, 200,
    222, 307, 311, 325, 330
O'Donnell, C. R., 231, 260
O'Donnell, L. O., 231, 260, 270, 281,
    282, 285
O'Donnell, P. R., 270, 281, 282, 285
O'Grady, K. E., 200, 223
O'Leary, A., 135, 152, 196, 201, 223
O'Malley, P. M., 307, 308, 329
Odaka, N., 308, 330
Oldenburg, B., 73, 83
Olson, J. M., 156, 180
Olszwski, L., 229, 230,
Omoto, A. M., 336, 337, 338, 339, 341,
    342, 343, 345, 346, 349, 350, 351,
    354, 355, 356
Or, J., 322, 330
Osmond, D. H., 230, 258
Ostrom, T. M., 100, 102, 103, 122, 161,
    181, 270, 285
Ostrow, D. G., 48, 52, 53, 55, 57, 60,
    66, 68, 69, 70, 72, 74, 75, 77, 82,
    83, 131, 150, 163, 168, 180, 200,
    201, 221, 222, 254, 257, 307, 311,
    325, 330
Ouellette-Kobasa, S. C., 342, 356

P

Padilla, E. R., 200, 223

Pagel, M. D., 59, 84
Paisley, W., 158, 180
Palmgreen, P., 163, 179
Panagis, D. M., 40, 57
Panem, S., 230, 260
Pappaioanou, M., 189, 224
Parisi, N., 231, 259, 336, 355
Parks, M. R., 118, 122
Pastore, N., 291, 302
Patterson, C., 267, 284
Paulker, S., 21, 37
Pavey, S., 336, 355
Paykel, E. S., 320, 331
Payne, S. F., 352, 355
Pearch, W. B., 87, 122
Pearlin, L. I., 313, 331
Peplau, L. A., 65, 67, 81, 96, 104, 121,
    345, 355
Perchacek, T., 41, 57
Perkins, C. I., 320, 330
Perlin, S., 321, 329
Perloff, L. S., 41, 51, 57, 75, 84, 176,
    180
Perper, T., 96, 122
Perry, R. B., 278, 286, 289, 290, 292,
    293, 296, 302
Pershing, A. L., 308, 329
Peters, S., 188, 189, 224
Peterson, D. R., 345, 355
Peterson, J. L., 65, 67, 81, 135, 152,
    193, 223
Peterson, M., 127, 150
Peterson, S., 89, 105, 123
Petit, C., 229, 260
Petromonaco, P., 276, 283
Pettigrew, T., 350, 354
Petty, R. E., 145, 152, 156, 161,
    164, 167, 168, 169, 170, 171,
    178, 179, 180, 181, 191, 192,
    223
Phair, J. P., 322, 325, 330, 331
Philliber, S., 198, 222
Phillips, L. D., 32, 37
Pines, A. M., 348, 356
Platt, L. P., 342, 356

Pleck, J. H., 65, 67, 84, 132, 152, 186, 187, 199, 223, 224, 231, 260, 270, 281, 285
Plichta, S., 65, 72, 84
Pokorny, A., 321, 329
Polk, B. F., 308, 322, 330, 331
Pollac, M. A., 201, 223
Pollack, L., 308, 331
Ponterotto, J. G., 282, 284
Powers, H., 322, 329
Pratkanis, A. R., 165, 181
Pratt, W. F., 186, 187, 223
Preister, J., 170, 181
Price, J. M., 199, 223
Price, V., 231, 253, 254, 260
Primavera, J., 199, 220
Proctor, D., 200, 224
Prohaska, T. R., 254, 257
Prusoff, B. A., 320, 331
Pryor, J. B., 97, 99, 122, 265, 266, 267, 268, 270, 272, 273, 274, 275, 276, 277, 279, 281, 284, 285, 292, 302, 336, 356
Puckett, S., 65, 67, 81, 200, 220
Pyle, C. R., 280, 285

Q

Quimby, E., 127, 152
Quinn, M. E., 318, 331
Quinn, S. C., 252, 260

R

Rabinowitz, P. C., 299, 301
Radius, S. M., 167, 181
Radloff, L. S., 322, 331
Raiffa, H., 5, 11, 13, 37
Ramsey, S. L., 282, 283
Rapoport, A., 32, 38
Read, S. E., 73, 82
Read, S. J., 87, 92, 93, 112, 113, 115, 116, 122, 123
Reardon, K. K., 155, 181
Redfield, R. R., 127, 150

Reeder, G. D., 265, 266, 268, 272, 273, 274, 275, 276, 279, 281, 285, 292, 302, 336, 356
Reinisch, J. M., 188, 223
Reis, H. T., 87, 123, 345, 354
Reisenberg, D. E., 307, 331
Reker, G. T., 349, 354
Renick, N. L., 165, 178
Rethans, A., 23, 37
Revenson, T. A., 313, 318, 330
Reynolds, K. D., 168, 181
Reznikoff, M., 318, 331
Rhodes, F., 136, 139, 152
Rhodes, N., 160, 181
Rice, D. P., 230, 260
Richard, R., 53, 57
Richmond, B., 89, 105, 123
Rickert, V. I., 205, 212, 223
Ridge, R. D., 342, 354
Ries, L. A., 27, 37
Rinaldo, C. R., 65, 67, 84, 128, 136, 153, 202, 224
Rippentoe, P. A., 40, 57
Roberts, N. E., 60, 84
Robinson, J. C., 65, 72, 84
Rodriguez, R., 77, 84, 314, 330
Roffman, R. E., 65, 67, 83, 127, 135, 151
Rogers, M. F., 12, 26, 27, 36
Rogers, R. W., 40, 57, 61, 83, 84, 169, 175, 181
Rogers, T. F., 159, 160, 181, 182, 230, 231, 260
Roman, S., 202, 206, 224
Ronen, J., 16, 37
Rook, K. S., 168, 181
Rosario, M., 205, 210, 223
Roscoe, B., 232, 258
Rose, R. M., 231, 260, 270, 281, 285
Rosenberg, C. E., 231, 249, 260
Rosenberg, M., 349, 356
Rosenstein, L. D., 232, 258, 298, 301
Rosenstock, I. M., 52, 56, 61, 84, 167, 173, 175, 181, 182, 307, 331
Rosoff, J. I., 186, 222

Ross, M. W., 73, 83, 132, 152
Rotheram-Borus, M. J., 128, 152, 194, 205, 209, 210, 223
Rothspan, S., 93, 94, 122
Rozin, P., 265, 267, 277, 285
Rummelhart, D. E., 104, 123
Rutherford, G. W., 352, 355

S

Saah, A. J., 322, 331
Safer, M. A., 40, 57
Saidi, P., 128, 150
Saika, G., 307, 331
Sandarelli, R., 42, 51, 57
Sande, M. A., 266, 285
Sanders, S. A., 188, 223
Sandman, P. M., 60, 84
Sants, H., 87, 121
Saracino, M., 163, 179
Sattath, S., 21, 37
Savage, L. J., 9, 37
Sax, D. S., 320, 332
Schaefer, C., 313, 330
Schank, R. C., 97, 113, 123
Scheibe, K. E., 336, 356
Scherbaum, C., 264, 283
Schifter, D. E., 196, 223
Schinke, S. P., 146, 153, 194, 205, 211, 212, 224
Schmidt, G., 278, 286, 295, 302
Schneider, S. G., 66, 71, 72, 77, 80, 81, 84, 163, 178, 309, 314, 320, 323, 329, 330, 332
Schneider, W., 231, 250, 260
Schoenfeld, M., 320, 332
Schooler, C., 313, 331
Schulman, R. E., 321, 329
Schumann, D., 171, 181
Schwalm, N. D., 16, 37
Schwartbaum, J., 279, 285
Schwartz, D., 186, 189, 221
Schwartz, K., 322, 329
Schwartzman, D. F., 168, 181
Schwarzer, R., 299, 300, 302

Scitovsky, A. A., 230, 260
Scott, R. A., 264, 266, 284
Scott, W., 187, 222
Searle, J. R., 87, 123
Sears, D. O., 281, 284, 286
Secord, P. F., 87, 121
Seiden, R. H., 321, 329
Seiter, J., 93, 94, 122
Selik, R. M., 189, 224
Seltzer, R., 193, 194, 203, 208, 221
Seropian, S., 231, 258
Serra, M., 270, 284
Sever, J. L., 322, 329
Shaffer, D., 156, 182
Shaklee, H., 16, 37, 45, 57
Shaver, P., 87, 123
Sheehan, E. P., 232, 249, 257, 259
Shepard, F. A., 73, 82
Sherman, S. J., 168, 181
Sherr, L., 163, 181
Shilts, R., 15, 37, 230, 260, 268, 269, 286
Shipp, E. R., 256, 260
Siegal, M., 267, 286
Siegel, D., 65, 67, 81
Siegel, K., 39, 41, 42, 44, 47, 48, 52, 55, 311, 332
Siegfried, A., 269, 286
Silver, R. C., 305, 332
Simon, H. A., 14, 37
Simon, W., 97, 123
Singer, E., 159, 60, 181, 182, 230, 231, 260
Skokan, L. A., 313, 318, 329
Slater, J., 320, 332
Slovic, P., 6, 14, 15, 16, 21, 32, 36, 37, 41, 57
Smith, E., 271, 286
Smith, J. E., 65, 67, 83, 128, 145, 152, 202, 222
Smith, M. B., 238, 260, 341, 356
Smith, M. J., 87, 123
Smith, P. J., 231, 258
Smith, S., 231, 259, 281, 284
Snarey, J., 231, 260, 270, 281, 282, 285

Snyder, L. B., 160, 182
Snyder, M. L., 281, 286, 336, 337, 338, 339, 341, 342, 343, 345, 346, 349, 350, 351, 354, 355, 356
Solomon, M. Z., 159, 182, 193, 194, 206, 207, 224
Sonanstein, F. L., 65, 67, 84, 132, 152, 186, 187, 199, 224
Sontag, S., 239, 260
Sorbom, D., 149, 151
Sorensen, J. L., 135, 151
Sorenson, J. R., 231, 261
Sorenson, R., 199, 224
Soskolne, C. L., 73, 82
Sotheran, J. L., 127, 150, 168, 179
Sox, H., Jr., 21, 37
Spanier, G., 198, 224
Spears, H., 204, 205, 222
Spira, T., 127, 150
Sprecher, S., 347, 354
Srull, T. K., 271, 286
St. Lawrence, J. S., 65, 67, 83, 128, 131, 132, 134, 135, 136, 139, 143, 146, 148, 151, 152, 153, 165, 180, 190, 202, 222, 231, 259, 312, 330
Staats, A. W., 165, 182
Staats, C., 165, 182
Stall, R. D., 127, 135, 152, 153, 156, 182, 307, 331, 332
Stasser, G., 100, 123
Stefanski, R., 42, 51, 57
Stehr-Green, J. K., 127, 153
Stephens, R., 202, 206, 224
Stepper, S., 42, 51, 57
Stevenson, L. Y., 128, 132, 145, 151, 152, 202, 222
Stewart, F. H., 185, 186, 221
Stewart, G. K., 185, 186, 221
Stipp, H., 231, 232, 254, 260
Stites, D. P., 202, 220, 221, 312, 329
Stoddard, A. M., 308, 331
Stoupakis, T., 313, 330
Strasser, J. A., 290, 302
Strathman, A., 156, 181
Strecher, V. J., 168, 175, 181, 182

Strenta, A., 281, 286
Strong, E. K., 156, 182
Strunin, L., 65, 83, 200, 201, 221
Suder, C., 199, 219
Sudman, S., 32, 37
Sugarman, D. B., 231, 232, 261, 344, 356
Sugrue, N. M., 254, 257
Sullivan, G., 66, 68, 69, 72, 83, 84, 163, 180, 308, 311, 330
Suls, J., 318, 332, 345, 356
Summala, H., 23, 37
Sutherland, E. M., 86, 121
Svenson, O., 23, 37, 41, 57
Syroit, J., 42, 51, 57

T

Tarfidd, K., 306, 320, 331
Taylor, D. A., 345, 353
Taylor, H., 186, 198, 224
Taylor, S. E., 47, 57, 66, 71, 72, 77, 80, 81, 84, 163, 178, 308, 309, 313, 314, 318, 320, 325, 329, 330, 332
Teitelbaum, M. A., 65, 72, 84
Temelso, T., 352, 355
Temoshok, L., 199, 221, 280, 286
Tesser, A., 156, 182
Thagard, P., 104, 113, 114, 123
Thalberg, S. P., 198, 220
Thomas, P., 127, 150
Thomas, S. B., 188, 224, 252, 260
Thompson, L., 198, 224
Thornberry, O. T., 5, 8, 11, 32, 37
Tierney, H., 306, 320, 331
Timko, C., 68, 77, 81
Traupmann, J., 347, 354
Trexler, L., 315, 323, 329
Triplet, R. G., 231, 232, 261, 344, 356
Trope, Y., 279, 286
Trout, D., 320, 325, 332
Trussell, J., 185, 186, 221
Turner, C. F., 129, 152
Tversky, A., 6, 13, 14, 15, 21, 28, 36, 37

U

Udry, J., 198, 220
Unnava, R., 156, 168, 178, 181
Utne, M., 347, 354

V

Valantinsen, B., 87, 121
Valdiserri, R. O., 66, 67, 84, 128, 136,
    153, 200, 202, 224, 268, 279, 286
van der Linden, M. M. D., 42, 56
van der Pligt, J., 42, 43, 44, 46, 48, 51,
    53, 56, 57, 58
van Doornum, G. J. J., 42, 56
Van Leeuwen, M. D., 282, 283
van Raden, M., 307, 329
Vercuso, P., 89, 105, 123
Verplane, B., 171, 182
Vinacco, R., 265, 266, 273, 279, 285,
    292, 302, 336, 356
Visintine, R., 127, 150
Visscher, B. R., 307, 322, 329
Vitaliano, P. P., 313, 330
von Winterfeldt, D., 5, 8, 11, 32, 38

W

Walder, L., 336, 355
Wallack, J. J., 231, 261
Wallack, L., 155, 175, 182
Wallsten, T., 32, 37, 38
Wallston, B. S., 59, 84
Wallston, K. A., 59, 84
Walsh, M. E., 267, 283
Walster, G. W., 347, 354
Warner, T. D., 42, 56, 65, 67, 73, 74,
    82
Warren, W. K., 128, 152, 200, 223
Washington, C., 93, 94, 122
Watkins, J. D., 333, 356
Wayment, H. A., 305, 332
Webber, A. W., 232, 261
Weber, J., 127, 150

Weiner, B., 231, 232, 261, 278, 286,
    289, 290, 291, 292, 293, 294, 295,
    296, 300, 302
Weinstein, N. D., 22, 23, 38, 40, 41, 42,
    44, 45, 46, 47, 50, 58, 60, 62, 75,
    76, 77, 80, 84, 176, 182, 255, 261
Weisfeld, G. E., 198, 221
Weisman, A. D., 313, 332
Weisman, C. S., 65, 72, 84
Weiss, D. L., 96, 122
Weissman, A., 315, 323, 329
Wells, G. A., 128, 152, 200, 223
Wells, G. L., 170, 181
Wemuth, L., 135, 151
Werth, J. L., 282, 286
Wertz, D. C., 231, 261
West, S. C., 282, 283
Westoff, C. F., 186, 222
Weston, R. E., 194, 205, 211, 212, 244
Wheat, J., 279, 285
White, H., 313, 330
White, K. P., 127, 152
White, L. A., 63, 73, 82, 84
White, R. W., 238, 260, 341, 356
Whiteley, S., 86, 120
Wilcox, J., 199, 221
Wilensky, R., 93, 123
Wiley, J. A., 135, 152, 307, 331
Wiley, K., 231, 261
Wilkie, P., 270, 284
Willenbring, K., 270, 284
Williams, J. G., 278, 285
Williams, M. J., 338, 356
Williams, R. L., 215, 224
Williams, S. S., 132, 135, 136, 142,
    143, 149, 151
Willoughby, A., 127, 151
Wills, T. A., 131, 135, 153, 345, 354
Willy, G., 42, 51, 57
Wilson, R. W., 32, 33, 38
Winett, R. A., 129, 153
Wing, D. L., 280, 286
Winkelstein, W., 127, 153
Winkler, R., 32, 37
Witt, L. A., 249, 261, 268, 286

Wittlin, B. J., 321, 329
Wolcott, D. L., 66, 68, 69, 72, 83, 84,
    163, 180, 308, 311, 330
Wolitski, R., 136, 139, 152
Wolkon, G. H., 268, 283
Wong, L. M., 342, 356
Wong, M., 313, 330, 332
Wong, P. T. P., 349, 354
Wood, J. V., 47, 57
Wood, W., 160, 181
Worden, J. W., 313, 332
Wormser, G. P., 231. 258
Wortman, C. B., 48, 52, 53, 55, 57, 66,
    68, 69, 70, 72, 74, 77, 82, 83, 163,
    168, 180, 200, 201, 221, 222, 307,
    311, 325, 330
Wulf, D., 186, 222
Wyatt, G. E., 188, 189, 224
Wyer, R. S., Jr., 271, 286

Y

Yancovitz, 127, 150
Yates, J. F., 32, 38
Young, R. K., 232, 258, 261, 298, 301

Z

Zabin, L., 198, 224
Zanna, M. P., 68, 82, 156, 177, 179,
    180
Zapka, J. G., 308, 331
Zelnik, M., 186, 187, 188, 224
Zich, J., 280, 286
Zielony, R. D., 131, 135, 153
Ziemba-Davis, M., 188, 223
Zorn, J., 199, 221
Zucker, G. S., 298, 302
Zuckerman, M., 163, 182
Zwick, R., 32, 38

Subject Index

A

Abortion, HIV and, 216
Adolescents
  condoms and, 186
  health messages and, 167
  interventions, 211, 212
  pregnancy, 186
  reliability of self-report, 73, 74
  risk assessment and, 62, 63
AIDS hotline, 147
AIDS Pragmatism scale, 234, 242, 244-
  246
AIDS prevention, irrelevancies, 131
AIDS risk
  as gay plague, 269
  overestimation of, 254, 255
  Pap tests and, 143
  public perception of, 29
  stigma, contamination reaction, 275,
    276, 280-282
AIDS risk-Reduction Behavior
  Sequence, 134, 135, 139
AIDS transmission, distrust of medical
  information, 266
AIDS
  attitudes of Blacks, 183-185, 251,
    254
  attribution theory, 288-301, see also
    AIDS, stigma
  avoiding information on, 159
  changing risk behavior, 127, 128
  changing stereotypes, 176
  dissipating fear, 109

  economic costs of, 230
  educating for risks of, 5, 234
  employment discrimination and, 229
  innocent victims of, 278, 293
  intelligence and, 215
  judging victims, 289, 290, 298-300
  mandatory HIV testing and naming,
    229, 234, 249
  origins of, 131, 268, 269, 290
  pediatric, 185
  perceived risk, 67
  personal controllability and, 291,
    297, 301
  prevention motivation, 137, 138
  public policy attitudes, 248-251
  public service announcements, 162
  quarantine, 234, 249
  racist plot, 189, 190, 215, 216, 273
  recognition-only information, 131
  risk perception, 5
  risk-reduction strategies, 5
  social contamination, 267
  sympathy for patients, 278
  symptom delay, 78
  testing by insurance companies, 229
  see HIV
AIDS, vs. other life threats, 77, 78
AIDS-related attitudes, 238, 255
AIDS-related stigma, 230, 231, 232,
  249, 255, 263, 264, 266-274
  see also, Volunteerism, Racism,
    Minorities
AIDS/HIV, child's concept of, 267
Alcohol, 143

sexual scripts and, 99
Altruism, 297, see Volunteerism
American Civil Liberties Union, 265
Americans with Disabilities Act
(ADA), 280, 281
Attitude Functions Inventory (AFI),
239
Attitude Toward Gay Men (ATG)
scale, 233, 234, 238
Attitudes Toward AIDS Preventive
Acts scale, 136

B

Behavior change, minorities and, 195,
196
Behavioral Intentions to Practice AIDS
Preventive Acts scale, 136
Bias
accumulation bias, 6
comparability of, 22-24, 27
cumulative risk and, 19, 31
decision, 14
in perception, 15-17
optimism and, 14, 24, 25, 52-54
probability bias, 15, 17
risk perceptions, 75
see also, Framing bias
Birth control, 63, see Condom use,
Contraception
Blacks
attitudes concerning AIDS, 251-253
risk behavior, 183, 186, 187, 194
views of homosexuality, 253
see also, Minorities
Blood donors, screening, 242
Blood, contaminated, 252, 272
Buddy system, 117, 334, 336, 340, 343,
347, 350, see Volunteerism

C

Casual Contact Beliefs scale, 233, 236,
241, 254

Census Bureau Current Population
Survey, 238
Center for Epidemiological Studies
Depression Scale (CES-D) 322
Civil Rights Act of 1964, 281
Cognitive bias, 6
Coherence, mental models and, 112-
115
College students
Interventions, 144-147
risk relevancy profile, 131, 140
unsafe sexual practices, 86, 94, 99
vulnerability to AIDS, 142
Communication, for safer sex, 87
see Negotiating safer sex
Computer simulations
coherence of, 113, 114
for safer sex, 100, 102
STELLA, 105-108
see Safer sex
Condom availability, 118
Condom use, 67
hedonism and, 200, 201, 207, 210,
214, 215
minorities and, 186, 196-198
negotiating, 200, 201
self-report, 137
teen survey, 156
validity of self-report, 73, 74, 76
Condoms
as health related, 173
bias and, 14, 15, 21, 22
changing attitudes, 145-147
computer simulation and, 104
coupon redemption and, 215, 217
eroticizing, 208, 212, 213
government distribution of, 234
partner discussion of, 99
purchasing, 94
religion and, 167, 172
risk levels and, 19
safer sex and, 53
social learning theory, 174, 186
women and, 141, 142
Contact Knowledge scores, 236, 241

Contraception, 63, 187, 198, 199,
see also, Condom use
Coping strategies, 305-309, 312-328
age and, 316, 317
emotional regulation, 313
HIV serostatus, 311, 312, 314, 316-319, 323, 324
problem solving efforts, 313
Coping With Thoughts of Developing AIDS scale, 315
Cross-sectional studies, 65-71
Cultural sensitivity, 189, 190, 192

D

Dating relationships, goals in, 92-94, 100, 101
Decision aids, 13
Decision theory
bias and, 14
concepts of, 6, 7, 11
HIV risk and, 7-10
Decision trees, 8, 9, 12-14
Decision, utility of, 10, 11
Decisions, consequences of, 9, 10
Defensive avoidance, 48, 49
Defensive coping, 47-50,
see Unrealistic optimism
Defensive denial, 51
Denial, of risk, 48-50
Discussion of Safer Sex with Partners, 137
Dynamic modeling, 105-110

E

Echo program, 115
Education programs, 116, 117
computer simulations, 118
video and, 117, 118
Egocentric bias, 45, 46, see Unrealistic optimism
Employment, AIDS discrimination and, 229, 266

Erotophobia, 63, 64, 73
Ethnic minorities, see Minorities, Risk behavior, Blacks, Hispanics
Ethnocentrism, interventions and, 189-194, 213
Evaluation research, see (IMB) model

F

Fear Drive Model, 40
Fear, 255
AIDS as threat, 292
AIDS messages and, 176
Framing bias, condoms and, 21, 22, 35

G

Gay Related Immune Deficiency (GRID), 269
Gays, high risk, 68, 69
lapse behavior, 90
see Homosexuality
Gender, 236, 237
condoms, 141, 142
intervention, 195, 197
power imbalance, 135
General AIDS Information Scale, 136

H

Health behavior survey, with embedded risk-reduction information, 148
Health Belief Model, 40, 61, 173, 201, 307
Health education programs
optimism and, 55
see Preventive programs
Health education, denial process and, 48
Hedonism, 200, 201, 207, 210, 214, 215, see Minorities
Helms, Jesse, 230
Hemophilia, 127, 272
Herpes, risk of, 31, see also Sexually transmitted diseases

High-risk males, 68, 69, *see* Risk
    behavior
Hispanics, risk behavior, 183-185, 187,
    189, 194
HIV, 5, 6
    Blacks and, 183-185
    children with, 273
    decision to test for, 7, 90
    in school, 274
    mother to child, 131, 210
    negative/positive, sex practices, 163
    risk estimates and, 26, 27, 31
    transmission, public policy
        decisions, 7
    Transmission Scale, 136
    see AIDS
Homophobia, 293, 294, 298, *see*
    Homosexuality, Gays
Homosexuality, 127,
    denial of, 189
    prejudice and, 231, 232, 256, 270,
        274, 276, 281
    risk-reduction behavior, 307, 308,
        311, 312
    self-acceptance/denial of, 159
    views of Blacks, 253
    see Gay males
Hopelessness Scale, 315, 322, 323

                    I

Information-Motivation-Behavioral
    Skills model (IMB), 129-131, 136-
    143, 146, 148
    evaluation of, 147, 148
Intervention components, 144-146
Intervention programs, 116, 117
    adolescents, 211, 212
    attitude formation, 163-168
    audience directed, 194, 208, 218,
        219
    college students, 144-147
    community on-site, 209, 210
    cultural relevance of, 201, 211, 255,
        256

diary use in, 117, 119
    ethnocentrism and, 189-192
    evaluating impact, 148, 149
    group specific, 143, 144
    "information only", 131
    irrelevancies, 131
    minority, 187, 189-195, 199, 200,
        201
    peer educators, 145, 146
    population specific, 139
    risk reduction, 128, 129
    role-playing in, 118, 119
    social comparison couples, 147
    teaching behavior skills, 135, 136
    understanding safe sex failures, 118
    video for, 147
    see Persuasion-based intervention
Intimate Contact Knowledge scale, 233
Intravenous drug users (IV), 43, 127,
    199, 202, 207, 268, 269
    needle exchange program, 234, 253,
        254
Invulnerability, to AIDS, 52, 75, 76

                    K

Kaposi's sarcoma, 269, 326

                    L

LaRouche, Lyndon, 229, 256
Loneliness, 109, 320, 222, 324, 344
    gay men and, 117
    UCLA Loneliness Scale, 322
    see Suicide ideation
Lying
    between partners, 39
    sexual histories and, 111

                    M

Medical decision analysis, 7, 8
Mental models, coherence of, 111-115
    see Computer simulations, Safe sex
Minorities, 127, 135

ethnic group differences, 201
hedonism and, 200, 207, 214, 215
peers and, 198
persuasion and, 192-194
racism and, 237
religion and, 244
risk behavior, 183, 185, 187-189,
191
views of homosexuality, 189
see Intervention programs, Racism,
Persuasion, Blacks
Morality, 279
AIDS as sin, 289, 292
see also, Religion
Mother-to-infant transmission, 131,
139, 210
Multicenter AIDS Cohort Study
(MACS), 67, 306, 308, 321
Multiple-encounter risk, 19, 20

N

National Survey of Adolescent Males,
199
National Survey of Female Growth,
187
National Survey of Young Women, 189
National Telephone Survey (1988),
237, 257
Natural History of AIDS—Psychoso-
cial Study (NHAPS), 306, 314, 321
Needle exchange program, 253, 254
see Intravenous drug users
Negotiating processes, 112
Negotiating safer sex, 147
between partners, 86, 87, 92, 100
computer simulation and, 100
Normative decision theory, 5-7, 13
Normative decisions, as predictors, 13

O

Optimism bias, 15, 24, 25
Optimism, 52-55

AIDS and, 40, 41, 42
bias and, 22-24, 27, 28, 35
health risks and, 28, 29
vulnerability and, 80

P

Peer health educators, 147
Peer Interventions, 145, 146, 172
Perceived control, 44, 45
see Unrealistic optimism
Perceived Difficulty of AIDS Preventive Behavior scale, 137
Preventive Behavior scale, 136
Perceived risk, 59, 163, 309, 311
assessment of, 6
emotional barriers, 78
for gay men, 163
optimism and, 55
worry and, 28, 29, 35
Perceived vulnerability, 59-62
changing, 81
see Persuasion-based interventions
Personal risk audit, 146
Persuasion, input/output model, 192,
193, 195
Persuasion, with minorities, 192-194
Persuasion-based interventions, 155,
156
attention guarantee, 159
attitude formation, 163, 165, 177
celebrities as models , 165
changing stereotypes, 176
cognitive response theory, 161, 162
communication/persuasion matrix,
156-169
demographic relevance, 167, 168
for long-lasting change, 176
intelligence and, 160
memory storage, 159, 160
perceived vulnerability, 168, 169
personal relevance, 167, 167
relevance to audience, 175-177
routes to, 164-166
social learning theory 174-175

Precaution Adoption Process, 62, 77, 80
Prejudice, and volunteerism, 352
President's Commission on AIDS, 280
Prevent AIDS Now Initiative Committee (PANIC), 229
Prevention Intervention scales, 136, 137
Preventive behavior, 68, 75
   determinents of, 131-133
   increasing, 76, 77
   modeling, 147
   optimism and, 55
   perceived vulnerability and, 59, 60
   public commitment to, 145
   sexuality and, 78, 79
   self-efficacy, 135
   see (IMB) model
Preventive programs, 39
Print media, 144
Profile of Mood States (POMS), 315, 323
Proposition 64, 229, 256
Proposition 96, 229, 230, 256
Proposition 102, 229, 256, 257
Prostitution, 43
Protection Motivation Theory, 40, 61
Public health strategy, see Intervention, Volunteerism
Public policy decisions
   AIDS education and, 7
   blood donors and, 7, 13
   funding and, 7
   HIV transmission and, 7
   preventive behavior and, 145
   treatment and, 7, 13
Public service announcements, persuasion messages, 162

Q

Qualitative/Quantitative risk assessment, 32-34
Questionnaires, 136, 142, 209, 307

R

Racism, AIDS and, 215, 216, 239, 281
Rehabilitation Act of 1973, 280, 281
Religion, 197
   AIDS and, 243, 253
   condoms and, 167, 172
   education in church, 256,
   punishment by God, 249, 252
Risk appraisals, 39
Risk Assessment Questionnaire, 24, 25, 27
Risk assessment scale, hierarchical nature of, 29-31
Risk behavior
   biases in, 5, 6
   change, model for, 129, 130
   controlling, 117
   cumulative stages of, 62
   decision making, 6
   determinants of, 183, 185, 191, 192
   invulnerability and, 52
   loneliness and, 117
   reducing, 69-72, 76, 77
   sex guilt and, 65
   unsafe sex and, 90
   vulnerability and, 59
Risk estimates, replicability of, 30
Risk factors, sensitivity to, 30, 31
Risk groups, measurement and, 54
Risk perception, 52, 53, 63, 68-72
   AIDS and, 5, 41, 43
   individual differences and, 81
   inherent bias, 75
   measuring, 72
   self-relevancy and, 173
   sexuality and, 79
   see Perceived risk
Risk prevention, irrelevancies in, 131
Risk reduction
   AIDS and, 41
   college students and, 72
   gay males and, 72
Risk taking behavior, 36
Risk

cumulative nature of, 15-17, 20, 21, 29
invulnerability, 40, 41, 42
measurement of, 6
messengers of, 29
misappraisal of, 39
perceived, 39, 40
sociopsychological variables and, 61
see Single-encounter risk, Multiple-encounter risk
Risk-avoiding strategies, 39
Risk-reducing behavior, 48, 307
behavior change, 142
gays and, 307, 308
serostatus and, 308, 311, 312
Risk-reduction interventions, 128-130, 146
barriers to, 307
minorities and, 193, 194
Risks
comparable nature of, 42, 43
measurability of, 41
vulnerability/unvulnerability and, 40, 41, 42
Role playing, 142

S

Safer sex, 53, 76
computer simulations, 102, 103
condom use and, 96
connectionist modeling tools, 103, 104, 113
goals and strategies, 88-90, 116, 117
initiating, 105
loneliness and, 89
negotiating, 85-120, 147
obstacles to, 92-95, 117
self-efficacy and, 201
sexual negotiation, 102
strategies, 105
San Diego AIDS Project, 334
Scale for Suicide Ideation, 323

Self-efficacy, sexual practices and, 53, 56
Self-esteem maintenance, 47, 50,
see Unrealistic optimism
Self-report, 137
diaries, 119
measurement, 74, 75
validity of, 73
Serostatus, 39, 79
Sex guilt, 63, 64, 73
Sexual behavior
cultural differences, 189, 193, 194
high risk, 67
minorities, 185-189
noncoital, 188, 189
Sexual encounters
coercion, 96, 97
deception, 96
strategies used, 95, 96
Sexual histories, lying and 111
Sexual partners, honesty of, 39
Sexual scripts, 92
fluctuations in, 119
inter/intrapersonal conflict, 94, 97, 98
nonverbal in nature, 99
pre-AIDS era, 117
rating partners and, 112
relationship building strategies, 97
subgoals, 116
Sexually transmitted diseases (STD), 186, 188
adolescents and, 209
minorities and, 209, 211
Single-encounter risk, 19
Smoking, risk behavior, 52
Social learning theory, 174, 175
Social psychological model for change, 129
Stereotyped beliefs, 46, see Unrealistic optimism
Stigma, AIDS and, 263-282
volunteers and, 336
see AIDS-related stigma
Subjective Norms Concerning AIDS

Preventive Acts scale, 136
Suicide ideation, 306, 319, 320, 321, 323-328
Support groups, 117
Surgeon General's report on AIDS, 243

T

Testing, for HIV, 7
Theory of Planned Behavior, 173
Theory of Reasoned Action, 77, 132, 133, 136, 140, 173, 192, 196, 197

U

U. S. Government Brochure, 158
Underaccumulation bias, 15, 17-19, 34
Unrealistic optimism, 51, 52
    consequences of, 52, 54
    causes of, 43-36, 49, 50
    reducing, 50, 51
    see Optimism
Unsafe sex,
    gays and, 163
    loneliness and, 109
    refusing, 147
    see Persuasion-based interventions
Utility theory, 14
Utility, measure of outcome, 10-12

V

Validity of self-report, 73, 74
Video intervention, 144-147, 194
    Blacks and, 207, 208, 213
    influence of family, 199, 213
    rap and, 194
Volunteerism, 333-353
    burnout, 348, 349
    motivation for, 351
    stigma, 352
    structuring patient contacts, 346, 347
Vulnerability
    to AIDS, 266, 282
    changing AIDS stereotypes, 176
    perceived, 71-73
    perceptions of, 73, 76
    precautionary behavior and, 62
    to pregnancy, 64
    problems of measurement, 80
    see Risk
Vulnerability/behavior link, 77, 79

W

Women, HIV and, 183-185
    Marines, 73, 75